D1600844

THE
APOSTOLIC FATHERS

THE
APOSTOLIC FATHERS

Revised Greek Texts
with
Introductions
and
English Translations

edited by

J. B. Lightfoot

and

J. R. Harmer

BAKER BOOK HOUSE
Grand Rapids, Michigan 49506

Reprinted 1984, 1987 by
Baker Book House Company
from the 1891 edition published by
Macmillan and Co., London

ISBN : 0-8010-5627-6

Printed and bound
in the United States of America

INTRODUCTORY NOTE

THE text of the Epistles of Clement, Ignatius and Polycarp and of the Martyrdom of Polycarp is taken from Bishop Lightfoot's larger work *The Apostolic Fathers, Part I. S. Clement of Rome* (2 vols., Macmillan & Co., 1890); *Part II. S. Ignatius, S. Polycarp* (2nd edition, 3 vols., Macmillan & Co., 1889). That of the Teaching of the Apostles was revised by him for this work. Mr Harmer contributes the text of the Epistle of Barnabas, the Shepherd of Hermas, and the Epistle to Diognetus. The Fragments of Papias and the Reliques of the Elders are taken from the printed editions referred to in each case.

No attempt has been made to give any apparatus criticus; but in passages where the reading of all the Greek authorities has been set aside for that of a version or patristic quotation, or for a conjectural emendation, the fact is stated in a footnote, and the authorities given.

The introductions throughout (with the exceptions of those which deal with the text, and the short prefatory note to the Fragments of Papias) were either written by Dr Lightfoot for this work, or are derived from his larger work referred to above.

The translations of the Epistles of Clement, Ignatius, and Polycarp and of the Martyrdom of Polycarp are reprinted from the larger edition. The rest of the translations are based upon rough notes found among his papers, but in the case of the Reliques of the Elders Keble's translation of Irenæus in the *Library of Fathers of the Holy Catholic Church* (Parker & Co., 1872) has been adopted with a few verbal alterations.

Mr Harmer alone has fulfilled the task of seeing the volume through the press, and the Trustees are indebted to him in this and in other works not only for critical skill and constant care, but also for great generosity which is not further referred to only in deference to his own firmly expressed wish. It should however be added that the Bishop himself recorded in a written memorandum 'his earnest desire that Mr Harmer's name should stand upon the title page, side by side with his own.'

It is hoped that an index of words and phrases will be published separately.

H. W. W.

May 25, 1891.

TABLE OF CONTENTS

TABLE OF CONTENTS

THE EPISTLES

OF

S. CLEMENT OF ROME

I. *GENUINE EPISTLE TO THE CORINTHIANS.*

II. *ANCIENT HOMILY, COMMONLY CALLED THE SECOND EPISTLE.*

S. CLEMENT OF ROME

1

THE EPISTLE was written in the name of the Roman Church to the Christian brotherhood at Corinth. The author was Clement, the Bishop of the Roman Christians, but he does not write in his own name. Hence it is mentioned by early Christian writers, sometimes as the work of the Roman Church, sometimes as written by or sent by the hand of Clement. Its date was nearly simultaneous with the close of Diocletian's persecution, when the emperor's cousin, Flavius Clemens, the namesake of the writer, perished during or immediately after the year of his consulate (A.D. 95), and his wife Domitilla, Domitian's own niece, was driven into banishment on charges apparently connected with Christianity.

A feud had broken out in the Church of Corinth. Presbyters appointed by Apostles, or their immediate successors, had been unlawfully deposed. A spirit of insubordination was rife. The letter of Clement was written to rebuke these irregularities. Allusion is made in it to the persecution at Rome, as an apology for the delay in attending to the matter. Some information is thus given incidentally respecting the character of the persecution in the course of the letter. But more precise and definite facts are contained elsewhere respecting the earlier and more severe assault on the Christians in the latter years of the reign of Nero, where reference is made especially to the martyrdoms of S. Peter and S. Paul.

2

Besides the patristic quotations more especially those in Clement of Alexandria, and in some later fathers, the text is mainly due to three sources.

(1) The famous Alexandrian uncial MS of the New Testament [A] in the British Museum, belonging to the fifth century, to which it is

added as a sort of appendix together with the spurious so-called Second Epistle of Clement to the Corinthians. This MS is mutilated at the close of both Epistles besides being torn or illegible in many passages of the first. From this was published the *Editio princeps* of Patricius Junius (1633).

(2) The Constantinopolitan or Hierosolymitan MS [C] belonging to the library of the Greek Patriarch of Jerusalem, whose chief residence is at Constantinople. From this the two Epistles of Clement (the Genuine and the Spurious) were first printed in full (1875) by Bryennios, then Metropolitan of Serræ, but now Patriarch of Nicomedia. This MS is dated A.D. 1056.

(3) The Syriac translation discovered a few years ago and now in the possession of the Cambridge University Library. This is not yet published, but all the various readings were given in Lightfoot's *S. Clement of Rome* Appendix, London, 1877. This Syriac Version bears a date corresponding to A.D. 1170.

The relations of these authorities are fully discussed in the larger edition of Clement. Here it is sufficient to say that A, as being the most ancient, is likewise far the best authority; but owing to the lacunae in it and other reasons the two other authorities are of the highest value in different ways.

Wherever the text is taken from any one or any combination of these three authorities, no notice is given of a various reading. But where the authority is patristic it is mentioned in the notes, and occasionally a reading is either adopted into the text, or recorded as highly probable in the footnote on conjecture, in which case the name of its author is given.

The square brackets [ ] throughout the book denote that a word so included is of doubtful authority and ought perhaps to be neglected; corruptions in the text are indicated by daggers † † placed on each side of the corrupt passage. A full list of symbols and abbreviations employed in dealing with the text is given at the end of the volume.

ΠΡΟΣ ΚΟΡΙΝΘΙΟΥΣ

Ἡ ᾿ΕΚΚΛΗΣΙΑ τοῦ Θεοῦ ἡ παροικοῦσα ῾Ρώμην τῇ ἐκκλησίᾳ τοῦ Θεοῦ τῇ παροικούσῃ Κόρινθον, κλητοῖς, ἡγιασμένοις ἐν θελήματι Θεοῦ διὰ τοῦ Κυρίου ἡμῶν Ἰησοῦ Χριστοῦ. χάρις ὑμῖν καὶ εἰρήνη ἀπὸ παντοκράτορος Θεοῦ διὰ Ἰησοῦ Χριστοῦ πληθυνθείη. I. Διὰ τὰς αἰφνιδίους καὶ ἐπαλλήλους γενομένας ἡμῖν συμφορὰς καὶ περιπτώσεις, ἀδελφοί, βράδιον νομίζομεν ἐπιστροφὴν πεποιῆσθαι περὶ τῶν ἐπιζητουμένων παρ᾽ ὑμῖν πραγμάτων, ἀγαπητοί, τῆς τε ἀλλοτρίας καὶ ξένης τοῖς ἐκλεκτοῖς τοῦ Θεοῦ, μιαρᾶς καὶ ἀνοσίου στάσεως, ἣν ὀλίγα πρόσωπα προπετῆ καὶ αὐθάδη ὑπάρχοντα εἰς τοσοῦτον ἀπονοίας ἐξέκαυσαν, ὥστε τὸ σεμνὸν καὶ περιβόητον καὶ πᾶσιν ἀνθρώποις ἀξιαγάπητον ὄνομα ὑμῶν μεγάλως βλασφημηθῆναι. 2. τίς γὰρ παρεπιδημήσας πρὸς ὑμᾶς τὴν πανάρετον καὶ βεβαίαν ὑμῶν πίστιν οὐκ ἐδοκίμασεν; τήν τε σώφρονα καὶ ἐπιεικῆ ἐν Χριστῷ εὐσέβειαν οὐκ ἐθαύμασεν; καὶ τὸ μεγαλοπρεπὲς τῆς φιλοξενίας ὑμῶν ἦθος οὐκ ἐκήρυξεν; καὶ τὴν τελείαν καὶ ἀσφαλῆ γνῶσιν οὐκ ἐμακάρισεν; 3. ἀπροσωπολήμπτως γὰρ πάντα ἐποιεῖτε, καὶ τοῖς νομίμοις τοῦ Θεοῦ ἐπορεύεσθε, ὑποτασσόμενοι τοῖς ἡγουμένοις ὑμῶν καὶ τιμὴν τὴν καθήκουσαν ἀπονέμοντες τοῖς παρ᾽ ὑμῖν πρεσβυτέροις· νέοις τε μέτρια καὶ σεμνὰ νοεῖν ἐπετρέπετε· γυναιξίν τε ἐν ἀμώμῳ καὶ σεμνῇ καὶ ἁγνῇ συνειδήσει πάντα ἐπιτελεῖν

---

i. 3 τοῖς νομίμοις] Clem. Alex.; τοῖς νόμοις AC; *in lege* S.

παρηγγέλλετε, στεργούσας καθηκόντως τοὺς ἄνδρας ἑαυτῶν· ἔν τε τῷ κανόνι τῆς ὑποταγῆς ὑπαρχούσας τὰ κατὰ τὸν οἶκον σεμνῶς οἰκουργεῖν ἐδιδάσκετε, πάνυ σωφρονούσας. II. Πάντες τε ἐταπεινοφρονεῖτε, μηδὲν ἀλαζονευόμενοι, ὑποτασσόμενοι μᾶλλον ἢ ὑποτάσσοντες, ἭΔΙΟΝ ΔΙΔόΝΤΕC ἢ λΑΜΒάΝΟΝΤΕC, τοῖς ἐφοδίοις τοῦ Θεοῦ ἀρκούμενοι· καὶ προσέχοντες τοὺς λόγους αὐτοῦ ἐπιμελῶς ἐνεστερνισμένοι ἦτε τοῖς σπλάγχνοις, καὶ τὰ παθήματα αὐτοῦ ἦν πρὸ ὀφθαλμῶν ὑμῶν. 2. Οὕτως εἰρήνη βαθεῖα καὶ λιπαρὰ ἐδέδοτο πᾶσιν καὶ ἀκόρεστος πόθος εἰς ἀγαθοποιΐαν, καὶ πλήρης πνεύματος ἁγίου ἔκχυσις ἐπὶ πάντας ἐγίνετο· 3. μεστοί τε ὁσίας βουλῆς ἐν ἀγαθῇ προθυμίᾳ μετ' εὐσεβοῦς πεποιθήσεως ἐξετείνατε τὰς χεῖρας ὑμῶν πρὸς τὸν παντοκράτορα Θεόν, ἱκετεύοντες αὐτὸν ἵλεως γενέσθαι, εἴ τι ἄκοντες ἡμάρτετε. 4. ἀγὼν ἦν ὑμῖν ἡμέρας τε καὶ νυκτὸς ὑπὲρ πάσης τῆς ἀδελφότητος, εἰς τὸ σώζεσθαι μετὰ δέους καὶ συνειδήσεως τὸν ἀριθμὸν τῶν ἐκλεκτῶν αὐτοῦ· 5. εἰλικρινεῖς καὶ ἀκέραιοι ἦτε καὶ ἀμνησίκακοι εἰς ἀλλήλους· 6. πᾶσα στάσις καὶ πᾶν σχίσμα βδελυκτὸν ὑμῖν· ἐπὶ τοῖς παραπτώμασιν τοῖς πλησίον ἐπενθεῖτε· τὰ ὑστερήματα αὐτῶν ἴδια ἐκρίνετε· 7. ἀμεταμέλητοι ἦτε ἐπὶ πάσῃ ἀγαθοποιΐα, ἕτοιμοι εἰc πᾶν ἔργον ἀγαθόν· 8. τῇ παναρέτῳ καὶ σεβασμίῳ πολιτείᾳ κεκοσμημένοι πάντα ἐν τῷ φόβῳ αὐτοῦ ἐπετελεῖτε· τὰ προστάγματα καὶ τὰ δικαιώματα τοῦ Κυρίου ἐπὶ τὰ πλάτη τῆc καρδίαc ὑμῶν ἐγέγραπτο. III. Πᾶσα δόξα καὶ πλατυσμὸς ἐδόθη ὑμῖν, καὶ ἐπετελέσθη τὸ γεγραμμένον· Ἔφαγεν καὶ ἔπιεν καὶ ἐπλατύνθη καὶ ἐπαχύνθη καὶ ἀπελάκτιςεν ὁ ἠγαπημένος. 2. Ἐκ τούτου ζῆλος καὶ φθόνος, [καὶ] ἔρις καὶ στάσις, διωγμὸς καὶ ἀκαταστασία, πόλεμος καὶ αἰχμαλωσία. 3. οὕτως ἐπηγέρθησαν οἱ ἄτιμοι ἐπὶ τοὺς ἐντίμουc, οἱ ἄδοξοι ἐπὶ τοὺς ἐνδόξους, οἱ ἄφρονες ἐπὶ τοὺς φρονίμους, οἱ νέοι ἐπὶ τοὺς πρεcβυτέρουc. 4. διὰ τοῦτο πόρρω ἄπεcτιν ἡ δικαιοcύνη καὶ εἰρήνη, ἐν τῷ ἀπολείπειν ἕκαστον τὸν φόβον τοῦ Θεοῦ καὶ ἐν τῇ πίστει αὐτοῦ ἀμβλυωπῆσαι μηδὲ ἐν τοῖς νομίμοις τῶν προσταγμάτων αὐτοῦ πο-

Acts xx. 35.

Titus iii. 1.

Prov. vii. 3.

Deut. xxxii. 15.

Is. iii. 5.

Is. lix. 14.

ρεύεσθαι μηδὲ πολιτεύεσθαι κατὰ τὸ καθῆκον τῷ Χριστῷ,
ἀλλὰ ἕκαστον βαδίζειν κατὰ τὰς ἐπιθυμίας τῆς καρδίας αὐτοῦ
τῆς πονηρᾶς, ζῆλον ἄδικον καὶ ἀσεβῆ ἀνειληφότας, δι' οὗ καὶ
θάνατος εἰσῆλθεν εἰς τὸν κόσμον.

IV. Γέγραπται γὰρ οὕτως· Καὶ ἐγένετο μεθ' ἡμέρας, ἤνεγκεν Κάϊν ἀπὸ τῶν καρπῶν τῆς γῆς θυσίαν τῷ Θεῷ, καὶ Ἄβελ
ἤνεγκεν καὶ αὐτὸς ἀπὸ τῶν πρωτοτόκων τῶν προβάτων καὶ ἀπὸ
τῶν στεάτων αὐτῶν. 2. καὶ ἐπεῖδεν ὁ Θεὸς ἐπὶ Ἄβελ καὶ ἐπὶ
τοῖς δώροις αὐτοῦ, ἐπὶ δὲ Κάϊν καὶ ἐπὶ ταῖς θυσίαις αὐτοῦ οὐ
προσέσχεν. 3. καὶ ἐλυπήθη Κάϊν λίαν καὶ συνέπεσεν τῷ προσώπῳ αὐτοῦ. 4. καὶ εἶπεν ὁ Θεὸς πρὸς Κάϊν· Ἵνα τί περίλυπος
ἐγένου; καὶ ἵνα τί συνέπεσεν τὸ πρόσωπόν σου; οὐκ ἐὰν ὀρθῶς
προσενέγκῃς ὀρθῶς δὲ μὴ διέλῃς, ἥμαρτες; 5. ἡσύχασον· πρὸς
σὲ ἡ ἀποστροφὴ αὐτοῦ, καὶ σὺ ἄρξεις αὐτοῦ. 6. καὶ εἶπεν Κάϊν
πρὸς Ἄβελ τὸν ἀδελφὸν αὐτοῦ· Διέλθωμεν εἰς τὸ πεδίον. καὶ
ἐγένετο ἐν τῷ εἶναι αὐτοὺς ἐν τῷ πεδίῳ ἀνέστη Κάϊν ἐπὶ Ἄβελ
τὸν ἀδελφὸν αὐτοῦ καὶ ἀπέκτεινεν αὐτόν. 7. Ὁρᾶτε, ἀδελφοί,
ζῆλος καὶ φθόνος ἀδελφοκτονίαν κατειργάσατο. 8. διὰ ζῆλος
ὁ πατὴρ ἡμῶν Ἰακὼβ ἀπέδρα ἀπὸ προσώπου Ἠσαῦ τοῦ
ἀδελφοῦ αὐτοῦ. 9. ζῆλος ἐποίησεν Ἰωσὴφ μέχρι θανάτου
διωχθῆναι καὶ μέχρι δουλείας εἰσελθεῖν. 10. ζῆλος φυγεῖν
ἠνάγκασεν Μωϋσῆν ἀπὸ προσώπου Φαραὼ βασιλέως Αἰγύπτου ἐν τῷ ἀκοῦσαι αὐτὸν ἀπὸ τοῦ ὁμοφύλου, Τίς σε κατέστησεν
κριτὴν ἢ δικαστὴν ἐφ' ἡμῶν; μὴ ἀνελεῖν με σὺ θέλεις, ὃν τρόπον ἀνεῖλες ἐχθὲς τὸν Αἰγύπτιον; 11. διὰ ζῆλος Ἀαρὼν καὶ
Μαριὰμ ἔξω τῆς παρεμβολῆς ηὐλίσθησαν. 12. ζῆλος Δαθὰν
καὶ Ἀβειρὼν ζῶντας κατήγαγεν εἰς ᾅδου, διὰ τὸ στασιάσαι
αὐτοὺς πρὸς τὸν θεράποντα τοῦ Θεοῦ Μωϋσῆν. 13. διὰ
ζῆλος Δαυεὶδ φθόνον ἔσχεν οὐ μόνον ὑπὸ τῶν ἀλλοφύλων,
ἀλλὰ καὶ ὑπὸ Σαοὺλ [βασιλέως Ἰσραὴλ] ἐδιώχθη.

V. Ἀλλ' ἵνα τῶν ἀρχαίων ὑποδειγμάτων παυσώμεθα,
ἔλθωμεν ἐπὶ τοὺς ἔγγιστα γενομένους ἀθλητάς· λάβωμεν τῆς
γενεᾶς ἡμῶν τὰ γενναῖα ὑποδείγματα. 2. Διὰ ζῆλον καὶ
φθόνον οἱ μέγιστοι καὶ δικαιότατοι στύλοι ἐδιώχθησαν καὶ

Wisd. ii.
24.
Gen. iv.
3—8.

Ex. ii. 14.

ἕως θανάτου ἤθλησαν. 3. Λάβωμεν πρὸ ὀφθαλμῶν ἡμῶν τοὺς ἀγαθοὺς ἀποστόλους· 4. Πέτρον, ὃς διὰ ζῆλον ἄδικον οὐχ ἕνα οὐδὲ δύο ἀλλὰ πλείονας ὑπήνεγκεν πόνους, καὶ οὕτω μαρτυρήσας ἐπορεύθη εἰς τὸν ὀφειλόμενον τόπον τῆς δόξης. 5. Διὰ ζῆλον καὶ ἔριν Παῦλος ὑπομονῆς βραβεῖον ὑπέδειξεν, 6. ἑπτάκις δεσμὰ φορέσας, φυγαδευθείς, λιθασθείς, κήρυξ γενόμενος ἔν τε τῇ ἀνατολῇ καὶ ἐν τῇ δύσει, τὸ γενναῖον τῆς πίστεως αὐτοῦ κλέος ἔλαβεν, 7. δικαιοσύνην διδάξας ὅλον τὸν κόσμον καὶ ἐπὶ τὸ τέρμα τῆς δύσεως ἐλθών· καὶ μαρτυρήσας ἐπὶ τῶν ἡγουμένων, οὕτως ἀπηλλάγη τοῦ κόσμου καὶ εἰς τὸν ἅγιον τόπον ἐπορεύθη, ὑπομονῆς γενόμενος μέγιστος ὑπογραμμός.

VI. Τούτοις τοῖς ἀνδράσιν ὁσίως πολιτευσαμένοις συνηθροίσθη πολὺ πλῆθος ἐκλεκτῶν, οἵτινες πολλαῖς αἰκίαις καὶ βασάνοις, διὰ ζῆλος παθόντες, ὑπόδειγμα κάλλιστον ἐγένοντο ἐν ἡμῖν. 2. Διὰ ζῆλος διωχθεῖσαι γυναῖκες, †Δαναΐδες καὶ Δίρκαι†, αἰκίσματα δεινὰ καὶ ἀνόσια παθοῦσαι, ἐπὶ τὸν τῆς πίστεως βέβαιον δρόμον κατήντησαν καὶ ἔλαβον γέρας γενναῖον αἱ ἀσθενεῖς τῷ σώματι. 3. ζῆλος ἀπηλλοτρίωσεν γαμετὰς ἀνδρῶν καὶ ἠλλοίωσεν τὸ ῥηθὲν ὑπὸ τοῦ πατρὸς Gen. ii. 23. ἡμῶν Ἀδάμ, Τοῦτο νῦν ὀστοῦν ἐκ τῶν ὀστέων μου καὶ σάρξ ἐκ τῆς σαρκός μου. 4. ζῆλος καὶ ἔρις πόλεις μεγάλας κατέστρεψεν καὶ ἔθνη μεγάλα ἐξερίζωσεν.

VII. Ταῦτα, ἀγαπητοί, οὐ μόνον ὑμᾶς νουθετοῦντες ἐπιστέλλομεν, ἀλλὰ καὶ ἑαυτοὺς †ὑπομνήσκοντες†· ἐν γὰρ τῷ αὐτῷ ἐσμὲν σκάμματι, καὶ ὁ αὐτὸς ἡμῖν ἀγὼν ἐπίκειται. 2. Διὸ ἀπολείπωμεν τὰς κενὰς καὶ ματαίας φροντίδας, καὶ ἔλθωμεν ἐπὶ τὸν εὐκλεῆ καὶ σεμνὸν τῆς παραδόσεως ἡμῶν κανόνα, 3. καὶ ἴδωμεν τί καλὸν καὶ τί τερπνὸν καὶ τί προσδεκτὸν ἐνώπιον τοῦ ποιήσαντος ἡμᾶς. 4. ἀτενίσωμεν εἰς τὸ αἷμα τοῦ Χριστοῦ καὶ γνῶμεν ὡς ἔστιν τίμιον τῷ πατρὶ αὐτοῦ, ὅτι διὰ τὴν ἡμετέραν σωτηρίαν ἐκχυθὲν παντὶ τῷ κόσμῳ μετανοίας χάριν ὑπήνεγκεν. 5. διέλθωμεν εἰς τὰς

vi. 2 Δαναΐδες καὶ Δίρκαι] ACS ; νεάνιδες παιδίσκαι conj. Wordsworth.

γενεὰς πάσας καὶ καταμάθωμεν ὅτι ἐν γενεᾷ καὶ γενεᾷ μετανοίας τόπον ἔδωκεν ὁ δεσπότης τοῖς βουλομένοις ἐπιστρα-
φῆναι ἐπ' αὐτόν.   6. Νῶε ἐκήρυξεν μετάνοιαν, καὶ οἱ ὑπα-
κούσαντες ἐσώθησαν.   7. Ἰωνᾶς Νινευίταις καταστροφὴν
ἐκήρυξεν, οἱ δὲ μετανοήσαντες ἐπὶ τοῖς ἁμαρτήμασιν αὐτῶν
ἐξιλάσαντο τὸν Θεὸν ἱκετεύσαντες καὶ ἔλαβον σωτηρίαν,
καίπερ ἀλλότριοι τοῦ Θεοῦ ὄντες.   VIII. Οἱ λειτουργοὶ τῆς χάριτος τοῦ Θεοῦ διὰ πνεύματος ἁγίου περὶ μετανοίας ἐλάλησαν, 2. καὶ αὐτὸς δὲ ὁ
δεσπότης τῶν ἁπάντων περὶ μετανοίας ἐλάλησεν μετὰ ὅρκου·
Ζῶ ΓᾸΡ ἐΓώ, λέΓει Κγριος, ΟΫ ΒΟγλΟΜΑΙ τὸΝ θάΝΑτΟΝ τΟΫ ἁΜΑΡτω-   Ezek.
λΟΫ, ὡΣ τΗΝ ΜετάΝΟΙΑΝ· προστιθεὶς καὶ γνώμην ἀγαθήν·   xxxiii. 11.
3. ΜετΑΝΟΉΣΑτε, ΟἶΚΟΣ ἸΣΡΑΉλ, ἀπὸ τΗ͂Σ ἀΝΟΜίΑΣ γΜῶΝ· εἶπΟΝ ps-Ezek.?
τΟῖΣ γἱΟῖΣ τΟΫ λΑΟΫ ΜΟγ· Ἐὰ̀Ν ὦΣΙΝ Αἱ ἁΜΑΡτίΑΙ γΜῶΝ ἀπὸ τΗ͂Σ Γῆ́Σ
ἔωΣ τΟΫ Οὐ̓ΡΑΝΟΫ, ΚΑὶ ἐὰΝ ὦΣΙΝ πγΡΡΌτεΡΑΙ ΚΌΚΚΟγ ΚΑὶ ΜελΑΝώ-
τεΡΑΙ ΣάΚΚΟγ, ΚΑὶ ἐπΙΣτΡΑφΗ͂τε πΡὸΣ Μὲ ἐΞ ὅλΗΣ τΗ͂Σ ΚΑΡδίΑΣ ΚΑὶ
εἴπΗτε, ΠάτεΡ, ἐπΑΚΟΎΣΟΜΑΙ γΜῶΝ ὡΣ λΑΟΫ ἁΓίΟγ.   4. καὶ ἐν
ἑτέρῳ τόπῳ λέγει οὕτως· λΟΎΣΑΣθε ΚΑὶ ΚΑθΑΡΟὶ Γέ́ΝεΣθε· ἀφέ-   Is. i. 16—
λεΣθε τὰΣ πΟΝΗΡίΑΣ ἀπὸ τῶΝ ψγχῶΝ γΜῶΝ ἀπέΝΑΝτΙ τῶΝ ὀφθΑλ-   20.
ΜῶΝ ΜΟγ· πΑΎΣΑΣθε ἀπὸ τῶΝ πΟΝΗΡῶΝ γΜῶΝ, Μάθετε ΚΑλὸΝ
πΟΙεῖΝ, ἐΚζΗτΉΣΑτε ΚΡίΣΙΝ, ῥΎΣΑΣθε ἀδΙΚΟΎΜεΝΟΝ, ΚΡίΝΑτε ὀΡφΑΝῶ
ΚΑὶ δΙΚΑΙώΣΑτε χΉΡᾳ, ΚΑὶ δεῦτε ΚΑὶ δΙελεΓχθῶΜεΝ, λέΓει· ΚΑὶ ἐὰΝ
ὦΣΙΝ Αἱ ἁΜΑΡτίΑΙ γΜῶΝ ὡΣ φΟΙΝΙΚΟΫΝ, ὡΣ χΙΌΝΑ λεγΚΑΝῶ· ἐὰΝ δὲ
ὦΣΙΝ ὡΣ ΚΌΚΚΙΝΟΝ, ὡΣ ἔΡΙΟΝ λεγΚΑΝῶ· ΚΑὶ ἐὰΝ θέλΗτε ΚΑὶ εἰΣΑ-
ΚΟΎΣΗτέ ΜΟγ, τὰ ἀΓΑθὰ τΗ͂Σ Γῆ́Σ φάΓεΣθε· ἐὰΝ δὲ ΜῊ θέλΗτε ΜΗδὲ
εἰΣΑΚΟΎΣΗτέ ΜΟγ, ΜάχΑΙΡΑ γΜᾶΣ ΚΑτέδετΑΙ· τὸ ΓὰΡ ΣτΌΜΑ Κγρίογ
ἐλάλΗΣεΝ τΑῦτΑ.   5. Πάντας οὖν τοὺς ἀγαπητοὺς αὐτοῦ βουλόμενος μετανοίας μετασχεῖν ἐστήριξεν τῷ παντοκρατορικῷ
βουλήματι αὐτοῦ.

IX. Διὸ ὑπακούσωμεν τῇ μεγαλοπρεπεῖ καὶ ἐνδόξῳ
βουλήσει αὐτοῦ, καὶ ἱκέται γενόμενοι τοῦ ἐλέους καὶ τῆς
χρηστότητος αὐτοῦ προσπέσωμεν καὶ ἐπιστρέψωμεν ἐπὶ τοὺς
οἰκτιρμοὺς αὐτοῦ, ἀπολιπόντες τὴν ματαιοπονίαν τήν τε ἔριν
καὶ τὸ εἰς θάνατον ἄγον ζῆλος.   2. Ἀτενίσωμεν εἰς τοὺς

τελείως λειτουργήσαντας τῇ μεγαλοπρεπεῖ δόξῃ αὐτοῦ. 3. λάβωμεν Ἐνώχ, ὃς ἐν ὑπακοῇ δίκαιος εὑρεθεὶς μετετέθη, καὶ οὐχ εὑρέθη αὐτοῦ θάνατος. 4. Νῶε πιστὸς εὑρεθεὶς διὰ τῆς λειτουργίας αὐτοῦ παλιγγενεσίαν κόσμῳ ἐκήρυξεν, καὶ διέσωσεν δι' αὐτοῦ ὁ δεσπότης τὰ εἰσελθόντα ἐν ὁμονοίᾳ ζῷα εἰς τὴν κιβωτόν.

X. Ἀβραάμ, ὁ φίλος προσαγορευθείς, πιστὸς εὑρέθη ἐν τῷ αὐτὸν ὑπήκοον γενέσθαι τοῖς ῥήμασιν τοῦ Θεοῦ. 2. οὗτος δι' ὑπακοῆς ἐξῆλθεν ἐκ τῆς γῆς αὐτοῦ καὶ ἐκ τῆς συγγενείας αὐτοῦ καὶ ἐκ τοῦ οἴκου τοῦ πατρὸς αὐτοῦ, ὅπως γῆν ὀλίγην καὶ συγγένειαν ἀσθενῆ καὶ οἶκον μικρὸν καταλιπὼν κληρονο-

Gen. xii. 1—3.

μήσῃ τὰς ἐπαγγελίας τοῦ Θεοῦ. λέγει γὰρ αὐτῷ· 3. Ἄπελθε ἐκ τῆϲ γῆϲ ϲογ καὶ ἐκ τῆϲ ϲγγγενείαϲ ϲογ καὶ ἐκ τογ οἴκογ τογ πατρόϲ ϲογ εἰϲ τὴν γῆν ἣν ἄν ϲοι δείξω, καὶ ποιήϲω ϲε εἰϲ ἔθνοϲ μέγα καὶ εγλογήϲω ϲε καὶ μεγαλγνῶ τὸ ὄνομά ϲογ, καὶ ἔϲῃ εγλογημένοϲ· καὶ εγλογήϲω τογϲ εγλογογντάϲ ϲε καὶ καταράϲομαι τογϲ καταρωμένογϲ ϲε, καὶ εγλογηθήϲονται ἐν ϲοὶ πᾶϲαι αἱ φγλαὶ τῆϲ γῆϲ. 4. καὶ πάλιν ἐν τῷ διαχωρισθῆναι αὐτὸν ἀπὸ Λὼτ

Gen. xiii. 14—16.

εἶπεν αὐτῷ ὁ Θεός· Ἀναβλέψαϲ τοῖϲ ὀφθαλμοῖϲ ϲογ, ἴδε ἀπὸ τογ τόπογ, ογ νγν ϲγ εἶ, πρὸϲ Βορρᾶν καὶ λίβα καὶ ἀνατολὰϲ καὶ θάλαϲϲαν· ὅτι πᾶϲαν τὴν γῆν, ἣν ϲγ ὁρᾷϲ, ϲοὶ δώϲω αγτὴν καὶ τῷ ϲπέρματί ϲογ ἕωϲ αἰῶνοϲ· 5. καὶ ποιήϲω τὸ ϲπέρμα ϲογ ὡϲ τὴν ἄμμον τῆϲ γῆϲ· εἰ δγναταί τιϲ ἐξαριθμῆϲαι τὴν ἄμμον τῆϲ γῆϲ, καὶ τὸ ϲπέρμα ϲογ ἐξαριθμηθήϲεται. 6. καὶ πάλιν λέγει·

Gen. xv. 5, 6.

Ἐξήγαγεν ὁ Θεὸϲ τὸν Ἀβραὰμ καὶ εἶπεν αγτῷ· Ἀνάβλεψον εἰϲ τὸν ογρανὸν καὶ ἀρίθμηϲον τογϲ ἀϲτέραϲ, εἰ δγνήϲῃ ἐξαριθμῆϲαι αγτογϲ· ογτωϲ ἔϲται τὸ ϲπέρμα ϲογ· ἐπίϲτεγϲεν δὲ Ἀβραὰμ τῷ Θεῷ, καὶ ἐλογίϲθη αγτῷ εἰϲ δικαιοϲγνην. 7. Διὰ πίϲτιν καὶ φιλοξενίαν ἐδόθη αὐτῷ υἱὸς ἐν γήρᾳ, καὶ δι' ὑπακοῆς προσήνεγκεν αὐτὸν θυσίαν τῷ Θεῷ πρὸς ἓν τῶν ὀρέων ὧν ἔδειξεν αὐτῷ.

XI. Διὰ φιλοξενίαν καὶ εὐσέβειαν Λὼτ ἐσώθη ἐκ Σοδόμων, τῆς περιχώρου πάσης κριθείσης διὰ πυρὸς καὶ θείου· πρόδηλον ποιήσας ὁ δεσπότης, ὅτι τοὺς ἐλπίζοντας ἐπ' αὐτὸν οὐκ ἐγκαταλείπει, τοὺς δὲ ἑτεροκλινεῖς ὑπάρχοντας εἰς κόλασιν καὶ αἰκισμὸν τίθησιν· 2. συνεξελθούσης γὰρ αὐτῷ τῆς γυναικός, ἑτερογνώμονος ὑπαρχούσης καὶ οὐκ ἐν ὁμονοίᾳ, εἰς τοῦτο σημεῖον ἐτέθη ὥστε γενέσθαι αὐτὴν στήλην ἁλὸς ἕως τῆς ἡμέρας ταύτης, εἰς τὸ γνωστὸν εἶναι πᾶσιν ὅτι οἱ δίψυχοι καὶ οἱ διστάζοντες περὶ τῆς τοῦ Θεοῦ δυνάμεως εἰς κρίμα καὶ εἰς σημείωσιν πάσαις ταῖς γενεαῖς γίνονται.

XII. Διὰ πίστιν καὶ φιλοξενίαν ἐσώθη Ῥαὰβ ἡ πόρνη· 2. ἐκπεμφθέντων γὰρ ὑπὸ Ἰησοῦ τοῦ τοῦ Ναυὴ κατασκόπων εἰς τὴν Ἱεριχώ, ἔγνω ὁ βασιλεὺς τῆς γῆς ὅτι ἥκασιν κατασκοπεῦσαι τὴν χώραν αὐτῶν, καὶ ἐξέπεμψεν ἄνδρας τοὺς συλλημψομένους αὐτούς, ὅπως συλλημφθέντες θανατωθῶσιν. 3. ἡ οὖν φιλόξενος Ῥαὰβ εἰσδεξαμένη αὐτοὺς ἔκρυψεν εἰς τὸ ὑπερῷον ὑπὸ τὴν λινοκαλάμην. 4. ἐπισταθέντων δὲ τῶν παρὰ τοῦ βασιλέως καὶ λεγόντων· Πρὸς σὲ εἰϲΗλθον οἱ κατά- Josh. ii. 6 sq. ϲκοποι τΗϲ ΓΗϲ ΗΜϢΝ· ἐϲάΓαΓε αὐτοὐϲ, ὁ ΓὰΡ Βαϲιλεὺϲ οὕτωϲ κελεὐει· ἡ δὲ ἀπεκρίθη· ΕἰϲΗλθον ΜὲΝ οἱ ἄΝΔΡεϲ, οὑϲ ζΗτεῖτε, πρόϲ Με, ἀλλὰ εὐθέωϲ ἀπΗλθον καὶ ποΡεὐοΝται τῇ ὁΔῷ· ὑποδεικνύουσα αὐτοῖς ἐναλλάξ. 5. Καὶ εἶπεν πρὸς τοὺς ἄνδρας· ΓιΝὡϲκογϲα ΓιΝὡϲκω ἐΓὼ ὅτι ΚὐΡιοϲ ὁ θεὸϲ ὑΜϢΝ παΡαΔίΔωϲιΝ ὑΜῖΝ τΗΝ πόλιΝ ταὐτΗΝ, ὁ ΓὰΡ φόΒοϲ καὶ ὁ τΡόΜοϲ ὑΜϢΝ ἐπέπεϲεΝ τοῖϲ κατοικοῦϲιΝ αὐτΗΝ. ὡϲ ἐὰΝ οὖΝ ΓέΝΗται λαΒεῖΝ αὐτΗΝ ὑΜᾶϲ, Διαϲὡϲατέ Με καὶ τὸΝ οἶκοΝ τοῦ πατΡόϲ Μογ. 6. καὶ εἶπαν αὐτῇ· Ἔϲται οὕτωϲ ὡϲ ἐλάλΗϲαϲ ΗΜῖΝ. ὡϲ ἐὰΝ οὖΝ ΓΝῷϲ παΡαΓιΝοΜέΝογϲ ΗΜᾶϲ, ϲγΝάζειϲ πάΝταϲ τογϲ ϲογϲ ὑπὸ τὸ τέΓοϲ ϲογ, καὶ ΔιαϲωθΗϲοΝται· ὅϲοι ΓὰΡ ἐὰΝ εὑΡεθῶϲιΝ ἔζω τΗϲ οἰκίαϲ, ἀπολοῦΝται. 7. καὶ προσέθεντο αὐτῇ δοῦναι σημεῖον, ὅπως κρεμάσῃ ἐκ τοῦ οἴκου αὐτῆς κόκκινον, πρόδηλον ποιοῦντες ὅτι διὰ τοῦ αἵματος τοῦ Κυρίου λύτρωσις ἔσται πᾶσιν τοῖς πιστεύουσιν καὶ ἐλπίζουσιν ἐπὶ τὸν Θεόν. 8. Ὁρᾶτε, ἀγαπητοί, οὐ μόνον πίστις ἀλλὰ προφητεία ἐν τῇ γυναικὶ γέγονεν.

XIII. Ταπεινοφρονήσωμεν οὖν, ἀδελφοί, ἀποθέμενοι πᾶσαν ἀλαζονείαν καὶ τῦφος καὶ ἀφροσύνην καὶ ὀργάς, καὶ ποιήσωμεν τὸ γεγραμμένον· λέγει γὰρ τὸ πνεῦμα τὸ ἅγιον·

1 Sam. ii. Μὴ καγχάcθω ὁ coφὸc ἐν τῇ coφίᾳ αὐτοῦ, μηδὲ ὁ ἰcχρὸc ἐν τῇ
10.
Jer. ix. ἰcχύϊ αὐτοῦ, μηδὲ ὁ πλούcιοc ἐν τῷ πλούτῳ αὐτοῦ, ἀλλ' ἢ ὁ καγ-
23,
24. χώμενοc ἐν Κυρίῳ καγχάcθω, τοῦ ἐκζητεῖν αὐτὸν καὶ ποιεῖν
κρίμα καὶ Δικαιοcύνηн· μάλιστα μεμνημένοι τῶν λόγων τοῦ
Κυρίου Ἰησοῦ, οὓς ἐλάλησεν διδάσκων ἐπιείκειαν καὶ μακρο-
S. Matt. v. θυμίαν· 2. οὕτως γὰρ εἶπεν· Ἐλεᾶτε ἵνα ἐλεηθῆτε, ἀφίετε
7, vi. 14,
vii. 1, 2. ἵνα ἀφεθῇ ὑμῖν· ὡc ποιεῖτε, οὕτω ποιηθήcεται ὑμῖν· ὡc δίδοτε,
S. Luke vi.
31,36—38. οὕτωc δοθήcεται ὑμῖν· ὡc κρίνετε, οὕτωc κριθήcεcθε· ὡc χρη-
cτεύεcθε, οὕτωc χρηcτευθήcεται ὑμῖν· ᾧ μέτρῳ μετρεῖτε, ἐν
αὐτῷ μετρηθήcεται ὑμῖν. 3. Ταύτῃ τῇ ἐντολῇ καὶ τοῖς παρ-
αγγέλμασιν τούτοις στηρίξωμεν ἑαυτοὺς εἰς τὸ πορεύεσθαι
ὑπηκόους ὄντας τοῖς ἁγιοπρεπέσι λόγοις αὐτοῦ, ταπεινοφρο-
Is. lxvi. 2. νοῦντες. φησὶν γὰρ ὁ ἅγιος λόγος· 4. Ἐπὶ τίνα ἐπιβλέψω,
ἀλλ' ἢ ἐπὶ τὸν πραΰν καὶ ἡcύχιον καὶ τρέμοντά μου τὰ λόγια ;

XIV. Δίκαιον οὖν καὶ ὅσιον, ἄνδρες ἀδελφοί, ὑπηκόους
ἡμᾶς μᾶλλον γενέσθαι τῷ Θεῷ ἢ τοῖς ἐν ἀλαζονείᾳ καὶ ἀκα-
ταστασίᾳ μυσεροῦ ζήλους ἀρχηγοῖς ἐξακολουθεῖν. 2. βλάβην γὰρ οὐ τὴν τυχοῦσαν, μᾶλλον δὲ κίνδυνον ὑποίσομεν
μέγαν, ἐὰν ῥιψοκινδύνως ἐπιδῶμεν ἑαυτοὺς τοῖς θελήμασιν
τῶν ἀνθρώπων, οἵτινες ἐξακοντίζουσιν εἰς ἔριν καὶ στάσεις
εἰς τὸ ἀπαλλοτριῶσαι ἡμᾶς τοῦ καλῶς ἔχοντος. 3. χρη-
στευσώμεθα αὐτοῖς κατὰ τὴν εὐσπλαγχνίαν καὶ γλυκύτητα
Prov. ii. τοῦ ποιήσαντος ἡμᾶς. 4. γέγραπται γάρ· Χρηcτοὶ ἔcονται
21, 22.
Ps. xxxvii. οἰκήτορεc γῆc, ἄκακοι δὲ ὑπολειφθήcονται ἐπ' αὐτῆc· οἱ δὲ παρα-
9, 38. νομοῦντεc ἐξολεθρευθήcονται ἀπ' αὐτῆc· 5. καὶ πάλιν λέγει·
Ps. xxxvii. Εἶδον ἀcεβῆ ὑπερυψούμενον καὶ ἐπαιρόμενον ὡc τὰc κέδρουc
35—37. τοῦ Λιβάνου, καὶ παρῆλθον καὶ ἰδοὺ οὐκ ἦν, καὶ ἐζεζήτηcα τὸν
τόπον αὐτοῦ καὶ οὐχ εὗρον. φύλαccε ἀκακίαν καὶ ἴδε εὐθύτητα, ὅτι
ἐcτὶν ἐγκατάλειμμα ἀνθρώπῳ εἰρηνικῷ.

XV. Τοίνυν κολληθῶμεν τοῖς μετ' εὐσεβείας εἰρηνεύουσιν, καὶ μὴ τοῖς μεθ' ὑποκρίσεως βουλομένοις εἰρήνην.

Is.xxix.13. 2. λέγει γάρ που· Οὗτος ὁ λαὸc τοῖc χείλεcίν με τιμᾷ, ἡ δὲ
Ps. lxii. 5. καρδία αὐτῶν πόρρω ἄπεcτιν ἀπ' ἐμοῦ. 3. καὶ πάλιν· Τῷ

cτόΜΑτι ΑϒτῶΝ ἐϒλοΓοϒcΑΝ, τῇ Δὲ ΚΑΡΔίᾳ ΑϒτῶΝ ΚΑτΗΡῶΝτο.
4. καὶ πάλιν λέγει· ἨΓάπΗcΑΝ ΑϒτόΝ τῷ cτόΜΑτι ΑϒτῶΝ ΚΑὶ τῇ Ps. lxxviii.
ΓλώccΗ ΑϒτῶΝ ἐΨεϒcΑΝτο ΑϒτόΝ, Ἡ Δὲ ΚΑΡΔίΑ ΑϒτῶΝ οϒΚ εϒθεῖΑ 36, 37.
Μετ᾽ Αϒτοϒ, οϒΔὲ ἐπιcτώθΗcΑΝ ἐΝ τῇ ΔιΑθΗΚῌ Αϒτοϒ. 5. ΔιὰPs.xxxi.19.
τοϒτο ἄλΑλΑ ΓεΝΗθΗτω τὰ χείλΗ τὰ ΔόλιΑ τὰ λΑλοϒΝτΑ ΚΑτὰ τοϒ
ΔιΚΑίοϒ ἀΝοΜίΑΝ· ΚΑὶ πάλιΝ· Ἐ
ξολεθΡεϒcΑι ΚϒΡιοc πάΝτΑ τὰ χείλΗ Ps. xii.
τὰ ΔόλιΑ, ΓλῶccΑΝ ΜεΓΑλοΡΗΜοΝΑ, τοϒc εἰπόΝτΑc· τΗΝ ΓλῶccΑΝ 4—6.
ἩΜῶΝ ΜεΓΑλϒΝωΜεΝ, τὰ χείλΗ ἩΜῶΝ πΑΡ᾽ ἩΜῖΝ ἐcτιΝ· τίc ἩΜῶΝ
ΚϒΡιόc ἐcτιΝ; 6. ἀπὸ τῆc τΑλΑιπωΡίΑc τῶΝ πτωχῶΝ ΚΑὶ ἀπὸ
τοϒ cτεΝΑΓΜοϒ τῶΝ πεΝΗτωΝ ΝϒΝ ἀΝΑcτΗcοΜΑι, λέΓει ΚϒΡιοc·
θΗcοΜΑι ἐΝ cωτΗΡίᾳ, 7. πΑΡΡΗcιάcοΜΑι ἐΝ Αϒτῷ.

XVI. Ταπεινοφρονούντων γάρ ἐστιν ὁ Χριστός, οὐκ
ἐπαιρομένων ἐπὶ τὸ ποίμνιον αὐτοῦ. 2. τὸ σκῆπτρον [τῆς
μεγαλωσύνης] τοῦ Θεοῦ, ὁ Κύριος [ἡμῶν] Χριστὸς Ἰησοῦς,
οὐκ ἦλθεν ἐν κόμπῳ ἀλαζονείας οὐδὲ ὑπερηφανίας, καίπερ
δυνάμενος, ἀλλὰ ταπεινοφρονῶν, καθὼς τὸ πνεῦμα τὸ ἅγιον
περὶ αὐτοῦ ἐλάλησεν· φησὶν γάρ· 3. Κύριε, τίc ἐπίcτεϒcεΝ Is. liii.
τῇ ἀΚοῇ ἩΜῶΝ; ΚΑὶ ὁ ΒΡΑχίωΝ ΚϒΡίοϒ τίΝι ἀπεΚΑλϒφθΗ; ἀΝΗΓ- 1—12.
ΓείλΑΜεΝ ἐΝΑΝτίοΝ Αϒτοϒ, ὡc πΑιΔίοΝ, ὡc ῥίζΑ ἐΝ Γῇ ΔιΨώcΗ· οϒΚ
ἔcτιΝ εἶΔοc Αϒτῷ, οϒΔὲ ΔόξΑ· ΚΑὶ εἴΔοΜεΝ ΑϒτόΝ, ΚΑὶ οϒΚ εἶχεΝ
εἶΔοc οϒΔὲ Κάλλοc, ἀλλὰ τὸ εἶΔοc Αϒτοϒ ἄτιΜοΝ, ἐΚλεῖποΝ πΑΡὰ
τὸ εἶΔοc τῶΝ ἀΝθΡώπωΝ· ἄΝθΡωποc ἐΝ πλΗΓῇ ὢΝ ΚΑὶ πόΝῳ ΚΑὶ
εἰΔὼc φέΡειΝ ΜΑλΑΚίΑΝ, ὅτι ἀπέcτΡΑπτΑι τὸ πΡόcωποΝ Αϒτοϒ, Ἡτι-
ΜάcθΗ ΚΑὶ οϒΚ ἐλοΓίcθΗ. 4. οϒτοc τὰc ἁΜΑΡτίΑc ἩΜῶΝ φέΡει ΚΑὶ
πεΡὶ ἩΜῶΝ ὀΔϒΝᾶτΑι, ΚΑὶ ἩΜεῖc ἐλοΓιcάΜεθΑ ΑϒτὸΝ εἶΝΑι ἐΝ πόΝῳ
ΚΑὶ ἐΝ πλΗΓῇ ΚΑὶ ἐΝ ΚΑΚώcει. 5. Αϒτὸc Δὲ ἐτΡΑϒΜΑτίcθΗ Διὰ τὰc
ἁΜΑΡτίΑc ἩΜῶΝ ΚΑὶ ΜεΜΑλάΚιcτΑι Διὰ τὰc ἀΝοΜίΑc ἩΜῶΝ. πΑιΔείΑ
εἰΡΗΝΗc ἩΜῶΝ ἐπ᾽ ΑϒτόΝ· τῷ Μώλωπι Αϒτοϒ ἩΜεῖc ἰάθΗΜεΝ.
6. πάΝτεc ὡc πΡόΒΑτΑ ἐπλΑΝΗθΗΜεΝ, ἄΝθΡωποc τῇ ὁΔῷ Αϒτοϒ
ἐπλΑΝΗθΗ· 7. ΚΑὶ ΚϒΡιοc πΑΡέΔωΚεΝ ΑϒτὸΝ ὑπὲΡ τῶΝ ἁΜΑΡτιῶΝ
ἩΜῶΝ, ΚΑὶ Αϒτὸc Διὰ τὸ ΚεΚΑΚῶcθΑι οϒΚ ἀΝοίΓει τὸ cτόΜΑ· ὡc
πΡόΒΑτοΝ ἐπὶ cφΑΓΗΝ ἤχθΗ, ΚΑὶ ὡc ἀΜΝὸc ἐΝΑΝτίοΝ τοϒ ΚείΡΑΝτοc
ἄφωΝοc, οϒτωc οϒΚ ἀΝοίΓει τὸ cτόΜΑ Αϒτοϒ. ἐΝ τῇ τΑπειΝώcει
Ἡ ΚΡίcιc Αϒτοϒ ἤΡθΗ· 8. τΗΝ ΓεΝεὰΝ Αϒτοϒ τίc ΔιΗΓΗcετΑι; ὅτι

αἴρεται ἀπὸ τῆϲ ΓΗϲ ἡ ζωὴ ἀϒτοϒ· 9. ἀπὸ τῶν ἀνομιῶν τοϒ
λαοϒ μοϒ ἥκει εἰϲ θάνατον.   10. καὶ Δώϲω τοϒϲ πονηροϒϲ ἀντὶ
τῆϲ ταφῆϲ ἀϒτοϒ καὶ τοϒϲ πλοϒϲίοϒϲ ἀντὶ τοϒ θανάτοϒ ἀϒτοϒ· ὅτι
ἀνομίαν οϒκ ἐποίηϲεν, οϒδὲ εϒρέθη Δόλοϲ ἐν τῷ ϲτόματι ἀϒτοϒ.
καὶ Κύριοϲ Βούλεται καθαρίϲαι ἀϒτὸν τῆϲ πληΓῆϲ·   11. ἐὰν Δῶτε
περὶ ἁμαρτίαϲ, ἡ ψϒχὴ ϒμῶν ὄψεται ϲπέρμα μακρύβιον.   12. καὶ
Κύριοϲ Βούλεται ἀφελεῖν ἀπὸ τοϒ πόνοϒ τῆϲ ψϒχῆϲ ἀϒτοϒ, Δεῖξαι
ἀϒτῷ φῶϲ καὶ πλάϲαι τῇ ϲϒνέϲει, Δικαιῶϲαι Δίκαιον εϒ̓ Δοϒλεϓοντα
πολλοῖϲ· καὶ τὰϲ ἁμαρτίαϲ ἀϒτῶν ἀϒτὸϲ ἀνοίϲει.   13. Διὰ τοϒτο
ἀϒτὸϲ κληρονομήϲει πολλοϒϲ καὶ τῶν ἰϲχϒρῶν μεριεῖ ϲκϒ̓λα· ἀνθ'
ῶν παρεΔόθη εἰϲ θάνατον ἡ ψϒχὴ ἀϒτοϒ καὶ τοῖϲ ἀνόμοιϲ ἐλο-
Γίϲθη·   14. καὶ ἀϒτὸϲ ἁμαρτίαϲ πολλῶν ἀνήνεΓκεν καὶ Διὰ τὰϲ

Ps. xxii
7—9. ἁμαρτίαϲ ἀϒτῶν παρεΔόθη.   15. *καὶ πάλιν αὐτός φησιν·* Ἐγὼ
Δέ εἰμι ϲκώληξ καὶ οϒκ ἄνθρωποϲ, ὄνειδοϲ ἀνθρώπων καὶ ἐξοϒ-
θένημα λαοϒ.   16. πάντεϲ οἱ θεωροϒντέϲ με ἐξεμϒκτήριϲάν με,
ἐλάληϲαν ἐν χείλεϲιν, ἐκίνηϲαν κεφαλήν, Ἤλπιϲεν ἐπὶ Κύριον,
ρϒϲάϲθω αϒτόν, ϲωϲάτω ἀϒτόν, ὅτι θέλει ἀϒτόν.   17. *Ὁρᾶτε,
ἄνδρες ἀγαπητοί, τίς ὁ ὑπογραμμὸς ὁ δεδομένος ἡμῖν· εἰ γὰρ
ὁ Κύριος οὕτως ἐταπεινοφρόνησεν, τί ποιήσωμεν ἡμεῖς οἱ ὑπὸ
τὸν ζυγὸν τῆς χάριτος αὐτοῦ δι' αὐτοῦ ἐλθόντες;*

XVII.   *Μιμηταὶ γενώμεθα κἀκείνων, οἵτινες ἐν δέρμασιν
αἰγείοις καὶ μηλωταῖς περιεπάτησαν κηρύσσοντες τὴν ἔλευσιν τοῦ Χριστοῦ· λέγομεν δὲ Ἠλίαν καὶ Ἐλισαιέ, ἔτι δὲ καὶ
Ἰεζεκιήλ, τοὺς προφήτας· πρὸς τούτοις καὶ τοὺς μεμαρτυρημένους.   2. ἐμαρτυρήθη μεγάλως Ἀβραὰμ καὶ φίλος
προσηγορεύθη τοῦ Θεοῦ, καὶ λέγει ἀτενίζων εἰς τὴν δόξαν*

Gen. xviii. *τοῦ Θεοῦ, ταπεινοφρονῶν·* Ἐγὼ Δέ εἰμι Γῆ καὶ ϲποΔόϲ.   3. *ἔτι
27.
Job i. 1. δὲ καὶ περὶ Ἰὼβ οὕτως γέγραπται·* Ἰὼβ Δὲ ἦν Δίκαιοϲ καὶ
ἄμεμπτοϲ, ἀληθινόϲ, θεοϲεβήϲ, ἀπεχόμενοϲ ἀπὸ παντὸϲ κακοϒ·
Job xiv.
4, 5. 4. *ἀλλ' αὐτὸς ἑαυτοῦ κατηγορεῖ λέγων·* Οϒδεὶϲ καθαρὸϲ ἀπὸ
ρύποϒ, οϒδ' ἂν μιᾶϲ ἡμέραϲ [ἦ] ἡ ζωὴ ἀϒτοϒ.   5. *Μωϋσῆς*
Numb. xii.
7. *πιϲτὸϲ ἐν ὅλῳ τῷ οἴκῳ αὐτοῦ ἐκλήθη, καὶ διὰ τῆς ὑπηρεσίας
αὐτοῦ ἔκρινεν ὁ Θεὸς Αἴγυπτον διὰ τῶν μαστίγων καὶ τῶν*

xvii. 4 ἦ] insert Lightfoot.

αἰκισμάτων αὐτῶν. ἀλλὰ κἀκεῖνος δοξασθεὶς μεγάλως οὐκ
ἐμεγαλορημόνησεν, ἀλλ᾽ εἶπεν, ἐπὶ τῆς βάτου χρηματισμοῦ
αὐτῷ διδομένου· Τίς εἰμι ἐγώ, ὅτι με πέμπεις; ἐγὼ δέ εἰμι   Ex. iii. 11,
ἰσχνόφωνος καὶ βραδύγλωσσος. 6. καὶ πάλιν λέγει, Ἐγὼ δέ   iv. 10.
εἰμι ἀτμὶς ἀπὸ κύθρας.   ?

XVIII. Τί δὲ εἴπωμεν ἐπὶ τῷ μεμαρτυρημένῳ Δαυείδ;
πρὸς ὃν εἶπεν ὁ Θεός, Εῖρον ἄνδρα κατὰ τὴν καρδίαν μου,   Ps. lxxxix.
Δαγεὶδ τὸν τοῦ Ἰεσσαί, ἐν ἐλέει αἰωνίῳ ἔχρισα αὐτόν. 2. ἀλλὰ   21.
                                                            1 Sam.
καὶ αὐτὸς λέγει πρὸς τὸν Θεόν· Ἐλέησόν με, ὁ Θεός, κατὰ τὸ   xiii. 14.
                                                            Ps. li. 3—
μέγα ἔλεός σου, καὶ κατὰ τὸ πλῆθος τῶν οἰκτιρμῶν σου ἐξά-   19.
λειψον τὸ ἀνόμημά μου. 3. ἐπὶ πλεῖον πλῦνόν με ἀπὸ τῆς
ἀνομίας μου, καὶ ἀπὸ τῆς ἀμαρτίας μου καθάρισόν με· ὅτι τὴν
ἀνομίαν μου ἐγὼ γινώσκω, καὶ ἡ ἁμαρτία μου ἐνώπιόν μού ἐστιν
διὰ παντός. 4. σοὶ μόνῳ ἥμαρτον, καὶ τὸ πονηρὸν ἐνώπιόν σου
ἐποίησα· ὅπως ἂν δικαιωθῇς ἐν τοῖς λόγοις σου, καὶ νικήσῃς ἐν
τῷ κρίνεσθαί σε. 5. ἰδοὺ γὰρ ἐν ἀνομίαις συνελήμφθην, καὶ ἐν
ἁμαρτίαις ἐκίσσησέν με ἡ μήτηρ μου. 6. ἰδοὺ γὰρ ἀλήθειαν ἠγά-
πησας· τὰ ἄδηλα καὶ τὰ κρύφια τῆς σοφίας σου ἐδήλωσάς μοι.
7. ῥαντιεῖς με ὑσσώπῳ, καὶ καθαρισθήσομαι· πλυνεῖς με, καὶ ὑπὲρ
χιόνα λευκανθήσομαι. 8. ἀκουτιεῖς με ἀγαλλίασιν καὶ εὐφροσύνην, ἀγαλλιάσονται ὀστᾶ τεταπεινωμένα. 9. ἀπόστρεψον τὸ
πρόσωπόν σου ἀπὸ τῶν ἁμαρτιῶν μου, καὶ πάσας τὰς ἀνομίας
μου ἐξάλειψον. 10. καρδίαν καθαρὰν κτίσον ἐν ἐμοί, ὁ Θεός,
καὶ πνεῦμα εὐθὲς ἐγκαίνισον ἐν τοῖς ἐγκάτοις μου. 11. μὴ ἀπο-
ρίψῃς με ἀπὸ τοῦ προσώπου σου, καὶ τὸ πνεῦμα τὸ ἅγιόν σου μὴ
ἀντανέλῃς ἀπ᾽ ἐμοῦ. 12. ἀπόδος μοι τὴν ἀγαλλίασιν τοῦ σωτη-
ρίου σου, καὶ πνεύματι ἡγεμονικῷ στήρισόν με. 13. διδάξω ἀνόμους τὰς ὁδούς σου, καὶ ἀσεβεῖς ἐπιστρέψουσιν ἐπὶ σέ. 14. ῥῦσαί
με ἐξ αἱμάτων, ὁ Θεός, ὁ Θεὸς τῆς σωτηρίας μου. 15. ἀγαλλιάσεται ἡ γλῶσσά μου τὴν δικαιοσύνην σου. Κύριε, τὸ στόμα μου
ἀνοίξεις, καὶ τὰ χείλη μου ἀναγγελεῖ τὴν αἴνεσίν σου. 16. ὅτι
εἰ ἠθέλησας θυσίαν, ἔδωκα ἄν· ὁλοκαυτώματα οὐκ εὐδοκήσεις.
17. θυσία τῷ Θεῷ πνεῦμα συντετριμμένον· καρδίαν συντε-
τριμμένην καὶ τεταπεινωμένην ὁ Θεὸς οὐκ ἐξουθενώσει.

XIX. Τῶν τοσούτων οὖν καὶ τοιούτων οὕτως μεμαρτυ-
ρημένων τὸ ταπεινοφρονοῦν καὶ τὸ ὑποδεὲς διὰ τῆς ὑπακοῆς
οὐ μόνον ἡμᾶς ἀλλὰ καὶ τὰς πρὸ ἡμῶν γενεὰς βελτίους ἐποίησεν, τούς τε καταδεξαμένους τὰ λόγια αὐτοῦ ἐν φόβῳ καὶ
ἀληθείᾳ. 2. Πολλῶν οὖν καὶ μεγάλων καὶ ἐνδόξων μετειλη-
φότες πράξεων, ἐπαναδράμωμεν ἐπὶ τὸν ἐξ ἀρχῆς παραδε-
δομένον ἡμῖν τῆς εἰρήνης σκοπόν, καὶ ἀτενίσωμεν εἰς τὸν
πατέρα καὶ κτίστην τοῦ σύμπαντος κόσμου, καὶ ταῖς μεγα-
λοπρεπέσι καὶ ὑπερβαλλούσαις αὐτοῦ δωρεαῖς τῆς εἰρήνης
εὐεργεσίαις τε κολληθῶμεν· 3. ἴδωμεν αὐτὸν κατὰ διάνοιαν
καὶ ἐμβλέψωμεν τοῖς ὄμμασιν τῆς ψυχῆς εἰς τὸ μακρόθυμον
αὐτοῦ βούλημα· νοήσωμεν πῶς ἀόργητος ὑπάρχει πρὸς
πᾶσαν τὴν κτίσιν αὐτοῦ.

XX. Οἱ οὐρανοὶ τῇ διοικήσει αὐτοῦ σαλευόμενοι ἐν
εἰρήνῃ ὑποτάσσονται αὐτῷ· 2. ἡμέρα τε καὶ νὺξ τὸν τεταγ-
μένον ὑπ' αὐτοῦ δρόμον διανύουσιν, μηδὲν ἀλλήλοις ἐμποδί-
ζοντα. 3. ἥλιός τε καὶ σελήνη ἀστέρων τε χοροὶ κατὰ τὴν
διαταγὴν αὐτοῦ ἐν ὁμονοίᾳ δίχα πάσης παρεκβάσεως ἐξελίσ-
σουσιν τοὺς ἐπιτεταγμένους αὐτοῖς ὁρισμούς. 4. γῆ κυοφο-
ροῦσα κατὰ τὸ θέλημα αὐτοῦ τοῖς ἰδίοις καιροῖς τὴν παν-
πληθῆ ἀνθρώποις τε καὶ θηρσὶν καὶ πᾶσιν τοῖς οὖσιν ἐπ'
αὐτὴν ζώοις ἀνατέλλει τροφήν, μὴ διχοστατοῦσα μηδὲ ἀλλοι-
οῦσά τι τῶν δεδογματισμένων ὑπ' αὐτοῦ. 5. ἀβύσσων τε
ἀνεξιχνίαστα καὶ νερτέρων ἀνεκδιήγητα †κρίματα† τοῖς αὐτοῖς
συνέχεται προστάγμασιν. 6. τὸ κύτος τῆς ἀπείρου θαλάσ-

Gen. i. 9. σης κατὰ τὴν δημιουργίαν αὐτοῦ συσταθὲν εἰc τὰc cΥΝΑΓωΓὰc
οὐ παρεκβαίνει τὰ περιτεθειμένα αὐτῇ κλεῖθρα, ἀλλὰ καθὼς
Job
xxxviii. 11. διέταξεν αὐτῇ, οὕτως ποιεῖ. 7. εἶπεν γάρ· Ἕωc ὧδε Ἥξειc,
καὶ τὰ κΥΜατά coy ἐν coὶ cΥΝτριβΗcεται. 8. ὠκεανὸς ἀνθρώποις
ἀπέρατος καὶ οἱ μετ' αὐτὸν κόσμοι ταῖς αὐταῖς ταγαῖς τοῦ
δεσπότου διευθύνονται. 9. καιροὶ ἐαρινοὶ καὶ θερινοὶ καὶ
μετοπωρινοὶ καὶ χειμερινοὶ ἐν εἰρήνῃ μεταπαραδιδόασιν ἀλλήλοις. 10. ἀνέμων σταθμοὶ κατὰ τὸν ἴδιον καιρὸν τὴν
λειτουργίαν αὐτῶν ἀπροσκόπως ἐπιτελοῦσιν· ἀέναοί τε πηγαὶ

πρὸς ἀπόλαυσιν καὶ ὑγείαν δημιουργηθεῖσαι δίχα ἐλλείψεως παρέχονται τοὺς πρὸς ζωῆς ἀνθρώποις μαζούς. τά τε ἐλάχιστα τῶν ζώων τὰς συνελεύσεις αὐτῶν ἐν ὁμονοίᾳ καὶ εἰρήνῃ ποιοῦνται. 11. Ταῦτα πάντα ὁ μέγας δημιουργὸς καὶ δεσπότης τῶν ἁπάντων ἐν εἰρήνῃ καὶ ὁμονοίᾳ προσέταξεν εἶναι, εὐεργετῶν τὰ πάντα, ὑπερεκπερισσῶς δὲ ἡμᾶς τοὺς προσπεφευγότας τοῖς οἰκτιρμοῖς αὐτοῦ διὰ τοῦ Κυρίου ἡμῶν Ἰησοῦ Χριστοῦ, 12. ᾧ ἡ δόξα καὶ ἡ μεγαλωσύνη εἰς τοὺς αἰῶνας τῶν αἰώνων. ἀμήν.

XXI. Ὁρᾶτε, ἀγαπητοί, μὴ αἱ εὐεργεσίαι αὐτοῦ αἱ πολλαὶ γένωνται εἰς κρίμα πᾶσιν ἡμῖν, ἐὰν μὴ ἀξίως αὐτοῦ πολιτευόμενοι τὰ καλὰ καὶ εὐάρεστα ἐνώπιον αὐτοῦ ποιῶμεν μεθ' ὁμονοίας. 2. λέγει γάρ που· Πνεῦμα Κυρίου λύχνος ἐρευνῶν τὰ ταμιεῖα τῆς γαστρός. 3. Ἴδωμεν πῶς ἐγγύς ἐστιν, καὶ ὅτι οὐδὲν λέληθεν αὐτὸν τῶν ἐννοιῶν ἡμῶν οὐδὲ τῶν διαλογισμῶν ὧν ποιούμεθα. 4. δίκαιον οὖν ἐστὶν μὴ λιποτακτεῖν ἡμᾶς ἀπὸ τοῦ θελήματος αὐτοῦ· 5. μᾶλλον ἀνθρώποις ἄφροσι καὶ ἀνοήτοις καὶ ἐπαιρομένοις καὶ ἐγκαυχωμένοις ἐν ἀλαζονείᾳ τοῦ λόγου αὐτῶν προσκόψωμεν ἢ τῷ Θεῷ. 6. τὸν Κύριον Ἰησοῦν [Χριστόν],οὗ τὸ αἷμα ὑπὲρ ἡμῶν ἐδόθη, ἐντραπῶμεν· τοὺς προηγουμένους ἡμῶν αἰδεσθῶμεν, τοὺς πρεσβυτέρους ἡμῶν τιμήσωμεν, τοὺς νέους παιδεύσωμεν τὴν παιδείαν τοῦ φόβου τοῦ Θεοῦ, τὰς γυναῖκας ἡμῶν ἐπὶ τὸ ἀγαθὸν διορθωσώμεθα· 7. τὸ ἀξιαγάπητον τῆς ἁγνείας ἦθος ἐνδειξάσθωσαν, τὸ ἀκέραιον τῆς πραΰτητος αὐτῶν βούλημα ἀποδειξάτωσαν, τὸ ἐπιεικὲς τῆς γλώσσης αὐτῶν διὰ τῆς σιγῆς φανερὸν ποιησάτωσαν· τὴν ἀγάπην αὐτῶν, μὴ κατὰ προσκλίσεις, ἀλλὰ πᾶσιν τοῖς φοβουμένοις τὸν Θεὸν ὁσίως ἴσην παρεχέτωσαν· 8. τὰ τέκνα ὑμῶν τῆς ἐν Χριστῷ παιδείας μεταλαμβανέτωσαν· μαθέτωσαν, τί ταπεινοφροσύνη παρὰ Θεῷ ἰσχύει, τί ἀγάπη ἁγνὴ παρὰ τῷ Θεῷ δύναται, πῶς ὁ φόβος αὐτοῦ καλὸς καὶ μέγας καὶ σώζων πάντας τοὺς ἐν αὐτῷ ὁσίως ἀναστρεφομένους ἐν καθαρᾷ διανοίᾳ· 9. ἐρευνητὴς γάρ ἐστιν ἐννοιῶν καὶ ἐνθυμήσεων· οὗ ἡ πνοὴ αὐτοῦ ἐν ἡμῖν ἐστίν, καὶ ὅταν θέλῃ ἀνελεῖ αὐτήν.

Prov. xx. 27.

XXII. Ταῦτα δὲ πάντα βεβαιοῖ ἡ ἐν Χριστῷ πίστις· καὶ γὰρ αὐτὸς διὰ τοῦ πνεύματος τοῦ ἁγίου οὕτως προσκαλεῖται ἡμᾶς· Δεῦτε τέκνα, ἀκούϲατέ μου, φόβον Κυρίου διδάξω ὑμᾶϲ. 2. τίϲ ἐϲτιν ἄνθρωποϲ ὁ θέλων ζωήν, ἀγαπῶν ἡμέραϲ ἰδεῖν ἀγαθάϲ; 3. παῦϲον τὴν γλῶϲϲάν ϲου ἀπὸ κακοῦ, καὶ χείλη τοῦ μὴ λαλῆϲαι δόλον· 4. ἔκκλινον ἀπὸ κακοῦ καὶ ποίηϲον ἀγαθόν· 5. ζήτηϲον εἰρήνην καὶ δίωξον αὐτήν. 6. ὀφθαλμοὶ Κυρίου ἐπὶ δικαίουϲ, καὶ ὦτα αὐτοῦ πρὸϲ δέηϲιν αὐτῶν· πρόϲωπον δὲ Κυρίου ἐπὶ ποιοῦντας κακὰ τοῦ ἐξολεθρεῦϲαι ἐκ γῆϲ τὸ μνημόϲυνον αὐτῶν. 7. ἐκέκραξεν ὁ δίκαιος, καὶ ὁ Κύριος εἰϲήκουϲεν αὐτοῦ καὶ ἐκ παϲῶν τῶν θλίψεων αὐτοῦ ἐρύϲατο αὐτόν. 8. πολλαὶ αἱ θλίψειϲ τοῦ δικαίου καὶ ἐκ παϲῶν αὐτῶν ῥύϲεται αὐτὸν ὁ Κύριος· εἶτα· Πολλαὶ αἱ μάϲτιγεϲ τοῦ ἁμαρτωλοῦ, τοὺϲ δὲ ἐλπίζονταϲ ἐπὶ Κύριον ἔλεοϲ κυκλώϲει.

XXIII. Ὁ οἰκτίρμων κατὰ πάντα καὶ εὐεργετικὸς πατὴρ ἔχει σπλάγχνα ἐπὶ τοὺς φοβουμένους αὐτόν, ἠπίως τε καὶ προσηνῶς τὰς χάριτας αὐτοῦ ἀποδιδοῖ τοῖς προσερχομένοις αὐτῷ ἁπλῇ διανοίᾳ. 2. διὸ μὴ διψυχῶμεν, μηδὲ ἰνδαλλέσθω ἡ ψυχὴ ἡμῶν ἐπὶ ταῖς ὑπερβαλλούσαις καὶ ἐνδόξοις δωρεαῖς αὐτοῦ. 3. πόρρω γενέσθω ἀφ᾽ ἡμῶν ἡ γραφὴ αὕτη, ὅπου λέγει· Ταλαίπωροί εἰϲιν οἱ δίψυχοι, οἱ διϲτάζοντεϲ τὴν ψυχήν, οἱ λέγοντεϲ, Ταῦτα ἠκούϲαμεν καὶ ἐπὶ τῶν πατέρων ἡμῶν, καὶ ἰδοὺ γεγηράκαμεν καὶ οὐδὲν ἡμῖν τούτων ϲυνβέβηκεν. 4. ὦ ἀνόητοι, ϲυμβάλετε ἑαυτοὺϲ ξύλῳ· λάβετε ἄμπελον· πρῶτον μὲν φυλλοροεῖ, εἶτα βλαϲτὸϲ γίνεται, εἶτα φύλλον, εἶτα ἄνθοϲ, καὶ μετὰ ταῦτα ὄμφαξ, εἶτα ϲταφυλὴ παρεϲτηκυῖα. Ὁρᾶτε ὅτι ἐν καιρῷ ὀλίγῳ εἰς πέπειρον καταντᾷ ὁ καρπὸς τοῦ ξύλου. 5. ἐπ᾽ ἀληθείας ταχὺ καὶ ἐξαίφνης τελειωθήσεται τὸ βούλημα αὐτοῦ, ϲυνεπιμαρτυρούϲηϲ καὶ τῆϲ γραφῆϲ ὅτι ταχὺ ἥξει καὶ οὐ χρονιεῖ, καὶ ἐξαίφνηϲ ἥξει ὁ Κύριοϲ εἰϲ τὸν ναὸν αὐτοῦ, καὶ ὁ ἅγιοϲ ὃν ὑμεῖϲ προϲδοκᾶτε.

XXIV. Κατανοήσωμεν, ἀγαπητοί, πῶς ὁ δεσπότης ἐπιδείκνυται διηνεκῶς ἡμῖν τὴν μέλλουσαν ἀνάστασιν ἔσεσθαι, ἧς τὴν ἀπαρχὴν ἐποιήσατο τὸν Κύριον Ἰησοῦν Χριστὸν ἐκ

Ps. xxxiv.
12—18, 20.

Ps. xxxii.
10.

? 'Eldad
and
Modad'.

Is. xiii. 22.
Mal. iii. 1.

νεκρῶν ἀναστήσας. 2. ἴδωμεν, ἀγαπητοί, τὴν κατὰ καιρὸν γινομένην ἀνάστασιν. 3. ἡμέρα καὶ νὺξ ἀνάστασιν ἡμῖν δηλοῦσιν· κοιμᾶται ἡ νύξ, ἀνίσταται ἡμέρα· ἡ ἡμέρα ἄπεισιν, νὺξ ἐπέρχεται. 4. λάβωμεν τοὺς καρπούς· ὁ σπόρος πῶς καὶ τίνα τρόπον γίνεται; 5. ἐξῆλθεν ὁ cπείρων καὶ ἔβαλεν εἰς τὴν γῆν ἕκαστον τῶν σπερμάτων, ἅτινα πεσόντα εἰς τὴν γῆν ξηρὰ καὶ γυμνὰ διαλύεται. εἶτ᾿ ἐκ τῆς διαλύσεως ἡ μεγαλειότης τῆς προνοίας τοῦ δεσπότου ἀνίστησιν αὐτά, καὶ ἐκ τοῦ ἑνὸς πλείονα αὔξει καὶ ἐκφέρει καρπόν.

S. Matt. xiii. 3.
S. Mark iv. 3.
S. Luke viii. 5.

XXV. Ἴδωμεν τὸ παράδοξον σημεῖον, τὸ γινόμενον ἐν τοῖς ἀνατολικοῖς τόποις, τουτέστιν τοῖς περὶ τὴν Ἀραβίαν. 2. ὄρνεον γάρ ἐστιν ὃ προσονομάζεται φοῖνιξ· τοῦτο μονογενὲς ὑπάρχον ζῇ ἔτη πεντακόσια· γενόμενόν τε ἤδη πρὸς ἀπόλυσιν τοῦ ἀποθανεῖν αὐτό, σηκὸν ἑαυτῷ ποιεῖ ἐκ λιβάνου καὶ σμύρνης καὶ τῶν λοιπῶν ἀρωμάτων, εἰς ὃν πληρωθέντος τοῦ χρόνου εἰσέρχεται καὶ τελευτᾷ. 3. σηπομένης δὲ τῆς σαρκὸς σκώληξ τις γεννᾶται, ὃς ἐκ τῆς ἰκμάδος τοῦ τετελευτηκότος ζῴου ἀνατρεφόμενος πτεροφυεῖ· εἶτα γενναῖος γενόμενος αἴρει τὸν σηκὸν ἐκεῖνον ὅπου τὰ ὀστᾶ τοῦ προγεγονότος ἐστίν, καὶ ταῦτα βαστάζων διανύει ἀπὸ τῆς Ἀραβικῆς χώρας ἕως τῆς Αἰγύπτου εἰς τὴν λεγομένην Ἡλιούπολιν· 4. καὶ ἡμέρας, βλεπόντων πάντων, ἐπιπτὰς ἐπὶ τὸν τοῦ ἡλίου βωμὸν τίθησιν αὐτά, καὶ οὕτως εἰς τοὐπίσω ἀφορμᾷ. 5. οἱ οὖν ἱερεῖς ἐπισκέπτονται τὰς ἀναγραφὰς τῶν χρόνων καὶ εὑρίσκουσιν αὐτὸν πεντακοσιοστοῦ ἔτους πεπληρωμένου ἐληλυθέναι.

XXVI. Μέγα καὶ θαυμαστὸν οὖν νομίζομεν εἶναι, εἰ ὁ δημιουργὸς τῶν ἁπάντων ἀνάστασιν ποιήσεται τῶν ὁσίως αὐτῷ δουλευσάντων ἐν πεποιθήσει πίστεως ἀγαθῆς, ὅπου καὶ δι᾿ ὀρνέου δείκνυσιν ἡμῖν τὸ μεγαλεῖον τῆς ἐπαγγελίας αὐτοῦ; 2. λέγει γάρ που· Καὶ ἐξαναcτήcειc με καὶ ἐξομολογήcομαί coι. καί· Ἐκοιμήθην καὶ ὕπνωcα, ἐξηγέρθην, ὅτι cὺ μετ᾿ ἐμοῦ εἶ. 3. καὶ πάλιν Ἰὼβ λέγει· Καὶ ἀναcτήcειc τὴν cάρκα μου ταύτην τὴν ἀναντλήcαcαν ταῦτα πάντα.

Ps. xxviii. 7.
Ps. iii. 6.
Ps. xxiii. 4.
Job xix. 26.

XXVII. Ταύτῃ οὖν τῇ ἐλπίδι προσδεδέσθωσαν αἱ ψυχαὶ ἡμῶν τῷ πιστῷ ἐν ταῖς ἐπαγγελίαις καὶ τῷ δικαίῳ ἐν τοῖς κρίμασιν. 2. ὁ παραγγείλας μὴ ψεύδεσθαι πολλῷ μᾶλλον αὐτὸς οὐ ψεύσεται· οὐδὲν γὰρ ἀδύνατον παρὰ τῷ Θεῷ, εἰ μὴ τὸ ψεύσασθαι. 3. ἀναζωπυρησάτω οὖν ἡ πίστις αὐτοῦ ἐν ἡμῖν, καὶ νοήσωμεν ὅτι πάντα ἐγγὺς αὐτῷ ἐστίν. 4. ἐν λόγῳ τῆς μεγαλωσύνης αὐτοῦ συνεστήσατο τὰ πάντα,

Wisd. xii. 12, xi. 22. καὶ ἐν λόγῳ δύναται αὐτὰ καταστρέψαι. 5. Τίς ἐρεῖ αὐτῷ· Τί ἐποίησας; ἢ τίς ἀντιστήσεται τῷ κράτει τῆς ἰσχύος αὐτοῦ; ὅτε θέλει καὶ ὡς θέλει ποιήσει πάντα, καὶ οὐδὲν μὴ παρέλθῃ τῶν δεδογματισμένων ὑπ' αὐτοῦ. 6. πάντα ἐνώπιον αὐτοῦ εἰσίν,

Ps. xix. 2—4. καὶ οὐδὲν λέληθεν τὴν βουλὴν αὐτοῦ, 7. εἰ Οἱ οὐρανοὶ διηγοῦνται δόξαν Θεοῦ, ποίησιν δὲ χειρῶν αὐτοῦ ἀναγγέλλει τὸ στερέωμα· ἡ ἡμέρα τῇ ἡμέρᾳ ἐρεύγεται ῥῆμα, καὶ νὺξ νυκτὶ ἀναγγέλλει γνῶσιν· καὶ οὐκ εἰσὶν λόγοι οὐδὲ λαλιαί, ὧν οὐχὶ ἀκούονται αἱ φωναὶ αὐτῶν.

XXVIII. Πάντων οὖν βλεπομένων καὶ ἀκουομένων, φοβηθῶμεν αὐτὸν καὶ ἀπολείπωμεν φαύλων ἔργων μιαρὰς ἐπιθυμίας, ἵνα τῷ ἐλέει αὐτοῦ σκεπασθῶμεν ἀπὸ τῶν μελλόντων κριμάτων. 2. ποῦ γάρ τις ἡμῶν δύναται φυγεῖν ἀπὸ τῆς κραταιᾶς χειρὸς αὐτοῦ; ποῖος δὲ κόσμος δέξεταί τινα τῶν αὐτομολούντων ἀπ' αὐτοῦ; λέγει γάρ που τὸ γραφεῖον·

Ps. cxxxix. 7—10. 3. Ποῦ ἀφήξω καὶ ποῦ κρυβήσομαι ἀπὸ τοῦ προσώπου σου; ἐὰν ἀναβῶ εἰς τὸν οὐρανόν, σὺ εἶ ἐκεῖ· ἐὰν ἀπέλθω εἰς τὰ ἔσχατα τῆς γῆς, ἐκεῖ ἡ δεξιά σου· ἐὰν καταστρώσω εἰς τὰς ἀβύσσους, ἐκεῖ τὸ πνεῦμά σου. 4. ποῖ οὖν τις ἀπέλθῃ ἢ ποῦ ἀποδράσῃ ἀπὸ τοῦ τὰ πάντα ἐμπεριέχοντος;

XXIX. Προσέλθωμεν οὖν αὐτῷ ἐν ὁσιότητι ψυχῆς, ἁγνὰς καὶ ἀμιάντους χεῖρας αἴροντες πρὸς αὐτόν, ἀγαπῶντες τὸν ἐπιεικῆ καὶ εὔσπλαγχνον πατέρα ἡμῶν ὃς ἐκλογῆς μέρος

Deut. xxxii. 8, 9. ἡμᾶς ἐποίησεν ἑαυτῷ. 2. Οὕτω γὰρ γέγραπται· Ὅτε διεμέριζεν ὁ ὕψιστος ἔθνη, ὡς διέσπειρεν υἱοὺς Ἀδάμ, ἔστησεν ὅρια ἐθνῶν κατὰ ἀριθμὸν ἀγγέλων Θεοῦ. ἐγενήθη μερὶς Κυρίου λαὸς αὐτοῦ Ἰακώβ, σχοίνισμα κληρονομίας αὐτοῦ Ἰσραήλ. 3. καὶ ἐν

Deut. iv. 34, xiv. 2. ἑτέρῳ τόπῳ λέγει· Ἰδοὺ Κύριος λαμβάνει ἑαυτῷ ἔθνος ἐκ μέσου

ἐθνῶν, ὥσπερ λαμβάνει ἄνθρωπος τὴν ἀπαρχὴν αὐτοῦ τῆς ἅλω, Numb.
καὶ ἐξελέγεται ἐκ τοῦ ἔθνους ἐκείνου ἅγια ἁγίων. xviii. 27.
2 Chron.

XXX. Ἁγίου οὖν μερὶς ὑπάρχοντες ποιήσωμεν τὰ τοῦ xxxi. 14.
Ezek.
ἁγιασμοῦ πάντα, φεύγοντες καταλαλιάς, μιαράς τε καὶ ἀν- xlviii. 12.
άγνους συμπλοκάς, μέθας τε καὶ νεωτερισμοὺς καὶ βδελυ-
κτὰς ἐπιθυμίας, μυσερὰν μοιχείαν, βδελυκτὴν ὑπερηφανίαν.
2. Θεὸς γάρ, φησίν, ὑπερηφάνοις ἀντιτάσσεται, ταπεινοῖς δὲ Prov. iii.
34.
δίδωσιν χάριν. 3. Κολληθῶμεν οὖν ἐκείνοις οἷς ἡ χάρις ἀπὸ James iv. 6.
τοῦ Θεοῦ δέδοται· ἐνδυσώμεθα τὴν ὁμόνοιαν, ταπεινοφρο- 1 Pet. v. 6.
νοῦντες, ἐγκρατευόμενοι, ἀπὸ παντὸς ψιθυρισμοῦ καὶ καταλαλιᾶς πόρρω ἑαυτοὺς ποιοῦντες, ἔργοις δικαιούμενοι καὶ μὴ
λόγοις. 4. λέγει γάρ· Ὁ τὰ πολλὰ λέγων καὶ ἀντακούσεται· ἢ Job xi. 2,
ὁ εὔλαλος οἴεται εἶναι δίκαιος ; 5. εὐλογημένος γεννητὸς γυναι- 3.
κὸς ὀλιγόβιος. μὴ πολὺς ἐν ῥήμασιν γίνου. 6. Ὁ ἔπαινος
ἡμῶν ἔστω ἐν Θεῷ καὶ μὴ ἐξ αὐτῶν, αὐτεπαινετοὺς γὰρ μισεῖ
ὁ Θεός. 7. ἡ μαρτυρία τῆς ἀγαθῆς πράξεως ἡμῶν διδόσθω
ὑπ᾽ ἄλλων, καθὼς ἐδόθη τοῖς πατράσιν ἡμῶν τοῖς δικαίοις.
8. θράσος καὶ αὐθάδεια καὶ τόλμα τοῖς κατηραμένοις ὑπὸ τοῦ
Θεοῦ· ἐπιείκεια καὶ ταπεινοφροσύνη καὶ πραΰτης παρὰ τοῖς
ηὐλογημένοις ὑπὸ τοῦ Θεοῦ.

XXXI. Κολληθῶμεν οὖν τῇ εὐλογίᾳ αὐτοῦ, καὶ ἴδωμεν
τίνες αἱ ὁδοὶ τῆς εὐλογίας. ἀνατυλίξωμεν τὰ ἀπ᾽ ἀρχῆς
γενόμενα. 2. τίνος χάριν ηὐλογήθη ὁ πατὴρ ἡμῶν Ἀβραάμ;
οὐχὶ δικαιοσύνην καὶ ἀλήθειαν διὰ πίστεως ποιήσας;
3. Ἰσαὰκ μετὰ πεποιθήσεως γινώσκων τὸ μέλλον ἡδέως
προσήγετο θυσία. 4. Ἰακὼβ μετὰ ταπεινοφροσύνης ἐξεχώρη-
σεν τῆς γῆς αὐτοῦ δι᾽ ἀδελφὸν καὶ ἐπορεύθη πρὸς Λαβὰν καὶ
ἐδούλευσεν, καὶ ἐδόθη αὐτῷ τὸ δωδεκάσκηπτρον τοῦ Ἰσραήλ.

XXXII. Ἐάν τις καθ᾽ ἓν ἕκαστον εἰλικρινῶς κατα-
νοήσῃ, ἐπιγνώσεται μεγαλεῖα τῶν ὑπ᾽ αὐτοῦ δεδομένων δωρεῶν. 2. ἐξ αὐτοῦ γὰρ ἱερεῖς καὶ λευῖται πάντες οἱ λειτουργοῦντες τῷ θυσιαστηρίῳ τοῦ Θεοῦ· ἐξ αὐτοῦ ὁ Κύριος
Ἰησοῦς τὸ κατὰ σάρκα· ἐξ αὐτοῦ βασιλεῖς καὶ ἄρχοντες καὶ

xxxii. 1 Ἐάν] conj. Lightfoot; Ὁ ἂν C; quae si S; def. A.

ἡγούμενοι, κατὰ τὸν Ἰούδαν· τὰ δὲ λοιπὰ σκῆπτρα αὐτοῦ
οὐκ ἐν μικρᾷ δόξῃ ὑπάρχουσιν, ὡς ἐπαγγειλαμένου τοῦ Θεοῦ
ὅτι Ἔσται τὸ σπέρμα coγ ὡc oἱ ἀcτέρεc τοῦ oὐρanoῦ. 3. Πάντες οὖν ἐδοξάσθησαν καὶ ἐμεγαλύνθησαν οὐ δι᾽ αὐτῶν ἢ τῶν
ἔργων αὐτῶν ἢ τῆς δικαιοπραγίας ἧς κατειργάσαντο, ἀλλὰ
διὰ τοῦ θελήματος αὐτοῦ. 4. καὶ ἡμεῖς οὖν, διὰ θελήματος
αὐτοῦ ἐν Χριστῷ Ἰησοῦ κληθέντες, οὐ δι᾽ ἑαυτῶν δικαιούμεθα
οὐδὲ διὰ τῆς ἡμετέρας σοφίας ἢ συνέσεως ἢ εὐσεβείας ἢ
ἔργων ὧν κατειργασάμεθα ἐν ὁσιότητι καρδίας, ἀλλὰ διὰ τῆς
πίστεως, δι᾽ ἧς πάντας τοὺς ἀπ᾽ αἰῶνος ὁ παντοκράτωρ Θεὸς
ἐδικαίωσεν· ᾧ ἔστω ἡ δόξα εἰς τοὺς αἰῶνας τῶν αἰώνων. ἀμήν.

XXXIII. Τί οὖν ποιήσωμεν, ἀδελφοί; ἀργήσωμεν ἀπὸ
τῆς ἀγαθοποιΐας καὶ ἐγκαταλείπωμεν τὴν ἀγάπην; μηθαμῶς
τοῦτο ἐάσαι ὁ δεσπότης ἐφ᾽ ἡμῖν γε γενηθῆναι, ἀλλὰ σπεύ-
σωμεν μετὰ ἐκτενείας καὶ προθυμίας πᾶν ἔργον ἀγαθὸν
ἐπιτελεῖν. 2. αὐτὸς γὰρ ὁ δημιουργὸς καὶ δεσπότης τῶν
ἁπάντων ἐπὶ τοῖς ἔργοις αὐτοῦ ἀγαλλιᾶται. 3. τῷ γὰρ
παμμεγεθεστάτῳ αὐτοῦ κράτει οὐρανοὺς ἐστήρισεν καὶ τῇ
ἀκαταλήπτῳ αὐτοῦ συνέσει διεκόσμησεν αὐτούς· γῆν τε
διεχώρισεν ἀπὸ τοῦ περιέχοντος αὐτὴν ὕδατος καὶ ἥδρασεν
ἐπὶ τὸν ἀσφαλῆ τοῦ ἰδίου βουλήματος θεμέλιον· τά τε ἐν
αὐτῇ ζῷα φοιτῶντα τῇ ἑαυτοῦ διατάξει ἐκέλευσεν εἶναι· θάλασσαν καὶ τὰ ἐν αὐτῇ ζῷα προδημιουργήσας ἐνέκλεισεν τῇ
ἑαυτοῦ δυνάμει. 4. ἐπὶ πᾶσι τὸ ἐξοχώτατον καὶ παμμέγεθες
κατὰ διάνοιαν, ἄνθρωπον ταῖς ἱεραῖς καὶ ἀμώμοις χερσὶν
ἔπλασεν τῆς ἑαυτοῦ εἰκόνος χαρακτῆρα. 5. οὕτως γάρ φησιν
ὁ Θεός· Ποιήcωμεν ἄνθρωπον κατ᾽ εἰκόνα καὶ καθ᾽ ὁμοίωcιν
ἡμετέραν. καὶ ἐποίηcεν ὁ Θεὸc τὸν ἄνθρωπον, ἄρcεν καὶ θῆλγ
ἐποίηcεν αὐτούc. 6. Ταῦτα οὖν πάντα τελειώσας ἐπήνεσεν
αὐτὰ καὶ ηὐλόγησεν καὶ εἶπεν· Αὐξάνεcθε καὶ πληθγνεcθε.
7. Εἴδομεν ὅτι ἐν ἔργοις ἀγαθοῖς πάντες ἐκοσμήθησαν οἱ
δίκαιοι· καὶ αὐτὸς οὖν ὁ Κύριος ἔργοις ἑαυτὸν κοσμήσας
ἐχάρη. 8. ἔχοντες οὖν τοῦτον τὸν ὑπογραμμὸν ἀόκνως προσ-

Gen. xv. 5,
xxii. 17.
Gen. i. 26, 27.
Gen. i. 28.

xxxiii. 7 Εἴδομεν] conj. Young; ἴδωμεν ACS.

ἔλθωμεν τῷ θελήματι αὐτοῦ, ἐξ ὅλης ἰσχύος ἡμῶν ἐργα-
σώμεθα ἔργον δικαιοσύνης.

XXXIV. Ὁ ἀγαθὸς ἐργάτης μετὰ παρρησίας λαμβάνει
τὸν ἄρτον τοῦ ἔργου αὐτοῦ, ὁ νωθρὸς καὶ παρειμένος οὐκ
ἀντοφθαλμεῖ τῷ ἐργοπαρέκτῃ αὐτοῦ. 2. δέον οὖν ἐστιν προ-
θύμους ἡμᾶς εἶναι εἰς ἀγαθοποιΐαν· ἐξ αὐτοῦ γάρ ἐστιν τὰ
πάντα. 3. προλέγει γὰρ ἡμῖν· Ἰδοὺ ὁ Κύριος, καὶ ὁ μισθὸς
αὐτοῦ πρὸ προσώπου αὐτοῦ, ἀποδοῦναι ἑκάστῳ κατὰ τὸ ἔργον
αὐτοῦ. 4. Προτρέπεται οὖν ἡμᾶς πιστεύοντας ἐξ ὅλης τῆς
καρδίας ἐπ᾽ αὐτῷ μὴ ἀργοὺς μηδὲ παρειμένους εἶναι ἐπὶ πᾶν
ἔργον ἀγαθόν· 5. τὸ καύχημα ἡμῶν καὶ ἡ παρρησία ἔστω
ἐν αὐτῷ· ὑποτασσώμεθα τῷ θελήματι αὐτοῦ· κατανοήσωμεν
τὸ πᾶν πλῆθος τῶν ἀγγέλων αὐτοῦ, πῶς τῷ θελήματι αὐτοῦ
λειτουργοῦσιν παρεστῶτες· 6. λέγει γὰρ ἡ γραφή· Μύριαι
μυριάδες παρειστήκεισαν αὐτῷ, καὶ χίλιαι χιλιάδες ἐλειτούργουν
αὐτῷ· καὶ ἐκέκραγον· Ἅγιος, ἅγιος, ἅγιος Κύριος Σαβαώθ, πλήρης
πᾶσα ἡ κτίσις τῆς δόξης αὐτοῦ. 7. Καὶ ἡμεῖς οὖν, ἐν ὁμονοίᾳ
ἐπὶ τὸ αὐτὸ συναχθέντες τῇ συνειδήσει, ὡς ἐξ ἑνὸς στόματος
βοήσωμεν πρὸς αὐτὸν ἐκτενῶς εἰς τὸ μετόχους ἡμᾶς γενέσθαι
τῶν μεγάλων καὶ ἐνδόξων ἐπαγγελιῶν αὐτοῦ. 8. λέγει γάρ·
Ὀφθαλμὸς οὐκ εἶδεν καὶ οὖς οὐκ ἤκουσεν, καὶ ἐπὶ καρδίαν ἀνθρώπου οὐκ ἀνέβη, ὅσα ἡτοίμασεν τοῖς ὑπομένουσιν αὐτόν.

XXXV. Ὡς μακάρια καὶ θαυμαστὰ τὰ δῶρα τοῦ Θεοῦ,
ἀγαπητοί. 2. ζωὴ ἐν ἀθανασίᾳ, λαμπρότης ἐν δικαιοσύνῃ,
ἀλήθεια ἐν παρρησίᾳ, πίστις ἐν πεποιθήσει, ἐγκράτεια ἐν
ἁγιασμῷ· καὶ ταῦτα ὑπέπιπτεν πάντα ὑπὸ τὴν διάνοιαν
ἡμῶν. 3. τίνα οὖν ἄρα ἐστὶν τὰ ἑτοιμαζόμενα τοῖς ὑπομένουσιν; ὁ δημιουργὸς καὶ πατὴρ τῶν αἰώνων ὁ πανάγιος
αὐτὸς γινώσκει τὴν ποσότητα καὶ τὴν καλλονὴν αὐτῶν.
4. ἡμεῖς οὖν ἀγωνισώμεθα εὑρεθῆναι ἐν τῷ ἀριθμῷ τῶν
ὑπομενόντων αὐτόν, ὅπως μεταλάβωμεν τῶν ἐπηγγελμένων
δωρεῶν. 5. πῶς δὲ ἔσται τοῦτο, ἀγαπητοί; ἐὰν ἐστηριγμένη
ᾖ ἡ διάνοια ἡμῶν διὰ πίστεως πρὸς τὸν Θεόν· ἐὰν ἐκζητῶμεν
τὰ εὐάρεστα καὶ εὐπρόσδεκτα αὐτῷ· ἐὰν ἐπιτελέσωμεν τὰ ἀνή-

Is. xl. 10,
lxii. 11.
Rev. xxii.
12.

Dan. vii.
10.
Is. vi. 3

Is. lxiv. 4,
lxv. 16, 17.
1 Cor. ii. 9.

κοντα τῇ ἀμώμῳ βουλήσει αὐτοῦ καὶ ἀκολουθήσωμεν τῇ ὁδῷ
τῆς ἀληθείας, ἀπορρίψαντες ἀφ᾽ ἑαυτῶν πᾶσαν ἀδικίαν καὶ
ἀνομίαν, πλεονεξίαν, ἔρεις, κακοηθείας τε καὶ δόλους, ψιθυ-
ρισμούς τε καὶ καταλαλιάς, θεοστυγίαν, ὑπερηφανίαν τε καὶ
ἀλαζονείαν, κενοδοξίαν τε καὶ ἀφιλοξενίαν. 6. ταῦτα γὰρ
οἱ πράσσοντες στυγητοὶ τῷ Θεῷ ὑπάρχουσιν· οὐ μόνον δὲ
οἱ πράσσοντες αὐτά, ἀλλὰ καὶ οἱ συνευδοκοῦντες αὐτοῖς.
7. λέγει γὰρ ἡ γραφή· Τῷ ΔΕ ἁΜΑΡΤωλῷ ΕἶπεΝ ὁ Θεόс· Ἵνα τί
сὺ ΔΙΗΓῇ τὰ ΔΙΚΑΙώΜΑΤά ΜΟΥ ΚΑὶ ἀΝΑλΑΜΒάΝΕΙС ΤὴΝ ΔΙΑΘήΚΗΝ ΜΟΥ
ἐπὶ СΤόΜΑΤός СΟΥ; 8. Сὺ Δὲ ἐΜίСΗСΑС ΠΑΙΔΕίΑΝ, ΚΑὶ ἐξέΒΑλλΕС
ΤΟὺС λόΓΟΥС ΜΟΥ Εἰς Τὰ ὀΠίСω. Εἰ ἐΘΕώΡΕΙС ΚλέπτΗΝ, СΥΝέΤΡΕΧΕС
ΑΥ̓Τῷ, ΚΑὶ ΜΕΤὰ ΜΟΙΧῶΝ ΤὴΝ ΜΕΡίΔΑ СΟΥ ἐΤίΘΕΙС· Τὸ СΤόΜΑ СΟΥ
ἐΚΠλΕόΝΑСΕΝ ΚΑΚίΑΝ, ΚΑὶ ἡ ΓλῶССά СΟΥ ΠΕΡΙέΠλΕΚΕΝ ΔΟλΙόΤΗΤΑ·
ΚΑΘήΜΕΝΟС ΚΑΤὰ ΤΟὗ ἀΔΕλφΟὗ СΟΥ ΚΑΤΕλάλΕΙС, ΚΑὶ ΚΑΤὰ ΤΟὗ ΥἱΟὗ
Τῆς ΜΗΤΡός СΟΥ ἐΤίΘΕΙС СΚάΝΔΑλΟΝ· 9. ΤΑῦΤΑ ἐΠΟίΗСΑС ΚΑὶ ἐСί-
ΓΗСΑ· ὑΠέλΑΒΕС, ἄΝΟΜΕ, ὅΤΙ ἔСΟΜΑί СΟΙ ὅΜΟΙΟС· 10. ἐλέΓξω СΕ ΚΑὶ
ΠΑΡΑСΤήСω СΕ ΚΑΤὰ ΠΡόСωΠόΝ СΟΥ. 11. С́ΥΝΕΤΕ Δὴ ΤΑῦΤΑ, Οἱ
ἐΠΙλΑΝΘΑΝόΜΕΝΟΙ ΤΟῦ Θεοῦ, ΜήΠΟΤΕ ἁΡΠάСῌ ὡс λέωΝ, ΚΑὶ Μὴ ᾖ ὁ
ῥΥόΜΕΝΟС. 12. ΘΥСίΑ ΑἰΝέСΕωС ΔΟξάСΕΙ ΜΕ, ΚΑὶ ἐΚΕῖ ὁΔός ἧ
ΔΕίξω ΑΥ̓Τῷ Τὸ СωΤήΡΙΟΝ ΤΟῦ Θεοῦ.

XXXVI. Αὕτη ἡ ὁδός, ἀγαπητοί, ἐν ᾗ εὕρομεν τὸ σωτή-
ριον ἡμῶν Ἰησοῦν Χριστὸν τὸν ἀρχιερέα τῶν προσφορῶν
ἡμῶν, τὸν προστάτην καὶ βοηθὸν τῆς ἀσθενείας ἡμῶν.
2. διὰ τούτου ἀτενίσωμεν εἰς τὰ ὕψη τῶν οὐρανῶν· διὰ
τούτου ἐνοπτριζόμεθα τὴν ἄμωμον καὶ ὑπερτάτην ὄψιν
αὐτοῦ· διὰ τούτου ἠνεῴχθησαν ἡμῶν οἱ ὀφθαλμοὶ τῆς
καρδίας· διὰ τούτου ἡ ἀσύνετος καὶ ἐσκοτωμένη διάνοια
ἡμῶν ἀναθάλλει εἰς τὸ φῶς· διὰ τούτου ἠθέλησεν ὁ δεσπότης τῆς ἀθανάτου γνώσεως ἡμᾶς γεύσασθαι· ὃс ὢΝ ἀπΑύ-
ΓΑСΜΑ Τῆс ΜΕΓΑλωСύΝΗс ΑΥ̓ΤΟῦ ΤΟСΟύΤῳ ΜΕίΖωΝ ἐСΤὶΝ ἀΓΓέλωΝ,
ὅСῳ ΔΙΑφΟΡώΤΕΡΟΝ ὄΝΟΜΑ ΚΕΚλΗΡΟΝόΜΗΚΕΝ. 3. ΓέΓΡΑΠΤΑΙ ΓὰΡ
Οὕτωс· Ὁ ΠΟΙῶΝ ΤΟὺс ἀΓΓέλΟΥс ΑΥ̓ΤΟῦ ΠΝΕύΜΑΤΑ ΚΑὶ ΤΟὺс λΕΙ-
ΤΟΥΡΓΟὺс ΑΥ̓ΤΟῦ ΠΥΡὸс φλόΓΑ. 4. Ἐπὶ Δὲ Τῷ Υἱῷ ΑΥ̓ΤΟῦ Οὕτωс
ΕἶπΕΝ ὁ ΔΕСΠόΤΗС· ΥἹός ΜΟΥ Εἶ Сύ, ἐΓὼ СήΜΕΡΟΝ ΓΕΓέΝΝΗΚά СΕ·

Ps. 1. 16—
23.
Heb. i. 3, 4.
Ps. civ. 4.
Heb. i. 7.
Ps. ii. 7, 8.
Heb. i. 5.

αἴτηϲαι παρ' ἐμοῦ, καὶ Δώϲω ϲοι ἔθνη τὴν κληρονομίαν ϲογ, καὶ
τὴν κατάϲχεϲίν ϲογ τὰ πέρατα τῆϲ γῆϲ. 5. καὶ πάλιν λέγει
πρὸς αὐτόν· Κάθου ἐκ Δεξιῶν μογ, ἕωϲ ἂν θῶ τοὺϲ ἐχθρούϲ ϲογ Ps. cx. I.
ὑποπόΔιον τῶν ποΔῶν ϲογ. 6. Τίνες οὖν οἱ ἐχθροί; οἱ φαῦλοι
καὶ ἀντιτασσόμενοι τῷ θελήματι αὐτοῦ. Heb. i. 13.

XXXVII. Στρατευσώμεθα οὖν, ἄνδρες ἀδελφοί, μετὰ
πάσης ἐκτενείας ἐν τοῖς ἀμώμοις προστάγμασιν αὐτοῦ·
2. κατανοήσωμεν τοὺς στρατευομένους τοῖς ἡγουμένοις ἡμῶν,
πῶς εὐτάκτως, πῶς εἰκτικῶς, πῶς ὑποτεταγμένως ἐπιτελοῦσιν
τὰ διατασσόμενα. 3. οὐ πάντες εἰσὶν ἔπαρχοι οὐδὲ χιλίαρχοι
οὐδὲ ἑκατόνταρχοι οὐδὲ πεντηκόνταρχοι οὐδὲ τὸ καθεξῆς·
ἀλλ' ἕκαστος ἐν τῷ ἰδίῳ τάγματι τὰ ἐπιτασσόμενα ὑπὸ τοῦ
βασιλέως καὶ τῶν ἡγουμένων ἐπιτελεῖ. 4. οἱ μεγάλοι δίχα τῶν
μικρῶν οὐ δύνανται εἶναι, οὔτε οἱ μικροὶ δίχα τῶν μεγάλων·
σύγκρασίς τίς ἐστιν ἐν πᾶσιν, καὶ ἐν τούτοις χρῆσις. 5. Λάβωμεν τὸ σῶμα ἡμῶν· ἡ κεφαλὴ δίχα τῶν ποδῶν οὐδέν ἐστιν,
οὕτως οὐδὲ οἱ πόδες δίχα τῆς κεφαλῆς· τὰ δὲ ἐλάχιστα μέλη
τοῦ σώματος ἡμῶν ἀναγκαῖα καὶ εὔχρηστά εἰσιν ὅλῳ τῷ
σώματι· ἀλλὰ πάντα συνπνεῖ καὶ ὑποταγῇ μιᾷ χρῆται εἰς τὸ
σώζεσθαι ὅλον τὸ σῶμα.

XXXVIII. Σωζέσθω οὖν ἡμῶν ὅλον τὸ σῶμα ἐν Χριστῷ
Ἰησοῦ, καὶ ὑποτασσέσθω ἕκαστος τῷ πλησίον αὐτοῦ, καθὼς
καὶ ἐτέθη ἐν τῷ χαρίσματι αὐτοῦ. 2. ὁ ἰσχυρὸς μὴ ἀτημε-
λείτω τὸν ἀσθενή, ὁ δὲ ἀσθενὴς ἐντρεπέσθω τὸν ἰσχυρόν· ὁ
πλούσιος ἐπιχορηγείτω τῷ πτωχῷ, ὁ δὲ πτωχὸς εὐχαριστείτω
τῷ Θεῷ, ὅτι ἔδωκεν αὐτῷ δι' οὗ ἀναπληρωθῇ αὐτοῦ τὸ ὑστέ-
ρημα. ὁ σοφὸς ἐνδεικνύσθω τὴν σοφίαν αὐτοῦ μὴ ἐν λόγοις
ἀλλ' ἐν ἔργοις ἀγαθοῖς· ὁ ταπεινοφρονῶν μὴ ἑαυτῷ μαρτυρείτω,
ἀλλ' ἐάτω ὑφ' ἑτέρου ἑαυτὸν μαρτυρεῖσθαι· ὁ ἁγνὸς ἐν τῇ
σαρκὶ ἤτω καὶ μὴ ἀλαζονευέσθω, γινώσκων ὅτι ἕτερός ἐστιν
ὁ ἐπιχορηγῶν αὐτῷ τὴν ἐγκράτειαν. 3. Ἀναλογισώμεθα
οὖν, ἀδελφοί, ἐκ ποίας ὕλης ἐγενήθημεν, ποῖοι καὶ τίνες εἰσήλ-

xxxviii. 2 μὴ ἀτημελείτω] conj. Lightfoot; μητμμελειτω (sic) A; τημελειτω
(om. μὴ) CS. ἤτω] insert Laurent.

θαμεν εἰς τὸν κόσμον· ἐκ ποίου τάφου καὶ σκότους ὁ πλάσας ἡμᾶς καὶ δημιουργήσας εἰσήγαγεν εἰς τὸν κόσμον αὐτοῦ, προετοιμάσας τὰς εὐεργεσίας αὐτοῦ πρὶν ἡμᾶς γεννηθῆναι. 4. ταῦτα οὖν πάντα ἐξ αὐτοῦ ἔχοντες ὀφείλομεν κατὰ πάντα εὐχαριστεῖν αὐτῷ· ᾧ ἡ δόξα εἰς τοὺς αἰῶνας τῶν αἰώνων. ἀμήν. XXXIX. Ἄφρονες καὶ ἀσύνετοι καὶ μωροὶ καὶ ἀπαίδευτοι χλευάζουσιν ἡμᾶς καὶ μυκτηρίζουσιν, ἑαυτοὺς βουλόμενοι ἐπαίρεσθαι ταῖς διανοίαις αὐτῶν. 2. τί γὰρ δύναται

Job iv. 16
—18, xv.
15, iv. 19
—v. 5.
θνητός; ἢ τίς ἰσχὺς γηγενοῦς; 3. γέγραπται γάρ· Οὐκ ἦν μορφὴ πρὸ ὀφθαλμῶν μου, ἀλλ᾽ ἢ αὔραν καὶ φωνὴν ἤκουον· 4. τί γάρ; μὴ καθαρὸς ἔσται βροτὸς ἔναντι Κυρίου; ἢ ἀπὸ τῶν ἔργων αὐτοῦ ἄμεμπτος ἀνήρ; εἰ κατὰ παίδων αὐτοῦ οὐ πιστεύει, κατὰ δὲ ἀγγέλων αὐτοῦ σκολιόν τι ἐπενόησεν· 5. οὐρανὸς δὲ οὐ καθαρὸς ἐνώπιον αὐτοῦ· ἔα δέ, οἱ κατοικοῦντες οἰκίας πηλίνας, ἐξ ὧν καὶ αὐτοὶ ἐκ τοῦ αὐτοῦ πηλοῦ ἐσμέν. ἔπαισεν αὐτοὺς σητὸς τρόπον, καὶ ἀπὸ πρωΐθεν ἕως ἑσπέρας οὐκ ἔτι εἰσίν· παρὰ τὸ μὴ δύνασθαι αὐτοὺς ἑαυτοῖς βοηθῆσαι ἀπώλοντο· 6. ἐνεφύσησεν αὐτοῖς καὶ ἐτελεύτησαν, παρὰ τὸ μὴ ἔχειν αὐτοὺς σοφίαν. 7. ἐπικάλεσαι δέ, εἴ τίς σοι ὑπακούσεται, ἢ εἴ τινα ἁγίων ἀγγέλων ὄψῃ· καὶ γὰρ ἄφρονα ἀναιρεῖ ὀργή, πεπλανημένον δὲ θανατοῖ ζῆλος. 8. ἐγὼ δὲ ἑώρακα ἄφρονας ῥίζας βαλόντας, ἀλλ᾽ εὐθέως ἐβρώθη αὐτῶν ἡ δίαιτα. 9. πόρρω γένοιντο οἱ υἱοὶ αὐτῶν ἀπὸ σωτηρίας· κολαβρισθείησαν ἐπὶ θύραις ἡσσόνων, καὶ οὐκ ἔσται ὁ ἐξαιρούμενος· ἃ γὰρ ἐκείνοις ἡτοίμασται, δίκαιοι ἔδονται· αὐτοὶ δὲ ἐκ κακῶν οὐκ ἐξαίρετοι ἔσονται.

XL. Προδήλων οὖν ἡμῖν ὄντων τούτων, καὶ ἐγκεκυφότες εἰς τὰ βάθη τῆς θείας γνώσεως, πάντα τάξει ποιεῖν ὀφείλομεν ὅσα ὁ δεσπότης ἐπιτελεῖν ἐκέλευσεν κατὰ καιροὺς τεταγμένους· 2. τάς τε προσφορὰς καὶ λειτουργίας ἐπιμελῶς ἐπιτελεῖσθαι καὶ οὐκ εἰκῆ ἢ ἀτάκτως ἐκέλευσεν γίνεσθαι, ἀλλ᾽ ὡρισμένοις καιροῖς καὶ ὥραις· 3. ποῦ τε καὶ διὰ τίνων ἐπιτελεῖσθαι θέλει, αὐτὸς ὥρισεν τῇ ὑπερτάτῳ αὐτοῦ βουλήσει· ἵν᾽ ὁσίως πάντα γινόμενα ἐν εὐδοκήσει εὐπρόσδεκτα

xl. 2 ἐπιμελῶς] insert Lightfoot.

εἴη τῷ θελήματι αὐτοῦ. 4. Οἱ οὖν τοῖς προστεταγμένοις καιροῖς ποιοῦντες τὰς προσφορὰς αὐτῶν εὐπρόσδεκτοί τε καὶ μακάριοι, τοῖς γὰρ νομίμοις τοῦ δεσπότου ἀκολουθοῦντες οὐ διαμαρτάνουσιν. 5. τῷ γὰρ ἀρχιερεῖ ἴδιαι λειτουργίαι δεδομέναι εἰσίν, καὶ τοῖς ἱερεῦσιν ἴδιος ὁ τόπος προστέτακται, καὶ λευΐταις ἴδιαι διακονίαι ἐπίκεινται· ὁ λαϊκὸς ἄνθρωπος τοῖς λαϊκοῖς προστάγμασιν δέδεται.

XLI. Ἕκαστος ὑμῶν, ἀδελφοί, ἐν τῷ ἰδίῳ τάγματι εὐχαριστείτω Θεῷ ἐν ἀγαθῇ συνειδήσει ὑπάρχων, μὴ παρεκβαίνων τὸν ὡρισμένον τῆς λειτουργίας αὐτοῦ κανόνα, ἐν σεμνότητι. 2. Οὐ πανταχοῦ, ἀδελφοί, προσφέρονται θυσίαι ἐνδελεχισμοῦ ἢ εὐχῶν ἢ περὶ ἁμαρτίας καὶ πλημμελείας, ἀλλ᾽ ἢ ἐν Ἱερουσαλὴμ μόνῃ· κἀκεῖ δὲ οὐκ ἐν παντὶ τόπῳ προσφέρεται, ἀλλ᾽ ἔμπροσθεν τοῦ ναοῦ πρὸς τὸ θυσιαστήριον, μωμοσκοπηθὲν τὸ προσφερόμενον διὰ τοῦ ἀρχιερέως καὶ τῶν προειρημένων λειτουργῶν. 3. οἱ οὖν παρὰ τὸ καθῆκον τῆς βουλήσεως αὐτοῦ ποιοῦντές τι θάνατον τὸ πρόστιμον ἔχουσιν. 4. Ὁρᾶτε, ἀδελφοί, ὅσῳ πλείονος κατηξιώθημεν γνώσεως, τοσούτῳ μᾶλλον ὑποκείμεθα κινδύνῳ.

XLII. Οἱ ἀπόστολοι ἡμῖν εὐηγγελίσθησαν ἀπὸ τοῦ Κυρίου Ἰησοῦ Χριστοῦ, Ἰησοῦς ὁ Χριστὸς ἀπὸ τοῦ Θεοῦ ἐξεπέμφθη. 2. ὁ Χριστὸς οὖν ἀπὸ τοῦ Θεοῦ, καὶ οἱ ἀπόστολοι ἀπὸ τοῦ Χριστοῦ· ἐγένοντο οὖν ἀμφότερα εὐτάκτως ἐκ θελήματος Θεοῦ. 3. παραγγελίας οὖν λαβόντες καὶ πληροφορηθέντες διὰ τῆς ἀναστάσεως τοῦ Κυρίου ἡμῶν Ἰησοῦ Χριστοῦ καὶ πιστωθέντες ἐν τῷ λόγῳ τοῦ Θεοῦ μετὰ πληροφορίας πνεύματος ἁγίου ἐξῆλθον, εὐαγγελιζόμενοι τὴν βασιλείαν τοῦ Θεοῦ μέλλειν ἔρχεσθαι. 4. κατὰ χώρας οὖν καὶ πόλεις κηρύσσοντες καθίστανον τὰς ἀπαρχὰς αὐτῶν, δοκιμάσαντες τῷ πνεύματι, εἰς ἐπισκόπους καὶ διακόνους τῶν μελλόντων πιστεύειν. 5. καὶ τοῦτο οὐ καινῶς, ἐκ γὰρ δὴ πολλῶν χρόνων ἐγέγραπτο περὶ ἐπισκόπων καὶ διακόνων· οὕτως γάρ που λέγει ἡ γραφή· Καταστήϲω τοὺϲ ἐπιϲκόπουϲ αὐτῶν ἐν Is. lx. 17. δικαιοϲύνῃ καὶ τοὺϲ διακόνουϲ αὐτῶν ἐν πίϲτει.

XLIII. Καὶ τί θαυμαστὸν εἰ οἱ ἐν Χριστῷ πιστευθέντες παρὰ Θεοῦ ἔργον τοιοῦτο κατέστησαν τοὺς προειρημένους; ὅπου καὶ ὁ μακάριος πιστὸc θεράπων ἐν ὅλῳ τῷ οἴκῳ Μωϋσῆς τὰ διατεταγμένα αὐτῷ πάντα ἐσημειώσατο ἐν ταῖς ἱεραῖς βίβλοις, ᾧ καὶ ἐπηκολούθησαν οἱ λοιποὶ προφῆται συνεπιμαρτυροῦντες τοῖς ὑπ' αὐτοῦ νενομοθετημένοις. 2. ἐκεῖνος γάρ, ζήλου ἐμπεσόντος περὶ τῆς ἱερωσύνης καὶ στασιαζουσῶν τῶν φυλῶν ὁποία αὐτῶν εἴη τῷ ἐνδόξῳ ὀνόματι κεκοσμημένη, ἐκέλευσεν τοὺς δώδεκα φυλάρχους προσενεγκεῖν αὐτῷ ῥάβδους ἐπιγεγραμμένας ἑκάστης φυλῆς κατ' ὄνομα· καὶ λαβὼν αὐτὰς ἔδησεν καὶ ἐσφράγισεν τοῖς δακτυλίοις τῶν φυλάρχων, καὶ ἀπέθετο αὐτὰς εἰς τὴν σκηνὴν τοῦ μαρτυρίου ἐπὶ τὴν τράπεζαν τοῦ Θεοῦ· 3. καὶ κλείσας τὴν σκηνὴν ἐσφράγισεν τὰς κλεῖδας ὡσαύτως καὶ τὰς θύρας· 4. καὶ εἶπεν αὐτοῖς· Ἄνδρες ἀδελφοί, ἧς ἂν φυλῆς ἡ ῥάβδος βλαστήσῃ, ταύτην ἐκλέλεκται ὁ Θεὸς εἰς τὸ ἱερατεύειν καὶ λειτουργεῖν αὐτῷ. 5. πρωΐας δὲ γενομένης συνεκάλεσεν πάντα τὸν Ἰσραήλ, τὰς ἑξακοσίας χιλιάδας τῶν ἀνδρῶν, καὶ ἐπεδείξατο τοῖς φυλάρχοις τὰς σφραγῖδας καὶ ἤνοιξεν τὴν σκηνὴν τοῦ μαρτυρίου καὶ προεῖλεν τὰς ῥάβδους· καὶ εὑρέθη ἡ ῥάβδος Ἀαρὼν οὐ μόνον βεβλαστηκυῖα ἀλλὰ καὶ καρπὸν ἔχουσα. 6. τί δοκεῖτε, ἀγαπητοί; οὐ προῄδει Μωϋσῆς τοῦτο μέλλειν ἔσεσθαι; μάλιστα ᾔδει· ἀλλ' ἵνα μὴ ἀκαταστασία γένηται ἐν τῷ Ἰσραήλ, οὕτως ἐποίησεν εἰς τὸ δοξασθῆναι τὸ ὄνομα τοῦ ἀληθινοῦ καὶ μόνου Κυρίου· ᾧ ἡ δόξα εἰς τοὺς αἰῶνας τῶν αἰώνων. ἀμήν.

XLIV. Καὶ οἱ ἀπόστολοι ἡμῶν ἔγνωσαν διὰ τοῦ Κυρίου ἡμῶν Ἰησοῦ Χριστοῦ ὅτι ἔρις ἔσται ἐπὶ τοῦ ὀνόματος τῆς ἐπισκοπῆς. 2. Διὰ ταύτην οὖν τὴν αἰτίαν πρόγνωσιν εἰληφότες τελείαν κατέστησαν τοὺς προειρημένους, καὶ μεταξὺ ἐπιμονὴν δεδώκασιν ὅπως, ἐὰν κοιμηθῶσιν, διαδέξωνται ἕτεροι δεδοκιμασμένοι ἄνδρες τὴν λειτουργίαν αὐτῶν. 3. Τοὺς

Numb. xii.
7.
Heb. iii. 5.

xliv. 2 ἐπιμονὴν] conj. Turner; ἐπινομὴν A; ἐπιδομὴν C; *super probatione* (ἐπὶ δοκιμῇ) S.

οὖν κατασταθέντας ὑπ' ἐκείνων ἢ μεταξὺ ὑφ' ἑτέρων ἐλλο-
γίμων ἀνδρῶν, συνευδοκησάσης τῆς ἐκκλησίας πάσης, καὶ
λειτουργήσαντας ἀμέμπτως τῷ ποιμνίῳ τοῦ Χριστοῦ μετὰ
ταπεινοφροσύνης ἡσύχως καὶ ἀβαναύσως, μεμαρτυρημένους
τε πολλοῖς χρόνοις ὑπὸ πάντων, τούτους οὐ δικαίως νομίζομεν ἀποβάλλεσθαι τῆς λειτουργίας. 4. ἁμαρτία γὰρ οὐ
μικρὰ ἡμῖν ἔσται, ἐὰν τοὺς ἀμέμπτως καὶ ὁσίως προσενεγκόν-
τας τὰ δῶρα τῆς ἐπισκοπῆς ἀποβάλωμεν. 5. μακάριοι οἱ
προοδοιπορήσαντες πρεσβύτεροι, οἵτινες ἔγκαρπον καὶ τελείαν ἔσχον τὴν ἀνάλυσιν· οὐ γὰρ εὐλαβοῦνται μή τις αὐτοὺς
μεταστήσῃ ἀπὸ τοῦ ἱδρυμένου αὐτοῖς τόπου. 6. ὁρῶμεν γὰρ
ὅτι ἐνίους ὑμεῖς μετηγάγετε καλῶς πολιτευομένους ἐκ τῆς
ἀμέμπτως αὐτοῖς †τετιμημένης† λειτουργίας.

XLV. Φιλόνεικοί ἐστε, ἀδελφοί, καὶ ζηλωταὶ περὶ τῶν
ἀνηκόντων εἰς σωτηρίαν. 2. ἐγκεκύφατε εἰς τὰς γραφάς, τὰς
ἀληθεῖς, τὰς[διὰ]τοῦ πνεύματος τοῦ ἁγίου· 3. ἐπίστασθε ὅτι
οὐδὲν ἄδικον οὐδὲ παραπεποιημένον γέγραπται ἐν αὐταῖς.
οὐχ εὑρήσετε δικαίους ἀποβεβλημένους ἀπὸ ὁσίων ἀνδρῶν.
4. ἐδιώχθησαν δίκαιοι, ἀλλ' ὑπὸ ἀνόμων· ἐφυλακίσθησαν,
ἀλλ' ὑπὸ ἀνοσίων· ἐλιθάσθησαν ὑπὸ παρανόμων· ἀπεκτάν-
θησαν ὑπὸ τῶν μιαρὸν καὶ ἄδικον ζῆλον ἀνειληφότων.
5. ταῦτα πάσχοντες εὐκλεῶς ἤνεγκαν. 6. Τί γὰρ εἴπωμεν,
ἀδελφοί; Δανιὴλ ὑπὸ τῶν φοβουμένων τὸν Θεὸν ἐβλήθη εἰς
λάκκον λεόντων; 7. ἢ Ἀνανίας καὶ Ἀζαρίας καὶ Μισαὴλ
ὑπὸ τῶν θρησκευόντων τὴν μεγαλοπρεπῆ καὶ ἔνδοξον θρησκείαν τοῦ ὑψίστου κατείρχθησαν εἰς κάμινον πυρός; μηθαμῶς τοῦτο γένοιτο. Τίνες οὖν οἱ ταῦτα δράσαντες; οἱ
στυγητοὶ καὶ πάσης κακίας πλήρεις εἰς τοσοῦτο ἐξήρισαν
θυμοῦ ὥστε τοὺς ἐν ὁσίᾳ καὶ ἀμώμῳ προθέσει δουλεύοντας
τῷ Θεῷ εἰς αἰκίαν†περιβαλεῖν†,μὴ εἰδότες ὅτι ὁ ὕψιστος
ὑπέρμαχος καὶ ὑπερασπιστής ἐστιν τῶν ἐν καθαρᾷ συνειδήσει
λατρευόντων τῷ παναρέτῳ ὀνόματι αὐτοῦ· ᾧ ἡ δόξα εἰς τοὺς
αἰῶνας τῶν αἰώνων. ἀμήν. 8. οἱ δὲ ὑπομένοντες ἐν πεποι-

θήσει δόξαν καὶ τιμὴν ἐκληρονόμησαν, ἐπήρθησάν τε καὶ
ἔγγραφοι ἐγένοντο ἀπὸ τοῦ Θεοῦ ἐν τῷ μνημοσύνῳ αὐτῶν
εἰς τοὺς αἰῶνας τῶν αἰώνων. ἀμήν. XLVI. Τοιούτοις οὖν ὑποδείγμασιν κολληθῆναι καὶ
ἡμᾶς δεῖ, ἀδελφοί. 2. γέγραπται γάρ· Κολλᾶсθε τοῖс ἁΓίοιс,
ὅτι οἱ κολλώμενοι αὐτοῖс ἁΓιαсθήсονται. 3. καὶ πάλιν ἐν ἑτέρῳ

Ps. xviii.
26, 27. τόπῳ λέγει· Μετὰ ἀνΔρὸс ἀθῴοΥ ἀθῷοс ἔсΗ καὶ μετὰ ἐκλεκτοῦ
ἐκλεκτὸс ἔсΗ καὶ μετὰ сτρεΒλοῦ Διαсτρέψειс. 4. κολληθῶμεν
οὖν τοῖς ἀθῴοις καὶ δικαίοις· εἰσὶν δὲ οὗτοι ἐκλεκτοὶ τοῦ
Θεοῦ. 5. Ἵνα τί ἔρεις καὶ θυμοὶ καὶ διχοστασίαι καὶ σχίσματα πόλεμός τε ἐν ὑμῖν; 6. ἢ οὐχὶ ἕνα Θεὸν ἔχομεν καὶ
ἕνα Χριστὸν καὶ ἓν πνεῦμα τῆς χάριτος τὸ ἐκχυθὲν ἐφ' ἡμᾶς;
καὶ μία κλῆσις ἐν Χριστῷ; 7. ἵνα τί διέλκομεν καὶ διασπῶ-
μεν τὰ μέλη τοῦ Χριστοῦ, καὶ στασιάζομεν πρὸς τὸ σῶμα τὸ
ἴδιον, καὶ εἰς τοσαύτην ἀπόνοιαν ἐρχόμεθα ὥστε ἐπιλαθέσθαι
ἡμᾶς ὅτι μέλη ἐσμὲν ἀλλήλων; μνήσθητε τῶν λόγων Ἰησοῦ

S. Matt.
xxvi. 24,
xviii. 6.
S. Mark
xiv. 21, ix.
42.
S. Luke
xxii. 22,
xvii. 1, 2. τοῦ Κυρίου ἡμῶν· 8. εἶπεν γάρ· ΟὐΑὶ τῷ ἀνθρώπῳ ἐκείνῳ·
καλὸν ἦν αὐτῷ εἰ οὐκ ἐΓεννήθη, ἢ ἕνα τῶν ἐκλεκτῶν μοΥ
сκανΔαλίсαι· κρεῖττον ἦν αὐτῷ περιτεθῆναι μΥλον καὶ κατα-
ποντιсθῆναι εἰс τὴν θάλαссαν, ἢ ἕνα τῶν ἐκλεκτῶν μοΥ Δια-
сτρέψαι. 9. τὸ σχίσμα ὑμῶν πολλοὺς διέστρεψεν, πολλοὺς
εἰς ἀθυμίαν ἔβαλεν, πολλοὺς εἰς δισταγμόν, τοὺς πάντας
ἡμᾶς εἰς λύπην· καὶ ἐπίμονος ὑμῶν ἐστὶν ἡ στάσις.

XLVII. Ἀναλάβετε τὴν ἐπιστολὴν τοῦ μακαρίου Παύλου τοῦ ἀποστόλου. 2. τί πρῶτον ὑμῖν ἐν ἀρχῇ τοῦ εὐαγγελίου ἔγραψεν; 3. ἐπ' ἀληθείας πνευματικῶς ἐπέστειλεν
ὑμῖν περὶ αὑτοῦ τε καὶ Κηφᾶ τε καὶ Ἀπολλώ, διὰ τὸ καὶ
τότε προσκλίσεις ὑμᾶς πεποιῆσθαι· 4. ἀλλ' ἡ πρόσκλισις
ἐκείνη ἥττονα ἁμαρτίαν ὑμῖν προσήνεγκεν· προσεκλίθητε γὰρ
ἀποστόλοις μεμαρτυρημένοις καὶ ἀνδρὶ δεδοκιμασμένῳ παρ'
αὐτοῖς. 5. νυνὶ δὲ κατανοήσατε τίνες ὑμᾶς διέστρεψαν καὶ
τὸ σεμνὸν τῆς περιβοήτου φιλαδελφίας ὑμῶν ἐμείωσαν.
6. αἰσχρά, ἀγαπητοί, καὶ λίαν αἰσχρά, καὶ ἀνάξια τῆς ἐν
Χριστῷ ἀγωγῆς, ἀκούεσθαι τὴν βεβαιοτάτην καὶ ἀρχαίαν

Κορινθίων ἐκκλησίαν δι' ἐν ᾗ δύο πρόσωπα στασιάζειν πρὸς τοὺς πρεσβυτέρους. 7. καὶ αὕτη ἡ ἀκοὴ οὐ μόνον εἰς ἡμᾶς ἐχώρησεν ἀλλὰ καὶ εἰς τοὺς ἑτεροκλινεῖς ὑπάρχοντας ἀφ' ἡμῶν, ὥστε καὶ βλασφημίας ἐπιφέρεσθαι τῷ ὀνόματι Κυρίου διὰ τὴν ὑμετέραν ἀφροσύνην, ἑαυτοῖς δὲ κίνδυνον ἐπεξεργάζεσθαι. XLVIII. Ἐξάρωμεν οὖν τοῦτο ἐν τάχει καὶ προσπέσωμεν τῷ δεσπότῃ καὶ κλαύσωμεν ἱκετεύοντες αὐτόν, ὅπως ἵλεως γενόμενος ἐπικαταλλαγῇ ἡμῖν καὶ ἐπὶ τὴν σεμνὴν τῆς φιλαδελφίας ἡμῶν ἀγνὴν ἀγωγὴν ἀποκαταστήσῃ ἡμᾶς. 2. πύλη γὰρ δικαιοσύνης ἀνεῳγυῖα εἰς ζωὴν αὕτη, καθὼς γέγραπται· Ἀνοίξατέ μοι πύλας Δικαιοϲύνηϲ, ἵνα εἰϲελθὼν ἐν αὐταῖϲ Ps. cxviii. ἐξομολογήϲωμαι τῷ Κυρίῳ· 3. αὕτη ἡ πύλη τοῦ Κυρίου, Δίκαιοι ¹⁹, ²⁰. εἰϲελεύϲονται ἐν αὐτῇ. 4. Πολλῶν οὖν πυλῶν ἀνεῳγυιῶν, ἡ ἐν δικαιοσύνῃ αὕτη ἐστὶν ἡ ἐν Χριστῷ, ἐν ᾗ μακάριοι πάντες οἱ εἰσελθόντες καὶ κατευθύνοντες τὴν πορείαν αὐτῶν ἐν ὁσιότητι καὶ δικαιοσύνῃ, ἀταράχως πάντα ἐπιτελοῦντες. 5. ἤτω τις πιστός, ἤτω δυνατὸς γνῶσιν ἐξειπεῖν, ἤτω σοφὸς ἐν διακρίσει λόγων, ἤτω γοργὸς ἐν ἔργοις, ἤτω ἁγνός. 6. τοσούτῳ γὰρ μᾶλλον ταπεινοφρονεῖν ὀφείλει, ὅσῳ δοκεῖ μᾶλλον μείζων εἶναι, καὶ ζητεῖν τὸ κοινωφελὲς πᾶσιν καὶ μὴ τὸ ἑαυτοῦ.

XLIX. Ὁ ἔχων ἀγάπην ἐν Χριστῷ ποιησάτω τὰ τοῦ Χριστοῦ παραγγέλματα. 2. τὸν δεσμὸν τῆς ἀγάπης τοῦ Θεοῦ τίς δύναται ἐξηγήσασθαι; 3. τὸ μεγαλεῖον τῆς καλλονῆς αὐτοῦ τίς ἀρκετὸς ἐξειπεῖν; 4. τὸ ὕψος εἰς ὃ ἀνάγει ἡ ἀγάπη ἀνεκδιήγητόν ἐστιν. 5. ἀγάπη κολλᾷ ἡμᾶς τῷ Θεῷ· ἀγάπη καλύπτει πλῆθος ἁμαρτιῶν· ἀγάπη πάντα ἀνέ- 1 Pet. iv. 8. χεται, πάντα μακροθυμεῖ· οὐδὲν βάναυσον ἐν ἀγάπῃ, οὐδὲν ὑπερήφανον· ἀγάπη σχίσμα οὐκ ἔχει, ἀγάπη οὐ στασιάζει, ἀγάπη πάντα ποιεῖ ἐν ὁμονοίᾳ· ἐν τῇ ἀγάπῃ ἐτελειώθησαν πάντες οἱ ἐκλεκτοὶ τοῦ Θεοῦ· δίχα ἀγάπης οὐδὲν εὐάρεστόν ἐστιν τῷ Θεῷ· 6. ἐν ἀγάπῃ προσελάβετο ἡμᾶς ὁ δεσπότης· διὰ τὴν ἀγάπην, ἣν ἔσχεν πρὸς ἡμᾶς, τὸ αἷμα αὐτοῦ ἔδωκεν

xlviii. 5 ἤτω γοργὸς ἐν ἔργοις, ἤτω ἁγνός] Clem. Alex.; ἤτω ἁγνὸς ἐν ἔργοις
ACS.

ὑπὲρ ἡμῶν Ἰησοῦς Χριστὸς ὁ Κύριος ἡμῶν ἐν θελήματι Θεοῦ, καὶ τὴν σάρκα ὑπὲρ τῆς σαρκὸς ἡμῶν καὶ τὴν ψυχὴν ὑπὲρ τῶν ψυχῶν ἡμῶν. L. Ὁρᾶτε, ἀγαπητοί, πῶς μέγα καὶ θαυμαστόν ἐστιν ἡ ἀγάπη, καὶ τῆς τελειότητος αὐτῆς οὐκ ἐστὶν ἐξήγησις· 2. τίς ἱκανὸς ἐν αὐτῇ εὑρεθῆναι, εἰ μὴ οὓς ἂν καταξιώσῃ ὁ Θεός; δεώμεθα οὖν καὶ αἰτώμεθα ἀπὸ τοῦ ἐλέους αὐτοῦ, ἵνα ἐν ἀγάπῃ εὑρεθῶμεν δίχα προσκλίσεως ἀνθρωπίνης ἄμωμοι. 3. Αἱ γενεαὶ πᾶσαι ἀπὸ Ἀδὰμ ἕως τῆσδε [τῆς] ἡμέρας παρῆλθον, ἀλλ' οἱ ἐν ἀγάπῃ τελειωθέντες κατὰ τὴν τοῦ Θεοῦ χάριν ἔχουσιν χῶρον εὐσεβῶν· οἳ φανερωθήσονται ἐν τῇ ἐπισκοπῇ τῆς βασιλείας τοῦ Θεοῦ. 4. γέγραπται γάρ·

Is.xxvi.20. Εἰσέλθετε εἰς τὰ ταμεῖα μικρὸν ὅσον ὅσον, ἕως οὗ παρέλθῃ ἡ
Ezek.
xxxvii. 12. ὀργὴ καὶ ὁ θυμός μου, καὶ μνησθήσομαι ἡμέρας ἀγαθῆς καὶ ἀναστήσω ὑμᾶς ἐκ τῶν θηκῶν ὑμῶν. 5. Μακάριοι ἦμεν, ἀγαπητοί, εἰ τὰ προστάγματα τοῦ Θεοῦ ἐποιοῦμεν ἐν ὁμονοίᾳ ἀγάπης, εἰς τὸ ἀφεθῆναι ἡμῖν δι' ἀγάπης τὰς ἁμαρτίας.

Ps. xxxii. 6. γέγραπται γάρ· Μακάριοι ὧν ἀφέθησαν αἱ ἀνομίαι καὶ ὧν
1, 2. ἐπεκαλύφθησαν αἱ ἁμαρτίαι· μακάριος ἀνὴρ οὗ οὐ μὴ λογίσηται Κύριος ἁμαρτίαν, οὐδέ ἐστιν ἐν τῷ στόματι αὐτοῦ δόλος. 7. Οὗτος ὁ μακαρισμὸς ἐγένετο ἐπὶ τοὺς ἐκλελεγμένους ὑπὸ τοῦ Θεοῦ διὰ Ἰησοῦ Χριστοῦ τοῦ Κυρίου ἡμῶν, ᾧ ἡ δόξα εἰς τοὺς αἰῶνας τῶν αἰώνων. ἀμήν.

LI. Ὅσα οὖν παρεπέσαμεν καὶ ἐποιήσαμεν διά τινος τῶν τοῦ ἀντικειμένου, ἀξιώσωμεν ἀφεθῆναι ἡμῖν· καὶ ἐκεῖνοι δὲ οἵτινες ἀρχηγοὶ στάσεως καὶ διχοστασίας ἐγενήθησαν, ὀφείλουσιν τὸ κοινὸν τῆς ἐλπίδος σκοπεῖν. 2. οἱ γὰρ μετὰ φόβου καὶ ἀγάπης πολιτευόμενοι ἑαυτοὺς θέλουσιν μᾶλλον αἰκίαις περιπίπτειν ἢ τοὺς πλησίον, μᾶλλον δὲ ἑαυτῶν κατάγνωσιν φέρουσιν ἢ τῆς παραδεδομένης ἡμῖν καλῶς καὶ δικαίως ὁμοφωνίας. 3. καλὸν γὰρ ἀνθρώπῳ ἐξομολογεῖσθαι περὶ τῶν παραπτωμάτων ἢ σκληρῦναι τὴν καρδίαν αὐτοῦ, καθὼς ἐσκληρύνθη ἡ καρδία τῶν στασιαζόντων πρὸς τὸν θεράποντα τοῦ Θεοῦ Μωϋσῆν· ὧν τὸ κρίμα πρόδηλον ἐγε-

νήθη. 4. κατέβησαν γὰρ εἰς ᾅδου ζῶντες, καὶ θάνατος ποι- Ps. xlix.
ΜΑΝΕῖ ΑΥΤΟΥϹ. 5. Φαραὼ καὶ ἡ στρατιὰ αὐτοῦ καὶ πάντες οἱ ¹⁵·
ἡγούμενοι Αἰγύπτου, τά τε ἅρματα καὶ οἱ ἀναΒάται αὐτῶν, οὐ δι' Ex. xiv.
ἄλλην τινὰ αἰτίαν ἐβυθίσθησαν εἰς θάλασσαν ἐρυθρὰν καὶ ²³, ²⁶, ²⁸,
xv. 19.
ἀπώλοντο, ἀλλὰ διὰ τὸ σκληρυνθῆναι αὐτῶν τὰς ἀσυνέτους
καρδίας μετὰ τὸ γενέσθαι τὰ σημεῖα καὶ τὰ τέρατα ἐν γῇ
Αἰγύπτου διὰ τοῦ θεράποντος τοῦ Θεοῦ Μωϋσέως.

LII. Ἀπροσδεής, ἀδελφοί, ὁ δεσπότης ὑπάρχει τῶν
ἁπάντων, οὐδὲν οὐδενὸς χρῄζει εἰ μὴ τὸ ἐξομολογεῖσθαι αὐτῷ.
2. φησὶν γὰρ ὁ ἐκλεκτὸς Δαυείδ· Ἐξομολογήϲομαι τῷ Κυρίῳ, Ps. lxix.
καὶ ἀρέϲει ΑΥΤῷ ὑπὲρ μόϲχον νέον κέρατα ἐκφέροντα καὶ ὁπλάϲ· ³¹—³³·
ἰΔέτωϲΑΝ πτωχοὶ καὶ ΕΥφρΑΝθήτωϲΑΝ. 3. καὶ πάλιν λέγει·
Θῦϲον τῷ Θεῷ θυϲίΑΝ αἰνέϲεωϲ καὶ ἀπόΔΟϹ τῷ ὑψίϲτῳ τὰϲ ΕΥχάϲ Ps. l. 14,
ϹΟΥ· καὶ ἐπικάλεϲαί με ἐν Ἡμέρᾳ θλίψεώϲ ϹΟΥ, καὶ ἐξελοῦμαί ϲε, ¹⁵·
καὶ δοξάϲειϲ Με. 4. θυϲία ΓᾺρ τῷ Θεῷ πνεῦμα ϲΥΝτετριμμένον. Ps. li. 19.

LIII. Ἐπίστασθε γὰρ καὶ καλῶς ἐπίστασθε τὰς ἱερὰς
γραφάς, ἀγαπητοί, καὶ ἐγκεκύφατε εἰς τὰ λόγια τοῦ Θεοῦ·
πρὸς ἀνάμνησιν οὖν ταῦτα γράφομεν. 2. Μωϋσέως γὰρ
ἀναβαίνοντος εἰς τὸ ὄρος καὶ ποιήσαντος τεσσεράκοντα ἡμέρας καὶ τεσσεράκοντα νύκτας ἐν νηστείᾳ καὶ ταπεινώσει,
εἶπεν πρὸς αὐτὸν ὁ Θεός· Μωγϲῆ, Μωγϲῆ, κατάΒΗθι τὸ τάχοϲ Deut. ix.
ἐντεῦθεν, ὅτι ἨΝόμΗϲεΝ ὁ λαόϲ ϹΟΥ ΟὛϹ ἐξήΓΑΓεϲ ἐκ Γῆϲ Αἰγύπ- ¹²—¹⁴·
τογ· πΑρέΒΗϲΑΝ τΑχΥ ἐκ τῆϲ ὁδοῦ ἧϲ ἐνετείλω ΑΥτοῖϲ, ἐποίΗϲΑΝ
ἑΑΥτοῖϲ χωνεΥμΑτΑ. 3. Καὶ εἶπεν Κύριοϲ πρὸϲ ΑΥτόν· ΛελΑ-
λΗκΑ πρόϲ ϲε ἅπΑξ καὶ δὶϲ λέγων, Ἑώρακα τὸν λαὸν τοῦτον, καὶ
ἰδογ ἐϲτιν ϲκληροτράχΗλοϲ· ἔΑϲόν με ἐξολεθρεῦϲΑι ΑΥτογϲ, καὶ
ἐξαλείψω τὸ ὄνομα ΑΥτῶν ὑποκάτωθεν τογ ΟΥρΑΝΟῦ καὶ ποιήϲω
ϲὲ εἰϲ ἔθνοϲ μέΓΑ καὶ θαυμαϲτὸν καὶ πολὺ μᾶλλον ἢ τοῦτο.
4. Καὶ εἶπε Μωϋσῆϲ· ΜΗθΑμῶϲ Κύριε· ἄφεϲ τὴν ἁμΑρτίαν τῷ Ex. xxxii.
λαῷ τούτῳ ἢ κἀμὲ ἐξάλειψον ἐκ Βίβλου ζώντων. 5. ὦ μεγάλης ³¹, ³²·
ἀγάπης, ὦ τελειότητος ἀνυπερβλήτου· παρρησιάζεται θεράπων πρὸς κύριον, αἰτεῖται ἄφεσιν τῷ πλήθει ἢ καὶ ἑαυτὸν
ἐξαλειφθῆναι μετ' αὐτῶν ἀξιοῖ.

LIV. Τίς οὖν ἐν ὑμῖν γενναῖος; τίς εὔσπλαγχνος; τίς

πεπληροφορημένος ἀγάπης; 2. εἰπάτω· Εἰ δι᾽ ἐμὲ στάσις καὶ ἔρις καὶ σχίσματα, ἐκχωρῶ, ἄπειμι οὗ ἐὰν βούλησθε, καὶ ποιῶ τὰ προστασσόμενα ὑπὸ τοῦ πλήθους· μόνον τὸ ποίμνιον τοῦ Χριστοῦ εἰρηνευέτω μετὰ τῶν καθεσταμένων πρεσβυτέρων. 3. τοῦτο ὁ ποιήσας ἑαυτῷ μέγα κλέος ἐν Χριστῷ Ps. xxiv. 1. περιποιήσεται, καὶ πᾶς τόπος δέξεται αὐτόν· τοῦ γὰρ Κυρίου ἡ γῆ καὶ τὸ πλήρωμα αὐτῆς. 4. ταῦτα οἱ πολιτευόμενοι τὴν ἀμεταμέλητον πολιτείαν τοῦ Θεοῦ ἐποίησαν καὶ ποιήσουσιν.

LV. Ἵνα δὲ καὶ ὑποδείγματα ἐθνῶν ἐνέγκωμεν· πολλοὶ βασιλεῖς καὶ ἡγούμενοι, λοιμικοῦ τινὸς ἐνστάντος καιροῦ, χρησμοδοτηθέντες παρέδωκαν ἑαυτοὺς εἰς θάνατον, ἵνα ῥύσωνται διὰ τοῦ ἑαυτῶν αἵματος τοὺς πολίτας. πολλοὶ ἐξεχώρησαν ἰδίων. πόλεων, ἵνα μὴ στασιάζωσιν ἐπὶ πλεῖον. 2. ἐπιστάμεθα πολλοὺς ἐν ἡμῖν παραδεδωκότας ἑαυτοὺς εἰς δεσμά, ὅπως ἑτέρους λυτρώσονται. πολλοὶ ἑαυτοὺς παρέδωκαν εἰς δουλείαν, καὶ λαβόντες τὰς τιμὰς αὐτῶν ἑτέρους ἐψώμισαν. 3. πολλαὶ γυναῖκες ἐνδυναμωθεῖσαι διὰ τῆς χάριτος τοῦ Θεοῦ ἐπετελέσαντο πολλὰ ἀνδρεῖα. 4. Ἰουδὶθ ἡ μακαρία, ἐν συγκλεισμῷ οὔσης τῆς πόλεως, ᾐτήσατο παρὰ τῶν πρεσβυτέρων ἐαθῆναι αὐτὴν ἐξελθεῖν εἰς τὴν παρεμβολὴν τῶν ἀλλοφύλων· 5. παραδοῦσα οὖν ἑαυτὴν τῷ κινδύνῳ ἐξῆλθεν δι᾽ ἀγάπην τῆς πατρίδος καὶ τοῦ λαοῦ τοῦ ὄντος ἐν συγκλεισμῷ, καὶ παρέδωκεν Κύριος Ὀλοφέρνην ἐν χειρὶ θηλείας. 6. οὐχ ἥττονι καὶ ἡ τελεία κατὰ πίστιν Ἐσθὴρ κινδύνῳ ἑαυτὴν παρέβαλεν, ἵνα, τὸ δωδεκάφυλον τοῦ Ἰσραὴλ μέλλον ἀπολέσθαι ῥύσηται· διὰ γὰρ τῆς νηστείας καὶ τῆς ταπεινώσεως αὐτῆς ἠξίωσεν τὸν παντεπόπτην δεσπότην, Θεὸν τῶν αἰώνων· ὃς ἰδὼν τὸ ταπεινὸν τῆς ψυχῆς αὐτῆς ἐρύσατο τὸν λαόν, ὧν χάριν ἐκινδύνευσεν.

LVI. Καὶ ἡμεῖς οὖν ἐντύχωμεν περὶ τῶν ἔν τινι παραπτώματι ὑπαρχόντων, ὅπως δοθῇ αὐτοῖς ἐπιείκεια καὶ ταπεινοφροσύνη εἰς τὸ εἶξαι αὐτοὺς μὴ ἡμῖν ἀλλὰ τῷ θελήματι τοῦ Θεοῦ.· οὕτως γὰρ ἔσται αὐτοῖς ἔγκαρπος καὶ τελεία ἡ πρὸς τὸν Θεὸν καὶ τοὺς ἁγίους μετ᾽ οἰκτιρμῶν μνεία. 2. ἀνα-

λάβωμεν παιδείαν, ἐφ᾽ ᾗ οὐδεὶς ὀφείλει ἀγανακτεῖν, ἀγαπητοί.
ἡ νουθέτησις, ἣν ποιούμεθα εἰς ἀλλήλους, καλή ἐστιν καὶ
ὑπεράγαν ὠφέλιμος· κολλᾷ γὰρ ἡμᾶς τῷ θελήματι τοῦ Θεοῦ.
3. οὕτως γάρ φησιν ὁ ἅγιος λόγος· Πλιδεγων ἐπλίδεγcέν με Ps. cxviii.
18.
ὁ ΚΥΡΙΟc, κλὶ τῷ θλνάτῳ ΟΥ πλρέΔωκέν με. 4. ὃν ΓΔρ ἀ̓Γλπᾷ Prov. iii.
12.
ΚΥΡΙΟc πλιΔεΥΕΙ, μλcΤΙΓΟῖ ΔΕ πάΝΤλ ΥἱὸΝ ὃΝ πλρλΔέχΕΤλι. 5. Πλι- Ps. cxli. 5.
ΔεΥcει με ΓΔρ, φησίν, ΔίκλΙΟc ἐΝ ἐλέΕΙ κλὶ ἐλέΓˉΖει με, † ἔλεΟc † ΔΕ
ἁμλρΤωλῶΝ μῊ λΙπλΝΔΤω ΤῊΝ κεφλλΉΝ μΟΥ. 6. Κλὶ πάλιΝ
λέΓει· ΜλκάριΟc ἄΝθρωπΟc ὃΝ ἬλεˉΖεΝ ὁ ΚΥΡΙΟc, ΝΟΥθέΤΗμλ ΔῈ Job v. 17—
26.
πλΝΤΟκράΤΟρΟc μῊ ἀπλΝλίΝΟΥ· λΥΤῸc ΓΔρ ἀλΓεῖΝ πΟΙεῖ, κλὶ πάλιΝ
ἀπΟκλθίcΤΗcΙΝ· 7. ἔπλιcεΝ, κλὶ λἱ χεῖρεc λΥΤΟΥ̑ ἰάcλΝΤΟ. 8. ἑˉΖάκιc
ἐˉΖ ἀΝλΓκῶΝ ἐˉΖελεῖΤλί cε, ἐΝ ΔῈ Τῷ ἑβΔΌμῳ ΟΥ̓χ ἄψΕΤλί cΟΥ κλκΌΝ·
9. ἐΝ λιμῷ ῥΎcεΤλί cε ἐκ θλνάΤΟΥ, ἐΝ πΟλέμῳ ΔῈ ἐκ χειρῸc
cιΔΉρΟΥ λΎcει cε· 10. κλὶ ἀπῸ μάcΤΙΓΟc ΓλώccΗc cε κρΎψει, κλὶ
ΟΥ̓ μῊ φΟβΗθΉcῃ κλκῶΝ ἐπερχΟμέΝωΝ· 11. ἀΔίκωΝ κλὶ ἀΝΌμωΝ
κλΤλΓελάcῃ, ἀπῸ ΔῈ θΗρίωΝ ἀΓρίωΝ ΟΥ̓ μῊ φΟβΗθΗ̑c. 12. θΗ̑ρεc
ΓΔρ ἄΓριΟΙ εἰρΗΝεΎcΟΥcίΝ cΟι· 13. εἶΤλ ΓΝώcῃ ὅΤι εἰρΗΝεΎcει cΟΥ
ὁ ΟἶκΟc· Ἠ ΔῈ Δίλιτλ ΤΗ̑c cκΗΝΗ̑c cΟΥ ΟΥ̓ μῊ ἁμάρΤῃ, 14. ΓΝώcῃ
ΔῈ ὅΤι πΟλῪ ΤῸ cπέρμλ cΟΥ, ΤΔ ΔῈ ΤέκΝλ cΟΥ ὥcπερ ΤῸ πλμβΌΤλ-
ΝΟΝ ΤΟΥ̑ ἀΓρΟΥ̑· 15. ἐλέΥcῃ ΔῈ ἐΝ Τάφῳ ὥcπερ cῖΤΟc ὥριμΟc
κλΤὰ κλιρὸΝ θεριζΌμεΝΟc, Ἢ ὥcπερ θΗμωΝιὰ ἅλωΝΟc κλθ᾽ ὥρλΝ
cΥΓκΟμιcθεῖcλ. 16. ΒλέπεΤε, ἀγαπητοί, πόσος ὑπερασπισμὸς
ἐστιν τοῖς παιδευομένοις ὑπὸ τοῦ δεσπότου· πατὴρ γὰρ ἀγαθὸς ὢν παιδεύει εἰς τὸ ἐλεηθῆναι ἡμᾶς διὰ τῆς ὁσίας παιδείας
αὐτοῦ.

LVII. Ὑμεῖς οὖν, οἱ τὴν καταβολὴν τῆς στάσεως ποιήσαντες, ὑποτάγητε τοῖς πρεσβυτέροις καὶ παιδεύθητε εἰς
μετάνοιαν, κάμψαντες τὰ γόνατα τῆς καρδίας ὑμῶν· 2. μάθετε ὑποτάσσεσθαι, ἀποθέμενοι τὴν ἀλαζόνα καὶ ὑπερήφανον
τῆς γλώσσης ὑμῶν αὐθάδειαν· ἄμεινον γάρ ἐστιν ὑμῖν ἐν τῷ
ποιμνίῳ τοῦ Χριστοῦ μικροὺς καὶ ἐλλογίμους εὑρεθῆναι,
ἢ καθ᾽ ὑπεροχὴν δοκοῦντας ἐκριφῆναι ἐκ τῆς ἐλπίδος αὐτοῦ.
3. οὕτως γὰρ λέγει ἡ πανάρετος σοφία· Ἰ̓ΔΟῪ πρΟΉcΟμλι ὙμῖΝ Prov. i. 23
—33.
ἐμΗ̑c πΝΟΗ̑c ῥΗ̑cιΝ, ΔιΔάˉΖω ΔῈ ὙμΔc ΤῸΝ ἐμῸΝ λΌΓΟΝ· 4. ἐπειΔῊ

ἐκάλογν καὶ ογχ ὑπηκούcατε, καὶ ἐΖέτεινον λόγογc καὶ ογ προcεί-
χετε, ἀλλὰ ἀκύρογc ἐποιεῖτε τὰc ἐμὰc Βογλὰc τοῖc Δὲ ἐμοῖc
ἐλέγχοιc Ηπειθήcατε· τοιγαρογ̂ν κἀγὼ τῇ ὑμετέρᾳ ἀπωλείᾳ ἐπιγε-
λάcομαι, καταχαρογ̂μαι Δὲ Ηνίκα ἂν ἔρχηται ὑμῖν ὄλεθρος καὶ ὡc
ἂν ἀφίκηται ὑμῖν ἄφνω θόργΒοc, Η Δὲ καταστροφΗ ὁμοία καταιγίΔι
παρῇ, Η ὅταν ἔρχηται ὑμῖν θλίψιc καὶ πολιορκία. 5. ἔcται γάρ,
ὅταν ἐπικαλέcηcθέ με, ἐγὼ Δὲ ογκ εἰcακούcομαι ὑμῶν· ζητήcογ-
cίν με κακοὶ καὶ ογχ εγρήcογcιν· ἐμίcηcαν γὰρ cοφίαν, τὸν Δὲ
φόΒον τογ̂ Κγρίογ ογ προείλαντο, ογΔὲ Ηθελον ἐμαῖc προcέχειν
Βογλαῖc, ἐμγκτήριζον Δὲ ἐμογ̂c ἐλέγχογc. 6. τοιγαρογ̂ν ἔΔονται
τΗc ἑαγτῶν ὁΔογ̂ τογ̂c καρπούc, καὶ τΗc ἑαγτῶν ἀceΒείαc πληcθή-
cονται. 7. ἀνθ' ὧν γὰρ ΗΔίκογν νηπίογc, φονεγθήcονται, καὶ
ἐΖεταcμὸc ἀceΒεῖc ὀλεῖ· ὁ Δὲ ἐμογ̂ ἀκούων καταcκηνώcει ἐπ'
ἐλπίΔι πεποιθώc, καὶ Ηcγχάcει ἀφόΒωc ἀπὸ παντὸc κακογ̂.

LVIII. Ὑπακούσωμεν οὖν τῷ παναγίῳ καὶ ἐνδόξῳ
ὀνόματι αὐτοῦ, φυγόντες τὰς προειρημένας διὰ τῆς σοφίας
τοῖς ἀπειθοῦσιν ἀπειλάς, ἵνα κατασκηνώσωμεν πεποιθότες
ἐπὶ τὸ ὁσιώτατον τῆς μεγαλωσύνης αὐτοῦ ὄνομα. 2. δέξασθε
τὴν συμβουλὴν ἡμῶν, καὶ ἔσται ἀμεταμέλητα ὑμῖν. ζῇ γὰρ
ὁ Θεὸς καὶ ζῇ ὁ Κύριος Ἰησοῦς Χριστὸς καὶ τὸ πνεῦμα τὸ
ἅγιον, ἥ τε πίστις καὶ ἡ ἐλπὶς τῶν ἐκλεκτῶν, ὅτι ὁ ποιήσας
ἐν ταπεινοφροσύνῃ μετ' ἐκτενοῦς ἐπιεικείας ἀμεταμελήτως
τὰ ὑπὸ τοῦ Θεοῦ δεδομένα δικαιώματα καὶ προστάγματα,
οὗτος ἐντεταγμένος καὶ ἐλλόγιμος ἔσται εἰς τὸν ἀριθμὸν τῶν
σωζομένων διὰ Ἰησοῦ Χριστοῦ, δι' οὗ ἐστιν αὐτῷ ἡ δόξα εἰς
τοὺς αἰῶνας τῶν αἰώνων. ἀμήν.

LIX. Ἐὰν δέ τινες ἀπειθήσωσιν τοῖς ὑπ' αὐτοῦ δι' ἡμῶν
εἰρημένοις, γινωσκέτωσαν ὅτι παραπτώσει καὶ κινδύνῳ οὐ
μικρῷ ἑαυτοὺς ἐνδήσουσιν, 2. ἡμεῖς δὲ ἀθῷοι ἐσόμεθα ἀπὸ
ταύτης τῆς ἁμαρτίας· καὶ αἰτησόμεθα, ἐκτενῆ τὴν δέησιν καὶ
ἱκεσίαν ποιούμενοι, ὅπως τὸν ἀριθμὸν τὸν κατηριθμημένον
τῶν ἐκλεκτῶν αὐτοῦ ἐν ὅλῳ τῷ κόσμῳ διαφυλάξῃ ἄθραυστον
ὁ δημιουργὸς τῶν ἁπάντων διὰ τοῦ ἠγαπημένου παιδὸς αὐτοῦ
Ἰησοῦ Χριστοῦ, δι' οὗ ἐκάλεσεν ἡμᾶς ἀπὸ σκότους εἰς φῶς,

ἀπὸ ἀγνωσίας εἰς ἐπίγνωσιν δόξης ὀνόματος αὐτοῦ. 3. [Δὸς
ἡμῖν, Κύριε], ἐλπίζειν ἐπὶ τὸ ἀρχέγονον πάσης κτίσεως ὄνομά
σου, ἀνοίξας τοὺς ὀφθαλμοὺς τῆς καρδίας ἡμῶν εἰς τὸ γινώσκειν σε, τὸν μόνον ὝΨΙϹΤΟΝ ἐν ὑΨΗλΟῖϲ ἅΓΙΟΝ ἐν ἁΓίΟΙϹ ἀΝΑ- Is. lvii. 15,
xiii. 11.
παγόΜΕΝΟΝ, τὸν ταπεινοῦντα ὕΒΡΙΝ ὑπερηφάνων, τὸν ΔΙΑλΓΟΝΤΑ Ps. xxxiii.
λΟΓΙϹΜΟΓϹ ἐθΝῶΝ, τὸν ποιοῦντα ταπεινΟΓϹ εἰϲ ὕΨΟϲ καὶ τοὺϲ Job v. 11.
ὑΨΗλΟΓϹ ταπεινΟῦΝΤΑ, τὸν πλΟΓΤίζΟΝΤΑ Καὶ πτωχίζΟΝΤΑ, τὸν ἀπο- Is. x. 33.
1 Sam. ii.7.
ΚΤΕίΝΟΝΤΑ Καὶ ζῆΝ ποιΟῦΝΤΑ, μόνον εὐεργέτην πνευμάτων καὶ Deut.
xxxii. 39.
Θεὸν πάσης σαρκός, τὸν ἐπιΒλέποντα ἐν ταῖϲ ἀΒΓϹϹΟΙϹ, τὸν Ecclus.
ἐπόπτην ἀνθρωπίνων ἔργων, τὸν τῶν κινδυνευόντων βοηθόν, xvi. 18, 19.
τὸν τῶν ἀπηλπιϹΜέΝΩΝ Ϲωτῆρα, τὸν παντὸς πνεύματος κτίστην Judith ix.
καὶ ἐπίσκοπον, τὸν πληθύνοντα ἔθνη ἐπὶ γῆς καὶ ἐκ πάντων 11.
ἐκλεξάμενον τοὺς ἀγαπῶντάς σε διὰ Ἰησοῦ Χριστοῦ τοῦ
ἠγαπημένου παιδός σου, δι᾽ οὗ ἡμᾶς ἐπαίδευσας, ἡγίασας,
ἐτίμησας. 4. Ἀξιοῦμέν σε, δέσποτα, ΒΟΗθόΝ γενέσθαι Καὶ Ps. cxix.
ἀΝΤΙλΗΠΤΟΡΑ ἡμῶν. τοὺς ἐν θλίψει ἡμῶν σῶσον· τοὺς ταπει- 114.
νοὺς ἐλέησον· τοὺς πεπτωκότας ἔγειρον· τοῖς δεομένοις ἐπι-
φάνηθι· τοὺς ἀσεβεῖς ἴασαι· τοὺς πλανωμένους τοῦ λαοῦ σου
ἐπίστρεψον· χόρτασον τοὺς πεινῶντας· λύτρωσαι τοὺς δεσ-
μίους ἡμῶν· ἐξανάστησον τοὺς ἀσθενοῦντας· παρακάλεσον
τοὺς ὀλιγοψυχοῦντας· ΓΝώΤΩϹΑΝ ἅπαντα τὰ ἔθνη, ὅτι ϲΓ εῖ 1 Kings
viii. 60.
ὁ Θεὸς Μόνος, καὶ Ἰησοῦς Χριστὸς ὁ παῖς σου, καὶ ἡΜΕῖϲ λαόϲ 2 Kings
ϹΟΓ Καὶ πρόΒΑΤΑ τῆϲ ΝΟΜῆϲ ϹΟΓ. xix. 19.
Ps. lxxix.
LX. Σὺ τὴν ἀέναον τοῦ κόσμου σύστασιν διὰ τῶν 13, c. 3.
ἐνεργουμένων ἐφανεροποίησας· σύ, Κύριε, τὴν οἰκουμένην
ἔκτισας, ὁ πιστὸς ἐν πάσαις ταῖς γενεαῖς, δίκαιος ἐν τοῖς
κρίμασιν, θαυμαστὸς ἐν ἰσχύϊ καὶ μεγαλοπρεπείᾳ, ὁ σοφὸς ἐν
τῷ κτίζειν καὶ συνετὸς ἐν τῷ τὰ γενόμενα ἑδράσαι, ὁ ἀγαθὸς
ἐν τοῖς ὁρωμένοις καὶ πιστὸς ἐν τοῖς πεποιθόσιν ἐπὶ σέ,
ἐλεῆΜΟΝ Καὶ ΟἰΚΤίρμΟΝ, ἄφες ἡμῖν τὰς ἀνομίας ἡμῶν καὶ τὰς Ecclus. ii.
ἀδικίας καὶ τὰ παραπτώματα καὶ πλημμελείας. 2. μὴ λο- 11.
γίσῃ πᾶσαν ἁμαρτίαν δούλων σου καὶ παιδισκῶν, ἀλλὰ

lix. 3 Δὸς ἡμῖν Κύριε] insert Lightfoot.   ὑψηλοῖς] LXX; ὑψίστοις C; def. A;
dub. S.

Ps. xl. 3.
1 Kings ix.
4.
Deut. xiii.
18.
Ps. lxvii. 1.
Ex. vi. 1.

Ps. cxlv.
18.

καθάρισον ἡμᾶς τὸν καθαρισμὸν τῆς σῆς ἀληθείας, καὶ
κατεγθγνον τὰ διαβήματα ἡμῶν ἐν ὁcιότητι καὶ δικαιοσύνη καὶ
ἁπλότητι καρδίας πορεγεcθαι καὶ ποιεῖν τὰ καλὰ καὶ εγάρεcτα
ἐνώπιόν cου καὶ ἐνώπιον τῶν ἀρχόντων ἡμῶν. 3. ναί, δέ-
cποτα, ἐπίφανον τὸ πρόcωπόν coγ ἐφ᾽ ἡμᾶc εἰς ἀγαθὰ ἐν
εἰρήνη, εἰς τὸ σκεπασθῆναι ἡμᾶς τῇ χειρί coγ τῇ κραταιᾷ καὶ
ῥυσθῆναι ἀπὸ πάσης ἁμαρτίας τῷ βραχίονί coγ τῷ γψηλῷ· καὶ
ῥῦσαι ἡμᾶς ἀπὸ τῶν μισούντων ἡμᾶς ἀδίκως. 4. δὸς ὁμόνοιαν καὶ εἰρήνην ἡμῖν τε καὶ πᾶσιν τοῖς κατοικοῦσιν τὴν
γῆν, καθὼς ἔδωκας τοῖς πατράσιν ἡμῶν, ἐπικαλογμένων σε
αὐτῶν ὁσίως ἐν πίcτει κὰι ἀληθείᾳ, [ὥστε σώζεσθαι ἡμᾶς]
ὑπηκόους γινομένους τῷ παντοκράτορι καὶ παναρέτῳ ὀνόματί
σου, τοῖς τε ἄρχουσιν καὶ ἡγουμένοις ἡμῶν ἐπὶ τῆς γῆς.

LXI. Σύ, δέσποτα, ἔδωκας τὴν ἐξουσίαν τῆς βασιλείας
αὐτοῖς διὰ τοῦ μεγαλοπρεποῦς καὶ ἀνεκδιηγήτου κράτους
σου, εἰς τὸ γινώσκοντας ἡμᾶς τὴν ὑπὸ σοῦ αὐτοῖς δεδομένην
δόξαν καὶ τιμὴν ὑποτάσσεσθαι αὐτοῖς, μηδὲν ἐναντιουμένους
τῷ θελήματί σου· οἷς δός, Κύριε, ὑγίειαν, εἰρήνην, ὁμόνοιαν,
εὐστάθειαν, εἰς τὸ διέπειν αὐτοὺς τὴν ὑπὸ σοῦ δεδομένην
αὐτοῖς ἡγεμονίαν ἀπροσκόπως. 2. σὺ γάρ, δέσποτα ἐπου-
ράνιε, βασιλεῦ τῶν αἰώνων, δίδως τοῖς υἱοῖς τῶν ἀνθρώπων
δόξαν καὶ τιμὴν καὶ ἐξουσίαν τῶν ἐπὶ τῆς γῆς ὑπαρχόντων·
σύ, Κύριε, διεύθυνον τὴν βουλὴν αὐτῶν κατὰ τὸ καλὸν καὶ
εὐάρεστον ἐνώπιόν σου, ὅπως διέποντες ἐν εἰρήνῃ καὶ πραΰτητι εὐσεβῶς τὴν ὑπὸ σοῦ αὐτοῖς δεδομένην ἐξουσίαν ἵλεώ
σου τυγχάνωσιν. 3. Ὁ μόνος δυνατὸς ποιῆσαι ταῦτα καὶ
περισσότερα ἀγαθὰ μεθ᾽ ἡμῶν, σοὶ ἐξομολογούμεθα διὰ τοῦ
ἀρχιερέως καὶ προστάτου τῶν ψυχῶν ἡμῶν Ἰησοῦ Χριστοῦ,
δι᾽ οὗ σοι ἡ δόξα καὶ ἡ μεγαλωσύνη καὶ νῦν καὶ εἰς γενεὰν
γενεῶν καὶ εἰς τοὺς αἰῶνας τῶν αἰώνων. ἀμήν.

LXII. Περὶ μὲν τῶν ἀνηκόντων τῇ θρησκείᾳ ἡμῶν, καὶ
τῶν ὠφελιμωτάτων εἰς ἐνάρετον βίον τοῖς θέλουσιν εὐσεβῶς

lx. 2 καθάρισον] conj. Lightfoot; καθαρεῖς C; purifica S; def. A.
lx. 4 ὥστε σώζεσθαι ἡμᾶς] insert Lightfoot.

καὶ δικαίως διευθύνειν [τὴν πορείαν αὐτῶν], ἱκανῶς ἐπεστεί-
λαμεν ὑμῖν, ἄνδρες ἀδελφοί. 2. περὶ γὰρ πίστεως καὶ μετανοίας καὶ γνησίας ἀγάπης καὶ ἐγκρατείας καὶ σωφροσύνης
καὶ ὑπομονῆς πάντα τόπον ἐψηλαφήσαμεν, ὑπομιμνήσκοντες
δεῖν ὑμᾶς ἐν δικαιοσύνη καὶ ἀληθείᾳ καὶ μακροθυμίᾳ τῷ
παντοκράτορι Θεῷ ὁσίως εὐαρεστεῖν, ὁμονοοῦντας ἀμνησι-
κάκως ἐν ἀγάπῃ καὶ εἰρήνῃ μετὰ ἐκτενοῦς ἐπιεικείας, καθὼς
καὶ οἱ προδεδηλωμένοι πατέρες ἡμῶν εὐηρέστησαν ταπεινο-
φρονοῦντες τὰ πρὸς τὸν πατέρα καὶ Θεὸν καὶ κτίστην καὶ
πρὸς πάντας ἀνθρώπους. 3. καὶ ταῦτα τοσούτῳ ἥδιον
ὑπεμνήσαμεν, ἐπειδὴ σαφῶς ᾔδειμεν γράφειν ἡμᾶς ἀνδράσιν
πιστοῖς καὶ ἐλλογιμωτάτοις καὶ ἐγκεκυφόσιν εἰς τὰ λόγια
τῆς παιδείας τοῦ Θεοῦ.

LXIII. Θεμιτὸν οὖν ἐστιν τοῖς τοιούτοις καὶ τοσούτοις
ὑποδείγμασιν προσελθόντας ὑποθεῖναι τὸν τράχηλον καὶ
τὸν τῆς ὑπακοῆς τόπον ἀναπληρώσαντας προσκλιθῆναι τοῖς
ὑπάρχουσιν ἀρχηγοῖς τῶν ψυχῶν ἡμῶν, ὅπως ἡσυχάσαντες
τῆς ματαίας στάσεως ἐπὶ τὸν προκείμενον ἡμῖν ἐν ἀληθείᾳ
σκοπὸν δίχα παντὸς μώμου καταντήσωμεν. 2. χαρὰν γὰρ
καὶ ἀγαλλίασιν ἡμῖν παρέξετε, ἐὰν ὑπήκοοι γενόμενοι τοῖς ὑφ'
ἡμῶν γεγραμμένοις διὰ τοῦ ἁγίου πνεύματος ἐκκόψητε τὴν
ἀθέμιτον τοῦ ζήλους ὑμῶν ὀργὴν κατὰ τὴν ἔντευξιν ἣν ἐποιη-
σάμεθα περὶ εἰρήνης καὶ ὁμονοίας ἐν τῇδε τῇ ἐπιστολῇ.
3. Ἐπέμψαμεν δὲ καὶ ἄνδρας πιστοὺς καὶ σώφρονας, ἀπὸ
νεότητος ἀναστραφέντας ἕως γήρους ἀμέμπτως ἐν ἡμῖν, οἵτινες
καὶ μάρτυρες ἔσονται μεταξὺ ὑμῶν καὶ ἡμῶν. 4. τοῦτο δὲ
ἐποιήσαμεν ἵνα εἰδῆτε ὅτι πᾶσα ἡμῖν φροντὶς καὶ γέγονεν
καὶ ἔστιν εἰς τὸ ἐν τάχει ὑμᾶς εἰρηνεῦσαι.

LXIV. Λοιπὸν ὁ παντεπόπτης Θεὸς καὶ δεσπότης τῶν
πνευμάτων καὶ Κύριος πάσης σαρκός, ὁ ἐκλεξάμενος τὸν
Κύριον Ἰησοῦν Χριστὸν καὶ ἡμᾶς δι' αὐτοῦ εἰς λαὸν περιού-
σιον, δῴη πάσῃ ψυχῇ ἐπικεκλημένῃ τὸ μεγαλοπρεπὲς καὶ
ἅγιον ὄνομα αὐτοῦ πίστιν, φόβον, εἰρήνην, ὑπομονήν, μακρο-

lxii. 1 τὴν πορείαν αὐτῶν] insert Lightfoot.

θυμίαν, ἐγκράτειαν, ἁγνείαν καὶ σωφροσύνην, εἰς εὐαρέστησιν τῷ ὀνόματι αὐτοῦ διὰ τοῦ ἀρχιερέως καὶ προστάτου ἡμῶν Ἰησοῦ Χριστοῦ· δι᾽ οὗ αὐτῷ δόξα καὶ μεγαλωσύνη, κράτος, τιμή, καὶ νῦν καὶ εἰς πάντας τοὺς αἰῶνας τῶν αἰώνων. ἀμήν.

LXV. Τοὺς δὲ ἀπεσταλμένους ἀφ᾽ ἡμῶν Κλαύδιον Ἔφηβον καὶ Οὐαλέριον Βίτωνα σὺν καὶ Φορτουνάτῳ ἐν εἰρήνῃ μετὰ χαρᾶς ἐν τάχει ἀναπέμψατε πρὸς ἡμᾶς, ὅπως θᾶττον τὴν εὐκταίαν καὶ ἐπιποθήτην ἡμῖν εἰρήνην καὶ ὁμόνοιαν ἀπαγγείλωσιν· εἰς τὸ τάχιον καὶ ἡμᾶς χαρῆναι περὶ τῆς εὐσταθείας ὑμῶν.

2. Ἡ χάρις τοῦ Κυρίου ἡμῶν Ἰησοῦ Χριστοῦ μεθ᾽ ὑμῶν καὶ μετὰ πάντων πανταχῇ τῶν κεκλημένων ὑπὸ τοῦ Θεοῦ καὶ δι᾽ αὐτοῦ· δι᾽ οὗ αὐτῷ δόξα, τιμή, κράτος καὶ μεγαλωσύνη, θρόνος αἰώνιος, ἀπὸ τῶν αἰώνων εἰς τοὺς αἰῶνας τῶν αἰώνων. ἀμήν.

AN ANCIENT HOMILY

UNKNOWN AUTHOR

THE so-called Second Epistle of S. Clement to the Corinthians follows immediately upon the first in all the three MS authorities, and is apparently ascribed to S. Clement by them. It has however no claim to this designation; for, although it was known to the Fathers of the fourth century and later, it is not quoted by early writers as being the work of S. Clement, and the internal evidence both of style and doctrine, so far as it goes, is distinctly against this conclusion. There are some indications (§ 7) that it was indeed written or spoken in the first instance to the Corinthians, but its language and character point to its being a homily rather than a letter. This view has been confirmed by the recent discovery of the latter half of the Epistle. The speaker addresses his hearers more than once towards the close as 'Brothers and sisters' (§§ 19, 20). Elsewhere he appeals to them in language which is quite explicit on the point at issue. 'Let us not think', he says, 'to give heed and believe now only, while we are being admonished by the presbyters; but likewise when we have departed home, let us remember the commandments of the Lord, etc.' (§ 17). We may therefore now definitely regard it as the earliest Christian homily extant. As a literary production it has no value, but it is at least interesting for the high moral tone and unswerving faith which it displays throughout. Its date may with some confidence be assigned to the first half of the second century, probably c. A.D. 120—140.

[ΠΡΟΣ ΚΟΡΙΝΘΙΟΥΣ Β.]

I. ᾿ΑΔΕΛΦΟΙ, οὕτως δεῖ ἡμᾶς φρονεῖν περὶ ᾿Ιησοῦ Χριστοῦ, ὡς περὶ Θεοῦ, ὡς περὶ κριτοῦ ζώντων καὶ νεκρῶν. καὶ οὐ δεῖ ἡμᾶς μικρὰ φρονεῖν περὶ τῆς σωτηρίας ἡμῶν· 2. ἐν τῷ γὰρ φρονεῖν ἡμᾶς μικρὰ περὶ αὐτοῦ, μικρὰ καὶ ἐλπίζομεν λαβεῖν. καὶ οἱ ἀκούοντες ὡς περὶ μικρῶν[ἁμαρτάνουσιν, καὶ ἡμεῖς]ἁμαρτάνομεν, οὐκ εἰδότες πόθεν ἐκλήθημεν καὶ ὑπὸ τίνος καὶ εἰς ὃν τόπον, καὶ ὅσα ὑπέμεινεν ᾿Ιησοῦς Χριστὸς παθεῖν ἕνεκα ἡμῶν. 3. τίνα οὖν ἡμεῖς αὐτῷ δώσομεν ἀντιμισθίαν; ἢ τίνα καρπὸν ἄξιον οὗ ἡμῖν αὐτὸς ἔδωκεν; πόσα δὲ αὐτῷ ὀφείλομεν ὅσια; 4. τὸ φῶς γὰρ ἡμῖν ἐχαρίσατο, ὡς πατὴρ υἱοὺς ἡμᾶς προσηγόρευσεν, ἀπολλυμένους ἡμᾶς ἔσωσεν. 5. ποῖον οὖν αἶνον αὐτῷ δώσωμεν ἢ μισθὸν ἀντιμισθίας ὧν ἐλάβομεν; 6. πηροὶ ὄντες τῇ διανοίᾳ, προσκυνοῦντες λίθους καὶ ξύλα καὶ χρυσὸν καὶ ἄργυρον καὶ χαλκόν, ἔργα ἀνθρώπων· καὶ ὁ βίος ἡμῶν ὅλος ἄλλο οὐδὲν ἦν εἰ μὴ θάνατος. ἀμαύρωσιν οὖν περικείμενοι καὶ τοιαύτης ἀχλύος γέμοντες ἐν τῇ ὁράσει, ἀνεβλέψαμεν ἀποθέμενοι ἐκεῖνο ὃ περικείμεθα νέφος τῇ αὐτοῦ θελήσει. 7. ἠλέησεν γὰρ ἡμᾶς καὶ σπλαγχνισθεὶς ἔσωσεν, θεασάμενος ἐν ἡμῖν πολλὴν πλάνην καὶ ἀπώλειαν, καὶ μηδεμίαν ἐλπίδα ἔχοντας σωτηρίας, εἰ μὴ τὴν παρ᾿ αὐτοῦ. 8. ἐκάλεσεν γὰρ ἡμᾶς οὐκ ὄντας καὶ ἠθέλησεν ἐκ μὴ ὄντος εἶναι ἡμᾶς.

II. ΕΥ̓ΦΡΑΝΘΗΤΙ, ϹΤΕΙ͂ΡΑ Ἠ ΟΥ̓ ΤΙΚΤΟΥϹΑ· ῬΑ͂ΖΟΝ ΚΑῚ ΒΟΗϹΟΝ, Ἠ Is. liv. 1. ΟΥ̓Κ ὨΔΙΝΟΥϹΑ, ὌΤΙ ΠΟΛΛᾺ ΤᾺ ΤΕΚΝΑ ΤΗ͂Ϲ ἘΡΗΜΟΥ ΜΑ͂ΛΛΟΝ Ἢ ΤΗ͂Ϲ ἘΧΟΥϹΗϹ ΤῸΝ ἌΝΔΡΑ. Ὁ εἶπεν εὐφράνθητι στεῖρα ἡ οὐ τίκτουσα, ἡμᾶς εἶπεν· στεῖρα γὰρ ἦν ἡ ἐκκλησία ἡμῶν πρὸ τοῦ δοθῆναι αὐτῇ τέκνα. 2. ὃ δὲ εἶπεν Βόησον ἡ ογκ ὠδίνογcα, τοῦτο λέγει· τὰς προσευχὰς ἡμῶν ἁπλῶς ἀναφέρειν πρὸς τὸν Θεὸν μή, ὡς αἱ ὠδίνουσαι, ἐγκακῶμεν. 3. ὃ δὲ εἶπεν ὅτι πολλὰ τὰ τέκνα τῆς ἐρήμογ μᾶλλον ἢ τῆς ἐχογ̓cηc τὸν ἄνδρα, ἐπεὶ ἔρημος ἐδόκει εἶναι ἀπὸ τοῦ Θεοῦ ὁ λαὸς ἡμῶν, νυνὶ δὲ πιστεύσαντες πλείονες ἐγενόμεθα τῶν δοκούντων ἔχειν Θεόν. 4. καὶ ἑτέρα

S. Matt. ix. 13. δὲ γραφὴ λέγει ὅτι Ογκ ἦλθον καλέcαι Δικαίογc, ἀλλὰ ἁμαρτω-
S. Mark ii. 17. λογc. 5. τοῦτο λέγει, ὅτι δεῖ τοὺς ἀπολλυμένους σώζειν· 6. ἐκεῖνο γάρ ἐστιν μέγα καὶ θαυμαστόν, οὐ τὰ ἑστῶτα στηρίζειν ἀλλὰ τὰ πίπτοντα. 7. οὕτως καὶ ὁ Χριστὸς ἠθέλησεν σῶσαι τὰ ἀπολλύμενα, καὶ ἔσωσεν πολλούς, ἐλθὼν καὶ καλέσας ἡμᾶς ἤδη ἀπολλυμένους.

III. Τοσοῦτον οὖν ἔλεος ποιήσαντος αὐτοῦ εἰς ἡμᾶς· πρῶτον μέν, ὅτι ἡμεῖς οἱ ζῶντες τοῖς νεκροῖς θεοῖς οὐ θύομεν καὶ οὐ προσκυνοῦμεν αὐτοῖς, ἀλλὰ ἔγνωμεν δι᾽ αὐτοῦ τὸν πατέρα τῆς ἀληθείας· τίς ἡ γνῶσις ἡ πρὸς αὐτόν, ἢ τὸ μὴ
S. Matt. x. 32. ἀρνεῖσθαι δι᾽ οὗ ἔγνωμεν αὐτόν; 2. λέγει δὲ καὶ αὐτός· Τὸν
S. Luke xii. 8. ὁμολογήcαντά με [ἐνώπιον τῶν ἀνθρώπων], ὁμολογήcω αγ̓τὸν ἐνώπιον τογ̓ πατρόc μογ. 3. Οὗτος οὖν ἐστιν ὁ μισθὸς ἡμῶν, ἐὰν οὖν ὁμολογήσωμεν δι᾽ οὗ ἐσώθημεν. 4. ἐν τίνι δὲ αὐτὸν ὁμολογοῦμεν; ἐν τῷ ποιεῖν ἃ λέγει καὶ μὴ παρακούειν αὐτοῦ
S. Mark xii. 30. Is. xxix. 13. τῶν ἐντολῶν, καὶ μὴ μόνον χείλεcιν αγ̓τὸν τιμᾶν ἀλλὰ ἐξ ὅλης καρδίαc καὶ ἐξ ὅλης τῆς διανοίαc. 5. λέγει δὲ καὶ ἐν τῷ Ἠσαΐᾳ· Ὁ λαὸς οὗτος τοῖς χείλεcίν με τιμᾷ, ἡ Δὲ καρΔία αγ̓τῶν πόρρω ἄπεcτιν ἀπ᾽ ἐμογ̓.

IV. Μὴ μόνον οὖν αὐτὸν καλῶμεν Κύριον, οὐ γὰρ τοῦτο
S. Matt. vii. 21. σώσει ἡμᾶς. 2. λέγει γάρ· Ογ̓ πᾶς ὁ λέγων μοι, Κύριε, Κύριε, cωθήcεται, ἀλλ᾽ ὁ ποιῶν τὴν Δικαιοcύνην. 3. ὥστε οὖν, ἀδελφοί, ἐν τοῖς ἔργοις αὐτὸν ὁμολογῶμεν, ἐν τῷ ἀγαπᾶν ἑαυτούς, ἐν τῷ μὴ μοιχᾶσθαι μηδὲ καταλαλεῖν ἀλλήλων μηδὲ ζηλοῦν, ἀλλ᾽ ἐγκρατεῖς εἶναι, ἐλεήμονας, ἀγαθούς· καὶ συμπάσχειν ἀλλήλοις ὀφείλομεν, καὶ μὴ φιλαργυρεῖν. ἐν τούτοις τοῖς ἔργοις ὁμολογῶμεν αὐτὸν καὶ μὴ ἐν τοῖς ἐναντίοις· 4. καὶ οὐ

δεῖ ἡμᾶς φοβεῖσθαι τοὺς ἀνθρώπους μᾶλλον ἀλλὰ τὸν Θεόν.

5. διὰ τοῦτο, ταῦτα ὑμῶν πρασσόντων, εἶπεν ὁ Κύριος· Ἐὰν ? The Gospel of the ῆτε μετ᾽ ἐμοῦ cynhΓμένοι ἐν τῷ κόλπῳ μογ καὶ μH ποιῆτε τὰc Egyptians. ἐντολάc μογ, ἀποβαλῶ ὑμᾶc καὶ ἐρῶ ὑμῖν· ὙπάΓετε ἀπ᾽ ἐμοῦ, οὐκ οἶδα ὑμᾶc πόθεν ἐcτέ, ἐρΓάται ἀνομίαc.

V. "Οθεν, ἀδελφοί, καταλείψαντες τὴν παροικίαν τοῦ κόσμου τούτου ποιήσωμεν τὸ θέλημα τοῦ καλέσαντος ἡμᾶς, καὶ μὴ φοβηθῶμεν ἐξελθεῖν ἐκ τοῦ κόσμου τούτου. 2. λέγει γὰρ ὁ Κύριος· Ἔcεcθε ὡς ἀρνία ἐν μέcῳ λύκων· 3. ἀποκριθεὶς ? The Gospel of the δὲ ὁ Πέτρος αὐτῷ λέγει· Ἐὰν οὖν διαcπαράξωcιν οἱ λύκοι τὰ Egyptians. ἀρνία; 4. εἶπεν ὁ Ἰησοῦς τῷ Πέτρῳ· ΜH φοβείcθωcαν τὰ ἀρνία τοὺc λύκουc μετὰ τὸ ἀποθανεῖν αὐτά. καὶ ὑμεῖc μH φο- βεῖcθε τοὺc ἀποκτέννοντας ὑμᾶc καὶ μHδὲν ὑμῖν δγναμένουc ποιεῖν, ἀλλὰ φοβεῖcθε τὸν μετὰ τὸ ἀποθανεῖν ὑμᾶc ἔχοντα ἐξογcίαν ψγχῆc καὶ cώματος, τοῦ βαλεῖν εἰc Γέενναν πγρόc. 5. Καὶ γινώσκετε, ἀδελφοί, ὅτι ἡ ἐπιδημία ἡ ἐν τῷ κόσμῳ τούτῳ τῆς σαρκὸς ταύτης μικρά ἐστιν καὶ ὀλιγοχρόνιος· ἡ δὲ ἐπαγγελία τοῦ Χριστοῦ μεγάλη καὶ θαυμαστή ἐστιν, καὶ ἀνάπαυσις τῆς μελλούσης βασιλείας καὶ ζωῆς αἰωνίου. 6. τί οὖν ἐστιν ποιήσαντας ἐπιτυχεῖν αὐτῶν, εἰ μὴ τὸ ὁσίως καὶ δικαίως ἀναστρέφεσθαι, καὶ τὰ κοσμικὰ ταῦτα ὡς ἀλλό- τρια ἡγεῖσθαι καὶ μὴ ἐπιθυμεῖν αὐτῶν; 7. ἐν γὰρ τῷ ἐπι- θυμεῖν ἡμᾶς κτήσασθαι ταῦτα ἀποπίπτομεν τῆς ὁδοῦ τῆς δικαίας.

VI. Λέγει δὲ ὁ Κύριος· Οὐδεὶc οἰκέτηc δύναται δγcὶ κγρίοιc S. Matt. vi. δογλεύειν. ἐὰν ἡμεῖς θέλωμεν καὶ Θεῷ δουλεύειν καὶ μαμωνᾶ, 24. S. Luke ἀσύμφορον ἡμῖν ἐστίν. 2. τί Γὰρ τὸ ὄφελος, ἐάν τιc τὸν xvi. 13. κόcμον ὅλον κερδHcH τHν δὲ ψγχHν ζημιωθῆ; 3. ἔστιν δὲ S. Matt. xvi. 26. οὗτος ὁ αἰὼν καὶ ὁ μέλλων δύο ἐχθροί· 4. οὗτος λέγει μοι- S. Mark viii. 36. χείαν καὶ φθορὰν καὶ φιλαργυρίαν καὶ ἀπάτην, ἐκεῖνος δὲ τούτοις ἀποτάσσεται. 5. οὐ δυνάμεθα οὖν τῶν δύο φίλοι εἶναι· δεῖ δὲ ἡμᾶς τούτῳ ἀποταξαμένους ἐκείνῳ χρᾶσθαι. 6. οἰώμεθα ὅτι βέλτιόν ἐστιν τὰ ἐνθάδε μισῆσαι, ὅτι μικρὰ καὶ ὀλιγοχρόνια καὶ φθαρτά· ἐκεῖνα δὲ ἀγαπῆσαι, τὰ ἀγαθὰ τὰ ἄφθαρτα. 7. ποιοῦντες γὰρ τὸ θέλημα τοῦ Χριστοῦ εὑρήσομεν ἀνάπαυσιν· εἰ δὲ μήγε, οὐδὲν ἡμᾶς ῥύσεται ἐκ τῆς αἰωνίου κολάσεως, ἐὰν παρακούσωμεν τῶν ἐντολῶν αὐτοῦ.

Ezek. xiv. 8. λέγει δὲ καὶ ἡ γραφὴ ἐν τῷ Ἰεζεκιὴλ ὅτι Ἐὰν ἀναστῇ Νῶε
14, 18. καὶ Ἰὼβ καὶ Δανιήλ, ΟΥ ῬΥCΟΝΤΑΙ ΤᾺ ΤΈΚΝΑ ΑΥΤῶΝ ἐν τῇ αἰχμαλωσίᾳ. 9. εἰ δὲ καὶ οἱ τοιοῦτοι δίκαιοι οὐ δύνανται ταῖς ἑαυτῶν δικαιοσύναις ῥύσασθαι τὰ τέκνα αὐτῶν· ἡμεῖς, ἐὰν μὴ τηρήσωμεν τὸ βάπτισμα ἁγνὸν καὶ ἀμίαντον, ποίᾳ πεποιθήσει εἰσελευσόμεθα εἰς τὸ βασίλειον τοῦ Θεοῦ; ἢ τίς ἡμῶν παράκλητος ἔσται, ἐὰν μὴ εὑρεθῶμεν ἔργα ἔχοντες ὅσια καὶ δίκαια;

VII. Ὥστε οὖν, ἀδελφοί μου, ἀγωνισώμεθα, εἰδότες ὅτι ἐν χερσὶν ὁ ἀγών, καὶ ὅτι εἰς τοὺς φθαρτοὺς ἀγῶνας καταπλέουσιν πολλοί, ἀλλ᾽ οὐ πάντες στεφανοῦνται, εἰ μὴ οἱ πολλὰ κοπιάσαντες καὶ καλῶς ἀγωνισάμενοι. 2. ἡμεῖς οὖν ἀγωνισώμεθα, ἵνα πάντες στεφανωθῶμεν. 3. ὥστε θέωμεν τὴν ὁδὸν τὴν εὐθεῖαν, ἀγῶνα τὸν ἄφθαρτον, καὶ πολλοὶ εἰς αὐτὸν καταπλεύσωμεν καὶ ἀγωνισώμεθα, ἵνα καὶ στεφανωθῶμεν· καὶ εἰ μὴ δυνάμεθα πάντες στεφανωθῆναι, κἂν ἐγγὺς τοῦ στεφάνου γενώμεθα. 4. εἰδέναι ἡμᾶς δεῖ, ὅτι ὁ τὸν φθαρτὸν ἀγῶνα ἀγωνιζόμενος, ἐὰν εὑρεθῇ φθείρων, μαστιγωθεὶς αἴρεται καὶ ἔξω βάλλεται τοῦ σταδίου. 5. τί δοκεῖτε; ὁ τὸν τῆς ἀφθαρσίας ἀγῶνα φθείρας, τί παθεῖται; 6. τῶν γὰρ μὴ
Is. lxvi. 24. τηρησάντων, φησίν, τὴν σφραγῖδα ὁ CΚΏΛΗΞ ΑΥΤῶΝ ΟΥ ΤΕΛΕΥΤΉCΕΙ ΚΑῚ ΤῸ ΠῦΡ ΑΥΤῶΝ ΟΥ CΒΕCΘΉCΕΤΑΙ, ΚΑῚ ἜCΟΝΤΑΙ ΕἸC ὍΡΑCΙΝ ΠΆCΗ CΑΡΚΊ.

VIII. Ὡς οὖν ἐσμὲν ἐπὶ γῆς, μετανοήσωμεν· 2. πηλὸς γάρ ἐσμεν εἰς τὴν χεῖρα τοῦ τεχνίτου. ὃν τρόπον γὰρ ὁ κεραμεύς, ἐὰν ποιῇ σκεῦος καὶ ἐν ταῖς χερσὶν αὐτοῦ διαστραφῇ ἢ συντριβῇ, πάλιν αὐτὸ ἀναπλάσσει· ἐὰν δὲ προφθάσῃ εἰς τὴν κάμινον τοῦ πυρὸς αὐτὸ βαλεῖν, οὐκέτι βοηθήσει αὐτῷ· οὕτως καὶ ἡμεῖς, ἕως ἐσμὲν ἐν τούτῳ τῷ κόσμῳ, ἐν τῇ σαρκὶ ἃ ἐπράξαμεν πονηρὰ μετανοήσωμεν ἐξ ὅλης τῆς καρδίας, ἵνα σωθῶμεν ὑπὸ τοῦ Κυρίου, ἕως ἔχομεν καιρὸν μετανοίας· 3. μετὰ γὰρ τὸ ἐξελθεῖν ἡμᾶς ἐκ τοῦ κόσμου, οὐκέτι δυνάμεθα ἐκεῖ ἐξομολογήσασθαι ἢ μετανοεῖν ἔτι. 4. ὥστε, ἀδελφοί, ποιήσαντες τὸ θέλημα τοῦ πατρὸς καὶ τὴν σάρκα ἁγνὴν τηρήσαντες καὶ τὰς ἐντολὰς τοῦ Κυρίου φυλάξαντες ληψόμεθα ζωὴν αἰώνιον. 5. λέγει γὰρ ὁ Κύριος ἐν τῷ εὐαγγελίῳ· Εἰ τὸ μικρὸν ογκ ἐτηρήσατε, τὸ μέγα τίς ὑμῖν δώσει; λέγω γὰρ ὑμῖν ὅτι ὁ πιστὸς ἐν ἐλαχίστῳ καὶ ἐν πολλῷ πιστός ἐστιν. 6. ἄρα οὖν τοῦτο λέγει· τηρήσατε τὴν σάρκα ἁγνὴν καὶ τὴν σφραγῖδα ἄσπιλον, ἵνα τὴν ζωὴν ἀπολάβωμεν.

S. Matt.
xxv. 21.
S. Luke
xvi. 10, 11.

IX. Καὶ μὴ λεγέτω τις ὑμῶν, ὅτι αὕτη ἡ σὰρξ οὐ κρίνεται οὐδὲ ἀνίσταται. 2. γνῶτε· ἐν τίνι ἐσώθητε, ἐν τίνι ἀνεβλέψατε, εἰ μὴ ἐν τῇ σαρκὶ ταύτῃ ὄντες; 3. δεῖ οὖν ἡμᾶς ὡς ναὸν Θεοῦ φυλάσσειν τὴν σάρκα· 4. ὃν τρόπον γὰρ ἐν τῇ σαρκὶ ἐκλήθητε, καὶ ἐν τῇ σαρκὶ ἐλεύσεσθε. 5. εἰ Χριστὸς ὁ Κύριος, ὁ σώσας ἡμᾶς, ὢν μὲν τὸ πρῶτον πνεῦμα, ἐγένετο σὰρξ καὶ οὕτως ἡμᾶς ἐκάλεσεν, οὕτως καὶ ἡμεῖς ἐν ταύτῃ τῇ σαρκὶ ἀποληψόμεθα τὸν μισθόν. 6. ἀγαπῶμεν οὖν ἀλλήλους, ὅπως ἔλθωμεν πάντες εἰς τὴν βασιλείαν τοῦ Θεοῦ. 7. ὡς ἔχομεν καιρὸν τοῦ ἰαθῆναι, ἐπιδῶμεν ἑαυτοὺς τῷ θεραπεύοντι Θεῷ, ἀντιμισθίαν αὐτῷ διδόντες· 8. ποίαν; τὸ μετανοῆσαι ἐξ εἰλικρινοῦς καρδίας· 9. προγνώστης γάρ ἐστιν τῶν πάντων καὶ εἰδὼς ἡμῶν τὰ ἐν καρδίᾳ. 10. δῶμεν οὖν αὐτῷ αἶνον αἰώνιον, μὴ ἀπὸ στόματος μόνον ἀλλὰ καὶ ἀπὸ καρδίας, ἵνα ἡμᾶς προσδέξηται ὡς υἱούς. 11. καὶ γὰρ εἶπεν ὁ Κύριος· Ἀδελφοί μου ογτοί εἰcιν οἱ ποιογντες τὸ θέλημα S. Matt. τογ πατρός μογ.

xii. 50.

X. Ὥστε, ἀδελφοί μου, ποιήσωμεν τὸ θέλημα τοῦ πατρὸς τοῦ καλέσαντος ἡμᾶς, ἵνα ζήσωμεν, καὶ διώξωμεν μᾶλλον τὴν ἀρετήν, τὴν δὲ κακίαν καταλείψωμεν ὡς προοδοιπόρον τῶν ἁμαρτιῶν ἡμῶν, καὶ φύγωμεν τὴν ἀσέβειαν, μὴ ἡμᾶς καταλάβῃ κακά. 2. ἐὰν γὰρ σπουδάσωμεν ἀγαθοποιεῖν, διώξεται ἡμᾶς εἰρήνη. 3. Διὰ ταύτην γὰρ τὴν αἰτίαν οὐκ ἔστιν †εὑρεῖν† ἄνθρωπον, οἵτινες παράγουσι φόβους ἀνθρωπίνους, προῃρημένοι μᾶλλον τὴν ἐνθάδε ἀπόλαυσιν ἢ τὴν μέλλουσαν ἐπαγγελίαν. 4. ἀγνοοῦσιν γὰρ ἡλίκην ἔχει βάσανον ἡ ἐνθάδε ἀπόλαυσις, καὶ οἵαν τρυφὴν ἔχει ἡ μέλλουσα ἐπαγγελία. 5. καὶ εἰ μὲν αὐτοὶ μόνοι ταῦτα ἔπρασσον, ἀνεκτὸν ἦν· νῦν δὲ ἐπιμένουσιν κακοδιδασκαλοῦντες τὰς ἀναιτίους ψυχάς, οὐκ εἰδότες ὅτι δισσὴν ἕξουσιν τὴν κρίσιν, αὐτοί τε καὶ οἱ ἀκούοντες αὐτῶν.

XI. Ἡμεῖς οὖν ἐν καθαρᾷ καρδίᾳ δουλεύσωμεν τῷ Θεῷ, καὶ ἐσόμεθα δίκαιοι· ἐὰν δὲ μὴ δουλεύσωμεν διὰ τοῦ μὴ πιστεύειν ἡμᾶς τῇ ἐπαγγελίᾳ τοῦ Θεοῦ, ταλαίπωροι ἐσόμεθα.

? Eldad and Modad. 2. λέγει γὰρ καὶ ὁ προφητικὸς λόγος· Ταλαίπωροί εἰcιν οἱ Δίψγχοι, οἱ Διcτάζοντεc τῇ καρΔίᾳ, οἱ λέγοντεc· Ταῦτα πάντα Ηκούcαμεν καὶ ἐπὶ τῶν πατέρων ἡμῶν, ἡμεῖc δὲ ἡμέραν ἐξ ἡμέρας προcδεχόμενοι οὐδὲν τούτων ἑωράκαμεν. 3. Ἀνόητοι, cγμβάλετε ἑαυτοὺc ξγλῳ, λάβετε ἄμπελον· πρῶτον μὲν φγλλοροεῖ, εἶτα βλαcτὸc γίνεται, μετὰ ταῦτα ὄμφαξ, εἶτα cταφγλὴ παρεcτηκγῖα· 4. οὕτωc καὶ ὁ λαόc μογ ἀκαταcταcίαc καὶ θλίψειc ἔcχεν, ἔπειτα ἀπολήψεται τὰ ἀγαθά. 5. Ὥστε, ἀδελφοί μου, μὴ διψυχῶμεν, ἀλλὰ ἐλπίσαντες ὑπομείνωμεν, ἵνα καὶ τὸν μισθὸν κομισώ-

Heb. x. 23. μεθα. 6. πιcτὸc γάρ ἐcτιν ὁ ἐπαγγειλάμενοc τὰς ἀντιμιcθίαc ἀποδιδόναι ἑκάcτῳ τῶν ἔργων αὐτοῦ. 7. ἐὰν οὖν ποιήσωμεν τὴν δικαιοσύνην ἐναντίον τοῦ Θεοῦ, εἰσήξομεν εἰς τὴν βασι-

1 Cor. ii. 9. λείαν αὐτοῦ καὶ ληψόμεθα τὰς ἐπαγγελίας ἃς οὖc οὐκ Ηκογcεν οὐδὲ ὀφθαλμὸc εἶδεν, οὐδὲ ἐπὶ καρδίαν ἀνθρώπογ ἀνέβη.

XII. Ἐκδεχώμεθα οὖν καθ᾽ ὥραν τὴν βασιλείαν τοῦ Θεοῦ ἐν ἀγάπῃ καὶ δικαιοσύνῃ, ἐπειδὴ οὐκ οἴδαμεν τὴν ἡμέραν τῆς ἐπιφανείας τοῦ Θεοῦ. 2. ἐπερωτηθεὶς γὰρ αὐτὸς ? The Gospel of the Egyptians. ὁ Κύριος ὑπό τινος, πότε ἥξει αὐτοῦ ἡ βασιλεία, εἶπεν· Ὅταν ἔcται τὰ Δγο ἕν, καὶ τὸ ἔξω ὡc τὸ ἔcω, καὶ τὸ ἄρcεν μετὰ τῆc θηλείαc, οὔτε ἄρcεν οὔτε θῆλγ. 3. τὰ δγο δὲ ἕν ἐcτιν, ὅταν λαλῶμεν ἑαυτοῖc ἀλήθειαν, καὶ ἐν δυσὶ σώμασιν ἀνυποκρίτως εἴη μία ψυχή. 4. καὶ τὸ ἔξω ὡc τὸ ἔcω, τοῦτο λέγει· τὴν ψυχὴν λέγει τὸ ἔσω, τὸ δὲ ἔξω τὸ σῶμα λέγει. ὃν τρόπον οὖν σου τὸ σῶμα φαίνεται, οὕτως καὶ ἡ ψυχή σου δῆλος ἔστω ἐν τοῖς καλοῖς ἔργοις. 5. καὶ τὸ ἄρϲεν μετὰ τῆϲ θηλείαϲ οὔτε ἄρϲεν οὔτε θῆλυ, τοῦτο λέγει, ἵνα ἀδελφὸς ἰδὼν ἀδελφὴν μηδὲν φρονῇ περὶ αὐτῆς θηλυκόν, μηδὲ φρονῇ τι περὶ αὐτοῦ ἀρσενικόν. 6. ταῦτα ὑμῶν ποιούντων, φησίν, ἐλεύσεται ἡ βασιλεία τοῦ πατρός μου.

XIII. Ἀδελφοὶ †οὖν† ἤδη ποτὲ μετανοήσωμεν· νήψωμεν ἐπὶ τὸ ἀγαθόν· μεστοὶ γάρ ἐσμεν πολλῆς ἀνοίας καὶ πονηρίας. ἐξαλείψωμεν ἀφ᾽ ἡμῶν τὰ πρότερα ἁμαρτήματα, καὶ μετανοήσαντες ἐκ ψυχῆς σωθῶμεν. καὶ μὴ γινώμεθα ἀνθρωπάρεσκοι· μηδὲ θέλωμεν μόνον ἑαυτοῖς ἀρέσκειν, ἀλλὰ καὶ τοῖς ἔξω ἀνθρώποις ἐπὶ τῇ δικαιοσύνῃ, ἵνα τὸ ὄνομα δι᾽ ἡμᾶς μὴ βλασφημῆται. 2. Λέγει γὰρ καὶ ὁ Κύριος· Διὰ Is. lii. 5. παντὸς τὸ ὄνομά μου βλαϲφημεῖται ἐν πᾶϲιν τοῖϲ ἔθνεϲιν· καὶ πάλιν· Οὐαὶ δι᾽ ὃν βλαϲφημεῖται τὸ ὄνομά μου· ἐν τίνι βλαϲ- Is. lii. 5. φημεῖται; ἐν τῷ μὴ ποιεῖν ὑμᾶς ἃ βούλομαι. 3. τὰ ἔθνη γάρ, ἀκούοντα ἐκ τοῦ στόματος ἡμῶν τὰ λόγια τοῦ Θεοῦ, ὡς καλὰ καὶ μεγάλα θαυμάζει· ἔπειτα, καταμαθόντα τὰ ἔργα ἡμῶν ὅτι οὐκ ἔστιν ἄξια τῶν ῥημάτων ὧν λέγομεν, ἔνθεν εἰς βλασφημίαν τρέπονται, λέγοντες εἶναι μῦθόν τινα καὶ πλάνην. 4. ὅταν γὰρ ἀκούσωσιν παρ᾽ ἡμῶν ὅτι λέγει ὁ Θεός· Οὐ χάριϲ ὑμῖν εἰ ἀγαπᾶτε τοὺϲ ἀγαπῶνταϲ ὑμᾶϲ, ἀλλὰ χάριϲ ὑμῖν S. Luke vi. εἰ ἀγαπᾶτε τοὺϲ ἐχθροὺϲ καὶ τοὺϲ μιϲοῦνταϲ ὑμᾶϲ· ταῦτα ὅταν 32, 35. ἀκούσωσιν, θαυμάζουσιν τὴν ὑπερβολὴν τῆς ἀγαθότητος· ὅταν δὲ ἴδωσιν ὅτι οὐ μόνον τοὺς μισοῦντας οὐκ ἀγαπῶμεν, ἀλλ᾽ ὅτι οὐδὲ τοὺς ἀγαπῶντας, καταγελῶσιν ἡμῶν, καὶ βλασφημεῖται τὸ ὄνομα.

XIV. Ὥστε, ἀδελφοί, ποιοῦντες τὸ θέλημα τοῦ πατρὸς ἡμῶν Θεοῦ ἐσόμεθα ἐκ τῆς ἐκκλησίας τῆς πρώτης, τῆς πνευματικῆς, τῆς πρὸ ἡλίου καὶ σελήνης ἐκτισμένης· ἐὰν δὲ μὴ ποιήσωμεν τὸ θέλημα Κυρίου, ἐσόμεθα ἐκ τῆς γραφῆς τῆς Jer. vii. 11. λεγούσης Ἐγενήθη ὁ οἶκόϲ μου ϲπήλαιον ληϲτῶν. ὥστε οὖν S. Matt. xxi. 13.

---

xii. 5 μηδὲν φρονῇ] conj. Lightfoot ; οὐδὲν φρονεῖ C ; def. A.
xiii. 1 οὖν] C; om. S; def A ; μου conj. Lightfoot. ·

αἱρετισώμεθα ἀπὸ τῆς ἐκκλησίας τῆς ζωῆς εἶναι, ἵνα σωθῶ-

Eph. i. 23. μεν. 2. οὐκ οἴομαι δὲ ὑμᾶς ἀγνοεῖν ὅτι ἐκκλησία ζῶσα cῶμά

Gen. i. 27. ἐϲτιν Χριϲτοῦ· λέγει γὰρ ἡ γραφή· Ἐποίηϲεν ὁ Θεὸϲ τὸν ἄνθρωπον ἄρϲεν καὶ θῆλυ· τὸ ἄρσεν ἐστὶν ὁ Χριστός, τὸ θῆλυ ἡ
ἐκκλησία· καὶ ὅτι τὰ βιβλία καὶ οἱ ἀπόστολοι τὴν ἐκκλησίαν οὐ νῦν εἶναι, ἀλλὰ ἄνωθεν [λέγουσιν, δῆλον]· ἦν γὰρ
πνευματική, ὡς καὶ ὁ Ἰησοῦς ἡμῶν, ἐφανερώθη δὲ ἐπ᾽ ἐσχάτων τῶν ἡμερῶν ἵνα ἡμᾶς σώσῃ· 3. ἡ ἐκκλησία δὲ πνευμα-
τικὴ οὖσα ἐφανερώθη ἐν τῇ σαρκὶ Χριστοῦ, δηλοῦσα ἡμῖν
ὅτι, ἐάν τις ἡμῶν τηρήσῃ αὐτὴν ἐν τῇ σαρκὶ καὶ μὴ φθείρῃ,
ἀπολήψεται αὐτὴν ἐν τῷ πνεύματι τῷ ἁγίῳ· ἡ γὰρ σὰρξ
αὕτη ἀντίτυπός ἐστιν τοῦ πνεύματος· οὐδεὶς οὖν τὸ ἀντί-
τυπον φθείρας τὸ αὐθεντικὸν μεταλήψεται. ἄρα οὖν τοῦτο
λέγει, ἀδελφοί, Τηρήσατε τὴν σάρκα ἵνα τοῦ πνεύματος μετα-
λάβητε. 4. εἰ δὲ λέγομεν εἶναι τὴν σάρκα τὴν ἐκκλησίαν
καὶ τὸ πνεῦμα Χριστόν, ἄρα οὖν ὁ ὑβρίσας τὴν σάρκα ὕβρι-
σεν τὴν ἐκκλησίαν. ὁ τοιοῦτος οὖν οὐ μεταλήψεται τοῦ
πνεύματος, ὅ ἐστιν ὁ Χριστός. 5. τοσαύτην δύναται ἡ σὰρξ
αὕτη μεταλαβεῖν ζωὴν καὶ ἀθανασίαν, κολληθέντος αὐτῇ τοῦ
πνεύματος τοῦ ἁγίου. οὔτε ἐξειπεῖν τις δύναται οὔτε λαλῆ-

1 Cor. ii. σαι ἃ ἡτοίμαϲεν ὁ Κύριος τοῖς ἐκλεκτοῖς αὐτοῦ.
9.   XV. Οὐκ οἴομαι δὲ ὅτι μικρὰν συμβουλίαν ἐποιησάμην
περὶ ἐγκρατείας, ἣν ποιήσας τις οὐ μετανοήσει, ἀλλὰ καὶ
ἑαυτὸν σώσει κἀμὲ τὸν συμβουλεύσαντα. μισθὸς γὰρ οὐκ
ἔστιν μικρὸς πλανωμένην ψυχὴν καὶ ἀπολλυμένην ἀποστρέ-
ψαι εἰς τὸ σωθῆναι. 2. ταύτην γὰρ ἔχομεν τὴν ἀντιμισθίαν
ἀποδοῦναι τῷ Θεῷ τῷ κτίσαντι ἡμᾶς, ἐὰν ὁ λέγων καὶ
ἀκούων μετὰ πίστεως καὶ ἀγάπης καὶ λέγῃ καὶ ἀκούῃ.
3. ἐμμείνωμεν οὖν ἐφ᾽ οἷς ἐπιστεύσαμεν δίκαιοι καὶ ὅσιοι, ἵνα

Is. lviii. 9. μετὰ παρρησίας αἰτῶμεν τὸν Θεὸν τὸν λέγοντα· Ἔτι λαλοῦντόϲ ϲου ἐρῶ Ἰδοὺ πάρειμι. 4. τοῦτο γὰρ τὸ ῥῆμα μεγάλης
ἐστὶν ἐπαγγελίας σημεῖον· ἑτοιμότερον γὰρ ἑαυτὸν λέγει ὁ
Κύριος εἰς τὸ διδόναι τοῦ αἰτοῦντος. 5. τοσαύτης οὖν χρη-

στότητος μεταλαμβάνοντες μὴ φθονήσωμεν ἑαυτοῖς τυχεῖν
τοσούτων ἀγαθῶν. ὅσην γὰρ ἡδονὴν ἔχει τὰ ῥήματα ταῦτα
τοῖς ποιήσασιν αὐτά, τοσαύτην κατάκρισιν ἔχει τοῖς παρα-
κούσασιν.

XVI. Ὥστε, ἀδελφοί, ἀφορμὴν λαβόντες· οὐ μικρὰν εἰς
τὸ μετανοῆσαι, καιρὸν ἔχοντες ἐπιστρέψωμεν ἐπὶ τὸν καλέ-
σαντα ἡμᾶς Θεόν, ἕως ἔτι ἔχομεν τὸν παραδεχόμενον ἡμᾶς. 2.
ἐὰν γὰρ ταῖς ἡδυπαθείαις ταύταις ἀποταξώμεθα καὶ τὴν
ψυχὴν ἡμῶν νικήσωμεν ἐν τῷ μὴ ποιεῖν τὰς ἐπιθυμίας αὐτῆς
τὰς πονηράς, μεταληψόμεθα τοῦ ἐλέους Ἰησοῦ. 3. Γινώσκετε δὲ ὅτι ἔρχεται ἤδη ἡ ἡμέρα τῆς κρίσεως ὡς κλίβανος Mal. iv. 1.
καιόμενος, καὶ τακήσονται [αἱ] δυνάμεις τῶν οὐρανῶν, καὶ πᾶσα Is. xxxiv.
ἡ γῆ ὡς μόλιβος ἐπὶ πυρὶ τηκόμενος, καὶ τότε φανήσεται τὰ ⁴·
κρύφια καὶ φανερὰ ἔργα τῶν ἀνθρώπων. 4. καλὸν οὖν
ἐλεημοσύνη ὡς μετάνοια ἁμαρτίας· κρείσσων νηστεία προσευχῆς, ἐλεημοσύνη δὲ ἀμφοτέρων· ἀγάπη δὲ καλύπτει πλῆθος Prov. x. 12.
ἁμαρτιῶν· προσευχὴ δὲ ἐκ καλῆς συνειδήσεως ἐκ θανάτου   1 Pet. iv. 8.
ῥύεται. μακάριος πᾶς ὁ εὑρεθεὶς ἐν τούτοις πλήρης· ἐλεημο-
σύνη γὰρ κούφισμα ἁμαρτίας γίνεται.

XVII. Μετανοήσωμεν οὖν ἐξ ὅλης καρδίας, ἵνα μή τις
ἡμῶν παραπόληται. εἰ γὰρ ἐντολὰς ἔχομεν, ἵνα καὶ τοῦτο
πράσσωμεν, ἀπὸ τῶν εἰδώλων ἀποσπᾶν καὶ κατηχεῖν, πόσῳ
μᾶλλον ψυχὴν ἤδη γινώσκουσαν τὸν Θεὸν οὐ δεῖ ἀπόλλυ-
σθαι; 2. συλλάβωμεν οὖν ἑαυτοῖς καὶ τοὺς ἀσθενοῦντας
ἀνάγειν περὶ τὸ ἀγαθόν, ὅπως σωθῶμεν ἅπαντες· καὶ ἐπιστρέψωμεν ἀλλήλους καὶ νουθετήσωμεν. 3. καὶ μὴ μόνον
ἄρτι δοκῶμεν προσέχειν καὶ πιστεύειν ἐν τῷ νουθετεῖσθαι
ἡμᾶς ὑπὸ τῶν πρεσβυτέρων, ἀλλὰ καὶ ὅταν εἰς οἶκον ἀπαλ-
λαγῶμεν, μνημονεύωμεν τῶν τοῦ Κυρίου ἐνταλμάτων, καὶ
μὴ ἀντιπαρελκώμεθα ἀπὸ τῶν κοσμικῶν ἐπιθυμιῶν, ἀλλὰ
πυκνότερον προσερχόμενοι πειρώμεθα προκόπτειν ἐν ταῖς
ἐντολαῖς τοῦ Κυρίου, ἵνα πάντες τὸ αὐτὸ φρονοῦντες συνηγ-
μένοι ὦμεν ἐπὶ τὴν ζωήν. 4. εἶπεν γὰρ ὁ Κύριος· Ἔρχομαι Is. lxvi. 18.

συναγαγεῖν πάντα τὰ ἔθνη, φυλὰς καὶ γλώσσας· τοῦτο δὲ λέγει
τὴν ἡμέραν τῆς ἐπιφανείας αὐτοῦ, ὅτε ἐλθὼν λυτρώσεται
Is. lxvi. 18. ἡμᾶς ἕκαστον κατὰ τὰ ἔργα αὐτοῦ. 5. καὶ ὄψονται τὴν δόξαν
αὐτοῦ καὶ τὸ κράτος οἱ ἄπιστοι, καὶ ξενισθήσονται ἰδόντες τὸ
βασίλειον τοῦ κόσμου ἐν τῷ Ἰησοῦ λέγοντες, Οὐαὶ ἡμῖν, ὅτι
σὺ ἧς καὶ οὐκ ᾔδειμεν καὶ οὐκ ἐπιστεύομεν, καὶ οὐκ ἐπειθό-
μεθα τοῖς πρεσβυτέροις τοῖς ἀναγγέλλουσιν ἡμῖν περὶ τῆς
Is. lxvi. 24. σωτηρίας ἡμῶν· καὶ Ὁ σκώληξ αὐτῶν οὐ τελευτήσει καὶ τὸ πῦρ
αὐτῶν οὐ σβεσθήσεται καὶ ἔσονται εἰς ὅρασιν πάσῃ σαρκί. 6. τὴν
ἡμέραν ἐκείνην λέγει τῆς κρίσεως, ὅταν ὄψονται τοὺς ἐν
ἡμῖν ἀσεβήσαντας καὶ παραλογισαμένους τὰς ἐντολὰς Ἰησοῦ
Χριστοῦ. 7. οἱ δὲ δίκαιοι εὐπραγήσαντες καὶ ὑπομείναντες
τὰς βασάνους καὶ μισήσαντες τὰς ἡδυπαθείας τῆς ψυχῆς,
ὅταν θεάσωνται τοὺς ἀστοχήσαντας καὶ ἀρνησαμένους διὰ
τῶν λόγων ἢ διὰ τῶν ἔργων τὸν Ἰησοῦν, ὅπως κολάζονται
δειναῖς βασάνοις πυρὶ ἀσβέστῳ, ἔσονται δόξαν διδόντες τῷ
Θεῷ αὐτῶν, λέγοντες ὅτι Ἔσται ἐλπὶς τῷ δεδουλευκότι Θεῷ
ἐξ ὅλης καρδίας.

XVIII. Καὶ ἡμεῖς οὖν γενώμεθα ἐκ τῶν εὐχαριστούν-
των, τῶν δεδουλευκότων τῷ Θεῷ, καὶ μὴ ἐκ τῶν κρινομένων
ἀσεβῶν. 2. καὶ γὰρ αὐτὸς πανθαμαρτωλὸς ὢν καὶ μήπω
φυγὼν τὸν πειρασμόν, ἀλλ' ἔτι ὢν ἐν μέσοις τοῖς ὀργάνοις
τοῦ διαβόλου, σπουδάζω τὴν δικαιοσύνην διώκειν, ὅπως
ἰσχύσω κἂν ἐγγὺς αὐτῆς γενέσθαι, φοβούμενος τὴν κρίσιν
τὴν μέλλουσαν.

XIX. Ὥστε, ἀδελφοὶ καὶ ἀδελφαί, μετὰ τὸν Θεὸν τῆς
ἀληθείας ἀναγινώσκω ὑμῖν ἔντευξιν εἰς τὸ προσέχειν τοῖς
γεγραμμένοις, ἵνα καὶ ἑαυτοὺς σώσητε καὶ τὸν ἀναγινώσκοντα
ἐν ὑμῖν· μισθὸν γὰρ αἰτῶ ὑμᾶς τὸ μετανοῆσαι ἐξ ὅλης καρδίας σωτηρίαν ἑαυτοῖς καὶ ζωὴν διδόντας. τοῦτο γὰρ ποιήσαντες σκοπὸν πᾶσιν τοῖς νέοις θήσομεν τοῖς βουλομένοις
περὶ τὴν εὐσέβειαν καὶ τὴν χρηστότητα τοῦ Θεοῦ φιλοπο-
νεῖν. 2. καὶ μὴ ἀηδῶς ἔχωμεν καὶ ἀγανακτῶμεν οἱ ἄσοφοι,
ὅταν τις ἡμᾶς νουθετῇ καὶ ἐπιστρέφῃ ἀπὸ τῆς ἀδικίας εἰς τὴν

δικαιοσύνην. ἐνίοτε γὰρ πονηρὰ πράσσοντες οὐ γινώσκομεν διὰ τὴν διψυχίαν καὶ ἀπιστίαν τὴν ἐνοῦσαν ἐν τοῖς στήθεσιν ἡμῶν, καὶ ἐϲκοτίϲμεθα τὴν Διάνοιαν ὑπὸ τῶν ἐπιθυμιῶν τῶν Eph.iv.17. ματαίων. 3. πράξωμεν οὖν τὴν δικαιοσύνην ἵνα εἰς τέλος σωθῶμεν. μακάριοι οἱ τούτοις ὑπακούοντες τοῖς προστάγμασιν· κἂν ὀλίγον χρόνον κακοπαθήσωσιν ἐν τῷ κόσμῳ, τὸν ἀθάνατον τῆς ἀναστάσεως καρπὸν τρυγήσουσιν. 4. μὴ οὖν λυπείσθω ὁ εὐσεβὴς ἐὰν ἐπὶ τοῖς νῦν χρόνοις ταλαιπωρῇ· μακάριος αὐτὸν ἀναμένει χρόνος· ἐκεῖνος ἄνω μετὰ τῶν πατέρων ἀναβιώσας εὐφρανθήσεται εἰς τὸν ἀλύπητον αἰῶνα.

XX. Ἀλλὰ μηδὲ ἐκεῖνο τὴν διάνοιαν ὑμῶν ταρασσέτω, ὅτι βλέπομεν τοὺς ἀδίκους πλουτοῦντας, καὶ στενοχωρουμένους τοὺς τοῦ Θεοῦ δούλους. 2. πιστεύωμεν οὖν, ἀδελφοὶ καὶ ἀδελφαί· Θεοῦ ζῶντος πεῖραν ἀθλοῦμεν, καὶ γυμναζόμεθα τῷ νῦν βίῳ ἵνα τῷ μέλλοντι στεφανωθῶμεν. 3. οὐδεὶς τῶν δικαίων ταχὺν καρπὸν ἔλαβεν, ἀλλ' ἐκδέχεται αὐτόν. 4. εἰ γὰρ τὸν μισθὸν τῶν δικαίων ὁ Θεὸς συντόμως ἀπεδίδου, εὐθέως ἐμπορίαν ἠσκοῦμεν καὶ οὐ θεοσέβειαν· ἐδοκοῦμεν γὰρ εἶναι δίκαιοι, οὐ τὸ εὐσεβὲς ἀλλὰ τὸ κερδαλέον διώκοντες· καὶ διὰ τοῦτο θεία κρίσις ἔβλαψεν πνεῦμα μὴ ὂν δίκαιον, καὶ ἐβάρυνεν δεσμοῖς.

5. Τῷ μόνῳ Θεῷ ἀοράτῳ, πατρὶ τῆς ἀληθείας, τῷ ἐξαποστείλαντι ἡμῖν τὸν σωτῆρα καὶ ἀρχηγὸν τῆς ἀφθαρσίας, δι' οὗ καὶ ἐφανέρωσεν ἡμῖν τὴν ἀλήθειαν καὶ τὴν ἐπουράνιον ζωήν, αὐτῷ ἡ δόξα εἰς τοὺς αἰῶνας τῶν αἰώνων. ἀμήν.

TRANSLATION

OF THE

EPISTLES OF S. CLEMENT

THE EPISTLE OF S. CLEMENT

TO

THE CORINTHIANS

THE Church of God which sojourneth in Rome to the Church of God which sojourneth in Corinth, to them which are called and sanctified by the will of God through our Lord Jesus Christ. Grace to you and peace from Almighty God through Jesus Christ be multiplied.

1. By reason of the sudden and repeated calamities and reverses which are befalling us, brethren, we consider that we have been somewhat tardy in giving heed to the matters of dispute that have arisen among you, dearly beloved, and to the detestable and unholy sedition, so alien and strange to the elect of God, which a few headstrong and self-willed persons have kindled to such a pitch of madness that your name, once revered and renowned and lovely in the sight of all men, hath been greatly reviled. For who that had sojourned among you did not approve your most virtuous and stedfast faith? Who did not admire your sober and forbearing piety in Christ? Who did not publish abroad your magnificent disposition of hospitality? Who did not congratulate you on your perfect and sound knowledge? For ye did all things without respect of persons, and ye walked after the ordinances of God, submitting yourselves to your rulers and rendering to the older men among you the honour which is their due. On the young too ye enjoined modest and seemly thoughts: and the women ye charged to perform all their duties in a blameless and seemly and pure conscience, cherishing their own husbands, as is meet; and ye taught them to keep in the rule of obedience, and to manage the affairs of their household in seemliness, with all discretion.

2. And ye were all lowly in mind and free from arrogance, yielding rather than claiming submission, *more glad to give than to receive,* and content with the provisions which God supplieth. And giving heed unto His words, ye laid them up diligently in your hearts, and His sufferings were before your eyes. Thus a profound and rich peace was given to all, and an insatiable desire of doing good. An abundant outpouring also of the Holy Spirit fell upon all; and, being full of holy counsel, in excellent zeal and with a pious confidence ye stretched out your hands to Almighty God, supplicating Him to be propitious, if unwillingly ye had committed any sin. Ye had conflict day and night for all the brotherhood, that the number of His elect might be saved with fearfulness and intentness of mind. Ye were sincere and simple and free from malice one towards another. Every sedition and every schism was abominable to you. Ye mourned over the transgressions of your neighbours : ye judged their shortcomings to be your own. Ye repented not of any well-doing, but were *ready unto every good work.* Being adorned with a most virtuous and honourable life, ye performed all your duties in the fear of Him. The commandments and the ordinances of the Lord were *written on the tables of your hearts.*

3. All glory and enlargement was given unto you, and that was fulfilled which is written ; *My beloved ate and drank and was enlarged and waxed fat and kicked.* Hence come jealousy and envy, strife and sedition, persecution and tumult, war and captivity. So men were stirred up, *the mean against the honourable,* the ill-reputed against the highly-reputed, the foolish against the wise, *the young against the elder.* For this cause *righteousness* and peace *stand aloof,* while each man hath forsaken the fear of the Lord and become purblind in the faith of Him, neither walketh in the ordinances of His commandments nor liveth according to that which becometh Christ, but each goeth after the lusts of his evil heart, seeing that they have conceived an unrighteous and ungodly jealousy, through which also *death entered into the world.*

4. For so it is written, *And it came to pass after certain days that Cain brought of the fruits of the earth a sacrifice unto God, and Abel he also brought of the firstlings of the sheep and of their fatness. And God looked upon Abel and upon his gifts, but unto Cain and unto his sacrifices He gave no heed. And Cain sorrowed exceedingly, and his countenance fell. And God said unto Cain, Wherefore art thou very sorrowful? and wherefore did thy countenance fall? If thou hast offered aright and hast not divided aright, didst thou not sin? Hold thy peace. Unto thee shall*

he turn, and thou shalt rule over him. And Cain said unto Abel his brother, Let us go over unto the plain. And it came to pass, while they were in the plain, that Cain rose up against Abel his brother and slew him. Ye see, brethren, jealousy and envy wrought a brother's murder. By reason of jealousy our father Jacob ran away from the face of Esau his brother. Jealousy caused Joseph to be persecuted even unto death, and to come even unto bondage. Jealousy compelled Moses to flee from the face of Pharaoh king of Egypt while it was said to him by his own countryman, *Who made thee a judge or a decider over us? Wouldest thou slay me, even as yesterday thou slewest the Egyptian?* By reason of jealousy Aaron and Miriam were lodged outside the camp. Jealousy brought Dathan and Abiram down alive to hades, because they made sedition against Moses the servant of God. By reason of jealousy David was envied not only by the Philistines, but was persecuted also by Saul[king of Israel].

5. But, to pass from the examples of ancient days, let us come to those champions who lived nearest to our time. Let us set before us the noble examples which belong to our generation. By reason of jealousy and envy the greatest and most righteous pillars of the Church were persecuted, and contended even unto death. Let us set before our eyes the good Apostles. There was Peter who by reason of unrighteous jealousy endured not one nor two but many labours, and thus having borne his testimony went to his appointed place of glory. By reason of jealousy and strife Paul by his example pointed out the prize of patient endurance. After that he had been seven times in bonds, had been driven into exile, had been stoned, had preached in the East and in the West, he won the noble renown which was the reward of his faith, having taught righteousness unto the whole world and having reached the farthest bounds of the West; and when he had borne his testimony before the rulers, so he departed from the world and went unto the holy place, having been found a notable pattern of patient endurance.

6. Unto these men of holy lives was gathered a vast multitude of the elect, who through many indignities and tortures, being the victims of jealousy, set a brave example among ourselves. By reason of jealousy women being persecuted, after that they had suffered cruel and unholy insults †as Danaids and Dircæ†, safely reached the goal in the race of faith, and received a noble reward, feeble though they were in body. Jealousy hath estranged wives from their husbands and

changed the saying of our father Adam, *This now is bone of my bones and flesh of my flesh.* Jealousy and strife have overthrown great cities and uprooted great nations.

7. These things, dearly beloved, we write, not only as admonishing you, but also as putting ourselves in remembrance. For we are in the same lists, and the same contest awaiteth us. Wherefore let us forsake idle and vain thoughts; and let us conform to the glorious and venerable rule which hath been handed down to us; and let us see what is good and what is pleasant and what is acceptable in the sight of Him that made us. Let us fix our eyes on the blood of Christ and understand how precious it is unto His Father, because being shed for our salvation it won for the whole world the grace of repentance. Let us review all the generations in turn, and learn how from generation to generation the Master hath given a place for repentance unto them that desire to turn to Him. Noah preached repentance, and they that obeyed were saved. Jonah preached destruction unto the men of Nineveh; but they, repenting of their sins, obtained pardon of God by their supplications and received salvation, albeit they were aliens from God.

8. The ministers of the grace of God through the Holy Spirit spake concerning repentance. Yea and the Master of the universe Himself spake concerning repentance with an oath; *For, as I live, saith the Lord, I desire not the death of the sinner, so much as his repentance;* and He added also a merciful judgment: *Repent ye, O house of Israel, of your iniquity; say unto the sons of My people, Though your sins reach from the earth even unto the heaven, and though they be redder than scarlet and blacker than sackcloth, and ye turn unto Me with your whole heart and say Father, I will give ear unto you as unto a holy people.* And in another place He saith on this wise, *Wash, be ye clean. Put away your iniquities from your souls out of My sight. Cease from your iniquities; learn to do good; seek out judgment; defend him that is wronged: give judgment for the orphan, and execute righteousness for the widow; and come and let us reason together, saith He; and though your sins be as crimson, I will make them white as snow; and though they be as scarlet, I will make them white as wool. And if ye be willing and will hearken unto Me, ye shall eat the good things of the earth; but if ye be not willing, neither hearken unto Me, a sword shall devour you; for the mouth of the Lord hath spoken these things.* Seeing then that He desireth all His beloved to be partakers of repentance, He confirmed it by an act of His almighty will.

9. Wherefore let us be obedient unto His excellent and glorious will; and presenting ourselves as suppliants of His mercy and goodness, let us fall down before Him and betake ourselves unto His compassions, forsaking the vain toil and the strife and the jealousy which leadeth unto death. Let us fix our eyes on them that ministered perfectly unto His excellent glory. Let us set before us Enoch, who being found righteous in obedience was translated, and his death was not found. Noah, being found faithful, by his ministration preached regeneration unto the world, and through him the Master saved the living creatures that entered into the ark in concord.

10. Abraham, who was called the 'friend,' was found faithful in that he rendered obedience unto the words of God. He through obedience went forth from his land and from his kindred and from his father's house, that leaving a scanty land and a feeble kindred and a mean house he might inherit the promises of God. For He saith unto him; *Go forth from thy land and from thy kindred and from thy father's house unto the land which I shall show thee, and I will make thee into a great nation, and I will bless thee and will magnify thy name, and thou shalt be blessed. And I will bless them that bless thee, and I will curse them that curse thee; and in thee shall all the tribes of the earth be blessed.* And again, when he was parted from Lot, God said unto him; *Look up with thine eyes, and behold from the place where thou now art, unto the north and the south and the sunrise and the sea; for all the land which thou seest, I will give it unto thee and to thy seed for ever; and I will make thy seed as the dust of the earth. If any man can count the dust of the earth, then shall thy seed also be counted.* And again He saith; *God led Abraham forth and said unto him, Look up unto the heaven and count the stars, and see whether thou canst number them. So shall thy seed be. And Abraham believed God, and it was reckoned unto him for righteousness.* For his faith and hospitality a son was given unto him in old age, and by obedience he offered him a sacrifice unto God on one of the mountains which He showed him.

11. For his hospitality and godliness Lot was saved from Sodom, when all the country round about was judged by fire and brimstone; the Master having thus foreshown that He forsaketh not them which set their hope on Him, but appointeth unto punishment and torment them which swerve aside. For when his wife had gone forth with him, being otherwise-minded and not in accord, she was appointed for a sign hereunto, so that she became a pillar of salt unto this day, that it might be

known unto all men that they which are double-minded and they which doubt concerning the power of God are set for a judgment and for a token unto all the generations. 12. For her faith and hospitality Rahab the harlot was saved. For when the spies were sent forth unto Jericho by Joshua the son of Nun, the king of the land perceived that they were come to spy out his country, and sent forth men to seize them, that being seized they might be put to death. So the hospitable Rahab received them and hid them in the upper chamber under the flax-stalks. And when the messengers of the king came near and said, *The spies of our land entered in unto thee: bring them forth, for the king so ordereth:* then she answered, *The men truly, whom ye seek, entered in unto me, but they departed forthwith and are journeying on the way;* and she pointed out to them the opposite road. And she said unto the men, *Of a surety I perceive that the Lord your God delivereth this city unto you; for the fear and the dread of you is fallen upon the inhabitants thereof. When therefore it shall come to pass that ye take it, save me and the house of my father.* And they said unto her, *It shall be even so as thou hast spoken unto us. Whensoever therefore thou perceivest that we are coming, thou shalt gather all thy folk beneath thy roof, and they shall be saved; for as many as shall be found without the house shall perish.* And moreover they gave her a sign, that she should hang out from her house a scarlet thread, thereby showing beforehand that through the blood of the Lord there shall be redemption unto all them that believe and hope on God. Ye see, dearly beloved, not only faith, but prophecy, is found in the woman.

13. Let us therefore be lowly-minded, brethren, laying aside all arrogance and conceit and folly and anger, and let us do that which is written. For the Holy Ghost saith, *Let not the wise man boast in his wisdom, nor the strong in his strength, neither the rich in his riches; but he that boasteth let him boast in the Lord, that he may seek Him out, and do judgment and righteousness;* most of all remembering the words of the Lord Jesus which He spake, teaching forbearance and long-suffering: for thus He spake; *Have mercy, that ye may receive mercy: forgive, that it may be forgiven to you. As ye do, so shall it be done to you. As ye give, so shall it be given unto you. As ye judge, so shall ye be judged. As ye show kindness, so shall kindness be showed unto you. With what measure ye mete, it shall be measured withal to you.* With this commandment and these precepts let us confirm ourselves, that we may walk in obedience to His hallowed words, with lowliness of mind. For

the holy word saith, *Upon whom shall I look, save upon him that is gentle and quiet and feareth Mine oracles?*

14. Therefore it is right and proper, brethren, that we should be obedient unto God, rather than follow those who in arrogance and unruliness have set themselves up as leaders in abominable jealousy. For we shall bring upon us no common harm, but rather great peril, if we surrender ourselves recklessly to the purposes of men who launch out into strife and seditions, so as to estrange us from that which is right. Let us be good one towards another according to the compassion and sweetness of Him that made us. For it is written : *The good shall be dwellers in the land, and the innocent shall be left on it; but they that transgress shall be destroyed utterly from it.* And again He saith ; *I saw the ungodly lifted up on high and exalted as the cedars of Lebanon. And I passed by, and behold he was not ; and I sought out his place, and I found it not. Keep innocence and behold uprightness; for there is a remnant for the peaceful man.*

15. Therefore let us cleave unto them that practise peace with godliness, and not unto them that desire peace with dissimulation. For He saith in a certain place ; *This people honoureth Me with their lips, but their heart is far from Me ;* and again, *They blessed with their mouth, but they cursed with their heart.* And again He saith, *They loved Him with their mouth, and with their tongue they lied unto Him ; and their heart was not upright with Him, neither were they stedfast in His covenant. For this cause let the deceitful lips be made dumb which speak iniquity against the righteous.* And again ; *May the Lord utterly destroy all the deceitful lips, the tongue that speaketh proud things, even them that say, Let us magnify our tongue ; our lips are our own ; who is lord over us? For the misery of the needy and for the groaning of the poor I will now arise, saith the Lord. I will set him in safety ; I will deal boldly by him.*

16. For Christ is with them that are lowly of mind, not with them that exalt themselves over the flock. The sceptre [of the majesty] of God, even our Lord Jesus Christ, came not in the pomp of arrogance or of pride, though He might have done so, but in lowliness of mind, according as the Holy Spirit spake concerning Him. For He saith ; *Lord, who believed our report? and to whom was the arm of the Lord revealed? We announced Him in His presence. As a child was He, as a root in a thirsty ground. There is no form in Him, neither glory. And we beheld Him, and He had no form nor comeliness, but His form was*

mean, lacking more than the form of men. He was a man of stripes and of toil, and knowing how to bear infirmity: for His face is turned away. He was dishonoured and held of no account. He beareth our sins and suffereth pain for our sakes: and we accounted Him to be in toil and in stripes and in affliction. And He was wounded for our sins and hath been afflicted for our iniquities. The chastisement of our peace is upon Him. With His bruises we were healed. We all went astray like sheep, each man went astray in his own path: and the Lord delivered Him over for our sins. And He openeth not His mouth, because He is afflicted. As a sheep He was led to slaughter; and as a lamb before his shearer is dumb, so openeth He not His mouth. In His humiliation His judgment was taken away. His generation who shall declare? For His life is taken away from the earth. For the iniquities of my people He is come to death. And I will give the wicked for His burial, and the rich for His death; for He wrought no iniquity, neither was guile found in His mouth. And the Lord desireth to cleanse Him from His stripes. If ye offer for sin, your soul shall see a long-lived seed. And the Lord desireth to take away from the toil of His soul, to show Him light and to mould Him with under-standing, to justify a Just One that is a good servant unto many. And He shall bear their sins. Therefore He shall inherit many, and shall divide the spoils of the strong; because His soul was delivered unto death, and He was reckoned unto the transgressors; and He bare the sins of many, and for their sins was He delivered up. And again He Himself saith; *But I am a worm and no man, a reproach of men and an outcast of the people. All they that beheld me mocked at me; they spake with their lips; they wagged their heads, saying, He hoped on the Lord; let Him deliver him, or let Him save him, for He desireth him.* Ye see, dearly beloved, what is the pattern that hath been given unto us; for, if the Lord was thus lowly of mind, what should we do, who through Him have been brought under the yoke of His grace?

17. Let us be imitators also of them which went about in goatskins and sheepskins, preaching the coming of Christ. We mean Elijah and Elisha and likewise Ezekiel, the prophets, and besides them those men also that obtained a good report. Abraham obtained an exceeding good report and was called the friend of God; and looking stedfastly on the glory of God, he saith in lowliness of mind, *But I am dust and ashes.* Moreover concerning Job also it is thus written; *And Job was righteous and unblameable, one that was true and honoured God and abstained from all evil.* Yet he himself accuseth himself saying, *No*

man is clean from filth ; no, not though his life be but for a day. Moses was called *faithful in all His house,* and through his ministration God judged Egypt with the plagues and the torments which befel them. Howbeit he also, though greatly glorified, yet spake no proud words, but said, when an oracle was given to him at the bush, *Who am I, that Thou sendest me? Nay, I am feeble of speech and slow of tongue.* And again he saith, *But I am smoke from the pot.*

18. But what must we say of David that obtained a good report? of whom God said, *I have found a man after My heart, David the son of Jesse: with eternal mercy have I anointed him.* Yet he too saith unto God ; *Have mercy upon me, O God, according to Thy great mercy; and according to the multitude of Thy compassions, blot out mine iniquity. Wash me yet more from mine iniquity, and cleanse me from my sin. For I acknowledge mine iniquity, and my sin is ever before me. Against Thee only did I sin, and I wrought evil in Thy sight; that Thou mayest be justified in Thy words, and mayest conquer in Thy pleading. For behold, in iniquities was I conceived, and in sins did my mother bear me. For behold Thou hast loved truth : the dark and hidden things of Thy wisdom hast Thou showed unto me. Thou shalt sprinkle me with hyssop, and I shall be made clean. Thou shalt wash me, and I shall become whiter than snow. Thou shalt make me to hear of joy and gladness. The bones which have been humbled shall rejoice. Turn away Thy face from my sins, and blot out all mine iniquities. Make a clean heart within me, O God, and renew a right spirit in mine inmost parts. Cast me not away from Thy presence, and take not Thy Holy Spirit from me. Restore unto me the joy of Thy salvation, and strengthen me with a princely spirit. I will teach sinners Thy ways, and godless men shall be converted unto Thee. Deliver me from bloodguiltiness, O God, the God of my salvation. My tongue shall rejoice in Thy righteousness. Lord, Thou shalt open my mouth, and my lips shall declare Thy praise. For, if Thou hadst desired sacrifice, I would have given it: in whole burnt-offerings Thou wilt have no pleasure. A sacrifice unto God is a contrite spirit; a contrite and humbled heart God will not despise.*

19. The humility therefore and the submissiveness of so many and so great men, who have thus obtained a good report, hath through obedience made better not only us but also the generations which were before us, even them that received His oracles in fear and truth. Seeing then that we have been partakers of many great and glorious doings, let us hasten to return unto the goal of peace which hath been handed

down to us from the beginning, and let us look stedfastly unto the
Father and Maker of the whole world, and cleave unto His splendid
and excellent gifts of peace and benefits.   Let us behold Him in our
mind, and let us look with the eyes of our soul unto His long-suffering
will.   Let us note how free from anger He is towards all His creatures.
      20.   The heavens are moved by His direction and obey Him in
peace.   Day and night accomplish the course assigned to them by
Him, without hindrance one to another.   The sun and the moon and
the dancing stars according to His appointment circle in harmony
within the bounds assigned to them, without any swerving aside.   The
earth, bearing fruit in fulfilment of His will at her proper seasons,
putteth forth the food that supplieth abundantly both men and beasts
and all living things which are thereupon, making no dissension, neither
altering anything which He hath decreed.   Moreover, the inscrutable
depths of the abysses and the unutterable †statutes† of the nether
regions are constrained by the same ordinances.   The basin of the
boundless sea, gathered together by His workmanship *into its reservoirs*,
passeth not the barriers wherewith it is surrounded; but even as He
ordered it, so it doeth.   For He said, *So far shalt thou come, and thy
waves shall be broken within thee*.   The ocean which is impassable for
men, and the worlds beyond it, are directed by the same ordinances of
the Master.   The seasons of spring and summer and autumn and
winter give way in succession one to another in peace.   The winds in
their several quarters at their proper season fulfil their ministry without
disturbance; and the everflowing fountains, created for enjoyment and
health, without fail give their breasts which sustain the life for men.
Yea, the smallest of living things come together in concord and peace.
All these things the great Creator and Master of the universe ordered
to be in peace and concord, doing good unto all things, but far beyond
the rest unto us who have taken refuge in His compassionate mercies
through our Lord Jesus Christ, to whom be the glory and the majesty
for ever and ever.   Amen.
      21.   Look ye, brethren, lest His benefits, which are many, turn unto
judgment to all of us, if we walk not worthily of Him, and do those
things which are good and well-pleasing in His sight with concord.
For He saith in a certain place, *The Spirit of the Lord is a lamp
searching the closets of the belly*.   Let us see how near He is, and how
that nothing escapeth Him of our thoughts or our devices which
we make.   It is right therefore that we should not be deserters from

His will. Let us rather give offence to foolish and senseless men who exalt themselves and boast in the arrogance of their words, than to God. Let us fear the Lord Jesus[Christ],whose blood was given for us. Let us reverence our rulers; let us honour our elders; let us instruct our young men in the lesson of the fear of God. Let us guide our women toward that which is good : let them show forth their lovely disposition of purity; let them prove their sincere affection of gentleness; let them make manifest the moderation of their tongue through their silence; let them show their love, not in factious preferences but without partiality towards all them that fear God, in holiness. Let our children be partakers of the instruction which is in Christ : let them learn how lowliness of mind prevaileth with God, what power chaste love hath with God, how the fear of Him is good and great and saveth all them that walk therein in a pure mind with holiness. For He is the searcher out of the intents and desires; whose breath is in us, and when He listeth, He shall take it away.

22. Now all these things the faith which is in Christ confirmeth : for He Himself through the Holy Spirit thus inviteth us : *Come, my children, hearken unto Me, I will teach you the fear of the Lord. What man is he that desireth life and loveth to see good days? Make thy tongue to cease from evil, and thy lips that they speak no guile. Turn aside from evil and do good. Seek peace and ensue it. The eyes of the Lord are over the righteous, and His ears are turned to their prayers. But the face of the Lord is upon them that do evil, to destroy their memorial from the earth. The righteous cried out, and the Lord heard him, and delivered him from all his troubles. Many are the troubles of the righteous, and the Lord shall deliver him from them all.* And again; *Many are the stripes of the sinner, but them that set their hope on the Lord mercy shall compass about.*

23. The Father, who is pitiful in all things, and ready to do good, hath compassion on them that fear Him, and kindly and lovingly bestoweth His favours on them that draw nigh unto Him with a single mind. Wherefore let us not be double-minded, neither let our soul indulge in idle humours respecting His exceeding and glorious gifts. Let this scripture be far from us where He saith; *Wretched are the double-minded, which doubt in their soul and say, These things we did hear in the days of our fathers also, and behold we have grown old, and none of these things hath befallen us. Ye fools, compare yourselves unto a tree; take a vine. First it sheddeth its leaves, then a shoot cometh, then a*

leaf, then a flower, and after these a sour berry, then a full ripe grape.
Ye see that in a little time the fruit of the tree attaineth unto mellow-
ness. Of a truth quickly and suddenly shall His will be accomplished,
the scripture also bearing witness to it, saying; *He shall come quickly
and shall not tarry ; and the Lord shall come suddenly into His temple,
even the Holy One, whom ye expect.*

24. Let us understand, dearly beloved, how the Master continually
showeth unto us the resurrection that shall be hereafter ; whereof He
made the Lord Jesus Christ the firstfruit, when He raised Him from the
dead. Let us behold, dearly beloved, the resurrection which happeneth
at its proper season. Day and night show unto us the resurrection.
The night falleth asleep, and day ariseth ; the day departeth, and
night cometh on. Let us mark the fruits, how and in what manner the
sowing taketh place. *The sower goeth forth* and casteth into the earth
each of the seeds ; and these falling into the earth dry and bare decay :
then out of their decay the mightiness of the Master's providence raiseth
them up, and from being one they increase manifold and bear fruit.

25. Let us consider the marvellous sign which is seen in the
regions of the east, that is, in the parts about Arabia. There is a bird,
which is named the phœnix. This, being the only one of its kind,
liveth for five hundred years; and when it hath now reached the time of
its dissolution that it should die, it maketh for itself a coffin of frankincense and myrrh and the other spices, into the which in the fulness of
time it entereth, and so it dieth. But, as the flesh rotteth, a certain
worm is engendered, which is nurtured from the moisture of the dead
creature and putteth forth wings. Then, when it is grown lusty,
it taketh up that coffin where are the bones of its parent, and carrying
them journeyeth from the country of Arabia even unto Egypt, to the
place called the City of the Sun ; and in the day time in the sight of all,
flying to the altar of the Sun, it layeth them thereupon ; and this done,
it setteth forth to return. So the priests examine the registers of the
times, and they find that it hath come when the five hundredth year is
completed.

26. Do we then think it to be a great and marvellous thing, if the
Creator of the universe shall bring about the resurrection of them that
have served Him with holiness in the assurance of a good faith, seeing
that He showeth to us even by a bird the magnificence of His promise?
For He saith in a certain place ; *And Thou shalt raise me up, and I will
praise Thee ;* and ; *I went to rest and slept, I was awaked, for Thou art*

with me. And again Job saith; *And Thou shalt raise this my flesh which hath endured all these things.*

27. With this hope therefore let our souls be bound unto Him that is faithful in His promises and that is righteous in His judgments. He that commanded not to lie, much more shall He Himself not lie: for nothing is impossible with God save to lie. Therefore let our faith in Him be kindled within us, and let us understand that all things are nigh unto Him. By a word of His majesty He compacted the universe; and by a word He can destroy it. *Who shall say unto Him, What hast thou done? or who shall resist the might of His strength?* When He listeth, and as He listeth, He will do all things; and nothing shall pass away of those things that He hath decreed. All things are in His sight, and nothing escapeth His counsel, seeing that *The heavens declare the glory of God, and the firmament proclaimeth His handiwork. Day uttereth word unto day, and night proclaimeth knowledge unto night; and there are neither words nor speeches, whose voices are not heard.*

28. Since therefore all things are seen and heard, let us fear Him and forsake the abominable lusts of evil works, that we may be shielded by His mercy from the coming judgments. For where can any of us escape from His strong hand? And what world will receive any of them that desert from His service? For the holy writing saith in a certain place; *Where shall I go, and where shall I be hidden from Thy face? If I ascend into the heaven, Thou art there; if I depart into the farthest parts of the earth, there is Thy right hand; if I make my bed in the depths, there is Thy Spirit.* Whither then shall one depart, or where shall one flee, from Him that embraceth the universe?

29. Let us therefore approach Him in holiness of soul, lifting up pure and undefiled hands unto Him, with love towards our gentle and compassionate Father who made us an elect portion unto Himself. For thus it is written: *When the Most High divided the nations, when He dispersed the sons of Adam, He fixed the boundaries of the nations according to the number of the angels of God. His people Jacob became the portion of the Lord, and Israel the measurement of His inheritance.* And in another place He saith; *Behold, the Lord taketh for Himself a nation out of the midst of the nations, as a man taketh the firstfruits of his threshing floor; and the holy of holies shall come forth from that nation.*

30. Seeing then that we are the special portion of a Holy God, let us do all things that pertain unto holiness, forsaking evil-speakings, abominable and impure embraces, drunkennesses and tumults and

hateful lusts, abominable adultery, hateful pride ; *For God*, He saith, *resisteth the proud, but giveth grace to the lowly.* Let us therefore cleave unto those to whom grace is given from God. Let us clothe ourselves in concord, being lowly-minded and temperate, holding ourselves aloof from all backbiting and evil speaking, being justified by works and not by words. For He saith ; *He that saith much shall hear also again. Doth the ready talker think to be righteous ? Blessed is the offspring of a woman that liveth but a short time. Be not thou abundant in words.* Let our praise be with God, and not of ourselves : for God hateth them that praise themselves. Let the testimony to our well-doing be given by others, as it was given unto our fathers who were righteous. Boldness and arrogance and daring are for them that are accursed of God ; but forbearance and humility and gentleness are with them that are blessed of God.

31. Let us therefore cleave unto His blessing, and let us see what are the ways of blessing. Let us study the records of the things that have happened from the beginning. Wherefore was our father Abraham blessed? Was it not because he wrought righteousness and truth through faith? Isaac with confidence, as knowing the future, was led a willing sacrifice. Jacob with humility departed from his land because of his brother, and went unto Laban and served ; and the twelve tribes of Israel were given unto him.

32. If any man will consider them one by one in sincerity, he shall understand the magnificence of the gifts that are given by Him. For of Jacob are all the priests and levites who minister unto the altar of God ; of him is the Lord Jesus as concerning the flesh ; of him are kings and rulers and governors in the line of Judah ; yea and the rest of his tribes are held in no small honour, seeing that God promised saying, *Thy seed shall be as the stars of heaven.* They all therefore were glorified and magnified, not through themselves or their own works or the righteous doing which they wrought, but through His will. And so we, having been called through His will in Christ Jesus, are not justified through ourselves or through our own wisdom or understanding or piety or works which we wrought in holiness of heart, but through faith, whereby the Almighty God justified all men that have been from the beginning ; to whom be the glory for ever and ever. Amen.

33. What then must we do, brethren ? Must we idly abstain from doing good, and forsake love? May the Master never allow this to befal us at least ; but let us hasten with instancy and zeal to accomplish

every good work. For the Creator and Master of the universe Himself rejoiceth in His works. For by His exceeding great might He established the heavens, and in His incomprehensible wisdom He set them in order. And the earth He separated from the water that surroundeth it, and He set it firm on the sure foundation of His own will; and the living creatures which walk upon it He commanded to exist by His ordinance. Having before created the sea and the living creatures therein, He enclosed it by His own power. Above all, as the most excellent and exceeding great work of His intelligence, with His sacred and faultless hands He formed man in the impress of His own image. For thus saith God; *Let us make man after our image and after our likeness. And God made man; male and female made He them.* So having finished all these things, He praised them and blessed them and said, *Increase and multiply.* We have seen that all the righteous were adorned in good works. Yea, and the Lord Himself having adorned Himself with works rejoiced. Seeing then that we have this pattern, let us conform ourselves with all diligence to His will; let us with all our strength work the work of righteousness.

34. The good workman receiveth the bread of his work with boldness, but the slothful and careless dareth not look his employer in the face. It is therefore needful that we should be zealous unto well-doing, for of Him are all things: since He forewarneth us saying, *Behold, the Lord, and His reward is before His face, to recompense each man according to his work.* He exhorteth us therefore to believe on Him with our whole heart, and to be not idle nor careless unto every good work. Let our boast and our confidence be in Him: let us submit ourselves to His will; let us mark the whole host of His angels, how they stand by and minister unto His will. For the scripture saith; *Ten thousands of ten thousands stood by Him, and thousands of thousands ministered unto Him: and they cried aloud, Holy, holy, holy is the Lord of Sabaoth; all creation is full of His glory.* Yea, and let us ourselves then, being gathered together in concord with intentness of heart, cry unto Him as from one mouth earnestly that we may be made partakers of His great and glorious promises. For He saith, *Eye hath not seen and ear hath not heard, and it hath not entered into the heart of man what great things He hath prepared for them that patiently await Him.*

35. How blessed and marvellous are the gifts of God, dearly beloved! Life in immortality, splendour in righteousness, truth in boldness, faith in confidence, temperance in sanctification! And all

these things fall under our apprehension. What then, think ye, are the things preparing for them that patiently await Him? The Creator and Father of the ages, the All-holy One Himself knoweth their number and their beauty. Let us therefore contend, that we may be found in the number of those that patiently await Him, to the end that we may be partakers of His promised gifts. But how shall this be, dearly beloved? If our mind be fixed through faith towards God; if we seek out those things which are well pleasing and acceptable unto Him; if we accomplish such things as beseem His faultless will, and follow the way of truth, casting off from ourselves all unrighteousness and iniquity, covetousness, strifes, malignities and deceits, whisperings and back-bitings, hatred of God, pride and arrogance, vainglory and inhospitality. For they that do these things are hateful to God; and not only they that do them, but they also that consent unto them. For the scripture saith; *But unto the sinner said God, Wherefore dost thou declare Mine ordinances, and takest My covenant upon thy lips? Yet thou didst hate instruction and didst cast away My words behind thee. If thou sawest a thief, thou didst keep company with him, and with the adulterers thou didst set thy portion. Thy mouth multiplied wickedness, and thy tongue wove deceit. Thou sattest and spakest against thy brother, and against the son of thy mother thou didst lay a stumbling-block. These things thou hast done, and I kept silence. Thou thoughtest, unrighteous man, that I should be like unto thee. I will convict thee and will set thee face to face with thyself. Now understand ye these things, ye that forget God, lest at any time He seize you as a lion, and there be none to deliver. The sacrifice of praise shall glorify Me, and there is the way wherein I will show him the salvation of God.*

36. This is the way, dearly-beloved, wherein we found our salvation, even Jesus Christ the High-priest of our offerings, the Guardian and Helper of our weakness. Through Him let us look stedfastly unto the heights of the heavens; through Him we behold as in a mirror His faultless and most excellent visage; through Him the eyes of our hearts were opened; through Him our foolish and darkened mind springeth up unto the light; through Him the Master willed that we should taste of the immortal knowledge; *Who being the brightness of His majesty is so much greater than angels, as He hath inherited a more excellent name.* For so it is written; *Who maketh His angels spirits and His ministers a flame of fire;* but of His Son the Master said thus; *Thou art My Son, I this day have begotten Thee. Ask of Me,*

and I will give Thee the Gentiles for Thine inheritance, and the ends of the earth for Thy possession. And again He saith unto Him ; *Sit Thou on My right hand, until I make Thine enemies a footstool for Thy feet.* Who then are these enemies? They that are wicked and resist His will.

37. Let us therefore enlist ourselves, brethren, with all earnestness in His faultless ordinances. Let us mark the soldiers that are enlisted under our rulers, how exactly, how readily, how submissively, they execute the orders given them. All are not prefects, nor rulers of thousands, nor rulers of hundreds, nor rulers of fifties, and so forth; but each man in his own rank executeth the orders given by the king and the governors. The great without the small cannot exist, neither the small without the great. There is a certain mixture in all things, and therein is utility. Let us take our body as an example. The head without the feet is nothing; so likewise the feet without the head are nothing: even the smallest limbs of our body are necessary and useful for the whole body: but all the members conspire and unite in subjection, that the whole body may be saved.

38. So in our case let the whole body be saved in Christ Jesus, and let each man be subject unto his neighbour, according as also he was appointed with his special grace. Let not the strong neglect the weak; and let the weak respect the strong. Let the rich minister aid to the poor; and let the poor give thanks to God, because He hath given him one through whom his wants may be supplied. Let the wise display his wisdom, not in words, but in good works. He that is lowly in mind, let him not bear testimony to himself, but leave testimony to be borne to him by his neighbour. He that is pure in the flesh, let him be so, and not boast, knowing that it is Another who bestoweth his continence upon him. Let us consider, brethren, of what matter we were made; who and what manner of beings we were, when we came into the world; from what a sepulchre and what darkness He that moulded and created us brought us into His world, having prepared His benefits aforehand ere ever we were born. Seeing therefore that we have all these things from Him, we ought in all things to give thanks to Him, to whom be the glory for ever and ever. Amen.

39. Senseless and stupid and foolish and ignorant men jeer and mock at us, desiring that they themselves should be exalted in their imaginations. For what power hath a mortal? or what strength hath a child of earth? For it is written; *There was no form before mine eyes; only I heard a breath and a voice. What then? Shall a mortal be clean*

in the sight of the Lord ; or shall a man be unblameable for his works?
seeing that He is distrustful against His servants and noteth some perversity
against His angels. Nay, the heaven is not clean in His sight. Away
then, ye that dwell in houses of clay, whereof, even of the same clay, we
ourselves are made. He smote them like a moth, and from morn to even
they are no more. Because they could not succour themselves, they
perished. He breathed upon them and they died, because they had no
wisdom. But call thou, if perchance one shall obey thee, or if thou shalt
see one of the holy angels. For wrath killeth the foolish man, and envy
slayeth him that is gone astray. And I have seen fools throwing out roots,
but forthwith their habitation was eaten up. Far be their sons from
safety. May they be mocked at the gates of inferiors, and there shall be
none to deliver them. For the things which are prepared for them, the
righteous shall eat ; but they themselves shall not be delivered from evils.

40. Forasmuch then as these things are manifest beforehand, and we have searched into the depths of the Divine knowledge, we ought to do all things in order, as many as the Master hath commanded us to perform at their appointed seasons. Now the offerings and ministrations He commanded to be performed with care, and not to be done rashly or in disorder, but at fixed times and seasons. And where and by whom He would have them performed, He Himself fixed by His supreme will : that all things being done with piety according to His good pleasure might be acceptable to His will. They therefore that make their offerings at the appointed seasons are acceptable and blessed : for while they follow the institutions of the Master they cannot go wrong. For unto the high-priest his proper services have been assigned, and to the priests their proper office is appointed, and upon the levites their proper ministrations are laid. The layman is bound by the layman's ordinances.

41. Let each of you, brethren, in his own order give thanks unto God, maintaining a good conscience and not transgressing the appointed rule of his service, but acting with all seemliness. Not in every place, brethren, are the continual daily sacrifices offered, or the freewill offerings, or the sin offerings and the trespass offerings, but in Jerusalem alone. And even there the offering is not made in every place, but before the sanctuary in the court of the altar ; and this too through the high-priest and the aforesaid ministers, after that the victim to be offered hath been inspected for blemishes. They therefore who do any thing contrary to the seemly ordinance of His will receive death as the

penalty. Ye see, brethren, in proportion as greater knowledge hath been vouchsafed unto us, so much the more are we exposed to danger.

42. The Apostles received the Gospel for us from the Lord Jesus Christ; Jesus Christ was sent forth from God. So then Christ is from God, and the Apostles are from Christ. Both therefore came of the will of God in the appointed order. Having therefore received a charge, and having been fully assured through the resurrection of our Lord Jesus Christ and confirmed in the word of God with full assurance of the Holy Ghost, they went forth with the glad tidings that the kingdom of God should come. So preaching everywhere in country and town, they appointed their first-fruits, when they had proved them by the Spirit, to be bishops and deacons unto them that should believe. And this they did in no new fashion; for indeed it had been written concerning bishops and deacons from very ancient times; for thus saith the scripture in a certain place, *I will appoint their bishops in righteousness and their deacons in faith.*

43. And what marvel, if they which were entrusted in Christ with such a work by God appointed the aforesaid persons? seeing that even the blessed Moses who was *a faithful servant in all His house* recorded for a sign in the sacred books all things that were enjoined upon him. And him also the rest of the prophets followed, bearing witness with him unto the laws that were ordained by him. For he, when jealousy arose concerning the priesthood, and there was dissension among the tribes which of them was adorned with the glorious name, commanded the twelve chiefs of the tribes to bring to him rods inscribed with the name of each tribe. And he took them and tied them and sealed them with the signet rings of the chiefs of the tribes, and put them away in the tabernacle of the testimony on the table of God. And having shut the tabernacle he sealed the keys and likewise also the doors. And he said unto them, Brethren, the tribe whose rod shall bud, this hath God chosen to be priests and ministers unto Him. Now when morning came, he called together all Israel, even the six hundred thousand men, and showed the seals to the chiefs of the tribes and opened the tabernacle of the testimony and drew forth the rods. And the rod of Aaron was found not only with buds, but also bearing fruit. What think ye, dearly beloved? Did not Moses know beforehand that this would come to pass? Assuredly he knew it. But that disorder might not arise in Israel, he did thus, to the end that the Name of the true and only God might be glorified : to whom be the glory for ever and ever. Amen.

44. And our Apostles knew through our Lord Jesus Christ that there would be strife over the name of the bishop's office. For this cause therefore, having received complete foreknowledge, they appointed the aforesaid persons, and afterwards they provided a continuance, that if these should fall asleep, other approved men should succeed to their ministration. Those therefore who were appointed by them, or afterward by other men of repute with the consent of the whole Church, and have ministered unblameably to the flock of Christ in lowliness of mind, peacefully and with all modesty, and for long time have borne a good report with all—these men we consider to be unjustly thrust out from their ministration. For it will be no light sin for us, if we thrust out those who have offered the gifts of the bishop's office unblameably and holily. Blessed are those presbyters who have gone before, seeing that their departure was fruitful and ripe : for they have no fear lest any one should remove them from their appointed place. For we see that ye have displaced certain persons, though they were living honourably, from the ministration which †had been respected by them† blamelessly.

45. Be ye contentious, brethren, and jealous about the things that pertain unto salvation. Ye have searched the scriptures, which are true, which were given through the Holy Ghost; and ye know that nothing unrighteous or counterfeit is written in them. Ye will not find that righteous persons have been thrust out by holy men. Righteous men were persecuted, but it was by the lawless; they were imprisoned, but it was by the unholy. They were stoned by transgressors : they were slain by those who had conceived a detestable and unrighteous jealousy. Suffering these things, they endured nobly. For what must we say, brethren? Was Daniel cast into the lions' den by them that feared God? Or were Ananias and Azarias and Misael shut up in the furnace of fire by them that professed the excellent and glorious worship of the Most High? Far be this from our thoughts. Who then were they that did these things? Abominable men and full of all wickedness were stirred up to such a pitch of wrath, as to bring cruel suffering upon them that served God in a holy and blameless purpose, not knowing that the Most High is the champion and protector of them that in a pure conscience serve His excellent Name : unto whom be the glory for ever and ever. Amen. But they that endured patiently in confidence inherited glory and honour; they were exalted, and had their names recorded by God in their memorial for ever and ever. Amen.

46. To such examples as these therefore, brethren, we also ought to cleave. For it is written; *Cleave unto the saints, for they that cleave unto them shall be sanctified.* And again He saith in another place; *With the guiltless man thou shalt be guiltless, and with the elect thou shalt be elect, and with the crooked thou shalt deal crookedly* Let us therefore cleave to the guiltless and righteous : and these are the elect of God. Wherefore are there strifes and wraths and factions and divisions and war among you? Have we not one God and one Christ and one Spirit of grace that was shed upon us? And is there not one calling in Christ? Wherefore do we tear and rend asunder the members of Christ, and stir up factions against our own body, and reach such a pitch of folly, as to forget that we are members one of another? Remember the words of Jesus our Lord : for He said, *Woe unto that man; it were good for him if he had not been born, rather than that he should offend one of Mine elect. It were better for him that a mill-stone were hanged about him, and he cast into the sea, than that he should pervert one of Mine elect.* Your division hath perverted many; it hath brought many to despair, many to doubting, and all of us to sorrow. And your sedition still continueth.

47. Take up the epistle of the blessed Paul the Apostle. What wrote he first unto you in the beginning of the Gospel? Of a truth he charged you in the Spirit concerning himself and Cephas and Apollos, because that even then ye had made parties. Yet that making of parties brought less sin upon you ; for ye were partisans of Apostles that were highly reputed, and of a man approved in their sight. But now mark ye, who they are that have perverted you and diminished the glory of your renowned love for the brotherhood. It is shameful, dearly beloved, yes, utterly shameful and unworthy of your conduct in Christ, that it should be reported that the very stedfast and ancient Church of the Corinthians, for the sake of one or two persons, maketh sedition against its presbyters. And this report hath reached not only us, but them also which differ from us, so that ye even heap blasphemies on the Name of the Lord by reason of your folly, and moreover create peril for yourselves.

48. Let us therefore root this out quickly, and let us fall down before the Master and entreat Him with tears, that He may show Himself propitious and be reconciled unto us, and may restore us to the seemly and pure conduct which belongeth to our love of the brethren. For this is a gate of righteousness opened unto life, as it is written;

Open me the gates of righteousness, that I may enter in thereby and praise the Lord. This is the gate of the Lord; the righteous shall enter in thereby. Seeing then that many gates are opened, this is that gate which is in righteousness, even that which is in Christ, whereby all are blessed that have entered in and direct their path in holiness and righteousness, performing all things without confusion. Let a man be faithful, let him be able to expound a deep saying, let him be wise in the discernment of words, let him be strenuous in deeds, let him be pure; for so much the more ought he to be lowly in mind, in proportion as he seemeth to be the greater; and he ought to seek the common advantage of all, and not his own.

49. Let him that hath love in Christ fulfil the commandments of Christ. Who can declare the bond of the love of God? Who is sufficient to tell the majesty of its beauty? The height, whereunto love exalteth, is unspeakable. Love joineth us unto God; *love covereth a multitude of sins;* love endureth all things, is long-suffering in all things. There is nothing coarse, nothing arrogant in love. Love hath no divisions, love maketh no seditions, love doeth all things in concord. In love were all the elect of God made perfect; without love nothing is well-pleasing to God: in love the Master took us unto Himself; for the love which He had toward us, Jesus Christ our Lord hath given His blood for us by the will of God, and His flesh for our flesh and His life for our lives.

50. Ye see, dearly beloved, how great and marvellous a thing is love, and there is no declaring its perfection. Who is sufficient to be found therein, save those to whom God shall vouchsafe it? Let us therefore entreat and ask of His mercy, that we may be found blameless in love, standing apart from the factiousness of men. All the generations from Adam unto this day have passed away: but they that by God's grace were perfected in love dwell in the abode of the pious; and they shall be made manifest in the visitation of the Kingdom of God. For it is written; *Enter into the closet for a very little while, until Mine anger and My wrath shall pass away, and I will remember a good day and will raise you from your tombs.* Blessed were we, dearly beloved, if we should be doing the commandments of God in concord of love, to the end that our sins may through love be forgiven us. For it is written; *Blessed are they whose iniquities are forgiven, and whose sins are covered. Blessed is the man to whom the Lord shall impute no sin, neither is guile in his mouth.* This declaration of blessedness was pronounced

upon them that have been elected by God through Jesus Christ our Lord, to whom be the glory for ever and ever. Amen.

51. For all our transgressions which we have committed through any of the wiles of the adversary, let us entreat that we may obtain forgiveness. Yea and they also, who set themselves up as leaders of faction and division, ought to look to the common ground of hope. For such as walk in fear and love desire that they themselves should fall into suffering rather than their neighbours; and they pronounce condemnation against themselves rather than against the harmony which hath been handed down to us nobly and righteously. For it is good for a man to make confession of his trespasses rather than to harden his heart, as the heart of those was hardened who made sedition against Moses the servant of God; whose condemnation was clearly manifest, for they went down to hades alive, and *Death shall be their shepherd*. Pharaoh and his host and all the rulers of Egypt, *their chariots and their horsemen*, were overwhelmed in the depths of the Red Sea, and perished for none other reason but because their foolish hearts were hardened after that the signs and the wonders had been wrought in the land of Egypt by the hand of Moses the servant of God.

52. The Master, brethren, hath need of nothing at all. He desireth not anything of any man, save to confess unto Him. For the elect David saith; *I will confess unto the Lord, and it shall please Him more than a young calf that groweth horns and hoofs. Let the poor see it, and rejoice.* And again He saith; *Sacrifice to God a sacrifice of praise, and pay thy vows to the Most High: and call upon Me in the day of thine affliction, and I will deliver thee, and thou shalt glorify Me. For a sacrifice unto God is a broken spirit.*

53. For ye know, and know well, the sacred scriptures, dearly beloved, and ye have searched into the oracles of God. We write these things therefore to put you in remembrance. When Moses went up into the mountain and had spent forty days and forty nights in fasting and humiliation, God said unto him; *Moses, Moses, come down quickly hence, for My people whom thou leddest forth from the land of Egypt have wrought iniquity: they have transgressed quickly out of the way which thou didst command unto them: they have made for themselves molten images. And the Lord said unto him; I have spoken unto thee once and twice, saying, I have seen this people, and behold it is stiff-necked. Let Me destroy them utterly, and I will blot out their name from under heaven, and I will make of thee a nation great and wonderful and numerous more*

than this. And Moses said; *Nay, not so, Lord. Forgive this people their sin, or blot me also out of the book of the living.* O mighty love! O unsurpassable perfection! The servant is bold with his Master; he asketh forgiveness for the multitude, or he demandeth that himself also be blotted out with them.

54. Who therefore is noble among you? Who is compassionate? Who is fulfilled with love? Let him say; If by reason of me there be faction and strife and divisions, I retire, I depart, whither ye will, and I do that which is ordered by the people: only let the flock of Christ be at peace with its duly appointed presbyters. He that shall have done this, shall win for himself great renown in Christ, and every place will receive him: for *the earth is the Lord's and the fulness thereof.* Thus have they done and will do, that live as citizens of that kingdom of God which bringeth no regrets.

55. But, to bring forward examples of Gentiles also; many kings and rulers, when some season of pestilence pressed upon them, being taught by oracles have delivered themselves over to death, that they might rescue their fellow citizens through their own blood. Many have retired from their own cities, that they might have no more seditions. We know that many among ourselves have delivered themselves to bondage, that they might ransom others. Many have sold themselves to slavery, and receiving the price paid for themselves have fed others. Many women being strengthened through the grace of God have performed many manly deeds. The blessed Judith, when the city was beleaguered, asked of the elders that she might be suffered to go forth into the camp of the aliens. So she exposed herself to peril and went forth for love of her country and of her people which were beleaguered; and the Lord delivered Holophernes into the hand of a woman. To no less peril did Esther also, who was perfect in faith, expose herself, that she might deliver the twelve tribes of Israel, when they were on the point to perish. For through her fasting and her humiliation she entreated the all-seeing Master, the God of the ages; and He, seeing the humility of her soul, delivered the people for whose sake she encountered the peril.

56. Therefore let us also make intercession for them that are in any transgression, that forbearance and humility may be given them, to the end that they may yield not unto us, but unto the will of God. For so shall the compassionate remembrance of them with God and the saints be fruitful unto them, and perfect. Let us accept chastisement,

whereat no man ought to be vexed, dearly beloved. The admonition which we give one to another is good and exceeding useful; for it joineth us unto the will of God. For thus saith the holy word; *The Lord hath indeed chastened me, and hath not delivered me over unto death. For whom the Lord loveth He chasteneth, and scourgeth every son whom He receiveth. For the righteous,* it is said, *shall chasten me in mercy and shall reprove me, but let not the †mercy† of sinners anoint my head.* And again He saith; *Blessed is the man whom the Lord hath reproved, and refuse not thou the admonition of the Almighty. For He causeth pain, and He restoreth again: He hath smitten, and His hands have healed. Six times shall He rescue thee from afflictions: and at the seventh no evil shall touch thee. In famine He shall deliver thee from death, and in war He shall release thee from the arm of the sword. And from the scourge of the tongue shall He hide thee, and thou shalt not be afraid when evils approach. Thou shalt laugh at the unrighteous and wicked, and of the wild beasts thou shalt not be afraid. For wild beasts shall be at peace with thee. Then shalt thou know that thy house shall be at peace: and the abode of thy tabernacle shall not go wrong, and thou shalt know that thy seed is many, and thy children as the plenteous herbage of the field. And thou shalt come to the grave as ripe corn reaped in due season, or as the heap of the threshing floor gathered together at the right time.* Ye see, dearly beloved, how great protection there is for them that are chastened by the Master: for being a kind father He chasteneth us to the end that we may obtain mercy through His holy chastisement.

57. Ye therefore that laid the foundation of the sedition, submit yourselves unto the presbyters and receive chastisement unto repentance, bending the knees of your heart. Learn to submit yourselves, laying aside the arrogant and proud stubbornness of your tongue. For it is better for you to be found little in the flock of Christ and to have your name on God's roll, than to be had in exceeding honour and yet be cast out from the hope of Him. For thus saith the All-virtuous Wisdom; *Behold I will pour out for you a saying of My breath, and I will teach you My word. Because I called and ye obeyed not, and I held out words and ye heeded not, but made My counsels of none effect, and were disobedient unto My reproofs; therefore I also will laugh at your destruction, and will rejoice over you when ruin cometh upon you, and when confusion overtaketh you suddenly, and your overthrow is at hand like a whirlwind, or when anguish and beleaguerment come upon you. For it shall be, when ye call upon Me, yet will I not hear you. Evil men*

shall seek Me and shall not find Me: for they hated wisdom, and chose not the fear of the Lord, neither would they give heed unto My counsels, but mocked at My reproofs. Therefore they shall eat the fruits of their own way, and shall be filled with their own ungodliness. For because they wronged babes, they shall be slain, and inquisition shall destroy the ungodly. But he that heareth Me shall dwell safely trusting in hope, and shall be quiet from fear of all evil.

58. Let us therefore be obedient unto His most holy and glorious Name, thereby escaping the threatenings which were spoken of old by the mouth of Wisdom against them which disobey, that we may dwell safely, trusting in the most holy Name of His majesty. Receive our counsel, and ye shall have no occasion of regret. For as God liveth, and the Lord Jesus Christ liveth, and the Holy Spirit, who are the faith and the hope of the elect, so surely shall he, who with lowliness of mind and instant in gentleness hath without regretfulness performed the ordinances and commandments that are given by God, be enrolled and have a name among the number of them that are saved through Jesus Christ, through whom is the glory unto Him for ever and ever. Amen.

59. But if certain persons should be disobedient unto the words spoken by Him through us, let them understand that they will entangle themselves in no slight transgression and danger; but we shall be guiltless of this sin. And we will ask, with instancy of prayer and supplication, that the Creator of the universe may guard intact unto the end the number that hath been numbered of His elect throughout the whole world, through His beloved Son Jesus Christ, through whom He called us from darkness to light, from ignorance to the full knowledge of the glory of His Name.

[Grant unto us, Lord,] that we may set our hope on Thy Name which is the primal source of all creation, and open the eyes of our hearts, that we may know Thee, who alone *abidest Highest in the lofty, Holy in the holy;* who *layest low the insolence of the proud,* who *scatterest the imaginings of nations;* who *settest the lowly on high,* and *bringest the lofty low;* who *makest rich and makest poor;* who *killest and makest alive;* who alone art the Benefactor of spirits and the God of all flesh; who *lookest into the abysses,* who scannest the works of man; the Succour of them that are in peril, the *Saviour of them that are in despair;* the Creator and Overseer of every spirit; who multipliest the nations upon earth, and hast chosen out from all men those that love Thee through Jesus Christ, Thy beloved Son, through whom Thou didst

instruct us, didst sanctify us, didst honour us. We beseech Thee, Lord
and Master, to be *our help and succour.* Save those among us who
are in tribulation; have mercy on the lowly; lift up the fallen; show
Thyself unto the needy; heal the ungodly; convert the wanderers of
Thy people; feed the hungry; release our prisoners; raise up the
weak; comfort the faint-hearted. *Let* all *the Gentiles know that Thou
art God alone,* and Jesus Christ is Thy Son, and *we are Thy people and
the sheep of Thy pasture.*

60. Thou through Thine operations didst make manifest the everlasting fabric of the world. Thou, Lord, didst create the earth. Thou
that art faithful throughout all generations, righteous in Thy judgments,
marvellous in strength and excellence, Thou that art wise in creating
and prudent in establishing that which Thou hast made, that art good
in the things which are seen and faithful with them that trust on Thee,
pitiful and compassionate, forgive us our iniquities and our unrighteous-
nesses and our transgressions and shortcomings. Lay not to our account
every sin of Thy servants and Thine handmaids, but cleanse us with
the cleansing of Thy truth, and *guide our steps to walk in holiness* and
righteousness and singleness *of heart* and *to do such things as are good
and well-pleasing in Thy sight* and in the sight of our rulers. Yea,
Lord, *make Thy face to shine upon us* in peace for our good, that we
may be sheltered *by Thy mighty hand and* delivered from every sin *by
Thine uplifted arm.* And deliver us from them that hate us wrongfully.
Give concord and peace to us and to all that dwell on the earth, as
Thou gavest to our fathers, *when they called on* Thee *in faith and truth*
with holiness, [that we may be saved,] while we render obedience to
Thine almighty and most excellent Name, and to our rulers and governors
upon the earth.

61. Thou, Lord and Master, hast given them the power of sovereignty
through Thine excellent and unspeakable might, that we knowing the
glory and honour which Thou hast given them may submit ourselves
unto them, in nothing resisting Thy will. Grant unto them therefore,
O Lord, health, peace, concord, stability, that they may administer the
government which Thou hast given them without failure. For Thou, O
heavenly Master, King of the ages, givest to the sons of men glory and
honour and power over all things that are upon the earth. Do Thou,
Lord, direct their counsel according to that which is good and well-
pleasing in Thy sight, that, administering in peace and gentleness with
godliness the power which Thou hast given them, they may obtain Thy

favour. O Thou, who alone art able to do these things and things far more exceeding good than these for us, we praise Thee through the High-priest and Guardian of our souls, Jesus Christ, through whom be the glory and the majesty unto Thee both now and for all generations and for ever and ever. Amen.

62. As touching those things which befit our religion and are most useful for a virtuous life to such as would guide [their steps] in holiness and righteousness, we have written fully unto you, brethren. For concerning faith and repentance and genuine love and temperance and sobriety and patience we have handled every argument, putting you in remembrance, that ye ought to please Almighty God in righteousness and truth and long-suffering with holiness, laying aside malice and pursuing concord in love and peace, being instant in gentleness; even as our fathers, of whom we spake before, pleased Him, being lowly-minded towards their Father and God and Creator and towards all men. And we have put you in mind of these things the more gladly, since we knew well that we were writing to men who are faithful and highly accounted and have diligently searched into the oracles of the teaching of God.

63. Therefore it is right for us to give heed to so great and so many examples and to submit the neck and occupying the place of obedience to take our side with them that are the leaders of our souls, that ceasing from this foolish dissension we may attain unto the goal which lieth before us in truthfulness, keeping aloof from every fault. For ye will give us great joy and gladness, if ye render obedience unto the things written by us through the Holy Spirit, and root out the unrighteous anger of your jealousy, according to the entreaty which we have made for peace and concord in this letter. And we have also sent faithful and prudent men that have walked among us from youth unto old age unblameably, who shall also be witnesses between you and us. And this we have done that ye might know that we have had, and still have, every solicitude that ye should be speedily at peace.

64. Finally may the All-seeing God and Master of spirits and Lord of all flesh, who chose the Lord Jesus Christ, and us through Him for a peculiar people, grant unto every soul that is called after His excellent and holy Name faith, fear, peace, patience, long-suffering, temperance, chastity and soberness, that they may be well-pleasing unto His Name through our High-priest and Guardian Jesus Christ, through whom

unto Him be glory and majesty, might and honour, both now and for ever and ever. Amen.

65. Now send ye back speedily unto us our messengers Claudius Ephebus and Valerius Bito, together with Fortunatus also, in peace and with joy, to the end that they may the more quickly report the peace and concord which is prayed for and earnestly desired by us, that we also may the more speedily rejoice over your good order.

The grace of our Lord Jesus Christ be with you and with all men in all places who have been called by God and through Him, through whom be glory and honour, power and greatness and eternal dominion, unto Him, from the ages past and for ever and ever. Amen.

AN ANCIENT HOMILY

BRETHREN, we ought so to think of Jesus Christ, as of God, as of the Judge of quick and dead. And we ought not to think mean things of our Salvation : for when we think mean things of Him, we expect also to receive mean things. And they that listen as concerning mean things do wrong; and we ourselves do wrong, not knowing whence and by whom and unto what place we were called, and how many things Jesus Christ endured to suffer for our sakes. What recompense then shall we give unto Him? or what fruit worthy of His own gift to us? And how many mercies do we owe to Him! For He bestowed the light upon us; He spake to us, as a father to his sons; He saved us, when we were perishing. What praise then shall we give to Him? or what payment of recompense for those things which we received? we who were maimed in our understanding, and worshipped stocks and stones and gold and silver and bronze, the works of men; and our whole life was nothing else but death. While then we were thus wrapped in darkness and oppressed with this thick mist in our vision, we recovered our sight, putting off by His will the cloud wherein we were wrapped. For He had mercy on us, and in His compassion saved us, having beheld in us much error and perdition, even when we had no hope of salvation, save that which came from Him. For He called us, when we were not, and from not being He willed us to be.

2. *Rejoice, thou barren that bearest not. Break out and cry, thou that travailest not ; for more are the children of the desolate than of her that hath the husband.* In that He said *Rejoice, thou barren that bearest not,* He spake of us : for our Church was barren, before that children were given unto her. And in that He said, *Cry aloud, thou that travailest not,* He meaneth this ; Let us not, like women in travail, grow weary of offering up our prayers with simplicity to God. Again, in that He said, *For the children of the desolate are more than of her that hath the*

husband, He so spake, because our people seemed desolate and forsaken of God, whereas now, having believed, we have become more than those who seemed to have God. Again another scripture saith, *I came not to call the righteous, but sinners.* He meaneth this ; that it is right to save them that are perishing. For this indeed is a great and marvellous work, to establish, not those things which stand, but those which are falling. So also Christ willed to save the things which were perishing. And He saved many, coming and calling us when we were even now perishing.

3. Seeing then that He bestowed so great mercy on us ; first of all, that we, who are living, do not sacrifice to these dead gods, neither worship them, but through Him have known the Father of truth. What else is this knowledge to Himward, but not to deny Him through whom we have known Him ? Yea, He Himself saith, *Whoso confesseth Me, Him will I confess before the Father.* This then is our reward, if verily we shall confess Him through whom we were saved. But wherein do we confess Him ? When we do that which He saith and are not disobedient unto His commandments, and not only *honour Him with our lips,* but *with our whole heart and with our whole mind.* Now He saith also in Isaiah, *This people honoureth Me with their lips, but their heart is far from Me.*

4. Let us therefore not only call Him Lord, for this will not save us: for He saith, *Not every one that saith unto Me, Lord, Lord, shall be saved, but he that doeth righteousness.* So then, brethren, let us confess Him in our works, by loving one another, by not committing adultery nor speaking evil one against another nor envying, but being temperate, merciful, kindly. And we ought to have fellow-feeling one with another and not to be covetous. By these works let us confess Him, and not by the contrary. And we ought not rather to fear men but God. For this cause, if ye do these things, the Lord said, *Though ye be gathered together with Me in My bosom, and do not My commandments, I will cast you away and will say unto you, Depart from Me, I know you not whence ye are, ye workers of iniquity.*

5. Wherefore, brethren, let us forsake our sojourn in this world and do the will of Him that called us, and let us not be afraid to depart out of this world. For the Lord saith, *Ye shall be as lambs in the midst of wolves.* But Peter answered and said unto Him, *What then, if the wolves should tear the lambs ?* Jesus said unto Peter, *Let not the lambs fear the wolves after they are dead ; and ye also, fear ye not them that kill*

you and are not able to do anything to you; but fear Him that after ye are
dead hath power over soul and body, to cast them into the gehenna of fire.
And ye know, brethren, that the sojourn of this flesh in this world is
mean and for a short time, but the promise of Christ is great and
marvellous, even the rest of the kingdom that shall be and of life
eternal. What then can we do to obtain them, but walk in holiness and
righteousness, and consider these worldly things as alien to us, and not
desire them? For when we desire to obtain these things we fall away
from the righteous path.

6. But the Lord saith, *No servant can serve two masters.* If we
desire to serve both God and mammon, it is unprofitable for us : *For
what advantage is it, if a man gain the whole world and forfeit his soul?*
Now this age and the future are two enemies. The one speaketh of
adultery and defilement and avarice and deceit, but the other biddeth
farewell to these. We cannot therefore be friends of the two, but must
bid farewell to the one and hold companionship with the other. Let us
consider that it is better to hate the things which are here, because they
are mean and for a short time and perishable, and to love the things
which are there, for they are good and imperishable. For, if we do the
will of Christ, we shall find rest ; but if otherwise, then nothing shall
deliver us from eternal punishment, if we should disobey His commandments. And the scripture also saith in Ezekiel, *Though Noah and Job
and Daniel should rise up, they shall not deliver their children* in the
captivity. But if even such righteous men as these cannot by their
righteous deeds deliver their children, with what confidence shall we, if
we keep not our baptism pure and undefiled, enter into the kingdom of
God? Or who shall be our advocate, unless we be found having holy
and righteous works?

7. So then, my brethren, let us contend, knowing that the contest
is nigh at hand, and that, while many resort to the corruptible contests,
yet not all are crowned, but only they that have toiled hard and
contended bravely. Let us then contend that we all may be crowned.
Wherefore let us run in the straight course, the incorruptible contest.
And let us resort to it in throngs and contend, that we may also be
crowned. And if we cannot all be crowned, let us at least come near
to the crown. We ought to know that he which contendeth in the corruptible contest, if he be found dealing corruptly with it, is first flogged,
and then removed and driven out of the race-course. What think ye?
What shall be done to him that hath dealt corruptly with the contest of

incorruption? For as concerning them that have not kept the seal, He saith, *Their worm shall not die, and their fire shall not be quenched, and they shall be for a spectacle unto all flesh.*

8. While we are on earth then, let us repent : for we are clay under the craftsman's hand. For in like manner as the potter, if he be making a vessel, and it get twisted or crushed in his hands, reshapeth it again ; but if he have once put it into the fiery oven, he shall no longer mend it : so also let us, while we are in this world, repent with our whole heart of the evil things which we have done in the flesh, that we may be saved by the Lord, while we have yet time for repentance. For after that we have departed out of the world, we can no more make confession there, or repent any more. Wherefore, brethren, if we shall have done the will of the Father and kept the flesh pure and guarded the commandments of the Lord, we shall receive life eternal. For the Lord saith in the Gospel, *If ye kept not that which is little, who shall give unto you that which is great? For I say unto you that he which is faithful in the least, is faithful also in much.* So then He meaneth this, Keep the flesh pure and the seal unstained, to the end that we may receive life.

9. And let not any one of you say that this flesh is not judged neither riseth again. Understand ye. In what were ye saved? In what did ye recover your sight? if ye were not in this flesh. We ought therefore to guard the flesh as a temple of God : for in like manner as ye were called in the flesh, ye shall come also in the flesh. If Christ the Lord who saved us, being first spirit, then became flesh, and so called us, in like manner also shall we in this flesh receive our reward. Let us therefore love one another, that we all may come unto the kingdom of God. While we have time to be healed, let us place our-selves in the hands of God the physician, giving Him a recompense. What recompense? Repentance from a sincere heart. For He dis-cerneth all things beforehand and knoweth what is in our heart. Let us therefore give unto Him eternal praise, not from our lips only, but also from our heart, that He may receive us as sons. For the Lord also said, *These are My brethren, which do the will of My Father.*

10. Wherefore, my brethren, let us do the will of the Father which called us, that we may live ; and let us the rather pursue virtue, but forsake vice as the forerunner of our sins, and let us flee from ungodli-ness, lest evils overtake us. For if we be diligent in doing good, peace will pursue us. For for this cause is a man unable to †attain happiness†,

seeing that they call in the fears of men, preferring rather the enjoyment which is here than the promise which is to come. For they know not how great torment the enjoyment which is here bringeth, and what delight the promise which is to come bringeth. And if verily they were doing these things by themselves alone, it had been tolerable : but now they continue teaching evil to innocent souls, not knowing that they shall have their condemnation doubled, both themselves and their hearers.

11. Let us therefore serve God in a pure heart, and we shall be righteous; but if we serve Him not, because we believe not the promise of God, we shall be wretched. For the word of prophecy also saith : *Wretched are the double-minded, that doubt in their heart and say, These things we heard of old in the days of our fathers also, yet we have waited day after day and have seen none of them. Ye fools! compare yourselves unto a tree ; take a vine. First it sheddeth its leaves, then a shoot cometh, after this a sour berry, then a full ripe grape. So likewise My people had tumults and afflictions : but afterward they shall receive good things.* Wherefore, my brethren, let us not be double-minded but endure patiently in hope, that we may also obtain our reward. *For faithful is He that promised* to pay to each man the recompense of his works. If therefore we shall have wrought righteousness in the sight of God, we shall enter into His kingdom and shall receive the promises which *ear hath not heard nor eye seen, neither hath it entered into the heart of man.*

12. Let us therefore await the kingdom of God betimes in love and righteousness, since we know not the day of God's appearing. For the Lord Himself, being asked by a certain person when His kingdom would come, said, *When the two shall be one, and the outside as the inside, and the male with the female, neither male nor female.* Now *the two* are *one*, when we speak truth among ourselves, and in two bodies there shall be one soul without dissimulation. And by *the outside as the inside* He meaneth this : by the inside He meaneth the soul and by the outside the body. Therefore in like manner as thy body appeareth, so also let thy soul be manifest in its good works. And by *the male with the female, neither male nor female,* He meaneth this ; that a brother seeing a sister should have no thought of her as of a female, and that a sister seeing a brother should not have any thought of him as of a male. These things if ye do, saith He, the kingdom of my Father shall come.

13. Therefore, brethren, let us repent forthwith. Let us be sober unto that which is good: for we are full of much folly and wickedness. Let us wipe away from us our former sins, and let us repent with our whole soul and be saved. And let us not be found men-pleasers. Neither let us desire to please one another only, but also those men that are without, by our righteousness, that the Name be not blasphemed by reason of us. For the Lord saith, *Every way My Name is blasphemed among all the Gentiles;* and again, *Woe unto him by reason of whom My Name is blasphemed.* Wherein is it blasphemed? In that ye do not the things which I desire. For the Gentiles, when they hear from our mouth the oracles of God, marvel at them for their beauty and greatness; then, when they discover that our works are not worthy of the words which we speak, forthwith they betake themselves to blasphemy, saying that it is an idle story and a delusion. For when they hear from us that God saith, *It is no thank unto you, if ye love them that love you, but this is thank unto you, if ye love your enemies and them that hate you;* when they hear these things, I say, they marvel at their exceeding goodness; but when they see that we not only do not love them that hate us, but not even them that love us, they laugh us to scorn, and the Name is blasphemed.

14. Wherefore, brethren, if we do the will of God our Father, we shall be of the first Church, which is spiritual, which was created before the sun and moon; but if we do not the will of the Lord, we shall be of the scripture that saith, *My house was made a den of robbers.* So therefore let us choose rather to be of the Church of life, that we may be saved. And I do not suppose ye are ignorant that the living Church is *the body of Christ:* for the scripture saith, *God made man, male and female.* The male is Christ and the female is the Church. And the Books and the Apostles plainly declare that the Church existeth not now for the first time, but hath been from the beginning: for she was spiritual, as our Jesus also was spiritual, but was manifested in the last days that He might save us. Now the Church, being spiritual, was manifested in the flesh of Christ, thereby showing us that, if any of us guard her in the flesh and defile her not, he shall receive her again in the Holy Spirit: for this flesh is the counterpart and copy of the spirit. No man therefore, when he hath defiled the copy, shall receive the original for his portion. This therefore is what He meaneth, brethren; Guard ye the flesh, that ye may partake of the spirit. But if we say that the flesh is the Church and the spirit is Christ, then he that hath

dealt wantonly with the flesh hath dealt wantonly with the Church. Such an one therefore shall not partake of the spirit, which is Christ. So excellent is the life and immortality which this flesh can receive as its portion, if the Holy Spirit be joined to it. No man can declare or tell *those things which the Lord hath prepared* for His elect.

15. Now I do not think that I have given any mean counsel respecting continence, and whosoever performeth it shall not repent thereof, but shall save both himself and me his counsellor. For it is no mean reward to convert a wandering and perishing soul, that it may be saved. For this is the recompense which we are able to pay to God who created us, if he that speaketh and heareth both speak and hear with faith and love. Let us therefore abide in the things which we believed, in righteousness and holiness, that we may with boldness ask of God who saith, *Whiles thou art still speaking I will say, Behold, I am here.* For this word is the token of a great promise : for the Lord saith of Himself that He is more ready to give than he that asketh to ask. Seeing then that we are partakers of so great kindness, let us not grudge ourselves the obtaining of so many good things. For in proportion as the pleasure is great which these words bring to them that have performed them, so also is the condemnation great which they bring to them that have been disobedient.

16. Therefore, brethren, since we have found no small opportunity for repentance, seeing that we have time, let us turn again unto God that called us, while we have still One that receiveth us. For if we bid farewell to these enjoyments and conquer our soul in refusing to fulfil its evil lusts, we shall be partakers of the mercy of Jesus. But ye know that the day of judgment cometh even now *as a burning oven, and the powers of the heavens shall melt,* and all the earth as lead melting on the fire, and then shall appear the secret and open works of men. Almsgiving therefore is a good thing, even as repentance from sin. Fasting is better than prayer, but almsgiving than both. And *love covereth a multitude of sins,* but prayer out of a good conscience delivereth from death. Blessed is every man that is found full of these. For almsgiving lifteth off the burden of sin.

17. Let us therefore repent with our whole heart, lest any of us perish by the way. For if we have received commands, that we should make this also our business, to tear men away from idols and to instruct them, how much more is it wrong that a soul which knoweth God already should perish ! Therefore let us assist one another, that

we may also lead the weak upward as touching that which is good, to the end that we all may be saved: and let us convert and admonish one another. And let us not think to give heed and believe now only, while we are admonished by the presbyters; but likewise when we have departed home, let us remember the commandments of the Lord, and not suffer ourselves to be dragged off the other way by our worldly lusts; but coming hither more frequently, let us strive to go forward in the commands of the Lord, that we all having the same mind may be gathered together unto life. For the Lord said, *I come to gather together all the nations, tribes, and languages.* Herein He speaketh of the day of His appearing, when He shall come and redeem us, each man according to his works. *And* the unbelievers *shall see His glory* and His might: and they shall be amazed when they see the kingdom of the world given to Jesus, saying, Woe unto us, for Thou wast, and we knew it not, and believed not; and we obeyed not the presbyters when they told us of our salvation. And *Their worm shall not die, and their fire shall not be quenched, and they shall be for a spectacle unto all flesh.* He speaketh of that day of judgment, when men shall see those among us that lived ungodly lives and dealt falsely with the commandments of Jesus Christ. But the righteous, having done good and endured torments and hated the pleasures of the soul, when they shall behold them that have done amiss and denied Jesus by their words or by their deeds, how that they are punished with grievous torments in unquenchable fire, shall give glory to God, saying, There will be hope for him that hath served God with his whole heart.

18. Therefore let us also be found among those that give thanks, among those that have served God, and not among the ungodly that are judged. For I myself too, being an utter sinner and not yet escaped from temptation, but being still amidst the engines of the devil, do my diligence to follow after righteousness, that I may prevail so far at least as to come near unto it, while I fear the judgment to come.

19. Therefore, brothers and sisters, after the God of truth hath been heard, I read to you an exhortation to the end that ye may give heed to the things which are written, so that ye may save both yourselves and him that readeth in the midst of you. For I ask of you as a reward that ye repent with your whole heart, and give salvation and life to yourselves. For doing this we shall set a goal for all the young who desire to toil in the study of piety and of the goodness of

God. And let us not be displeased and vexed, fools that we are, whensoever any one admonisheth us and turneth us aside from unrighteousness unto righteousness. For sometimes while we do evil things, we perceive it not by reason of the double-mindedness and unbelief which is in our breasts, and *we are darkened in our understanding* by our vain lusts. Let us therefore practise righteousness that we may be saved unto the end. Blessed are they that obey these ordinances. Though they may endure affliction for a short time in the world, they will gather the immortal fruit of the resurrection. Therefore let not the godly be grieved, if he be miserable in the times that now are : a blessed time awaiteth him. He shall live again in heaven with the fathers, and shall have rejoicing throughout a sorrowless eternity.

20. Neither suffer ye this again to trouble your mind, that we see the unrighteous possessing wealth, and the servants of God straitened. Let us then have faith, brothers and sisters. We are contending in the lists of a living God ; and we are trained by the present life, that we may be crowned with the future. No righteous man hath reaped fruit quickly, but waiteth for it. For if God had paid the recompense of the righteous speedily, then straightway we should have been training ourselves in merchandise, and not in godliness ; for we should seem to be righteous, though we were pursuing not that which is godly, but that which is gainful. And for this cause Divine judgment overtaketh a spirit that is not just, and loadeth it with chains.

To the only God invisible, the Father of truth, who sent forth unto us the Saviour and Prince of immortality, through whom also He made manifest unto us the truth and the heavenly life, to Him be the glory for ever and ever. Amen.

THE EPISTLES

OF

S. IGNATIUS

A MAP TO ILLUSTRATE THE EPISTLES OF S. IGNATIUS.

Scale of English Miles.

London: Macmillan & Co.

Stanford's Geog.l Estab.t

Route (or alternative routes) of S. Ignatius ——

Route of the Messengers & Delegates - - - - -

THE EPISTLES OF S. IGNATIUS

I

THESE seven epistles were written in the early years of the second century, when the writer was on his way from Antioch to Rome, having been condemned to death and expecting to be thrown to the wild beasts in the amphitheatre on his arrival. They fall into two groups, written at two different halting-places on his way. The letters to the Ephesians, Magnesians, Trallians, and Romans, were sent from *Smyrna*, while Ignatius was staying there and was in personal communication with Polycarp the bishop. The three remaining letters, to the Philadelphians, to the Smyrnæans, and to Polycarp, were written at a subsequent stage in his journey, at *Alexandria Troas*, where again he halted for a time, before crossing the sea for Europe. The place of writing in every case is determined from notices in the epistles themselves.

The order in which they are printed here is the order given by Eusebius (*H. E.* iii. 36). Whether he found them in this order in his manuscript, or whether he determined the places of writing (as we might determine them) from internal evidence and arranged the epistles accordingly, may be questioned. So arranged, they fall into two groups, according to the place of writing. The letters themselves however contain no indication of their chronological order in their respective groups; and, unless Eusebius simply followed his manuscript, he must have exercised his judgment in the sequence adopted in each group, e.g. Ephesians, Magnesians, Trallians, and Romans.

The two groups, besides having been written at different places, are separated from each other by another distinctive feature. All the epistles written from Smyrna are addressed to churches which he had not visited in person but knew only through their delegates. On the other hand all the epistles written from Troas are addressed to those, whether churches (as in the case of the Philadelphians and Smyrnæans) or individuals (as in the case of Polycarp), with whom he had already held personal communication at some previous stage in his journey.

At some point in his journey (probably Laodicea on the Lycus), where there was a choice of roads, his guards selected the northern road through Philadelphia and Sardis to Smyrna[1]. If they had taken the southern route instead, they would have passed in succession through Tralles, Magnesia, and Ephesus, before they reached their goal. It is probable that, at the point where the roads diverged, the Christian brethren sent messengers to the churches lying on the southern road, apprising them of the martyr's destination; so that these churches would despatch their respective delegates without delay, and thus they would arrive at Smyrna as soon as, or even before, Ignatius himself.

The first group then consists of letters to these three churches, whose delegates had thus met him at Smyrna, together with a fourth to the Roman Christians apprising them of his speedy arrival among them—this last probably having been called forth by some opportunity (such as was likely to occur at Smyrna) of communicating with the metropolis. The three are arranged in a topographical order (Ephesus, Magnesia, Tralles) according to the distances of these cities from Smyrna, which is taken as the starting-point.

The second group consists of a letter to the Philadelphians whom he had visited on his way to Smyrna, and another to the Smyrnæans with whom he had stayed before going to Troas, together with a third to his friend Polycarp closing the series.

The order however in the Greek MS and in the versions (so far as it can be traced) is quite different, and disregards the places of writing. In these documents they stand in the following order:

1.	Smyrnæans	5.	Philadelphians
2.	Polycarp	6.	Trallians
3.	Ephesians	7.	Romans.
4.	Magnesians		

This sequence is consistent with the supposition that we have here the collection of the martyr's letters made at the time by Polycarp, who writing to the Philippians says 'The Epistles of Ignatius which were sent to us by him, and others as many as we had with us, we send

---

[1] See the map facing p. 97.

to you, even as ye directed : they are subjoined to this letter' (§ 13). But though this order, which is given in the documents, has high claims for consideration as representing the earliest form of the collected epistles, I have substituted the chronological arrangement of Eusebius as more instructive for purposes of continuous reading.

2

Our documents are as follows.

1. The *Manuscript of the Greek Original* (G), the famous Medicean MS at Florence, from which Voss published the *editio princeps* in 1646. It is incomplete at the end, and does not contain the Epistle to the Romans. If this MS had been, as Turrianus described it, ' emendatissimus ', we should have had no further trouble about the text. But since this is far from being the case, the secondary authorities are of the highest moment in settling the readings.

2. Among these the *Latin Version* (L) holds the first place, as being an extremely literal rendering of the original. The history of this version is especially interesting to Englishmen. It was discovered by Ussher in English libraries in two MSS, one of which has been since lost, and was given to the world by him in 1644. It was certainly translated in England, probably by Robert Grosseteste, Bishop of Lincoln (c. A.D. 1250), or his immediate circle. It exhibits a much purer form of the text, being free from several corruptions and a few interpolations and omissions which disfigure the Greek. At the same time however it is clear, both from the contents of the collection and from other indications, that this version was translated from a Greek MS of the same type as the extant Greek MS ; and therefore its value, as a check upon the readings of this MS, is limited. Whenever GL coincide, they must be regarded as one witness, not as two.

3. The *Syriac Version* (S) would therefore have been invaluable as an independent check, if we had possessed it entire, since it cannot have been made later than the fourth or fifth century, and would have exhibited the text much nearer to the fountain-head than either the Greek or the Latin. Unfortunately however only a few fragments (S_1, S_2, S_3, S_4) belonging to this version are preserved. But this defect is made up to a considerable extent in two ways. *First.* We have a rough *Abridgment* or *Collection of Excerpts* (Σ) from this Syriac Version

for three epistles (Ephesians, Romans, Polycarp) together with a fragment of a fourth (Trallians), preserving whole sentences and even paragraphs in their original form or with only slight changes. *Secondly*. There is extant also an *Armenian Version* (A) of the whole, made from the Syriac (S). This last however has passed through so many vicissitudes, that it is often difficult to discern the original Greek reading underlying its tertiary text. It will thus be seen that AΣ have no independent authority, where S is otherwise known, and that SAΣ must be regarded as one witness, not as three.

4. There is likewise extant a fragment of a *Coptic Version* (C), in the Sahidic (Thebaic) dialect of the Egyptian language, comprising the first six chapters of the Epistle to the Smyrnæans, besides the end of the spurious Epistle to Hero. The date of this version is uncertain, though probably early; but the text appears to be quite independent of our other authorities, and it is therefore much to be regretted that so little is preserved.

5. Another and quite independent witness is the *Greek Text of the Long Recension* (g) of the Ignatian Epistles. This Long Recension consists of the seven genuine Epistles but interpolated throughout, together with six additional Epistles (Mary to Ignatius, Ignatius to Mary, to the Tarsians, to the Philippians, to the Antiochenes and to Hero). The *Latin Version* (l) of the Long Recension has no independent value, and is only important as assisting in determining the original form of this recension. The practice of treating it as an independent authority is altogether confusing. The text of the Long Recension, once launched into the world, had its own history, which should be kept quite distinct from that of the genuine Epistles of Ignatius. For the purpose of determining the text of the latter, we are only concerned with its original form.

The Long Recension was constructed by some unknown author, probably in the latter half of the fourth century, from the genuine Ignatian Epistles by interpolation, alteration, and omission. If therefore we can ascertain in any given passage the Greek text of the genuine epistles which this author had before him, we have traced the reading back to an earlier point in the stream than the direct Greek and Latin authorities, probably even than the Syriac Version. This however it is not always easy to do, by reason of the freedom and capriciousness of the changes. No rule of universal application can be laid down. But the interpolator is obviously much more given to change at some times than at others; and, where the fit is upon him, no stress can be laid on minor variations. On the other hand, where he adheres pretty closely to the text of the genuine Ignatius, as for instance through great parts of the Epistles to Polycarp and to the Romans, the readings of this recension deserve every consideration.

Thus it will be seen that though this witness is highly important, because it cannot be suspected of collusion with other witnesses, yet it must be subject to careful cross-examination, before the truth underlying its statements can be ascertained.

6. Besides manuscripts and versions, we have a fair number of *Quotations*, of which the value will vary according to their age and independence.

From the above statement it will be seen that, though each authority separately may be regarded as more or less unsatisfactory, yet, as they are very various in kind, they act as checks one upon another, the one frequently supplying just that element of certainty which is lacking to the other, so that the result is fairly adequate. Thus A will often give what g withholds, and conversely. Moreover it will appear from what has been said that a combination of the secondary and capricious authorities must often decide a reading against the direct and primary. For instance, the combination Ag is, as a rule, decisive in favour of a reading, as against the more direct witnesses GL, notwithstanding that A singly, or g singly, is liable to any amount of aberration, though in different directions.

The foregoing account applies to six out of the seven letters. The text of the *Epistle to the Romans* has had a distinct history and is represented by separate authorities of its own. This epistle was at an early date incorporated into the Antiochene Acts of Martyrdom of Ignatius, and thus dissociated from the other six. In its new connexion, it was disseminated and translated separately. It so happens that the Greek MSS which contain this epistle (the Colbertine, 18 *S. Sab.*, and 519 *Sin.*) are even less satisfactory than the Greek MS of the other six (the Medicean); but on the other hand we have more than compensation for this inferiority in the fact that the Acts of Martyrdom (with the incorporated epistle) were translated independently both into Syriac (S_m) and into Armenian (A_m); and these two versions, which are extant, furnish two additional authorities for the text. Moreover the Metaphrast, who compiled his Acts of Ignatius from this and another

Martyrology, has retained the Epistle to the Romans in his text, though in an abridged and altered form.

From this account it will be seen that the authorities for the Epistle to the Romans fall into three classes.

(1) Those authorities, which contain the epistle as part of the Martyrology. These are the Greek (G), the Latin (L), the Syriac (S$_m$), and the Armenian (A$_m$), besides the Metaphrast (M). These authorities however are of different values. When the epistle was first incorporated in the Acts of Martyrdom, it still preserved a comparatively pure form. When it has arrived at the stage in which it appears in the extant Greek MS (G), it is very corrupt. In this last form, among other corruptions, it exhibits interpolations and alterations which have been introduced from the Long Recension (g). The MS used by the Metaphrast exhibited a text essentially the same as that of G.

(2) The independent *Syriac Version* (S) of which only a few fragments remain, but which is represented, as before, by the *Syriac Abridgment* (Σ) and the *Armenian Version* (A).

(3) The *Long Recension* (g), which in great parts of this epistle keeps close to the text of the original Ignatius.

3

Though the principles on which a text of the Seven Epistles should be constructed are sufficiently obvious, they have been strangely overlooked.

The first period in the history of the text of the genuine Ignatius commences with the publication of the Latin Version by Ussher (1644), and of the Greek original by Isaac Voss (1646). The Greek of the Epistle to the Romans was first published by Ruinart (1689). The text of Voss was a very incorrect transcript of the Medicean MS, and in this respect subsequent collations have greatly improved on his *editio princeps*. But beyond this next to nothing was done to emend the Greek text. Though some very obvious corrections are suggested by the Latin Version, these were either neglected altogether by succeeding editors or were merely indicated by them in their notes without being introduced into the text. There was the same neglect also of the aid which might have been derived from the Long Recension. Moreover the practice of treating the several MSS and the Latin Version of the Long Recension independently of one another and recording them co-ordinately with the Greek and Latin of the genuine Ignatius (instead of using them apart to ascertain the original form of the Long Recension, and then employing the text of this Recension, when thus ascertained, as a single authority) threw the criticism of the text into great confusion. Nor was any attention paid to the quotations, which in several instances have the highest value. Hence it happened that during this period which extended over two centuries from Voss to Hefele (ed. 1, 1839; ed. 3, 1847) and Jacobson (ed. 1, 1838; ed. 3, 1847) inclusive, nothing or next to nothing (beyond the more accurate collation of the Medicean MS) was done for the Greek text.

The second period dates from the publication of the Oriental versions—the Syriac Abridgment with the Syriac Fragments by Cureton (1845, 1849), and the Armenian Version by Petermann (1849)[1]. New materials of the highest value were thus placed in the hands of critics; but, notwithstanding the interest which the Ignatian question excited, nearly thirty years elapsed before any proper use was made of them. In some cases the failure was due, at least in part, to a false solution of the Ignatian question. The text of Bunsen (1847), Cureton (1849), and Lipsius (1859), which started from the assumption that the Syriac Abridgment represented the genuine Ignatius, must necessarily have foundered on this rock, even if the principles adopted had been sound in other respects. Petermann and Dressel (1857) however maintained the priority of the Seven Epistles of the Vossian text to the Three of the Curetonian; and so far they built upon the true basis. But Petermann contented himself with a casual emendation of the text here and there from the versions; while Dressel neglected them altogether. Jacobson (ed. 4, 1863) and Hefele (ed. 4, 1855) also, in their more recent editions which have appeared since the Oriental versions were rendered accessible, have been satisfied with recording some of the phenomena of these versions in their notes without applying them to the correction of the text, though they also were unhampered by the false theory which maintained the priority of the Curetonian Abridgment. It was reserved for the most recent editors, Zahn (1876), and Funk (1878), to make use of all the available materials

---

[1] The editio princeps of the Armenian was published at Constantinople in 1783; but this version was practically unknown to scholars until Petermann's edition appeared.

and to reconstruct the text for the first time on sound and intelligible principles.

The text which I have given was constructed independently of both these editions, and before I had seen them, but the main principles are the same. Indeed these principles must be sufficiently obvious to those who have investigated the materials with any care. In the details however my views frequently differ from theirs, as must necessarily be the case with independent editors; and in some respects I have had the advantage of more complete or more accurate materials than were accessible to them.

ΠΡΟΣ ΕΦΕΣΙΟΥΣ

ΙΓΝΑΤΙΟΣ, ὁ καὶ Θεοφόρος, τῇ εὐλογημένῃ ἐν μεγέθει Θεοῦ πατρὸς πληρώματι, τῇ προωρισμένῃ πρὸ αἰώνων εἶναι διὰ παντὸς εἰς δόξαν παράμονον ἄτρεπτον, ἡνωμένῃ καὶ ἐκλελεγμένῃ ἐν πάθει ἀληθινῷ ἐν θελήματι τοῦ πατρὸς καὶ Ἰησοῦ Χριστοῦ τοῦ Θεοῦ ἡμῶν, τῇ ἐκκλησίᾳ τῇ ἀξιομακαρίστῳ τῇ οὔσῃ ἐν Ἐφέσῳ [τῆς Ἀσίας], πλεῖστα ἐν Ἰησοῦ Χριστῷ καὶ ἐν ἀμώμῳ χαρᾷ χαίρειν.

I. Ἀποδεξάμενος [ὑμῶν] ἐν Θεῷ τὸ πολυαγάπητον ὄνομα, ὃ κέκτησθε φύσει [ἐν γνώμῃ ὀρθῇ καὶ] δικαίᾳ κατὰ πίστιν καὶ ἀγάπην ἐν Χριστῷ Ἰησοῦ τῷ σωτῆρι ἡμῶν· μιμηταὶ ὄντες Θεοῦ, ἀναζωπυρήσαντες ἐν αἵματι Θεοῦ, τὸ συγγενικὸν ἔργον τελείως ἀπηρτίσατε· 2. ἀκούσαντες γὰρ δεδεμένου ἀπὸ Συρίας ὑπὲρ τοῦ κοινοῦ ὀνόματος καὶ ἐλπίδος, ἐλπίζοντα τῇ προσευχῇ ὑμῶν ἐπιτυχεῖν ἐν Ῥώμῃ θηριομαχῆσαι, ἵνα διὰ τοῦ ἐπιτυχεῖν δυνηθῶ μαθητὴς εἶναι, ἱστορῆσαι ἐσπουδάσατε. 3. ἐπεὶ οὖν τὴν πολυπλήθειαν ὑμῶν ἐν ὀνόματι Θεοῦ ἀπείληφα ἐν Ὀνησίμῳ, τῷ ἐπ' ἀγάπῃ ἀδιηγήτῳ, ὑμῶν δὲ [ἐν σαρκὶ] ἐπισκόπῳ· ὃν εὔχομαι κατὰ Ἰησοῦν Χριστὸν ὑμᾶς ἀγαπᾶν, καὶ πάντας ὑμᾶς αὐτῷ ἐν ὁμοιότητι εἶναι· εὐλογητὸς γὰρ ὁ χαρισάμενος ὑμῖν ἀξίοις οὖσιν τοιοῦτον ἐπίσκοπον κεκτῆσθαι.

II. Περὶ δὲ τοῦ συνδούλου μου Βούρρου τοῦ κατὰ Θεὸν διακόνου ὑμῶν [καὶ] ἐν πᾶσιν εὐλογημένου, εὔχομαι παραμεῖναι αὐτὸν εἰς τιμὴν ὑμῶν καὶ τοῦ ἐπισκόπου. καὶ Κρόκος δὲ ὁ Θεοῦ ἄξιος καὶ ὑμῶν, ὃν ἐξεμπλάριον τῆς ἀφ' ὑμῶν ἀγάπης ἀπέλαβον, κατὰ πάντα με ἀνέπαυσεν, ὡς καὶ αὐτὸν ὁ πατὴρ Ἰησοῦ Χριστοῦ ἀναψύξαι, ἅμα Ὀνησίμῳ καὶ Βούρρῳ καὶ Εὔπλῳ καὶ Φρόντωνι, δι᾽ ὧν πάντας ὑμᾶς κατὰ ἀγάπην εἶδον· 2. ὀναίμην ὑμῶν διὰ παντός, ἐάνπερ ἄξιος ὦ. πρέπον οὖν ἐστιν κατὰ πάντα τρόπον δοξάζειν Ἰησοῦν Χριστὸν τὸν δοξάσαντα ὑμᾶς· ἵνα ἐν μιᾷ ὑποταγῇ κατηρτισμένοι, ὑποτασσόμενοι τῷ ἐπισκόπῳ καὶ τῷ πρεσβυτερίῳ, κατὰ πάντα ἦτε ἡγιασμένοι.

III. Οὐ διατάσσομαι ὑμῖν, ὡς ὤν τι· εἰ γὰρ καὶ δέδεμαι ἐν τῷ ὀνόματι, οὔπω ἀπήρτισμαι ἐν Ἰησοῦ Χριστῷ· νῦν [γὰρ] ἀρχὴν ἔχω τοῦ μαθητεύεσθαι καὶ προσλαλῶ ὑμῖν ὡς συνδιδασκαλίταις μου· ἐμὲ γὰρ ἔδει ὑφ᾽ ὑμῶν ὑπαλειφθῆναι πίστει, νουθεσίᾳ, ὑπομονῇ, μακροθυμίᾳ. 2. ἀλλ᾽ ἐπεὶ ἡ ἀγάπη οὐκ ἐᾷ με σιωπᾶν περὶ ὑμῶν, διὰ τοῦτο προέλαβον παρακαλεῖν ὑμᾶς, ὅπως συντρέχητε τῇ γνώμῃ τοῦ Θεοῦ. καὶ γὰρ Ἰησοῦς Χριστός, τὸ ἀδιάκριτον ἡμῶν ζῆν, τοῦ πατρὸς ἡ γνώμη, ὡς καὶ οἱ ἐπίσκοποι οἱ κατὰ τὰ πέρατα ὁρισθέντες ἐν Ἰησοῦ Χριστοῦ γνώμῃ εἰσίν.

IV. Ὅθεν πρέπει ὑμῖν συντρέχειν τῇ τοῦ ἐπισκόπου γνώμῃ· ὅπερ καὶ ποιεῖτε. τὸ γὰρ ἀξιονόμαστον ὑμῶν πρεσβυτέριον, τοῦ Θεοῦ ἄξιον, οὕτως συνήρμοσται τῷ ἐπισκόπῳ ὡς χορδαὶ κιθάρᾳ. διὰ τοῦτο ἐν τῇ ὁμονοίᾳ ὑμῶν καὶ συμφώνῳ ἀγάπῃ Ἰησοῦς Χριστὸς ᾄδεται. 2. καὶ οἱ κατ᾽ ἄνδρα δὲ χορὸς γίνεσθε, ἵνα σύμφωνοι ὄντες ἐν ὁμονοίᾳ, χρῶμα Θεοῦ λαβόντες, ἐν ἑνότητι ᾄδητε ἐν φωνῇ μιᾷ διὰ Ἰησοῦ Χριστοῦ τῷ πατρί, ἵνα ὑμῶν καὶ ἀκούσῃ καὶ ἐπιγινώσκῃ, δι᾽ ὧν εὖ πράσσετε, μέλη ὄντας τοῦ υἱοῦ αὐτοῦ. χρήσιμον οὖν ἐστιν ὑμᾶς ἐν ἀμώμῳ ἑνότητι εἶναι, ἵνα καὶ Θεοῦ πάντοτε μετέχητε.

V. Εἰ γὰρ ἐγὼ ἐν μικρῷ χρόνῳ τοιαύτην συνήθειαν ἔσχον πρὸς τὸν ἐπίσκοπον ὑμῶν, οὐκ ἀνθρωπίνην οὖσαν ἀλλὰ πνευματικήν, πόσῳ μᾶλλον ὑμᾶς μακαρίζω τοὺς ἀνακεκραμένους οὕτως, ὡς ἡ ἐκκλησία Ἰησοῦ Χριστῷ καὶ ὡς Ἰησοῦς Χριστὸς τῷ πατρί, ἵνα πάντα ἐν ἑνότητι σύμφωνα ᾖ. 2. μηδεὶς πλανάσθω· ἐὰν μή τις ᾖ ἐντὸς τοῦ θυσιαστηρίου, ὑστερεῖται τοῦ ἄρτου [τοῦ Θεοῦ]. εἰ γὰρ ἑνὸς καὶ δευτέρου

προσευχὴ τοσαύτην ἰσχὺν ἔχει, πόσῳ μᾶλλον ἥ τε τοῦ
ἐπισκόπου καὶ πάσης τῆς ἐκκλησίας. 3. ὁ οὖν μὴ ἐρχόμενος
ἐπὶ τὸ αὐτὸ οὗτος ἤδη ὑπερηφανεῖ καὶ ἑαυτὸν διέκρινεν· Prov. iii.
γέγραπται γάρ, ὙπΕΡΗΦΆΝΟΙC ὁ ΘΕὸC ἈΝΤΙΤΆCCΕΤΑΙ. σπου- 34·
δάσωμεν οὖν μὴ ἀντιτάσσεσθαι τῷ ἐπισκόπῳ, ἵνα ὦμεν Θεοῦ 1 Pet. v. 5. James iv. 6.
ὑποτασσόμενοι.

VI. Καὶ ὅσον βλέπει τις σιγῶντα ἐπίσκοπον, πλειόνως
αὐτὸν φοβείσθω. πάντα γὰρ ὃν πέμπει ὁ οἰκοδεσπότης εἰς
ἰδίαν οἰκονομίαν, οὕτως δεῖ ἡμᾶς αὐτὸν δέχεσθαι, ὡς αὐτὸν
τὸν πέμψαντα. τὸν οὖν ἐπίσκοπον δηλονότι ὡς αὐτὸν τὸν
Κύριον δεῖ προσβλέπειν. 2. αὐτὸς μὲν οὖν Ὀνήσιμος ὑπερε-
παινεῖ ὑμῶν τὴν ἐν Θεῷ εὐταξίαν, ὅτι πάντες κατὰ ἀλήθειαν
ζῆτε καὶ ὅτι ἐν ὑμῖν οὐδεμία αἵρεσις κατοικεῖ· ἀλλ' οὐδὲ
ἀκούετέ τινος πλέον ἢ περὶ Ἰησοῦ Χριστοῦ λαλοῦντος ἐν
ἀληθείᾳ.

VII. Εἰώθασιν γάρ τινες δόλῳ πονηρῷ τὸ ὄνομα περι-
φέρειν, ἄλλα τινὰ πράσσοντες ἀνάξια Θεοῦ· οὓς δεῖ ὑμᾶς ὡς
θηρία ἐκκλίνειν· εἰσὶν γὰρ κύνες λυσσῶντες, λαθροδῆκται,
οὓς δεῖ ὑμᾶς φυλάσσεσθαι ὄντας δυσθεραπεύτους. 2. εἷς
ἰατρός ἐστιν, σαρκικὸς καὶ πνευματικός, γεννητὸς καὶ ἀγέννη-
τος, ἐν ἀνθρώπῳ Θεός, ἐν θανάτῳ ζωὴ ἀληθινή, καὶ ἐκ
Μαρίας καὶ ἐκ Θεοῦ, πρῶτον παθητὸς καὶ τότε ἀπαθής,
Ἰησοῦς Χριστὸς ὁ Κύριος ἡμῶν.

VIII. Μὴ οὖν τις ὑμᾶς ἐξαπατάτω, ὥσπερ οὐδὲ ἐξα-
πατᾶσθε, ὅλοι ὄντες Θεοῦ. ὅταν γὰρ μηδεμία ἐπιθυμία
ἐνήρεισται ἐν ὑμῖν ἡ δυναμένη ὑμᾶς βασανίσαι, ἄρα κατὰ
Θεὸν ζῆτε. περίψημα ὑμῶν καὶ ἁγνίζομαι ὑμῶν Ἐφεσίων
ἐκκλησίας τῆς διαβοήτου τοῖς αἰῶσιν. 2. οἱ σαρκικοὶ τὰ
πνευματικὰ πράσσειν οὐ δύνανται οὐδὲ οἱ πνευματικοὶ τὰ
σαρκικά, ὥσπερ οὐδὲ ἡ πίστις τὰ τῆς ἀπιστίας οὐδὲ ἡ ἀπι-
στία τὰ τῆς πίστεως. ἃ δὲ καὶ κατὰ σάρκα πράσσετε, ταῦτα
πνευματικά ἐστιν· ἐν Ἰησοῦ γὰρ Χριστῷ πάντα πράσσετε.

vii. 2 ἐν ἀνθρώπῳ Θεός] Fathers [A]; ἐν σαρκὶ γενόμενος Θεός GL ; al. g.
ἐν θανάτῳ ζωὴ ἀληθινή] Fathers [A] ; ἐν ἀθανάτῳ ζωῇ ἀληθινῇ GL ; al. g.

IX. Ἔγνων δὲ παροδεύσαντάς τινας ἐκεῖθεν, ἔχοντας
κακὴν διδαχήν· οὓς οὐκ εἰάσατε σπεῖραι εἰς ὑμᾶς, βύσαντες
τὰ ὦτα εἰς τὸ μὴ παραδέξασθαι τὰ σπειρόμενα ὑπ' αὐτῶν·
ὡς ὄντες λίθοι ναοῦ προητοιμασμένοι εἰς οἰκοδομὴν Θεοῦ
πατρός, ἀναφερόμενοι εἰς τὰ ὕψη διὰ τῆς μηχανῆς Ἰησοῦ
Χριστοῦ, ὅς ἐστιν σταυρός, σχοινίῳ χρώμενοι τῷ πνεύματι
τῷ ἁγίῳ· ἡ δὲ πίστις ὑμῶν ἀναγωγεὺς ὑμῶν, ἡ δὲ ἀγάπη
ὁδὸς ἡ ἀναφέρουσα εἰς Θεόν. 2. ἐστὲ οὖν καὶ σύνοδοι
πάντες, θεοφόροι καὶ ναοφόροι, χριστοφόροι, ἁγιοφόροι, κατὰ
πάντα κεκοσμημένοι ἐν ἐντολαῖς Ἰησοῦ Χριστοῦ· οἷς καὶ
ἀγαλλιώμενος ἠξιώθην, δι' ὧν γράφω, προσομιλῆσαι ὑμῖν,
καὶ συγχαρῆναι ὅτι κατ' ἀνθρώπων βίον οὐδὲν ἀγαπᾶτε, εἰ
μὴ μόνον τὸν Θεόν.

X. Καὶ ὑπὲρ τῶν ἄλλων δὲ ἀνθρώπων ἀδιαλείπτως
προσεύχεσθε· ἔστιν γὰρ [ἐν] αὐτοῖς ἐλπὶς μετανοίας, ἵνα
Θεοῦ τύχωσιν. ἐπιτρέψατε οὖν αὐτοῖς κἂν ἐκ τῶν ἔργων
ὑμῖν μαθητευθῆναι. 2. πρὸς τὰς ὀργὰς αὐτῶν ὑμεῖς πραεῖς,
πρὸς τὰς μεγαλορημοσύνας αὐτῶν ὑμεῖς ταπεινόφρονες, πρὸς
τὰς βλασφημίας αὐτῶν ὑμεῖς τὰς προσευχάς, πρὸς τὴν

Col. i. 23. πλάνην αὐτῶν ὑμεῖς ἑδραῖοι τῇ πίϲτει, πρὸς τὸ ἄγριον αὐτῶν
ὑμεῖς ἥμεροι· μὴ σπουδάζοντες ἀντιμιμήσασθαι αὐτούς.
3. ἀδελφοὶ αὐτῶν εὑρεθῶμεν τῇ ἐπιεικείᾳ· μιμηταὶ δὲ τοῦ
Κυρίου σπουδάζωμεν εἶναι, τίς πλέον ἀδικηθῇ, τίς ἀποστε-
ρηθῇ, τίς ἀθετηθῇ· ἵνα μὴ τοῦ διαβόλου βοτάνη τις εὑρεθῇ
ἐν ὑμῖν· ἀλλ' ἐν πάσῃ ἁγνείᾳ καὶ σωφροσύνῃ μένετε ἐν
Χριστῷ Ἰησοῦ σαρκικῶς καὶ πνευματικῶς.

XI. Ἔσχατοι καιροί. λοιπὸν αἰσχυνθῶμεν, φοβηθῶμεν
τὴν μακροθυμίαν τοῦ Θεοῦ, ἵνα μὴ ἡμῖν εἰς κρῖμα γένηται.
ἢ γὰρ τὴν μέλλουσαν ὀργὴν φοβηθῶμεν ἢ τὴν ἐνεστῶσαν
χάριν ἀγαπήσωμεν, ἓν τῶν δύο· μόνον ἐν Χριστῷ Ἰησοῦ
εὑρεθῆναι εἰς τὸ ἀληθινὸν ζῆν. 2. χωρὶς τούτου μηδὲν ὑμῖν

---

ix. 1 προητοιμασμένοι] conj. Lightfoot, Markland; πατρὸς (written π̄ρ̄σ̄)
ἠτοιμασμένοι GLA [Σ]; al. g.   2 κατ' ἀνθρώπων βίον] conj. Lightfoot [g];
κατ' ἄλλον βίον GL; al. A.

πρεπέτω, ἐν ᾧ τὰ δεσμὰ περιφέρω, τοὺς πνευματικοὺς μαρ-
γαρίτας· ἐν οἷς γένοιτό μοι ἀναστῆναι τῇ προσευχῇ ὑμῶν, ἧς
γένοιτό μοι ἀεὶ μέτοχον εἶναι, ἵνα ἐν κλήρῳ Ἐφεσίων εὑρεθῶ
τῶν Χριστιανῶν, οἳ καὶ τοῖς ἀποστόλοις πάντοτε συνήνεσαν
ἐν δυνάμει Ἰησοῦ Χριστοῦ. XII. Οἶδα τίς εἰμι καὶ τίσιν γράφω. ἐγὼ κατάκριτος,
ὑμεῖς ἠλεημένοι· ἐγὼ ὑπὸ κίνδυνον, ὑμεῖς ἐστηριγμένοι. 2.
πάροδός ἐστε τῶν εἰς Θεὸν ἀναιρουμένων, Παύλου συμ-
μύσται τοῦ ἡγιασμένου, τοῦ μεμαρτυρημένου, ἀξιομακαρί-
στου, οὗ γένοιτό μοι ὑπὸ τὰ ἴχνη εὑρεθῆναι, ὅταν Θεοῦ
ἐπιτύχω· ὃς ἐν πάσῃ ἐπιστολῇ μνημονεύει ὑμῶν ἐν Χριστῷ
Ἰησοῦ. XIII. Σπουδάζετε οὖν πυκνότερον συνέρχεσθαι εἰς εὐχαριστίαν Θεοῦ καὶ εἰς δόξαν· ὅταν γὰρ πυκνῶς ἐπὶ τὸ αὐτὸ
γίνεσθε, καθαιροῦνται αἱ δυνάμεις τοῦ Σατανᾶ, καὶ λύεται
ὁ ὄλεθρος αὐτοῦ ἐν τῇ ὁμονοίᾳ ὑμῶν τῆς πίστεως. 2. οὐδέν
ἐστιν ἄμεινον εἰρήνης, ἐν ᾗ πᾶς πόλεμος καταργεῖται ἐπουρανίων καὶ ἐπιγείων. XIV. Ὧν οὐδὲν λανθάνει ὑμᾶς, ἐὰν τελείως εἰς Ἰησοῦν
Χριστὸν ἔχητε τὴν πίστιν καὶ τὴν ἀγάπην· ἥτις ἐστὶν ἀρχὴ
ζωῆς καὶ τέλος· ἀρχὴ μὲν πίστις, τέλος δὲ ἀγάπη· τὰ δὲ δύο
ἐν ἑνότητι γενόμενα Θεός ἐστιν, τὰ δὲ ἄλλα πάντα εἰς καλο-
καγαθίαν ἀκόλουθά ἐστιν. 2. οὐδεὶς πίστιν ἐπαγγελλόμενος
ἁμαρτάνει οὐδὲ ἀγάπην κεκτημένος μισεῖ. ΦΑΝΕΡΟΝ ΤΟ ΔΕΝ- S. Matt.
ΔΡΟΝ ἈΠΟ ΤΟΥ ΚΑΡΠΟΥ ΑΥΤΟΥ· οὕτως οἱ ἐπαγγελλόμενοι Χριστοῦ xii. 33.
εἶναι, δι᾽ ὧν πράσσουσιν ὀφθήσονται. οὐ γὰρ νῦν ἐπαγγελίας
τὸ ἔργον, ἀλλ᾽ ἐν δυνάμει πίστεως ἐάν τις εὑρεθῇ εἰς τέλος. XV. Ἄμεινόν ἐστιν σιωπᾶν καὶ εἶναι ἢ λαλοῦντα μὴ
εἶναι· καλὸν τὸ διδάσκειν, ἐὰν ὁ λέγων ποιῇ. εἷς οὖν διδά-
σκαλος, ὃς εἶπεν καὶ ἐγένετο· καὶ ἃ σιγῶν δὲ πεποίηκεν ἄξια Ps. xxxiii.
τοῦ πατρός ἐστιν. 2. ὁ λόγον Ἰησοῦ κεκτημένος ἀληθῶς 9.
δύναται καὶ τῆς ἡσυχίας αὐτοῦ ἀκούειν, ἵνα τέλειος ᾖ· ἵνα δι᾽
ὧν λαλεῖ πράσσῃ καὶ δι᾽ ὧν σιγᾷ γινώσκηται. 3. οὐδὲν
λανθάνει τὸν Κύριον, ἀλλὰ καὶ τὰ κρυπτὰ ἡμῶν ἐγγὺς αὐτῷ

ἐστιν. πάντα οὖν ποιῶμεν, ὡς αὐτοῦ ἐν ἡμῖν κατοικοῦντος, ἵνα ὦμεν αὐτοῦ ναοὶ καὶ αὐτὸς ᾖ ἐν ἡμῖν Θεός· ὅπερ καὶ ἔστιν καὶ φανήσεται πρὸ προσώπου ἡμῶν, ἐξ ὧν δικαίως ἀγαπῶμεν αὐτόν.

1 Cor. vi.   XVI. Μὴ πλανᾶσθε, ἀδελφοί μου· οἱ οἰκοφθόροι Βαcι-
9, 10.
Gal. v. 21.   λεÍαν Θεοῦ οὐ κληρονομήcουcιν. 2. εἰ οὖν οἱ κατὰ σάρκα ταῦτα πράσσοντες ἀπέθανον, πόσῳ μᾶλλον ἐὰν πίστιν Θεοῦ ἐν κακοδιδασκαλίᾳ φθείρῃ, ὑπὲρ ἧς Ἰησοῦς Χριστὸς ἐσταυρώθη. ὁ τοιοῦτος ῥυπαρὸς γενόμενος εἰς τὸ πῦρ τὸ ἄσβεστον χωρήσει, ὁμοίως καὶ ὁ ἀκούων αὐτοῦ.

XVII. Διὰ τοῦτο μύρον ἔλαβεν ἐπὶ τῆς κεφαλῆς [αὐτοῦ] ὁ Κύριος, ἵνα πνέῃ τῇ ἐκκλησίᾳ ἀφθαρσίαν. μὴ ἀλείφεσθε δυσωδίαν τῆς διδασκαλίας τοῦ ἄρχοντος τοῦ αἰῶνος τούτου, μὴ αἰχμαλωτίσῃ ὑμᾶς ἐκ τοῦ προκειμένου ζῆν. 2. διὰ τί δὲ οὐ πάντες φρόνιμοι γινόμεθα λαβόντες Θεοῦ γνῶσιν, ὅ ἐστιν Ἰησοῦς Χριστός; τί μωρῶς ἀπολλύμεθα ἀγνοοῦντες τὸ χάρισμα ὃ πέπομφεν ἀληθῶς ὁ Κύριος;

XVIII. Περίψημα τὸ ἐμὸν πνεῦμα τοῦ σταυροῦ, ὅ ἐστιν σκάνδαλον τοῖς ἀπιστοῦσιν, ἡμῖν δὲ σωτηρία καὶ ζωὴ αἰώ-
1 Cor. i. 20.   νιος. ποῦ coφόc; ποῦ cυzητητής; ποῦ καύχησις τῶν λεγομένων συνετῶν; 2. ὁ γὰρ Θεὸς ἡμῶν Ἰησοῦς ὁ Χριστὸς ἐκυοφορήθη ὑπὸ Μαρίας κατ᾽ οἰκονομίαν, ἐκ σπέρματος μὲν Δαυεὶδ πνεύματος δὲ ἁγίου· ὃς ἐγεννήθη καὶ ἐβαπτίσθη ἵνα τῷ πάθει τὸ ὕδωρ καθαρίσῃ.

XIX. Καὶ ἔλαθεν τὸν ἄρχοντα τοῦ αἰῶνος τούτου ἡ παρθενία Μαρίας καὶ ὁ τοκετὸς αὐτῆς, ὁμοίως καὶ ὁ θάνατος τοῦ Κυρίου· τρία μυστήρια κραυγῆς, ἅτινα ἐν ἡσυχίᾳ Θεοῦ ἐπράχθη. 2. πῶς οὖν ἐφανερώθη τοῖς αἰῶσιν; ἀστὴρ ἐν οὐρανῷ ἔλαμψεν ὑπὲρ πάντας τοὺς ἀστέρας, καὶ τὸ φῶς αὐτοῦ ἀνεκλάλητον ἦν, καὶ ξενισμὸν παρεῖχεν ἡ καινότης αὐτοῦ· τὰ δὲ λοιπὰ πάντα ἄστρα ἅμα ἡλίῳ καὶ σελήνῃ χορὸς ἐγένετο τῷ ἀστέρι, αὐτὸς δὲ ἦν ὑπερβάλλων τὸ φῶς αὐτοῦ ὑπὲρ πάντα· ταραχή τε ἦν πόθεν ἡ καινότης ἡ ἀνόμοιος αὐτοῖς. 3. ὅθεν ἐλύετο πᾶσα μαγεία καὶ πᾶς δεσμός, ἠφανί-

ζετο κακίας ἄγνοια, καθῃρεῖτο παλαιὰ βασιλεία, [διεφθεί-
ρετο], Θεοῦ ἀνθρωπίνως φανερουμένου εἰς ⲕⲁⲓⲛⲟⲧⲏⲧⲁ ἀϊδίου Rom. vi. 4.
ⲍⲱⲏⲥ· ἀρχὴν δὲ ἐλάμβανεν τὸ παρὰ Θεῷ ἀπηρτισμένον.
ἔνθεν τὰ πάντα συνεκινεῖτο διὰ τὸ μελετᾶσθαι θανάτου
κατάλυσιν.

XX. Ἐάν με καταξιώσῃ Ἰησοῦς Χριστὸς ἐν τῇ προσευχῇ ὑμῶν, καὶ θέλημα ᾖ, ἐν τῷ δευτέρῳ βιβλιδίῳ, ὃ μέλλω
γράφειν ὑμῖν, προσδηλώσω ὑμῖν ἧς ἠρξάμην οἰκονομίας εἰς
τὸν καινὸν ἄνθρωπον Ἰησοῦν Χριστόν, ἐν τῇ αὐτοῦ πίστει
καὶ ἐν τῇ αὐτοῦ ἀγάπῃ, ἐν πάθει αὐτοῦ καὶ ἀναστάσει,
μάλιστα ἐὰν ὁ Κύριός μοι ἀποκαλύψῃ· †ὅτι† οἱ κατ' ἄνδρα
κοινῇ πάντες ἐν χάριτι ἐξ ὀνόματος συνέρχεσθε ἐν μιᾷ
πίστει καὶ ἑνὶ Ἰησοῦ Χριστῷ τῷ κατὰ σάρκα ἐκ γένους
Δαυείδ, τῷ υἱῷ ἀνθρώπου καὶ υἱῷ Θεοῦ, εἰς τὸ ὑπακούειν
ὑμᾶς τῷ ἐπισκόπῳ καὶ τῷ πρεσβυτερίῳ ἀπερισπάστῳ δια-
νοίᾳ· ἕνα ἄρτον κλῶντες, ὅ ἐστιν φάρμακον ἀθανασίας, ἀντί-
δοτος τοῦ μὴ ἀποθανεῖν ἀλλὰ ζῆν ἐν Ἰησοῦ Χριστῷ διὰ
παντός.

XXI. Ἀντίψυχον ὑμῶν ἐγώ, καὶ ὧν ἐπέμψατε εἰς Θεοῦ
τιμὴν εἰς Σμύρναν· ὅθεν καὶ γράφω ὑμῖν εὐχαριστῶν τῷ
Κυρίῳ, ἀγαπῶν Πολύκαρπον ὡς καὶ ὑμᾶς. μνημονεύετέ μου,
ὡς καὶ ὑμῶν Ἰησοῦς Χριστός. 2. προσεύχεσθε ὑπὲρ τῆς
ἐκκλησίας τῆς ἐν Συρίᾳ, ὅθεν δεδεμένος εἰς Ῥώμην ἀπάγομαι,
ἔσχατος ὢν τῶν ἐκεῖ πιστῶν, ὥσπερ ἠξιώθην εἰς τιμὴν Θεοῦ
εὑρεθῆναι. ἔρρωσθε ἐν Θεῷ πατρὶ καὶ ἐν Ἰησοῦ Χριστῷ τῇ
κοινῇ ἐλπίδι ἡμῶν.

xx. ἑνὶ Ἰησοῦ Χριστῷ] Theodt. Gelas.; ἐν Ἰησοῦ Χριστῷ GLS₂ ; al. Ag.

ΠΡΟΣ ΤΟΥΣ ΕΝ ΜΑΓΝΗΣΙΑΙ

ΙΓΝΑΤΙΟΣ ὁ καὶ Θεοφόρος, τῇ εὐλογημένῃ ἐν χάριτι
Θεοῦ πατρὸς ἐν Χριστῷ Ἰησοῦ τῷ σωτῆρι [ἡμῶν], ἐν ᾧ
ἀσπάζομαι τὴν ἐκκλησίαν τὴν οὖσαν ἐν Μαγνησίᾳ τῇ πρὸς
Μαιάνδρῳ, καὶ εὔχομαι ἐν Θεῷ πατρὶ καὶ ἐν Ἰησοῦ Χριστῷ
πλεῖστα χαίρειν. I. Γνοὺς ὑμῶν τὸ πολυεύτακτον τῆς κατὰ Θεὸν ἀγάπης,
ἀγαλλιώμενος προειλάμην ἐν πίστει Ἰησοῦ Χριστοῦ προσ-
λαλῆσαι ὑμῖν. 2. καταξιωθεὶς γὰρ ὀνόματος θεοπρεπεστά-
του, ἐν οἷς περιφέρω δεσμοῖς ᾄδω τὰς ἐκκλησίας, ἐν αἷς
ἕνωσιν εὔχομαι σαρκὸς καὶ πνεύματος Ἰησοῦ Χριστοῦ τοῦ
διὰ παντὸς ἡμῶν ζῆν, πίστεώς τε καὶ ἀγάπης, ἧς οὐδὲν προκέκριται, τὸ δὲ κυριώτερον, Ἰησοῦ καὶ πατρός· 3. ἐν ᾧ
ὑπομένοντες τὴν πᾶσαν ἐπήρειαν τοῦ ἄρχοντος τοῦ αἰῶνος
τούτου καὶ διαφυγόντες Θεοῦ τευξόμεθα.

II. Ἐπεὶ οὖν ἠξιώθην ἰδεῖν ὑμᾶς διὰ Δαμᾶ τοῦ ἀξιοθέου
ὑμῶν ἐπισκόπου καὶ πρεσβυτέρων ἀξίων Βάσσου καὶ Ἀπολ-
λωνίου καὶ τοῦ συνδούλου μου διακόνου Ζωτίωνος, οὗ ἐγὼ
ὀναίμην, ὅτι ὑποτάσσεται τῷ ἐπισκόπῳ ὡς χάριτι Θεοῦ καὶ
τῷ πρεσβυτερίῳ ὡς νόμῳ Ἰησοῦ Χριστοῦ.

III. Καὶ ὑμῖν δὲ πρέπει μὴ συγχρᾶσθαι τῇ ἡλικίᾳ τοῦ
ἐπισκόπου, ἀλλὰ κατὰ δύναμιν Θεοῦ πατρὸς πᾶσαν ἐντροπὴν
αὐτῷ ἀπονέμειν, καθὼς ἔγνων καὶ τοὺς ἁγίους πρεσβυτέρους
οὐ προσειληφότας τὴν φαινομένην νεωτερικὴν τάξιν, ἀλλ᾽ ὡς
φρονίμῳ ἐν Θεῷ συγχωροῦντας αὐτῷ· οὐκ αὐτῷ δέ, ἀλλὰ τῷ
πατρὶ Ἰησοῦ Χριστοῦ τῷ πάντων ἐπισκόπῳ. 2. εἰς τιμὴν
οὖν ἐκείνου τοῦ θελήσαντος ὑμᾶς πρέπον ἐστὶν ὑπακούειν
κατὰ μηδεμίαν ὑπόκρισιν· ἐπεὶ οὐχ ὅτι τὸν ἐπίσκοπον τοῦτον
τὸν βλεπόμενον πλανᾷ τις, ἀλλὰ τὸν ἀόρατον παραλογίζεται·
τὸ δὲ τοιοῦτον, οὐ πρὸς σάρκα ὁ λόγος ἀλλὰ πρὸς Θεὸν τὸν
τὰ κρύφια εἰδότα.

IV. Πρέπον οὖν ἐστιν μὴ μόνον καλεῖσθαι Χριστιανοὺς ἀλλὰ καὶ εἶναι· ὥσπερ καί τινες ἐπίσκοπον μὲν καλοῦσιν. χωρὶς δὲ αὐτοῦ πάντα πράσσουσιν. οἱ τοιοῦτοι [δὲ] οὐκ εὐσυνείδητοί μοι εἶναι φαίνονται διὰ τὸ μὴ βεβαίως κατ᾽ ἐντολὴν συναθροίζεσθαι.

V. Ἐπεὶ οὖν τέλος τὰ πράγματα ἔχει, καὶ πρόκειται τὰ δύο ὁμοῦ, ὅ τε θάνατος καὶ ἡ ζωή, καὶ ἕκαστος εἰς τὸν ἴδιον   Acts i. 25. τόπον μέλλει χωρεῖν· 2. ὥσπερ γάρ ἐστιν νομίσματα δύο, ὃ μὲν Θεοῦ ὃ δὲ κόσμου, καὶ ἕκαστον αὐτῶν ἴδιον χαρακτῆρα ἐπικείμενον ἔχει, οἱ ἄπιστοι τοῦ κόσμου τούτου, οἱ δὲ πιστοὶ ἐν ἀγάπῃ χαρακτῆρα Θεοῦ πατρὸς διὰ Ἰησοῦ Χριστοῦ, δι᾽ οὗ ἐὰν μὴ αὐθαιρέτως ἔχωμεν τὸ ἀποθανεῖν εἰς τὸ αὐτοῦ πάθος, τὸ ζῆν αὐτοῦ οὐκ ἔστιν ἐν ἡμῖν.

VI. Ἐπεὶ οὖν ἐν τοῖς προγεγραμμένοις προσώποις τὸ πᾶν πλῆθος ἐθεώρησα ἐν πίστει καὶ ἠγάπησα, παραινῶ ἐν ὁμονοίᾳ Θεοῦ σπουδάζετε πάντα πράσσειν, προκαθημένου τοῦ ἐπισκόπου εἰς τύπον Θεοῦ καὶ τῶν πρεσβυτέρων εἰς τύπον συνεδρίου τῶν ἀποστόλων, καὶ τῶν διακόνων τῶν ἐμοὶ γλυκυτάτων, πεπιστευμένων διακονίαν Ἰησοῦ Χριστοῦ, ὃς πρὸ αἰώνων παρὰ πατρὶ ἦν καὶ ἐν τέλει ἐφάνη. 2. πάντες οὖν ὁμοήθειαν Θεοῦ λαβόντες ἐντρέπεσθε ἀλλήλους, καὶ μηδεὶς κατὰ σάρκα βλεπέτω τὸν πλησίον, ἀλλ᾽ ἐν Ἰησοῦ Χριστῷ ἀλλήλους διὰ παντὸς ἀγαπᾶτε. μηδὲν ἔστω ἐν ὑμῖν ὃ δυνήσεται ὑμᾶς μερίσαι, ἀλλ᾽ ἑνώθητε τῷ ἐπισκόπῳ καὶ τοῖς προκαθημένοις εἰς τύπον καὶ διδαχὴν ἀφθαρσίας.

VII. Ὥσπερ οὖν ὁ Κύριος ἄνευ τοῦ πατρὸς οὐδὲν ἐποίησεν [ἡνωμένος ὤν], οὔτε δι᾽ ἑαυτοῦ οὔτε διὰ τῶν ἀποστόλων, οὕτως μηδὲ ὑμεῖς ἄνευ τοῦ ἐπισκόπου καὶ τῶν πρεσβυτέρων μηδὲν πράσσετε· μηδὲ πειράσητε εὔλογόν τι φαίνεσθαι ἰδίᾳ ὑμῖν· ἀλλ᾽ ἐπὶ τὸ αὐτὸ μία προσευχή, μία δέησις, εἷς νοῦς, μία ἐλπίς, ἐν ἀγάπῃ, ἐν τῇ χαρᾷ τῇ ἀμώμῳ, ὅς ἐστιν Ἰησοῦς Χριστός, οὗ ἄμεινον οὐθέν ἐστιν. 2. πάντες ὡς εἰς ἕνα ναὸν συντρέχετε †Θεοῦ†, ὡς ἐπὶ ἓν θυσιαστήριον, ἐπὶ ἕνα Ἰησοῦν

vii. 1 ὅς ἐστιν] conj. Lightfoot; εἷς ἐστιν G ; ὅ ἐστιν L Antioch:; al. Ag.

Χριστὸν τὸν ἀφ' ἑνὸς πατρὸς προελθόντα καὶ εἰς ἕνα ὄντα
καὶ χωρήσαντα.

VIII. Μὴ πλανᾶσθε ταῖς ἑτεροδοξίαις μηδὲ μυθεύμασιν
τοῖς παλαιοῖς ἀνωφελέσιν οὖσιν· εἰ γὰρ μέχρι νῦν κατὰ ἰουδαϊσμὸν ζῶμεν, ὁμολογοῦμεν χάριν μὴ εἰληφέναι. 2. οἱ γὰρ
θειότατοι προφῆται κατὰ Χριστὸν Ἰησοῦν ἔζησαν. διὰ τοῦτο
καὶ ἐδιώχθησαν, ἐμπνεόμενοι ὑπὸ τῆς χάριτος [αὐτοῦ] εἰς τὸ
πληροφορηθῆναι τοὺς ἀπειθοῦντας, ὅτι εἷς Θεός ἐστιν ὁ φανε-
ρώσας ἑαυτὸν διὰ Ἰησοῦ Χριστοῦ τοῦ υἱοῦ αὐτοῦ, ὅς ἐστιν
αὐτοῦ λόγος ἀπὸ σιγῆς προελθών, ὃς κατὰ πάντα εὐηρέστη-
σεν τῷ πέμψαντι αὐτόν.

IX. Εἰ οὖν οἱ ἐν παλαιοῖς πράγμασιν ἀναστραφέντες
εἰς καινότητα ἐλπίδος ἦλθον, μηκέτι σαββατίζοντες ἀλλὰ
κατὰ κυριακὴν ζῶντες, ἐν ᾗ καὶ ἡ ζωὴ ἡμῶν ἀνέτειλεν δι'
αὐτοῦ καὶ τοῦ θανάτου αὐτοῦ, 2. ὅν τινες ἀρνοῦνται· δι' οὗ
μυστηρίου ἐλάβομεν τὸ πιστεύειν, καὶ διὰ τοῦτο ὑπομένομεν,
ἵνα εὑρεθῶμεν μαθηταὶ Ἰησοῦ Χριστοῦ τοῦ μόνου διδασκάλου
ἡμῶν· πῶς ἡμεῖς δυνησόμεθα ζῆσαι χωρὶς αὐτοῦ; 3. οὗ καὶ
οἱ προφῆται μαθηταὶ ὄντες τῷ πνεύματι ὡς διδάσκαλον αὐτὸν
προσεδόκων. καὶ διὰ τοῦτο, ὃν δικαίως ἀνέμενον, παρὼν ἤγειρεν αὐτοὺς ἐκ νεκρῶν.

X. Μὴ οὖν ἀναισθητῶμεν τῆς χρηστότητος αὐτοῦ. ἂν
γὰρ ἡμᾶς μιμήσηται καθὰ πράσσομεν, οὐκέτι ἐσμέν. διὰ
τοῦτο, μαθηταὶ αὐτοῦ γενόμενοι, μάθωμεν κατὰ χριστιανισμὸν ζῆν. ὃς γὰρ ἄλλῳ ὀνόματι καλεῖται πλέον τούτου, οὐκ
ἔστιν τοῦ Θεοῦ. 2. ὑπέρθεσθε οὖν τὴν κακὴν ζύμην τὴν
παλαιωθεῖσαν καὶ ἐνοξίσασαν, καὶ μεταβάλεσθε εἰς νέαν
ζύμην, ὅς ἐστιν Ἰησοῦς Χριστός. ἁλίσθητε ἐν αὐτῷ, ἵνα μὴ
διαφθαρῇ τις ἐν ὑμῖν, ἐπεὶ ἀπὸ τῆς ὀσμῆς ἐλεγχθήσεσθε.
3. ἄτοπόν ἐστιν Ἰησοῦν Χριστὸν λαλεῖν καὶ ἰουδαΐζειν. ὁ
γὰρ χριστιανισμὸς οὐκ εἰς ἰουδαϊσμὸν ἐπίστευσεν, ἀλλ' ἰου-
Is. lxvi. 18. δαϊσμὸς εἰς χριστιανισμόν, ᾧ πᾶσα ϲλῶϲϲα πιστεύσασα εἰς
Θεὸν ϲγΝΗχθΗ.

XI. Ταῦτα δέ, ἀγαπητοί μου, οὐκ ἐπεὶ ἔγνων τινὰς ἐξ

ὑμῶν οὕτως ἔχοντας, ἀλλ' ὡς μικρότερος ὑμῶν θέλω προφυ-
λάσσεσθαι ὑμᾶς μὴ ἐμπεσεῖν εἰς τὰ ἄγκιστρα τῆς κενοδοξίας,
ἀλλὰ πεπληροφόρησθε ἐν τῇ γεννήσει καὶ τῷ πάθει καὶ τῇ
ἀναστάσει τῇ γενομένῃ ἐν καιρῷ τῆς ἡγεμονίας Ποντίου
Πιλάτου· πραχθέντα ἀληθῶς καὶ βεβαίως ὑπὸ Ἰησοῦ Χριστοῦ, τῆς ἐλπίδος ἡμῶν, ἧς ἐκτραπῆναι μηδενὶ ὑμῶν γένοιτο.
XII. Ὀναίμην ὑμῶν κατὰ πάντα, ἐάνπερ ἄξιος ὦ. εἰ
γὰρ καὶ δέδεμαι, πρὸς ἕνα τῶν λελυμένων ὑμῶν οὐκ εἰμί.
οἶδα ὅτι οὐ φυσιοῦσθε· Ἰησοῦν γὰρ Χριστὸν ἔχετε ἐν ἑαυτοῖς.
καὶ μᾶλλον, ὅταν ἐπαινῶ ὑμᾶς, οἶδα ὅτι ἐντρέπεσθε· ὡς
γέγραπται ὅτι ὁ Δίκαιος ἑαυτοῦ κατήγορος.   Prov. xviii.
XIII. Σπουδάζετε οὖν βεβαιωθῆναι ἐν τοῖς δόγμασιν   17.
τοῦ Κυρίου καὶ τῶν ἀποστόλων, ἵνα πάντα ὅσα ποιεῖτε Ps. i. 3.
κατευοδωθῆτε σαρκὶ καὶ πνεύματι, πίστει καὶ ἀγάπῃ, ἐν υἱῷ
καὶ πατρὶ καὶ ἐν πνεύματι, ἐν ἀρχῇ καὶ ἐν τέλει, μετὰ τοῦ
ἀξιοπρεπεστάτου ἐπισκόπου ὑμῶν καὶ ἀξιοπλόκου πνευμα-
τικοῦ στεφάνου τοῦ πρεσβυτερίου ὑμῶν καὶ τῶν κατὰ Θεὸν
διακόνων. 2. ὑποτάγητε τῷ ἐπισκόπῳ καὶ ἀλλήλοις, ὡς
Ἰησοῦς Χριστὸς τῷ πατρὶ [κατὰ σάρκα] καὶ οἱ ἀπόστολοι
τῷ Χριστῷ καὶ τῷ πατρί, ἵνα ἕνωσις ᾖ σαρκική τε καὶ πνευματική.
XIV. Εἰδὼς ὅτι Θεοῦ γέμετε, συντόμως παρεκάλεσα
ὑμᾶς. μνημονεύετέ μου ἐν ταῖς προσευχαῖς ὑμῶν, ἵνα Θεοῦ
ἐπιτύχω, καὶ τῆς ἐν Συρίᾳ ἐκκλησίας, ὅθεν οὐκ ἄξιός εἰμι
καλεῖσθαι. ἐπιδέομαι γὰρ τῆς ἡνωμένης ὑμῶν ἐν Θεῷ προσευχῆς καὶ ἀγάπης εἰς τὸ ἀξιωθῆναι τὴν ἐν Συρίᾳ ἐκκλησίαν
διὰ τῆς ἐκτενείας ὑμῶν δροσισθῆναι.
XV. Ἀσπάζονται ὑμᾶς Ἐφέσιοι ἀπὸ Σμύρνης, ὅθεν καὶ
γράφω ὑμῖν, παρόντες εἰς δόξαν Θεοῦ, ὥσπερ καὶ ὑμεῖς, οἳ
κατὰ πάντα με ἀνέπαυσαν, ἅμα Πολυκάρπῳ ἐπισκόπῳ Σμυρναίων. καὶ αἱ λοιπαὶ δὲ ἐκκλησίαι ἐν τιμῇ Ἰησοῦ Χριστοῦ
ἀσπάζονται ὑμᾶς. ἔρρωσθε ἐν ὁμονοίᾳ Θεοῦ, κεκτημένοι
ἀδιάκριτον πνεῦμα, ὅς ἐστιν Ἰησοῦς Χριστός.

xiv. ἐκτενείας] conj. Lightfoot [A] ; ἐκκλησίας GL ; εὐταξίας g.

ΠΡΟΣ ΤΡΑΛΛΙΑΝΟΥΣ

ΙΓΝΑΤΙΟΣ, ὁ καὶ Θεοφόρος, ἠγαπημένῃ Θεῷ πατρὶ Ἰησοῦ Χριστοῦ, ἐκκλησίᾳ ἁγίᾳ τῇ οὔσῃ ἐν Τράλλεσιν τῆς Ἀσίας, ἐκλεκτῇ καὶ ἀξιοθέῳ, εἰρηνευούσῃ ἐν σαρκὶ καὶ πνεύματι τῷ πάθει Ἰησοῦ Χριστοῦ τῆς ἐλπίδος ἡμῶν ἐν τῇ εἰς αὐτὸν ἀναστάσει· ἣν καὶ ἀσπάζομαι ἐν τῷ πληρώματι ἐν ἀποστολικῷ χαρακτῆρι, καὶ εὔχομαι πλεῖστα χαίρειν.

I. Ἄμωμον διάνοιαν καὶ ἀδιάκριτον ἐν ὑπομονῇ ἔγνων ὑμᾶς ἔχοντας, οὐ κατὰ χρῆσιν ἀλλὰ κατὰ φύσιν· καθὼς ἐδήλωσέν μοι Πολύβιος ὁ ἐπίσκοπος ὑμῶν, ὃς παρεγένετο θελήματι Θεοῦ καὶ Ἰησοῦ Χριστοῦ ἐν Σμύρνῃ, καὶ οὕτως μοι συνεχάρη δεδεμένῳ ἐν Χριστῷ Ἰησοῦ, ὥστε με τὸ πᾶν πλῆθος ὑμῶν ἐν αὐτῷ θεωρῆσαι. 2. ἀποδεξάμενος οὖν τὴν κατὰ Θεὸν εὔνοιαν δι' αὐτοῦ, ἐδόξασα εὑρὼν ὑμᾶς, ὡς ἔγνων, μιμητὰς ὄντας Θεοῦ.

II. Ὅταν γὰρ τῷ ἐπισκόπῳ ὑποτάσσησθε ὡς Ἰησοῦ Χριστῷ, φαίνεσθέ μοι οὐ κατὰ ἀνθρώπους ζῶντες, ἀλλὰ κατὰ Ἰησοῦν Χριστόν, τὸν δι' ἡμᾶς ἀποθανόντα ἵνα πιστεύσαντες εἰς τὸν θάνατον αὐτοῦ τὸ ἀποθανεῖν ἐκφύγητε. 2. ἀναγκαῖον οὖν ἐστιν, ὥσπερ ποιεῖτε, ἄνευ τοῦ ἐπισκόπου μηδὲν πράσσειν ὑμᾶς· ἀλλ' ὑποτάσσεσθε καὶ τῷ πρεσβυτερίῳ, ὡς [τοῖς] ἀποστόλοις Ἰησοῦ Χριστοῦ, τῆς ἐλπίδος ἡμῶν, ἐν ᾧ διάγοντες [ἐν αὐτῷ] εὑρεθησόμεθα. 3. δεῖ δὲ καὶ τοὺς διακόνους ὄντας μυστηρίων Ἰησοῦ Χριστοῦ κατὰ πάντα τρόπον πᾶσιν ἀρέσκειν· οὐ γὰρ βρωμάτων καὶ ποτῶν εἰσιν διάκονοι, ἀλλ' ἐκκλησίας Θεοῦ ὑπηρέται· δέον οὖν αὐτοὺς φυλάσσεσθαι τὰ ἐγκλήματα ὡς πῦρ.

III. Ὁμοίως πάντες ἐντρεπέσθωσαν τοὺς διακόνους ὡς Ἰησοῦν Χριστόν, ὡς καὶ τὸν ἐπίσκοπον ὄντα τύπον τοῦ πατρός, τοὺς δὲ πρεσβυτέρους ὡς συνέδριον Θεοῦ καὶ [ὡς] σύνδεσμον ἀποστόλων· χωρὶς τούτων ἐκκλησία οὐ καλεῖται.

2. περὶ ὧν πέπεισμαι ὑμᾶς οὕτως ἔχειν· τὸ γὰρ ἐξεμπλάριον τῆς ἀγάπης ὑμῶν ἔλαβον καὶ ἔχω μεθ' ἑαυτοῦ ἐν τῷ ἐπισκόπῳ ὑμῶν, οὗ αὐτὸ τὸ κατάστημα μεγάλη μαθητεία, ἡ δὲ πραότης αὐτοῦ δύναμις· ὃν λογίζομαι καὶ τοὺς ἀθέους ἐντρέπεσθαι. 3. ἀγαπῶν ὑμᾶς οὕτως φείδομαι, συντονώτερον δυνάμενος γράφειν ὑπὲρ τούτου· [ἀλλ' οὐχ ἱκανὸν ἑαυτὸν] εἰς τοῦτο ᾠήθην, ἵνα ὢν κατάκριτος ὡς ἀπόστολος ὑμῖν διατάσσωμαι.

IV. Πολλὰ φρονῶ ἐν Θεῷ· ἀλλ' ἐμαυτὸν μετρῶ, ἵνα μὴ ἐν καυχήσει ἀπόλωμαι· νῦν γάρ με δεῖ πλέον φοβεῖσθαι καὶ μὴ προσέχειν τοῖς φυσιοῦσίν με· οἱ γὰρ λέγοντές μοι μαστιγοῦσίν με. 2. ἀγαπῶ μὲν γὰρ τὸ παθεῖν, ἀλλ' οὐκ οἶδα εἰ ἄξιός εἰμι· τὸ γὰρ ζῆλος πολλοῖς μὲν οὐ φαίνεται, ἐμὲ δὲ [πλέον] πολεμεῖ. χρήζω οὖν πραότητος, ἐν ᾗ καταλύεται ὁ ἄρχων τοῦ αἰῶνος τούτου.

V. Μὴ οὐ δύναμαι ὑμῖν τὰ ἐπουράνια γράψαι; ἀλλὰ φοβοῦμαι μὴ νηπίοις οὖσιν ὑμῖν βλάβην παραθῶ. καὶ συγγνωμονεῖτέ μοι, μήποτε οὐ δυνηθέντες χωρῆσαι στραγγαλωθῆτε. 2. καὶ γὰρ ἐγώ, οὐ καθότι δέδεμαι καὶ δύναμαι νοεῖν τὰ ἐπουράνια καὶ τὰς τοποθεσίας τὰς ἀγγελικὰς καὶ τὰς συστάσεις τὰς ἀρχοντικάς, ὁρατά τε καὶ ἀόρατα, παρὰ τοῦτο ἤδη καὶ μαθητής εἰμι· πολλὰ γὰρ ἡμῖν λείπει, ἵνα Θεοῦ μὴ λειπώμεθα.

VI. Παρακαλῶ οὖν ὑμᾶς, οὐκ ἐγὼ ἀλλ' ἡ ἀγάπη Ἰησοῦ Χριστοῦ, μόνῃ τῇ Χριστιανῇ τροφῇ χρῆσθε, ἀλλοτρίας δὲ βοτάνης ἀπέχεσθε, ἥτις ἐστὶν αἵρεσις· 2. οἳ καὶ ἰῷ παρεμπλέκουσιν Ἰησοῦν Χριστόν, καταξιοπιστευόμενοι, ὥσπερ θανάσιμον φάρμακον διδόντες μετὰ οἰνομέλιτος, ὅπερ ὁ ἀγνοῶν ἀδεῶς λαμβάνει ἐν ἡδονῇ κακῇ τὸ ἀποθανεῖν.

VII. Φυλάττεσθε οὖν τοὺς τοιούτους. τοῦτο δὲ ἔσται

iii. 3 ἀγαπῶν ὑμᾶς οὕτως φείδομαι] conj. Lightfoot [Ag]; ἀγαπῶντας ὡς οὐ φείδομαι GL.   ἀλλ' οὐχ ἱκανὸν ἑαυτὸν] insert Lightfoot [A].

vi. 2 οἳ καὶ ἰῷ παρεμπλέκουσιν] conj. Lightfoot; οἱ καιροὶ παρεμπλέκουσιν G; καὶ τὸν ἰὸν προσπλέκοντες g; οἳ καὶ ῥυπαρ' ἐμπλέκουσιν L; οἳ καὶ παρεμπλέκουσιν S₁A.   ἀδεῶς] conj. Lightfoot [g]; ἡδέως GLS₁A.

ὑμῖν μὴ φυσιουμένοις καὶ οὖσιν ἀχωρίστοις [Θεοῦ] Ἰησοῦ Χριστοῦ καὶ τοῦ ἐπισκόπου καὶ τῶν διαταγμάτων τῶν ἀποστόλων. 2. ὁ ἐντὸς θυσιαστηρίου ὢν καθαρός ἐστιν, ὁ δὲ ἐκτὸς θυσιαστηρίου ὢν οὐ καθαρός ἐστιν· τουτέστιν, ὁ χωρὶς ἐπισκόπου καὶ πρεσβυτερίου καὶ διακόνων πράσσων τι, οὗτος οὐ καθαρός ἐστιν τῇ συνειδήσει. VIII. Οὐκ ἐπεὶ ἔγνων τοιοῦτόν τι ἐν ὑμῖν, ἀλλὰ προφυλάσσω ὑμᾶς ὄντας μου ἀγαπητούς, προορῶν τὰς ἐνέδρας τοῦ διαβόλου. ὑμεῖς οὖν τὴν πραϋπάθειαν ἀναλαβόντες ἀνακτήσασθε ἑαυτοὺς ἐν πίστει, ὅ ἐστιν σὰρξ τοῦ Κυρίου, καὶ ἐν ἀγάπῃ, ὅ ἐστιν αἷμα Ἰησοῦ Χριστοῦ. 2. μηδεὶς ὑμῶν κατὰ τοῦ πλησίον ἐχέτω· μὴ ἀφορμὰς δίδοτε τοῖς ἔθνεσιν, ἵνα μὴ δι᾽ ὀλίγους ἄφρονας τὸ ἔνθεον πλῆθος βλασφημῆται· Οὐαὶ γὰρ δι᾽ οὗ ἐπὶ ματαιότητι τὸ ὄνομά μου ἐπί τινων βλασφημεῖται.

IX. Κωφώθητε οὖν, ὅταν ὑμῖν χωρὶς Ἰησοῦ Χριστοῦ λαλῇ τις, τοῦ ἐκ γένους Δαυείδ, τοῦ ἐκ Μαρίας, ὃς ἀληθῶς ἐγεννήθη, ἔφαγέν τε καὶ ἔπιεν, ἀληθῶς ἐδιώχθη ἐπὶ Ποντίου Πιλάτου, ἀληθῶς ἐσταυρώθη καὶ ἀπέθανεν, βλεπόντων [τῶν] ἐπουρανίων καὶ ἐπιγείων καὶ ὑποχθονίων· 2. ὃς καὶ ἀληθῶς ἠγέρθη ἀπὸ νεκρῶν, ἐγείραντος αὐτὸν τοῦ πατρὸς αὐτοῦ, κατὰ τὸ ὁμοίωμα ὃς καὶ ἡμᾶς τοὺς πιστεύοντας αὐτῷ οὕτως ἐγερεῖ ὁ πατὴρ αὐτοῦ ἐν Χριστῷ Ἰησοῦ, οὗ χωρὶς τὸ ἀληθινὸν ζῆν οὐκ ἔχομεν.

X. Εἰ δέ, ὥσπερ τινὲς ἄθεοι ὄντες, τουτέστιν ἄπιστοι, λέγουσιν τὸ δοκεῖν πεπονθέναι αὐτόν, αὐτοὶ ὄντες τὸ δοκεῖν, ἐγὼ τί δέδεμαι; τί δὲ καὶ εὔχομαι θηριομαχῆσαι; δωρεὰν οὖν ἀποθνήσκω. ἄρα οὖν καταψεύδομαι τοῦ Κυρίου.

XI. Φεύγετε οὖν τὰς κακὰς παραφυάδας τὰς γεννώσας καρπὸν θανατηφόρον, οὗ ἐὰν γεύσηταί τις, παραυτὰ ἀποθνήσκει. οὗτοι γὰρ οὔκ εἰσιν φυτεία πατρός· 2. εἰ γὰρ ἦσαν, ἐφαίνοντο ἂν κλάδοι τοῦ σταυροῦ, καὶ ἦν ἂν ὁ καρπὸς αὐτῶν

viii. 1 ἀνακτήσασθε] conj. Cotelier; ἀνακτίσασθε G; dub. LS₁A.   2 ἔνθεον] Dam-Vat.; ἐν Θεῷ GL; dub. Ag.

ἄφθαρτος· δι’ οὗ ἐν τῷ πάθει αὐτοῦ προσκαλεῖται ὑμᾶς, ὄντας μέλη αὐτοῦ. οὐ δύναται οὖν κεφαλὴ χωρὶς γεννηθῆναι ἄνευ μελῶν, τοῦ Θεοῦ ἕνωσιν ἐπαγγελλομένου, ὅς ἐστιν αὐτός.

XII. Ἀσπάζομαι ὑμᾶς ἀπὸ Σμύρνης, ἅμα ταῖς συμπα- ρούσαις μοι ἐκκλησίαις τοῦ Θεοῦ, οἳ κατὰ πάντα με ἀνέ- παυσαν σαρκί τε καὶ πνεύματι. 2. παρακαλεῖ ὑμᾶς τὰ δεσμά μου, ἃ ἕνεκεν Ἰησοῦ Χριστοῦ περιφέρω, αἰτούμενος Θεοῦ ἐπιτυχεῖν· διαμένετε ἐν τῇ ὁμονοίᾳ ὑμῶν καὶ τῇ μετ’ ἀλλήλων προσευχῇ. πρέπει γὰρ ὑμῖν τοῖς καθ’ ἕνα, ἐξαιρέ- τως καὶ τοῖς πρεσβυτέροις, ἀναψύχειν τὸν ἐπίσκοπον εἰς τιμὴν πατρὸς [καὶ εἰς τιμὴν] Ἰησοῦ Χριστοῦ καὶ τῶν ἀποσ- τόλων. 3. εὔχομαι ὑμᾶς ἐν ἀγάπῃ ἀκοῦσαί μου, ἵνα μὴ εἰς μαρτύριον ᾧ [ἐν] ὑμῖν γράψας. καὶ περὶ ἐμοῦ δὲ προσ- εύχεσθε, τῆς ἀφ’ ὑμῶν ἀγάπης χρῄζοντος ἐν τῷ ἐλέει τοῦ Θεοῦ, εἰς τὸ καταξιωθῆναί με τοῦ κλήρου οὗπερ ἔγκειμαι ἐπιτυχεῖν, ἵνα μὴ ἀδόκιμος εὑρεθῶ.

XIII. Ἀσπάζεται ὑμᾶς ἡ ἀγάπη Σμυρναίων καὶ Ἐφε- σίων. μνημονεύετε ἐν ταῖς προσευχαῖς ὑμῶν τῆς ἐν Συρίᾳ ἐκκλησίας· ὅθεν [καὶ] οὐκ ἄξιός εἰμι λέγεσθαι, ὢν ἔσχατος ἐκείνων. 2. ἔρρωσθε ἐν Ἰησοῦ Χριστῷ, ὑποτασσόμενοι τῷ ἐπισκόπῳ ὡς τῇ ἐντολῇ, ὁμοίως καὶ τῷ πρεσβυτερίῳ· καὶ οἱ κατ’ ἄνδρα ἀλλήλους ἀγαπᾶτε ἐν ἀμερίστῳ καρδίᾳ. 3. ἁγ- νίζεται ὑμῶν τὸ ἐμὸν πνεῦμα, οὐ μόνον νῦν ἀλλὰ καὶ ὅταν Θεοῦ ἐπιτύχω. ἔτι γὰρ ὑπὸ κίνδυνόν εἰμι· ἀλλὰ πιστὸς ὁ πατὴρ ἐν Ἰησοῦ Χριστῷ πληρῶσαί μου τὴν αἴτησιν καὶ ὑμῶν· ἐν ᾧ εὑρεθείημεν ἄμωμοι.

ΠΡΟΣ ΡΩΜΑΙΟΥΣ

ΙΓΝΑΤΙΟΣ, ὁ καὶ Θεοφόρος, τῇ ἠλεημένῃ ἐν μεγαλειότητι πατρὸς ὑψίστου καὶ Ἰησοῦ Χριστοῦ, τοῦ μόνου υἱοῦ αὐτοῦ, ἐκκλησίᾳ ἠγαπημένῃ καὶ πεφωτισμένῃ ἐν θελήματι τοῦ θελή- σαντος τὰ πάντα ἃ ἔστιν, κατὰ πίστιν καὶ ἀγάπην Ἰησοῦ

Χριστοῦ τοῦ Θεοῦ ἡμῶν, ἥτις καὶ προκάθηται ἐν τόπῳ χωρίου
Ῥωμαίων, ἀξιόθεος, ἀξιοπρεπής, ἀξιομακάριστος, ἀξιέπαινος,
ἀξιοεπίτευκτος, ἀξίαγνος, καὶ προκαθημένη τῆς ἀγάπης, χρι-
στόνομος, πατρώνυμος· ἣν καὶ ἀσπάζομαι ἐν ὀνόματι Ἰησοῦ
Χριστοῦ υἱοῦ πατρός· κατὰ σάρκα καὶ πνεῦμα ἡνωμένοις
πάσῃ ἐντολῇ αὐτοῦ, πεπληρωμένοις χάριτος Θεοῦ ἀδιακρίτως καὶ ἀποδιυλισμένοις ἀπὸ παντὸς ἀλλοτρίου χρώματος,
πλεῖστα ἐν Ἰησοῦ Χριστῷ τῷ Θεῷ ἡμῶν ἀμώμως χαίρειν.

I.   Ἐπεὶ εὐξάμενος Θεῷ ἐπέτυχον ἰδεῖν ὑμῶν τὰ ἀξιόθεα
πρόσωπα, ὡς καὶ πλέον ἢ ᾐτούμην λαβεῖν· δεδεμένος γὰρ ἐν
Χριστῷ Ἰησοῦ ἐλπίζω ὑμᾶς ἀσπάσασθαι, ἐάνπερ θέλημα
ᾖ τοῦ ἀξιωθῆναί με εἰς τέλος εἶναι· 2. ἡ μὲν γὰρ ἀρχὴ
εὐοικονόμητός ἐστιν, ἐὰν πέρατος ἐπιτύχω εἰς τὸ τὸν κλῆρόν
μου ἀνεμποδίστως ἀπολαβεῖν.   φοβοῦμαι γὰρ τὴν ὑμῶν
ἀγάπην, μὴ αὐτή με ἀδικήσῃ· ὑμῖν γὰρ εὐχερές ἐστιν, ὃ
θέλετε ποιῆσαι, ἐμοὶ δὲ δύσκολόν ἐστιν τοῦ Θεοῦ ἐπιτυχεῖν,
ἐάνπερ ὑμεῖς μὴ φείσησθέ μου.

II.   Οὐ γὰρ θέλω ὑμᾶς ἀνθρωπαρεσκῆσαι ἀλλὰ Θεῷ
ἀρέσαι, ὥσπερ καὶ ἀρέσκετε.   οὔτε γὰρ ἐγώ ποτε ἕξω καιρὸν
τοιοῦτον Θεοῦ ἐπιτυχεῖν· οὔτε ὑμεῖς, ἐὰν σιωπήσητε, κρείττονι
ἔργῳ ἔχετε ἐπιγραφῆναι.   ἐὰν γὰρ σιωπήσητε ἀπ’ ἐμοῦ,
ἐγὼ λόγος Θεοῦ· ἐὰν δὲ ἐρασθῆτε τῆς σαρκός μου, πάλιν
ἔσομαι φωνή.   2. πλέον [δέ] μοι μὴ παράσχησθε τοῦ σπον-
δισθῆναι Θεῷ, ὡς ἔτι θυσιαστήριον ἕτοιμόν ἐστιν· ἵνα ἐν
ἀγάπῃ χορὸς γενόμενοι ᾄσητε τῷ πατρὶ ἐν Ἰησοῦ Χριστῷ,
ὅτι τὸν ἐπίσκοπον Συρίας κατηξίωσεν ὁ Θεὸς εὑρεθῆναι εἰς
δύσιν, ἀπὸ ἀνατολῆς μεταπεμψάμενος.   καλὸν τὸ δῦναι ἀπὸ
κόσμου πρὸς Θεόν, ἵνα εἰς αὐτὸν ἀνατείλω.

III.   Οὐδέποτε ἐβασκάνατε οὐδενί· ἄλλους ἐδιδάξατε.
ἐγὼ δὲ θέλω ἵνα κἀκεῖνα βέβαια ᾖ ἃ μαθητεύοντες ἐντέλ-
λεσθε.   2. μόνον μοι δύναμιν αἰτεῖσθε ἔσωθέν τε καὶ ἔξωθεν,
ἵνα μὴ μόνον λέγω ἀλλὰ καὶ θέλω· ἵνα μὴ μόνον λέγωμαι
Χριστιανός, ἀλλὰ καὶ εὑρεθῶ.   ἐὰν γὰρ εὑρεθῶ, καὶ λέγεσθαι

i. 1 ἢ] insert Lightfoot [Aₘ]; om. GLAgSₘ; def. ΣM.

δύναμαι, καὶ τότε πιστὸς εἶναι, ὅταν κόσμῳ μὴ φαίνωμαι.
3. οὐδὲν φαινόμενον καλόν. ὁ γὰρ Θεὸς ἡμῶν Ἰησοῦς
Χριστός, ἐν πατρὶ ὤν, μᾶλλον φαίνεται. οὐ πεισμονῆς τὸ
ἔργον ἀλλὰ μεγέθους ἐστὶν ὁ χριστιανισμός, ὅταν μισῆται
ὑπὸ κόσμου. IV. Ἐγὼ γράφω πάσαις ταῖς ἐκκλησίαις, καὶ ἐντέλλομαι πᾶσιν ὅτι [ἐγὼ] ἑκὼν ὑπὲρ Θεοῦ ἀποθνήσκω, ἐάνπερ
ὑμεῖς μὴ κωλύσητε. παρακαλῶ ὑμᾶς, μὴ εὔνοια ἄκαιρος
γένησθέ μοι. ἄφετέ με θηρίων εἶναι, δι᾽ ὧν [ἔν-]εστιν Θεοῦ
ἐπιτυχεῖν. σῖτός εἰμι Θεοῦ, καὶ δι᾽ ὀδόντων θηρίων ἀλήθο-
μαι, ἵνα καθαρὸς ἄρτος εὑρεθῶ [τοῦ Χριστοῦ]. 2. μᾶλλον
κολακεύσατε τὰ θηρία, ἵνα μοι τάφος γένωνται, καὶ μηθὲν
καταλίπωσιν τῶν τοῦ σώματός μου, ἵνα μὴ κοιμηθεὶς βαρύς
τινι γένωμαι. τότε ἔσομαι μαθητὴς ἀληθῶς Ἰησοῦ Χριστοῦ,
ὅτε οὐδὲ τὸ σῶμά μου ὁ κόσμος ὄψεται. λιτανεύσατε τὸν
Κύριον ὑπὲρ ἐμοῦ, ἵνα διὰ τῶν ὀργάνων τούτων Θεοῦ θυσία
εὑρεθῶ. 3. οὐχ ὡς Πέτρος καὶ Παῦλος διατάσσομαι ὑμῖν·
ἐκεῖνοι ἀπόστολοι, ἐγὼ κατάκριτος· ἐκεῖνοι ἐλεύθεροι, ἐγὼ δὲ
μέχρι νῦν δοῦλος. ἀλλ᾽ ἐὰν πάθω, ἀπελεύθερος Ἰησοῦ
Χριστοῦ, καὶ ἀναστήσομαι ἐν αὐτῷ ἐλεύθερος. νῦν μανθάνω
δεδεμένος μηδὲν ἐπιθυμεῖν. V. Ἀπὸ Συρίας μέχρι Ῥώμης θηριομαχῶ, διὰ γῆς καὶ
θαλάσσης, νυκτὸς καὶ ἡμέρας, ἐνδεδεμένος δέκα λεοπάρδοις,
ὅ ἐστιν στρατιωτικὸν τάγμα, οἳ καὶ εὐεργετούμενοι χείρους
γίνονται. ἐν δὲ τοῖς ἀδικήμασιν αὐτῶν μᾶλλον μαθη-
τεύομαι· ἀλλ᾽ οὐ παρὰ τοῦτο δεδικαίωμαι. 2. ὀναίμην τῶν 1 Cor. iv. 4.
θηρίων τῶν ἐμοὶ ἡτοιμασμένων, ἃ καὶ εὔχομαι σύντομά μοι
εὑρεθῆναι· ἃ καὶ κολακεύσω συντόμως με καταφαγεῖν, οὐχ
ὥσπερ τινῶν δειλαινόμενα οὐχ ἥψαντο· κἂν αὐτὰ δὲ ἑκόντα
μὴ θέλῃ, ἐγὼ προσβιάσομαι. 3. συγγνώμην μοι ἔχετε· τί
μοι συμφέρει ἐγὼ γινώσκω· νῦν ἄρχομαι μαθητὴς εἶναι· μηθέν
με ζηλῶσαι τῶν ὁρατῶν καὶ τῶν ἀοράτων, ἵνα Ἰησοῦ Χριστοῦ
ἐπιτύχω. πῦρ καὶ σταυρὸς θηρίων τε συστάσεις, [ἀνατομαί,
διαιρέσεις], σκορπισμοὶ ὀστέων, συγκοπαὶ μελῶν, ἀλεσμοὶ

ὅλου τοῦ σώματος, κακαὶ κολάσεις τοῦ διαβόλου ἐπ᾽ ἐμὲ
ἐρχέσθωσαν· μόνον ἵνα Ἰησοῦ Χριστοῦ ἐπιτύχω.

VI. Οὐδέν με ὠφελήσει τὰ πέρατα τοῦ κόσμου, οὐδὲ
αἱ βασιλεῖαι τοῦ αἰῶνος τούτου· καλόν μοι ἀποθανεῖν διὰ
Ἰησοῦν Χριστόν, ἢ βασιλεύειν τῶν περάτων τῆς γῆς. ἐκεῖνον
ζητῶ, τὸν ὑπὲρ ἡμῶν ἀποθανόντα· ἐκεῖνον θέλω, τὸν [δι᾽
ἡμᾶς] ἀναστάντα. ὁ τοκετός μοι ἐπίκειται. 2. σύγγνωτέ μοι,
ἀδελφοί· μὴ ἐμποδίσητέ μοι ζῆσαι, μὴ θελήσητέ με ἀποθανεῖν.
τὸν τοῦ Θεοῦ θέλοντα εἶναι κόσμῳ μὴ χαρίσησθε, μηδὲ ὕλῃ
κολακεύσητε. ἄφετέ με καθαρὸν φῶς λαβεῖν· ἐκεῖ παραγενό-
μενος ἄνθρωπος ἔσομαι. 3. ἐπιτρέψατέ μοι μιμητὴν εἶναι τοῦ
πάθους τοῦ Θεοῦ μου. εἴ τις αὐτὸν ἐν ἑαυτῷ ἔχει, νοησάτω
ὃ θέλω καὶ συμπαθείτω μοι εἰδὼς τὰ συνέχοντά με.

VII. Ὁ ἄρχων τοῦ αἰῶνος τούτου διαρπάσαι με βούλεται καὶ τὴν εἰς Θεόν μου γνώμην διαφθεῖραι. μηδεὶς οὖν
τῶν παρόντων ὑμῶν βοηθείτω αὐτῷ· μᾶλλον ἐμοῖ γίνεσθε,
τουτέστιν τοῦ Θεοῦ. μὴ λαλεῖτε Ἰησοῦν Χριστὸν κόσμον δὲ
ἐπιθυμεῖτε. 2. βασκανία ἐν ὑμῖν μὴ κατοικείτω· μηδ᾽ ἂν
ἐγὼ παρὼν παρακαλῶ ὑμᾶς, πείσθητέ μοι, τούτοις δὲ μᾶλλον
πιστεύσατε, οἷς γράφω ὑμῖν. ζῶν [γὰρ] γράφω ὑμῖν, ἐρῶν τοῦ
ἀποθανεῖν· ὁ ἐμὸς ἔρως ἐσταύρωται, καὶ οὐκ ἔστιν ἐν ἐμοὶ
πῦρ φιλόϋλον, ὕδωρ δὲ ζῶν †καὶ λαλοῦν† ἐν ἐμοί, ἔσωθέν
μοι λέγον· Δεῦρο πρὸς τὸν πατέρα. 3. οὐχ ἥδομαι τροφῇ
φθορᾶς οὐδὲ ἡδοναῖς τοῦ βίου τούτου· ἄρτον Θεοῦ θέλω, ὅ
ἐστιν σὰρξ τοῦ Χριστοῦ τοῦ ἐκ σπέρματος Δαυείδ, καὶ πόμα
θέλω τὸ αἷμα αὐτοῦ, ὅ ἐστιν ἀγάπη ἄφθαρτος.

VIII. Οὐκέτι θέλω κατὰ ἀνθρώπους ζῆν· τοῦτο δὲ ἔσται,
ἐὰν ὑμεῖς θελήσητε. θελήσατε, ἵνα καὶ ὑμεῖς θεληθῆτε.
2. δι᾽ ὀλίγων γραμμάτων αἰτοῦμαι ὑμᾶς· πιστεύσατέ μοι.
Ἰησοῦς δὲ Χριστὸς ὑμῖν ταῦτα φανερώσει, ὅτι ἀληθῶς λέγω·
τὸ ἀψευδὲς στόμα, ἐν ᾧ ὁ πατὴρ ἐλάλησεν [ἀληθῶς]. 3. αἰ-
τήσασθε περὶ ἐμοῦ, ἵνα ἐπιτύχω [ἐν πνεύματι ἁγίῳ]. οὐ
κατὰ σάρκα ὑμῖν ἔγραψα, ἀλλὰ κατὰ γνώμην Θεοῦ. ἐὰν
πάθω, ἠθελήσατε· ἐὰν ἀποδοκιμασθῶ, ἐμισήσατε.

IX. Μνημονεύετε ἐν τῇ προσευχῇ ὑμῶν τῆς ἐν Συρίᾳ ἐκκλησίας, ἥτις ἀντὶ ἐμοῦ ποιμένι τῷ Θεῷ χρῆται· μόνος αὐτὴν Ἰησοῦς Χριστὸς ἐπισκοπήσει καὶ ἡ ὑμῶν ἀγάπη. 2. ἐγὼ δὲ αἰσχύνομαι ἐξ αὐτῶν λέγεσθαι· οὐδὲ γὰρ ἄξιός εἰμι, ὢν ἔσχατος αὐτῶν καὶ ἔκτρωμα· ἀλλ᾽ ἠλέημαί τις εἶναι, ἐὰν Θεοῦ ἐπιτύχω. 3. ἀσπάζεται ὑμᾶς τὸ ἐμὸν πνεῦμα καὶ ἡ ἀγάπη τῶν ἐκκλησιῶν τῶν δεξαμένων με εἰς ὄνομα Ἰησοῦ Χριστοῦ, οὐχ ὡς παροδεύοντα· καὶ γὰρ αἱ μὴ προσήκουσαί μοι τῇ ὁδῷ τῇ κατὰ σάρκα κατὰ πόλιν με προῆγον. X. Γράφω δὲ ὑμῖν ταῦτα ἀπὸ Σμύρνης δι᾽ Ἐφεσίων τῶν ἀξιομακαρίστων. ἔστιν δὲ καὶ ἅμα ἐμοὶ σὺν ἄλλοις πολλοῖς καὶ Κρόκος, τὸ ποθητόν [μοι] ὄνομα. 2. περὶ τῶν προελθόντων με ἀπὸ Συρίας εἰς Ῥώμην εἰς δόξαν [τοῦ] Θεοῦ πιστεύω ὑμᾶς ἐπεγνωκέναι. οἷς καὶ δηλώσατε ἐγγύς με ὄντα· πάντες γάρ εἰσιν ἄξιοι [τοῦ] Θεοῦ καὶ ὑμῶν· οὓς πρέπον ὑμῖν ἐστιν κατὰ πάντα ἀναπαῦσαι. 3. ἔγραψα δὲ ὑμῖν ταῦτα τῇ πρὸ ἐννέα καλανδῶν Σεπτεμβρίων. ἔρρωσθε εἰς τέλος ἐν ὑπομονῇ Ἰησοῦ Χριστοῦ.

ΠΡΟΣ ΦΙΛΑΔΕΛΦΕΙΣ

ἸΓΝΑΤΙΟΣ, ὁ καὶ Θεοφόρος, ἐκκλησίᾳ Θεοῦ πατρὸς καὶ Ἰησοῦ Χριστοῦ τῇ οὔσῃ ἐν Φιλαδελφίᾳ τῆς Ἀσίας, ἠλεημένῃ καὶ ἡδρασμένῃ ἐν ὁμονοίᾳ Θεοῦ καὶ ἀγαλλιωμένῃ ἐν τῷ πάθει τοῦ Κυρίου ἡμῶν ἀδιακρίτως καὶ ἐν τῇ ἀναστάσει αὐτοῦ, πεπληροφορημένῃ ἐν παντὶ ἐλέει· ἣν ἀσπάζομαι ἐν αἵματι Ἰησοῦ Χριστοῦ, ἥτις ἐστὶν χαρὰ αἰώνιος καὶ παράμονος· μάλιστα ἐὰν ἐν ἑνὶ ὦσιν σὺν τῷ ἐπισκόπῳ καὶ τοῖς σὺν αὐτῷ πρεσβυτέροις καὶ διακόνοις ἀποδεδειγμένοις ἐν γνώμῃ Ἰησοῦ Χριστοῦ, οὓς κατὰ τὸ ἴδιον θέλημα ἐστήριξεν ἐν βεβαιωσύνῃ τῷ ἁγίῳ αὐτοῦ πνεύματι.

I. Ὃν ἐπίσκοπον ἔγνων οὐκ ἀφ᾽ ἑαυτοῦ οὐδὲ δι᾽ ἀνθρώπων κεκτῆσθαι τὴν διακονίαν τὴν εἰς τὸ κοινὸν ἀνήκουσαν,
οὐδὲ κατὰ κενοδοξίαν, ἀλλ᾽ ἐν ἀγάπῃ Θεοῦ πατρὸς καὶ Κυρίου
Ἰησοῦ Χριστοῦ· οὗ καταπέπληγμαι τὴν ἐπιείκειαν, ὃς σιγῶν
πλείονα δύναται τῶν λαλούντων. 2. συνευρύθμισται γὰρ
ταῖς ἐντολαῖς, ὡς χορδαῖς κιθάρα. διὸ μακαρίζει μου ἡ ψυχὴ
τὴν εἰς Θεὸν αὐτοῦ γνώμην, ἐπιγνοὺς ἐνάρετον καὶ τέλειον
οὖσαν, τὸ ἀκίνητον αὐτοῦ καὶ τὸ ἀόργητον [αὐτοῦ] ἐν πάσῃ
ἐπιεικείᾳ Θεοῦ ζῶντος.

II. Τέκνα οὖν [φωτὸς] ἀληθείας, φεύγετε τὸν μερισμὸν
καὶ τὰς κακοδιδασκαλίας· ὅπου δὲ ὁ ποιμήν ἐστιν, ἐκεῖ
ὡς πρόβατα ἀκολουθεῖτε· 2. πολλοὶ γὰρ λύκοι ἀξιόπιστοι
ἡδονῇ κακῇ αἰχμαλωτίζουσιν τοὺς θεοδρόμους· ἀλλ᾽ ἐν τῇ
ἑνότητι ὑμῶν οὐχ ἕξουσιν τόπον.

III. Ἀπέχεσθε τῶν κακῶν βοτανῶν, ἅστινας οὐ γεωργεῖ
Ἰησοῦς Χριστός, διὰ τὸ μὴ εἶναι αὐτοὺς φυτείαν πατρός. οὐχ
ὅτι παρ᾽ ὑμῖν μερισμὸν εὗρον, ἀλλ᾽ ἀποδιϋλισμόν. 2. ὅσοι
γὰρ Θεοῦ εἰσιν καὶ Ἰησοῦ Χριστοῦ, οὗτοι μετὰ τοῦ ἐπισκόπου
εἰσίν· καὶ ὅσοι ἂν μετανοήσαντες ἔλθωσιν ἐπὶ τὴν ἑνότητα
τῆς ἐκκλησίας, καὶ οὗτοι Θεοῦ ἔσονται, ἵνα ὦσιν κατὰ Ἰησοῦν
Χριστὸν ζῶντες. 3. μὴ πλανᾶσθε, ἀδελφοί μου· εἴ τις
1 Cor. vi. 9. σχίζοντι ἀκολουθεῖ, Βασιλείαν Θεοῦ οὐ κληρονομεῖ· εἴ τις ἐν
ἀλλοτρίᾳ γνώμῃ περιπατεῖ, οὗτος τῷ πάθει οὐ συγκατατί-
θεται.

IV. Σπουδάσατε οὖν μιᾷ εὐχαριστίᾳ χρῆσθαι· μία γὰρ
σάρξ τοῦ Κυρίου ἡμῶν Ἰησοῦ Χριστοῦ, καὶ ἓν ποτήριον εἰς
ἕνωσιν τοῦ αἵματος αὐτοῦ· ἓν θυσιαστήριον, ὡς εἷς ἐπίσκοπος,
ἅμα τῷ πρεσβυτερίῳ καὶ διακόνοις τοῖς συνδούλοις μου· ἵνα,
ὃ ἐὰν πράσσητε, κατὰ Θεὸν πράσσητε.

V. Ἀδελφοί μου, λίαν ἐκκέχυμαι ἀγαπῶν ὑμᾶς, καὶ
ὑπεραγαλλόμενος ἀσφαλίζομαι ὑμᾶς· οὐκ ἐγὼ δέ, ἀλλ᾽ Ἰησοῦς Χριστός, ἐν ᾧ δεδεμένος φοβοῦμαι μᾶλλον, ὡς ἔτι ὢν
ἀναπάρτιστος. ἀλλ᾽ ἡ προσευχὴ ὑμῶν [εἰς Θεόν] με ἀπαρ-
τίσει, ἵνα ἐν ᾧ κλήρῳ ἠλεήθην ἐπιτύχω, προσφυγὼν τῷ

εὐαγγελίῳ ὡς σαρκὶ Ἰησοῦ καὶ τοῖς ἀποστόλοις ὡς πρεσβυτερίῳ ἐκκλησίας. 2. καὶ τοὺς προφήτας δὲ ἀγαπῶμεν, διὰ τὸ καὶ αὐτοὺς εἰς τὸ εὐαγγέλιον κατηγγελκέναι καὶ εἰς αὐτὸν ἐλπίζειν καὶ αὐτὸν ἀναμένειν· ἐν ᾧ καὶ πιστεύσαντες ἐσώθησαν ἐν ἑνότητι Ἰησοῦ Χριστοῦ, ὄντες ἀξιαγάπητοι καὶ ἀξιοθαύμαστοι ἅγιοι, ὑπὸ Ἰησοῦ Χριστοῦ μεμαρτυρημένοι καὶ συνηριθμημένοι ἐν τῷ εὐαγγελίῳ τῆς κοινῆς ἐλπίδος.

VI. Ἐὰν δέ τις ἰουδαϊσμὸν ἑρμηνεύῃ ὑμῖν, μὴ ἀκούετε αὐτοῦ. ἄμεινον γάρ ἐστιν παρὰ ἀνδρὸς περιτομὴν ἔχοντος χριστιανισμὸν ἀκούειν ἢ παρὰ ἀκροβύστου ἰουδαϊσμόν. ἐὰν δὲ ἀμφότεροι περὶ Ἰησοῦ Χριστοῦ μὴ λαλῶσιν, οὗτοι ἐμοὶ στῆλαί εἰσιν καὶ τάφοι νεκρῶν, ἐφ᾽ οἷς γέγραπται μόνον ὀνόματα ἀνθρώπων. 2. φεύγετε οὖν τὰς κακοτεχνίας καὶ ἐνέδρας τοῦ ἄρχοντος τοῦ αἰῶνος τούτου, μήποτε θλιβέντες τῇ γνώμῃ αὐτοῦ ἐξασθενήσητε ἐν τῇ ἀγάπῃ· ἀλλὰ πάντες ἐπὶ τὸ αὐτὸ γίνεσθε ἐν ἀμερίστῳ καρδίᾳ. 3. εὐχαριστῶ δὲ τῷ Θεῷ μου, ὅτι εὐσυνείδητός εἰμι ἐν ὑμῖν, καὶ οὐκ ἔχει τις καυχήσασθαι οὔτε λάθρα οὔτε φανερῶς, ὅτι ἐβάρησά τινα ἐν μικρῷ ἢ ἐν μεγάλῳ. καὶ πᾶσι δέ, ἐν οἷς ἐλάλησα, εὔχομαι ἵνα μὴ εἰς μαρτύριον αὐτὸ κτήσωνται.

VII. Εἰ γὰρ καὶ κατὰ σάρκα μέ τινες ἠθέλησαν πλανῆσαι, ἀλλὰ τὸ πνεῦμα οὐ πλανᾶται, ἀπὸ Θεοῦ ὄν· οἶδεν γὰρ S. John iii. 8. πόθεν ἔρχεται καὶ ποῦ ὑπάγει, καὶ τὰ κρυπτὰ ἐλέγχει. ἐκραύγασα μεταξὺ ὤν, ἐλάλουν μεγάλῃ φωνῇ, Θεοῦ φωνῇ· Τῷ ἐπισκόπῳ προσέχετε καὶ τῷ πρεσβυτερίῳ καὶ διακόνοις. 2. οἱ δ᾽ ὑποπτεύσαντές με, ὡς προειδότα τὸν μερισμόν τινων, λέγειν ταῦτα. μάρτυς δέ μοι ἐν ᾧ δέδεμαι, ὅτι ἀπὸ σαρκὸς ἀνθρωπίνης οὐκ ἔγνων· τὸ δὲ πνεῦμα ἐκήρυσσεν, λέγον τάδε· Χωρὶς τοῦ ἐπισκόπου μηδὲν ποιεῖτε· τὴν σάρκα ὑμῶν ὡς ναὸν Θεοῦ τηρεῖτε· τὴν ἕνωσιν ἀγαπᾶτε· τοὺς μερισμοὺς φεύγετε· μιμηταὶ γίνεσθε Ἰησοῦ Χριστοῦ, ὡς καὶ αὐτὸς τοῦ πατρὸς αὐτοῦ.

VIII. Ἐγὼ μὲν οὖν τὸ ἴδιον ἐποίουν, ὡς ἄνθρωπος εἰς ἕνωσιν κατηρτισμένος. οὗ δὲ μερισμός ἐστιν καὶ ὀργή, Θεὸς

οὐ κατοικεῖ. πᾶσιν οὖν μετανοοῦσιν ἀφίει ὁ Κύριος, ἐὰν
μετανοήσωσιν εἰς ἑνότητα Θεοῦ καὶ συνέδριον τοῦ ἐπισκόπου.
πιστεύω τῇ χάριτι Ἰησοῦ Χριστοῦ, ὃς λύσει ἀφ' ὑμῶν πάντα
δεσμόν· 2. παρακαλῶ δὲ ὑμᾶς, μηδὲν κατ' ἐρίθειαν πράσσετε ἀλλὰ κατὰ χριστομαθίαν. ἐπεὶ ἤκουσά τινων λεγόντων
ὅτι Ἐὰν μὴ ἐν τοῖς ἀρχείοις εὕρω, ἐν τῷ εὐαγγελίῳ οὐ
πιστεύω· καὶ λέγοντός μου αὐτοῖς ὅτι Γέγραπται, ἀπεκρί-
θησάν μοι ὅτι Πρόκειται. ἐμοὶ δὲ ἀρχεῖά ἐστιν Ἰησοῦς
Χριστός, τὰ ἄθικτα ἀρχεῖα ὁ σταυρὸς αὐτοῦ καὶ ὁ θάνατος
καὶ ἡ ἀνάστασις αὐτοῦ καὶ ἡ πίστις ἡ δι' αὐτοῦ· ἐν οἷς θέλω
ἐν τῇ προσευχῇ ὑμῶν δικαιωθῆναι.

IX. Καλοὶ καὶ οἱ ἱερεῖς· κρεῖσσον δὲ ὁ ἀρχιερεὺς ὁ
πεπιστευμένος τὰ ἅγια τῶν ἁγίων, ὃς μόνος πεπίστευται τὰ
κρυπτὰ τοῦ Θεοῦ· αὐτὸς ὢν θύρα τοῦ πατρός, δι' ἧς εἰσέρ-
χονται Ἀβραὰμ καὶ Ἰσαὰκ καὶ Ἰακὼβ καὶ οἱ προφῆται καὶ
οἱ ἀπόστολοι καὶ ἡ ἐκκλησία. πάντα ταῦτα εἰς ἑνότητα
Θεοῦ. 2. ἐξαίρετον δέ τι ἔχει τὸ εὐαγγέλιον, τὴν παρουσίαν
τοῦ σωτῆρος, Κυρίου ἡμῶν Ἰησοῦ Χριστοῦ, τὸ πάθος αὐτοῦ,
τὴν ἀνάστασιν. οἱ γὰρ ἀγαπητοὶ προφῆται κατήγγειλαν εἰς
αὐτόν· τὸ δὲ εὐαγγέλιον ἀπάρτισμά ἐστιν ἀφθαρσίας. πάντα
ὁμοῦ καλά ἐστιν, ἐὰν ἐν ἀγάπῃ πιστεύητε.

X. Ἐπειδὴ κατὰ τὴν προσευχὴν ὑμῶν, καὶ κατὰ τὰ
σπλάγχνα ἃ ἔχετε ἐν Χριστῷ Ἰησοῦ, ἀπηγγέλη μοι εἰρη-
νεύειν τὴν ἐκκλησίαν τὴν ἐν Ἀντιοχείᾳ τῆς Συρίας· πρέπον
ἐστὶν ὑμῖν, ὡς ἐκκλησίᾳ Θεοῦ, χειροτονῆσαι διάκονον εἰς τὸ
πρεσβεῦσαι ἐκεῖ Θεοῦ πρεσβείαν, εἰς τὸ συγχαρῆναι αὐτοῖς
ἐπὶ τὸ αὐτὸ γενομένοις καὶ δοξάσαι τὸ ὄνομα· 2. μακάριος
ἐν Χριστῷ Ἰησοῦ, ὃς καταξιωθήσεται τῆς τοιαύτης διακονίας·
καὶ ὑμεῖς δοξασθήσεσθε. θέλουσιν δὲ ὑμῖν οὐκ ἔστιν ἀδύνατον ὑπὲρ ὀνόματος Θεοῦ· ὡς καὶ αἱ ἔγγιστα ἐκκλησίαι ἔπεμ-
ψαν ἐπισκόπους, αἱ δὲ πρεσβυτέρους καὶ διακόνους.

XI. Περὶ δὲ Φίλωνος τοῦ διακόνου ἀπὸ Κιλικίας, ἀνδρὸς
μεμαρτυρημένου, ὃς καὶ νῦν ἐν λόγῳ Θεοῦ ὑπηρετεῖ μοι, ἅμα
Ῥαΐῳ Ἀγαθόποδι, ἀνδρὶ ἐκλεκτῷ, ὃς ἀπὸ Συρίας μοι ἀκο-

λουθεῖ ἀποταξάμενος τῷ βίῳ· οἳ καὶ μαρτυροῦσιν ὑμῖν.
κἀγὼ τῷ Θεῷ εὐχαριστῶ ὑπὲρ ὑμῶν, ὅτι ἐδέξασθε αὐτούς, ὡς
καὶ ὑμᾶς ὁ Κύριος. οἱ δὲ ἀτιμάσαντες αὐτοὺς λυτρωθείησαν
ἐν τῇ χάριτι Ἰησοῦ Χριστοῦ. 2. ἀσπάζεται ὑμᾶς ἡ ἀγάπη
τῶν ἀδελφῶν τῶν ἐν Τρωάδι· ὅθεν καὶ γράφω ὑμῖν διὰ Βούρρου πεμφθέντος ἅμα ἐμοὶ ἀπὸ Ἐφεσίων καὶ Σμυρναίων εἰς
λόγον τιμῆς. τιμήσει αὐτοὺς ὁ Κύριος Ἰησοῦς Χριστός,
εἰς ὃν ἐλπίζουσιν σαρκί, ψυχῇ, πνεύματι, πίστει, ἀγάπῃ,
ὁμονοίᾳ. ἔρρωσθε ἐν Χριστῷ Ἰησοῦ, τῇ κοινῇ ἐλπίδι ἡμῶν.

ΠΡΟΣ ΣΜΥΡΝΑΙΟΥΣ

ἸΓΝΑΤΙΟΣ, ὁ καὶ Θεοφόρος, ἐκκλησίᾳ Θεοῦ πατρὸς καὶ
τοῦ ἠγαπημένου Ἰησοῦ Χριστοῦ, ἠλεημένῃ ἐν παντὶ χαρίσματι, πεπληρωμένῃ ἐν πίστει καὶ ἀγάπῃ, ἀνυστερήτῳ οὔσῃ
παντὸς χαρίσματος, θεοπρεπεστάτῃ καὶ ἁγιοφόρῳ, τῇ οὔσῃ
ἐν Σμύρνῃ τῆς Ἀσίας, ἐν ἀμώμῳ πνεύματι καὶ λόγῳ Θεοῦ
πλεῖστα χαίρειν.

I. Δοξάζω Ἰησοῦν Χριστὸν τὸν Θεὸν τὸν οὕτως ὑμᾶς
σοφίσαντα· ἐνόησα γὰρ ὑμᾶς κατηρτισμένους ἐν ἀκινήτῳ
πίστει, ὥσπερ καθηλωμένους ἐν τῷ σταυρῷ τοῦ Κυρίου
Ἰησοῦ Χριστοῦ, σαρκί τε καὶ πνεύματι, καὶ ἡδρασμένους ἐν
ἀγάπῃ ἐν τῷ αἵματι Χριστοῦ, πεπληροφορημένους εἰς τὸν
Κύριον ἡμῶν ἀληθῶς ὄντα ἐκ γένους Δαυεὶδ κατὰ σάρκα, υἱὸν
Θεοῦ κατὰ θέλημα καὶ δύναμιν, γεγεννημένον ἀληθῶς ἐκ
παρθένου, βεβαπτισμένον ὑπὸ Ἰωάννου ἵνα πληρωθῇ πᾶϲα S. Matt.
ΔΙΚΑΙΟϹΎΝΗ ὑπ᾽ αὐτοῦ, 2. ἀληθῶς ἐπὶ Ποντίου Πιλάτου καὶ iii. 15.
Ἡρώδου τετράρχου καθηλωμένον ὑπὲρ ἡμῶν ἐν σαρκί· ἀφ᾽
οὗ καρποῦ ἡμεῖς ἀπὸ τοῦ θεομακαρίστου αὐτοῦ πάθους· ἵνα
ἄΡΗ ϹΎϹϹΗΜΟΝ εἰς τοὺς αἰῶνας διὰ τῆς ἀναστάσεως εἰς τοὺς Is. v. 26,
ἁγίους καὶ πιστοὺς αὐτοῦ, εἴτε ἐν Ἰουδαίοις εἴτε ἐν ἔθνεσιν, xlix. 22.
ἐν ἑνὶ σώματι τῆς ἐκκλησίας αὐτοῦ.

II. Ταῦτα γὰρ πάντα ἔπαθεν δι' ἡμᾶς [ἵνα σωθῶμεν]·
καὶ ἀληθῶς ἔπαθεν, ὡς καὶ ἀληθῶς ἀνέστησεν ἑαυτόν· οὐχ
ὥσπερ ἄπιστοί τινες λέγουσιν τὸ δοκεῖν αὐτὸν πεπονθέναι,
αὐτοὶ τὸ δοκεῖν ὄντες· καὶ καθὼς φρονοῦσιν, καὶ συμβήσεται
αὐτοῖς, οὖσιν ἀσωμάτοις καὶ δαιμονικοῖς.

III. Ἐγὼ γὰρ καὶ μετὰ τὴν ἀνάστασιν ἐν σαρκὶ αὐτὸν
οἶδα καὶ πιστεύω ὄντα· 2. καὶ ὅτε πρὸς τοὺς περὶ Πέτρον

? 'The
Teaching
of Peter.'
ἦλθεν, ἔφη αὐτοῖς· Λάβετε, ψηλαφήσατέ με, καὶ ἴδετε ὅτι οὐκ
εἰμὶ δαιμόνιον ἀσώματον. καὶ εὐθὺς αὐτοῦ ἥψαντο, καὶ ἐπίστευσαν κραθέντες τῇ σαρκὶ αὐτοῦ καὶ τῷ αἵματι. διὰ τοῦτο
καὶ θανάτου κατεφρόνησαν, ηὑρέθησαν δὲ ὑπὲρ θάνατον.
3. μετὰ δὲ τὴν ἀνάστασιν [καὶ] συνέφαγεν αὐτοῖς καὶ συνέ-
πιεν ὡς σαρκικός, καίπερ πνευματικῶς ἡνωμένος τῷ πατρί.

IV. Ταῦτα δὲ παραινῶ ὑμῖν, ἀγαπητοί, εἰδὼς ὅτι καὶ
ὑμεῖς οὕτως ἔχετε· προφυλάσσω δὲ ὑμᾶς ἀπὸ τῶν θηρίων
τῶν ἀνθρωπομόρφων, οὓς οὐ μόνον δεῖ ὑμᾶς μὴ παραδέχεσθαι,
ἀλλ', εἰ δυνατόν, μηδὲ συναντᾶν [αὐτοῖς]· μόνον δὲ προσεύχεσθε ὑπὲρ αὐτῶν, ἐάν πως μετανοήσωσιν, ὅπερ δύσκολον·
τούτου δὲ ἔχει ἐξουσίαν Ἰησοῦς Χριστός, τὸ ἀληθινὸν ἡμῶν
ζῆν. 2. εἰ γὰρ τὸ δοκεῖν ταῦτα ἐπράχθη ὑπὸ τοῦ Κυρίου
ἡμῶν, κἀγὼ τὸ δοκεῖν δέδεμαι. τί δὲ καὶ ἑαυτὸν ἔκδοτον
δέδωκα τῷ θανάτῳ, πρὸς πῦρ, πρὸς μάχαιραν, πρὸς θηρία;
ἀλλ' ὁ ἐγγὺς μαχαίρας, ἐγγὺς Θεοῦ· μεταξὺ θηρίων, μεταξὺ
Θεοῦ· μόνον ἐν τῷ ὀνόματι Ἰησοῦ Χριστοῦ εἰς τὸ συμπαθεῖν
αὐτῷ. πάντα ὑπομένω, αὐτοῦ με ἐνδυναμοῦντος τοῦ τελείου
ἀνθρώπου.

V. Ὅν τινες ἀγνοοῦντες ἀρνοῦνται, μᾶλλον δὲ ἠρνήθη-
σαν ὑπ' αὐτοῦ, ὄντες συνήγοροι τοῦ θανάτου μᾶλλον ἢ τῆς
ἀληθείας· οὓς οὐκ ἔπεισαν αἱ προφητεῖαι οὐδὲ ὁ νόμος Μω-
σέως, ἀλλ' οὐδὲ μέχρι νῦν τὸ εὐαγγέλιον, οὐδὲ τὰ ἡμέτερα τῶν
κατ' ἄνδρα παθήματα· 2. καὶ γὰρ περὶ ἡμῶν τὸ αὐτὸ φρονοῦσιν. τί γάρ [με] ὠφελεῖ, εἰ ἐμὲ ἐπαινεῖ τις, τὸν δὲ Κύριόν
μου βλασφημεῖ, μὴ ὁμολογῶν αὐτὸν σαρκοφόρον; ὁ δὲ τοῦτο
μὴ λέγων τελείως αὐτὸν ἀπήρνηται, ὢν νεκροφόρος. 3. τὰ δὲ

ὀνόματα αὐτῶν, ὄντα ἄπιστα, οὐκ ἔδοξέν μοι ἐγγράψαι· ἀλλὰ
μηδὲ γένοιτό μοι αὐτῶν μνημονεύειν, μέχρις οὗ μετανοήσωσιν
εἰς τὸ πάθος, ὅ ἐστιν ἡμῶν ἀνάστασις. VI. Μηδεὶς πλανάσθω.
καὶ τὰ ἐπουράνια καὶ ἡ δόξα
τῶν ἀγγέλων καὶ οἱ ἄρχοντες ὁρατοί τε καὶ ἀόρατοι, ἐὰν μὴ
πιστεύσωσιν εἰς τὸ αἷμα Χριστοῦ [τοῦ Θεοῦ], κἀκείνοις κρίσις ἐστίν. ὁ χωρῶν χωρείτω. τόπος μηδένα φυσιούτω· τὸ S. Matt.
γὰρ ὅλον ἐστὶν πίστις καὶ ἀγάπη, ὧν οὐδὲν προκέκριται. xix. 12.
2. καταμάθετε δὲ τοὺς ἑτεροδοξοῦντας εἰς τὴν χάριν Ἰησοῦ
Χριστοῦ τὴν εἰς ἡμᾶς ἐλθοῦσαν, πῶς ἐναντίοι εἰσὶν τῇ γνώμῃ
τοῦ Θεοῦ. περὶ ἀγάπης οὐ μέλει αὐτοῖς, οὐ περὶ χήρας, οὐ
περὶ ὀρφανοῦ, οὐ περὶ θλιβομένου, οὐ περὶ δεδεμένου [ἢ
λελυμένου], οὐ περὶ πεινῶντος ἢ διψῶντος· εὐχαριστίας καὶ
προσευχῆς ἀπέχονται διὰ τὸ μὴ ὁμολογεῖν τὴν εὐχαριστίαν
σάρκα εἶναι τοῦ σωτῆρος ἡμῶν Ἰησοῦ Χριστοῦ, τὴν ὑπὲρ τῶν
ἁμαρτιῶν ἡμῶν παθοῦσαν, ἣν τῇ χρηστότητι ὁ πατὴρ ἤγειρεν.

VII. Οἱ οὖν ἀντιλέγοντες τῇ δωρεᾷ τοῦ Θεοῦ συζητοῦν-
τες ἀποθνήσκουσιν. συνέφερεν δὲ αὐτοῖς ἀγαπᾶν, ἵνα καὶ
ἀναστῶσιν. 2. πρέπον [οὖν] ἐστὶν ἀπέχεσθαι τῶν τοιούτων,
καὶ μήτε κατ' ἰδίαν περὶ αὐτῶν λαλεῖν μήτε κοινῇ· προσέχειν
δὲ τοῖς προφήταις, ἐξαιρέτως δὲ τῷ εὐαγγελίῳ, ἐν ᾧ τὸ πάθος
ἡμῖν δεδήλωται καὶ ἡ ἀνάστασις τετελείωται.

VIII. Τοὺς [δὲ] μερισμοὺς φεύγετε, ὡς ἀρχὴν κακῶν.
πάντες τῷ ἐπισκόπῳ ἀκολουθεῖτε, ὡς Ἰησοῦς Χριστὸς τῷ
πατρί, καὶ τῷ πρεσβυτερίῳ ὡς τοῖς ἀποστόλοις· τοὺς δὲ
διακόνους ἐντρέπεσθε ὡς Θεοῦ ἐντολήν. μηδεὶς χωρὶς ἐπισκόπου τι πρασσέτω τῶν ἀνηκόντων εἰς τὴν ἐκκλησίαν.
ἐκείνη βεβαία εὐχαριστία ἡγείσθω ἡ ὑπὸ τὸν ἐπίσκοπον
οὖσα, ἢ ᾧ ἂν αὐτὸς ἐπιτρέψῃ. 2. ὅπου ἂν φανῇ ὁ ἐπίσκοπος,
ἐκεῖ τὸ πλῆθος ἔστω, ὥσπερ ὅπου ἂν ᾖ Χριστὸς Ἰησοῦς, ἐκεῖ
ἡ καθολικὴ ἐκκλησία. οὐκ ἐξόν ἐστιν χωρὶς τοῦ ἐπισκόπου
οὔτε βαπτίζειν οὔτε ἀγάπην ποιεῖν· ἀλλ' ὃ ἂν ἐκεῖνος δοκι-

vi. 1 τοῦ Θεοῦ] Timoth. Anon-Syr.₂; om. GLAC; al. g.

μάσῃ, τοῦτο καὶ τῷ Θεῷ εὐάρεστον, ἵνα ἀσφαλὲς ᾖ καὶ βέβαιον πᾶν ὃ πράσσετε.

IX. Εὔλογόν ἐστιν λοιπὸν ἀνανῆψαι ἡμᾶς, ὡς [ἔτι] καιρὸν ἔχομεν εἰς Θεὸν μετανοεῖν. καλῶς ἔχει Θεὸν καὶ ἐπίσκοπον εἰδέναι. ὁ τιμῶν ἐπίσκοπον ὑπὸ Θεοῦ τετίμηται· ὁ λάθρα ἐπισκόπου τι πράσσων τῷ διαβόλῳ λατρεύει. 2. πάντα οὖν ὑμῖν ἐν χάριτι περισσευέτω, ἄξιοι γάρ ἐστε. κατὰ πάντα με ἀνεπαύσατε, καὶ ὑμᾶς Ἰησοῦς Χριστός. ἀπόντα με καὶ παρόντα ἠγαπήσατε· ἀμείβοι ὑμῖν Θεός, δι᾽ ὃν πάντα ὑπομένοντες αὐτοῦ τεύξεσθε.

X. Φίλωνα καὶ Ῥαῖον Ἀγαθόπουν, οἳ ἐπηκολούθησάν μοι εἰς λόγον Θεοῦ, καλῶς ἐποιήσατε ὑποδεξάμενοι ὡς διακόνους [Χριστοῦ] Θεοῦ· οἳ καὶ εὐχαριστοῦσιν τῷ Κυρίῳ ὑπὲρ ὑμῶν, ὅτι αὐτοὺς ἀνεπαύσατε κατὰ πάντα τρόπον. οὐδὲν ὑμῖν οὐ μὴ ἀπολεῖται. 2. ἀντίψυχον ὑμῶν τὸ πνεῦμά μου, καὶ τὰ δεσμά μου ἃ οὐχ ὑπερηφανήσατε οὐδὲ ἐπῃσχύνθητε· οὐδὲ ὑμᾶς ἐπαισχυνθήσεται ἡ τελεία πίστις, Ἰησοῦς Χριστός.

XI. Ἡ προσευχὴ ὑμῶν ἀπῆλθεν ἐπὶ τὴν ἐκκλησίαν τὴν ἐν Ἀντιοχείᾳ τῆς Συρίας· ὅθεν δεδεμένος θεοπρεπεστάτοις δεσμοῖς πάντας ἀσπάζομαι, οὐκ ὢν ἄξιος ἐκεῖθεν εἶναι, ἔσχατος αὐτῶν ὤν· κατὰ θέλημα κατηξιώθην, οὐκ ἐκ συνειδότος, ἀλλ᾽ ἐκ χάριτος Θεοῦ, ἣν εὔχομαι τελείαν μοι δοθῆναι, ἵνα ἐν τῇ προσευχῇ ὑμῶν Θεοῦ ἐπιτύχω. 2. ἵνα οὖν τέλειον ὑμῶν γένηται τὸ ἔργον καὶ ἐπὶ γῆς καὶ ἐν οὐρανῷ, πρέπει εἰς τιμὴν Θεοῦ χειροτονῆσαι τὴν ἐκκλησίαν ὑμῶν θεοπρεσβύτην εἰς τὸ γενόμενον ἕως Συρίας συγχαρῆναι αὐτοῖς ὅτι εἰρηνεύουσιν καὶ ἀπέλαβον τὸ ἴδιον μέγεθος καὶ ἀπεκατεστάθη αὐτοῖς τὸ ἴδιον σωματεῖον. 3. ἐφάνη μοι οὖν ἄξιον πρᾶγμα πέμψαι τινὰ τῶν ὑμετέρων μετ᾽ ἐπιστολῆς, ἵνα συνδοξάσῃ τὴν κατὰ Θεὸν αὐτοῖς γενομένην εὐδίαν, καὶ ὅτι λιμένος ἤδη ἐτύγχανον τῇ προσευχῇ ὑμῶν. τέλειοι ὄντες τέλεια καὶ φρονεῖτε· θέλουσιν γὰρ ὑμῖν εὖ πράσσειν Θεὸς ἕτοιμος εἰς τὸ παρασχεῖν.

XII. Ἀσπάζεται ὑμᾶς ἡ ἀγάπη τῶν ἀδελφῶν τῶν ἐν Τρωάδι, ὅθεν καὶ γράφω ὑμῖν διὰ Βούρρου, ὃν ἀπεστείλατε

μετ' ἐμοῦ ἅμα Ἐφεσίοις τοῖς ἀδελφοῖς ὑμῶν· ὃς κατὰ πάντα
με ἀνέπαυσεν. καὶ ὄφελον πάντες αὐτὸν ἐμιμοῦντο, ὄντα
ἐξεμπλάριον Θεοῦ διακονίας. ἀμείψεται αὐτὸν ἡ χάρις κατὰ
πάντα. 2. ἀσπάζομαι τὸν ἀξιόθεον ἐπίσκοπον καὶ θεοπρε-
πὲς πρεσβυτέριον, [καὶ] τοὺς συνδούλους μου διακόνους καὶ
τοὺς κατ' ἄνδρα καὶ κοινῇ πάντας, ἐν ὀνόματι Ἰησοῦ Χριστοῦ,
καὶ τῇ σαρκὶ αὐτοῦ καὶ τῷ αἵματι, πάθει τε καὶ ἀναστάσει
σαρκικῇ τε καὶ πνευματικῇ, ἐν ἑνότητι Θεοῦ καὶ ὑμῶν. χάρις
ὑμῖν, ἔλεος, εἰρήνη, ὑπομονὴ διὰ παντός.

XIII. Ἀσπάζομαι τοὺς οἴκους τῶν ἀδελφῶν μου σὺν
γυναιξὶν καὶ τέκνοις, καὶ τὰς παρθένους τὰς λεγομένας χήρας.
ἔρρωσθέ μοι ἐν δυνάμει πατρός. ἀσπάζεται ὑμᾶς Φίλων,
σὺν ἐμοὶ ὤν. 2. ἀσπάζομαι τὸν οἶκον Γαουΐας, ἣν εὔχομαι
ἑδρᾶσθαι πίστει καὶ ἀγάπῃ σαρκικῇ τε καὶ πνευματικῇ.
ἀσπάζομαι Ἄλκην, τὸ ποθητόν μοι ὄνομα, καὶ Δάφνον τὸν
ἀσύγκριτον καὶ Εὔτεκνον καὶ πάντας κατ' ὄνομα. ἔρρωσθε
ἐν χάριτι Θεοῦ.

ΠΡΟΣ ΠΟΛΥΚΑΡΠΟΝ

ΙΓΝΑΤΙΟΣ ὁ καὶ Θεοφόρος, Πολυκάρπῳ ἐπισκόπῳ
ἐκκλησίας Σμυρναίων, μᾶλλον ἐπισκοπημένῳ ὑπὸ Θεοῦ
πατρὸς καὶ Ἰησοῦ Χριστοῦ, πλεῖστα χαίρειν.

I. Ἀποδεχόμενός σου τὴν ἐν Θεῷ γνώμην ἡδρασμένην
ὡς ἐπὶ πέτραν ἀκίνητον, ὑπερδοξάζω καταξιωθεὶς τοῦ προσώπου σου τοῦ ἀμώμου, οὗ ὀναίμην ἐν Θεῷ. 2. παρακαλῶ
σε ἐν χάριτι ᾗ ἐνδέδυσαι προσθεῖναι τῷ δρόμῳ σου, καὶ
πάντας παρακαλεῖν ἵνα σώζωνται. ἐκδίκει σου τὸν τόπον
ἐν πάσῃ ἐπιμελείᾳ σαρκικῇ τε καὶ πνευματικῇ. τῆς ἑνώσεως
φρόντιζε, ἧς οὐδὲν ἄμεινον· πάντας βάσταζε, ὡς καί σε ὁ
Κύριος· πάντων ἀνέχου ἐν ἀγάπῃ, ὥσπερ καὶ ποιεῖς· 3. προσευχαῖς σχόλαζε ἀδιαλείπτοις· αἰτοῦ σύνεσιν πλείονα ἧς
ἔχεις· γρηγόρει ἀκοίμητον πνεῦμα κεκτημένος· τοῖς κατ'

ἄνδρα κατὰ ὁμοήθειαν Θεοῦ λάλει· πάντων τὰς νόσους βάσταζε, ὡς τέλειος ἀθλητής· ὅπου πλείων κόπος, πολὺ κέρδος.
II. Καλοὺς μαθητὰς ἐὰν φιλῇς, χάρις σοι οὐκ ἔστιν·
μᾶλλον τοὺς λοιμοτέρους ἐν πραΰτητι ὑπότασσε. οὐ πᾶν
τραῦμα τῇ αὐτῇ ἐμπλάστρῳ θεραπεύεται· τοὺς παροξυσμοὺς

ἐμβροχαῖς παῦε. 2. φρόνιμοϲ γίνου ὡϲ ὁ ὄφιϲ ἐν πᾶϲιν κⲁὶ
ἀκέρⲁιοϲ εἰϲαεὶ ὡϲ ἡ περιϲτερά. διὰ τοῦτο σαρκικὸς εἶ καὶ
πνευματικός, ἵνα τὰ φαινόμενά σου εἰς πρόσωπον κολακεύῃς·
τὰ δὲ ἀόρατα αἴτει ἵνα σοι φανερωθῇ· ἵνα μηδενὸς λείπῃ, καὶ
παντὸς χαρίσματος περισσεύῃς. 3. ὁ καιρὸς ἀπαιτεῖ σε, ὡς
κυβερνῆται ἀνέμους καὶ ὡς χειμαζόμενος λιμένα, εἰς τὸ Θεοῦ
ἐπιτυχεῖν. νῆφε, ὡς Θεοῦ ἀθλητής· τὸ θέμα ἀφθαρσία καὶ
ζωὴ αἰώνιος, περὶ ἧς καὶ σὺ πέπεισαι. κατὰ πάντα σου
ἀντίψυχον ἐγὼ καὶ τὰ δεσμά μου ἃ ἠγάπησας.

III. Οἱ δοκοῦντες ἀξιόπιστοι εἶναι καὶ ἑτεροδιδασκα-
λοῦντες μή σε καταπλησσέτωσαν. στῆθι ἑδραῖος, ὡς ἄκμων
τυπτόμενος. μεγάλου ἐστὶν ἀθλητοῦ [τὸ] δέρεσθαι καὶ νικᾶν.
μάλιστα δὲ ἕνεκεν Θεοῦ πάντα ὑπομένειν ἡμᾶς δεῖ, ἵνα καὶ
αὐτὸς ἡμᾶς ὑπομείνῃ. 2. πλέον σπουδαῖος γίνου οὗ εἶ. τοὺς
καιροὺς καταμάνθανε· τὸν ὑπὲρ καιρὸν προσδόκα, τὸν ἄχρο-
νον, τὸν ἀόρατον, τὸν δι᾽ ἡμᾶς ὁρατόν, τὸν ἀψηλάφητον, τὸν
ἀπαθῆ, τὸν δι᾽ ἡμᾶς παθητόν, τὸν κατὰ πάντα τρόπον δι᾽
ἡμᾶς ὑπομείναντα.

IV. Χῆραι μὴ ἀμελείσθωσαν· μετὰ τὸν Κύριον σὺ αὐτῶν
φροντιστὴς ἔσο. μηδὲν ἄνευ γνώμης σου γινέσθω, μηδὲ σὺ
ἄνευ Θεοῦ γνώμης τι πρᾶσσε· ὅπερ οὐδὲ πράσσεις. εὐστάθει.
2. πυκνότερον συναγωγαὶ γινέσθωσαν· ἐξ ὀνόματος πάντας
ζήτει. 3. δούλους καὶ δούλας μὴ ὑπερηφάνει· ἀλλὰ μηδὲ
αὐτοὶ φυσιούσθωσαν, ἀλλ᾽ εἰς δόξαν Θεοῦ πλέον δουλευέτω-
σαν, ἵνα κρείττονος ἐλευθερίας ἀπὸ Θεοῦ τύχωσιν· μὴ ἐρά-
τωσαν ἀπὸ τοῦ κοινοῦ ἐλευθεροῦσθαι, ἵνα μὴ δοῦλοι εὑρεθῶσιν
ἐπιθυμίας.

V. Τὰς κακοτεχνίας φεῦγε, μᾶλλον δὲ περὶ τούτων
ὁμιλίαν ποιοῦ. ταῖς ἀδελφαῖς μου προσλάλει ἀγαπᾶν τὸν

Κύριον καὶ τοῖς συμβίοις ἀρκεῖσθαι σαρκὶ καὶ πνεύματι. ὁμοίως καὶ τοῖς ἀδελφοῖς μου παράγγελλε ἐν ὀνόματι Ἰησοῦ Χριστοῦ ἀγαπᾶν τὰς συμβίους, ὡς ὁ Κύριος τὴν ἐκκλησίαν. Eph. v. 29. 2. εἴ τις δύναται ἐν ἁγνείᾳ μένειν εἰς τιμὴν τῆς σαρκὸς τοῦ Κυρίου, ἐν ἀκαυχησίᾳ μενέτω· ἐὰν καυχήσηται, ἀπώλετο· καὶ ἐὰν γνωσθῇ πλέον τοῦ ἐπισκόπου, ἔφθαρται.   πρέπει δὲ τοῖς γαμοῦσι καὶ ταῖς γαμούσαις μετὰ γνώμης τοῦ ἐπισκόπου τὴν ἕνωσιν ποιεῖσθαι, ἵνα ὁ γάμος ᾖ κατὰ Κύριον καὶ μὴ κατ᾽ ἐπιθυμίαν.   πάντα εἰς τιμὴν Θεοῦ γινέσθω.

VI. Τῷ ἐπισκόπῳ προσέχετε, ἵνα καὶ ὁ Θεὸς ὑμῖν. ἀντίψυχον ἐγὼ τῶν ὑποτασσομένων [τῷ] ἐπισκόπῳ, πρεσβυτέροις, διακόνοις· μετ᾽ αὐτῶν μοι τὸ μέρος γένοιτο σχεῖν παρὰ Θεῷ.   συγκοπιᾶτε ἀλλήλοις, συναθλεῖτε, συντρέχετε, συμπάσχετε, συγκοιμᾶσθε, συνεγείρεσθε, ὡς Θεοῦ οἰκονόμοι καὶ πάρεδροι καὶ ὑπηρέται.   2. ἀρέσκετε ᾧ στρατεύεσθε, ἀφ᾽ οὗ καὶ τὰ ὀψώνια κομίζεσθε.   μήτις ὑμῶν δεσέρτωρ εὑρεθῇ. τὸ βάπτισμα ὑμῶν μενέτω ὡς ὅπλα, ἡ πίστις ὡς περικεφαλαία, ἡ ἀγάπη ὡς δόρυ, ἡ ὑπομονὴ ὡς πανοπλία· τὰ δεπόσιτα ὑμῶν τὰ ἔργα ὑμῶν, ἵνα τὰ ἄκκεπτα ὑμῶν ἄξια κομίσησθε. μακροθυμήσατε οὖν μετ᾽ ἀλλήλων ἐν πραΰτητι, ὡς ὁ Θεὸς μεθ᾽ ὑμῶν.   ὀναίμην ὑμῶν διὰ παντός.

VII. Ἐπειδὴ ἡ ἐκκλησία ἡ ἐν Ἀντιοχείᾳ τῆς Συρίας εἰρηνεύει, ὡς ἐδηλώθη μοι, διὰ τῆς προσευχῆς ὑμῶν, κἀγὼ εὐθυμότερος ἐγενόμην ἐν ἀμεριμνίᾳ Θεοῦ, ἐάνπερ διὰ τοῦ παθεῖν Θεοῦ ἐπιτύχω, εἰς τὸ εὑρεθῆναί με ἐν τῇ αἰτήσει ὑμῶν μαθητήν.   2. πρέπει, Πολύκαρπε θεομακαριστότατε, συμβούλιον ἀγαγεῖν θεοπρεπέστατον καὶ χειροτονῆσαί τινα ὃν ἀγαπητὸν λίαν ἔχετε καὶ ἄοκνον, ὃς δυνήσεται θεοδρόμος καλεῖσθαι· τοῦτον καταξιῶσαι, ἵνα πορευθεὶς εἰς Συρίαν δοξάσῃ ὑμῶν τὴν ἄοκνον ἀγάπην εἰς δόξαν Θεοῦ.   3. Χριστιανὸς ἑαυτοῦ ἐξουσίαν οὐκ ἔχει ἀλλὰ Θεῷ σχολάζει.   τοῦτο τὸ ἔργον Θεοῦ ἐστιν καὶ ὑμῶν, ὅταν αὐτὸ ἀπαρτίσητε. πιστεύω γὰρ τῇ χάριτι, ὅτι ἕτοιμοί ἐστε εἰς εὐποιΐαν Θεῷ ἀνήκουσαν. εἰδὼς ὑμῶν τὸ σύντονον τῆς ἀληθείας δι᾽ ὀλίγων ὑμᾶς γραμμάτων παρεκάλεσα.

VIII. Ἐπεὶ πάσαις ταῖς ἐκκλησίαις οὐκ ἠδυνήθην γράψαι διὰ τὸ ἐξαίφνης πλεῖν με ἀπὸ Τρωάδος εἰς Νεάπολιν, ὡς τὸ θέλημα προστάσσει, γράψεις ταῖς ἔμπροσθεν ἐκκλησίαις, ὡς Θεοῦ γνώμην κεκτημένος, εἰς τὸ καὶ αὐτοὺς τὸ αὐτὸ ποιῆσαι—οἱ μὲν δυνάμενοι πεζοὺς πέμψαι, οἱ δὲ ἐπιστολὰς διὰ τῶν ὑπό σου πεμπομένων, ἵνα δοξασθῆτε αἰωνίῳ ἔργῳ— ὡς ἄξιος ὤν.

2. Ἀσπάζομαι πάντας ἐξ ὀνόματος, καὶ τὴν τοῦ Ἐπιτρόπου σὺν ὅλῳ τῷ οἴκῳ αὐτῆς καὶ τῶν τέκνων· ἀσπάζομαι Ἄτταλον τὸν ἀγαπητόν μου· ἀσπάζομαι τὸν μέλλοντα καταξιοῦσθαι τοῦ εἰς Συρίαν πορεύεσθαι· ἔσται ἡ χάρις μετ᾽ αὐτοῦ διὰ παντός, καὶ τοῦ πέμποντος αὐτὸν Πολυκάρπου. 3. ἐρρῶσθαι ὑμᾶς διὰ παντὸς ἐν Θεῷ ἡμῶν Ἰησοῦ Χριστῷ εὔχομαι, ἐν ᾧ διαμείνητε ἐν ἑνότητι Θεοῦ καὶ ἐπισκοπῇ. ἀσπάζομαι Ἄλκην τὸ ποθητόν μοι ὄνομα. ἔρρωσθε ἐν Κυρίῳ.

TRANSLATION

EPISTLES OF S. IGNATIUS

EPISTLES OF S. IGNATIUS

I

TO THE EPHESIANS

IGNATIUS, who is also Theophorus, unto her which hath been blessed in greatness through the plenitude of God the Father; which hath been foreordained before the ages to be for ever unto abiding and unchangeable glory, united and elect in a true passion, by the will of the Father and of Jesus Christ our God; even unto the church which is in Ephesus [of Asia], worthy of all felicitation: abundant greeting in Christ Jesus and in blameless joy.

1. While I welcomed in God [your] well-beloved name which ye bear by natural right, [in an upright and virtuous mind], by faith and love in Christ Jesus our Saviour—being imitators of God, and having your hearts kindled in the blood of God, ye have perfectly fulfilled your congenial work—for when ye heard that I was on my way from Syria, in bonds for the sake of the common Name and hope, and was hoping through your prayers to succeed in fighting with wild beasts in Rome, that by so succeeding I might have power to be a disciple, ye were eager to visit me:—seeing then that in God's name I have received your whole multitude in the person of Onesimus, whose love passeth utterance and who is moreover your bishop [in the flesh]—and I pray that ye may love him according to Jesus Christ and that ye all may be like him; for blessed is He that granted unto you according to your deserving to have such a bishop:—

2. But as touching my fellow-servant Burrhus, who by the will of God is your deacon blessed in all things, I pray that he may remain with me to the honour of yourselves and of your bishop. Yea, and Crocus also, who is worthy of God and of you, whom I received as an ensample of the love which ye bear me, hath relieved me in all ways—

even so may the Father of Jesus Christ refresh him—together with Onesimus and Burrhus and Euplus and Fronto; in whom I saw you all with the eyes of love. May I have joy of you always, if so be I am worthy of it. It is therefore meet for you in every way to glorify Jesus Christ who glorified you; that being perfectly joined together in one submission, submitting yourselves to your bishop and presbytery, ye may be sanctified in all things.

3. I do not command you, as though I were somewhat. For even though I am in bonds for the Name's sake, I am not yet perfected in Jesus Christ. [For] now am I beginning to be a disciple; and I speak to you as to my school-fellows. For I ought to be trained by you for the contest in faith, in admonition, in endurance, in long-suffering. But, since love doth not suffer me to be silent concerning you, therefore was I forward to exhort you, that ye run in harmony with the mind of God: for Jesus Christ also, our inseparable life, is the mind of the Father, even as the bishops that are settled in the farthest parts of the earth are in the mind of Jesus Christ.

4. So then it becometh you to run in harmony with the mind of the bishop; which thing also ye do. For your honourable presbytery, which is worthy of God, is attuned to the bishop, even as its strings to a lyre. Therefore in your concord and harmonious love Jesus Christ is sung. And do ye, each and all, form yourselves into a chorus, that being harmonious in concord and taking the key note of God ye may in unison sing with one voice through Jesus Christ unto the Father, that He may both hear you and acknowledge you by your good deeds to be members of His Son. It is therefore profitable for you to be in blameless unity, that ye may also be partakers of God always.

5. For if I in a short time had such converse with your bishop, which was not after the manner of men but in the Spirit, how much more do I congratulate you who are closely joined with him as the Church is with Jesus Christ and as Jesus Christ is with the Father, that all things may be harmonious in unity. Let no man be deceived. If any one be not within the precinct of the altar, he lacketh the bread [of God]. For, if the prayer of one and another hath so great force, how much more that of the bishop and of the whole Church. Whosoever therefore cometh not to the congregation, he doth thereby show his pride and hath separated himself; for it is written, *God resisteth the proud.* Let us therefore be careful not to resist the bishop, that by our submission we may give ourselves to God.

6. And in proportion as a man seeth that his bishop is silent, let him fear him the more. For every one whom the Master of the household sendeth to be steward over His own house, we ought so to receive as Him that sent him. Plainly therefore we ought to regard the bishop as the Lord Himself. Now Onesimus of his own accord highly praiseth your orderly conduct in God, for that ye all live according to truth, and that no heresy hath a home among you: nay, ye do not so much as listen to any one, if he speak of aught else save concerning Jesus Christ in truth.

7. For some are wont of malicious guile to hawk about the Name, while they do certain other things unworthy of God. These men ye ought to shun, as wild-beasts; for they are mad dogs, biting by stealth; against whom ye ought to be on your guard, for they are hard to heal. There is one only physician, of flesh and of spirit, generate and ingenerate, God in man, true Life in death, Son of Mary and Son of God, first passible and then impassible, Jesus Christ our Lord.

8. Let no one therefore deceive you, as indeed ye are not deceived, seeing that ye belong wholly to God. For when no lust is established in you, which hath power to torment you, then truly ye live after God. I devote myself for you, and I dedicate myself as an offering for the church of you Ephesians which is famous unto all the ages. They that are of the flesh cannot do the things of the Spirit, neither can they that are of the Spirit do the things of the flesh; even as faith cannot do the things of unfaithfulness, neither unfaithfulness the things of faith. Nay, even those things which ye do after the flesh are spiritual; for ye do all things in Jesus Christ.

9. But I have learned that certain persons passed through you from yonder, bringing evil doctrine; whom ye suffered not to sow seed in you, for ye stopped your ears, so that ye might not receive the seed sown by them; forasmuch as ye are stones of a temple, which were prepared beforehand for a building of God the Father, being hoisted up to the heights through the engine of Jesus Christ, which is the Cross, and using for a rope the Holy Spirit; while your faith is your windlass, and love is the way that leadeth up to God. So then ye are all companions in the way, carrying your God and your shrine, your Christ and your holy things, being arrayed from head to foot in the commandments of Jesus Christ. And I too, taking part in the festivity, am permitted by letter to bear you company and to rejoice with you, that ye set not your love on anything after the common life of men, but only on God.

10. And pray ye also without ceasing for the rest of mankind (for there is in them a hope of repentance), that they may find God. Therefore permit them to take lessons at least from your works. Against their outbursts of wrath be ye meek; against their proud words be ye humble; against their railings set ye your prayers; against their errors be ye *stedfast in the faith*; against their fierceness be ye gentle. And be not zealous to imitate them by requital. Let us show ourselves their brothers by our forbearance; but let us be zealous to be imitators of the Lord, vying with each other who shall suffer the greater wrong, who shall be defrauded, who shall be set at nought; that no herb of the devil be found in you: but in all purity and temperance abide ye in Christ Jesus, with your flesh and with your spirit.

11. These are the last times. Henceforth let us have reverence; let us fear the long-suffering of God, lest it turn into a judgment against us. For either let us fear the wrath which is to come or let us love the grace which now is—the one or the other; provided only that we be found in Christ Jesus unto true life. Let nothing glitter in your eyes apart from Him, in whom I carry about my bonds, my spiritual pearls in which I would fain rise again through your prayer, whereof may it be my lot to be always a partaker, that I may be found in the company of those Christians of Ephesus who moreover were ever of one mind with the Apostles in the power of Jesus Christ.

12. I know who I am and to whom I write. I am a convict, ye have received mercy: I am in peril, ye are established. Ye are the high-road of those that are on their way to die unto God. Ye are associates in the mysteries with Paul, who was sanctified, who obtained a good report, who is worthy of all felicitation; in whose foot-steps I would fain be found treading, when I shall attain unto God; who in every letter maketh mention of you in Christ Jesus.

13. Do your diligence therefore to meet together more frequently for thanksgiving to God and for His glory. For when ye meet together frequently, the powers of Satan are cast down; and his mischief cometh to nought in the concord of your faith. There is nothing better than peace, in which all warfare of things in heaven and things on earth is abolished.

14. None of these things is hidden from you, if ye be perfect in your faith and love toward Jesus Christ, for these are the beginning and end of life—faith is the beginning and love is the end—and the two being found in unity are God, while all things else follow in their train

unto true nobility. No man professing faith sinneth, and no man possessing love hateth. *The tree is manifest from its fruit;* so they that profess to be Christ's shall be seen through their actions. For the Work is not a thing of profession now, but is seen then when one is found in the power of faith unto the end.

15. It is better to keep silence and to be, than to talk and not to be. It is a fine thing to teach, if the speaker practise. Now there is one teacher, who *spake and it came to pass* : yea and even the things which He hath done in silence are worthy of the Father. He that truly possesseth the word of Jesus is able also to hearken unto His silence, that he may be perfect; that through his speech he may act and through his silence he may be known. Nothing is hidden from the Lord, but even our secrets are nigh unto Him. Let us therefore do all things as knowing that He dwelleth in us, to the end that we may be His temples and He Himself may be in us as our God. This is so, and it will also be made clear in our sight from the love which we rightly bear towards Him.

16. Be not deceived, my brethren. Corrupters of houses *shall not inherit the kingdom of God.* If then they which do these things after the flesh are put to death, how much more if a man through evil doctrine corrupt the faith of God for which Jesus Christ was crucified. Such a man, having defiled himself, shall go into the unquenchable fire ; and in like manner also shall he that hearkeneth unto him.

17. For this cause the Lord received ointment on His head, that He might breathe incorruption upon the Church. Be not anointed with the ill odour of the teaching of the prince of this world, lest he lead you captive and rob you of the life which is set before you. And wherefore do we not all walk prudently, receiving the knowledge of God, which is Jesus Christ? Why perish we in our folly, not knowing the gift of grace which the Lord hath truly sent?

18. My spirit is made an offscouring for the Cross, which is a stumbling-block to them that are unbelievers, but to us salvation and life eternal. *Where is the wise ? Where is the disputer ?* Where is the boasting of them that are called prudent? For our God, Jesus the Christ, was conceived in the womb by Mary according to a dispensation, of the seed of David but also of the Holy Ghost; and He was born and was baptized that by His passion He might cleanse water.

19. And hidden from the prince of this world were the virginity of Mary and her child-bearing and likewise also the death of the Lord—

three mysteries to be cried aloud—the which were wrought in the silence of God. How then were they made manifest to the ages? A star shone forth in the heaven above all the stars; and its light was unutterable, and its strangeness caused amazement; and all the rest of the constellations with the sun and moon formed themselves into a chorus about the star; but the star itself far outshone them all; and there was perplexity to know whence came this strange appearance which was so unlike them. From that time forward every sorcery and every spell was dissolved, the ignorance of wickedness vanished away, the ancient kingdom was pulled down, when God appeared in the likeness of man unto *newness of* everlasting *life;* and that which had been perfected in the counsels of God began to take effect. Thence all things were perturbed, because the abolishing of death was taken in hand.

20. If Jesus Christ should count me worthy through your prayer, and it should be the Divine will, in my second tract, which I intend to write to you, I will further set before you the dispensation whereof I have begun to speak, relating to the new man Jesus Christ, which consisteth in faith towards Him and in love towards Him, in His passion and resurrection, especially if the Lord should reveal aught to me. Assemble yourselves together in common, every one of you severally, man by man, in grace, in one faith and one Jesus Christ, who after the flesh was of David's race, who is Son of Man and Son of God, to the end that ye may obey the bishop and the presbytery without distraction of mind; breaking one bread, which is the medicine of immortality and the antidote that we should not die but live for ever in Jesus Christ.

21. I am devoted to you and to those whom for the honour of God ye sent to Smyrna; whence also I write unto you with thanksgiving to the Lord, having love for Polycarp as I have for you also. Remember me, even as I would that Jesus Christ may also remember you. Pray for the church which is in Syria, whence I am led a prisoner to Rome— I who am the very last of the faithful there; according as I was counted worthy to be found unto the honour of God. Fare ye well in God the Father and in Jesus Christ our common hope.

2

TO THE MAGNESIÁNS

I GNATIUS, who is also Theophorus, unto her which hath been blessed through the grace of God the Father in Christ Jesus our Saviour, in whom I salute the church which is in Magnesia on the Mæander, and I wish her abundant greeting in God the Father and in Jesus Christ.

1. When I learned the exceeding good order of your love in the ways of God, I was gladdened and I determined to address you in the faith of Jesus Christ. For being counted worthy to bear a most godly name, in these bonds, which I carry about, I sing the praise of the churches; and I pray that there may be in them union of the flesh and of the spirit which are Jesus Christ's, our never-failing life—an union of faith and of love which is preferred before all things, and—what is more than all—an union with Jesus and with the Father; in whom if we endure patiently all the despite of the prince of this world and escape therefrom, we shall attain unto God.

2. Forasmuch then as I was permitted to see you in the person of Damas your godly bishop and your worthy presbyters Bassus and Apollonius and my fellow-servant the deacon Zotion, of whom I would fain have joy, for that he is subject to the bishop as unto the grace of God and to the presbytery as unto the law of Jesus Christ:—

3. Yea, and it becometh you also not to presume upon the youth of your bishop, but according to the power of God the Father to render unto him all reverence, even as I have learned that the holy presbyters also have not taken advantage of his outwardly youthful estate, but give place to him as to one prudent in God; yet not to him, but to the Father of Jesus Christ, even to the Bishop of all. For the honour therefore of Him that desired you, it is meet that ye should be obedient without dissimulation. For a man doth not so much deceive this bishop who is seen, as cheat that other who is invisible; and in such a case he must reckon not with flesh but with God who knoweth the hidden things.

4. It is therefore meet that we not only be called Christians, but also be such; even as some persons have the bishop's name on their

lips, but in everything act apart from him. Such men appear to me not to keep a good conscience, forasmuch as they do not assemble themselves together lawfully according to commandment.

5. Seeing then that all things have an end, and these two—life and death—are set before us together, and each man shall go *to his own place;* for just as there are two coinages, the one of God and the other of the world, and each of them hath its proper stamp impressed upon it, the unbelievers the stamp of this world, but the faithful in love the stamp of God the Father through Jesus Christ, through whom unless of our own free choice we accept to die unto His passion, His life is not in us :—

6. Seeing then that in the aforementioned persons I beheld your whole people in faith and embraced them, I advise you, be ye zealous to do all things in godly concord, the bishop presiding after the likeness of God and the presbyters after the likeness of the council of the Apostles, with the deacons also who are most dear to me, having been entrusted with the diaconate of Jesus Christ, who was with the Father before the worlds and appeared at the end of time. Therefore do ye all study conformity to God and pay reverence one to another; and let no man regard his neighbour after the flesh, but love ye one another in Jesus Christ always. Let there be nothing among you which shall have power to divide you, but be ye united with the bishop and with them that preside over you as an ensample and a lesson of incorruptibility.

7. Therefore as the Lord did nothing without the Father, [being united with Him], either by Himself or by the Apostles, so neither do ye anything without the bishop and the presbyters. And attempt not to think anything right for yourselves apart from others : but let there be one prayer in common, one supplication, one mind, one hope, in love and in joy unblameable, which is Jesus Christ, than whom there is nothing better. Hasten to come together all of you, as to one temple, even God ; as to one altar, even to one Jesus Christ, who came forth from One Father and is with One and departed unto One.

8. Be not seduced by strange doctrines nor by antiquated fables, which are profitless. For if even unto this day we live after the manner of Judaism, we avow that we have not received grace : for the divine prophets lived after Christ Jesus. For this cause also they were persecuted, being inspired by His grace to the end that they which are disobedient might be fully persuaded that there is one God who manifested Himself through Jesus Christ His Son, who is His Word that

proceeded from silence, who in all things was well-pleasing unto Him that sent Him.

9. If then those who had walked in ancient practices attained unto newness of hope, no longer observing sabbaths but fashioning their lives after the Lord's day, on which our life also arose through Him and through His death which some men deny—a mystery whereby we attained unto belief, and for this cause we endure patiently, that we may be found disciples of Jesus Christ our only teacher—if this be so, how shall we be able to live apart from Him? seeing that even the prophets, being His disciples, were expecting Him as their teacher through the Spirit. And for this cause He whom they rightly awaited, when He came, raised them from the dead.

10. Therefore let us not be insensible to His goodness. For if He should imitate us according to our deeds, we are lost. For this cause, seeing that we are become His disciples, let us learn to live as beseemeth Christianity. For whoso is called by another name besides this, is not of God. Therefore put away the vile leaven which hath waxed stale and sour, and betake yourselves to the new leaven, which is Jesus Christ. Be ye salted in Him, that none among you grow putrid, seeing that by your savour ye shall be proved. It is monstrous to talk of Jesus Christ and to practise Judaism. For Christianity did not believe in Judaism, but Judaism in Christianity, wherein *every tongue* believed and *was gathered together* unto God.

11. Now these things I say, my dearly beloved, not because I have learned that any of you are so minded ; but as being less than any of you, I would have you be on your guard betimes, that ye fall not into the snares of vain doctrine ; but be ye fully persuaded concerning the birth and the passion and the resurrection, which took place in the time of the governorship of Pontius Pilate ; for these things were truly and certainly done by Jesus Christ our hope ; from which hope may it not befal any of you to be turned aside.

12. Let me have joy of you in all things, if I be worthy. For even though I am in bonds, yet am I not comparable to one of you who are at liberty. I know that ye are not puffed up ; for ye have Jesus Christ in yourselves. And, when I praise you, I know that ye only feel the more shame ; as it is written *The righteous man is a self-accuser*.

13. Do your diligence therefore that ye be confirmed in the ordinances of the Lord and of the Apostles, that ye may *prosper in all*

things whatsoever ye do in flesh and spirit, by faith and by love, in the Son and Father and in the Spirit, in the beginning and in the end, with your revered bishop, and with the fitly wreathed spiritual circlet of your presbytery, and with the deacons who walk after God. Be obedient to the bishop and to one another, as Jesus Christ was to the Father [according to the flesh], and as the Apostles were to Christ and to the Father, that there may be union both of flesh and of spirit.

14. Knowing that ye are full of God, I have exhorted you briefly. Remember me in your prayers, that I may attain unto God; and remember also the church which is in Syria, whereof I am not worthy to be called a member. For I have need of your united prayer and love in God, that it may be granted to the church which is in Syria to be refreshed by the dew of your fervent supplication.

15. The Ephesians from Smyrna salute you, from whence also I write to you. They are here with me for the glory of God, as also are ye; and they have comforted me in all things, together with Polycarp bishop of the Smyrnæans. Yea, and all the other churches salute you in the honour of Jesus Christ. Fare ye well in godly concord, and possess ye a stedfast spirit, which is Jesus Christ.

3

TO THE TRALLIANS

IGNATIUS, who is also Theophorus, unto her that is beloved by God the Father of Jesus Christ; to the holy church which is in Tralles of Asia, elect and worthy of God, having peace in flesh and spirit through the passion of Jesus Christ, who is our hope through our resurrection unto Him; which church also I salute in the Divine plenitude after the apostolic fashion, and I wish her abundant greeting.

1. I have learned that ye have a mind unblameable and stedfast in patience, not from habit, but by nature, according as Polybius your bishop informed me, who by the will of God and of Jesus Christ visited me in Smyrna; and so greatly did he rejoice with me in my bonds in Christ Jesus, that in him I beheld the whole multitude of you. Having therefore received your godly benevolence at his hands, I gave glory,

forasmuch as I had found you to be imitators of God, even as I had learned.

2. For when ye are obedient to the bishop as to Jesus Christ, it is evident to me that ye are living not after men but after Jesus Christ, who died for us, that believing on His death ye might escape death. It is therefore necessary, even as your wont is, that ye should do nothing without the bishop; but be ye obedient also to the presbytery, as to the Apostles of Jesus Christ our hope; for if we live in Him, we shall also be found in Him. And those likewise who are deacons of the mysteries of Jesus Christ must please all men in all ways. For they are not deacons of meats and drinks but servants of the Church of God. It is right therefore that they should beware of blame as of fire.

3. In like manner let all men respect the deacons as Jesus Christ, even as they should respect the bishop as being a type of the Father and the presbyters as the council of God and as the college of Apostles. Apart from these there is not even the name of a church. And I am persuaded that ye are so minded as touching these matters: for I received the ensample of your love, and I have it with me, in the person of your bishop, whose very demeanour is a great lesson, while his gentleness is power—a man to whom I think even the godless pay reverence. Seeing that I love you I thus spare you, though I might write more sharply on his behalf: but I did not think myself competent for this, that being a convict I should order you as though I were an Apostle.

4. I have many deep thoughts in God: but I take the measure of myself, lest I perish in my boasting. For now I ought to be the more afraid and not to give heed to those that would puff me up: for they that say these things to me are a scourge to me. For though I desire to suffer, yet I know not whether I am worthy: for the envy of the devil is unseen indeed by many, but against me it wages the fiercer war. So then I crave gentleness, whereby the prince of this world is brought to nought.

5. Am I not able to write to you of heavenly things? But I fear lest I should cause you harm being babes. So bear with me, lest not being able to take them in, ye should be choked. For I myself also, albeit I am in bonds and can comprehend heavenly things and the arrays of the angels and the musterings of the principalities, things visible and things invisible—I myself am not yet by reason of this a disciple. For we lack many things, that God may not be lacking to us.

6. I exhort you therefore—yet not I, but the love of Jesus Christ—take ye only Christian food, and abstain from strange herbage, which is heresy: for these men do even mingle poison with Jesus Christ, imposing upon others by a show of honesty, like persons administering a deadly drug with honied wine, so that one who knoweth it not, fearing nothing, drinketh in death with a baneful delight.

7. Be ye therefore on your guard against such men. And this will surely be, if ye be not puffed up and if ye be inseparable from [God] Jesus Christ and from the bishop and from the ordinances of the Apostles. He that is within the sanctuary is clean; but he that is without the sanctuary is not clean, that is, he that doeth aught without the bishop and presbytery and deacons, this man is not clean in his conscience.

8. Not indeed that I have known of any such thing among you, but I keep watch over you betimes, as my beloved, for I foresee the snares of the devil. Do ye therefore arm yourselves with gentleness and recover yourselves in faith which is the flesh of the Lord, and in love which is the blood of Jesus Christ. Let none of you bear a grudge against his neighbour. Give no occasion to the Gentiles, lest by reason of a few foolish men the godly multitude be blasphemed: for *Woe unto him through whom My name is vainly blasphemed before some.*

9. Be ye deaf therefore, when any man speaketh to you apart from Jesus Christ, who was of the race of David, who was the Son of Mary, who was truly born and ate and drank, was truly persecuted under Pontius Pilate, was truly crucified and died in the sight of those in heaven and those on earth and those under the earth; who moreover was truly raised from the dead, His Father having raised Him, who in the like fashion will so raise us also who believe on Him—His Father, I say, will raise us—in Christ Jesus, apart from whom we have not true life.

10. But if it were as certain persons who are godless, that is unbelievers, say, that He suffered only in semblance, being themselves mere semblance, why am I in bonds? And why also do I desire to fight with wild beasts? So I die in vain. Truly then I lie against the Lord.

11. Shun ye therefore those vile offshoots that gender a deadly fruit, whereof if a man taste, forthwith he dieth. For these men are not the Father's planting: for if they had been, they would have been

seen to be branches of the Cross, and their fruit imperishable—the Cross whereby He through His passion inviteth us, being His members. Now it cannot be that a head should be found without members, seeing that God promiseth union, and this union is Himself.

12. I salute you from Smyrna, together with the churches of God that are present with me; men who refreshed me in all ways both in flesh and in spirit. My bonds exhort you, which for Jesus Christ's sake I bear about, entreating that I may attain unto God; abide ye in your concord and in prayer one with another. For it becometh you severally, and more especially the presbyters, to cheer the soul of your bishop unto the honour of the Father [and to the honour] of Jesus Christ and of the Apostles. I pray that ye may hearken unto me in love, lest I be for a testimony against you by having so written. And pray ye also for me who have need of your love in the mercy of God, that I may be vouchsafed the lot which I am eager to attain, to the end that I be not found reprobate.

13. The love of the Smyrnæans and Ephesians saluteth you. Remember in your prayers the church which is in Syria; whereof [also] I am not worthy to be called a member, being the very last of them. Fare ye well in Jesus Christ, submitting yourselves to the bishop as to the commandment, and likewise also to the presbytery; and each of you severally love one another with undivided heart. My spirit is offered up for you, not only now, but also when I shall attain unto God. For I am still in peril; but the Father is faithful in Jesus Christ to fulfil my petition and yours. May we be found unblameable in Him.

4

TO THE ROMANS

IGNATIUS, who is also Theophorus, unto her that hath found mercy in the bountifulness of the Father Most High and of Jesus Christ His only Son; to the church that is beloved and enlightened through the will of Him who willed all things that are, by faith and love towards Jesus Christ our God; even unto her that hath the presidency in the country of the region of the Romans, being worthy of God, worthy of honour, worthy of felicitation, worthy of praise, worthy of success, worthy in purity, and having the presidency of love, walking in the law of Christ and bearing the Father's name; which church also I salute in the name of Jesus Christ the Son of the Father; unto them that in flesh and spirit are united unto His every commandment, being filled with the grace of God without wavering, and filtered clear from every foreign stain; abundant greeting in Jesus Christ our God in blamelessness.

1. Forasmuch as in answer to my prayer to God it hath been granted me to see your godly countenances, so that I have obtained even more than I asked; for wearing bonds in Christ Jesus I hope to salute you, if it be the Divine will that I should be counted worthy to reach unto the end; for the beginning verily is well ordered, if so be I shall attain unto the goal, that I may receive mine inheritance without hindrance. For I dread your very love, lest it do me an injury; for it is easy for you to do what ye will, but for me it is difficult to attain unto God, unless ye shall spare me.

2. For I would not have you to be men-pleasers but to please God, as indeed ye do please Him. For neither shall I myself ever find an opportunity such as this to attain unto God, nor can ye, if ye be silent, win the credit of any nobler work. For, if ye be silent and leave me alone, I am a word of God; but if ye desire my flesh, then shall I be again a mere cry. [Nay] grant me nothing more than that I be poured out a libation to God, while there is still an altar ready; that forming yourselves into a chorus in love ye may sing to the Father in Jesus Christ, for that God hath vouchsafed that the bishop from Syria should be found in the West, having summoned him from the East. It is good to set from the world unto God, that I may rise unto Him.

3. Ye never grudged any one; ye were the instructors of others. And my desire is that those lessons shall hold good which as teachers ye enjoin. Only pray that I may have power within and without, so that I may not only say it but also desire it; that I may not only be called a Christian, but also be found one. For if I shall be found so, then can I also be called one, and be faithful then, when I am no more visible to the world. Nothing visible is good. For our God Jesus Christ, being in the Father, is the more plainly visible. The Work is not of persuasiveness, but Christianity is a thing of might, whensoever it is hated by the world.

4. I write to all the churches, and I bid all men know, that of my own free will I die for God, unless ye should hinder me. I exhort

you, be ye not an unseasonable kindness to me. Let me be given to the wild beasts, for through them I can attain unto God. I am God's wheat, and I am ground by the teeth of wild beasts that I may be found pure bread [of Christ]. Rather entice the wild beasts, that they may become my sepulchre and may leave no part of my body behind, so that I may not, when I am fallen asleep, be burdensome to any one. Then shall I be truly a disciple of Jesus Christ, when the world shall not so much as see my body. Supplicate the Lord for me, that through these instruments I may be found a sacrifice to God. I do not enjoin you, as Peter and Paul did. They were Apostles, I am a convict; they were free, but I am a slave to this very hour. Yet if I shall suffer, then am I a freed-man of Jesus Christ, and I shall rise free in Him. Now I am learning in my bonds to put away every desire.

5. From Syria even unto Rome I fight with wild beasts, by land and sea, by night and by day, being bound amidst ten leopards, even a company of soldiers, who only wax worse when they are kindly treated. Howbeit through their wrong doings I become more completely a disciple; *yet am I not hereby justified.* May I have joy of the beasts that have been prepared for me; and I pray that I may find them prompt; nay I will entice them that they may devour me promptly, not as they have done to some, refusing to touch them through fear. Yea though of themselves they should not be willing while I am ready, I myself will force them to it. Bear with me. I know what is expedient for me. Now am I beginning to be a disciple. May naught of things visible and things invisible envy me; that I may attain unto Jesus Christ. Come fire and cross and grapplings with wild beasts, [cuttings and manglings,] wrenching of bones, hacking of limbs, crushings of my whole body, come cruel tortures of the devil to assail me. Only be it mine to attain unto Jesus Christ.

6. The farthest bounds of the universe shall profit me nothing, neither the kingdoms of this world. It is good for me to die for Jesus Christ rather than to reign over the farthest bounds of the earth. Him I seek, who died on our behalf; Him I desire, who rose again [for our sake]. The pangs of a new birth are upon me. Bear with me, brethren. Do not hinder me from living; do not desire my death. Bestow not on the world one who desireth to be God's, neither allure him with material things. Suffer me to receive the pure light. When I am come thither, then shall I be a man. Permit me to be an imitator of the passion of my God. If any man hath Him within himself,

let him understand what I desire, and let him have fellow-feeling with me, for he knoweth the things which straiten me.

7. The prince of this world would fain tear me in pieces and corrupt my mind to Godward. Let not any of you therefore who are near abet him. Rather stand ye on my side, that is on God's side. Speak not of Jesus Christ and withal desire the world. Let not envy have a home in you. Even though I myself, when I am with you, should beseech you, obey me not; but rather give credence to these things which I write to you. [For] I write to you in the midst of life, yet lusting after death. My lust hath been crucified, and there is no fire of material longing in me, but only water living †and speaking† in me, saying within me, Come to the Father. I have no delight in the food of corruption or in the delights of this life. I desire the bread of God, which is the flesh of Christ who was of the seed of David; and for a draught I desire His blood, which is love incorruptible.

8. I desire no longer to live after the manner of men; and this shall be, if ye desire it. Desire ye, that ye yourselves also may be desired. In a brief letter I beseech you; believe me. And Jesus Christ shall make manifest unto you these things, that I speak the truth—Jesus Christ, the unerring mouth in whom the Father hath spoken [truly]. Entreat ye for me, that I may attain [through the Holy Spirit]. I write not unto you after the flesh, but after the mind of God. If I shall suffer, it was your desire; if I shall be rejected, it was your hatred.

9. Remember in your prayers the church which is in Syria, which hath God for its shepherd in my stead. Jesus Christ alone shall be its bishop—He and your love. But for myself I am ashamed to be called one of them; for neither am I worthy, being the very last of them and an untimely birth: but I have found mercy that I should be some one, if so be I shall attain unto God. My spirit saluteth you, and the love of the churches which received me in the name of Jesus Christ, not as a mere wayfarer: for even those churches which did not lie on my route after the flesh went before me from city to city.

10. Now I write these things to you from Smyrna by the hand of the Ephesians who are worthy of all felicitation. And Crocus also, a name very dear to me, is with me, with many others besides.

As touching those who went before me from Syria to Rome unto the glory of God, I believe that ye have received instructions; whom also apprise that I am near; for they all are worthy of God and of you, and it becometh you to refresh them in all things. These things I write to you on the 9th before the Kalends of September. Fare ye well unto the end in the patient waiting for Jesus Christ.

5

TO THE PHILADELPHIANS

IGNATIUS, who is also Theophorus, to the church of God the Father and of Jesus Christ, which is in Philadelphia of Asia, which hath found mercy and is firmly established in the concord of God and rejoiceth in the passion of our Lord and in His resurrection without wavering, being fully assured in all mercy; which church I salute in the blood of Jesus Christ, that is eternal and abiding joy; more especially if they be at one with the bishop and the presbyters who are with him, and with the deacons that have been appointed according to the mind of Jesus Christ, whom after His own will He confirmed and established by His Holy Spirit.

1. This your bishop I have found to hold the ministry which pertaineth to the common weal, not of himself or through men, nor yet for vain glory, but in the love of God the Father and the Lord Jesus Christ. And I am amazed at his forbearance; whose silence is more powerful than others' speech. For he is attuned in harmony with the commandments, as a lyre with its strings. Wherefore my soul blesseth his godly mind, for I have found that it is virtuous and perfect —even the imperturbable and calm temper which he hath, while living in all godly forbearance.

2. As children therefore [of the light] of the truth, shun division and wrong doctrines; and where the shepherd is, there follow ye as sheep. For many specious wolves with baneful delights lead captive the runners in God's race; but, where ye are at one, they will find no place.

3. Abstain from noxious herbs, which are not the husbandry of Jesus Christ, because they are not the planting of the Father. Not that I have found division among you, but filtering. For as many as are of God and of Jesus Christ, they are with the bishop; and as many as shall repent and enter into the unity of the Church, these also

shall be of God, that they may be living after Jesus Christ. Be not deceived, my brethren. If any man followeth one that maketh a schism, *he doth not inherit the kingdom of God.* If any man walketh in strange doctrine, he hath no fellowship with the passion.

4. Be ye careful therefore to observe one eucharist (for there is one flesh of our Lord Jesus Christ and one cup unto union in His blood; there is one altar, as there is one bishop, together with the presbytery and the deacons my fellow-servants), that whatsoever ye do, ye may do it after God.

5. My brethren, my heart overfloweth altogether in love towards you; and rejoicing above measure I watch over your safety; yet not I, but Jesus Christ, wearing whose bonds I am the more afraid, because I am not yet perfected. But your prayer will make me perfect [unto God], that I may attain unto the inheritance wherein I have found mercy, taking refuge in the Gospel as the flesh of Jesus and in the Apostles as the presbytery of the Church. Yea, and we love the prophets also, because they too pointed to the Gospel in their preaching and set their hope on Him and awaited Him; in whom also having faith they were saved in the unity of Jesus Christ, being worthy of all love and admiration as holy men, approved of Jesus Christ and numbered together in the Gospel of our common hope.

6. But if any one propound Judaism unto you, hear him not: for it is better to hear Christianity from a man who is circumcised than Judaism from one uncircumcised. But if either the one or the other speak not concerning Jesus Christ, I look on them as tombstones and graves of the dead, whereon are inscribed only the names of men. Shun ye therefore the wicked arts and plottings of the prince of this world, lest haply ye be crushed by his devices, and wax weak in your love. But assemble yourselves all together with undivided heart. And I give thanks to my God, that I have a good conscience in my dealings with you, and no man can boast either in secret or openly, that I was burdensome to any one in small things or in great. Yea and for all among whom I spoke, it is my prayer that they may not turn it into a testimony against themselves.

7. For even though certain persons desired to deceive me after the flesh, yet the spirit is not deceived, being from God; for *it knoweth whence it cometh and where it goeth,* and it searcheth out the hidden things. I cried out, when I was among you; I spake with a loud voice, with God's own voice, Give ye heed to the bishop and the

presbytery and deacons. Howbeit there were those who suspected me of saying this, because I knew beforehand of the division of certain persons. But He in whom I am bound is my witness that I learned it not from flesh of man; it was the preaching of the Spirit who spake on this wise; Do nothing without the bishop; keep your flesh as a temple of God; cherish union ; shun divisions; be imitators of Jesus Christ, as He Himself also was of His Father.

8. I therefore did my own part, as a man composed unto union. But where there is division and anger, there God abideth not. Now the Lord forgiveth all men when they repent, if repenting they return to the unity of God and to the council of the bishop. I have faith in the grace of Jesus Christ, who shall strike off every fetter from you; and I entreat you, Do ye nothing in a spirit of factiousness but after the teaching of Christ. For I heard certain persons saying, If I find it not in the charters, I believe it not in the Gospel. And when I said to them, It is written, they answered me That is the question. But as for me, my charter is Jesus Christ, the inviolable charter is His cross and His death and His resurrection, and faith through Him ; wherein I desire to be justified through your prayers.

9. The priests likewise were good, but better is the High-priest to whom is committed the holy of holies ; for to Him alone are committed the hidden things of God; He Himself being the door of the Father, through which Abraham and Isaac and Jacob enter in, and the Prophets and the Apostles and the whole Church; all these things combine in the unity of God. But the Gospel hath a singular preeminence in the advent of the Saviour, even our Lord Jesus Christ, and His passion and resurrection. For the beloved Prophets in their preaching pointed to Him ; but the Gospel is the completion of immortality. All things together are good, if ye believe through love.

10. Seeing that in answer to your prayer and to the tender sympathy which ye have in Christ Jesus, it hath been reported to me that the church which is in Antioch of Syria hath peace, it is becoming for you, as a church of God, to appoint a deacon to go thither as God's ambassador, that he may congratulate them when they are assembled together, and may glorify the Name. Blessed in Jesus Christ is he that shall be counted worthy of such a ministration ; and ye yourselves shall be glorified. Now if ye desire it, it is not impossible for you to do this for the name of God ; even as the churches which are nearest have sent bishops, and others presbyters and deacons.

11. But as touching Philo the deacon from Cilicia, a man of good report, who now also ministereth to me in the word of God, together with Rhaius Agathopus, an elect one who followeth me from Syria, having bidden farewell to this present life; the same who also bear witness to you—and I myself thank God on your behalf, because ye received them, as I trust the Lord will receive you. But may those who treated them with dishonour be redeemed through the grace of Jesus Christ. The love of the brethren which are in Troas saluteth you; from whence also I write to you by the hand of Burrhus, who was sent with me by the Ephesians and Smyrnæans as a mark of honour. The Lord shall honour them, even Jesus Christ, on whom their hope is set in flesh and soul and spirit, by faith, by love, by concord. Fare ye well in Christ Jesus our common hope.

6

TO THE SMYRNÆANS

IGNATIUS, who is also Theophorus, to the church of God the Father and of Jesus Christ the Beloved, which hath been mercifully endowed with every grace, being filled with faith and love and lacking in no grace, most reverend and bearing holy treasures; to the church which is in Smyrna of Asia, in a blameless spirit and in the word of God abundant greeting.

1. I give glory to Jesus Christ the God who bestowed such wisdom upon you; for I have perceived that ye are established in faith immovable, being as it were nailed on the cross of the Lord Jesus Christ, in flesh and in spirit, and firmly grounded in love in the blood of Christ, fully persuaded as touching our Lord that He is truly of the race of David according to the flesh, but Son of God by the Divine will and power, truly born of a virgin and baptized by John that *all righteousness might be fulfilled* by Him, truly nailed up in the flesh for our sakes under Pontius Pilate and Herod the tetrarch (of which fruit are we—that is, of His most blessed passion); that *He might set up an ensign* unto all the ages through His resurrection, for His saints and faithful people, whether among Jews or among Gentiles, in one body of His Church.

2. For He suffered all these things for our sakes [that we might be saved]; and He suffered truly, as also He raised Himself truly; not as

certain unbelievers say, that He suffered in semblance, being themselves mere semblance. And according as their opinions are, so shall it happen to them, for they are without body and demon-like.

3. For I know and believe that He was in the flesh even after the resurrection; and when He came to Peter and his company, He said to them, *Lay hold and handle me, and see that I am not a demon without body.* And straightway they touched Him, and they believed, being joined unto His flesh and His blood. Wherefore also they despised death, nay they were found superior to death. And after His resurrection He [both] ate with them and drank with them as one in the flesh, though spiritually He was united with the Father.

4. But these things I warn you, dearly beloved, knowing that ye yourselves are so minded. Howbeit I watch over you betimes to protect you from wild beasts in human form—men whom not only should ye not receive, but, if it were possible, not so much as meet [them]; only pray ye for them, if haply they may repent. This indeed is difficult, but Jesus Christ, our true life, hath power over it. For if these things were done by our Lord in semblance, then am I also a prisoner in semblance. And why then have I delivered myself over to death, unto fire, unto sword, unto wild beasts? But near to the sword, near to God; in company with wild beasts, in company with God. Only let it be in the name of Jesus Christ, so that we may suffer together with Him. I endure all things, seeing that He Himself enableth me, who is perfect Man.

5. But certain persons ignorantly deny Him, or rather have been denied by Him, being advocates of death rather than of the truth; and they have not been persuaded by the prophecies nor by the law of Moses, nay nor even to this very hour by the Gospel, nor by the sufferings of each of us severally; for they are of the same mind also concerning us. For what profit is it [to me], if a man praiseth me, but blasphemeth my Lord, not confessing that He was a bearer of flesh? Yet he that affirmeth not this, doth thereby deny Him altogether, being himself a bearer of a corpse. But their names, being unbelievers, I have not thought fit to record in writing; nay, far be it from me even to remember them, until they repent and return to the passion, which is our resurrection.

6. Let no man be deceived. Even the heavenly beings and the glory of the angels and the rulers visible and invisible, if they believe not in the blood of Christ [who is God], judgment awaiteth them also.

He that receiveth let him receive. Let not office puff up any man; for faith and love are all in all, and nothing is preferred before them. But mark ye those who hold strange doctrine touching the grace of Jesus Christ which came to us, how that they are contrary to the mind of God. They have no care for love, none for the widow, none for the orphan, none for the afflicted, none for the prisoner, none for the hungry or thirsty. They abstain from eucharist (thanksgiving) and prayer, because they allow not that the eucharist is the flesh of our Saviour Jesus Christ, which flesh suffered for our sins, and which the Father of His goodness raised up.

7. They therefore that gainsay the good gift of God perish by their questionings. But it were expedient for them to have love, that they may also rise again. It is therefore meet that ye should abstain from such, and not speak of them either privately or in public; but should give heed to the Prophets, and especially to the Gospel, wherein the passion is shown unto us and the resurrection is accomplished.

8. [But] shun divisions, as the beginning of evils. Do ye all follow your bishop, as Jesus Christ followed the Father, and the presbytery as the Apostles; and to the deacons pay respect, as to God's commandment. Let no man do aught of things pertaining to the Church apart from the bishop. Let that be held a valid eucharist which is under the bishop or one to whom he shall have committed it. Wheresoever the bishop shall appear, there let the people be; even as where Jesus may be, there is the universal Church. It is not lawful apart from the bishop either to baptize or to hold a love-feast; but whatsoever he shall approve, this is well-pleasing also to God; that everything which ye do may be sure and valid.

9. It is reasonable henceforth that we wake to soberness, while we have [still] time to repent and turn to God. It is good to recognise God and the bishop. He that honoureth the bishop is honoured of God; he that doeth aught without the knowledge of the bishop rendereth service to the devil. May all things therefore abound unto you in grace, for ye are worthy. Ye refreshed me in all things, and Jesus Christ shall refresh you. In my absence and in my presence ye cherished me. May God recompense you; for whose sake if ye endure all things, ye shall attain unto Him.

10. Philo and Rhaius Agathopus, who followed me in the cause of God, ye did well to receive as ministers of [Christ] God; who also give thanks to the Lord for you, because ye refreshed them in every

way. Nothing shall be lost to you. My spirit is devoted for you, as also are my bonds, which ye despised not, neither were ashamed of them. Nor shall He, who is perfect faithfulness, be ashamed of you, even Jesus Christ.

11. Your prayer sped forth unto the church which is in Antioch of Syria; whence coming a prisoner in most godly bonds I salute all men, though I am not worthy to belong to it, being the very last of them. By the Divine will was this vouchsafed to me, not of my own complicity, but by God's grace, which I pray may be given to me perfectly, that through your prayers I may attain unto God. Therefore that your work may be perfected both on earth and in heaven, it is meet that your church should appoint, for the honour of God, an ambassador of God that he may go as far as Syria and congratulate them because they are at peace, and have recovered their proper stature, and their proper bulk hath been restored to them. It seemed to me therefore a fitting thing that ye should send one of your own people with a letter, that he might join with them in giving glory for the calm which by God's will had overtaken them, and because they were already reaching a haven through your prayers. Seeing ye are perfect, let your counsels also be perfect; for if ye desire to do well, God is ready to grant the means.

12. The love of the brethren which are in Troas saluteth you; from whence also I write to you by the hand of Burrhus, whom ye sent with me jointly with the Ephesians your brethren. He hath refreshed me in all ways. And I would that all imitated him, for he is an ensample of the ministry of God. The Divine grace shall requite him in all things. I salute your godly bishop and your venerable presbytery [and] my fellow-servants the deacons, and all of you severally and in a body, in the name of Jesus Christ, and in His flesh and blood, in His passion and resurrection, which was both carnal and spiritual, in the unity of God and of yourselves. Grace to you, mercy, peace, patience, always.

13. I salute the households of my brethren with their wives and children, and the virgins who are called widows. I bid you farewell in the power of the Father. Philo, who is with me, saluteth you. I salute the household of Gavia, and I pray that she may be grounded in faith and love both of flesh and of spirit. I salute Alce, a name very dear to me, and Daphnus the incomparable, and Eutecnus, and all by name. Fare ye well in the grace of God.

7

TO S. POLYCARP

IGNATIUS, who is also Theophorus, unto Polycarp who is bishop of the church of the Smyrnæans or rather who hath for his bishop God the Father and Jesus Christ, abundant greeting.

1. Welcoming thy godly mind which is grounded as it were on an immovable rock, I give exceeding glory that it hath been vouchsafed me to see thy blameless face, whereof I would fain have joy in God. I exhort thee in the grace wherewith thou art clothed to press forward in thy course and to exhort all men that they may be saved. Vindicate thine office in all diligence of flesh and of spirit. Have a care for union, than which there is nothing better. Bear all men, as the Lord also beareth thee. Suffer all men in love, as also thou doest. Give thyself to unceasing prayers. Ask for larger wisdom than thou hast. Be watchful, and keep thy spirit from slumbering. Speak to each man severally after the manner of God. Bear the maladies of all, as a perfect athlete. Where there is more toil, there is much gain.

2. If thou lovest good scholars, this is not thankworthy in thee. Rather bring the more pestilent to submission by gentleness. All wounds are not healed by the same salve. Allay sharp pains by fomentations. *Be thou prudent as the serpent* in all things *and guileless* always *as the dove.* Therefore art thou made of flesh and spirit, that thou mayest humour the things which appear before thine eyes; and as for the invisible things, pray thou that they may be revealed unto thee; that thou mayest be lacking in nothing, but mayest abound in every spiritual gift. The season requireth thee, as pilots require winds or as a storm-tossed mariner a haven, that it may attain unto God. Be sober, as God's athlete. The prize is incorruption and life eternal, concerning which thou also art persuaded. In all things I am devoted to thee—I and my bonds which thou didst cherish.

3. Let not those that seem to be plausible and yet teach strange doctrine dismay thee. Stand thou firm, as an anvil when it is smitten. It is the part of a great athlete to receive blows and be victorious. But especially must we for God's sake endure all things, that He also may endure us. Be thou more diligent than thou art. Mark the seasons.

Await Him that is above every season, the Eternal, the Invisible, who became visible for our sake, the Impalpable, the Impassible, who suffered for our sake, who endured in all ways for our sake.

4. Let not widows be neglected. After the Lord be thou their protector. Let nothing be done without thy consent; neither do thou anything without the consent of God, as indeed thou doest not. Be stedfast. Let meetings be held more frequently. Seek out all men by name. Despise not slaves, whether men or women. Yet let not these again be puffed up, but let them serve the more faithfully to the glory of God, that they may obtain a better freedom from God. Let them not desire to be set free at the public cost, lest they be found slaves of lust.

5. Flee evil arts, or rather hold thou discourse about these. Tell my sisters to love the Lord and to be content with their husbands in flesh and in spirit. In like manner also charge my brothers in the name of Jesus Christ to love their wives, *as the Lord loved the Church.* If any one is able to abide in chastity to the honour of the flesh of the Lord, let him so abide without boasting. If he boast, he is lost; and if it be known beyond the bishop, he is polluted. It becometh men and women too, when they marry, to unite themselves with the consent of the bishop, that the marriage may be after the Lord and not after concupiscence. Let all things be done to the honour of God.

6. Give ye heed to the bishop, that God also may give heed to you. I am devoted to those who are subject to the bishop, the presbyters, the deacons. May it be granted me to have my portion with them in the presence of God. Toil together one with another, struggle together, run together, suffer together, lie down together, rise up together, as God's stewards and assessors and ministers. Please the Captain in whose army ye serve, from whom also ye will receive your pay. Let none of you be found a deserter. Let your baptism abide with you as your shield; your faith as your helmet; your love as your spear; your patience as your body armour. Let your works be your deposits, that ye may receive your assets due to you. Be ye therefore long-suffering one with another in gentleness, as God is with you. May I have joy of you always.

7. Seeing that the church which is in Antioch of Syria hath peace, as it hath been reported to me, through your prayers, I myself also have been the more comforted since God hath banished my care; if so be I may through suffering attain unto God, that I may be found a disciple

through your intercession. It becometh thee, most blessed Polycarp, to call together a godly council and to elect some one among you who is very dear to you and zealous also, who shall be fit to bear the name of God's courier—to appoint him, I say, that he may go to Syria and glorify your zealous love unto the glory of God. A Christian hath no authority over himself, but giveth his time to God. This is God's work, and yours also, when ye shall complete it: for I trust in the Divine grace, that ye are ready for an act of well-doing which is meet for God. Knowing the fervour of your sincerity, I have exhorted you in a short letter.

8. Since I have not been able to write to all the churches, by reason of my sailing suddenly from Troas to Neapolis, as the Divine will enjoineth, thou shalt write to the churches in front, as one possessing the mind of God, to the intent that they also may do this same thing—let those who are able send messengers, and the rest letters by the persons who are sent by thee, that ye may be glorified by an ever memorable deed—for this is worthy of thee.

I salute all by name, and especially the wife of Epitropus with her whole household and her children's. I salute Attalus my beloved. I salute him that shall be appointed to go to Syria. Grace shall be with him always, and with Polycarp who sendeth him. I bid you farewell always in our God Jesus Christ, in whom abide ye in the unity and supervision of God. I salute Alce, a name very dear to me. Fare ye well in the Lord.

THE EPISTLE

OF

S. POLYCARP

THE EPISTLE OF S. POLYCARP

I

THE Epistle of Polycarp was written in reply to a communication from the Philippians. They had invited him to address words of exhortation to them (§ 3); they had requested him to forward by his own messenger the letter which they had addressed to the Syrian Church (§ 13); and they had asked him to send them any epistles of Ignatius which he might have in his hands (*ib.*).

This epistle is intimately connected with the letters and martyrdom of Ignatius himself. The Philippians had recently welcomed and escorted on their way certain saints who were in bonds (§ 1). From a later notice in the epistle it appears that Ignatius was one of these (§ 9). Two others besides are mentioned by name, Zosimus and Rufus (*ib.*). A not improbable conjecture makes these persons Bithynian Christians who had been sent by Pliny to Rome to be tried there and had joined Ignatius at Philippi. In this case they would be placed under the same escort with Ignatius, and proceed with him to Rome in the custody of the 'ten leopards' (Ign. *Rom.* 5). It is clear that Ignatius—probably by word of mouth—had given to the Philippians the same injunction which he gave to the churches generally (*Philad.* 10, *Smyrn.* 11, *Polyc.* 7), that they should send letters, and (where possible) representatives also, to congratulate the Church of Antioch on the restoration of peace. Hence the request of the Philippians, seconded by Ignatius himself, that Polycarp would forward their letter to Syria. It is plain likewise, that they had heard, either from Ignatius himself or from those about him, of the epistles which he had addressed to the Churches of Asia Minor, more especially to Smyrna. Hence their further petition that Polycarp would send them such of these letters as were in his possession. The visit of Ignatius had been recent—so recent indeed, that Polycarp, though he assumes that the saint has suffered martyrdom, is yet without any certain knowledge of the fact. He therefore asks the Philippians, who are some stages nearer to Rome than Smyrna, to communicate to him any information which they may have received respecting the saint and his companions (§ 13).

Beyond these references to Ignatius there is not much of personal matter in the letter. Polycarp refers to S. Paul's communications with the Philippians, both written and oral (§§ 3, 11). He mentions the fame of the Philippian Church in the primitive days of the Gospel, and he congratulates them on sustaining their early reputation (§§ 1, 11). Incidentally he states that the Philippians were converted to the Gospel before the Smyrnæans (§ 11)—a statement which entirely accords with the notices of the two churches in the New Testament.

The fair fame of the Philippian Church however had been sullied by the sin of one unworthy couple. Valens and his wife—the Ananias and Sapphira of the Philippian community—had been guilty of some act of greed, perhaps of fraud and dishonesty. Valens was one of their presbyters, and thus the church was more directly responsible for his crime. Polycarp expresses himself much grieved. Though the incident itself is only mentioned in one passage, it has plainly made a deep impression on him. The sin of avarice is denounced again and again in the body of the letter (§§ 2, 4, 6, 11).

The letter is sent by the hand of one Crescens. The sister of Crescens also, who purposes visiting Philippi, is commended to them (§ 14).

2

The authorities for the text are as follows.

(1) GREEK MANUSCRIPTS (G). These are nine in number (*Vaticanus* 859 [v], *Ottobonianus* 348 [o], *Florentinus Laur.* vii. 21 [f], *Parisiensis Graec.* 937 [p], *Casanatensis* G. v. 14 [c], *Theatinus* [t], *Neapolitanus Mus. Nat.* II. A. 17 [n], *Salmasianus* [s], *Andrius* [a]), and all belong to the same family, as appears from the fact that the Epistle of Polycarp runs on continuously into the Epistle of Barnabas without any break, the mutilated ending of Polycarp § 9 ἀποθανόντα καὶ δι' ἡμᾶς ὑπὸ being

followed by the mutilated beginning of Barnabas § 5 τὸν λαὸν τὸν καινὸν κ.τ.λ. Within this family however the MSS fall into two subdivisions : (1) *vopf*, all MSS in which the Epistle of Polycarp is attached
to the pseudo-Ignatian letters ; and (2) *ctna* (to which we may probably
add *s*), where it stands alone. In the first subdivision, *opf* have no
independent authority, being derived directly or indirectly from *v*. Of
the two subdivisions the former is slightly superior to the latter.

(2) LATIN VERSION (L). In the earlier part of the epistle this
version is sometimes useful for correcting the text of the extant Greek
MSS ; for, though very paraphrastic, it was made from an older form of
the Greek than these. But the two are closely allied, as appears from
the fact that this version is always found in connexion with the Latin
of the pseudo-Ignatian letters and seems to have been translated from
the same volume which contained them. For the latter part of the
epistle, from § 10 onward, it is the sole authority; with the exception
of portions of § 12, which are preserved in Syriac in passages of
Timotheus and Severus or elsewhere, and nearly the whole of § 13,
which is given by Eusebius in his *Ecclesiastical History*. The MSS of
which collations have been made for this part either by myself or by
others are nine in number (*Reginensis* 81 [r], *Trecensis* 412 [t], *Parisiensis* 1639, formerly *Colbertinus* 1039 [c], *Bruxellensis* 5510 [b], *Oxon.
Balliolensis* 229 [o], *Palatinus* 150 [p], *Florentinus Laur.* xxiii. 20 [f],
Vindobonensis 1068 [v], *Oxon. Magdalenensis* 78 [m]).

It will have been seen that, so far as regards the Greek and Latin
MSS, the Epistle of Polycarp is closely connected with the Long Recension of the Ignatian Epistles. This fact, if it had stood by itself, would
have thrown some discredit on the integrity of the text. It might have
been suspected that the same hand which interpolated the Ignatian
Epistles had tampered with this also. But the internal evidence, and
especially the allusiveness of the references to the Ignatian Epistles, is
decisive in favour of its genuineness. As regards external evidence,
not only does Irenæus, a pupil of Polycarp, allude to 'the very adequate
epistle of Polycarp written to the Philippians,' but the quotations of
Eusebius, Timotheus, and Severus, with the other Syriac fragments, are
a highly important testimony. They show that, wherever we have
opportunity of testing the text of the Greek and Latin copies, its general
integrity is vindicated.

ΠΡΟΣ ΦΙΛΙΠΠΗΣΙΟΥΣ

ΠΟΛΥΚΑΡΠΟΣ καὶ οἱ σὺν αὐτῷ πρεσβύτεροι τῇ ἐκκλησίᾳ τοῦ Θεοῦ τῇ παροικούσῃ Φιλίππους· ἔλεος ὑμῖν καὶ εἰρήνη παρὰ Θεοῦ παντοκράτορος καὶ Ἰησοῦ Χριστοῦ τοῦ σωτῆρος ἡμῶν πληθυνθείη.

I. Συνεχάρην ὑμῖν μεγάλως ἐν Κυρίῳ ἡμῶν Ἰησοῦ Χριστῷ, δεξαμένοις τὰ μιμήματα τῆς ἀληθοῦς ἀγάπης καὶ προπέμψασιν, ὡς ἐπέβαλεν ὑμῖν, τοὺς ἐνειλημένους τοῖς ἁγιοπρεπέσιν δεσμοῖς, ἅτινά ἐστιν διαδήματα τῶν ἀληθῶς ὑπὸ Θεοῦ καὶ τοῦ Κυρίου ἡμῶν ἐκλελεγμένων· 2. καὶ ὅτι ἡ βεβαία τῆς πίστεως ὑμῶν ῥίζα, ἐξ ἀρχαίων καταγγελλομένη χρόνων, μέχρι νῦν διαμένει καὶ καρποφορεῖ εἰς τὸν Κύριον ἡμῶν Ἰησοῦν Χριστόν, ὃς ὑπέμεινεν ὑπὲρ τῶν ἁμαρτιῶν ἡμῶν ἕως θανάτου καταντῆσαι, ὃν ἬΓΕΙΡΕΝ ὁ Θεὸς ΛΎϹΑϹ ΤᾺϹ ὠΔῖΝΑϹ ΤΟΥ̑ ᾅΔΟΥ· 3. εἰς ὃΝ ΟΥ̓Κ ἰΔΌΝΤΕϹ ΠΙϹΤΕΎΕΤΕ χαρᾷ ἀνεκλαλήτῳ ΚΑὶ ΔΕΔΟΖΑϹΜΕΝΗ εἰς ἣν πολλοὶ ἐπιθυμοῦσιν εἰσελθεῖν, εἰΔΌΤΕϹ ὅΤΙ χΆΡΙΤΪ ἐϹΤΕ ϹΕϹΩϹΜΕΝΟΙ, ΟΥ̓Κ ἐΖ ἔΡΓΩΝ, ἀλλὰ θελήματι Θεοῦ διὰ Ἰησοῦ Χριστοῦ.

II. Διὸ ἀΝΑΖΩϹΆΜΕΝΟΙ ΤᾺϹ ὀϹΦΎΑϹ ΔΟΥΛΕΎϹΑΤΕ τῷ Θεῷ ἐΝ φόβῳ καὶ ἀληθείᾳ, ἀπολιπόντες τὴν κενὴν ματαιολογίαν καὶ τὴν τῶν πολλῶν πλάνην, ΠΙϹΤΕΎϹΑΝΤΕϹ εἰϹ ΤὸΝ ἐγείΡΑΝΤΑ ΤὸΝ ΚΎΡΙΟΝ ἡΜῺΝ Ἰ̈ΗϹΟΥ̑Ν ΧΡΙϹΤὸΝ ἐΚ ΝΕΚΡΩ̑Ν ΚΑὶ ΔόΝΤΑ ΑΥ̓ΤΩ̑ ΔόΖΑΝ καὶ θρόνον ἐκ δεξιῶν αὐτοῦ· ᾧ ὑπετάγη τὰ πάντα ἐπουράνια καὶ ἐπίγεια, ᾧ πᾶσα πνοὴ λατρεύει, ὃς ἔρχεται ΚΡΙΤῊϹ ΖΏΝΤΩΝ ΚΑὶ ΝΕΚΡΩ̑Ν, οὗ τὸ αἷμα ἐκζητήσει ὁ Θεὸς ἀπὸ τῶν ἀπειθούντων αὐτῷ. 2. ὁ δὲ ἐγείΡΑϹ αὐτὸν ἐκ νεκρῶν καὶ

Acts ii. 24.
I Pet. i. 8.
Eph. ii. 8,
9.
I Pet. i. 13.
Ps. ii. 11.
I Pet. i. 21.
Acts x. 42.
2 Cor. iv.
14.

ἡμᾶς ἐγερεῖ, ἐὰν ποιῶμεν αὐτοῦ τὸ θέλημα καὶ πορευώμεθα ἐν ταῖς ἐντολαῖς αὐτοῦ καὶ ἀγαπῶμεν ἃ ἠγάπησεν, ἀπεχόμενοι πάσης ἀδικίας, πλεονεξίας, φιλαργυρίας, καταλαλιᾶς, ψευδο- μαρτυρίας· ΜΗ ἀποΔιΔόντες κακὸν ἀντὶ κακοῦ ἢ λοιΔορίαν ἀντὶ 1 Pet. iii. 9, λοιΔορίας ἢ γρόνθον ἀντὶ γρόνθου ἢ κατάραν ἀντὶ κατάρας, 3. μνημονεύοντες δὲ ὧν εἶπεν ὁ Κύριος διδάσκων· ΜΗ κρίνετε, S.Matt.vii. ἵνα ΜΗ κριθῆτε· ἀφίετε, καὶ ἀφεθήσεται ὑμῖν· ἐλεᾶτε, ἵνα ἐλεη- S. Luke vi. θῆτε· ᾧ μέτρῳ μετρεῖτε, ἀντιμετρηθήσεται ὑμῖν· καὶ ὅτι Μακά- 36—38. S. Matt. v. ριοι οἱ πτωχοὶ καὶ οἱ Διωκόμενοι ἕνεκεν ΔικαιοσύνΗς, ὅτι αὐτῶν 3, 10. ἐστὶν Η Βασιλεία τοῦ Θεοῦ.

III. Ταῦτα, ἀδελφοί, οὐκ ἐμαυτῷ ἐπιτρέψας γράφω ὑμῖν περὶ τῆς δικαιοσύνης, ἀλλ᾽ ἐπεὶ ὑμεῖς προεπεκαλέσασθέ με. 2. οὔτε γὰρ ἐγὼ οὔτε ἄλλος ὅμοιος ἐμοὶ δύναται κατακολου- θῆσαι τῇ σοφίᾳ τοῦ μακαρίου καὶ ἐνδόξου Παύλου, ὃς γενό- μενος ἐν ὑμῖν κατὰ πρόσωπον τῶν τότε ἀνθρώπων ἐδίδαξεν ἀκριβῶς καὶ βεβαίως τὸν περὶ ἀληθείας λόγον, ὃς καὶ ἀπὼν ὑμῖν ἔγραψεν ἐπιστολάς, εἰς ἃς ἐὰν ἐγκύπτητε, δυνηθήσεσθε οἰκοδομεῖσθαι εἰς τὴν δοθεῖσαν ὑμῖν πίστιν· 3. ἥτις ἐστὶν Gal. iv. 26. μήτηρ πάντων ἡμῶν, ἐπακολουθούσης τῆς ἐλπίδος, προαγού- σης τῆς ἀγάπης τῆς εἰς Θεὸν καὶ Χριστὸν καὶ εἰς τὸν πλησίον. ἐὰν γάρ τις τούτων ἐντὸς ᾖ, πεπλήρωκεν ἐντολὴν δικαιοσύνης· ὁ γὰρ ἔχων ἀγάπην μακράν ἐστιν πάσης ἁμαρ- τίας.

IV. Ἀρχὴ Δὲ πάντων χαλεπῶν φιλαργυρία. εἰδότες οὖν 1 Tim. vi. ὅτι οὐΔὲν εἰσΗνέγκαμεν εἰς τὸν κόσμον, ἀλλ᾽ οὐΔὲ ἐξενεγκεῖν τι 7, 10. ἔχομεν, ὁπλισώμεθα τοῖς ὅπλοις τῆς δικαιοσύνης καὶ διδάξω- μεν ἑαυτοὺς πρῶτον πορεύεσθαι ἐν τῇ ἐντολῇ τοῦ Κυρίου· 2. ἔπειτα καὶ τὰς γυναῖκας ὑμῶν ἐν τῇ δοθείσῃ αὐταῖς πίστει καὶ ἀγάπῃ καὶ ἁγνείᾳ, στεργούσας τοὺς ἑαυτῶν ἄνδρας ἐν πάσῃ ἀληθείᾳ καὶ ἀγαπώσας πάντας ἐξ ἴσου ἐν πάσῃ ἐγκρα- τείᾳ, καὶ τὰ τέκνα παιδεύειν τὴν παιδείαν τοῦ φόβου τοῦ Θεοῦ· 3. τὰς χήρας σωφρονούσας περὶ τὴν τοῦ Κυρίου πίστιν, ἐντυγχανούσας ἀδιαλείπτως περὶ πάντων, μακρὰν οὔσας πάσης διαβολῆς, καταλαλιᾶς, ψευδομαρτυρίας, φιλαργυρίας,

καὶ παντὸς κακοῦ· γινωσκούσας ὅτι εἰσὶ θυσιαστήριον Θεοῦ,
καὶ ὅτι πάντα μωμοσκοπεῖται, καὶ λέληθεν αὐτὸν οὐδὲν οὔτε
1 Cor. xiv. λογισμῶν οὔτε ἐννοιῶν, οὔτε τι τῶν κρυπτῶν τῆς καρδίας.
25.
Gal. vi. 7.   V. Εἰδότες οὖν ὅτι Θεὸς οὐ μυκτηρίζεται, ὀφείλομεν ἀξίως
τῆς ἐντολῆς αὐτοῦ καὶ δόξης περιπατεῖν. 2. ὁμοίως διάκονοι
ἄμεμπτοι κατενώπιον αὐτοῦ τῆς δικαιοσύνης, ὡς Θεοῦ καὶ
Χριστοῦ διάκονοι, καὶ οὐκ ἀνθρώπων· μὴ διάβολοι, μὴ δί-
λογοι, ἀφιλάργυροι, ἐγκρατεῖς περὶ πάντα, εὔσπλαγχνοι,
ἐπιμελεῖς, πορευόμενοι κατὰ τὴν ἀλήθειαν τοῦ Κυρίου, ὃς
S. Mark ix. ἐγένετο διάκονος πάντων· ᾧ ἐὰν εὐαρεστήσωμεν ἐν τῷ νῦν
35·   αἰῶνι, ἀποληψόμεθα καὶ τὸν μέλλοντα, καθὼς ὑπέσχετο
ἡμῖν ἐγεῖραι ἡμᾶς ἐκ νεκρῶν καὶ ὅτι, ἐὰν πολιτευσώμεθα
2 Tim. ii. ἀξίως αὐτοῦ, καὶ συμβασιλεύσομεν αὐτῷ, εἴγε πιστεύομεν.
12.   3. ὁμοίως καὶ νεώτεροι ἄμεμπτοι ἐν πᾶσιν, πρὸ παντὸς προνοοῦντες ἁγνείας καὶ χαλιναγωγοῦντες ἑαυτοὺς ἀπὸ παντὸς
κακοῦ. καλὸν γὰρ τὸ ἀνακόπτεσθαι ἀπὸ τῶν ἐπιθυμιῶν ἐν
1 Pet. ii. 11. τῷ κόσμῳ, ὅτι πᾶσα ἐπιθυμία κατὰ τοῦ πνεύματος στρατεύεται,
Gal. v. 17.
1 Cor. vi. καὶ οὔτε πόρνοι οὔτε μαλακοὶ οὔτε ἀρσενοκοῖται βασιλείαν Θεοῦ
9, 10.   κληρονομήσουσιν, οὔτε οἱ ποιοῦντες τὰ ἄτοπα. διὸ δέον ἀπέχεσθαι ἀπὸ πάντων τούτων, ὑποτασσομένους τοῖς πρεσβυτέροις καὶ διακόνοις ὡς Θεῷ καὶ Χριστῷ· τὰς παρθένους ἐν
ἀμώμῳ καὶ ἁγνῇ συνειδήσει περιπατεῖν.

VI. Καὶ οἱ πρεσβύτεροι δὲ εὔσπλαγχνοι, εἰς πάντας
Ezek. ἐλεήμονες, ἐπιστρέφοντες τὰ ἀποπεπλανημένα, ἐπισκεπτόμενοι
xxxiv. 4. πάντας ἀσθενεῖς, μὴ ἀμελοῦντες χήρας ἢ ὀρφανοῦ ἢ πένητος,
2 Cor. viii. ἀλλὰ προνοοῦντες ἀεὶ τοῦ καλοῦ ἐνώπιον Θεοῦ καὶ ἀνθρώπων,
21.   ἀπεχόμενοι πάσης ὀργῆς, προσωποληψίας, κρίσεως ἀδίκου,
μακρὰν ὄντες πάσης φιλαργυρίας, μὴ ταχέως πιστεύοντες
κατά τινος, μὴ ἀπότομοι ἐν κρίσει, εἰδότες ὅτι πάντες ὀφει-
λέται ἐσμὲν ἁμαρτίας. 2. εἰ οὖν δεόμεθα τοῦ Κυρίου ἵνα
ἡμῖν ἀφῇ, ὀφείλομεν καὶ ἡμεῖς ἀφιέναι· ἀπέναντι γὰρ τῶν
Rom. xiv. τοῦ Κυρίου καὶ Θεοῦ ἐσμὲν ὀφθαλμῶν, καὶ πάντας δεῖ παρα-
10, 12.   στῆναι τῷ βήματι τοῦ Χριστοῦ, καὶ ἕκαστον ὑπὲρ ἑαυτοῦ λόγον
δοῦναι. 3. οὕτως οὖν δουλεύσωμεν αὐτῷ μετὰ φόβου καὶ

πάσης εὐλαβείας, καθὼς αὐτὸς ἐνετείλατο καὶ οἱ εὐαγγελισάμενοι ἡμᾶς ἀπόστολοι καὶ οἱ προφῆται οἱ προκηρύξαντες
τὴν ἔλευσιν τοῦ Κυρίου ἡμῶν, ζηλωταὶ περὶ τὸ καλόν, ἀπεχόμενοι τῶν σκανδάλων καὶ τῶν ψευδαδέλφων καὶ τῶν ἐν
ὑποκρίσει φερόντων τὸ ὄνομα τοῦ Κυρίου, οἵτινες ἀποπλα-
νῶσι κενοὺς ἀνθρώπους. VII. Πᾶς γάρ, ὃс ἂν μὴ ὁμολογῇ Ἰησοῦν Χριστὸν ἐν сαρκὶ 1 John iv.
ἐληλυθέναι, ἀντίχριστός ἐστιν. καὶ ὃς ἂν μὴ ὁμολογῇ τὸ μαρ- 2, 3.
τύριον τοῦ σταυροῦ, ἐκ τοῦ διαβόλου ἐστίν· καὶ ὃς ἂν μεθο-
δεύῃ τὰ λόγια τοῦ Κυρίου πρὸς τὰς ἰδίας ἐπιθυμίας, καὶ
λέγει μήτε ἀνάστασιν μήτε κρίσιν, οὗτος πρωτότοκός ἐστι
τοῦ Σατανᾶ. 2. διὸ ἀπολιπόντες τὴν ματαιότητα τῶν πολλῶν καὶ τὰς ψευδοδιδασκαλίας ἐπὶ τὸν ἐξ ἀρχῆς ἡμῖν παραδοθέντα λόγον ἐπιστρέψωμεν, νήφοντες πρὸс τὰс εὐχὰс καὶ 1 Pet. iv. 7.
προσκαρτεροῦντες νηστείαις, δεήσεσιν αἰτούμενοι τὸν παντεπόπτην Θεὸν μὴ εἰсενεγκεῖν ἡμᾶс εἰс πειρασμόν, καθὼς εἶπεν S. Matt. vi.
ὁ Κύριος· τὸ μὲν πνεῦμα πρόθυμον, ἡ δὲ сὰρξ ἀσθενής. 13.
S. Matt.
VIII. Ἀδιαλείπτως οὖν προσκαρτερῶμεν τῇ ἐλπίδι xxvi. 41.
S. Mark
ἡμῶν καὶ τῷ ἀρραβῶνι τῆς δικαιοσύνης ἡμῶν, ὅς ἐστι xiv. 38.
Χριστὸς Ἰησοῦς, ὃс ἀνήνεγκεν ἡμῶν τὰс ἁμαρτίαс τῷ ἰδίῳ 1 Pet. ii.
сώματι ἐπὶ τὸ ξύλον, ὃс ἁμαρτίαν οὐκ ἐποίηсεν, οὐδὲ εὑρέθη 22, 24.
δόλος ἐν τῷ στόματι αὐτοῦ· ἀλλὰ δι' ἡμᾶς, ἵνα ζήσωμεν ἐν
αὐτῷ, πάντα ὑπέμεινεν. 2. μιμηταὶ οὖν γενώμεθα τῆς ὑπομονῆς [αὐτοῦ]· καὶ ἐὰν πάσχωμεν διὰ τὸ ὄνομα αὐτοῦ, δοξά-
ζωμεν αὐτόν. τοῦτον γὰρ ἡμῖν τὸν ὑπογραμμὸν ἔθηκε δι'
ἑαυτοῦ, καὶ ἡμεῖς τοῦτο ἐπιστεύσαμεν.

IX. Παρακαλῶ οὖν πάντας ὑμᾶς πειθαρχεῖν τῷ λόγῳ
τῆς δικαιοσύνης καὶ ἀσκεῖν πᾶσαν ὑπομονήν, ἣν καὶ εἴδατε
κατ' ὀφθαλμοὺς οὐ μόνον ἐν τοῖς μακαρίοις Ἰγνατίῳ καὶ
Ζωσίμῳ καὶ Ῥούφῳ, ἀλλὰ καὶ ἐν ἄλλοις τοῖς ἐξ ὑμῶν καὶ ἐν
αὐτῷ Παύλῳ καὶ τοῖς λοιποῖς ἀποστόλοις· 2. πεπεισμένους,
ὅτι οὗτοι πάντες οὐκ εἰс κενὸν ἔδραμον, ἀλλ' ἐν πίστει καὶ Phil. ii. 16.
δικαιοσύνῃ, καὶ ὅτι εἰς τὸν ὀφειλόμενον αὐτοῖς τόπον εἰσὶ
παρὰ τῷ Κυρίῳ, ᾧ καὶ συνέπαθον. οὐ γὰρ τὸν νῦν ἠγάπη- 2 Tim. iv.
10.

cαn αἰῶnα, ἀλλὰ τὸν ὑπὲρ ἡμῶν ἀποθανόντα καὶ δι' ἡμᾶς ὑπὸ τοῦ Θεοῦ ἀναστάντα.

1 Cor. xv. 58.
1 Pet. ii.
17.
Rom. xii.
10.
Prov. iii. 28.
Tobit iv. 10.
Eph. v. 21.
1 Pet. ii. 12.

X. In his ergo state et Domini exemplar sequimini, *firmi in fide* et *immutabiles, fraternitatis amatores diligentes invicem*, in veritate sociati, mansuetudinem Domini *alterutri praestolantes*, nullum despicientes. 2. *Cum potestis bene- facere*, nolite differre, quia *Eleemosyna de morte liberat. Omnes vobis invicem subiecti estote, conversationem vestram* irreprehensibilem *habentes in gentibus, ut ex bonis operibus vestris* et vos laudem accipiatis et Dominus in vobis non

Ign. *Trall.* 8.

blasphemetur. 3. *Vae* autem *per quem nomen Domini blasphematur.* Sobrietatem ergo docete omnes, in qua et vos conversamini.

XI. Nimis contristatus sum pro Valente, qui presbyter factus est aliquando apud vos, quod sic ignoret is locum qui datus est ei. Moneo itaque vos, ut abstineatis vos ab avaritia et sitis casti veraces. Abstinete vos ab omni malo. 2. Qui autem non potest se in his gubernare, quo- modo alii pronuntiat hoc? Si quis non se abstinuerit ab avaritia, ab idololatria coinquinabitur, et tanquam inter

Jer. v. 4.
1 Cor. vi. 2.

gentes iudicabitur, qui *ignorant iudicium Domini. Aut nescimus, quia sancti mundum iudicabunt?* sicut Paulus docet. 3. Ego autem nihil tale sensi in vobis vel audivi, in quibus laboravit beatus Paulus, qui estis in principio

2 Cor. iii. 2.
2 Thess. i. 4.

epistulae eius : *de vobis* etenim *gloriatur in* omnibus *ecclesiis,* quae solae tunc Dominum cognoverant ; nos autem non- dum cognoveramus. 4. Valde ergo, fratres, contristor pro illo et pro coniuge eius, quibus det Dominus poenitentiam

2 Thess. iii. 15.

veram. Sobrii ergo estote et vos in hoc; *et non sicut inimicos tales existimetis,* sed sicut passibilia membra et errantia eos revocate, ut omnium vestrum corpus salvetis. Hoc enim agentes, vos ipsos aedificatis.

XII. Confido enim vos bene exercitatos esse in sacris literis, et nihil vos latet ; mihi autem non est concessum.

Modo, ut his scripturis dictum est, *Irascimini et nolite* Ps. iv. 5.
peccare, et *Sol non occidat super iracundiam vestram.* Eph.iv.26.
Beatus, qui meminerit; quod ego credo esse in vobis.
2. Deus autem et pater Domini nostri Jesu Christi et ipse
sempiternus pontifex, Dei filius Jesus Christus, aedificet
vos in fide et veritate et in omni mansuetudine et sine
iracundia et in patientia et in longanimitate et tolerantia
et castitate; et det vobis sortem et partem inter sanctos
suos, et nobis vobiscum, et omnibus qui sunt sub caelo,
qui credituri sunt in Dominum nostrum et Deum Jesum
Christum et in ipsius patrem *qui resuscitavit eum a mortuis.* Gal. i. 1.
3. *Pro omnibus sanctis orate.* Orate etiam *pro regibus* et $\begin{smallmatrix}\text{Eph.vi.18.}\\\text{1 Tim.ii.1.}\end{smallmatrix}$
potestatibus et principibus atque *pro persequentibus* et S. Matt. v.
odientibus *vos* et pro *inimicis crucis*, ut fructus vester Phil.iii.18.
manifestus sit in omnibus, ut sitis in illo perfecti. $\begin{smallmatrix}\text{1 Tim. iv.}\\\text{15.}\end{smallmatrix}$

XIII. Ἐγράψατέ μοι καὶ ὑμεῖς καὶ Ἰγνάτιος ἵνα, ἐάν
τις ἀπέρχηται εἰς Συρίαν, καὶ τὰ παρ᾽ ὑμῶν ἀποκομίσῃ
γράμματα· ὅπερ ποιήσω, ἐὰν λάβω καιρὸν εὔθετον, εἴτε ἐγὼ
εἴτε ὃν πέμψω πρεσβεύσοντα καὶ περὶ ὑμῶν. 2. τὰς ἐπιστολὰς Ἰγνατίου τὰς πεμφθείσας ἡμῖν ὑπ᾽ αὐτοῦ, καὶ ἄλλας
ὅσας εἴχομεν παρ᾽ ἡμῖν, ἐπέμψαμεν ὑμῖν, καθὼς ἐνετείλασθε·
αἵτινες ὑποτεταγμέναι εἰσὶ τῇ ἐπιστολῇ ταύτῃ· ἐξ ὧν μεγάλα
ὠφεληθῆναι δυνήσεσθε. περιέχουσι γὰρ πίστιν καὶ ὑπομο-
νὴν καὶ πᾶσαν οἰκοδομὴν τὴν εἰς τὸν Κύριον ἡμῶν ἀνήκουσαν.
et de ipso Ignatio et de his qui cum eo sunt, quod certius
agnoveritis, significate.

XIV. Haec vobis scripsi per Crescentem, quem in
praesenti commendavi vobis, et nunc commendo: con-
versatus est enim nobiscum inculpabiliter, credo autem
quia et vobiscum similiter. Sororem autem eius habebitis
commendatam, cum venerit ad vos. Incolumes estote in
Domino Jesu Christo in gratia cum omnibus vestris.
Amen.

xii. 2 Dei filius] L (but add *eius* rpmf); *Deus* Tim. Sev.

TRANSLATION

EPISTLE OF S. POLYCARP

THE EPISTLE OF S. POLYCARP

POLYCARP and the presbyters that are with him unto the Church of God which sojourneth at Philippi; mercy unto you and peace from God Almighty and Jesus Christ our Saviour be multiplied.

1. I rejoiced with you greatly in our Lord Jesus Christ, for that ye received the followers of the true Love and escorted them on their way, as befitted you—those men encircled in saintly bonds which are the diadems of them that be truly chosen of God and our Lord; and that the stedfast root of your faith which was famed from primitive times abideth until now and beareth fruit unto our Lord Jesus Christ, who endured to face even death for our sins, *whom God raised, having loosed the pangs of Hades; on whom, though ye saw Him not, ye believe with joy unutterable and full of glory;* unto which joy many desire to enter in; forasmuch as ye know that it is *by grace ye are saved, not of works,* but by the will of God through Jesus Christ.

2. *Wherefore gird up your loins and serve God in fear* and truth, forsaking the vain and empty talking and the error of the many, *for that ye have believed on Him that raised our Lord Jesus Christ from the dead and gave unto Him glory* and a throne on His right hand; unto whom all things were made subject that are in heaven and that are on the earth; to whom every creature that hath breath doeth service; who cometh as *judge of quick and dead;* whose blood God will require of them that are disobedient unto Him. Now *He that raised Him* from the dead *will raise us also;* if we do His will and walk in His commandments and love the things which He loved, abstaining from all unrighteousness, covetousness, love of money, evil speaking, false witness; *not rendering evil for evil or railing for railing* or blow for blow or cursing for cursing; but remembering the words which the Lord spake, as He taught; *Judge not that ye be not judged.*

Forgive, and it shall be forgiven to you.   Have mercy that ye may receive mercy.   With what measure ye mete, it shall be measured to you again ; and again *Blessed are the poor and they that are persecuted for righteousness' sake, for theirs is the kingdom of God.*

3. These things, brethren, I write unto you concerning righteousness, not because I laid this charge upon myself, but because ye invited me.   For neither am I, nor is any other like unto me, able to follow the wisdom of the blessed and glorious Paul, who when he came among you taught face to face with the men of that day the word which concerneth truth carefully and surely; who also, when he was absent, wrote a letter unto you, into the which if ye look diligently, ye shall be able to be builded up unto the faith given to you, *which is the mother of us all,* while hope followeth after and love goeth before—love toward God and Christ and toward our neighbour.   For if any man be occupied with these, he hath fulfilled the commandment of righteousness ; for he that hath love is far from all sin.

4. *But the love of money is the beginning of all troubles.*   Knowing therefore that *we brought nothing into the world neither can we carry anything out,* let us arm ourselves with the armour of righteousness, and let us teach ourselves first to walk in the commandment of the Lord ; and then our wives also, to walk in the faith that hath been given unto them and in love and purity, cherishing their own husbands in all truth and loving all men equally in all chastity, and to train their children in the training of the fear of God.   Our widows must be sober-minded as touching the faith of the Lord, making intercession without ceasing for all men, abstaining from all calumny, evil speaking, false witness, love of money, and every evil thing, knowing that they are God's altar, and that all sacrifices are carefully inspected, and nothing escapeth Him either of their thoughts or intents or any of the secret things of the heart.

5. Knowing then that *God is not mocked,* we ought to walk worthily of His commandment and His glory.   In like manner deacons should be blameless in the presence of His righteousness, as deacons of God and Christ and not of men ; not calumniators, not double-tongued, not lovers of money, temperate in all things, compassionate, diligent, walking according to the truth of the Lord who became *a minister (deacon) of all.*   For if we be well pleasing unto Him in this present world, we shall receive the future world also, according as He promised

us to raise us from the dead, and that if we conduct ourselves worthily of Him *we shall also reign with Him*, if indeed we have faith. In like manner also the younger men must be blameless in all things, caring for purity before everything and curbing themselves from every evil. For it is a good thing to refrain from lusts in the world, for every *lust warreth against the Spirit*, and *neither whoremongers nor effeminate persons nor defilers of themselves with men shall inherit the kingdom of God*, neither they that do untoward things. Wherefore it is right to abstain from all these things, submitting yourselves to the presbyters and deacons as to God and Christ. The virgins must walk in a blameless and pure conscience.

6. And the presbyters also must be compassionate, merciful towards all men, *turning back the sheep that are gone astray*, visiting all the infirm, not neglecting a widow or an orphan or a poor man : but *providing always for that which is honorable in the sight of God and of men*, abstaining from all anger, respect of persons, unrighteous judgment, being far from all love of money, not quick to believe anything against any man, not hasty in judgment, knowing that we all are debtors of sin. If then we entreat the Lord that He would forgive us, we also ought to forgive : for we are before the eyes of our Lord and God, and we must *all stand at the judgment-seat of Christ*, and *each man must give an account of himself.* Let us therefore so serve Him with fear and all reverence, as He himself gave commandment and the Apostles who preached the Gospel to us and the prophets who proclaimed beforehand the coming of our Lord ; being zealous as touching that which is good, abstaining from offences and from the false brethren and from them that bear the name of the Lord in hypocrisy, who lead foolish men astray.

7. For every one *who shall not confess that Jesus Christ is come in the flesh, is antichrist:* and whosoever shall not confess the testimony of the Cross, is of the devil ; and whosoever shall pervert the oracles of the Lord to his own lusts and say that there is neither resurrection nor judgment, that man is the first-born of Satan. Wherefore let us forsake the vain doing of the many and their false teachings, and turn unto the word which was delivered unto us from the beginning, *being sober unto prayer* and constant in fastings, entreating the all-seeing God with supplications that He *bring us not into temptation*, according as the Lord said, *The spirit indeed is willing, but the flesh is weak.*

8. Let us therefore without ceasing hold fast by our hope and by the earnest of our righteousness, which is Jesus Christ who *took up our sins in His own body upon the tree, who did no sin, neither was guile found in His mouth*, but for our sakes He endured all things, that we might live in Him. Let us therefore become imitators of His endurance; and if we should suffer for His name's sake, let us glorify Him. For He gave this example to us in His own person, and we believed this.

9. I exhort you all therefore to be obedient unto the word of righteousness and to practise all endurance, which also ye saw with your own eyes in the blessed Ignatius and Zosimus and Rufus, yea and in others also who came from among yourselves, as well as in Paul himself and the rest of the Apostles; being persuaded that all these *ran not in vain* but in faith and righteousness, and that they are in their due place in the presence of the Lord, with whom also they suffered. For they *loved not the present world*, but Him that died for our sakes and was raised by God for us.

10. Stand fast therefore in these things and follow the example of the Lord, *being firm in the faith* and *immovable, in love of the brotherhood kindly affectioned one to another*, partners with the truth, *forestalling one another* in the gentleness of the Lord, despising no man. *When ye are able to do good*, defer it not, for *Pitifulness delivereth from death*. *Be ye all subject one to another, having your conversation* unblameable *among the Gentiles, that from your good works* both ye may receive praise and the Lord may not be blasphemed in you. But *woe to him through whom the name of the Lord is blasphemed*. Therefore teach all men soberness, in which ye yourselves also walk.

11. I was exceedingly grieved for Valens, who aforetime was a presbyter among you, because he is so ignorant of the office which was given unto him. I warn you therefore that ye refrain from covetousness, and that ye be pure and truthful. Refrain from all evil. But he who cannot govern himself in these things, how doth he enjoin this upon another? If a man refrain not from covetousness, he shall be defiled by idolatry, and shall be judged as one of the Gentiles who *know not the judgment of the Lord*. *Nay, know we not, that the saints shall judge the world*, as Paul teacheth? But I have not found any such thing in you, neither have heard thereof, among whom the blessed Paul laboured, who were his *letters* in the beginning. For *he boasteth of you in* all those *churches* which alone at that time knew God; for we

knew Him not as yet. Therefore I am exceedingly grieved for him and for his wife, unto whom may the Lord grant true repentance. Be ye therefore yourselves also sober herein, and *hold not such as enemies*, but restore them as frail and erring members, that ye may save the whole body of you. For so doing, ye do edify one another.

12. For I am persuaded that ye are well trained in the sacred writings, and nothing is hidden from you. But to myself this is not granted. Only, as it is said in these scriptures, *Be ye angry and sin not*, and *Let not the sun set on your wrath*. Blessed is he that remembereth this; and I trust that this is in you. Now may the God and Father of our Lord Jesus Christ, and the eternal High-priest Himself, the [Son of] God Jesus Christ, build you up in faith and truth, and in all gentleness and in all avoidance of wrath and in forbearance and long suffering and in patient endurance and in purity; and may He grant unto you a lot and portion among His saints, and to us with you, and to all that are under heaven, who shall believe on our Lord and God Jesus Christ and on His Father *that raised Him from the dead. Pray for all the saints.* Pray also *for kings* and powers and princes, and *for them that persecute* and hate *you*, and for *the enemies of the cross*, that your fruit may be *manifest among all men*, that ye may be perfect in Him.

13. Ye wrote to me, both ye yourselves and Ignatius, asking that if any one should go to Syria he might carry thither the letters from you. And this I will do, if I get a fit opportunity, either I myself, or he whom I shall send to be ambassador on your behalf also. The letters of Ignatius which were sent to us by him, and others as many as we had by us, we send unto you, according as ye gave charge; the which are subjoined to this letter; from which ye will be able to gain great advantage. For they comprise faith and endurance and every kind of edification, which pertaineth unto our Lord. Moreover concerning Ignatius himself and those that were with him, if ye have any sure tidings, certify us.

14. I write these things to you by Crescens, whom I commended to you recently and now commend unto you: for he hath walked blamelessly with us; and I believe also with you in like manner. But ye shall have his sister commended, when she shall come to you. Fare ye well in the Lord Jesus Christ in grace, ye and all yours. Amen.

THE MARTYRDOM

OF

S. POLYCARP

THE MARTYRDOM OF POLYCARP

I

THE document which gives an account of Polycarp's martyrdom is in the form of a letter addressed by the Church of Smyrna to the Church of Philomelium. It was however intended for much wider circulation, and at the close (§ 20) directions are given to secure its being so circulated. The letter seems to have been written shortly after the martyrdom itself, which happened A.D. 155 or 156. It consists of two parts, (1) the main body of the letter ending with the twentieth chapter, and (2) a number of supplementary paragraphs, comprising the twenty-first and twenty-second chapters. In point of form these supplementary paragraphs are separable from the rest of the letter. Indeed, as Eusebius, our chief witness to the genuineness of the documents, ends his quotations and paraphrases before he reaches the close of the main body of the letter, we cannot say confidently whether he had or had not the supplementary paragraphs. The genuineness of the two parts therefore must be considered separately.

For the genuineness of the main document there is abundant evidence. A quarter of a century after the occurrence Irenæus and a little later Polycrates bear testimony to the fact of Polycarp's martyrdom. Further the Letter of the Gallican Churches (c. A.D. 177) presents striking coincidences with the language of the Letter of the Smyrnæans, and unless several points of resemblance are accidental, Lucian in his account of Peregrinus Proteus (c. A.D. 165) must have been acquainted with the document. At the beginning of the fourth century Eusebius directly refers to it in his Chronicon, and again in his Ecclesiastical History (iv. 15), where he quotes and paraphrases nearly the whole of it, intimating that it was the earliest written record of a martyrdom with which he was acquainted. At the close of the same century the author of the Pionian Life of Polycarp inserts the letter in his work. The internal evidence likewise is clearly in favour of the genuineness; and the adverse argument based upon the miraculous element in the story falls to the ground when the incident of the dove (§ 16) is proved to be a later interpolation.

The supplementary paragraphs present a more difficult problem. They fall into three parts, separate in form the one from the other, and not improbably written by different hands; (i) The Chronological Appendix (§ 21); (ii) The Commendatory Postscript (§ 22. 1); (iii) The History of the Transmission (§ 22. 2, 3).

The first of these closes with a paragraph which is copied from the close of the Epistle of S. Clement, just as the opening of the Smyrnæan Letter is modelled on the opening of S. Clement's Epistle. The obligation being the same in kind at the beginning and at the end of the letter, the obvious inference is that they were penned by the same hand. And when the historical references contained in this appendix are found upon examination not only not to contradict history, but, as in the case of Philip the Trallian, to be confirmed by fresh accessions to our knowledge of the archæology and chronology of the age, the conclusion becomes irresistible that § 21 formed part of the original document.

The Commendatory Postscript is omitted in the Moscow MS and in the Latin version, but it may well have been a postscript added by the Philomelian Church, when they forwarded copies of the letter, as they were charged to do (§ 20), to churches more distant from Smyrna than themselves.

The History of the Transmission occurs in an expanded form in the Moscow MS, but in each edition it ends with a note purporting to be written by one Pionius. He tells us that he copied it from the transcript of the last-mentioned transcriber, and that Polycarp revealed its locality to him in a vision of which he promises to give an account in the sequel. Now the Acts are extant of a Pionius who was martyred under Decius (A.D. 250) while celebrating the birthday of Polycarp. There is also a Life of Polycarp extant (incorporating this very Letter of the Smyrnæans), which purports to have been written by this Pionius, but is manifestly the work of a forger of the fifth century. This life is incomplete, otherwise doubtless it would have contained the account of the vision of Pionius promised in the sequel. The writer of the Pionian Life is therefore the author of the History of the Transmission. One further fact remains to be recorded. Not only do the Pionian Life and the History of the Transmission appeal without scruple to ancient documents which have no existence. They abound largely in the supernatural. Now our extant MSS of the Smyrnæan Epistle have the Pionian postscript and therefore represent the Pionian edition of that Letter. Eusebius alone of all extant authorities is prior to the false Pionius and gives an independent text. Now our spurious Pionius was before all things a miracle-monger. Among other miracles he relates that on the eve of Polycarp's appointment to the episcopate a dove hovered round his head. So also in the Letter of the Smyrnæans a dove is found leaving his body when his spirit is wafted to heaven (§ 16). But this miracle appears only in the Pionian copies, not in Eusebius. Moreover, by the abruptness of its appearance an interpolation is suggested. Is it not the same dove which appears on the two occasions, and was it not uncaged and let fly by the same hand? We cannot resist the suspicion that our spurious Pionius was responsible for both these appearances.

2

The authorities for the text are threefold.

1. The GREEK MANUSCRIPTS [G], five in number, viz. (1) *Mosquensis* 160 (now 159) [m] which omits the first paragraph § 22 and amplifies the remaining part of this same chapter. This, though of the thirteenth century, is the most important of the Greek manuscripts. (2) *Barroccianus* 238 [b] in the Bodleian Library, an eleventh century MS from which Ussher derived his text. (3) *Paris. Bibl. Nat. Graec.* 1452 [p] of the tenth century, called by Halloix *Mediceus*. (4) *Vindob. Hist. Graec. Eccl.* iii. [v] an eleventh or early twelfth century MS betraying marks of an arbitrary literary revision; and (5) *S. Sep. Hierosol.* 1 fol. 136 [s] a tenth century MS of the same group as bpv, discovered quite recently in the Library of the Holy Sepulchre at Jerusalem by Professor Rendel Harris.

2. EUSEBIUS [E]. The extracts found in *Hist. Eccl.* iv. 15; not only the earliest, but also the most valuable authority.

3. The LATIN VERSION [L] in three forms; (*a*) as given in Rufinus' translation of Eusebius, which is probably the version of the martyrdom read, as we learn from Gregory of Tours that it was read, in the Churches of Gaul; (*b*) an independent Latin Version very loose and paraphrastic; (*c*) a combination of the two preceding forms. The MSS of the Latin Version are numerous.

There are also a Syriac Version and a Coptic Version in the Memphitic dialect; but both of these, like the Rufinian form, are made not from the document itself, but from the account in Eusebius. They do not therefore constitute fresh authorities.

ΜΑΡΤΥΡΙΟΝ ΠΟΛΥΚΑΡΠΟΥ

Ἡ ΕΚΚΛΗΣΙΑ τοῦ Θεοῦ ἡ παροικοῦσα Σμύρναν, τῇ ἐκκλησίᾳ τοῦ Θεοῦ τῇ παροικούσῃ ἐν Φιλομηλίῳ καὶ πάσαις ταῖς κατὰ πάντα τόπον τῆς ἁγίας καὶ καθολικῆς ἐκκλησίας παροικίαις, ἔλεος καὶ εἰρήνη καὶ ἀγάπη Θεοῦ πατρὸς καὶ [τοῦ] Κυρίου ἡμῶν Ἰησοῦ Χριστοῦ πληθυνθείη.

I. Ἐγράψαμεν ὑμῖν, ἀδελφοί, τὰ κατὰ τοὺς μαρτυρήσαντας καὶ τὸν μακάριον Πολύκαρπον, ὅστις ὥσπερ ἐπισφραγίσας διὰ τῆς μαρτυρίας αὐτοῦ κατέπαυσε τὸν διωγμόν. σχεδὸν γὰρ πάντα τὰ προάγοντα ἐγένετο, ἵνα ἡμῖν ὁ Κύριος ἄνωθεν ἐπιδείξῃ τὸ κατὰ τὸ εὐαγγέλιον μαρτύριον. 2. περιέμενεν γὰρ ἵνα παραδοθῇ, ὡς καὶ ὁ Κύριος, ἵνα μιμηταὶ καὶ ἡμεῖς αὐτοῦ γενώμεθα, ΜΗ μόνον ϲκοποῦντεϲ τὸ καθ᾽ ἑαυτοὺϲ Phil. ii. 4. ἀλλὰ καὶ τὸ κατὰ τοὺϲ πέλαϲ. ἀγάπης γὰρ ἀληθοῦς καὶ βεβαίας ἐστὶν μὴ μόνον ἑαυτὸν θέλειν σώζεσθαι ἀλλὰ καὶ πάντας τοὺς ἀδελφούς.

II. Μακάρια μὲν οὖν καὶ γενναῖα τὰ μαρτύρια πάντα [τὰ] κατὰ τὸ θέλημα τοῦ Θεοῦ γεγονότα· δεῖ γὰρ εὐλαβεστέρους ἡμᾶς ὑπάρχοντας τῷ Θεῷ τὴν κατὰ πάντων ἐξουσίαν ἀνατιθέναι. 2. τὸ γὰρ γενναῖον αὐτῶν καὶ ὑπομονητικὸν καὶ φιλοδέσποτον τίς οὐκ ἂν θαυμάσειεν; οἳ μάστιξι μὲν καταξανθέντες, ὥστε μέχρι τῶν ἔσω φλεβῶν καὶ ἀρτηριῶν τὴν τῆς σαρκὸς οἰκονομίαν θεωρεῖσθαι, ὑπέμειναν, ὡς καὶ τοὺς περιεστῶτας ἐλεεῖν καὶ ὀδύρεσθαι· τοὺς δὲ καὶ εἰς τοσοῦτον

---

1. 2. τοὺς πέλας] conj. Ussher; τοῦ πέλας mb; τοὺς παῖδας vs; τοὺς πλείονας p; al. L.

γενναιότητος ἐλθεῖν ὥστε μήτε γρύξαι μήτε στενάξαι τινὰ
αὐτῶν, ἐπιδεικνυμένους ἅπασιν ἡμῖν ὅτι ἐκείνῃ τῇ ὥρᾳ βασανιζόμενοι τῆς σαρκὸς ἀπεδήμουν οἱ μάρτυρες τοῦ Χριστοῦ,
μᾶλλον δὲ ὅτι παρεστὼς ὁ Κύριος ὡμίλει αὐτοῖς. 3. καὶ
προσέχοντες τῇ τοῦ Χριστοῦ χάριτι τῶν κοσμικῶν κατεφρό-
νουν βασάνων, διὰ μιᾶς ὥρας τὴν αἰώνιον κόλασιν ἐξαγορα-
ζόμενοι. καὶ τὸ πῦρ ἦν αὐτοῖς ψυχρὸν τὸ τῶν ἀπανθρώπων
βασανιστῶν· πρὸ ὀφθαλμῶν γὰρ εἶχον φυγεῖν τὸ αἰώνιον
καὶ μηδέποτε σβεννύμενον, καὶ τοῖς τῆς καρδίας ὀφθαλμοῖς
Is. lxiv. 4. ἀνέβλεπον τὰ τηρούμενα τοῖς ὑπομείνασιν ἀγαθά, ἃ ογτε ογϲ
1 Cor. ii. 9. ΗΚΟΥϹΕΝ ΟΥΤΕ ὀφθαλμὸϲ εἶΔΕΝ, ΟΥΤΕ ἐπὶ ΚΑΡΔΙΑΝ ἀΝθΡΩΠΟΥ
ἀΝΕΒΗ, ἐκείνοις δὲ ὑπεδείκνυτο ὑπὸ τοῦ Κυρίου, οἵπερ μηκέτι
ἄνθρωποι ἀλλ᾽ ἤδη ἄγγελοι ἦσαν. 4. ὁμοίως δὲ καὶ οἱ εἰς
τὰ θηρία κριθέντες ὑπέμειναν δεινὰς κολάσεις, κήρυκας μὲν
ὑποστρωννύμενοι καὶ ἄλλαις ποικίλων βασάνων ἰδέαις κολα-
φιζόμενοι, ἵνα, εἰ δυνηθείη, διὰ τῆς ἐπιμόνου κολάσεως εἰς
ἄρνησιν αὐτοὺς τρέψῃ· πολλὰ γὰρ ἐμηχανᾶτο κατ᾽ αὐτῶν ὁ
διάβολος.

III. Ἀλλὰ χάρις τῷ Θεῷ· κατὰ πάντων γὰρ οὐκ ἴσχυ-
σεν. ὁ γὰρ γενναιότατος Γερμανικὸς ἐπερρώννυεν αὐτῶν τὴν
δειλίαν διὰ τῆς ἐν αὐτῷ ὑπομονῆς· ὃς καὶ ἐπισήμως ἐθηριο-
μάχησεν. βουλομένου γὰρ τοῦ ἀνθυπάτου πείθειν αὐτὸν καὶ
λέγοντος τὴν ἡλικίαν αὐτοῦ κατοικτεῖραι, ἑαυτῷ ἐπεσπάσατο
τὸ θηρίον προσβιασάμενος, τάχιον τοῦ ἀδίκου καὶ ἀνόμου
βίου αὐτῶν ἀπαλλαγῆναι βουλόμενος. ἐκ τούτου οὖν πᾶν τὸ
πλῆθος, θαυμάσαν τὴν γενναιότητα τοῦ θεοφιλοῦς καὶ θεοσε-
βοῦς γένους τῶν Χριστιανῶν, ἐπεβόησεν· Αἶρε τοὺς ἀθέους,
ζητείσθω Πολύκαρπος.

IV. Εἷς δὲ ὀνόματι Κόϊντος, Φρὺξ προσφάτως ἐληλυ-
θὼς ἀπὸ τῆς Φρυγίας, ἰδὼν τὰ θηρία ἐδειλίασεν. οὗτος δὲ ἦν
ὁ παραβιασάμενος ἑαυτόν τε καί τινας προσελθεῖν ἑκόντας.
τοῦτον ὁ ἀνθύπατος πολλὰ ἐκλιπαρήσας ἔπεισεν ὀμόσαι καὶ
ἐπιθῦσαι. διὰ τοῦτο οὖν, ἀδελφοί, οὐκ ἐπαινοῦμεν τοὺς προ-
διδόντας ἑαυτούς, ἐπειδὴ οὐχ οὕτως διδάσκει τὸ εὐαγγέλιον.

V. Ὁ δὲ θαυμασιώτατος Πολύκαρπος τὸ μὲν πρῶτον
ἀκούσας οὐκ ἐταράχθη, ἀλλ᾽ ἐβούλετο κατὰ πόλιν μένειν· οἱ
δὲ πλείους ἔπειθον αὐτὸν ὑπεξελθεῖν. καὶ ὑπεξῆλθεν εἰς
ἀγρίδιον οὐ μακρὰν ἀπέχον ἀπὸ τῆς πόλεως, καὶ διέτριβε
μετ᾽ ὀλίγων, νύκτα καὶ ἡμέραν οὐδὲν ἕτερον ποιῶν ἢ προσευχόμενος περὶ πάντων καὶ τῶν κατὰ τὴν οἰκουμένην ἐκκλη-
σιῶν· ὅπερ ἦν σύνηθες αὐτῷ. 2. καὶ προσευχόμενος ἐν
ὀπτασίᾳ γέγονεν πρὸ τριῶν ἡμερῶν τοῦ συλληφθῆναι αὐτόν,
καὶ εἶδεν τὸ προσκεφάλαιον αὐτοῦ ὑπὸ πυρὸς κατακαιόμενον·
καὶ στραφεὶς εἶπεν πρὸς τοὺς σὺν αὐτῷ, Δεῖ με ζῶντα καῆναι.

VI. Καὶ ἐπιμενόντων τῶν ζητούντων αὐτόν, μετέβη εἰς
ἕτερον ἀγρίδιον· καὶ εὐθέως ἐπέστησαν οἱ ζητοῦντες αὐτόν.
καὶ μὴ εὑρόντες συνελάβοντο παιδάρια δύο, ὧν τὸ ἕτερον
βασανιζόμενον ὡμολόγησεν· ἦν γὰρ καὶ ἀδύνατον λαθεῖν
αὐτόν, ἐπεὶ καὶ οἱ προδιδόντες αὐτὸν οἰκεῖοι ὑπῆρχον. 2. καὶ
ὁ εἰρήναρχος, ὁ κεκληρωμένος τὸ αὐτὸ ὄνομα, Ἡρώδης ἐπι-
λεγόμενος, ἔσπευδεν εἰς τὸ στάδιον αὐτὸν εἰσαγαγεῖν, ἵνα
ἐκεῖνος μὲν τὸν ἴδιον κλῆρον ἀπαρτίσῃ, Χριστοῦ κοινωνὸς
γενόμενος, οἱ δὲ προδόντες αὐτὸν τὴν αὐτοῦ τοῦ Ἰούδα ὑπό-
σχοιεν τιμωρίαν.

VII. Ἔχοντες οὖν τὸ παιδάριον, τῇ παρασκευῇ περὶ
δείπνου ὥραν ἐξῆλθον διωγμῖται καὶ ἱππεῖς μετὰ τῶν συνή-
θων αὐτοῖς ὅπλων, ὡς ἐπὶ λῃcτὴν τρέχοντες. καὶ ὀψὲ τῆς S. Matt.
ὥρας συνεπελθόντες, ἐκεῖνον μὲν εὗρον ἔν τινι δωματίῳ κατα- xxvi. 55.
κείμενον ὑπερῴῳ· κἀκεῖθεν δὲ ἠδύνατο εἰς ἕτερον χωρίον
ἀπελθεῖν, ἀλλ᾽ οὐκ ἠβουλήθη, εἰπών· Τὸ θέλημα τοῦ Θεοῦ Acts xxi.
 γενέσθω. 2. ἀκούσας οὖν [αὐτοὺς] παρόντας, καταβὰς διε- 14.
λέχθη αὐτοῖς, θαυμαζόντων τῶν παρόντων τὴν ἡλικίαν αὐτοῦ
καὶ τὸ εὐσταθές, [καὶ] εἰ τοσαύτη σπουδὴ ἦν τοῦ συλληφθῆναι τοιοῦτον πρεσβύτην ἄνδρα. εὐθέως οὖν αὐτοῖς ἐκέλευσε παρατεθῆναι φαγεῖν καὶ πιεῖν ἐν ἐκείνῃ τῇ ὥρᾳ, ὅσον
ἂν βούλωνται· ἐξητήσατο δὲ αὐτούς, ἵνα δῶσιν αὐτῷ ὥραν
πρὸς τὸ προσεύξασθαι ἀδεῶς. τῶν δὲ ἐπιτρεψάντων, σταθεὶς προσηύξατο πλήρης ὢν τῆς χάριτος τοῦ Θεοῦ οὕτως, ὡς

ἐπὶ δύο ὥρας μὴ δύνασθαι σιγῆσαι, καὶ ἐκπλήττεσθαι τοὺς ἀκούοντας, πολλούς τε μετανοεῖν ἐπὶ τῷ ἐληλυθέναι ἐπὶ τοιοῦτον θεοπρεπῆ πρεσβύτην.

VIII. Ἐπεὶ δέ ποτε κατέπαυσε τὴν προσευχήν, μνημονεύσας ἁπάντων καὶ τῶν πώποτε συμβεβληκότων αὐτῷ, μικρῶν τε καὶ μεγάλων, ἐνδόξων τε καὶ ἀδόξων, καὶ πάσης τῆς κατὰ τὴν οἰκουμένην καθολικῆς ἐκκλησίας, τῆς ὥρας ἐλθούσης τοῦ ἐξιέναι, ὄνῳ καθίσαντες αὐτὸν ἤγαγον εἰς τὴν πόλιν, ὄντος σαββάτου μεγάλου. 2. καὶ ὑπήντα αὐτῷ ὁ εἰρήναρχος Ἡρώδης καὶ ὁ πατὴρ αὐτοῦ Νικήτης, οἳ καὶ μεταθέντες αὐτὸν ἐπὶ τὴν καροῦχαν ἔπειθον παρακαθεζόμενοι καὶ λέγοντες· Τί γὰρ κακόν ἐστιν εἰπεῖν, Κύριος Καῖσαρ, καὶ ἐπιθῦσαι, καὶ τὰ τούτοις ἀκόλουθα, καὶ διασώζεσθαι; ὁ δὲ τὰ μὲν πρῶτα οὐκ ἀπεκρίνατο αὐτοῖς, ἐπιμενόντων δὲ αὐτῶν ἔφη· Οὐ μέλλω ποιεῖν ὃ συμβουλεύετέ μοι. 3. οἱ δέ, ἀποτυχόντες τοῦ πεῖσαι αὐτόν, δεινὰ ῥήματα ἔλεγον καὶ μετὰ σπουδῆς καθῆρουν αὐτόν, ὡς κατιόντα ἀπὸ τῆς καρούχας ἀποσῦραι τὸ ἀντικνήμιον. καὶ μὴ ἐπιστραφείς, ὡς οὐδὲν πεπονθώς, προθύμως μετὰ σπουδῆς ἐπορεύετο, ἀγόμενος εἰς τὸ στάδιον, θορύβου τηλικούτου ὄντος ἐν τῷ σταδίῳ ὡς μηδὲ ἀκουσθῆναί τινα δύνασθαι.

IX. Τῷ δὲ Πολυκάρπῳ εἰσιόντι εἰς τὸ στάδιον φωνὴ ἐξ οὐρανοῦ ἐγένετο· Ἴσχυε Πολύκαρπε καὶ ἀνδρίζου. καὶ τὸν μὲν εἰπόντα οὐδεὶς εἶδεν, τὴν δὲ φωνὴν τῶν ἡμετέρων οἱ παρόντες ἤκουσαν. καὶ λοιπὸν προσαχθέντος αὐτοῦ θόρυβος ἦν μέγας ἀκουσάντων ὅτι Πολύκαρπος συνείληπται. 2. προσαχθέντα οὖν αὐτὸν ἀνηρώτα ὁ ἀνθύπατος, εἰ αὐτὸς εἴη· τοῦ δὲ ὁμολογοῦντος, ἔπειθεν ἀρνεῖσθαι λέγων, Αἰδέσθητί σου τὴν ἡλικίαν, καὶ ἕτερα τούτοις ἀκόλουθα, ὡς ἔθος αὐτοῖς λέγειν· Ὄμοσον τὴν Καίσαρος τύχην, μετανόησον, εἶπον, Αἶρε τοὺς ἀθέους. ὁ δὲ Πολύκαρπος ἐμβριθεῖ τῷ προσώπῳ εἰς πάντα τὸν ὄχλον τὸν ἐν τῷ σταδίῳ ἀνόμων ἐθνῶν ἐμβλέψας καὶ ἐπισείσας αὐτοῖς τὴν χεῖρα, στενάξας τε καὶ ἀναβλέψας εἰς τὸν οὐρανόν, εἶπεν· Αἶρε τοὺς ἀθέους. 3. ἐγκειμένου δὲ τοῦ

ἀνθυπάτου καὶ λέγοντος· Ὄμοσον, καὶ ἀπολύω σε· λοιδόρη-
σον τὸν Χριστόν· ἔφη ὁ Πολύκαρπος· Ὀγδοήκοντα καὶ ἓξ
ἔτη [ἔχω] δουλεύω[ν] αὐτῷ, καὶ οὐδέν με ἠδίκησεν· καὶ πῶς
δύναμαι βλασφημῆσαι τὸν βασιλέα μου, τὸν σώσαντά με;
X. Ἐπιμένοντος δὲ πάλιν αὐτοῦ καὶ λέγοντος, Ὄμοσον
τὴν Καίσαρος τύχην, ἀπεκρίνατο· Εἰ κενοδοξεῖς ἵνα ὀμόσω
τὴν Καίσαρος τύχην, ὡς σὺ λέγεις, προσποιεῖ δὲ ἀγνοεῖν με
τίς εἰμι, μετὰ παρρησίας ἄκουε, Χριστιανός εἰμι. εἰ δὲ θέλεις
τὸν τοῦ χριστιανισμοῦ μαθεῖν λόγον, δὸς ἡμέραν καὶ ἄκουσον.
2. ἔφη ὁ ἀνθύπατος· Πεῖσον τὸν δῆμον. ὁ δὲ Πολύκαρπος
εἶπεν· Σὲ μὲν κἂν λόγου ἠξίωσα· δεδιδάγμεθα γὰρ ἀρχαῖς
καὶ ἐξουσίαις ὑπὸ Θεοῦ τεταγμέναις τιμὴν κατὰ τὸ προσῆκον
τὴν μὴ βλάπτουσαν ἡμᾶς, ἀπονέμειν· ἐκείνους δὲ οὐκ ἀξίους
ἡγοῦμαι τοῦ ἀπολογεῖσθαι αὐτοῖς.

XI. Ὁ δὲ ἀνθύπατος εἶπεν· Θηρία ἔχω, τούτοις σε
παραβαλῶ, ἐὰν μὴ μετανοήσῃς. ὁ δὲ εἶπεν· Κάλει· ἀμετά-
θετος γὰρ ἡμῖν ἡ ἀπὸ τῶν κρειττόνων ἐπὶ τὰ χείρω μετάνοια·
καλὸν δὲ μετατίθεσθαι ἀπὸ τῶν χαλεπῶν ἐπὶ τὰ δίκαια.
2. ὁ δὲ πάλιν πρὸς αὐτόν· Πυρί σε ποιῶ δαπανηθῆναι, εἰ
τῶν θηρίων καταφρονεῖς, ἐὰν μὴ μετανοήσῃς. ὁ δὲ Πολύ-
καρπος· Πῦρ ἀπειλεῖς τὸ πρὸς ὥραν καιόμενον καὶ μετ᾽
ὀλίγον σβεννύμενον· ἀγνοεῖς γὰρ τὸ τῆς μελλούσης κρίσεως
καὶ αἰωνίου κολάσεως τοῖς ἀσεβέσι τηρούμενον πῦρ. ἀλλὰ
τί βραδύνεις; φέρε ὃ βούλει.

XII. Ταῦτα δὲ καὶ ἕτερα πλείονα λέγων, θάρσους καὶ
χαρᾶς ἐνεπίμπλατο, καὶ τὸ πρόσωπον αὐτοῦ χάριτος ἐπλη-
ροῦτο, ὥστε οὐ μόνον μὴ συμπεσεῖν ταραχθέντα ὑπὸ τῶν
λεγομένων πρὸς αὐτόν, ἀλλὰ τοὐναντίον τὸν ἀνθύπατον ἐκ-
στῆναι πέμψαι τε τὸν ἑαυτοῦ κήρυκα, ἐν μέσῳ τῷ σταδίῳ
κηρῦξαι τρίς· Πολύκαρπος ὡμολόγησεν ἑαυτὸν Χριστιανὸν
εἶναι. 2. τούτου λεχθέντος ὑπὸ τοῦ κήρυκος, ἅπαν τὸ πλῆθος ἐθνῶν τε καὶ Ἰουδαίων τῶν τὴν Σμύρναν κατοικούντων
ἀκατασχέτῳ θυμῷ καὶ μεγάλῃ φωνῇ ἐπεβόα· Οὗτός ἐστιν
ὁ τῆς Ἀσίας διδάσκαλος, ὁ πατὴρ τῶν Χριστιανῶν, ὁ τῶν

ἡμετερων θεῶν καθαιρέτης, ὁ πολλοὺς διδάσκων μὴ θύειν μηδὲ προσκυνεῖν. ταῦτα λέγοντες ἐπεβόων καὶ ἠρώτων τὸν Ἀσιάρχην Φίλιππον, ἵνα ἐπαφῇ τῷ Πολυκάρπῳ λέοντα. ὁ δὲ ἔφη μὴ εἶναι ἐξὸν αὐτῷ, ἐπειδὴ πεπληρώκει τὰ κυνηγέσια. 3. τότε ἔδοξεν αὐτοῖς ὁμοθυμαδὸν ἐπιβοῆσαι, ὥστε τὸν Πολύκαρπον ζῶντα κατακαῦσαι. ἔδει γὰρ τὸ τῆς φανερωθείσης ἐπὶ τοῦ προσκεφαλαίου ὀπτασίας πληρωθῆναι, ὅτε ἰδὼν αὐτὸ καιόμενον προσευχόμενος εἶπεν ἐπιστραφεὶς τοῖς σὺν αὐτῷ πιστοῖς προφητικῶς· Δεῖ με ζῶντα καῆναι.

XIII. Ταῦτα οὖν μετὰ τοσούτου τάχους ἐγένετο, θᾶττον ἢ ἐλέγετο, τῶν ὄχλων παραχρῆμα συναγόντων ἔκ τε τῶν ἐργαστηρίων καὶ βαλανείων ξύλα καὶ φρύγανα, μάλιστα Ἰουδαίων προθύμως, ὡς ἔθος αὐτοῖς, εἰς ταῦτα ὑπουργούντων. 2. ὅτε δὲ ἡ πυρκαϊὰ ἡτοιμάσθη, ἀποθέμενος ἑαυτῷ πάντα τὰ ἱμάτια καὶ λύσας τὴν ζώνην, ἐπειρᾶτο καὶ ὑπολύειν ἑαυτόν, μὴ πρότερον τοῦτο ποιῶν διὰ τὸ ἀεὶ ἕκαστον τῶν πιστῶν σπουδάζειν ὅστις τάχιον τοῦ χρωτὸς αὐτοῦ ἅψηται· [ἐν] παντὶ γὰρ ἀγαθῆς ἕνεκεν πολιτείας καὶ πρὸ τῆς πολιᾶς ἐκεκόσμητο. 3. εὐθέως οὖν αὐτῷ περιετίθετο τὰ πρὸς τὴν πυρὰν ἡρμοσμένα ὄργανα. μελλόντων δὲ αὐτῶν καὶ προσηλοῦν εἶπεν· Ἄφετέ με οὕτως· ὁ γὰρ δοὺς ὑπομεῖναι τὸ πῦρ δώσει καὶ χωρὶς τῆς ὑμετέρας ἐκ τῶν ἥλων ἀσφαλείας ἄσκυλτον ἐπιμεῖναι τῇ πυρᾷ.

XIV. Οἱ δὲ οὐ καθήλωσαν μέν, προσέδησαν δὲ αὐτόν. ὁ δὲ ὀπίσω τὰς χεῖρας ποιήσας καὶ προσδεθείς, ὥσπερ κριὸς ἐπίσημος ἐκ μεγάλου ποιμνίου εἰς προσφοράν, ὁλοκαύτωμα δεκτὸν τῷ Θεῷ ἡτοιμασμένον, ἀναβλέψας εἰς τὸν οὐρανὸν εἶπεν· Κύριε ὁ Θεὸς ὁ παντοκράτωρ, ὁ τοῦ ἀγαπητοῦ καὶ εὐλογητοῦ παιδός σου Ἰησοῦ Χριστοῦ πατήρ, δι' οὗ τὴν περὶ σοῦ ἐπίγνωσιν εἰλήφαμεν, ὁ Θεὸς [ὁ] ἀγγέλων καὶ δυνάμεων καὶ πάσης κτίσεως παντός τε τοῦ γένους τῶν δικαίων οἳ ζῶσιν ἐνώπιόν σου· 2. εὐλογῶ σε, ὅτι κατηξίωσάς με τῆς ἡμέρας καὶ ὥρας ταύτης, τοῦ λαβεῖν με μέρος ἐν ἀριθμῷ τῶν μαρτύρων ἐν τῷ ποτηρίῳ τοῦ Χριστοῦ [σου]

εἰ**c** ἀ**ν**ά**c**τα**c**ι**ν** ζω**c** αἰωνίου ψυχῆς τε καὶ σώματος ἐν S. John v.
ἀφθαρσίᾳ πνεύματος ἁγίου· ἐν οἷς προσδεχθείην ἐνώπιόν 29.
σου σήμερον ἐν θυσίᾳ πίονι καὶ προσδεκτῇ, καθὼς προη-
τοίμασας καὶ προεφανέρωσας καὶ ἐπλήρωσας, ὁ ἀψευδὴς
καὶ ἀληθινὸς Θεός. 3. διὰ τοῦτο καὶ περὶ πάντων σε αἰνῶ,
σὲ εὐλογῶ, σὲ δοξάζω διὰ τοῦ αἰωνίου καὶ ἐπουρανίου ἀρχιερέως Ἰησοῦ Χριστοῦ, ἀγαπητοῦ σου παιδός, δι' οὗ σοι σὺν
αὐτῷ καὶ πνεύματι ἁγίῳ [ἡ] δόξα καὶ νῦν [καὶ ἀεὶ] καὶ εἰς
τοὺς μέλλοντας αἰῶνας. ἀμήν.

XV. Ἀναπέμψαντος δὲ αὐτοῦ τὸ ἀμὴν καὶ πληρώσαντος
τὴν εὐχήν, οἱ τοῦ πυρὸς ἄνθρωποι ἐξῆψαν τὸ πῦρ. μεγάλης
δὲ ἐκλαμψάσης φλογός, θαῦμα εἴδομεν, οἷς ἰδεῖν ἐδόθη· οἳ
καὶ ἐτηρήθημεν εἰς τὸ ἀναγγεῖλαι τοῖς λοιποῖς τὰ γενόμενα.
2. τὸ γὰρ πῦρ καμάρας εἶδος ποιῆσαν, ὥσπερ ὀθόνη πλοίου
ὑπὸ πνεύματος πληρουμένη, κύκλῳ περιετείχισεν τὸ σῶμα
τοῦ μάρτυρος· καὶ ἦν μέσον, οὐχ ὡς σὰρξ καιομένη, ἀλλ' ὡς
[ἄρτος ὀπτώμενος, ἢ ὡς] χρυσὸς καὶ ἄργυρος ἐν καμίνῳ
πυρούμενος. καὶ γὰρ εὐωδίας τοσαύτης ἀντελαβόμεθα, ὡς
λιβανωτοῦ πνέοντος ἢ ἄλλου τινὸς τῶν τιμίων ἀρωμάτων.

XVI. Πέρας οὖν ἰδόντες οἱ ἄνομοι μὴ δυνάμενον αὐτοῦ
τὸ σῶμα ὑπὸ τοῦ πυρὸς δαπανηθῆναι, ἐκέλευσαν προσελ-
θόντα αὐτῷ κομφέκτορα παραβῦσαι ξιφίδιον. καὶ τοῦτο
ποιήσαντος, ἐξῆλθε [περιστερὰ καὶ] πλῆθος αἵματος, ὥστε
κατασβέσαι τὸ πῦρ καὶ θαυμάσαι πάντα τὸν ὄχλον, εἰ τοσαύτη τις διαφορὰ μεταξὺ τῶν τε ἀπίστων καὶ τῶν ἐκλεκτῶν·
2. ὧν εἷς καὶ οὗτος γεγόνει ὁ θαυμασιώτατος [Πολύκαρπος],
ἐν τοῖς καθ' ἡμᾶς χρόνοις διδάσκαλος ἀποστολικὸς καὶ προφητικὸς γενόμενος, ἐπίσκοπος τῆς ἐν Σμύρνῃ ἁγίας ἐκκλη-
σίας· πᾶν γὰρ ῥῆμα, ὃ ἀφῆκεν ἐκ τοῦ στόματος αὐτοῦ,
ἐτελειώθη καὶ τελειωθήσεται.

XVII. Ὁ δὲ ἀντίζηλος καὶ βάσκανος καὶ πονηρός, ὁ
ἀντικείμενος τῷ γένει τῶν δικαίων, ἰδὼν τό τε μέγεθος αὐτοῦ
τῆς μαρτυρίας καὶ τὴν ἀπ' ἀρχῆς ἀνεπίληπτον πολιτείαν,

xvi. 1 περιστερὰ καὶ] περὶ στύρακα conj. Wordsworth.

ἐστεφανωμένον τε τὸν τῆς ἀφθαρσίας στέφανον καὶ βραβεῖον ἀναντίρρητον ἀπενηνεγμένον, ἐπετήδευσεν ὡς μηδὲ τὸ σωμάτιον αὐτοῦ ὑφ᾽ ἡμῶν ληφθῆναι, καίπερ πολλῶν ἐπιθυμούντων τοῦτο ποιῆσαι καὶ κοινωνῆσαι τῷ ἁγίῳ αὐτοῦ σαρκίῳ. 2. ὑπέβαλεν γοῦν Νικήτην τὸν τοῦ Ἡρώδου πατέρα, ἀδελφὸν δὲ Ἄλκης, ἐντυχεῖν τῷ ἄρχοντι ὥστε μὴ δοῦναι αὐτοῦ τὸ σῶμα, μή, φησίν, ἀφέντες τὸν ἐσταυρωμένον, τοῦτον ἄρξωνται σέβεσθαι· καὶ ταῦτα [εἶπον] ὑποβαλλόντων καὶ ἐνισχυόντων τῶν Ἰουδαίων, οἳ καὶ ἐτήρησαν, μελλόντων ἡμῶν ἐκ τοῦ πυρὸς αὐτὸν λαμβάνειν, ἀγνοοῦντες ὅτι οὔτε τὸν Χριστόν ποτε καταλιπεῖν δυνησόμεθα, τὸν ὑπὲρ τῆς τοῦ παντὸς κόσμου τῶν σωζομένων σωτηρίας παθόντα, ἄμωμον ὑπὲρ ἁμαρτωλῶν, οὔτε ἕτερόν τινα σέβεσθαι. 3. τοῦτον μὲν γὰρ υἱὸν ὄντα τοῦ Θεοῦ προσκυνοῦμεν, τοὺς δὲ μάρτυρας ὡς μαθητὰς καὶ μιμητὰς τοῦ Κυρίου ἀγαπῶμεν ἀξίως ἕνεκεν εὐνοίας ἀνυπερβλήτου τῆς εἰς τὸν ἴδιον βασιλέα καὶ διδάσκαλον· ὧν γένοιτο καὶ ἡμᾶς συγκοινωνούς τε καὶ συμμαθητὰς γενέσθαι.

XVIII. Ἰδὼν οὖν ὁ κεντυρίων τὴν τῶν Ἰουδαίων γενομένην φιλονεικίαν, θεὶς αὐτὸν ἐν μέσῳ, ὡς ἔθος αὐτοῖς, ἔκαυσεν. οὕτως τε ἡμεῖς ὕστερον ἀνελόμενοι τὰ τιμιώτερα λίθων πολυτελῶν καὶ δοκιμώτερα ὑπὲρ χρυσίον ὀστᾶ αὐτοῦ, ἀπεθέμεθα ὅπου καὶ ἀκόλουθον ἦν. 2. ἔνθα ὡς δυνατὸν ἡμῖν συναγομένοις ἐν ἀγαλλιάσει καὶ χαρᾷ παρέξει ὁ Κύριος ἐπιτελεῖν τὴν τοῦ μαρτυρίου αὐτοῦ ἡμέραν γενέθλιον, εἴς τε τὴν τῶν προηθληκότων μνήμην καὶ τῶν μελλόντων ἄσκησίν τε καὶ ἑτοιμασίαν.

XIX. Τοιαῦτα τὰ κατὰ τὸν μακάριον Πολύκαρπον, ὃς σὺν τοῖς ἀπὸ Φιλαδελφίας δωδέκατος ἐν Σμύρνῃ μαρτυρήσας μόνος ὑπὸ πάντων [μᾶλλον] μνημονεύεται, ὥστε καὶ ὑπὸ τῶν ἐθνῶν ἐν παντὶ τόπῳ λαλεῖσθαι, οὐ μόνον διδάσκαλος γενόμενος ἐπίσημος, ἀλλὰ καὶ μάρτυς ἔξοχος, οὗ τὸ μαρτύριον πάντες ἐπιθυμοῦσιν μιμεῖσθαι, κατὰ τὸ εὐαγγέλιον Χριστοῦ γενόμενον. 2. διὰ τῆς ὑπομονῆς καταγωνισάμενος τὸν ἄδικον

ἄρχοντα καὶ οὕτως τὸν τῆς ἀφθαρσίας στέφανον ἀπολαβών,
σὺν τοῖς ἀποστόλοις καὶ πᾶσιν δικαίοις ἀγαλλιώμενος δοξάζει τὸν Θεὸν καὶ πατέρα παντοκράτορα καὶ εὐλογεῖ [τὸν]
Κύριον [ἡμῶν] Ἰησοῦν Χριστόν, τὸν σωτῆρα τῶν ψυχῶν
ἡμῶν καὶ κυβερνήτην τῶν σωμάτων ἡμῶν καὶ ποιμένα τῆς
κατὰ τὴν οἰκουμένην καθολικῆς ἐκκλησίας.

XX. Ὑμεῖς μὲν οὖν ἠξιώσατε διὰ πλειόνων δηλωθῆναι
ὑμῖν τὰ γενόμενα· ἡμεῖς δὲ κατὰ τὸ παρὸν ὡς ἐν κεφαλαίῳ
μεμηνύκαμεν διὰ τοῦ ἀδελφοῦ ἡμῶν Μαρκιανοῦ. μαθόντες
οὖν ταῦτα καὶ τοῖς ἐπέκεινα ἀδελφοῖς τὴν ἐπιστολὴν διαπέμ-
ψασθε, ἵνα καὶ ἐκεῖνοι δοξάσωσι τὸν Κύριον τὸν ἐκλογὰς
ποιούμενον τῶν ἰδίων δούλων.

2. Τῷ δὲ δυναμένῳ πάντας ἡμᾶς εἰσαγαγεῖν [ἐν] τῇ
αὐτοῦ χάριτι καὶ δωρεᾷ εἰς τὴν ἐπουράνιον αὐτοῦ βασιλείαν,
διὰ παιδὸς αὐτοῦ, τοῦ μονογενοῦς Ἰησοῦ Χριστοῦ, δόξα, τιμή,
κράτος, μεγαλωσύνη, εἰς τοὺς αἰῶνας. προσαγορεύετε πάντας τοὺς ἁγίους. ὑμᾶς οἱ σὺν ἡμῖν προσαγορεύουσιν καὶ
Εὐάρεστος ὁ γράψας πανοικεί.

XXI. Μαρτυρεῖ δὲ ὁ μακάριος Πολύκαρπος μηνὸς
Ξανθικοῦ δευτέρᾳ ἱσταμένου, πρὸ ἑπτὰ καλανδῶν Μαρτίων,
σαββάτῳ μεγάλῳ, ὥρᾳ ὀγδόῃ· συνελήφθη ὑπὸ Ἡρώδου ἐπὶ
ἀρχιερέως Φιλίππου Τραλλιανοῦ, ἀνθυπατεύοντος Στατίου
Κοδράτου, βασιλεύοντος δὲ εἰς τοὺς αἰῶνας Ἰησοῦ Χριστοῦ·
ᾧ ἡ δόξα, τιμή, μεγαλωσύνη, θρόνος αἰώνιος, ἀπὸ γενεᾶς εἰς
γενεάν. ἀμήν.

XXII. [Ἐρρῶσθαι ὑμᾶς εὐχόμεθα, ἀδελφοί, στοιχοῦν-
τας τῷ κατὰ τὸ εὐαγγέλιον λόγῳ Ἰησοῦ Χριστοῦ· μεθ᾽
οὗ δόξα τῷ Θεῷ ἐπὶ σωτηρίᾳ τῇ τῶν ἁγίων ἐκλεκτῶν·
καθὼς ἐμαρτύρησεν ὁ μακάριος Πολύκαρπος, οὗ γένοιτο ἐν
τῇ βασιλείᾳ Ἰησοῦ Χριστοῦ πρὸς τὰ ἴχνη εὑρεθῆναι
ἡμᾶς.]

2. Ταῦτα μετεγράψατο μὲν Γάϊος ἐκ τῶν Εἰρηναίου
μαθητοῦ τοῦ Πολυκάρπου, ὃς καὶ συνεπολιτεύσατο τῷ Εἰρηναίῳ.

3. Ἐγὼ δὲ Σωκράτης ἐν Κορίνθῳ ἐκ τῶν Γαΐου ἀντιγράφων ἔγραψα. ἡ χάρις μετὰ πάντων.

4. Ἐγὼ δὲ πάλιν Πιόνιος ἐκ τοῦ προγεγραμμένου ἔγραψα ἀναζητήσας αὐτά, κατὰ ἀποκάλυψιν φανερώσαντός μοι τοῦ μακαρίου Πολυκάρπου, καθὼς δηλώσω ἐν τῷ καθεξῆς, συναγαγὼν αὐτὰ ἤδη σχεδὸν ἐκ τοῦ χρόνου κεκμηκότα,˙ ἵνα κἀμὲ συναγάγῃ ὁ Κύριος Ἰησοῦς Χριστὸς μετὰ τῶν ἐκλεκτῶν αὐτοῦ εἰς τὴν ἐπουράνιον βασιλείαν αὐτοῦ, ᾧ ἡ δόξα σὺν πατρὶ καὶ ἁγίῳ πνεύματι εἰς τοὺς αἰῶνας τῶν αἰώνων. ἀμήν.

[*The three preceding paragraphs as read in the Moscow MS.*]

2. Ταῦτα μετεγράψατο μὲν Γάϊος ἐκ τῶν Εἰρηναίου συγγραμμάτων ὃς καὶ συνεπολιτεύσατο τῷ Εἰρηναίῳ, μαθητῇ γεγονότι τοῦ ἁγίου Πολυκάρπου. οὗτος γὰρ ὁ Εἰρηναῖος, κατὰ τὸν καιρὸν τοῦ μαρτυρίου τοῦ ἐπισκόπου Πολυκάρπου γενόμενος ἐν Ῥώμῃ, πολλοὺς ἐδίδαξεν· οὗ καὶ πολλὰ αὐτοῦ συγγράμματα κάλλιστα καὶ ὀρθότατα φέρεται· ἐν οἷς μέμνηται Πολυκάρπου, ὅτι παρ' αὐτοῦ ἔμαθεν· ἱκανῶς τε πᾶσαν αἵρεσιν ἤλεγξεν, καὶ τὸν ἐκκλησιαστικὸν κανόνα καὶ καθολικόν, ὡς παρέλαβεν παρὰ τοῦ ἁγίου, καὶ παρέδωκεν. λέγει δὲ καὶ τοῦτο, ὅτι συναντήσαντός ποτε τῷ ἁγίῳ Πολυκάρπῳ Μαρκίωνος, ἀφ' οὗ οἱ λεγόμενοι Μαρκιωνισταί, καὶ εἰπόντος, Ἐπιγίνωσκε ἡμᾶς, Πολύκαρπε, εἶπεν αὐτὸς τῷ Μαρκίωνι, Ἐπιγινώσκω, ἐπιγινώσκω τὸν πρωτότοκον τοῦ Σατανᾶ. καὶ τοῦτο δὲ φέρεται ἐν τοῖς τοῦ Εἰρηναίου συγγράμμασιν, ὅτι ᾗ ἡμέρα καὶ ὥρα ἐν Σμύρνῃ ἐμαρτύρησεν ὁ Πολύκαρπος, ἤκουσεν φωνὴν ἐν τῇ Ῥωμαίων πόλει ὑπάρχων ὁ Εἰρηναῖος, ὡς σάλπιγγος λεγούσης, Πολύκαρπος ἐμαρτύρησεν.

xxii. 2 ὀρθότατα] ὀρθώτατα m.   Μαρκίωνος] μαρκίων m.   εἶπεν] εἰπεῖν m.   πόλει] πόλι m.   ἐμαρτύρησεν] ἐμαρτύρϊσεν m.

3. Ἐκ τούτων οὖν, ὡς προλέλεκται, τῶν τοῦ Εἰρηναίου συγγραμμάτων Γάϊος μετεγράψατο, ἐκ δὲ τῶν Γαΐου ἀντιγράφων Ἰσοκράτης ἐν Κορίνθῳ.

4. Ἐγὼ δὲ πάλιν Πιόνιος ἐκ τῶν Ἰσοκράτους ἀντιγράφων ἔγραψα, κατὰ ἀποκάλυψιν τοῦ ἁγίου Πολυκάρπου ζητήσας αὐτά, συναγαγὼν αὐτὰ ἤδη σχεδὸν ἐκ τοῦ χρόνου κεκμηκότα, ἵνα κἀμὲ συναγάγῃ ὁ Κύριος Ἰησοῦς Χριστὸς μετὰ τῶν ἐκλεκτῶν αὐτοῦ εἰς τὴν ἐπουράνιον αὐτοῦ βασιλείαν· ᾧ ἡ δόξα σὺν τῷ πατρὶ καὶ τῷ υἱῷ καὶ τῷ ἁγίῳ πνεύματι εἰς τοὺς αἰῶνας τῶν αἰώνων. ἀμήν.

3 τούτων] τούτου m.   Εἰρηναίου] εἰρηναῖος m.

TRANSLATION

OF THE

LETTER OF THE SMYRNÆANS

LETTER OF THE SMYRNÆANS

THE CHURCH OF GOD which sojourneth at Smyrna to the Church of God which sojourneth in Philomelium and to all the brotherhoods of the holy and universal Church sojourning in every place ; mercy and peace and love from God the Father and our Lord Jesus Christ be multiplied.

1. We write unto you, brethren, an account of what befel those that suffered martyrdom and especially the blessed Polycarp, who stayed the persecution, having as it were set his seal upon it by his martyrdom. For nearly all the foregoing events came to pass that the Lord might show us once more an example of martyrdom which is conformable to the Gospel. For he lingered that he might be delivered up, even as the Lord did, to the end that we too might be imitators of him, *not looking* only *to that which concerneth ourselves, but also to that which concerneth our neighbours.* For it is the office of true and stedfast love, not only to desire that oneself be saved, but all the brethren also.

2. Blessed therefore and noble are all the martyrdoms which have taken place according to the will of God (for it behoveth us to be very scrupulous and to assign to God the power over all things). For who could fail to admire their nobleness and patient endurance and loyalty to the Master ? seeing that when they were so torn by lashes that the mechanism of their flesh was visible even as far as the inward veins and arteries, they endured patiently, so that the very bystanders had pity and wept ; while they themselves reached such a pitch of bravery that none of them uttered a cry or a groan, thus showing to us all that at that hour the martyrs of Christ being tortured were absent from the flesh, or rather that the Lord was standing by and conversing with them. And giving heed unto the grace of Christ they despised the tortures of

this world, purchasing at the cost of one hour a release from eternal punishment. And they found the fire of their inhuman torturers cold: for they set before their eyes the escape from the eternal fire which is never quenched; while with the eyes of their heart they gazed upon the good things which are reserved for those that endure patiently, things *which neither ear hath heard nor eye hath seen, neither have they entered into the heart of man*, but were shown by the Lord to them, for they were no longer men but angels already. And in like manner also those that were condemned to the wild beasts endured fearful punishments, being made to lie on sharp shells and buffeted with other forms of manifold tortures, that the devil might, if possible, by the persistence of the punishment bring them to a denial; for he tried many wiles against them.

3. But thanks be to God; for He verily prevailed against all. For the right noble Germanicus encouraged their timorousness through the constancy which was in him; and he fought with the wild beasts in a signal way. For when the proconsul wished to prevail upon him and bade him have pity on his youth, he used violence and dragged the wild beast towards him, desiring the more speedily to obtain a release from their unrighteous and lawless life. So after this all the multitude, marvelling at the bravery of the God-beloved and God-fearing people of the Christians, raised a cry, 'Away with the atheists; let search be made for Polycarp.'

4. But one man, Quintus by name, a Phrygian newly arrived from Phrygia, when he saw the wild beasts, turned coward. He it was who had forced himself and some others to come forward of their own free will. This man the proconsul by much entreaty persuaded to swear the oath and to offer incense. For this cause therefore, brethren, we praise not those who deliver themselves up, since the Gospel doth not so teach us.

5. Now the glorious Polycarp at the first, when he heard it, so far from being dismayed, was desirous of remaining in town; but the greater part persuaded him to withdraw. So he withdrew to a farm not far distant from the city; and there he stayed with a few companions, doing nothing else night and day but praying for all men and for the churches throughout the world; for this was his constant habit. And while praying he falleth into a trance three days before his apprehension; and he saw his pillow burning with fire. And he turned and said unto those that were with him: 'It must needs be that I shall be burned alive.'

6. And as those that were in search of him persisted, he departed to another farm; and forthwith they that were in search of him came up; and not finding him, they seized two slave lads, one of whom confessed under torture; for it was impossible for him to lie concealed, seeing that the very persons who betrayed him were people of his own household. And the captain of the police, who chanced to have the very name, being called Herod, was eager to bring him into the stadium, that he himself might fulfil his appointed lot, being made a partaker with Christ, while they—his betrayers—underwent the punishment of Judas himself.

7. So taking the lad with them, on the Friday about the supper hour, the gendarmes and horsemen went forth with their accustomed arms, hastening *as against a robber*. And coming up in a body late in the evening, they found the man himself in bed in an upper chamber in a certain cottage; and though he might have departed thence to another place, he would not, saying, *The will of God be done*. So when he heard that they were come, he went down and conversed with them, the bystanders marvelling at his age and his constancy, and wondering how there should be so much eagerness for the apprehension of an old man like him. Thereupon forthwith he gave orders that a table should be spread for them to eat and drink at that hour, as much as they desired. And he persuaded them to grant him an hour that he might pray unmolested; and on their consenting, he stood up and prayed, being so full of the grace of God, that for two hours he could not hold his peace, and those that heard were amazed, and many repented that they had come against such a venerable old man.

8. But when at length he brought his prayer to an end, after remembering all who at any time had come in his way, small and great, high and low, and all the universal Church throughout the world, the hour of departure being come, they seated him on an ass and brought him into the city, it being a high sabbath. And he was met by Herod the captain of police and his father Nicetes, who also removed him to their carriage and tried to prevail upon him, seating themselves by his side and saying, 'Why what harm is there in saying, Cæsar is Lord, and offering incense', with more to this effect, 'and saving thyself?' But he at first gave them no answer. When however they persisted, he said, 'I am not going to do what ye counsel me.' Then they, failing to persuade him, uttered threatening words and made him dismount with speed, so that he bruised his shin, as he got down from the carriage.

And without even turning round, he went on his way promptly and with speed, as if nothing had happened to him, being taken to the stadium; there being such a tumult in the stadium that no man's voice could be so much as heard.

9. But as Polycarp entered into the stadium, a voice came to him from heaven; 'Be strong, Polycarp, and play the man.' And no one saw the speaker, but those of our people who were present heard the voice. And at length, when he was brought up, there was a great tumult, for they heard that Polycarp had been apprehended. When then he was brought before him, the proconsul enquired whether he were the man. And on his confessing that he was, he tried to persuade him to a denial saying, 'Have respect to thine age,' and other things in accordance therewith, as it is their wont to say; 'Swear by the genius of Cæsar; repent and say, Away with the atheists.' Then Polycarp with solemn countenance looked upon the whole multitude of lawless heathen that were in the stadium, and waved his hand to them; and groaning and looking up to heaven he said, 'Away with the atheists.' But when the magistrate pressed him hard and said, 'Swear the oath, and I will release thee; revile the Christ,' Polycarp said, 'Fourscore and six years have I been His servant, and He hath done me no wrong. How then can I blaspheme my King who saved me?'

10. But on his persisting again and saying, 'Swear by the genius of Cæsar,' he answered, 'If thou supposest vainly that I will swear by the genius of Cæsar, as thou sayest, and feignest that thou art ignorant who I am, hear thou plainly, I am a Christian. But if thou wouldest learn the doctrine of Christianity, assign a day and give me a hearing.' The proconsul said; 'Prevail upon the people.' But Polycarp said; 'As for thyself, I should have held thee worthy of discourse; for we have been taught to render, as is meet, to princes and authorities appointed by God such honour as does us no harm; but as for these, I do not hold them worthy, that I should defend myself before them.'

11. Whereupon the proconsul said; 'I have wild beasts here and I will throw thee to them, except thou repent.' But he said, 'Call for them: for the repentance from better to worse is a change not permitted to us; but it is a noble thing to change from untowardness to righteousness.' Then he said to him again, 'I will cause thee to be consumed by fire, if thou despisest the wild beasts, unless thou repent.' But Polycarp said; 'Thou threatenest that fire which burneth for a season and after a little while is quenched: for thou art ignorant of the

fire of the future judgment and eternal punishment, which is reserved for the ungodly. But why delayest thou? Come, do what thou wilt.'

12. Saying these things and more besides, he was inspired with courage and joy, and his countenance was filled with grace, so that not only did it not drop in dismay at the things which were said to him, but on the contrary the proconsul was astounded and sent his own herald to proclaim three times in the midst of the stadium, 'Polycarp hath confessed himself to be a Christian.' When this was proclaimed by the herald, the whole multitude both of Gentiles and of Jews who dwelt in Smyrna cried out with ungovernable wrath and with a loud shout, 'This is the teacher of Asia, the father of the Christians, the puller down of our gods, who teacheth numbers not to sacrifice nor worship.' Saying these things, they shouted aloud and asked the Asiarch Philip to let a lion loose upon Polycarp. But he said that it was not lawful for him, since he had brought the sports to a close. Then they thought fit to shout out with one accord that Polycarp should be burned alive. For it must needs be that the matter of the vision should be fulfilled, which was shown him concerning his pillow, when he saw it on fire while praying, and turning round he said prophetically to the faithful who were with him, 'I must needs be burned alive.'

13. These things then happened with so great speed, quicker than words could tell, the crowds forthwith collecting from the workshops and baths timber and faggots, and the Jews more especially assisting in this with zeal, as is their wont. But when the pile was made ready, divesting himself of all his upper garments and loosing his girdle, he endeavoured also to take off his shoes, though not in the habit of doing this before, because all the faithful at all times vied eagerly who should soonest touch his flesh. For he had been treated with all honour for his holy life even before his gray hairs came. Forthwith then the instruments that were prepared for the pile were placed about him; and as they were going likewise to nail him to the stake, he said; 'Leave me as I am; for He that hath granted me to endure the fire will grant me also to remain at the pile unmoved, even without the security which ye seek from the nails.'

14. So they did not nail him, but tied him. Then he, placing his hands behind him and being bound to the stake, like a noble ram out of a great flock for an offering, a burnt sacrifice made ready and acceptable to God, looking up to heaven said; 'O Lord God Almighty,

the Father of Thy beloved and blessed Son Jesus Christ, through whom we have received the knowledge of Thee, the God of angels and powers and of all creation and of the whole race of the righteous, who live in Thy presence; I bless Thee for that Thou hast granted me this day and hour, that I might receive a portion amongst the number of martyrs in the cup of [Thy] Christ unto resurrection of eternal life, both of soul and of body, in the incorruptibility of the Holy Spirit. May I be received among these in Thy presence this day, as a rich and acceptable sacrifice, as Thou didst prepare and reveal it beforehand, and hast accomplished it, Thou that art the faithful and true God. For this cause, yea and for all things, I praise Thee, I bless Thee, I glorify Thee, through the eternal and heavenly High-priest, Jesus Christ, Thy beloved Son, through whom with Him and the Holy Spirit be glory both now [and ever] and for the ages to come. Amen.'

15. When he had offered up the Amen and finished his prayer, the firemen lighted the fire. And, a mighty flame flashing forth, we to whom it was given to see, saw a marvel, yea and we were preserved that we might relate to the rest what happened. The fire, making the appearance of a vault, like the sail of a vessel filled by the wind, made a wall round about the body of the martyr; and it was there in the midst, not like flesh burning, but like [a loaf in the oven or like] gold and silver refined in a furnace. For we perceived such a fragrant smell, as if it were the wafted odour of frankincense or some other precious spice.

16. So at length the lawless men, seeing that his body could not be consumed by the fire, ordered an executioner to go up to him and stab him with a dagger. And when he had done this, there came forth [a dove and] a quantity of blood, so that it extinguished the fire; and all the multitude marvelled that there should be so great a difference between the unbelievers and the elect. In the number of these was this man, the glorious martyr Polycarp, who was found an apostolic and prophetic teacher in our own time, a bishop of the holy Church which is in Smyrna. For every word which he uttered from his mouth was accomplished and will be accomplished.

17. But the jealous and envious Evil One, the adversary of the family of the righteous, having seen the greatness of his martyrdom and his blameless life from the beginning, and how he was crowned with the crown of immortality and had won a reward which none could gainsay, managed that not even his poor body should be taken away

by us, although many desired to do this and to touch his holy flesh. So he put forward Nicetes, the father of Herod and brother of Alce, to plead with the magistrate not to give up his body, 'lest,' so it was said, 'they should abandon the crucified one and begin to worship this man'—this being done at the instigation and urgent entreaty of the Jews, who also watched when we were about to take it from the fire, not knowing that it will be impossible for us either to forsake at any time the Christ who suffered for the salvation of the whole world of those that are saved—suffered though faultless for sinners—nor to worship any other.   For Him, being the Son of God, we adore, but the martyrs as disciples and imitators of the Lord we cherish as they deserve for their matchless affection towards their own King and Teacher.   May it be our lot also to be found partakers and fellow-disciples with them.

18.   The centurion therefore, seeing the opposition raised on the part of the Jews, set him in the midst and burnt him after their custom. And so we afterwards took up his bones which are more valuable than precious stones and finer than refined gold, and laid them in a suitable place; where the Lord will permit us to gather ourselves together, as we are able, in gladness and joy, and to celebrate the birth-day of his martyrdom for the commemoration of those that have already fought in the contest, and for the training and preparation of those that shall do so hereafter.

19.   So it befel the blessed Polycarp, who having with those from Philadelphia suffered martyrdom in Smyrna—twelve in all—is especially remembered more than the others by all men, so that he is talked of even by the heathen in every place : for he showed himself not only a notable teacher, but also a distinguished martyr, whose martyrdom all desire to imitate, seeing that it was after the pattern of the Gospel of Christ.   Having by his endurance overcome the unrighteous ruler in the conflict and so received the crown of immortality, he rejoiceth in company with the Apostles and all righteous men, and glorifieth the Almighty God and Father, and blesseth our Lord Jesus Christ, the saviour of our souls and helmsman of our bodies and shepherd of the universal Church which is throughout the world.

20.   Ye indeed required that the things which happened should be shown unto you at greater length : but we for the present have certified you as it were in a summary through our brother Marcianus. When then ye have informed yourselves of these things, send the letter

about likewise to the brethren which are farther off, that they also may glorify the Lord, who maketh election from His own servants. Now unto Him that is able to bring us all by His grace and bounty unto His eternal kingdom, through His only-begotten Son Jesus Christ, be glory, honour, power, and greatness for ever. Salute all the saints. They that are with us salute you, and Euarestus, who wrote the letter, with his whole house.

21.   Now the blessed Polycarp was martyred on the second day of the first part of the month Xanthicus, on the seventh before the kalends of March, on a great sabbath, at the eighth hour. He was apprehended by Herodes, when Philip of Tralles was high-priest, in the proconsulship of Statius Quadratus, but in the reign of the Eternal King Jesus Christ. To whom be the glory, honour, greatness, and eternal throne, from generation to generation. Amen.

22.   (1) We bid you God speed, brethren, while ye walk by the word of Jesus Christ which is according to the Gospel; with whom be glory to God for the salvation of His holy elect; even as the blessed Polycarp suffered martyrdom, in whose footsteps may it be our lot to be found in the kingdom of Jesus Christ.

(2)   This account Gaius copied from the papers of Irenæus, a disciple of Polycarp. The same also lived with Irenæus.

(3)   And I Socrates wrote it down in Corinth from the copy of Gaius. Grace be with all men.

(4)   And I Pionius again wrote it down from the aforementioned copy, having searched it out (for the blessed Polycarp showed me in a revelation, as I will declare in the sequel), gathering it together when it was now well nigh worn out by age, that the Lord Jesus Christ may gather me also with His elect into His heavenly kingdom; to whom be the glory with the Father and the Holy Spirit for ever and ever. Amen.

The three preceding paragraphs as read in the Moscow MS.

(2)   This account Gaius copied from the papers of Irenæus. The same lived with Irenæus who had been a disciple of the holy Polycarp. For this Irenæus, being in Rome at the time of the martyrdom of the bishop Polycarp, instructed many; and many most excellent and orthodox treatises by him are in circulation. In these he makes

mention of Polycarp, saying that he was taught by him. And he ably refuted every heresy, and handed down the catholic rule of the Church just as he had received it from the saint. He mentions this fact also, that when Marcion, after whom the Marcionites are called, met the holy Polycarp on one occasion, and said 'Recognize us, Polycarp,' he said in reply to Marcion, 'Yes indeed, I recognize the firstborn of Satan.' The following statement also is made in the writings of Irenæus, that on the very day and hour when Polycarp was martyred in Smyrna Irenæus being in the city of the Romans heard a voice as of a trumpet saying, 'Polycarp is martyred.'

(3) From these papers of Irenæus then, as has been stated already, Gaius made a copy, and from the copy of Gaius Isocrates made another in Corinth.

(4) And I Pionius again wrote it down from the copy of Isocrates, having searched for it in obedience to a revelation of the holy Polycarp, gathering it together, when it was well nigh worn out by age, that the Lord Jesus Christ may gather me also with His elect into His heavenly kingdom; to whom be the glory with the Father and the Son and the Holy Spirit for ever and ever. Amen.

THE DIDACHE

OR

TEACHING OF THE APOSTLES

THE TEACHING OF THE
APOSTLES

I

THE Didache is a church-manual of primitive Christianity or of some section of it. It is called 'The Teaching of the Apostles' or 'The Teaching of the Twelve Apostles.' The latter appears in the manuscript; but the former is the designation in several ancient writers who refer to it. It is therefore adopted as the title here. The manual consists of two parts: (1) a moral treatise founded on an ancient work called 'The Two Ways,' and setting forth the paths of righteousness and unrighteousness, of life and death respectively. This first part is not necessarily altogether of Christian origin; indeed there is reason to believe that some portions of it were known to the Jews, and perhaps also to the Greeks, though it has undoubtedly gathered by accretions. (2) The second part gives directions affecting church rites and orders. It treats of baptism, prayer and fasting, the eucharist and agape, the treatment of apostles and prophets, of bishops and deacons, the whole closing with a solemn warning to watchfulness in view of the second coming of Christ.

The work is obviously of very early date, as is shown by the internal evidence of language and subject-matter. Thus for instance the itinerant prophetic order has not yet been displaced by the permanent localized ministry, but exists side by side with it as in the lifetime of S. Paul (Eph. iv. 11, 1 Cor. xii. 28). Secondly, episcopacy has apparently not yet become universal; the word 'bishop' is still used as synonymous with 'presbyter,' and the writer therefore couples 'bishops' with 'deacons' (§ 15) as S. Paul does (1 Tim. iii. 1—8, Phil. i. 1) under similar circumstances. Thirdly, from the expression in § 10 'after ye have been filled' it appears that the agape still remains part of the Lord's Supper. Lastly, the archaic simplicity of its practical suggestions is only consistent with the early infancy of a church. These indications point to the first or the beginning of the second century as the date of the work in its present form.

As regards the place of writing, opinion in the first instance had been strongly in favour of Egypt, because the Teaching was early quoted by Egyptian writers; but from the casual allusion in § 9 to the 'corn scattered upon the mountains' it will appear to have been written either in Syria or Palestine.

2

The Didache was discovered by Bryennios in the same MS with the complete copy of the Epistle of Clement mentioned above (p. 4) and called the Constantinopolitan or Hierosolymitan MS. Besides the Teaching and the Genuine and Spurious Epistles of Clement in full, this document contained Chrysostom's Synopsis of the Old and New Testament (incomplete), the Epistle of Barnabas, and the Long Recension of the Ignatian Epistles. The MS is dated A.D. 1056. But though a list of the contents of this document was announced by Bryennios in 1875, eight years elapsed before the Didache itself was published. Meanwhile, as a work of this name is mentioned by Eusebius and others among early apocryphal writings, a hope was excited in the minds of those interested in such studies that this might be the book alluded to, and that it would throw some light on the vexed question of the origin of the Apostolical Constitutions. When at length in 1883 it was given to the world, its interest and importance were proved to exceed the highest expectations. It has been generally admitted to be the work mentioned by Eusebius and also quoted by Clement of Alexandria as 'scripture.' It is the basis of the seventh book of the Apostolical Constitutions. In language and subject-matter it presents close affinities to many other early documents, notably the Ecclesiastical Canons and the Epistle of Barnabas. A fragment of a Latin translation has also been discovered by Gebhardt, and is printed below (p. 225). Thus though there is but one extant MS of the Didache in its present form, the incorporation of a great part of it into patristic writings and early church-manuals renders the problem of its origin and development a peculiarly interesting one.

ΔΙΔΑΧΗ ΤΩΝ ΑΠΟΣΤΟΛΩΝ

ΔΙΔΑΧΗ Κυρίου διὰ τῶν δώδεκα ἀποστόλων τοῖς
ἔθνεσιν. I. Ὁδοὶ δύο εἰσί, μία τῆς ζωῆς καὶ μία τοῦ θανάτου,
διαφορὰ δὲ πολλὴ μεταξὺ τῶν δύο ὁδῶν. 2. Ἡ μὲν οὖν ὁδὸς Jer. xxi. 8.
τῆϲ ζωῆϲ ἐϲτὶν αὕτη· πρῶτον, ἀϲαπήϲειϲ τὸν Θεὸν τὸν S. Matt.
ποιήϲαντά ϲε· δεύτερον, τὸν πληϲίον ϲογ ὡϲ ϲεαγτόν· πάντα xxii. 37,39.
Lev. xix.
δὲ ὅϲα ἐὰν θελήϲηϲ μὴ ϲίνεϲθαί ϲοι, καὶ ϲγ ἄλλῳ μὴ ποίει. 18.
Tobit iv.
3. τούτων δὲ τῶν λόγων ἡ διδαχή ἐστιν αὕτη· Εϲλοϲεῖτε 15.
τογϲ καταρωμένογϲ γμῖν καὶ προϲεγχεϲθε ὑπὲρ τῶν ἐχθρῶν S. Matt. v.
44, 46.
ὑμῶν, νηϲτεύετε δὲ γπὲρ τῶν Διωκόντων γμᾶϲ. ποία ϲὰρ χάριϲ, S. Luke
vi. 27, 28,
ἐὰν ἀϲαπᾶτε τογϲ ἀϲαπῶνταϲ γμᾶϲ; ογχὶ καὶ τὰ ἔθνη τὸ αγτὸ 32, 33, 35.
ποιογϲιν; γμεῖϲ Δὲ ἀϲαπᾶτε τογϲ μιϲογνταϲ γμᾶϲ καὶ ογχ ἕξετε
ἐχθρόν. 4. ἀπέχου τῶν σαρκικῶν καὶ σωματικῶν ἐπιθυμιῶν.
ἐὰν τιϲ ϲοι Δῷ ῥάπιϲμα εἰϲ τὴν Δεξιὰν ϲιαϲονα, ϲτρέψον αγτῷ S. Matt.
καὶ τὴν ἄλλην, καὶ ἔϲη τέλειοϲ· ἐὰν ἀϲϲαρεγϲῃ ϲέ τιϲ μίλιον ἕν, v. 39—42.
S. Luke
γπαϲε μετ' αγτογ Δγο· ἐὰν ἄρη τιϲ τὸ ἱμάτιόν ϲου, Δὸϲ αγτῷ vi. 29, 30.
καὶ τὸν χιτῶνα· ἐὰν λάβη τιϲ ἀπό ϲου τὸ ϲόν, μὴ ἀπαίτει·
ογδὲ ϲὰρ δύναϲαι. 5. παντὶ τῷ αἰτογντί ϲε Δίδογ καὶ μὴ
ἀπαίτει· πᾶϲι ϲὰρ θέλει δίδοϲθαι ὁ πατὴρ ἐκ τῶν ἰδίων
χαρισμάτων. μακάριος ὁ διδοὺς κατὰ τὴν ἐντολήν· ἀθῷος
ϲάρ ἐϲτιν. ογαὶ τῷ λαμβάνοντι· εἰ μὲν ϲὰρ χρείαν ἔχων
λαμβάνει τις, ἀθῷος ἔϲται· ὁ δὲ μὴ χρείαν ἔχων δώϲει
δίκην, ἵνα τί ἔλαβε καὶ εἰς τί· ἐν ϲυνοχῇ δὲ ϲενόμενος
ἐξεταϲθήϲεται περὶ ὧν ἔπραξε καὶ ογκ ἐξελεγϲεται ἐκεῖθεν, S. Matt.
μέχριϲ ογ ἀποδῷ τὸν ἔϲχατον κοΔράντην. 6. ἀλλὰ καὶ περὶ v. 26.

τούτου δὲ εἴρηται· Ἱδρωτάτω ἡ ἐλεημοcύνη coy εἰc τὰc χεῖράc
coy, μέχριc ἂν γνῷc τίνι Δῷc.   II. Δευτέρα δὲ ἐντολὴ τῆς διδαχῆς· 2. Οὐ φονεύcειc, οὐ
μοιχεύcειc, οὐ παιδοφθορήσεις, οὐ πορνεύσεις, οὐ κλέψειc, οὐ
μαγεύσεις, οὐ φαρμακεύσεις, οὐ φονεύσεις τέκνον ἐν φθορᾷ
οὐδὲ γεννηθέντα ἀποκτενεῖς, οὐκ ἐπιθυμήcειc τὰ τοῦ πληcίον,
3. οὐκ ἐπιορκήcειc, οὐ ψεγΔομαρτγρήcειc, οὐ κακολογήσεις, οὐ
μνησικακήσεις· 4. οὐκ ἔσῃ διγνώμων οὐδὲ δίγλωσσος· παγὶς
γὰρ θανάτου ἡ διγλωσσία. 5. οὐκ ἔσται ὁ λόγος σου ψευδής,
οὐ κενός, ἀλλὰ μεμεστωμένος πράξει. 6. οὐκ ἔσῃ πλεονέκτης
οὐδὲ ἅρπαξ οὐδὲ ὑποκριτὴς οὐδὲ κακοήθης οὐδὲ ὑπερήφανος.
οὐ λήψῃ βουλὴν πονηρὰν κατὰ τοῦ πλησίον σου. 7. οὐ
μιcήcειc πάντα ἄνθρωπον, ἀλλὰ οὓc μὲν ἐλέγξειc, περὶ δὲ ὧν
προσεύξῃ, οὓc Δὲ ἀγαπήcειc ὑπὲρ τὴν ψυχήν σου.

III. Τέκνον μου, φεῦγε ἀπὸ παντὸς πονηροῦ καὶ ἀπὸ
παντὸς ὁμοίου αὐτοῦ. 2. μὴ γίνου ὀργίλος· ὁδηγεῖ γὰρ ἡ
ὀργὴ πρὸς τὸν φόνον· μηδὲ ζηλωτὴς μηδὲ ἐριστικὸς μηδὲ
θυμικός· ἐκ γὰρ τούτων ἁπάντων φόνοι γεννῶνται. 3. τέκνον
μου, μὴ γίνου ἐπιθυμητής· ὁδηγεῖ γὰρ ἡ ἐπιθυμία πρὸς τὴν
πορνείαν· μηδὲ αἰσχρολόγος μηδὲ ὑψηλόφθαλμος· ἐκ γὰρ
τούτων ἁπάντων μοιχεῖαι γεννῶνται. 4. τέκνον μου, μὴ
γίνογ οἰωνοσκόπος· ἐπειδὴ ὁδηγεῖ εἰς τὴν εἰδωλολατρίαν·
μηδὲ ἐπαοιδὸς μηδὲ μαθηματικὸς μηδὲ περικαθαίρων μηδὲ
θέλε αὐτὰ βλέπειν· ἐκ γὰρ τούτων ἁπάντων εἰδωλολατρία
γεννᾶται. 5. τέκνον μου, μὴ γίνου ψεύστης· ἐπειδὴ ὁδηγεῖ
τὸ ψεῦσμα εἰς τὴν κλοπήν· μηδὲ φιλάργυρος μηδὲ κενόδοξος·
ἐκ γὰρ τούτων ἁπάντων κλοπαὶ γεννῶνται. 6. τέκνον μου,
μὴ γίνου γόγγυσος· ἐπειδὴ ὁδηγεῖ εἰς τὴν βλασφημίαν· μηδὲ
αὐθάδης μηδὲ πονηρόφρων· ἐκ γὰρ τούτων ἁπάντων βλα-
σφημίαι γεννῶνται. 7. ἴσθι δὲ πραΰς· ἐπεὶ οἱ πραεῖc κληρο-
νομήcογcι τὴν γῆν. 8. γίνου μακρόθυμος καὶ ἐλεήμων καὶ
ἄκακος καὶ ἡcύχιος καὶ ἀγαθὸς καὶ τρέμων τοὺc λόγογc διὰ

? | Ex. xx. 13—17. | S. Matt. v. 33. | Lev. xix. 17, 18. Jude 22. | Lev. xix. 26. | S. Matt. v. 5. | Is. lxvi. 2.

iii. 2 ὀργίλος] conj. Bryennios; ὀργῖλος MS.   3 γεννῶνται] conj.
Bryennios; γενῶνται MS.

παντός, οὓς ἤκουσας. 9. οὐχ ὑψώσεις σεαυτὸν οὐδὲ δώσεις
τῇ ψυχῇ σου θράσος. οὐ κολληθήσεται ἡ ψυχή σου μετὰ
ὑψηλῶν, ἀλλὰ μετὰ δικαίων καὶ ταπεινῶν ἀναστραφήσῃ.
10. τὰ συμβαίνοντά σοι ἐνεργήματα ὡς ἀγαθὰ προσδέξῃ,
εἰδὼς ὅτι ἄτερ Θεοῦ οὐδὲν γίνεται. IV. Τέκνον μου, τοῦ λαλοῦντόϲ ϲοι τὸν λόγον τοῦ Θεοῦ
μνηϲθήϲη νυκτὸς καὶ ἡμέρας· τιμήσεις δὲ αὐτὸν ὡς Κύριον·
ὅθεν γὰρ ἡ κυριότης λαλεῖται, ἐκεῖ Κύριός ἐστιν. 2. ἐκζητήσεις δὲ καθ' ἡμέραν τὰ πρόσωπα τῶν ἁγίων, ἵνα ἐπαναπαῇς
τοῖς λόγοις αὐτῶν. 3. οὐ ποιήσεις σχίσμα, εἰρηνεύσεις δὲ
μαχομένους. κρινεῖς δικαίως, οὐ λήψῃ πρόσωπον ἐλέγξαι
ἐπὶ παραπτώμασιν. 4. οὐ διψυχήσεις, πότερον ἔσται ἢ οὔ.
5. μὴ γίνου πρὸϲ μὲν τὸ λαβεῖν ἐκτείνων τὰϲ χεῖραϲ, πρὸϲ δὲ
τὸ δοῦναι ϲυϲπῶν· 6. ἐὰν ἔχῃς διὰ τῶν χειρῶν σου, δώσεις
λύτρωσιν ἁμαρτιῶν σου. 7. οὐ διστάσεις δοῦναι οὐδὲ διδοὺς
γογγύσεις· γνώσῃ γὰρ τίς ἐστιν ὁ τοῦ μισθοῦ καλὸς ἀνταποδότης. 8. οὐκ ἀποστραφήσῃ τὸν ἐνδεόμενον, συγκοινωνήσεις
δὲ πάντα τῷ ἀδελφῷ σου καὶ οὐκ ἐρεῖς ἴδια εἶναι· εἰ γὰρ ἐν
τῷ ἀθανάτῳ κοινωνοί ἐστε, πόσῳ μᾶλλον ἐν τοῖς θνητοῖς;
9. οὐκ ἀρεῖς τὴν χεῖρά σου ἀπὸ τοῦ υἱοῦ σου ἢ ἀπὸ τῆς
θυγατρός σου, ἀλλὰ ἀπὸ νεότητος διδάξεις τὸν φόβον τοῦ
Θεοῦ. 10. οὐκ ἐπιτάξεις δούλῳ σου ἢ παιδίσκῃ, τοῖς ἐπὶ τὸν
αὐτὸν Θεὸν ἐλπίζουσιν, ἐν πικρίᾳ σου, μήποτε οὐ μὴ φοβηθή-
σονται τὸν ἐπ' ἀμφοτέροις Θεόν· οὐ γὰρ ἔρχεται κατὰ πρόσωπον καλέσαι, ἀλλ' ἐφ' οὓς τὸ πνεῦμα ἡτοίμασεν. 11. ὑμεῖς
δὲ οἱ δοῦλοι ὑποταγήσεσθε τοῖς κυρίοις ὑμῶν ὡς τύπῳ Θεοῦ
ἐν αἰσχύνῃ καὶ φόβῳ. 12. μισήσεις πᾶσαν ὑπόκρισιν καὶ
πᾶν ὃ μὴ ἀρεστὸν τῷ Κυρίῳ. 13. οὐ μὴ ἐγκαταλίπῃς
ἐντολὰς Κυρίου, φυλάξεις δὲ ἃ παρέλαβες, μήτε προστιθεὶς
μήτε ἀφαιρῶν. 14. ἐν ἐκκλησίᾳ ἐξομολογήσῃ τὰ παραπτώ-
ματά σου, καὶ οὐ προσελεύσῃ ἐπὶ προσευχήν σου ἐν συνειδήσει πονηρᾷ. αὕτη ἐστὶν ἡ ὁδὸς τῆς ζωῆς.

Heb. xiii. 7.

Ecclus. iv. 31.

Acts iv. 32.

V. Ἡ δὲ τοῦ θανάτου ὁδός ἐστιν αὕτη· πρῶτον πάντων πονηρά ἐστι καὶ κατάρας μεστή· φόνοι, μοιχεῖαι, ἐπιθυμίαι, πορνεῖαι, κλοπαί, εἰδωλολατρίαι, μαγεῖαι, φαρμακίαι, ἁρπαγαί, ψευδομαρτυρίαι, ὑποκρίσεις, διπλοκαρδία, δόλος, ὑπερηφανία, κακία, αὐθάδεια, πλεονεξία, αἰσχρολογία, ζηλοτυπία, θρασύτης, ὕψος, ἀλαζονεία· 2. διῶκται ἀγαθῶν, μισοῦντες ἀλήθειαν, ἀγαπῶντες ψεῦδος, οὐ γινώσκοντες μισθὸν δικαιο-

σύνης, οὐ κολλώμενοι ἀγαθῷ οὐδὲ κρίσει δικαίᾳ, ἀγρυπνοῦντες οὐκ εἰς τὸ ἀγαθόν, ἀλλ᾽ εἰς τὸ πονηρόν· ὧν μακρὰν πραΰτης καὶ ὑπομονή, μάταια ἀγαπῶντες, διώκοντες ἀνταπόδομα, οὐκ ἐλεοῦντες πτωχόν, οὐ πονοῦντες ἐπὶ καταπονουμένῳ, οὐ γινώσκοντες τὸν ποιήσαντα αὐτούς, φονεῖς τέκνων, φθορεῖς πλάσματος Θεοῦ, ἀποστρεφόμενοι τὸν ἐνδεόμενον, καταπονοῦντες τὸν θλιβόμενον, πλουσίων παράκλητοι, πενήτων ἄνομοι κριταί, πανθαμάρτητοι· ῥυσθείητε, τέκνα, ἀπὸ τούτων ἁπάντων.

VI. Ὅρα μή τις σε πλανήσῃ ἀπὸ ταύτης τῆς ὁδοῦ τῆς διδαχῆς, ἐπεὶ παρεκτὸς Θεοῦ σε διδάσκει. 2. εἰ μὲν γὰρ δύνασαι βαστάσαι ὅλον τὸν ζυγὸν τοῦ Κυρίου, τέλειος ἔσῃ· εἰ δ᾽ οὐ δύνασαι, ὃ δύνῃ τοῦτο ποίει.

3. Περὶ δὲ τῆς βρώσεως, ὃ δύνασαι βάστασον· ἀπὸ δὲ τοῦ εἰδωλοθύτου λίαν πρόσεχε· λατρεία γάρ ἐστιν θεῶν νεκρῶν.

VII. Περὶ δὲ τοῦ βαπτίσματος, οὕτω βαπτίσατε· ταῦτα
πάντα προειπόντες βαπτίσατε εἰς τὸ ὄνομα τοῦ Πατρὸς καὶ τοῦ Υἱοῦ καὶ τοῦ ἁγίου Πνεύματος ἐν ὕδατι ζῶντι. 2. ἐὰν δὲ μὴ ἔχῃς ὕδωρ ζῶν, εἰς ἄλλο ὕδωρ βάπτισον· εἰ δ᾽ οὐ δύνασαι ἐν ψυχρῷ, ἐν θερμῷ. 3. ἐὰν δὲ ἀμφότερα μὴ ἔχῃς, ἔκχεον εἰς τὴν κεφαλὴν τρὶς ὕδωρ εἰς ὄνομα Πατρὸς καὶ Υἱοῦ καὶ ἁγίου Πνεύματος. 4. πρὸ δὲ τοῦ βαπτίσματος προνηστευσάτω ὁ βαπτίζων καὶ ὁ βαπτιζόμενος καὶ εἴ τινες ἄλλοι δύνανται. κελεύεις δὲ νηστεῦσαι τὸν βαπτιζόμενον πρὸ μιᾶς ἢ δύο.

VIII. Αἱ δὲ νηστεῖαι ὑμῶν μὴ ἔστωσαν μετὰ τῶν ὑπο-

κριτῶν· νηστεύουσι γὰρ δευτέρᾳ σαββάτων καὶ πέμπτῃ·
ὑμεῖς δὲ νηστεύσατε τετράδα καὶ παρασκευήν. 2. μηδὲ προσεύχεσθε ὡς οἱ ὑποκριταί, ἀλλ᾽ ὡς ἐκέλευσεν ὁ Κύριος ἐν τῷ S. Matt.
εὐαγγελίῳ αὐτοῦ, ΟΥ̓ΤΩϹ ΠΡΟϹΕΎΧΕϹΘΕ· Πάτερ ἡΜῶΝ ὁ ἐΝ Τῷ S. Matt.
ΟΥ̓ΡΑΝῷ, ἁΓΙΑϹΘΉΤΩ Τὸ ὄΝΟΜΆ ϹΟΥ, ἐ̓ΛΘΈΤΩ ἡ ΒΑϹΙΛΕΊΑ ϹΟΥ, ΓΕΝΗ- vi. 9—13.
ΘΉΤΩ Τὸ ΘΈΛΗΜΆ ϹΟΥ ὡϹ ἐΝ ΟΥ̓ΡΑΝῷ ΚΑὶ ἐΠὶ ΓΗϹ· Τὸ́Ν ἄΡΤΟΝ xi. 2—4.
ἡΜῶΝ Τὸ́Ν ἐΠΙΟΎϹΙΟΝ Δὸϲ ἡΜῖΝ ϹΉΜΕΡΟΝ, ΚΑὶ ἄΦΕϹ ἡΜῖΝ ΤΉΝ
ὀΦΕΙΛΉΝ ἡΜῶΝ ὡϲ ΚΑὶ ἡΜΕῖϲ ἀΦΊΕΜΕΝ ΤΟῖϲ ὀΦΕΙΛΈΤΑΙϲ ἡΜῶΝ,
ΚΑὶ ΜῊ ΕἰϹΕΝΈΓΚΗϲ ἡΜᾶϲ Εἰϲ ΠΕΙΡΑϹΜΌΝ, ἀΛΛὰ ῥῦϹΑΙ ἡΜᾶϲ ἀΠὸ ΤΟῦ
ΠΟΝΗΡΟῦ· ὅΤΙ ϹΟῦ ἐϲΤΙΝ ἡ ΔΎΝΑΜΙϲ ΚΑὶ ἡ ΔΌΞΑ Εἰϲ ΤΟὺϲ ΑἰῶΝΑϲ.
3. τρὶς τῆς ἡμέρας οὕτω προσεύχεσθε.

IX. Περὶ δὲ τῆς εὐχαριστίας, οὕτω εὐχαριστήσατε·
2. πρῶτον περὶ τοῦ ποτηρίου· Εὐχαριστοῦμέν σοι, Πάτερ
ἡμῶν, ὑπὲρ τῆς ἁγίας ἀμπέλου Δαυεὶδ τοῦ παιδός σου, ἧς
ἐγνώρισας ἡμῖν διὰ Ἰησοῦ τοῦ παιδός σου· σοὶ ἡ δόξα εἰς
τοὺς αἰῶνας. 3. περὶ δὲ τοῦ κλάσματος· Εὐχαριστοῦμέν
σοι, Πάτερ ἡμῶν, ὑπὲρ τῆς ζωῆς καὶ γνώσεως, ἧς ἐγνώρισας
ἡμῖν διὰ Ἰησοῦ τοῦ παιδός σου· σοὶ ἡ δόξα εἰς τοὺς αἰῶνας.
4. ὥσπερ ἦν τοῦτο τὸ κλάσμα διεσκορπισμένον ἐπάνω τῶν
ὀρέων καὶ συναχθὲν ἐγένετο ἕν, οὕτω συναχθήτω σου ἡ
ἐκκλησία ἀπὸ τῶν περάτων τῆς γῆς εἰς τὴν σὴν βασιλείαν·
ὅτι σοῦ ἐστὶν ἡ δόξα καὶ ἡ δύναμις διὰ Ἰησοῦ Χριστοῦ εἰς
τοὺς αἰῶνας. 5. μηδεὶς δὲ φαγέτω μηδὲ πιέτω ἀπὸ τῆς
εὐχαριστίας ὑμῶν, ἀλλ᾽ οἱ βαπτισθέντες εἰς ὄνομα Κυρίου.
καὶ γὰρ περὶ τούτου εἴρηκεν ὁ Κύριος· ΜῊ Δῶτε Τὸ ἅΓΙΟΝ S. Matt.
ΤΟῖϲ ΚΥϹΊ.　vii. 6.

X. Μετὰ δὲ τὸ ἐμπλησθῆναι οὕτως εὐχαριστήσατε·
2. Εὐχαριστοῦμέν σοι, Πάτερ ἅγιε, ὑπὲρ τοῦ ἁγίου ὀνόματός
σου, οὗ κατεσκήνωσας ἐν ταῖς καρδίαις ἡμῶν, καὶ ὑπὲρ τῆς
γνώσεως καὶ πίστεως καὶ ἀθανασίας, ἧς ἐγνώρισας ἡμῖν διὰ
Ἰησοῦ τοῦ παιδός σου· σοὶ ἡ δόξα εἰς τοὺς αἰῶνας. 3. σύ,
δέσποτα παντοκράτορ, ἔκτισας τὰ πάντα ἕνεκεν τοῦ ὀνόμα-

---

viii. 2 γενηθήτω] conj. Bryennios; γεννηθήτω MS.　　ix. 4 τὸ] insert
Gebhardt after τοῦτο.　　x. 2 ἡμῶν] conj. Bryennios; ὑμῶν MS.

τός σου, τροφήν τε καὶ ποτὸν ἔδωκας τοῖς ἀνθρώποις εἰς
ἀπόλαυσιν ἵνα σοι εὐχαριστήσωσιν, ἡμῖν δὲ ἐχαρίσω πνευ-
ματικὴν τροφὴν καὶ ποτὸν καὶ ζωὴν αἰώνιον διὰ τοῦ παιδός
σου. 4. πρὸ πάντων εὐχαριστοῦμέν σοι ὅτι δυνατὸς εἶ σύ·
σοὶ ἡ δόξα εἰς τοὺς αἰῶνας. 5. μνήσθητι, Κύριε, τῆς ἐκκλησίας σου τοῦ ῥύσασθαι αὐτὴν ἀπὸ παντὸς πονηροῦ καὶ
τελειῶσαι αὐτὴν ἐν τῇ ἀγάπῃ σου, καὶ ϲΥΝΑΞΟΝ αὐτὴν ἀπὸ
τῶν τεϲϲάρων ἀνέμων, τὴν ἁγιασθεῖσαν εἰς τὴν σὴν βασιλείαν, ἣν ἡτοίμασας αὐτῇ· ὅτι σοῦ ἐστὶν ἡ δύναμις καὶ ἡ
δόξα εἰς τοὺς αἰῶνας. 6. ἐλθέτω χάρις καὶ παρελθέτω ὁ
κόσμος οὗτος. ὡσαννὰ τῷ θεῷ Δαυείδ. εἴ τις ἅγιός ἐστιν,
ἐρχέσθω· εἴ τις οὐκ ἐστί, μετανοείτω. ΜΑΡᾺΝ ἀθά. ἀμήν.
7. τοῖς δὲ προφήταις ἐπιτρέπετε εὐχαριστεῖν ὅσα θέλουσιν.

XI. Ὃς ἂν οὖν ἐλθὼν διδάξῃ ὑμᾶς ταῦτα πάντα τὰ
προειρημένα, δέξασθε αὐτόν· 2. ἐὰν δὲ αὐτὸς ὁ διδάσκων
στραφεὶς διδάσκῃ ἄλλην διδαχὴν εἰς τὸ καταλῦσαι, μὴ αὐτοῦ
ἀκούσητε· εἰς δὲ τὸ προσθεῖναι δικαιοσύνην καὶ γνῶσιν
Κυρίου, δέξασθε αὐτὸν ὡς Κύριον. 3. Περὶ δὲ τῶν ἀποστόλων καὶ προφητῶν κατὰ τὸ δόγμα τοῦ εὐαγγελίου οὕτως
ποιήσατε. 4. πᾶς δὲ ἀπόστολος ἐρχόμενος πρὸς ὑμᾶς
δεχθήτω ὡς Κύριος· 5. οὐ μενεῖ δὲ εἰ μὴ ἡμέραν μίαν· ἐὰν
δὲ ᾖ χρεία, καὶ τὴν ἄλλην· τρεῖς δὲ ἐὰν μείνῃ, ψευδοπροφήτης ἐστίν· 6. ἐξερχόμενος δὲ ὁ ἀπόστολος μηδὲν λαμ-
βανέτω εἰ μὴ ἄρτον, ἕως οὗ αὐλισθῇ· ἐὰν δὲ ἀργύριον αἰτῇ,
ψευδοπροφήτης ἐστί. 7. καὶ πάντα προφήτην λαλοῦντα ἐν
πνεύματι οὐ πειράσετε οὐδὲ διακρινεῖτε· πᾶσα γὰρ ἁμαρτία
ἀφεθήσεται, αὕτη δὲ ἡ ἁμαρτία οὐκ ἀφεθήσεται. 8. οὐ πᾶς
δὲ ὁ λαλῶν ἐν πνεύματι προφήτης ἐστίν, ἀλλ' ἐὰν ἔχῃ τοὺς
τρόπους Κυρίου. Ἀπὸ οὖν τῶν τρόπων γνωσθήσεται ὁ
ψευδοπροφήτης καὶ ὁ προφήτης. 9. καὶ πᾶς προφήτης
ὁρίζων τράπεζαν ἐν πνεύματι οὐ φάγεται ἀπ' αὐτῆς· εἰ δὲ
μήγε, ψευδοπροφήτης ἐστίν. 10. πᾶς δὲ προφήτης διδά-

Marginalia left: i Joh. iv. 18. S. Matt. xxiv. 31. — i Cor. xvi. 22.

σκων τὴν ἀλήθειαν εἰ ἃ διδάσκει οὐ ποιεῖ, ψευδοπροφήτης ἐστίν, 11. πᾶς δὲ προφήτης δεδοκιμασμένος ἀληθινὸς ποιῶν εἰς μυστήριον κοσμικὸν ἐκκλησίας, μὴ διδάσκων δὲ ποιεῖν ὅσα αὐτὸς ποιεῖ, οὐ κριθήσεται ἐφ' ὑμῶν· μετὰ Θεοῦ γὰρ ἔχει τὴν κρίσιν· ὡσαύτως γὰρ ἐποίησαν καὶ οἱ ἀρχαῖοι προφῆται. 12. ὃς δ' ἂν εἴπῃ ἐν πνεύματι· Δός μοι ἀργύρια ἢ ἕτερά τινα, οὐκ ἀκούσεσθε αὐτοῦ· ἐὰν δὲ περὶ ἄλλων ὑστερούντων εἴπῃ δοῦναι, μηδεὶς αὐτὸν κρινέτω.

XII. Πᾶς δὲ ὁ ἐρχόμενος ἐν ὀνόματι Κυρίου δεχθήτω· ἔπειτα δὲ δοκιμάσαντες αὐτὸν γνώσεσθε. σύνεσιν γὰρ ἕξετε δεξιὰν καὶ ἀριστεράν. 2. εἰ μὲν παρόδιός ἐστιν ὁ ἐρχόμενος, βοηθεῖτε αὐτῷ ὅσον δύνασθε· οὐ μενεῖ δὲ πρὸς ὑμᾶς εἰ μὴ δύο ἢ τρεῖς ἡμέρας, ἐὰν ᾖ ἀνάγκη. 3. εἰ δὲ θέλει πρὸς ὑμᾶς καθῆσθαι, τεχνίτης ὤν, ἐργαζέσθω καὶ φαγέτω. 4. εἰ δὲ οὐκ ἔχει τέχνην, κατὰ τὴν σύνεσιν ὑμῶν προνοήσατε, πῶς μὴ ἀργὸς μεθ' ὑμῶν ζήσεται Χριστιανός. 5. εἰ δ' οὐ θέλει οὕτω ποιεῖν, χριστέμπορός ἐστιν· προσέχετε ἀπὸ τῶν τοιούτων.

Ps. cxviii. (cxvii) 26. S. Matt. xxi. 9. S. Mark xi. 9. S. Luke xix. 38.

XIII. Πᾶς δὲ προφήτης ἀληθινὸς θέλων καθῆσθαι πρὸς ὑμᾶς ἄξιός ἐστιν τῆς τροφῆς αὐτοῦ. 2. ὡσαύτως διδάσκαλος ἀληθινός ἐστιν ἄξιος καὶ αὐτός, ὥσπερ ὁ ἐργάτης, τῆς τροφῆς αὐτοῦ. 3. πᾶσαν οὖν ἀπαρχὴν γεννημάτων ληνοῦ καὶ ἅλωνος, βοῶν τε καὶ προβάτων λαβὼν δώσεις τὴν ἀπαρχὴν τοῖς προφήταις· αὐτοὶ γάρ εἰσιν οἱ ἀρχιερεῖς ὑμῶν. 4. ἐὰν δὲ μὴ ἔχητε προφήτην, δότε τοῖς πτωχοῖς. 5. ἐὰν σιτίαν ποιῇς, τὴν ἀπαρχὴν λαβὼν δὸς κατὰ τὴν ἐντολήν. 6. ὡσαύτως κεράμιον οἴνου ἢ ἐλαίου ἀνοίξας τὴν ἀπαρχὴν λαβὼν δὸς τοῖς προφήταις· 7. ἀργυρίου δὲ καὶ ἱματισμοῦ καὶ παντὸς κτήματος λαβὼν τὴν ἀπαρχήν, ὡς ἄν σοι δόξῃ, δὸς κατὰ τὴν ἐντολήν.

S. Matt. x. 10.

XIV. Κατὰ κυριακὴν δὲ Κυρίου συναχθέντες κλάσατε ἄρτον καὶ εὐχαριστήσατε προεξομολογησάμενοι τὰ παραπτώματα ὑμῶν, ὅπως καθαρὰ ἡ θυσία ὑμῶν ᾖ. 2. πᾶς δὲ

---

xii. 1 ἕξετε] conj. Bryennios; ἕξεται MS.   xiv. 1 προεξομολογησάμενοι] conj. Hilgenfeld; προσεξομολογησάμενοι MS.   ὑμῶν sec.] conj. Bryennios; ἡμῶν MS.

ἔχων τὴν ἀμφιβολίαν μετὰ τοῦ ἑταίρου αὐτοῦ μὴ συνελθέτω
ὑμῖν, ἕως οὗ διαλλαγῶσιν, ἵνα μὴ κοινωθῇ ἡ θυσία ὑμῶν.

3. αὕτη γάρ ἐστιν ἡ ῥηθεῖσα ὑπὸ Κυρίου· Ἐν παντὶ τόπῳ καὶ χρόνῳ προσφέρειν μοι θυσίαν καθαράν· ὅτι Βασιλεὺς
μέγας εἰμί, λέγει Κύριος, καὶ τὸ ὄνομά μου θαυμαστὸν ἐν τοῖς
ἔθνεσι.

XV. Χειροτονήσατε οὖν ἑαυτοῖς ἐπισκόπους καὶ διακόνους ἀξίους τοῦ Κυρίου, ἄνδρας πραεῖς καὶ ἀφιλαργύρους καὶ
ἀληθεῖς καὶ δεδοκιμασμένους· ὑμῖν γὰρ λειτουργοῦσι καὶ
αὐτοὶ τὴν λειτουργίαν τῶν προφητῶν καὶ διδασκάλων. 2. μὴ οὖν ὑπερίδητε αὐτούς· αὐτοὶ γάρ εἰσιν οἱ τετιμημένοι
ὑμῶν μετὰ τῶν προφητῶν καὶ διδασκάλων. 3. Ἐλέγχετε δὲ ἀλλήλους μὴ ἐν ὀργῇ, ἀλλ' ἐν εἰρήνῃ,
ὡς ἔχετε ἐν τῷ εὐαγγελίῳ· καὶ παντὶ ἀστοχοῦντι κατὰ τοῦ
ἑτέρου μηδεὶς λαλείτω μηδὲ παρ' ὑμῶν ἀκουέτω, ἕως οὗ μετανοήσῃ. 4. τὰς δὲ εὐχὰς ὑμῶν καὶ τὰς ἐλεημοσύνας καὶ
πάσας τὰς πράξεις οὕτως ποιήσατε, ὡς ἔχετε ἐν τῷ εὐαγγελίῳ τοῦ Κυρίου ἡμῶν.

XVI. Γρηγορεῖτε ὑπὲρ τῆς ζωῆς ὑμῶν· οἱ λύχνοι ὑμῶν
μὴ σβεσθήτωσαν, καὶ αἱ ὀσφύες ὑμῶν μὴ ἐκλυέσθωσαν, ἀλλὰ
γίνεσθε ἕτοιμοι· οὐ γὰρ οἴδατε τὴν ὥραν, ἐν ᾗ ὁ Κύριος ἡμῶν
ἔρχεται. 2. πυκνῶς δὲ συναχθήσεσθε ζητοῦντες τὰ ἀνήκοντα
ταῖς ψυχαῖς ὑμῶν. οὐ γὰρ ὠφελήσει ὑμᾶς ὁ πᾶς χρόνος
τῆς πίστεως ὑμῶν, ἐὰν μὴ ἐν τῷ ἐσχάτῳ καιρῷ τελειωθῆτε.

3. ἐν γὰρ ταῖς ἐσχάταις ἡμέραις πληθυνθήσονται οἱ ψευδο-
προφῆται καὶ οἱ φθορεῖς, καὶ στραφήσονται τὰ πρόβατα εἰς
λύκους, καὶ ἡ ἀγάπη στραφήσεται εἰς μῖσος· 4. αὐξανούσης

γὰρ τῆς ἀνομίας μισήσουσιν ἀλλήλους καὶ διώξουσιν καὶ παρα-
δώσουσι. καὶ τότε φανήσεται ὁ κοσμοπλανὴς ὡς υἱὸς Θεοῦ καὶ
ποιήσει σημεῖα καὶ τέρατα, καὶ ἡ γῆ παραδοθήσεται εἰς χεῖρας
αὐτοῦ, καὶ ποιήσει ἀθέμιτα, ἃ οὐδέποτε γέγονεν ἐξ αἰῶνος.
5. τότε ἥξει ἡ κτίσις τῶν ἀνθρώπων εἰς τὴν πύρωσιν τῆς
δοκιμασίας, καὶ σκανδαλισθήσονται πολλοὶ καὶ ἀπολοῦνται,

οἱ δὲ ὑπομείναντες ἐν τῇ πίστει αὐτῶν σωθήσονται ὑπ' αὐτοῦ

τοῦ καταθέματος. 6. καὶ τότε φανήσεται τὰ σημεῖα τῆς ἀλη- S. Matt.
θείας· πρῶτον σημεῖον ἐκπετάσεως ἐν οὐρανῷ, εἶτα σημεῖον ^{xxiv. 30.}
φωνῆς σάλπιγγος, καὶ τὸ τρίτον ἀνάστασις νεκρῶν· οὐ πάν-
των δέ, ἀλλ' ὡς ἐρρέθη· Ἥξει ὁ Κύριος καὶ πάντες οἱ ἅγιοι μετ' Zech. xiv.
αὐτοῦ. 7. τότε ὄψεται ὁ κόσμος τὸν Κύριον ἐρχόμενον ἐπάνω 5.
τῶν νεφελῶν τοῦ οὐρανοῦ. S. Matt.
xxiv. 30.

DOCTRINA APOSTOLORUM.

Viae duae sunt in seculo, vitae et mortis, lucis et tene-
brarum. In his constituti sunt angeli duo, unus aequi-
tatis, alter iniquitatis. Distantia autem magna est duarum
viarum. Via ergo vitae haec est : Primo diliges Deum
aeternum, qui te fecit. Secundo proximum tuum, ut te
ipsum. Omne autem, quod tibi non vis fieri, alii ne feceris.
Interpretatio autem horum verborum haec est : non moe-
chaberis, non homicidium facies, non falsum testimonium
dices, non puerum violaveris, non fornicaveris, non ¹male-
facies, non medicamenta mala facies ; non occides filium in
abortum, nec natum succides. Non concupisces quidquam
de re proximi tui. Non perjurabis, non male loqueris, non
eris memor malorum factorum. Non eris duplex in consilium dandum, neque bilinguis ; tendiculum enim mortis
est lingua. Non erit verbum tuum vacuum nec mendax.
Non eris cupidus, nec avarus, nec rapax, nec ²adulator
nec... (*the MS here breaks off.*)

---

¹ malefacies] maofacies MS.   ² adulator] adolator MS.

TRANSLATION

TEACHING OF THE APOSTLES

THE TEACHING OF THE LORD TO THE GENTILES
BY THE TWELVE APOSTLES

1. THERE are two ways, one of life and one of death, and there is a great difference between the two ways. *The way of life is* this. First of all, *thou shalt love the God* that made thee ; secondly, *thy neighbour as thyself. And all things whatsoever thou wouldest not have befal thyself, neither do thou unto another.* Now of these words the doctrine is this. *Bless them that curse you, and pray for* your enemies and fast for *them that persecute you ; for what thank is it, if ye love them that love you ? Do not even the Gentiles the same ? But do ye love them that hate you,* and ye shall not have an enemy. Abstain thou from fleshly and bodily lusts. *If any man give thee a blow on thy right cheek, turn to him the other also,* and thou shalt be perfect ; *if a man impress thee to go with him one mile, go with him twain ; if a man take away thy cloak, give him thy coat also ; if a man take away from thee that which is thine own, ask it not back,* for neither art thou able. *To every man that asketh of thee give, and ask not back ;* for the Father desireth that gifts be given to all from His own bounties. Blessed is he that giveth according to the commandment ; for he is guiltless. Woe to him that receiveth ; for, if a man receiveth having need, he is guiltless ; but he that hath no need shall give satisfaction why and wherefore he received ; and being put in confinement he shall be examined concerning the deeds that he hath done, and *he shall not come out thence until he hath given back the last farthing.* Yea, as touching this also it is said ; *Let thine alms sweat into thine hands, until thou shalt have learnt to whom to give.*

2. And this is the second commandment of the teaching. *Thou shalt do no murder, thou shalt not commit adultery,* thou shalt not corrupt boys, thou shalt not commit fornication, *thou shalt not steal,* thou shalt

not deal in magic, thou shalt do no sorcery, thou shalt not murder a child by abortion nor kill them when born, *thou shalt not covet thy neighbour's goods, thou shalt not perjure thyself, thou shalt not bear false witness,* thou shalt not speak evil, thou shalt not cherish a grudge, thou shalt not be double-minded nor double-tongued; for the double tongue is a snare of death. Thy word shall not be false or empty, but fulfilled by action. Thou shalt not be avaricious nor a plunderer nor a hypocrite nor ill-tempered nor proud. Thou shalt not entertain an evil design against thy neighbour. *Thou shalt not hate* any man, *but some thou shalt reprove,* and for others thou shalt pray, *and others thou shalt love* more than thy life.

3. My child, flee from every evil and everything that resembleth it. Be not angry, for anger leadeth to murder, nor jealous nor contentious nor wrathful; for of all these things murders are engendered. My child, be not lustful, for lust leadeth to fornication, neither foul-speaking neither with uplifted eyes; for of all these things adulteries are engendered. My child, *be no dealer in omens,* since it leads to idolatry, nor an enchanter nor an astrologer nor a magician, neither be willing to look at them; for from all these things idolatry is engendered. My child, be not a liar, since lying leads to theft, neither avaricious neither vainglorious; for from all these things thefts are engendered. My child, be not a murmurer, since it leadeth to blasphemy, neither self-willed neither a thinker of evil thoughts; for from all these things blasphemies are engendered. But be meek, since *the meek shall inherit the earth.* Be long-suffering and pitiful and guileless and *quiet* and kindly *and* always *fearing the words* which thou hast heard. Thou shalt not exalt thyself, neither shalt thou admit boldness into thy soul. Thy soul shall not cleave together with the lofty, but with the righteous and humble shalt thou walk. The accidents that befal thee thou shalt receive as good, knowing that nothing is done without God.

4. My child, *thou shalt remember him that speaketh unto thee the word of God* night and day, and shalt honour him as the Lord; for whencesoever the Lordship speaketh, there is the Lord. Moreover thou shalt seek out day by day the persons of the saints, that thou mayest find rest in their words. Thou shalt not make a schism, but thou shalt pacify them that contend; thou shalt judge righteously, thou shalt not make a difference in a person to reprove him for transgressions. Thou shalt not doubt whether a thing shall be or not be.

Be not thou found holding out thy hands to receive, but drawing them in as to giving. If thou hast ought passing through thy hands, thou shalt give a ransom for thy sins. Thou shalt not hesitate to give, neither shalt thou murmur when giving; for thou shalt know who is the good paymaster of thy reward. Thou shalt not turn away from him that is in want, but shalt make thy brother partaker in all things, and shalt not say *that anything is thine own.* For if ye are fellow-partakers in that which is imperishable, how much rather in the things which are perishable?

Thou shalt not withhold thy hand from thy son or from thy daughter, but from their youth thou shalt teach them the fear of God. Thou shalt not command thy bondservant or thine handmaid in thy bitterness, who trust in the same God as thyself, lest haply they should cease to fear the God who is over both of you; for He cometh, not to call men with respect of persons, but He cometh to those whom the Spirit hath prepared. But ye, servants, shall be subject unto your masters, as to a type of God, in shame and fear.

Thou shalt hate all hypocrisy, and everything that is not pleasing to the Lord. Thou shalt never forsake the commandments of the Lord; but shalt keep those things which thou hast received, neither adding to them nor taking away from them. In church thou shalt confess thy transgressions, and shalt not betake thyself to prayer with an evil conscience. This is the way of life.

5. But the way of death is this. First of all, it is evil and full of a curse; murders, adulteries, lusts, fornications, thefts, idolatries, magical arts, witchcrafts, plunderings, false witnessings, hypocrisies, doubleness of heart, treachery, pride, malice, stubbornness, covetousness, foul-speaking, jealousy, boldness, exaltation, boastfulness; persecutors of good men, hating truth, loving a lie, not perceiving the reward of righteousness, not *cleaving to the good* nor to righteous judgment, wakeful not for that which is good but for that which is evil; from whom gentleness and forbearance stand aloof; loving vain things, pursuing a recompense, not pitying the poor man, not toiling for him that is oppressed with toil, not recognizing Him that made them, murderers of children, corrupters of the creatures of God, turning away from him that is in want, oppressing him that is afflicted, advocates of the wealthy, unjust judges of the poor, altogether sinful. May ye be delivered, my children, from all these things.

6. See lest any man lead you astray from this way of righteousness, for he teacheth thee apart from God. For if thou art able to bear the

whole yoke of the Lord, thou shalt be perfect; but if thou art not able, do that which thou art able.

But concerning eating, bear that which thou art able; yet abstain by all means from meat sacrificed to idols; for it is the worship of dead gods.

7. But concerning baptism, thus shall ye baptize. Having first recited all these things, baptize *in the name of the Father and of the Son and of the Holy Spirit* in living (running) water. But if thou hast not living water, then baptize in other water; and if thou art not able in cold, then in warm. But if thou hast neither, then pour water on the head thrice in the name of the Father and of the Son and of the Holy Spirit. But before the baptism let him that baptizeth and him that is baptized fast, and any others also who are able; and thou shalt order him that is baptized to fast a day or two before.

8. And let not your fastings be with the hypocrites, for they fast on the second and the fifth day of the week; but do ye keep your fast on the fourth and on the preparation (the sixth) day. Neither pray ye *as the hypocrites*, but as the Lord commanded in His Gospel, *thus pray ye: Our Father, which art in heaven, hallowed be Thy name; Thy kingdom come; Thy will be done, as in heaven, so also on earth; give us this day our daily bread; and forgive us our debt, as we also forgive our debtors; and lead us not into temptation, but deliver us from the evil one;* for Thine is the power and the glory for ever and ever. Three times in the day pray ye so.

9. But as touching the eucharistic thanksgiving give ye thanks thus. First, as regards the cup: We give Thee thanks, O our Father, for the holy vine of Thy son David, which Thou madest known unto us through Thy Son Jesus; Thine is the glory for ever and ever. Then as regards the broken bread: We give Thee thanks, O our Father, for the life and knowledge which Thou didst make known unto us through Thy Son Jesus; Thine is the glory for ever and ever. As this broken bread was scattered upon the mountains and being gathered together became one, so may Thy Church be gathered together from the ends of the earth into Thy kingdom; for Thine is the glory and the power through Jesus Christ for ever and ever. But let no one eat or drink of this eucharistic thanksgiving, but they that have been baptized into the name of the Lord; for concerning this also the Lord hath said: *Give not that which is holy to the dogs.*

10. And after ye are satisfied thus give ye thanks: We give Thee

thanks, Holy Father, for Thy holy name, which Thou hast made to tabernacle in our hearts, and for the knowledge and faith and immortality, which Thou hast made known unto us through Thy Son Jesus; Thine is the glory for ever and ever. Thou, Almighty Master, didst create all things for Thy name's sake, and didst give food and drink unto men for enjoyment, that they might render thanks to Thee; but didst bestow upon us spiritual food and drink and eternal life through Thy Son. Before all things we give Thee thanks that Thou art powerful; Thine is the glory for ever and ever. Remember, Lord, Thy Church to deliver it from all evil and to perfect it in Thy love; and *gather it together from the four winds*—even the Church which has been sanctified—into Thy kingdom which Thou hast prepared for it; for Thine is the power and the glory for ever and ever. May grace come and may this world pass away. Hosanna to the God of David. If any man is holy, let him come; if any man is not, let him repent. Maran Atha. Amen.

But permit the prophets to offer thanksgiving as much as they desire.

11. Whosoever therefore shall come and teach you all these things that have been said before, receive him; but if the teacher himself be perverted and teach a different doctrine to the destruction thereof, hear him not; but if to the increase of righteousness and the knowledge of the Lord, receive him as the Lord.

But concerning the apostles and prophets, so do ye according to the ordinance of the Gospel. Let every apostle, when he cometh to you, be received as the Lord; but he shall not abide more than a single day, or if there be need, a second likewise; but if he abide three days, he is a false prophet. And when he departeth let the apostle receive nothing save bread, until he findeth shelter; but if he ask money, he is a false prophet. And any prophet speaking in the Spirit ye shall not try neither discern; for every sin shall be forgiven, but this sin shall not be forgiven. Yet not every one that speaketh in the Spirit is a prophet, but only if he have the ways of the Lord. From his ways therefore the false prophet and the prophet shall be recognized. And no prophet when he ordereth a table in the Spirit shall eat of it; otherwise he is a false prophet. And every prophet teaching the truth, if he doeth not what he teacheth, is a false prophet. And every prophet approved and found true, if he doeth ought as an outward mystery typical of the Church, and yet teacheth you not to do all that he himself doeth, shall not be judged before you; he hath his judgment in the presence of God; for in like manner also did the prophets of old time. And whosoever shall say in the Spirit, Give me silver or anything else, ye shall not listen to him; but if he tell you to give on behalf of others that are in want, let no man judge him.

12. But let every one *that cometh in the name of the Lord* be received; and then when ye have tested him ye shall know him, for ye shall have understanding on the right hand and on the left. If the comer is a traveller, assist him, so far as ye are able; but he shall not stay with you more than two or three days, if it be necessary. But if he wishes to settle with you, being a craftsman, let him work for and eat his bread. But if he has no craft, according to your wisdom provide how he shall live as a Christian among you, but not in idleness. If he will not do this, he is trafficking upon Christ. Beware of such men.

13. But every true prophet desiring to settle among you *is worthy of his food.* In like manner a true teacher *is* also *worthy,* like *the workman, of his food.* Every firstfruit then of the produce of the wine-vat and of the threshing-floor, of thy oxen and of thy sheep, thou shalt take and give as the firstfruit to the prophets; for they are your chief-priests. But if ye have not a prophet, give them to the poor. If thou makest bread, take the firstfruit and give according to the commandment. In like manner, when thou openest a jar of wine or of oil, take the firstfruit and give to the prophets; yea and of money and raiment and every possession take the firstfruit, as shall seem good to thee, and give according to the commandment.

14. And on the Lord's own day gather yourselves together and break bread and give thanks, first confessing your transgressions, that your sacrifice may be pure. And let no man, having his dispute with his fellow, join your assembly until they have been reconciled, that your sacrifice may not be defiled; for this sacrifice it is that was spoken of by the Lord; *In every place and at every time offer Me a pure sacrifice; for I am a great king, saith the Lord, and My name is wonderful among the nations.*

15. Appoint for yourselves therefore bishops and deacons worthy of the Lord, men who are meek and not lovers of money, and true and approved; for unto you they also perform the service of the prophets and teachers. Therefore despise them not; for they are your honourable men along with the prophets and teachers.

And reprove one another, not in anger but in peace, as ye find in the Gospel; and let no one speak to any that has gone wrong towards his neighbour, neither let him hear a word from you, until he repent. But your prayers and your almsgivings and all your deeds so do ye as ye find it in the Gospel of our Lord.

16. *Be watchful* for your life; *let your lamps not be quenched and your loins not ungirded, but be ye ready; for ye know not the hour in which our Lord cometh.* And ye shall gather yourselves together frequently, seeking what is fitting for your souls; for the whole time of your faith shall not profit you, if ye be not perfected at the last season. For in the last days *the false prophets* and corrupters shall be multiplied, and the sheep shall be turned into wolves, and love shall be turned into hate. For as lawlessness increaseth, *they shall hate one another and shall persecute and betray. And then* the world-deceiver *shall appear* as a son of God; *and shall work signs and wonders,* and the earth shall be delivered into his hands; and he shall do unholy things, which have never been since the world began. Then all created mankind shall come to the fire of testing, and many shall be offended and perish; *but they that endure* in their faith *shall be saved* by the Curse Himself. *And then shall the signs* of the truth *appear*; first a sign of a rift in the heaven, then a sign of a voice of a trumpet, and thirdly a resurrection of the dead; yet not of all, but as it was said : *The Lord shall come and all His saints with Him. Then shall* the world *see the Lord coming upon the clouds of heaven.*

THE EPISTLE

OF

BARNABAS

THE EPISTLE OF BARNABAS

I

THE Epistle which bears the name of Barnabas stands alone in the literature of the early Church. The writer is an uncompromising antagonist of Judaism, but beyond this antagonism he has nothing in common with the Antijudaic heresies of the second century. Unlike Marcion, he postulates no opposition between the Old Testament and the New. On the contrary he sees Christianity everywhere in the Lawgiver and the Prophets, and treats them with a degree of respect which would have satisfied the most devout rabbi. He quotes them profusely as authoritative. Only he accuses the Jews of misunderstanding them from beginning to end, and intimates that the ordinances of circumcision, of the sabbath, of the distinctions of meats clean and unclean, were never intended to be literally observed, but had throughout a spiritual and mystical significance.

Who then was the writer of this Epistle? At the close of the second century Clement of Alexandria quotes it frequently, and ascribes it to the 'Apostle,' or the 'Prophet Barnabas,' identifying the author with 'Barnabas who himself also preached with the Apostle' (i.e. St Paul) 'in the ministry of the Gentiles.' Yet elsewhere he does not hesitate to criticize the work, and clearly therefore did not regard it as final and authoritative. A few years later, Origen cites the Epistle with the introductory words, 'It is written in the catholic (i.e. general) Epistle of Barnabas.' The earliest notices however are confined to the Alexandrian fathers, and the presumption is that it was written in Alexandria itself.

It will be observed that the writer nowhere claims to be the Apostle Barnabas; indeed his language is such as to suggest that he was wholly unconnected with the Apostles. The work therefore is in no sense apocryphal, if by apocryphal we mean fictitious. How the name of Barnabas came to be associated with it, it is impossible to say. An early tradition, or fiction, represents Barnabas as residing at Alexandria;

but this story might have been the consequence, rather than the cause, of the name attached to the letter. Possibly its author was some unknown namesake of the 'Son of Consolation.'

That Alexandria, the place of its earliest reception, was also the place of its birth, is borne out by the internal evidence of style and interpretation, which is Alexandrian throughout. The picture too which it presents of feuds between Jews and Christians is in keeping with the state of the population of that city, the various elements of which were continually in conflict. But the problem of the date is a more difficult one. The Epistle was certainly written after the first destruction of Jerusalem under Titus, to which it alludes; but, had it been composed after the war under Hadrian ending in the second devastation, it could hardly have failed to refer to that event. The possible limits therefore are A.D. 70 and A.D. 132. But within this period of sixty years the most various dates have been assigned to it. The conclusion depends mainly on the interpretation put upon two passages which treat of quotations from the prophets. (1) The first is in § 4, where Daniel vii. 7 sq is quoted as illustrating the great scandal or offence which, according to the writer, is at hand. The date will depend on the interpretation put upon the 'three kings in one' (τρεῖς ὑφ' ἓν τῶν βασιλέων), or 'three great horns in one' (ὑφ' ἓν τρία τῶν μεγάλων κεράτων) and 'the little excrescence' or 'offshoot horn' (μικρὸν κέρας παραφυάδιον). And here no theory yet propounded appears quite satisfactory. Weizsäcker, who dates the Epistle in Vespasian's reign (A.D. 70—79), is compelled to consider that emperor as at once one of the great horns and the little horn; Hilgenfeld, who places it under Nerva (A.D. 96—98), arbitrarily omits Julius and Vitellius from the list of Cæsars, that he may make Domitian the tenth king; while both alike fail to recognize in Daniel's little horn a prophecy of Antichrist and therefore a persecuting emperor. Volkmar's date (A.D. 119—132), besides other serious objections, depends upon the enumeration of the three kings over and above the ten, whereas the language suggests that they were in some sense comprised within the ten. The solution, which follows, and which we are disposed to adopt provisionally, has not, we believe, been offered before. We enumerate the ten Cæsars in their natural sequence, with Weizsäcker, and arrive at Vespasian as the tenth. We regard the three Flavii as the three kings destined to be humiliated, with Hilgenfeld. We do not however with him contemplate them as three separate emperors, but explain the language as referring to the association with himself by Vespasian of his two sons Titus and Domitian in the exercise of supreme power. So close a connexion of three in one was never seen in the history of the empire, until a date too late to enter into consideration. The significance of this association is commemorated in several types of coins, which exhibit Vespasian on the obverse and Titus and Domitian on the reverse in various attitudes and with various legends. Lastly, with Volkmar, we interpret the little horn as symbolizing Antichrist, and explain it by the expectation of Nero's reappearance which we know to have been rife during the continuation of the Flavian dynasty. (2) The second passage is the interpretation in § 16 given to Isaiah xlix. 17, where it is foretold to the Jews that 'those who pulled down this temple themselves shall build it up,' and the interpretation goes on to say that 'this is taking place (γίνεται). Because they went to war it was pulled down by their enemies ; now also the very subjects (ὑπηρέται) of their enemies (the Romans) shall build it up !' This is taken by interpreters generally to refer to the material temple at Jerusalem, and they explain it of the expectations of the Jews at one epoch or another that the Romans would rebuild the temple—the epoch generally chosen being the conquest of Hadrian, at which point consequently very many place the writing of the Epistle. This conflicts with any natural interpretation of the three horns and the little horn. But (i) no satisfactory evidence has been adduced that Hadrian had any such intention, or that the Jews had any such expectation in his time ; and (ii) there is the still more formidable objection that this interpretation runs counter to the general teaching of this writer, who reproaches the Jews with their material interpretations of prophecy, and to the whole context, which is conceived in his usual vein. He explains at the outset that the Jews are wrong in setting their hope on the material building. Yet here, if this interpretation be correct, he tells them to do this very thing. Moreover, lest there should be any mistake, he assures them that there *is* a temple, but this temple of the Lord, predicted by the prophets, is a spiritual temple ; for it is either the Church of Christ, or the soul of the individual believer, wherein the Lord dwells. Whether with ℵ we read a second καὶ after αὐτοὶ or not, this spiritual interpretation must be correct ; but the context suggests its omission. Thus the passage has no bearing at all on the date. For these reasons we should probably place the date of the so-called Epistle of Barnabas between A.D. 70—79 ; but the ultimate decision must be affected by the view which shall commend itself of the origin of those chapters, which the epistle has in common with the Teaching of the Apostles.

2

The authorities for the text are as follows:

(I) GREEK MANUSCRIPTS.

1.   The famous Sinaitic MS (ℵ) of the fourth century, where, in company with the Shepherd of Hermas, it occurs in a complete form, following the Apocalypse, as a sort of appendix to the sacred volume.

2.   The Constantinopolitan MS (C) of Bryennios, an eleventh century document (see above, pp. 4, 216); here also the epistle is found complete.

3.   The series of nine Greek MSS (G), all of one family, enumerated above, p. 166 sq; in this collection of manuscripts the first four chapters and part of the fifth are wanting.

There is also (II) a LATIN VERSION (L) extant in a MS of the ninth or tenth century (*Petropolitanus* Q. v. I. 39, formerly *Corbeiensis*). This MS omits the last four chapters, which apparently formed no part of the version in question.

Lastly, the quotations in Clement of Alexandria, comprising as they do portions of §§ 1, 4, 6, 9, 10, 11, 16, 21, and those passages in §§ 18—21 which this Epistle has in common with the Didache and other documents, open out additional considerations which must not be disregarded in the formation of the text.

ΒΑΡΝΑΒΑ ΕΠΙΣΤΟΛΗ

I. ΧΑΙΡΕΤΕ, υἱοὶ καὶ θυγατέρες, ἐν ὀνόματι Κυρίου τοῦ ἀγαπήσαντος ἡμᾶς, ἐν εἰρήνῃ. 2. Μεγάλων μὲν ὄντων καὶ πλουσίων τῶν τοῦ Θεοῦ δικαιωμάτων εἰς ὑμᾶς, ὑπέρ τι καὶ καθ' ὑπερβολὴν ὑπερευφραίνομαι ἐπὶ τοῖς μακαρίοις καὶ ἐνδόξοις ὑμῶν πνεύμασιν· οὕτως ἔμφυτον τῆς δωρεᾶς πνευματικῆς χάριν εἰλήφατε. 3. διὸ καὶ μᾶλλον συνχαίρω ἐμαυτῷ ἐλπίζων σωθῆναι, ὅτι ἀληθῶς βλέπω ἐν ὑμῖν ἐκκεχυμένον ἀπὸ τοῦ πλουσίου τῆς πηγῆς Κυρίου πνεῦμα ἐφ' ὑμᾶς. οὕτω με ἐξέπληξεν ἐπὶ ὑμῶν ἡ ἐπιποθήτη ὄψις ὑμῶν. 4. πεπεισμένος οὖν τοῦτο καὶ συνειδὼς ἐμαυτῷ, ὅτι ἐν ὑμῖν λαλήσας πολλὰ ἐπίσταμαι ὅτι ἐμοὶ συνώδευσεν ἐν ὁδῷ δικαιοσύνης Κύριος, καὶ πάντως ἀναγκάζομαι κἀγὼ εἰς τοῦτο, ἀγαπᾶν ὑμᾶς ὑπὲρ τὴν ψυχήν μου· ὅτι μεγάλη πίστις καὶ ἀγάπη ἐγκατοικεῖ ἐν ὑμῖν ἐλπίδι ζωῆς αὐτοῦ. 5. λογισάμενος οὖν τοῦτο, ὅτι ἐὰν μελήσῃ μοι περὶ ὑμῶν τοῦ μέρος τι μεταδοῦναι ἀφ' οὗ ἔλαβον, ὅτι ἔσται μοι τοιούτοις πνεύμασιν ὑπηρετήσαντι εἰς μισθόν, ἐσπούδασα κατὰ μικρὸν ὑμῖν πέμπειν, ἵνα μετὰ τῆς πίστεως ὑμῶν τελείαν ἔχητε τὴν γνῶσιν. 6. Τρία οὖν δόγματά ἐστιν Κυρίου· †ζωῆς ἐλπίς, ἀρχὴ καὶ τέλος πίστεως ἡμῶν· καὶ δικαιοσύνη, κρίσεως ἀρχὴ καὶ τέλος· ἀγάπη εὐφροσύνης καὶ ἀγαλλιάσεως, ἔργων δικαιοσύνης μαρτυρία†. 7. ἐγνώρισεν γὰρ ἡμῖν ὁ δεσπότης διὰ τῶν προφητῶν τὰ παρεληλυθότα καὶ τὰ ἐνεστῶτα, καὶ τῶν μελλόντων δοὺς ἀπαρχὰς ἡμῖν γεύσεως. ὧν

i. 2 οὕτως] conj. Hilgenfeld; οὖ τὸ ℵC; sic L.

τὰ καθ' ἕκαστα βλέποντες ἐνεργούμενα, καθὼς ἐλάλησεν, ὀφείλομεν πλουσιώτερον καὶ ὑψηλότερον προσάγειν τῷ φόβῳ αὐτοῦ. 8. ἐγὼ δὲ οὐχ ὡς διδάσκαλος ἀλλ' ὡς εἷς ἐξ ὑμῶν ὑποδείξω ὀλίγα, δι' ὧν ἐν τοῖς παροῦσιν εὐφρανθήσεσθε.

II. Ἡμερῶν οὖν οὐσῶν πονηρῶν καὶ αὐτοῦ τοῦ ἐνεργοῦντος ἔχοντος τὴν ἐξουσίαν, ὀφείλομεν ἑαυτοῖς προσέχοντες ἐκζητεῖν τὰ δικαιώματα Κυρίου. 2. τῆς οὖν πίστεως ἡμῶν εἰσὶν βοηθοὶ φόβος καὶ ὑπομονή, τὰ δὲ συνμαχοῦντα ἡμῖν μακροθυμία καὶ ἐγκράτεια· 3. τούτων μενόντων τὰ πρὸς Κύριον ἁγνῶς, συνευφραίνονται αὐτοῖς σοφία, σύνεσις, ἐπιστήμη, γνῶσις. 4. πεφανέρωκεν γὰρ ἡμῖν διὰ πάντων τῶν προφητῶν ὅτι οὔτε θυσιῶν οὔτε ὁλοκαυτωμάτων οὔτε προσ-

Is. i. 11—13. φορῶν χρῄζει, λέγων ὁτὲ μέν· 5. Τί μοι πλῆθος τῶν θγϲιῶν ὑμῶν; λέγει Κύριοϲ. πλΗρΗϲ εἰμὶ ὁλοκαγτωμάτων, καὶ ϲτέαρ ἀρνῶν καὶ αἷμα ταγρων καὶ τράγων ογ Βογλομαι, ογδ' ἂν ἔρχΗϲθε ὀφθΗναί μοι. τίϲ γὰρ ἐξεζΗτΗϲεν ταγτα ἐκ τῶν χειρῶν ὑμῶν; πατεῖν μογ τΗν αγλΗν ογ προϲθΗϲεϲθε· Ἐὰν φέρΗτε ϲεμίδαλιν, μάταιον· θγμίαμα, Βδέλγγμά μοί ἐϲτιν· τὰϲ νεομΗνίαϲ ὑμῶν καὶ τὰ ϲάββατα ογκ ἀνέχομαι. 6. ταῦτα οὖν κατήργησεν, ἵνα ὁ καινὸς νόμος τοῦ Κυρίου ἡμῶν Ἰησοῦ Χριστοῦ, ἄνευ ζυγοῦ ἀνάγκης ὤν, μὴ ἀνθρωποποίητον ἔχῃ τὴν προσφοράν. 7. λέ-

Jer. vii. 22, 23. γει δὲ πάλιν πρὸς αὐτούς· ΜΗ ἐγὼ ἐνετειλάμΗν τοῖϲ πατράϲιν ὑμῶν ἐκπορεγομένοιϲ ἐκ γΗϲ Αἰγύπτογ, προϲενέγκαι μοι ὁλοκαγ-

Zech. viii. 17. τώματα καὶ θγϲίαϲ; 8. ἀλλ' Η τοῦτο ἐνετειλάμΗν αγτοῖϲ· Ἕκαϲτοϲ ὑμῶν κατὰ τογ πλΗϲίον ἐν τῇ καρδίᾳ αγτογ κακίαν μΗ μνΗϲικακείτω, καὶ ὅρκον ψεγδΗ μΗ ἀγαπᾶτε. 9. Αἰσθάνεσθαι οὖν ὀφείλομεν, μὴ ὄντες ἀσύνετοι, τὴν γνώμην τῆς ἀγαθωσύνης τοῦ πατρὸς ἡμῶν· ὅτι ἡμῖν λέγει, θέλων ἡμᾶς μὴ ὁμοίως πλανωμένους ἐκείνοις ζητεῖν πῶς προσάγωμεν αὐτῷ. 10. ἡμῖν

Ps. li. 19. ? οὖν οὕτως λέγει· Θγϲία τῷ Θεῷ καρδία ϲγντετριμμένΗ, ὀϲμΗ εγωδίαϲ τῷ Κγρίῳ καρδία δοξάζογϲα τὸν πεπλακότα αγτΗν. ἀκριβεύεσθαι οὖν ὀφείλομεν, ἀδελφοί, περὶ τῆς σωτηρίας ἡμῶν, ἵνα μὴ ὁ πονηρὸς παρείσδυσιν πλάνης ποιήσας ἐν ἡμῖν ἐκσφενδονήσῃ ἡμᾶς ἀπὸ τῆς ζωῆς ἡμῶν.

III. Λέγει οὖν πάλιν περὶ τούτων πρὸς αὐτούς· Ἵνα τί Is. lviii.
μοι νηστεύετε, λέγει Κύριος, ὡς σήμερον ἀκουσθῆναι ἐν κραυγῇ 4—10.
τὴν φωνὴν ὑμῶν; οὐ ταύτην τὴν νηστείαν ἐγὼ ἐξελεξάμην,
λέγει Κύριος, οὐκ ἄνθρωπον ταπεινοῦντα τὴν ψυχὴν αὐτοῦ,
2. οὐδ᾽ ἂν κάμψητε ὡς κρίκον τὸν τράχηλον ὑμῶν, καὶ σάκκον
ἐνδύσησθε καὶ σποδὸν ὑποστρώσητε, οὐδ᾽ οὕτως καλέσετε νηστείαν δεκτήν. 3. πρὸς ἡμᾶς δὲ λέγει· Ἰδοὺ αὕτη ἡ νηστεία ἣν
ἐγὼ ἐξελεξάμην, λέγει Κύριος· λύε πᾶν σύνδεσμον ἀδικίας, διάλυε
στραγγαλιὰς βιαίων συναλλαγμάτων, ἀπόστελλε τεθραυσμένους ἐν
ἀφέσει, καὶ πᾶσαν ἄδικον συγγραφὴν διάσπα. διάθρυπτε πεινῶσιν
τὸν ἄρτον σου, καὶ γυμνὸν ἐὰν ἴδῃς, περίβαλε· ἀστέγους εἴσαγε
εἰς τὸν οἶκόν σου, καὶ ἐὰν ἴδῃς ταπεινόν, οὐχ ὑπερόψῃ αὐτόν,
οὐδὲ ἀπὸ τῶν οἰκείων τοῦ σπέρματός σου. 4. τότε ῥαγήσεται
πρώϊμον τὸ φῶς σου, καὶ τὰ ἰάματά σου ταχέως ἀνατελεῖ, καὶ
προπορεύσεται ἔμπροσθέν σου ἡ δικαιοσύνη, καὶ ἡ δόξα τοῦ Θεοῦ
περιστελεῖ σε· 5. τότε βοήσεις, καὶ ὁ Θεὸς ἐπακούσεταί σου, ἔτι
λαλοῦντός σου ἐρεῖ, Ἰδοὺ πάρειμι· ἐὰν ἀφέλῃς ἀπὸ σοῦ σύνδεσμον
καὶ χειροτονίαν καὶ ῥῆμα γογγυσμοῦ, καὶ δῷς πεινῶντι τὸν ἄρτον
σου ἐκ ψυχῆς σου, καὶ ψυχὴν τεταπεινωμένην ἐλεήσῃς. 6. εἰς
τοῦτο οὖν, ἀδελφοί, ὁ μακρόθυμος προβλέψας ὡς ἐν ἀκεραιοσύνῃ πιστεύσει ὁ λαὸς ὃν ἡτοίμασεν ἐν τῷ ἠγαπημένῳ αὐτοῦ,
προεφανέρωσεν ἡμῖν περὶ πάντων, ἵνα μὴ προσρησσώμεθα
ὡς ἐπήλυτοι τῷ ἐκείνων νόμῳ.

IV. Δεῖ οὖν ἡμᾶς περὶ τῶν ἐνεστώτων ἐπιπολὺ ἐραυ-
νῶντας ἐκζητεῖν τὰ δυνάμενα ἡμᾶς σώζειν. φύγωμεν οὖν
τελείως ἀπὸ πάντων τῶν ἔργων τῆς ἀνομίας, μήποτε καταλάβῃ ἡμᾶς τὰ ἔργα τῆς ἀνομίας· καὶ μισήσωμεν τὴν πλάνην
τοῦ νῦν καιροῦ, ἵνα εἰς τὸν μέλλοντα ἀγαπηθῶμεν. 2. μὴ
δῶμεν τῇ ἑαυτῶν ψυχῇ ἄνεσιν, ὥστε ἔχειν αὐτὴν ἐξουσίαν
μετὰ ἁμαρτωλῶν καὶ πονηρῶν συντρέχειν, μήποτε ὁμοιω-
θῶμεν αὐτοῖς. 3. τὸ τέλειον σκάνδαλον ἤγγικεν, περὶ οὗ
γέγραπται, ὡς Ἐνὼχ λέγει. εἰς τοῦτο γὰρ ὁ δεσπότης
συντέτμηκεν τοὺς καιροὺς καὶ τὰς ἡμέρας, ἵνα ταχύνῃ ὁ
ἠγαπημένος αὐτοῦ καὶ ἐπὶ τὴν κληρονομίαν ἥξῃ. 4. λέγει

Dan. vii.
24.

δὲ οὕτως καὶ ὁ προφήτης· Βαϲιλεῖαι δέκα ἐπὶ τῆϲ γῆϲ Βαϲιλεύ-
ϲουϲιν, καὶ ἐξαναϲτήϲεται ὄπιϲθεν αὐτῶν μικρὸϲ Βαϲιλεύϲ, ὃϲ
ταπεινώϲει τρεῖϲ ὑφ᾽ ἓν τῶν Βαϲιλέων. 5. ὁμοίως περὶ τοῦ

Dan. vii.
7, 8.

αὐτοῦ λέγει Δανιήλ· Καὶ εἶδον τὸ τέταρτον θηρίον πονηρὸν
καὶ ἰϲχυρὸν καὶ χαλεπώτερον παρὰ πάντα τὰ θηρία τῆϲ γῆϲ, καὶ
ὡϲ ἐξ αὐτοῦ ἀνέτειλεν δέκα κέρατα, καὶ ἐξ αὐτῶν μικρὸν
κέραϲ παραφυάδιον, καὶ ὡϲ ἐταπείνωϲεν ὑφ᾽ ἓν τρία τῶν μεγάλων κεράτων. 6. συνιέναι οὖν ὀφείλετε. Ἔτι δὲ καὶ τοῦτο
ἐρωτῶ ὑμᾶς ὡς εἷς ἐξ ὑμῶν ὤν, ἰδίως δὲ καὶ πάντας ἀγαπῶν
ὑπὲρ τὴν ψυχήν μου, προσέχειν νῦν ἑαυτοῖς καὶ μὴ ὁμοιοῦσθαί
τισιν, ἐπισωρεύοντας ταῖς ἁμαρτίαις ὑμῶν, λέγοντας ὅτι ἡ διαθήκη ἡμῶν μένει ἐκείνοις· ἡμῶν μέν· ἀλλ᾽ ἐκεῖνοι οὕτως εἰς
τέλος ἀπώλεσαν αὐτήν, λαβόντος ἤδη τοῦ Μωϋσέως. 7. λέγει

Ex. xxxi.
18, xxxiv.
28.

γὰρ ἡ γραφή· Καὶ ἦν Μωϋϲῆϲ ἐν τῷ ὄρει νηϲτεύων ἡμέραϲ τεϲϲεράκοντα καὶ νύκταϲ τεϲϲεράκοντα, καὶ ἔλαβεν τὴν διαθήκην ἀπὸ
τοῦ Κυρίου, πλάκαϲ λιθίναϲ γεγραμμέναϲ τῷ δακτύλῳ τῆϲ χειρὸϲ
τοῦ Κυρίου. 8. ἀλλὰ ἐπιστραφέντες ἐπὶ τὰ εἴδωλα ἀπώλεσαν

Ex. xxxii.
7.
Deut. ix.
12.

αὐτήν· λέγει γὰρ οὕτως Κύριος· Μωϋϲῆ Μωϋϲῆ, κατάβηθι
τὸ τάχοϲ, ὅτι ἠνόμηϲεν ὁ λαόϲ ϲου, οὓϲ ἐξήγαγεϲ ἐκ γῆϲ Αἰγύπτου.
καὶ συνῆκεν Μωϋσῆς καὶ ἔριψεν τὰς δύο πλάκας ἐκ τῶν
χειρῶν αὐτοῦ· καὶ συνετρίβη αὐτῶν ἡ διαθήκη, ἵνα ἡ τοῦ
ἠγαπημένου Ἰησοῦ ἐνκατασφραγισθῇ εἰς τὴν καρδίαν ἡμῶν
ἐν ἐλπίδι τῆς πίστεως αὐτοῦ. 9. Πολλὰ δὲ θέλων γράφειν,
οὐχ ὡς διδάσκαλος, ἀλλ᾽ ὡς πρέπει ἀγαπῶντι ἀφ᾽ ὧν ἔχομεν
μὴ ἐλλείπειν, γράφειν ἐσπούδασα, περίψημα ὑμῶν. διὸ
προσέχωμεν ἐν ταῖς ἐσχάταις ἡμέραις. οὐδὲν γὰρ ὠφελήσει
ἡμᾶς ὁ πᾶς χρόνος τῆς πίστεως ἡμῶν, ἐὰν μὴ νῦν ἐν τῷ
ἀνόμῳ καιρῷ καὶ τοῖς μέλλουσιν σκανδάλοις, ὡς πρέπει
υἱοῖς Θεοῦ, ἀντιστῶμεν, ἵνα μὴ σχῇ παρείσδυσιν ὁ μέλας.
10. φύγωμεν ἀπὸ πάσης ματαιότητος, μισήσωμεν τελείως τὰ
ἔργα τῆς πονηρᾶς ὁδοῦ. Μὴ καθ᾽ ἑαυτοὺς ἐνδύνοντες μονά-
ζετε ὡς ἤδη δεδικαιωμένοι, ἀλλ᾽ ἐπὶ τὸ αὐτὸ συνερχόμενοι

iv. 6 ἡμῶν μένει ἐκείνοις· ἡμῶν μέν] conj. Harmer; ἡμῶν μέν ℵ; ὑμῶν ὑμῖν
μένει C; illorum et nostrum est. nostrum est autem L.

συνζητεῖτε περὶ τοῦ κοινῇ συμφέροντος. 11. λέγει γὰρ ἡ γραφή· Οὐαὶ οἱ ϲγνετοὶ ἑαγτοῖϲ καὶ ἐνώπιον ἑαγτῶν ἐπιϲτήμονεϲ. Is. v. 21. γενώμεθα πνευματικοί, γενώμεθα ναὸς τέλειος τῷ Θεῷ. ἐφ᾽ ὅσον ἐστὶν ἐν ἡμῖν, μελετῶμεν τὸν φόβον τοῦ Θεοῦ [καὶ] φυλάσσειν ἀγωνιζώμεθα τὰς ἐντολὰς αὐτοῦ, ἵνα ἐν τοῖς δικαιώμασιν αὐτοῦ εὐφρανθῶμεν. 12. ὁ Κύριος ἀπροσω-πολήμπτως κρινεῖ τὸν κόσμον. ἕκαστος καθὼς ἐποίησεν κομιεῖται. ἐὰν ᾖ ἀγαθός, ἡ δικαιοσύνη αὐτοῦ προηγήσεται αὐτοῦ· ἐὰν ᾖ πονηρός, ὁ μισθὸς τῆς πονηρίας ἔμπροσθεν αὐτοῦ· 13. ἵνα μήποτε ἐπαναπαυόμενοι ὡς κλητοὶ ἐπικαθυ-πνώσωμεν ταῖς ἁμαρτίαις ἡμῶν, καὶ ὁ πονηρὸς ἄρχων λαβὼν τὴν καθ᾽ ἡμῶν ἐξουσίαν ἀπώσηται ἡμᾶς ἀπὸ τῆς βασιλείας τοῦ Κυρίου. 14. Ἔτι δὲ κἀκεῖνο, ἀδελφοί μου, νοεῖτε· ὅταν βλέπετε μετὰ τηλικαῦτα σημεῖα καὶ τέρατα γεγονότα ἐν τῷ Ἰσραὴλ καὶ οὕτως ἐνκαταλελεῖφθαι αὐτούς· προσέχωμεν μήποτε, ὡς γέγραπται, πολλοὶ κλητοί, ὀλίγοι δὲ ἐκλεκτοὶ S. Matt. εὑρεθῶμεν. xxii. 14.

V. Εἰς τοῦτο γὰρ ὑπέμεινεν ὁ Κύριος παραδοῦναι τὴν σάρκα εἰς καταφθοράν, ἵνα τῇ ἀφέσει τῶν ἁμαρτιῶν ἁγνισθῶ-μεν, ὅ ἐστιν ἐν τῷ αἵματι τοῦ ῥαντίσματος αὐτοῦ. 2. γέγραπ-ται γὰρ περὶ αὐτοῦ ἃ μὲν πρὸς τὸν Ἰσραήλ, ἃ δὲ πρὸς ἡμᾶς. λέγει δὲ οὕτως· Ἐτραγματίϲθη διὰ τὰϲ ἀνομίαϲ ἡμῶν Is. liii. 5, καὶ μεμαλάκιϲται διὰ τὰϲ ἁμαρτίαϲ ἡμῶν, τῷ μώλωπι αγτοῦ ἡμεῖϲ 7· ἰάθημεν. ὡϲ πρόβατον ἐπὶ ϲφαγὴν ἤχθη καὶ ὡϲ ἀμνὸϲ ἄφωνοϲ ἐναντίον τοῦ κείραντοϲ αγτόν. 3. οὐκοῦν ὑπερευχαριστεῖν ὀφείλομεν τῷ Κυρίῳ, ὅτι καὶ τὰ παρεληλυθότα ἡμῖν ἐγνώ-ρισεν, καὶ ἐν τοῖς ἐνεστῶσιν ἡμᾶς ἐσόφισεν, καὶ εἰς τὰ μέλλοντα οὐκ ἐσμὲν ἀσύνετοι. 4. λέγει δὲ ἡ γραφή· Οὐκ Prov. i. 17. ἀδίκως ἐκτείνεται δίκτγα πτερωτοῖϲ. τοῦτο λέγει ὅτι δικαίως ἀπολεῖται ἄνθρωπος, ὃς ἔχων ὁδοῦ δικαιοσύνης γνῶσιν, ἑαυτὸν εἰς ὁδὸν σκότους ἀποσυνέχει. 5. Ἔτι δὲ καὶ τοῦτο, ἀδελφοί μου· εἰ ὁ Κύριος ὑπέμεινεν παθεῖν περὶ τῆς ψυχῆς ἡμῶν, ὢν παντὸς τοῦ κόσμου Κύριος, ᾧ εἶπεν ὁ Θεὸς ἀπὸ καταβολῆς κόσμου· Ποιήϲωμεν ἄνθρωπον κατ᾽ εἰκόνα καὶ καθ᾽ Gen. i. 26.

ὁμοίωcιν ἡμετέρΑΝ· πῶς οὖν ὑπέμεινεν ὑπὸ χειρὸς ἀνθρώπων παθεῖν; μάθετε. 6. οἱ προφῆται, ἀπ᾽ αὐτοῦ ἔχοντες τὴν χάριν, εἰς αὐτὸν ἐπροφήτευσαν. αὐτὸς δὲ ἵνα καταργήσῃ τὸν θάνατον καὶ τὴν ἐκ νεκρῶν ἀνάστασιν δείξῃ, ὅτι ἐν σαρκὶ ἔδει αὐτὸν φανερωθῆναι, ὑπέμεινεν, 7. ἵνα καὶ τοῖς πατράσιν τὴν ἐπαγγελίαν ἀποδῷ καὶ αὐτὸς ἑαυτῷ τὸν λαὸν τὸν καινὸν ἑτοιμάζων ἐπιδείξῃ, ἐπὶ τῆς γῆς ὤν, ὅτι τὴν ἀνάστασιν αὐτὸς ποιήσας κρινεῖ. 8. πέρας γέ τοι διδάσκων τὸν Ἰσραὴλ καὶ τηλικαῦτα τέρατα καὶ σημεῖα ποιῶν ἐκήρυσσεν, καὶ ὑπερηγάπησεν αὐτόν. 9. ὅτε δὲ τοὺς ἰδίους ἀποστόλους τοὺς μέλλοντας κηρύσσειν τὸ εὐαγγέλιον αὐτοῦ ἐξελέξατο,

S. Matt.
ix. 13.
ὄντας ὑπὲρ πᾶσαν ἁμαρτίαν ἀνομωτέρους, ἵνα δείξῃ ὅτι ογκ ἦλθεν καλέcαι Δικαίογc ἀλλὰ ἁμαρτωλογc, τότε ἐφανέρωσεν ἑαυτὸν εἶναι υἱὸν Θεοῦ. 10. Εἰ γὰρ μὴ ἦλθεν ἐν σαρκί, οὐδ᾽ ἄν πως οἱ ἄνθρωποι ἐσώθησαν βλέποντες αὐτόν· ὅτε τὸν μέλλοντα μὴ εἶναι ἥλιον, ἔργον τῶν χειρῶν αὐτοῦ ὑπάρχοντα, ἐμβλέποντες οὐκ ἰσχύουσιν εἰς τὰς ἀκτῖνας αὐτοῦ ἀντοφθαλμῆσαι. 11. οὐκοῦν ὁ υἱὸς τοῦ Θεοῦ εἰς τοῦτο ἐν σαρκὶ ἦλθεν, ἵνα τὸ τέλειον τῶν ἁμαρτιῶν ἀνακεφαλαιώσῃ τοῖς διώξασιν ἐν θανάτῳ τοὺς προφήτας αὐτοῦ. 12. οὐκοῦν εἰς τοῦτο ὑπέμεινεν. λέγει γὰρ ὁ Θεὸς τὴν πληγὴν τῆς σαρκὸς

Zech. xiii.
7.
S. Matt.
xxvi. 31.
αὐτοῦ ὅτι ἐξ αὐτῶν· Ὅταν πατάξωcιν τὸν ποιμένα ἐλγτῶν, τότε ἀπολεῖται τὰ πρόβατα τῆc ποίμνηc. 13. Αὐτὸς δὲ ἠθέλησεν

Ps. xxii.
21, cxix.
120, xxii.
17.
Is. l. 6, 7.
οὕτω παθεῖν. ἔδει γὰρ ἵνα ἐπὶ ξύλου πάθῃ. λέγει γὰρ ὁ προφητεύων ἐπ᾽ αὐτῷ· Φεῖcαί μογ τῆc ψγχῆc ἀπὸ ῥομφαίαc· καί· Καθήλωcόν μογ τὰc cάρκαc, ὅτι πονηρεγομένων cγναγωγαὶ ἐπανέcτηcάν μοι. 14. καὶ πάλιν λέγει· Ἰδογ τέθεικά μογ τὸν νῶτον εἰς μάcτιγας, τὰc δὲ cιαγόναc μογ εἰς ῥαπίcματα, τὸ δὲ πρόcωπόν μογ ἔθηκα ὡc cτερεὰν πέτραν.

Is. l. 8, 9.
VI. Ὅτε οὖν ἐποίησεν τὴν ἐντολήν, τί λέγει; Τίc ὁ κρινόμενόc μοι; ἀντιcτήτω μοι· ἢ τίc ὁ Δικαιογμενόc μοι; ἐγγιcάτω τῷ παιδὶ Κγρίογ. 2. ογαὶ ὑμῖν, ὅτι ὑμεῖc πάντεc ὡc ἰμάτιον παλαιωθήcεcθε, καὶ cὴc καταφάγεται ὑμᾶc. καὶ πάλιν λέγει ὁ

Is. xxviii.
16.
προφήτης, ἐπεὶ ὡς λίθος ἰσχυρὸς ἐτέθη εἰς συντριβήν· Ἰδογ

ἐμβαλῶ εἰc τὰ θεμέλια Σιὼν λίθον πολυτελῆ, ἐκλεκτόν, ἀκρογω-
νιαῖον, ἔντιμον. 3. εἶτα τί λέγει; Καὶ ὃc ἐλπίcει ἐπ᾽ αὐτὸν
ζήcεται εἰc τὸν αἰῶνα. ἐπὶ λίθον οὖν ἡμῶν ἡ ἐλπίς; μὴ γένοιτο. ἀλλ᾽ ἐπεὶ ἐν ἰσχύι τέθεικεν τὴν σάρκα αὐτοῦ Κύριος.
λέγει γάρ· Καὶ ἔθηκέν με ὡc cτερεὰν πέτραν. 4. λέγει δὲ Is. l. 7.
πάλιν ὁ προφήτης· Λίθον ὃν ἀπεδοκίμαcαν οἱ οἰκοδομοῦντεc, Ps. cxviii.
οὗτοc ἐγενήθη εἰc κεφαλὴν γωνίαc. καὶ πάλιν λέγει· Αὕτη Ps. cxviii.
ἐcτὶν ἡ ἡμέρα ἡ μεγάλη καὶ θαυμαcτή, ἣν ἐποίηcεν ὁ Κύριοc. 24·
5. Ἁπλούστερον ὑμῖν γράφω, ἵνα συνίητε, ἐγὼ περίψημα
τῆς ἀγάπης ὑμῶν. 6. τί οὖν λέγει πάλιν ὁ προφήτης; Περι- Ps. xxii. 17,
ἔcχεν με cυναγωγὴ πονηρευομένων, ἐκύκλωcάν με ὡcεὶ μέλιc- cxviii. 12.
cαι κηρίον· καί· Ἐπὶ τὸν ἱματιcμόν μου ἔβαλον κλῆρον. 7. ἐν Ps. xxii. 19.
σαρκὶ οὖν αὐτοῦ μέλλοντος φανεροῦσθαι καὶ πάσχειν, προε-
φανερώθη τὸ πάθος. λέγει γὰρ ὁ προφήτης ἐπὶ τὸν Ἰσραήλ·
Οὐαὶ τῇ ψυχῇ αὐτῶν, ὅτι βεβούλευνται βουλὴν πονηρὰν καθ᾽ ἑαυ- Is. iii. 9,
τῶν, εἰπόντεc· Δήcωμεν τὸν δίκαιον, ὅτι δύcχρηcτοc ἡμῖν ἐcτίν. 10.
8. τί λέγει ὁ ἄλλος προφήτης Μωϋσῆς αὐτοῖς; Ἰδοὺ τάδε Ex. xxxiii.
λέγει Κύριος ὁ Θεός· Εἰcέλθατε εἰc τὴν γῆν τὴν ἀγαθήν, ἣν 1, 3·
ὤμοcεν Κύριοc τῷ Ἀβραὰμ καὶ Ἰcαὰκ καὶ Ἰακώβ, καὶ κατακληρο-
νομήcατε αὐτήν, γῆν ῥέουcαν γάλα καὶ μέλι. 9. τί δὲ λέγει ἡ
γνῶσις; μάθετε. ἐλπίσατε ἐπὶ τὸν ἐν σαρκὶ μέλλοντα φανεροῦσθαι ὑμῖν Ἰησοῦν. ἄνθρωπος γὰρ γῆ ἐστὶν πάσχουσα·
ἀπὸ προσώπου γὰρ τῆς γῆς ἡ πλάσις τοῦ Ἀδὰμ ἐγένετο.
10. τί οὖν λέγει· Εἰc τὴν γῆν τὴν ἀγαθήν, γῆν ῥέουcαν γάλα Ex. xxxiii.
καὶ μέλι; εὐλογητὸς ὁ Κύριος ἡμῶν, ἀδελφοί, ὁ σοφίαν καὶ 3·
νοῦν θέμενος ἐν ἡμῖν τῶν κρυφίων αὐτοῦ. λέγει γὰρ ὁ
προφήτης παραβολὴν Κυρίου· τίς νοήσει, εἰ μὴ σοφὸς καὶ
ἐπιστήμων καὶ ἀγαπῶν τὸν Κύριον αὐτοῦ; 11. Ἐπεὶ οὖν
ἐκαίνισεν ἡμᾶς ἐν τῇ ἀφέσει τῶν ἁμαρτιῶν, ἐποίησεν ἡμᾶς
ἄλλον τύπον, ὡς παιδίων ἔχειν τὴν ψυχήν, ὡς ἂν δὴ ἀνα-
πλάσσοντος αὐτοῦ ἡμᾶς. 12. λέγει γὰρ ἡ γραφὴ περὶ ἡμῶν,
ὡς λέγει τῷ υἱῷ· Ποιήcωμεν κατ᾽ εἰκόνα καὶ καθ᾽ ὁμοίωcιν Gen. i. 26.
ἡμῶν τὸν ἄνθρωπον, καὶ ἀρχέτωcαν τῶν θηρίων τῆc γῆc καὶ
τῶν πετεινῶν τοῦ οὐρανοῦ καὶ τῶν ἰχθύων τῆc θαλάccηc. καὶ

Gen. i. 28. εἶπεν Κύριος ἰδὼν τὸ καλὸν πλάσμα ἡμῶν· Αὐξάνεσθε καὶ
πληθύνεσθε καὶ πληρώσατε τὴν ΓΗΝ. ταῦτα πρὸς τὸν υἱόν.
13. πάλιν σοι ἐπιδείξω πῶς πρὸς ἡμᾶς λέγει [Κύριος]. δευ-
? S. Matt. τέραν πλάσιν ἐπ᾽ ἐσχάτων ἐποίησεν. λέγει δὲ Κύριος· Ἰδοὺ
xx. 16. ποιῶ τὰ ἔσχατα ὡς τὰ πρῶτα. εἰς τοῦτο οὖν ἐκήρυξεν ὁ προ-
Ex. xxxiii. φήτης· Εἰσέλθατε εἰς ΓΗΝ ῥέουσαν ΓΑΛΑ καὶ ΜΕΛΙ, καὶ κατακυριεύ-
1, 3. σατε αὐτῆς. 14. ἴδε οὖν ἡμεῖς ἀναπεπλάσμεθα, καθὼς πάλιν
Ez. xi. 19, ἐν ἑτέρῳ προφήτῃ λέγει· Ἰδού, λέγει Κύριος, ἐξελῶ τούτων,
xxxvi. 26. τουτέστιν ὧν προέβλεπεν τὸ πνεῦμα Κυρίου, τὰς λιθίνας
καρδίας καὶ ἐμβαλῶ σαρκίνας. ὅτι αὐτὸς ἐν σαρκὶ ἔμελλεν
φανεροῦσθαι καὶ ἐν ἡμῖν κατοικεῖν. 15. ναὸς γὰρ ἅγιος,
ἀδελφοί μου, τῷ Κυρίῳ τὸ κατοικητήριον ἡμῶν τῆς καρδίας.
Ps. xlii. 3. 16. λέγει γὰρ Κύριος πάλιν· Καὶ ἐν τίνι ὀφθήσομαι τῷ Κυρίῳ
Ps. xxii. 23. τῷ Θεῷ μου καὶ δοξασθήσομαι; Ἐξομολογήσομαί σοι ἐν ἐκκλησίᾳ
ἀδελφῶν μου καὶ ψαλῶ σοι ἀναμέσον ἐκκλησίας ἁγίων. οὐκοῦν
ἡμεῖς ἐσμεν οὓς εἰσήγαγεν εἰς τὴν γῆν τὴν ἀγαθήν. 17. τί
οὖν τὸ γάλα καὶ τὸ μέλι; ὅτι πρῶτον τὸ παιδίον μέλιτι, εἶτα
γάλακτι ζωοποιεῖται. οὕτως οὖν καὶ ἡμεῖς τῇ πίστει τῆς
ἐπαγγελίας καὶ τῷ λόγῳ ζωοποιούμενοι ζήσομεν κατακυριεύ-
Gen. i. 28. οντες τῆς γῆς. 18. προειρήκαμεν δὲ ἐπάνω· Καὶ αὐξανέσθω-
σαν καὶ πληθυνέσθωσαν καὶ ἀρχέτωσαν τῶν ἰχθύων. τίς οὖν ὁ
δυνάμενος [νῦν] ἄρχειν θηρίων ἢ ἰχθύων ἢ πετεινῶν τοῦ
οὐρανοῦ; αἰσθάνεσθαι γὰρ ὀφείλομεν ὅτι τὸ ἄρχειν ἐξουσίας
ἐστίν, ἵνα τις ἐπιτάξας κυριεύσῃ. 19. εἰ οὖν οὐ γίνεται
τοῦτο νῦν, ἄρα ἡμῖν εἴρηκεν πότε· ὅταν καὶ αὐτοὶ τελειωθῶ-
μεν κληρονόμοι τῆς διαθήκης Κυρίου γενέσθαι.

VII. Οὐκοῦν νοεῖτε, τέκνα εὐφροσύνης, ὅτι πάντα ὁ
καλὸς Κύριος προεφανέρωσεν ἡμῖν, ἵνα γνῶμεν ᾧ κατὰ
πάντα εὐχαριστοῦντες ὀφείλομεν αἰνεῖν. 2. εἰ οὖν ὁ υἱὸς
τοῦ Θεοῦ, ὢν Κύριος καὶ μέλλων κρίνειν ζῶντας καὶ νεκρούς,
ἔπαθεν ἵνα ἡ πληγὴ αὐτοῦ ζωοποιήσῃ ἡμᾶς, πιστεύσωμεν ὅτι
ὁ υἱὸς τοῦ Θεοῦ οὐκ ἠδύνατο παθεῖν εἰ μὴ δι᾽ ἡμᾶς. 3. Ἀλλὰ
καὶ σταυρωθεὶς ἐποτίζετο ὄξει καὶ χολῇ. ἀκούσατε πῶς περὶ
τούτου πεφανέρωκαν οἱ ἱερεῖς τοῦ ναοῦ. γεγραμμένης ἐντο-

λῆς· Ὃс ἂν μὴ νηстεύсῃ τὴν νηстείαν, θανάτῳ ἐξολεθρεγθή- Lev. xxiii.
сεται, ἐνετείλατο Κύριος, ἐπεὶ καὶ αὐτὸς ὑπὲρ τῶν ἡμετέρων ²⁹·
ἁμαρτιῶν ἔμελλεν τὸ σκεῦος τοῦ πνεύματος προσφέρειν θυσίαν, ἵνα καὶ ὁ τύπος ὁ γενόμενος ἐπὶ Ἰσαὰκ τοῦ προσενεχ-
θέντος ἐπὶ τὸ θυσιαστήριον τελεσθῇ. 4. τί οὖν λέγει ἐν τῷ
προφήτῃ; Καὶ φαγέτωсαν ἐκ τοῦ τράγογ τοῦ προсφερομένογ τῇ   ?
νηстείᾳ ὑπὲρ παсῶν τῶν ἁμαρτιῶν. προσέχετε ἀκριβῶς· Καὶ   ?
φαγέτωсαν οἱ ἱερεῖс μόνοι πάντεс τὸ ἔντερον ἄπλγτον μετὰ
ὄξογс. 5. πρὸς τί; ἐπειδὴ ἐμέ, ὑπὲρ ἁμαρτιῶν μέλλοντα
τοῦ λαοῦ μου τοῦ καινοῦ προσφέρειν τὴν σάρκα μου, μέλλετε
ποτίζειν χολὴν μετὰ ὄξους, φάγετε ὑμεῖς μόνοι, τοῦ λαοῦ
νηστεύοντος καὶ κοπτομένου ἐπὶ σάκκου καὶ σποδοῦ· ἵνα
δείξῃ ὅτι δεῖ αὐτὸν παθεῖν ὑπ' αὐτῶν. 6. ἃ ἐνετείλατο προσ-
έχετε· Λάβετε δύο τράγογс καλογς καὶ ὁμοίογс καὶ προсενέγκατε, Lev. xvi. 7,
καὶ λαβέτω ὁ ἱερεγς τὸν ἕνα εἰс ὁλοκαγτωμα ὑπὲρ ἁμαρτιῶν. ⁹·
7. τὸν δὲ ἕνα τί ποιήσωσιν; Ἐπικατάρατος, φησίν, ὁ εἷс. Lev. xvi. 8.
προσέχετε πῶς ὁ τύπος τοῦ Ἰησοῦ φανεροῦται· 8. Καὶ ἐμπτύ-
сατε πάντεс καὶ κατακεντήсατε, καὶ περίθετε τὸ ἔριον τὸ κόκ-   ?
κινον περὶ τὴν κεφαλὴν αγτοῦ, καὶ ογτωс εἰс ἔρημον βληθήτω.
καὶ ὅταν γένηται οὕτως, ἄγει ὁ βαστάζων τὸν τράγον εἰς τὴν
ἔρημον, καὶ ἀφαιρεῖ τὸ ἔριον καὶ ἐπιτίθησιν αὐτὸ ἐπὶ φρύ-
γανον τὸ λεγόμενον ῥαχία, οὗ καὶ τοὺς βλαστοὺς εἰώθαμεν
τρώγειν ἐν τῇ χώρᾳ εὑρίσκοντες. οὕτω μόνης τῆς ῥάχου οἱ
καρποὶ γλυκεῖς εἰσίν. 9. τί οὖν τοῦτό ἐστιν; προσέχετε·
Τὸν μὲν ἕνα ἐπὶ τὸ θγсιαстήριον, τὸν δὲ ἕνα ἐπικατάρατον, καὶ Lev. xvi. 8.
ὅτι τὸν ἐπικατάρατον ἐστεφανωμένον· ἐπειδὴ ὄψονται αὐτὸν
τότε τῇ ἡμέρᾳ τὸν ποδήρη ἔχοντα τὸν κόκκινον περὶ τὴν
σάρκα, καὶ ἐροῦσιν· Οὐχ οὗτός ἐστιν ὅν ποτε ἡμεῖς ἐσταυρώ-
σαμεν καὶ ἐξουθενήσαμεν ἐμπτύσαντες; ἀληθῶς οὗτος ἦν ὁ
τότε λέγων ἑαυτὸν υἱὸν τοῦ Θεοῦ εἶναι. 10. πῶς γὰρ ὅμοιος
ἐκείνῳ; εἰς τοῦτο ὁμοίογс τογς τράγογς, καλογς, ἴсογс, ἵνα ὅταν
ἴδωσιν αὐτὸν τότε ἐρχόμενον, ἐκπλαγῶσιν ἐπὶ τῇ ὁμοιότητι

vii. 8 ῥαχία] conj. Gebhardt; ῥαχήλ ℵ; ῥαχή C; ῥαχίλ G; rubus L.
ῥάχου] conj. Voss; ῥάχους ℵG; ῥαχῆς C; al. L.

τοῦ τράγου. οὐκοῦν ἴδε τὸν τύπον τοῦ μέλλοντος πάσχειν Ἰησοῦ. 11. Τί δὲ ὅτι τὸ ἔριον μέσον τῶν ἀκανθῶν τιθέασιν; τύπος ἐστὶν τοῦ Ἰησοῦ τῇ ἐκκλησίᾳ θέμενος, ὅτι ὃς ἐὰν θέλῃ τὸ ἔριον ἆραι τὸ κόκκινον, ἔδει αὐτὸν πολλὰ παθεῖν διὰ τὸ εἶναι φοβερὰν τὴν ἄκανθαν, καὶ θλιβέντα κυριεῦσαι αὐτοῦ. Οὕτω, φησίν, οἱ θέλοντές με ἰδεῖν καὶ ἅψασθαί μου τῆς βασιλείας ὀφείλουσιν θλιβέντες καὶ παθόντες λαβεῖν με. VIII. Τίνα δὲ δοκεῖτε τύπον εἶναι, ὅτι ἐντέταλται τῷ Ἰσραὴλ προσφέρειν δάμαλιν τοὺς ἄνδρας ἐν οἷς εἰσὶν ἁμαρτίαι τέλειαι, καὶ σφάξαντας κατακαίειν, καὶ αἴρειν τότε τὰ παιδία σποδὸν καὶ βάλλειν εἰς ἄγγη, καὶ περιτιθέναι τὸ ἔριον τὸ κόκκινον ἐπὶ ξύλον (ἴδε πάλιν ὁ τύπος ὁ τοῦ σταυροῦ καὶ τὸ ἔριον τὸ κόκκινον) καὶ τὸ ὕσσωπον, καὶ οὕτως ῥαντίζειν τὰ παιδία καθ᾽ ἕνα τὸν λαόν, ἵνα ἁγνίζωνται ἀπὸ τῶν ἁμαρτιῶν; 2. νοεῖτε πῶς ἐν ἁπλότητι λέγεται ὑμῖν· ὁ μόσχος Ἰησοῦς ἐστίν, οἱ προσφέροντες ἄνδρες ἁμαρτωλοὶ οἱ προσενέγκαντες αὐτὸν ἐπὶ τὴν σφαγήν. † εἶτα οὐκέτι ἄνδρες, οὐκέτι ἁμαρτωλῶν ἡ δόξα.† 3. Οἱ ῥαντίζοντες παῖδες οἱ εὐαγγελισάμενοι ἡμῖν τὴν ἄφεσιν τῶν ἁμαρτιῶν καὶ τὸν ἁγνισμὸν τῆς καρδίας, οἷς ἔδωκεν τοῦ εὐαγγελίου τὴν ἐξουσίαν, οὖσιν δεκαδύο εἰς μαρτύριον τῶν φυλῶν (ὅτι δεκαδύο φυλαὶ τοῦ Ἰσραήλ), εἰς τὸ κηρύσσειν. 4. διατί δὲ τρεῖς παῖδες οἱ ῥαντίζοντες; εἰς μαρτύριον Ἀβραάμ, Ἰσαάκ, Ἰακώβ, ὅτι οὗτοι μεγάλοι τῷ Θεῷ. 5. Ὅτι δὲ τὸ ἔριον ἐπὶ τὸ ξύλον· ὅτι ἡ βασιλεία Ἰησοῦ ἐπὶ ξύλου, καὶ ὅτι οἱ ἐλπίζοντες ἐπ᾽ αὐτὸν ζήσονται εἰς τὸν αἰῶνα. 6. Διατί δὲ ἅμα τὸ ἔριον καὶ τὸ ὕσσωπον; ὅτι ἐν τῇ βασιλείᾳ αὐτοῦ ἡμέραι ἔσονται πονηραὶ καὶ ῥυπαραί, ἐν αἷς ἡμεῖς σωθησόμεθα· ὅτι ὁ ἀλγῶν σάρκα διὰ τοῦ ῥύπου τοῦ ὑσσώπου ἰᾶται. 7. καὶ διὰ τοῦτο οὕτως γενόμενα ἡμῖν μέν ἐστιν φανερά, ἐκείνοις δὲ σκοτεινά, ὅτι οὐκ ἤκουσαν φωνῆς Κυρίου.

IX. Λέγει γὰρ πάλιν περὶ τῶν ὠτίων, πῶς περιέτεμεν ἡμῶν τὴν καρδίαν. λέγει Κύριος ἐν τῷ προφήτῃ· Εἰc ἀκοὴν ὠτίου ὑπήκουcάν μου. καὶ πάλιν λέγει· Ἀκοῇ ἀκούcονται οἱ

Ps. xviii.
45.
Is. xxxiii.
13.

πόρρωθεν, ἃ ἐποίησα γνώσονται· καί· Περιτμήθητε, λέγει Κύ- Jer. iv. 4.
ριος, τὰς καρδίας ὑμῶν. 2. καὶ πάλιν λέγει· Ἄκουε, Ἰσραήλ, Jer. vii. 2,
ὅτι τάδε λέγει Κύριος ὁ Θεός σου. Τίς ἐστιν ὁ θέλων ζῆσαι εἰς Ps. xxxiv. 3.
τὸν αἰῶνα; ἀκοῇ ἀκουσάτω τῆς φωνῆς τοῦ παιδός μου. 3. καὶ Ex. xv. 26. 13.
πάλιν λέγει· Ἄκουε οὐρανέ, καὶ ἐνωτίζου γῆ, ὅτι Κύριος ἐλάλη- Is. i. 2.
σεν ταῦτα εἰς μαρτύριον. καὶ πάλιν λέγει· Ἀκούσατε λόγον Is. i. 10.
Κυρίου, ἄρχοντες τοῦ λαοῦ τούτου. καὶ πάλιν λέγει· Ἀκούσατε, Is. xl. 3.
τέκνα, φωνῆς βοῶντος ἐν τῇ ἐρήμῳ. 4. οὐκοῦν περιέτεμεν
ἡμῶν τὰς ἀκοάς, ἵνα ἀκούσαντες λόγον πιστεύσωμεν ἡμεῖς.
Ἀλλὰ καὶ ἡ περιτομὴ ἐφ᾽ ᾗ πεποίθασιν κατήργηται· περιτομὴν γὰρ εἴρηκεν οὐ σαρκὸς γενηθῆναι. ἀλλὰ παρέβησαν,
ὅτι ἄγγελος πονηρὸς ἐσόφιζεν αὐτούς. 5. λέγει πρὸς αὐτούς·
Τάδε λέγει Κύριος ὁ Θεὸς ὑμῶν (ὧδε εὑρίσκω ἐντολήν)· Μὴ Jer. iv. 3, 4.
σπείρετε ἐπ᾽ ἀκάνθαις, περιτμήθητε τῷ Κυρίῳ ὑμῶν. καὶ τί
λέγει; Περιτμήθητε τὴν σκληροκαρδίαν ὑμῶν, καὶ τὸν τράχηλον Deut. x.
ὑμῶν οὐ σκληρυνεῖτε. λάβε πάλιν· Ἰδού, λέγει Κύριος, πάντα Jer. ix. 26. 16.
τὰ ἔθνη [ἀπερίτμητα] ἀκροβυστίαν, ὁ δὲ λαὸς οὗτος ἀπερίτμητος
καρδίας. 6. ἀλλ᾽ ἐρεῖς· Καὶ μὴν περιτέτμηται ὁ λαὸς εἰς
σφραγῖδα. ἀλλὰ καὶ πᾶς Σύρος καὶ Ἄραψ καὶ πάντες οἱ
ἱερεῖς τῶν εἰδώλων. ἆρα οὖν κἀκεῖνοι ἐκ τῆς διαθήκης αὐτῶν
εἰσίν; ἀλλὰ καὶ οἱ Αἰγύπτιοι ἐν περιτομῇ εἰσίν. 7. Μάθετε
οὖν, τέκνα ἀγάπης, περὶ πάντων πλουσίως, ὅτι Ἀβραὰμ
πρῶτος περιτομὴν δοὺς ἐν πνεύματι προβλέψας εἰς τὸν Ἰησοῦν περιέτεμεν, λαβὼν τριῶν γραμμάτων δόγματα. 8. λέγει γάρ· Καὶ περιέτεμεν Ἀβραὰμ ἐκ τοῦ οἴκου αὐτοῦ ἄνδρας Gen. xiv.
δεκαοκτὼ καὶ τριακοσίους. τίς οὖν ἡ δοθεῖσα αὐτῷ γνῶσις; 23. 14, xvii.
μάθετε ὅτι τοὺς δεκαοκτὼ πρώτους, καὶ διάστημα ποιήσας
λέγει τριακοσίους. τὸ δεκαοκτὼ [Ι δέκα, Η ὀκτώ]· ἔχεις
Ἰησοῦν. ὅτι δὲ ὁ σταυρὸς ἐν τῷ Τ ἤμελλεν ἔχειν τὴν χάριν,
λέγει καὶ τριακοσίους. δηλοῖ οὖν τὸν μὲν Ἰησοῦν ἐν τοῖς
δυσὶν γράμμασιν, καὶ ἐν τῷ ἑνὶ τὸν σταυρόν. 9. οἶδεν ὁ τὴν
ἔμφυτον δωρεὰν τῆς διαθήκης αὐτοῦ θέμενος ἐν ἡμῖν· οὐδεὶς
γνησιώτερον ἔμαθεν ἀπ᾽ ἐμοῦ λόγον· ἀλλὰ οἶδα ὅτι ἄξιοί
ἐστε ὑμεῖς.

Lev. xi. 7,
10,13—15.
Deut. xiv.
8, 10,
12—14.
Deut. iv.
10, 13.

X. "Οτι δὲ Μωϋσῆς εἶπεν· Οὐ φάγεσθε χοῖρον οὔτε ἀετὸν οὔτε ὀξύπτερον οὔτε κόρακα, οὔτε πάντα ἰχθὺν ὃς οὐκ ἔχει λεπίδα ἐν ἑαυτῷ, τρία ἔλαβεν ἐν τῇ συνέσει δόγματα. 2. πέρας γέ τοι λέγει αὐτοῖς ἐν τῷ Δευτερονομίῳ· Καὶ διαθήσομαι πρὸς τὸν λαὸν τοῦτον τὰ δικαιώματά μου. ἆρα οὖν οὐκ ἔστιν ἐντολὴ Θεοῦ τὸ μὴ τρώγειν, Μωϋσῆς δὲ ἐν πνεύματι ἐλάλησεν. 3. τὸ οὖν χοιρίον πρὸς τοῦτο εἶπεν· οὐ κολληθήσῃ, φησίν, ἀνθρώποις τοιούτοις, οἵτινές εἰσιν ὅμοιοι χοίρων· τουτέστιν ὅταν σπαταλῶσιν, ἐπιλανθάνονται τοῦ Κυρίου, ὅταν δὲ ὑστεροῦνται, ἐπιγινώσκουσιν τὸν Κύριον, ὡς καὶ ὁ χοῖρος ὅταν τρώγει τὸν κύριον οὐκ οἶδεν, ὅταν δὲ πεινᾷ κραυ-

Lev. xi.
13—15.
Deut. xiv.
12—14.

γάζει, καὶ λαβὼν πάλιν σιωπᾷ. 4. Οὔτε φάγῃ τὸν ἀετὸν οὐδὲ τὸν ὀξύπτερον οὐδὲ τὸν ἰκτῖνα οὐδὲ τὸν κόρακα· οὐ μή, φησίν, κολληθήσῃ οὐδὲ ὁμοιωθήσῃ ἀνθρώποις τοιούτοις, οἵτινες οὐκ οἴδασιν διὰ κόπου καὶ ἱδρῶτος ἑαυτοῖς πορίζειν τὴν τροφήν, ἀλλὰ ἁρπάζουσιν τὰ ἀλλότρια ἐν ἀνομίᾳ αὐτῶν καὶ ἐπιτηροῦσιν, ἐν ἀκεραιοσύνῃ περιπατοῦντες, καὶ περιβλέπονται τίνα ἐκδύσωσιν διὰ τὴν πλεονεξίαν, ὡς καὶ τὰ ὄρνεα ταῦτα μόνα ἑαυτοῖς οὐ πορίζει τὴν τροφήν, ἀλλὰ ἀργὰ καθήμενα ἐκζητεῖ πῶς ἀλλοτρίας σάρκας φάγῃ, ὄντα λοιμὰ τῇ

?

πονηρίᾳ αὐτῶν. 5. Καὶ οὐ φάγῃ, φησίν, σμύραιναν οὐδὲ πώλυπα οὐδὲ σηπίαν· οὐ μή, φησίν, ὁμοιωθήσῃ ἀνθρώποις τοιούτοις, οἵτινες εἰς τέλος εἰσὶν ἀσεβεῖς καὶ κεκριμένοι ἤδη τῷ θανάτῳ, ὡς καὶ ταῦτα τὰ ἰχθύδια μόνα ἐπικατάρατα ἐν τῷ βυθῷ νήχεται, μὴ κολυμβῶντα ὡς τὰ λοιπά, ἀλλὰ ἐν τῇ γῇ

Lev. xi. 5.

κάτω τοῦ βυθοῦ κατοικεῖ. 6. Ἀλλὰ καὶ τὸν δασύποδα οὐ μὴ φάγῃ. πρὸς τί; οὐ μὴ γένῃ παιδοφθόρος, οὐδὲ ὁμοιωθήσῃ τοῖς τοιούτοις. ὅτι ὁ λαγωὸς κατ' ἐνιαυτὸν πλεονεκτεῖ τὴν ἀφόδευσιν· ὅσα γὰρ ἔτη ζῇ, τοσαύτας ἔχει τρύπας. 7. Ἀλλὰ

?

οὐδὲ τὴν ὕαιναν φάγῃ· οὐ μή, φησίν, γένῃ μοιχὸς οὐδὲ φθορεύς, οὐδὲ ὁμοιωθήσῃ τοῖς τοιούτοις. πρὸς τί; ὅτι τὸ ζῷον τοῦτο παρ' ἐνιαυτὸν ἀλλάσσει τὴν φύσιν, καὶ ποτὲ μὲν ἄρρεν, ποτὲ δὲ θῆλυ γίνεται. 8. Ἀλλὰ καὶ τὴν γαλῆν ἐμίσησεν καλῶς. οὐ μή, φησίν, γενηθῇς τοιοῦτος, οἵους ἀκούομεν ἀνο-

μίαν ποιοῦντας ἐν τῷ στόματι δι' ἀκαθαρσίαν, οὐδὲ κολληθήσῃ ταῖς ἀκαθάρτοις ταῖς τὴν ἀνομίαν ποιούσαις ἐν τῷ
στόματι. τὸ γὰρ ζῷον τοῦτο τῷ στόματι κύει. 9. περὶ μὲν
τῶν βρωμάτων λαβὼν Μωϋσῆς τρία δόγματα οὕτως ἐν πνεύματι ἐλάλησεν, οἱ δὲ κατ' ἐπιθυμίαν τῆς σαρκὸς ὡς περὶ
βρώσεως προσεδέξαντο. 10. Λαμβάνει δὲ τῶν αὐτῶν τριῶν
δογμάτων γνῶσιν Δαυείδ, καὶ λέγει· Μακάριος ἀνὴρ ὃς ογκ Ps. i. 1.
ἐπορεγθη ἐν βογλῆ ἀςεβῶν, καθὼς καὶ οἱ ἰχθύες πορεύονται
ἐν σκότει εἰς τὰ βάθη, καὶ ἐν ὁδῷ ἁμαρτωλῶν ογκ ἔςτη, καθὼς
οἱ δοκοῦντες φοβεῖσθαι τὸν Κύριον ἁμαρτάνουσιν ὡς ὁ χοῖρος,
καὶ ἐπὶ καθέδραν λοιμῶν ογκ ἐκάθιςεν, καθὼς τὰ πετεινὰ τὰ
καθήμενα εἰς ἁρπαγήν. ἔχετε τελείως καὶ περὶ τῆς βρώσεως. 11. Πάλιν λέγει Μωϋσῆς· Φάγεςθε πᾶν διχηλογν καὶ Lev. xi. 3.
Deut. xiv.
μαργκώμενον. τί λέγει; ὁ τὴν τροφὴν λαμβάνων οἶδεν τὸν 6.
τρέφοντα αὐτόν, καὶ ἐπ' αὐτῷ ἀναπαυόμενος εὐφραίνεσθαι
δοκεῖ. καλῶς εἶπεν βλέπων τὴν ἐντολήν. τί οὖν λέγει;
κολλᾶσθε μετὰ τῶν φοβουμένων τὸν Κύριον, μετὰ τῶν μελε-
τώντων ὃ ἔλαβον διάσταλμα ῥήματος ἐν τῇ καρδίᾳ, μετὰ τῶν
λαλούντων τὰ δικαιώματα Κυρίου καὶ τηρούντων, μετὰ τῶν
εἰδότων ὅτι ἡ μελέτη ἐστὶν ἔργον εὐφροσύνης καὶ ἀναμαρυ-
κωμένων τὸν λόγον Κυρίου. τί δὲ τὸ διχηλοῦν; ὅτι ὁ δίκαιος
καὶ ἐν τούτῳ τῷ κόσμῳ περιπατεῖ καὶ τὸν ἅγιον αἰῶνα ἐκδέχεται. βλέπετε πῶς ἐνομοθέτησεν Μωϋσῆς καλῶς. 12. ἀλλὰ
πόθεν ἐκείνοις ταῦτα νοῆσαι ἢ συνιέναι; ἡμεῖς δὲ δικαίως
νοήσαντες τὰς ἐντολάς, λαλοῦμεν ὡς ἠθέλησεν ὁ Κύριος. διὰ
τοῦτο περιέτεμεν τὰς ἀκοὰς ἡμῶν καὶ τὰς καρδίας, ἵνα συνίω-
μεν ταῦτα.

XI. Ζητήσωμεν δὲ εἰ ἐμέλησεν τῷ Κυρίῳ προφανερῶσαι
περὶ τοῦ ὕδατος καὶ περὶ τοῦ σταυροῦ. περὶ μὲν τοῦ ὕδατος
γέγραπται ἐπὶ τὸν Ἰσραήλ, πῶς τὸ βάπτισμα τὸ φέρον ἄφεσιν ἁμαρτιῶν οὐ μὴ προσδέξονται, ἀλλ' ἑαυτοῖς οἰκοδομή-
σουσιν. 2. λέγει γὰρ ὁ προφήτης· Ἔκςτηθι ογρανέ, καὶ ἐπὶ Jer. ii. 12,
τογτῳ πλεῖον φριζάτω ἡ γῆ, ὅτι δγο καὶ πονηρὰ ἐποίηςεν ὁ λαὸς 13.
ογτος· ἐμὲ ἐγκατέλιπον πηγὴν ζωῆς, καὶ ἑαγτοῖς ὤργξαν βόθρον

Is. xvi.
1, 2.

Is. xlv.
2, 3.

Is. xxxiii.
16—18.

Ps. i. 3—6.

? Zeph. iii.
19.

Ez. xlvii.
1, 7, 12.
Cf. S. John
vi. 51.

θανάτου. 3. Μὴ πέτρα ἔρημός ἐστιν τὸ ὄρος τὸ ἅγιόν μου
Σινᾶ; ἔσεσθε γὰρ ὡς πετεινοῦ νοσσοὶ ἀνιπτάμενοι νοσσιᾶς ἀφῃ-
ρημένοι. 4. καὶ πάλιν λέγει ὁ προφήτης· Ἐγὼ πορεύσομαι
ἔμπροσθέν σου, καὶ ὄρη ὁμαλιῶ καὶ πύλας χαλκᾶς συντρίψω καὶ
μοχλοὺς σιδηροῦς συγκλάσω, καὶ δώσω σοι θησαυροὺς σκοτεινούς,
ἀποκρύφους, ἀοράτους, ἵνα γνῶσιν ὅτι ἐγὼ Κύριος ὁ Θεός. καί·
Κατοικήσεις ἐν ὑψηλῷ σπηλαίῳ πέτρας ἰσχυρᾶς. 5. καί· Τὸ
ὕδωρ αὐτοῦ πιστόν· Βασιλέα μετὰ δόξης ὄψεσθε, καὶ ἡ ψυχὴ ὑμῶν
μελετήσει φόβον Κυρίου. 6. καὶ πάλιν ἐν ἄλλῳ προφήτῃ
λέγει· Καὶ ἔσται ὁ ταῦτα ποιῶν ὡς τὸ ξύλον τὸ πεφυτευμένον
παρὰ τὰς διεξόδους τῶν ὑδάτων, ὃ τὸν καρπὸν αὐτοῦ δώσει ἐν
καιρῷ αὐτοῦ, καὶ τὸ φύλλον αὐτοῦ οὐκ ἀπορυήσεται, καὶ πάντα
ὅσα ἂν ποιῇ κατευοδωθήσεται. 7. οὐχ οὕτως οἱ ἀσεβεῖς, οὐχ
οὕτως, ἀλλ' ἢ ὡς ὁ χνοῦς ὃν ἐκρίπτει ὁ ἄνεμος ἀπὸ προσώπου
τῆς γῆς. διὰ τοῦτο οὐκ ἀναστήσονται [οἱ] ἀσεβεῖς ἐν κρίσει, οὐδὲ
ἁμαρτωλοὶ ἐν βουλῇ δικαίων· ὅτι γινώσκει Κύριος ὁδὸν δικαίων,
καὶ ὁδὸς ἀσεβῶν ἀπολεῖται. 8. αἰσθάνεσθε πῶς τὸ ὕδωρ καὶ
τὸν σταυρὸν ἐπὶ τὸ αὐτὸ ὥρισεν. τοῦτο γὰρ λέγει· Μακάριοι
οἳ ἐπὶ τὸν σταυρὸν ἐλπίσαντες κατέβησαν εἰς τὸ ὕδωρ· ὅτι
τὸν μὲν μισθὸν λέγει ἐν καιρῷ αὐτοῦ· τότε, φησίν, ἀποδώσω.
νῦν δὲ ὃ λέγει· Τὰ φύλλα οὐκ ἀπορυήσεται, τοῦτο λέγει ὅτι
πᾶν ῥῆμα ὃ ἐὰν ἐξελεύσεται ἐξ ὑμῶν διὰ τοῦ στόματος ὑμῶν
ἐν πίστει καὶ ἀγάπῃ, ἔσται εἰς ἐπιστροφὴν καὶ ἐλπίδα πολλοῖς. 9. καὶ πάλιν ἕτερος προφήτης λέγει· Καὶ ἦν ἡ γῆ τοῦ
Ἰακὼβ ἐπαινουμένη παρὰ πᾶσαν τὴν γῆν. τοῦτο λέγει· τὸ
σκεῦος τοῦ πνεύματος αὐτοῦ δοξάζει. 10. εἶτα τί λέγει; Καὶ
ἦν ποταμὸς ἕλκων ἐκ δεξιῶν, καὶ ἀνέβαινεν ἐξ αὐτοῦ δένδρα
ὡραῖα· καὶ ὃς ἂν φάγῃ ἐξ αὐτῶν ζήσεται εἰς τὸν αἰῶνα.
11. τοῦτο λέγει ὅτι ἡμεῖς μὲν καταβαίνομεν εἰς τὸ ὕδωρ
γέμοντες ἁμαρτιῶν καὶ ῥύπου, καὶ ἀναβαίνομεν καρποφο-
ροῦντες ἐν τῇ καρδίᾳ, [καὶ] τὸν φόβον καὶ τὴν ἐλπίδα εἰς τὸν
Ἰησοῦν ἐν τῷ πνεύματι ἔχοντες. Καὶ ὃς ἂν φάγῃ ἀπὸ τούτων
ζήσεται εἰς τὸν αἰῶνα, τοῦτο λέγει· ὃς ἄν, φησίν, ἀκούσῃ τούτων λαλουμένων καὶ πιστεύσῃ, ζήσεται εἰς τὸν αἰῶνα.

XII. Ὁμοίως πάλιν περὶ τοῦ σταυροῦ ὁρίζει ἐν ἄλλῳ
προφήτῃ λέγοντι· Καὶ πότε ταῦτα ϲγντελεϲθήϲεται; λέγει Κγριοϲ· 4 Esr. v. 5.
Ὅταν ξγλον κλιθῇ καὶ ἀναϲτῇ, καὶ ὅταν ἐκ ξγλογ αἷμα ϲτάξη.
ἔχεις πάλιν περὶ τοῦ σταυροῦ καὶ τοῦ σταυροῦσθαι μέλλοντος. 2. λέγει δὲ πάλιν [ἐν] τῷ Μωϋσῇ, πολεμουμένου τοῦ
Ἰσραὴλ ὑπὸ τῶν ἀλλοφύλων, καὶ ἵνα ὑπομνήσῃ αὐτοὺς
πολεμουμένους ὅτι διὰ τὰς ἁμαρτίας αὐτῶν παρεδόθησαν
εἰς θάνατον· λέγει εἰς τὴν καρδίαν Μωϋσέως τὸ πνεῦμα,
ἵνα ποιήσῃ τύπον σταυροῦ καὶ τοῦ μέλλοντος πάσχειν, ὅτι
ἐὰν μή, φησίν, ἐλπίσωσιν ἐπ᾿ αὐτῷ, εἰς τὸν αἰῶνα πολεμηθή-
σονται. τίθησιν οὖν Μωϋσῆς ἓν ἐφ᾿ ἓν ὅπλον ἐν μέσῳ τῆς
πυγμῆς, καὶ ὑψηλότερος σταθεὶς πάντων ἐξέτεινεν τὰς χεῖρας·
καὶ οὕτως πάλιν ἐνίκα ὁ Ἰσραήλ. εἶτα, ὁπόταν καθεῖλεν,
ἐθανατοῦντο. 3. πρὸς τί; ἵνα γνῶσιν ὅτι οὐ δύνανται σωθῆναι, ἐὰν μὴ ἐπ᾿ αὐτῷ ἐλπίσωσιν. 4. καὶ πάλιν ἐν ἑτέρῳ
προφήτῃ λέγει· Ὅλην τὴν ἡμέραν ἐξεπέταϲα τὰϲ χεῖράϲ μογ Is. lxv. 2.
πρὸϲ λαὸν ἀπειθῆ καὶ ἀντιλέγοντα ὁδῷ δικαίᾳ μογ. 5. Πάλιν
Μωϋσῆς ποιεῖ τύπον τοῦ Ἰησοῦ, ὅτι δεῖ αὐτὸν παθεῖν καὶ
αὐτὸς ζωοποιήσει ὃν δόξουσιν ἀπολωλεκέναι ἐν σημείῳ, πίπ-
τοντος τοῦ Ἰσραήλ. ἐποίησεν γὰρ Κύριος πάντα ὄφιν δάκνειν
αὐτούς, καὶ ἀπέθνησκον (ἐπειδὴ ἡ παράβασις διὰ τοῦ ὄφεως
ἐν Εὔᾳ ἐγένετο), ἵνα ἐλέγξῃ αὐτοὺς ὅτι διὰ τὴν παράβασιν
αὐτῶν εἰς θλῖψιν θανάτου παραδοθήσονται. 6. πέρας γέ
τοι αὐτὸς Μωϋσῆς ἐντειλάμενος· Ογκ ἔϲται ὑμῖν ογτε χωνεγτὸν Deut.
ογτε γλγπτὸν εἰϲ θεὸν ὑμῖν, αὐτὸς ποιεῖ, ἵνα τύπον τοῦ Ἰησοῦ xxvii. 15.
δείξῃ. ποιεῖ οὖν Μωϋσῆς χαλκοῦν ὄφιν καὶ τίθησιν ἐνδόξως,
καὶ κηρύγματι καλεῖ τὸν λαόν. 7. ἐλθόντες οὖν ἐπὶ τὸ
αὐτὸ ἐδέοντο Μωϋσέως ἵνα περὶ αὐτῶν ἀνενέγκῃ δέησιν περὶ
τῆς ἰάσεως αὐτῶν. εἶπεν δὲ πρὸς αὐτοὺς Μωϋσῆς· Ὅταν,
φησίν, δηχθῇ τις ὑμῶν, ἐλθέτω ἐπὶ τὸν ὄφιν τὸν ἐπὶ τοῦ
ξύλου ἐπικείμενον, καὶ ἐλπισάτω πιστεύσας ὅτι αὐτὸς ὢν
νεκρὸς δύναται ζωοποιῆσαι, καὶ παραχρῆμα σωθήσεται. καὶ
οὕτως ἐποίουν. ἔχεις πάλιν καὶ ἐν τούτοις τὴν δόξαν τοῦ
Ἰησοῦ, ὅτι ἐν αὐτῷ πάντα καὶ εἰς αὐτόν. 8. Τί λέγει πάλιν

Μωϋσῆς Ἰησοῦ υἱῷ Ναυή, ἐπιθεὶς αὐτῷ τοῦτο τὸ ὄνομα,
ὄντι προφήτῃ, ἵνα μόνον ἀκούσῃ πᾶς ὁ λαὸς ὅτι ὁ πατὴρ
πάντα φανεροῖ περὶ τοῦ υἱοῦ Ἰησοῦ; 9. λέγει οὖν Μωϋσῆς
Ἰησοῦ υἱῷ Ναυή, ἐπιθεὶς τοῦτο ὄνομα, ὁπότε ἔπεμψεν αὐτὸν
κατάσκοπον τῆς γῆς· Λάβε βιβλίον εἰς τὰς χεῖράς coy καὶ γράψον
ἃ λέγει Κύριος, ὅτι ἐκκόψει ἐκ ῥιζῶν τὸν οἶκον πάντα τοῦ
Ἀμαλήκ ὁ υἱὸς τοῦ Θεοῦ ἐπ᾽ ἐσχάτων τῶν ἡμερῶν. 10. ἴδε
πάλιν Ἰησοῦς, οὐχὶ υἱὸς ἀνθρώπου ἀλλὰ υἱὸς τοῦ Θεοῦ,
τύπῳ δὲ ἐν σαρκὶ φανερωθείς. Ἐπεὶ οὖν μέλλουσιν λέγειν
ὅτι Χριστὸς υἱὸς Δαυείδ ἐστιν, αὐτὸς προφητεύει Δαυείδ,
φοβούμενος καὶ συνίων τὴν πλάνην τῶν ἁμαρτωλῶν· Εἶπεν
Κύριος τῷ Κυρίῳ μου· Κάθου ἐκ δεξιῶν μου ἕως ἂν θῶ τοὺς
ἐχθρούς coy ὑποπόδιον τῶν ποδῶν coy. 11. καὶ πάλιν λέγει
οὕτως Ἡσαΐας· Εἶπεν Κύριος τῷ Χριστῷ μου Κυρίῳ, οὗ ἐκρά-
τησα τῆς δεξιᾶς αὐτοῦ, ἐπακοῦσαι ἔμπροσθεν αὐτοῦ ἔθνη, καὶ
ἰσχὺν βασιλέων διαρρήξω. ἴδε πῶς Δαγείδ λέγει αὐτὸν Κύριον,
καὶ υἱὸν οὐ λέγει.

XIII. Ἴδωμεν δὲ εἰ οὗτος ὁ λαὸς κληρονομεῖ ἢ ὁ πρῶτος,
καὶ ἡ διαθήκη εἰς ἡμᾶς ἢ εἰς ἐκείνους. 2. ἀκούσατε οὖν
περὶ τοῦ λαοῦ τί λέγει ἡ γραφή· Ἐδεῖτο δὲ Ἰσαὰκ περὶ Ῥεβέκ-
κας τῆς γυναικὸς αὐτοῦ, ὅτι στεῖρα ἦν. καὶ συνέλαβεν. εἶτα
ἐξῆλθεν Ῥεβέκκα πυθέσθαι παρὰ Κυρίου. καὶ εἶπεν Κύριος πρὸς
αὐτήν· Δύο ἔθνη ἐν τῇ γαστρί coy καὶ δύο λαοὶ ἐν τῇ κοιλίᾳ
coy, καὶ ὑπερέξει λαὸς λαοῦ, καὶ ὁ μείζων δουλεύσει τῷ ἐλάσσονι.
3. αἰσθάνεσθαι ὀφείλετε τίς ὁ Ἰσαὰκ καὶ τίς ἡ Ῥεβέκκα,
καὶ ἐπὶ τίνων δέδειχεν ὅτι μείζων ὁ λαὸς οὗτος ἢ ἐκεῖνος.
4. Καὶ ἐν ἄλλῃ προφητείᾳ λέγει φανερώτερον ὁ Ἰακὼβ
πρὸς Ἰωσὴφ τὸν υἱὸν αὐτοῦ, λέγων· Ἰδού, οὐκ ἐστέρησέν
με Κύριος τοῦ προσώπου coy· προσάγαγέ μοι τοὺς υἱούς coy, ἵνα
εὐλογήσω αὐτούς. 5. καὶ προσήγαγεν Ἐφραὶμ καὶ Μανασσῆ,
τὸν Μανασσῆ θέλων ἵνα εὐλογηθῇ, ὅτι πρεσβύτερος ἦν· ὁ
γὰρ Ἰωσὴφ προσήγαγεν εἰς τὴν δεξιὰν χεῖρα τοῦ πατρὸς
Ἰακώβ. εἶδεν δὲ Ἰακὼβ τύπον τῷ πνεύματι τοῦ λαοῦ τοῦ
μεταξύ. καὶ τί λέγει; Καὶ ἐποίησεν Ἰακὼβ ἐναλλὰξ τὰς χεῖρας

Ex. xvii. 14.

Ps. cx. 1.
S. Matt. xxii. 44.

Is. xlv. 1.

S. Matt. xxii. 45.

Gen. xxv. 21—23.

Gen. xlviii. 11, 9.

Gen. xlviii. 14, 18, 19.

αὐτοῦ, καὶ ἐπέθηκεν τὴν Δεξιὰν ἐπὶ τὴν κεφαλὴν Ἐφραὶμ τοῦ
Δεγτέρογ καὶ νεωτέρογ, καὶ εγλόγηcεν αγτόν. καὶ εἶπεν Ἰωcὴφ
πρὸς Ἰακώβ· Μετάθες cογ τὴν Δεξιὰν ἐπὶ τὴν κεφαλὴν Μαναccῆ,
ὅτι πρωτότοκόc μογ γιός ἐcτιν. καὶ εἶπεν Ἰακὼβ πρὸc Ἰωcήφ·
ΟἶΔα, τέκνον, οἶΔα· ἀλλ᾿ ὁ μείzων Δογλεγcει τῷ ἐλάccονι. καὶ
οῦτοc Δὲ εγλογηθήcεται. 6. Βλέπετε ἐπὶ τίνων τέθεικεν, τὸν
λαὸν τοῦτον εἶναι πρῶτον καὶ τῆς διαθήκης κληρονόμον. 7. εἰ
οὖν ἔτι καὶ διὰ τοῦ Ἀβραὰμ ἐμνήσθη, ἀπέχομεν τὸ τέλειον
τῆς γνώσεως ἡμῶν. τί οὖν λέγει τῷ Ἀβραάμ, ὅτε μόνος
πιστεύσας ἐτέθη εἰς δικαιοσύνην; Ἰδοὴ τέθεικά cε, Ἀβραάμ, Gen. xv. 6,
πατέρα ἐθνῶν τῶν πιcτεγόντων Δι᾿ ἀκροβγcτίαc τῷ Θεῷ. xvii. 5.
Rom.iv.11.

XIV. Ναί. ἀλλὰ ἴδωμεν τὴν διαθήκην ἣν ὤμοσεν τοῖς
πατράσι δοῦναι τῷ λαῷ, εἰ δέδωκεν. δέδωκεν· αὐτοὶ δὲ οὐκ
ἐγένοντο ἄξιοι λαβεῖν διὰ τὰς ἁμαρτίας αὐτῶν. 2. λέγει
γὰρ ὁ προφήτης· Καὶ ἧν Μωγcῆc νηcτεγων ἐν ὄρει Cινᾶ, τοῦ Ex. xxiv.
λαβεῖν τὴν Διαθήκην Κγρίογ πρὸc τὸν λαόν, ἡμέραc τεccεράκοντα 18.
καὶ νγκταc τεccεράκοντα. καὶ ἔλαβεν [Μωγcῆc] παρὰ Κγρίογ Ex. xxxi.
τὰc Δγο πλάκαc τὰc γεγραμμέναc τῷ Δακτγλῳ τῆc χειρὸc Κγρίογ 18.
ἐν πνεγματι. καὶ λαβὼν Μωϋcῆs κατέφερεν πρὸς τὸν λαὸν
δοῦναι. 3. καὶ εἶπεν Κύριος πρὸς Μωϋcῆν· Μωῦcῆ Μωῦcῆ, Ex. xxxii.
κατάβηθι τὸ τάχοc, ὅτι ὁ λαόc cογ ὃν ἐξήγαγεc ἐκ γῆc Αἰγγπτογ 7, 8, 19.
ἠνόμηcεν. καὶ cγνῆκεν Μωγcῆc ὅτι ἐποίηcαν ἑαγτοῖc πάλιν
χωνεγματα, καὶ ἔριψεν ἐκ τῶν χειρῶν, καὶ cγνετρίβηcαν αἱ
πλάκεc τῆc διαθήκηc Κγρίογ. 4. Μωϋσῆς μὲν ἔλαβεν, αὐτοὶ
δὲ οὐκ ἐγένοντο ἄξιοι. πῶς δὲ ἡμεῖς ἐλάβομεν; μάθετε.
Μωϋσῆς θεράπων ὢν ἔλαβεν, αὐτὸς δὲ Κύριος ἡμῖν ἔδωκεν
εἰς λαὸν κληρονομίας, δι᾿ ἡμᾶς ὑπομείνας. 5. ἐφανερώθη δὲ
ἵνα κἀκεῖνοι τελειωθῶσιν τοῖς ἁμαρτήμασιν καὶ ἡμεῖς διὰ
τοῦ κληρονομοῦντος διαθήκην Κυρίου Ἰησοῦ λάβωμεν, ὃς
εἰς τοῦτο ἡτοιμάσθη, ἵνα αὐτὸς φανεὶς τὰς ἤδη δεδαπανημένας
ἡμῶν καρδίας τῷ θανάτῳ καὶ παραδεδομένας τῇ τῆς πλάνης
ἀνομίᾳ λυτρωσάμενος ἐκ τοῦ σκότους, διάθηται ἐν ἡμῖν διαθήκην λόγῳ. 6. γέγραπται γὰρ πῶς αὐτῷ ὁ πατὴρ ἐντέλλεται,
λυτρωσάμενον ἡμᾶς ἐκ τοῦ σκότους, ἑτοιμάσαι ἑαυτῷ λαὸν

ἅγιον. 7. λέγει οὖν ὁ προφήτης· Ἐγὼ Κύριος ὁ Θεός coy
ἐκάλεcά cε ἐν Δικαιοcύνῃ, καὶ κρατήcω τῆc χειρόc coy καὶ
ἐνιcχύcω cε, καὶ ἔλωκά cε εἰc Διαθήκην γένουc, εἰc φῶc ἐθνῶν,
ἀνοῖξαι ὀφθαλμοὺc τυφλῶν, καὶ ἐξαγαγεῖν ἐκ Δεcμῶν πεπεδη-
μένουc καὶ ἐξ οἴκου φυλακῆc καθημένουc ἐν cκότει. γινώσκομεν

οὖν πόθεν ἐλυτρώθημεν. 8. πάλιν ὁ προφήτης λέγει· Ἰδοὺ
τέθεικά cε εἰc φῶc ἐθνῶν, τοῦ εἶναί cε εἰc cωτηρίαν ἕωc ἐcχάτου
τῆc γῆc· οὕτωc λέγει Κύριος ὁ λυτρωcάμενόc cε Θεός. 9. πάλιν

ὁ προφήτης λέγει· Πνεῦμα Κυρίου ἐπ' ἐμέ, οὗ εἵνεκεν ἔχριcέν
με εὐαγγελίcαcθαι ταπεινοῖc, ἀπέcταλκέν με ἰάcαcθαι τοὺc cυντε-
τριμμένουc τὴν καρδίαν, κηρῦξαι αἰχμαλώτοιc ἄφεcιν καὶ τυφλοῖc
ἀνάβλεψιν, καλέcαι ἐνιαυτὸν Κυρίου Δεκτὸν καὶ ἡμέραν ἀντα-
ποδόcεωc, παρακαλέcαι πάντας τοὺc πενθοῦντας.

XV. Ἔτι οὖν καὶ περὶ τοῦ σαββάτου γέγραπται ἐν
τοῖς δέκα λόγοις, ἐν οἷς ἐλάλησεν ἐν τῷ ὄρει Σινᾶ πρὸς

Μωϋσῆν κατὰ πρόσωπον· Καὶ ἁγιάcατε τὸ cάββατον Κυρίου
χερcὶν καθαραῖc καὶ καρδίᾳ καθαρᾷ. 2. καὶ ἐν ἑτέρῳ λέγει·

Ἐὰν φυλάξωcιν οἱ υἱοί μου τὸ cάββατον, τότε ἐπιθήcω τὸ ἔλεόc
μου ἐπ' αὐτούc. 3. τὸ σάββατον λέγει ἐν ἀρχῇ τῆς κτίσεως·

Καὶ ἐποίηcεν ὁ Θεὸc ἐν ἓξ ἡμέραιc τὰ ἔργα τῶν χειρῶν αὐτοῦ,
καὶ cυνετέλεcεν ἐν τῇ ἡμέρᾳ τῇ ἑβδόμῃ καὶ κατέπαυcεν ἐν
αὐτῇ, καὶ ἡγίαcεν αὐτήν. 4. προσέχετε, τέκνα, τί λέγει τό·
Συνετέλεcεν ἐν ἓξ ἡμέραιc. τοῦτο λέγει ὅτι ἐν ἑξακιcχιλίοιc
ἔτεσιν συντελέσει Κύριος τὰ σύνπαντα. ἡ γὰρ ἡμέρα παρ'
αὐτῷ [σημαίνει] χίλια ἔτη. αὐτὸς δέ μοι μαρτυρεῖ λέγων·

Ἰδοὺ ἡμέρα Κυρίου ἔcται ὡc χίλια ἔτη. οὐκοῦν, τέκνα, ἐν ἓξ
ἡμέραις, ἐν τοῖς ἑξακιcχιλίοις ἔτεσιν συντελεσθήσεται τὰ
σύνπαντα. 5. Καὶ κατέπαυcεν τῇ ἡμέρᾳ τῇ ἑβδόμῃ. τοῦτο
λέγει· ὅταν ἐλθὼν ὁ υἱὸς αὐτοῦ καταργήcει τὸν καιρὸν τοῦ
ἀνόμου καὶ κρινεῖ τοὺς ἀσεβεῖς καὶ ἀλλάξει τὸν ἥλιον καὶ
τὴν σελήνην καὶ τοὺς ἀστέρας, τότε καλῶς καταπαύσεται
ἐν τῇ ἡμέρᾳ τῇ ἑβδόμῃ. 6. πέρας γέ τοι λέγει· Ἁγιάcειc
αὐτὴν χερcὶν καθαραῖc καὶ καρδίᾳ καθαρᾷ. εἰ οὖν ἦν ὁ Θεὸς
ἡμέραν ἡγίαcεν, νῦν τις δύναται ἁγιάσαι καθαρὸς ὢν τῇ

καρδίᾳ, ἐν πᾶσιν πεπλανήμεθα. 7. εἰ δὲ οὖν ἄρα τότε καλῶς καταπαυόμενοι ἁγιάσομεν αὐτήν, ὅτε δυνησόμεθα αὐτοὶ δικαιωθέντες καὶ ἀπολαβόντες τὴν ἐπαγγελίαν, μηκέτι οὔσης τῆς ἀνομίας, καινῶν δὲ γεγονότων πάντων ὑπὸ Κυρίου, τότε δυνησόμεθα αὐτὴν ἁγιάσαι, αὐτοὶ ἁγιασθέντες πρῶτον. 8. πέρας γέ τοι λέγει αὐτοῖς· Τὰϲ νεομηνίαϲ ὑμῶν καὶ τὰ Is. i. 13. ϲάββατα οὐκ ἀνέχομαι. ὁρᾶτε πῶς λέγει· Οὐ τὰ νῦν σάββατα [ἐμοὶ] δεκτά, ἀλλὰ ὃ πεποίηκα, ἐν ᾧ καταπαύσας τὰ πάντα ἀρχὴν ἡμέρας ὀγδόης ποιήσω, ὅ ἐστιν ἄλλου κόσμου ἀρχήν. 9. διὸ καὶ ἄγομεν τὴν ἡμέραν τὴν ὀγδόην εἰς εὐφροσύνην, ἐν ᾗ καὶ ὁ Ἰησοῦς ἀνέστη ἐκ νεκρῶν καὶ φανερωθεὶς ἀνέβη εἰς οὐρανούς.

XVI. Ἔτι δὲ καὶ περὶ τοῦ ναοῦ ἐρῶ ὑμῖν, πῶς πλανώμενοι οἱ ταλαίπωροι εἰς τὴν οἰκοδομὴν ἤλπισαν, καὶ οὐκ ἐπὶ τὸν Θεὸν αὐτῶν τὸν ποιήσαντα αὐτούς, ὡς ὄντα οἶκον Θεοῦ. 2. σχεδὸν γὰρ ὡς τὰ ἔθνη ἀφιέρωσαν αὐτὸν ἐν τῷ ναῷ. ἀλλὰ πῶς λέγει Κύριος καταργῶν αὐτόν; μάθετε· Τίϲ ἐμέ- Is. xl. 12. τρηϲεν τὸν οὐρανὸν ϲπιθαμῇ, ἢ τὴν γῆν δρακί; οὐκ ἐγώ; λέγει Is. lxvi. 1. Κύριοϲ· Ὁ οὐρανόϲ μοι θρόνοϲ, ἡ δὲ γῆ ὑποπόδιον τῶν ποδῶν μου· ποῖον οἶκον οἰκοδομήϲετέ μοι; ἢ τίϲ τόποϲ τῆϲ καταπαύϲεώϲ μου; ἐγνώκατε ὅτι ματαία ἡ ἐλπὶς αὐτῶν. 3. πέρας γέ τοι πάλιν λέγει· Ἰδοὺ οἱ καθελόντεϲ τὸν ναὸν τοῦτον, αὐτοὶ Is. xlix. 17. αὐτὸν οἰκοδομήϲουϲιν. 4. γίνεται. διὰ γὰρ τὸ πολεμεῖν αὐτοὺς καθῃρέθη ὑπὸ τῶν ἐχθρῶν. νῦν καὶ αὐτοὶ οἱ τῶν ἐχθρῶν ὑπηρέται ἀνοικοδομήσουσιν αὐτόν. 5. πάλιν ὡς ἔμελλεν ἡ πόλις καὶ ὁ ναὸς καὶ ὁ λαὸς Ἰσραὴλ παραδίδοσθαι, ἐφανερώθη. λέγει γὰρ ἡ γραφή· Καὶ ἔϲται ἐπ' ἐϲχάτων τῶν ἡμερῶν, Enoch καὶ παραδώϲει Κύριοϲ τὰ πρόβατα τῆϲ νομῆϲ καὶ τὴν μάνδραν lxxxix. 56, καὶ τὸν πύργον αὐτῶν εἰϲ καταφθοράν. καὶ ἐγένετο καθ' ἃ 66. ἐλάλησεν Κύριος. 6. ζητήσωμεν δὲ εἰ ἔστιν ναὸς Θεοῦ. ἔστιν, ὅπου αὐτὸς λέγει ποιεῖν καὶ καταρτίζειν. γέγραπται γάρ· Καὶ ἔϲται τῆϲ ἑβδομάδοϲ ϲυντελουμένηϲ, οἰκοδομηθήϲεται Dan. ix. 24. ναὸϲ Θεοῦ ἐνδόξωϲ ἐπὶ τῷ ὀνόματι Κυρίου. 7. εὑρίσκω οὖν ὅτι ἐστὶν ναός. πῶς οὖν οἰκοδομηθήσεται ἐπὶ τῷ ὀνόματι

Κυρίου; μάθετε. πρὸ τοῦ ἡμᾶς πιστεῦσαι τῷ Θεῷ ἦν ἡμῶν τὸ κατοικητήριον τῆς καρδίας φθαρτὸν καὶ ἀσθενές, ὡς ἀληθῶς οἰκοδομητὸς ναὸς διὰ χειρός· ὅτι ἦν πλήρης μὲν εἰδωλολατρείας καὶ ἦν οἶκος δαιμονίων, διὰ τὸ ποιεῖν ὅσα ἦν ἐναντία τῷ Θεῷ. 8. οἰκοδομηθήcεται δὲ ἐπὶ τῷ ὀνόματι Κγρίογ. προσέχετε δέ, ἵνα ὁ ναὸς τοῦ Κυρίου ἐνδόξως οἰκοδομηθῇ. πῶς; μάθετε. λαβόντες τὴν ἄφεσιν τῶν ἁμαρτιῶν καὶ ἐλπίσαντες ἐπὶ τὸ ὄνομα ἐγενόμεθα καινοί, πάλιν ἐξ ἀρχῆς κτιζόμενοι· διὸ ἐν τῷ κατοικητηρίῳ ἡμῶν ἀληθῶς ὁ Θεὸς κατοικεῖ ἐν ἡμῖν. 9. πῶς; ὁ λόγος αὐτοῦ τῆς πίστεως, ἡ κλῆσις αὐτοῦ τῆς ἐπαγγελίας, ἡ σοφία τῶν δικαιωμάτων, αἱ ἐντολαὶ τῆς διδαχῆς, αὐτὸς ἐν ἡμῖν προφητεύων, αὐτὸς ἐν ἡμῖν κατοικῶν, τοῖς τῷ θανάτῳ δεδουλωμένοις ἀνοίγων ἡμῖν τὴν θύραν τοῦ ναοῦ, ὅ ἐστιν στόμα, μετάνοιαν διδοὺς ἡμῖν εἰσάγει εἰς τὸν ἄφθαρτον ναόν. 10. ὁ γὰρ ποθῶν σωθῆναι βλέπει οὐκ εἰς τὸν ἄνθρωπον ἀλλὰ εἰς τὸν ἐν αὐτῷ κατοικοῦντα καὶ λαλοῦντα, ἐπ᾽ αὐτῷ ἐκπλησσόμενος ἐπὶ τῷ μηδέποτε μήτε τοῦ λέγοντος τὰ ῥήματα ἀκηκοέναι ἐκ τοῦ στόματος μήτε αὐτός ποτε ἐπιτεθυμηκέναι ἀκούειν. τοῦτό ἐστιν πνευματικὸς ναὸς οἰκοδομούμενος τῷ Κυρίῳ.

XVII. Ἐφ᾽ ὅσον ἦν ἐν δυνατῷ καὶ ἁπλότητι δηλῶσαι ὑμῖν, ἐλπίζει μου ἡ ψυχὴ [τῇ ἐπιθυμίᾳ μου] μὴ παραλελοιπέναι τι [τῶν ἀνηκόντων εἰς σωτηρίαν]. 2. ἐὰν γὰρ περὶ τῶν ἐνεστώτων ἢ μελλόντων γράφω ὑμῖν, οὐ μὴ νοήσητε διὰ τὸ ἐν παραβολαῖς κεῖσθαι. ταῦτα μὲν οὕτως.

XVIII. Μεταβῶμεν δὲ καὶ ἐπὶ ἑτέραν γνῶσιν καὶ διδαχήν. Ὁδοὶ δύο εἰσὶν διδαχῆς καὶ ἐξουσίας, ἥ τε τοῦ φωτὸς καὶ ἡ τοῦ σκότους. διαφορὰ δὲ πολλὴ τῶν δύο ὁδῶν. ἐφ᾽ ἧς μὲν γάρ εἰσιν τεταγμένοι φωταγωγοὶ ἄγγελοι τοῦ Θεοῦ, ἐφ᾽ ἧς δὲ ἄγγελοι τοῦ Σατανᾶ. 2. καὶ ὁ μέν ἐστιν Κύριος ἀπὸ αἰώνων καὶ εἰς τοὺς αἰῶνας, ὁ δὲ ἄρχων καιροῦ τοῦ νῦν τῆς ἀνομίας.

XIX. Ἡ οὖν ὁδὸς τοῦ φωτός ἐστιν αὕτη· ἐάν τις θέλων ὁδὸν ὁδεύειν ἐπὶ τὸν ὡρισμένον τόπον σπεύσῃ τοῖς ἔργοις

αὐτοῦ. ἔστιν οὖν ἡ δοθεῖσα ἡμῖν γνῶσις τοῦ περιπατεῖν ἐν
αὐτῇ τοιαύτη· 2. Ἀγαπήσεις τὸν ποιήσαντά σε, φοβηθήσῃ
τόν σε πλάσαντα, δοξάσεις τόν σε λυτρωσάμενον ἐκ θανάτου·
ἔσῃ ἁπλοῦς τῇ καρδίᾳ καὶ πλούσιος τῷ πνεύματι· οὐ κολληθήσῃ μετὰ πορευομένων ἐν ὁδῷ θανάτου, μισήσεις πᾶν ὃ οὐκ
ἔστιν ἀρεστὸν τῷ Θεῷ, μισήσεις πᾶσαν ὑπόκρισιν· οὐ μὴ
ἐγκαταλίπῃς ἐντολὰς Κυρίου. 3. οὐχ ὑψώσεις σεαυτόν, ἔσῃ
δὲ ταπεινόφρων κατὰ πάντα. οὐκ ἀρεῖς ἐπὶ σεαυτὸν δόξαν.
οὐ λήμψῃ βουλὴν πονηρὰν κατὰ τοῦ πλησίον σου· οὐ δώσεις
τῇ ψυχῇ σου θράσος. 4. οὐ πορνεύσεις, οὐ μοιχεύσεις, οὐ Ex. xx. 14.
παιδοφθορήσεις. οὐ μή σου ὁ λόγος τοῦ Θεοῦ ἐξέλθῃ ἐν
ἀκαθαρσίᾳ τινῶν. οὐ λήμψῃ πρόσωπον ἐλέγξαι τινὰ ἐπὶ
παραπτώματι. ἔσῃ πραΰς, ἔσῃ ἡσύχιος, ἔσῃ τρέμων τοὺς Is. lxvi. 2.
λόγους οὓς ἤκουσας. οὐ μνησικακήσεις τῷ ἀδελφῷ σου.
5. οὐ μὴ διψυχήσῃς πότερον ἔσται ἢ οὔ. οὐ μὴ λάβῃς ἐπὶ Ex. xx. 7.
ματαίῳ τὸ ὄνομα Κυρίου. ἀγαπήσεις τὸν πλησίον σου ὑπὲρ
τὴν ψυχήν σου. οὐ φονεύσεις τέκνον ἐν φθορᾷ, οὐδὲ πάλιν
γεννηθὲν ἀποκτενεῖς. οὐ μὴ ἄρῃς τὴν χεῖρά σου ἀπὸ τοῦ
υἱοῦ σου ἢ ἀπὸ τῆς θυγατρός σου, ἀλλὰ ἀπὸ νεότητος διδάξεις φόβον Θεοῦ. 6. οὐ μὴ γένῃ ἐπιθυμῶν τὰ τοῦ πλησίον
σου, οὐ μὴ γένῃ πλεονέκτης. οὐδὲ κολληθήσῃ ἐκ ψυχῆς σου
μετὰ ὑψηλῶν, ἀλλὰ μετὰ ταπεινῶν καὶ δικαίων ἀναστραφήσῃ. τὰ συμβαίνοντά σοι ἐνεργήματα ὡς ἀγαθὰ προσδέξῃ,
εἰδὼς ὅτι ἄνευ Θεοῦ οὐδὲν γίνεται. 7. οὐκ ἔσῃ διγνώμων
οὐδὲ δίγλωσσος. ὑποταγήσῃ κυρίοις ὡς τύπῳ Θεοῦ ἐν αἰσχύνῃ
καὶ φόβῳ. οὐ μὴ ἐπιτάξῃς δούλῳ σου ἢ παιδίσκῃ ἐν πικρίᾳ,
τοῖς ἐπὶ τὸν αὐτὸν Θεὸν ἐλπίζουσιν, μήποτε οὐ μὴ φοβηθή-
σονται τὸν ἐπ᾽ ἀμφοτέροις Θεόν· ὅτι ἦλθεν οὐ κατὰ πρόσωπον καλέσαι, ἀλλ᾽ ἐφ᾽ οὓς τὸ πνεῦμα ἡτοίμασεν. 8. κοινω-
νήσεις ἐν πᾶσιν τῷ πλησίον σου, καὶ οὐκ ἐρεῖς ἴδια εἶναι· εἰ Acts iv. 32.
γὰρ ἐν τῷ ἀφθάρτῳ κοινωνοί ἐστε, πόσῳ μᾶλλον ἐν τοῖς
φθαρτοῖς. οὐκ ἔσῃ πρόγλωσσος· παγὶς γὰρ τὸ στόμα θανάτου. ὅσον δύνασαι ὑπὲρ τῆς ψυχῆς σου ἁγνεύσεις. 9. μὴ Ecclus. iv.
γίνου πρὸς μὲν τὸ λαβεῖν ἐκτείνων τὰς χεῖρας, πρὸς δὲ τὸ δοῦναι 31.

ϲΥϲΠῶΝ. ἀγαπήσεις ὡς κόρην τοῦ ὀφθαλμοῦ σου πάντα τὸν λαλοῦντά ϲοι τὸν λόγον Κγρίογ. 10. μΝΗϲθΗϲΗ ἡμέραν κρίσεως νυκτὸς καὶ ἡμέρας, καὶ ἐκζητήσεις καθ᾽ ἑκάστην ἡμέραν τὰ πρόσωπα τῶν ἁγίων, ἢ διὰ λόγου κοπιῶν καὶ πορευόμενος εἰς τὸ παρακαλέσαι καὶ μελετῶν εἰς τὸ σῶσαι ψυχὴν τῷ λόγῳ, ἢ διὰ τῶν χειρῶν σου ἐργάσῃ εἰς λύτρον ἁμαρτιῶν σου. 11. οὐ διστάσεις δοῦναι οὐδὲ διδοὺς γογγύσεις, γνώσῃ δὲ τίς ὁ τοῦ μισθοῦ καλὸς ἀνταποδότης. φυλάξεις ἃ παρέλαβες, μήτε προστιθεὶς μήτε ἀφαιρῶν. εἰς τέλος μισήσεις τὸν πονηρόν. κρινεῖς δικαίως. 12. οὐ ποιήσεις σχίσμα, εἰρηνεύσεις δὲ μαχομένους συναγαγών. ἐξομολογήσῃ ἐπὶ ἁμαρτίαις σου. οὐ προσήξεις ἐπὶ προσευχὴν ἐν συνειδήσει πονηρᾷ. αὕτη ἐστὶν ἡ ὁδὸς τοῦ φωτός.

XX. Ἡ δὲ τοῦ μέλανος ὁδός ἐστιν σκολιὰ καὶ κατάρας μεστή. ὁδὸς γάρ ἐστιν θανάτου αἰωνίου μετὰ τιμωρίας, ἐν ᾗ ἐστιν τὰ ἀπολλύντα τὴν ψυχὴν αὐτῶν· εἰδωλολατρεία, θρασύτης, ὕψος δυνάμεως, ὑπόκρισις, διπλοκαρδία, μοιχεία, φόνος, ἁρπαγή, ὑπερηφανία, παράβασις, δόλος, κακία, αὐθάδεια, φαρμακεία, μαγεία, πλεονεξία, ἀφοβία Θεοῦ. 2. διῶκται τῶν ἀγαθῶν, μισοῦντες ἀλήθειαν, ἀγαπῶντες ψεύδη, οὐ γινώσκοντες μισθὸν δικαιοσύνης, οὐ κολλώμεΝοι ἀγαθῷ, οὐ κρίσει δικαίᾳ, χήρᾳ καὶ ὀρφανῷ οὐ προσέχοντες, ἀγρυπνοῦντες οὐκ εἰς φόβον Θεοῦ ἀλλὰ ἐπὶ τὸ πονηρόν, ὧν μακρὰν καὶ πόρρω πραΰτης καὶ ὑπομονή, ἀγαπῶντες μάταια, διώκοντες ἀνταπόδομα, οὐκ ἐλεῶντες πτωχόν, οὐ πονοῦντες ἐπὶ καταπονουμένῳ, εὐχερεῖς ἐν καταλαλιᾷ, οὐ γινώσκοντες τὸν ποιήσαντα αὐτούς, φονεῖς τέκνων, φθορεῖς πλάσματος Θεοῦ, ἀποστρεφόμενοι τὸν ἐνδεόμενον, καταπονοῦντες τὸν θλιβόμενον, πλουσίων παράκλητοι, πενήτων ἄνομοι κριταί, πανθαμάρτητοι.

XXI. Καλὸν οὖν ἐστιν μαθόντα τὰ δικαιώματα τοῦ Κυρίου, ὅσα γέγραπται, ἐν τούτοις περιπατεῖν. ὁ γὰρ ταῦτα ποιῶν ἐν τῇ βασιλείᾳ τοῦ Θεοῦ δοξασθήσεται· ὁ ἐκεῖνα ἐκλεγόμενος μετὰ τῶν ἔργων αὐτοῦ συναπολεῖται. διὰ τοῦτο ἀνάστασις, διὰ τοῦτο ἀνταπόδομα. 2. Ἐρωτῶ τοὺς ὑπερέχοντας, εἴ τινά μου γνώμης ἀγαθῆς λαμβάνετε συμβουλίαν· ἔχετε μεθ᾽ ἑαυτῶν εἰς οὓς ἐργάσησθε τὸ καλόν· μὴ ἐλλείπητε. 3. ἐγγὺς ἡ ἡμέρα ἐν ᾗ συναπολεῖται πάντα τῷ πονηρῷ. ἐγγὺϲ ὁ Κⳙριοϲ κⲁⲓ ὁ μιϲθὸϲ ⲁⳙτοⳙ. 4. ἔτι καὶ ἔτι ἐρωτῶ ὑμᾶς· ἑαυτῶν γίνεσθε νομοθέται ἀγαθοί, ἑαυτῶν μένετε σύμβουλοι πιστοί, ἄρατε ἐξ ὑμῶν πᾶσαν ὑπόκρισιν. 5. ὁ δὲ Θεός, ὁ τοῦ παντὸς κόσμου κυριεύων, δῴη ὑμῖν σοφίαν, σύνεσιν, ἐπιστήμην, γνῶσιν τῶν δικαιωμάτων αὐτοῦ, ὑπομονήν. 6. γίνεσθε δὲ θεοδίδακτοι, ἐκζητοῦντες τί ζητεῖ Κύριος ἀφ᾽ ὑμῶν, καὶ ποιεῖτε ἵνα εὑρεθῆτε ἐν ἡμέρᾳ κρίσεως. 7. εἰ δέ τίς ἐστιν ἀγαθοῦ μνεία, μνημονεύετέ μου μελετῶντες ταῦτα, ἵνα καὶ ἡ ἐπιθυμία καὶ ἡ ἀγρυπνία εἴς τι ἀγαθὸν χωρήσῃ. ἐρωτῶ ὑμᾶς, χάριν αἰτούμενος. 8. ἕως ἔτι τὸ καλὸν σκεῦός ἐστιν μεθ᾽ ὑμῶν, μὴ ἐλλείπητε μηδενὶ ἑαυτῶν, ἀλλὰ συνεχῶς ἐκζητεῖτε ταῦτα καὶ ἀναπληροῦτε πᾶσαν ἐντολήν· ἔστιν γὰρ ἄξια. 9. διὸ μᾶλλον ἐσπούδασα γράψαι ἀφ᾽ ὧν ἠδυνήθην, εἰς τὸ εὐφρᾶναι ὑμᾶς. Σώζεσθε, ἀγάπης τέκνα καὶ εἰρήνης. ὁ Κύριος τῆς δόξης καὶ πάσης χάριτος μετὰ τοῦ πνεύματος ὑμῶν.

Is. xl. 10.
Apoc. xxii. 12.

TRANSLATION

OF THE

EPISTLE OF BARNABAS

THE EPISTLE OF BARNABAS

1. I BID you greeting, sons and daughters, in the name of the Lord that loved us, in peace.

Seeing that the ordinances of God are great and rich unto you, I rejoice with an exceeding great and overflowing joy at your blessed and glorious spirits; so innate is the grace of the spiritual gift that ye have received. Wherefore also I the more congratulate myself hoping to be saved, for that I truly see the Spirit poured out among you from the riches of the fount of the Lord. So greatly did the much-desired sight of you astonish me respecting you. Being therefore persuaded of this, and being conscious with myself that having said much among you I know that the Lord journeyed with me on the way of righteousness, and am wholly constrained also myself to this, to love you more than my own soul (for great faith and love dwelleth in you through the hope of the life which is His)—considering this therefore, that, if it shall be my care to communicate to you some portion of that which I received, it shall turn to my reward for having ministered to such spirits, I was eager to send you a trifle, that along with your faith ye might have your knowledge also perfect. Well then, there are three ordinances of the Lord; †the hope of life, which is the beginning and end of our faith; and righteousness, which is the beginning and end of judgment; love shown in gladness and exultation, the testimony of works of righteousness †. For the Lord made known to us by His prophets things past and present, giving us likewise the firstfruits of the taste of things future. And seeing each of these things severally coming to pass, according as He spake, we ought to offer a richer and higher offering to the fear of Him. But I, not as though I were a teacher, but as one of yourselves, will show forth a few things, whereby ye shall be gladdened in the present circumstances.

2. Seeing then that the days are evil, and that the Active One himself has the authority, we ought to give heed to ourselves and to seek out the ordinances of the Lord. The aids of our faith then are fear and patience, and our allies are long-suffering and self-restraint. While these abide in a pure spirit in matters relating to the Lord, wisdom, understanding, science, knowledge rejoice with them. For He hath made manifest to us by all the prophets that He wanteth neither sacrifices nor whole burnt-offerings nor oblations, saying at one time; *What to Me is the multitude of your sacrifices, saith the Lord? I am full of whole burnt-offerings, and the fat of lambs and the blood of bulls and of goats I desire not, not though ye should come to be seen of Me. For who required these things at your hands? Ye shall continue no more to tread My court. If ye bring fine flour, it is vain; incense is an abomination to Me; your new moons and your sabbaths I cannot away with.* These things therefore He annulled, that the new law of our Lord Jesus Christ, being free from the yoke of constraint, might have its oblation not made by human hands. And He saith again unto them; *Did I command your fathers when they went forth from the land of Egypt to bring Me whole burnt-offerings and sacrifices? Nay, this was My command unto them, Let none of you bear a grudge of evil against his neighbour in his heart, and love you not a false oath.* So we ought to perceive, unless we are without understanding, the mind of the goodness of our Father; for He speaketh to us, desiring us not to go astray like them but to seek how we may approach Him. Thus then speaketh He to us; *The sacrifice unto God is a broken heart, the smell of a sweet savour unto the Lord is a heart that glorifies its Maker.* We ought therefore, brethren, to learn accurately concerning our salvation, lest the Evil One having effected an entrance of error in us should fling us away from our life.

3. He speaketh again therefore to them concerning these things; *Wherefore fast ye for Me, saith the Lord, so that your voice is heard this day crying aloud? This is not the fast which I have chosen, saith the Lord; not a man abasing his soul; not though ye should bend your neck as a hoop, and put on sackcloth and make your bed of ashes, not even so shall ye call a fast that is acceptable.* But unto us He saith; *Behold, this is the fast which I have chosen, saith the Lord; loosen every band of wickedness, untie the tightened cords of forcible contracts, send away the broken ones released and tear in pieces every unjust bond. Break thy bread to the hungry, and if thou seest one naked clothe him; bring the shelterless into thy house, and if thou seest a humble man, thou shalt*

not despise him, neither shall any one of thy household and of thine own seed. Then shall thy light break forth in the morning, and thy healing shall arise quickly, and righteousness shall go before thy face, and the glory of God shall environ thee. Then shalt thou cry out and God shall hear thee; while thou art still speaking, He shall say, 'Lo, I am here'; if thou shalt take away from thee the yoke and the stretching forth of the finger and the word of murmuring, and shalt give thy bread to the hungry heartily, and shalt pity the abased soul. To this end therefore, my brethren, He that is long-suffering, foreseeing that the people whom He had prepared in His well-beloved would believe in simplicity, manifested to us beforehand concerning all things, that we might not as novices shipwreck ourselves upon their law.

4. It behoves us therefore to investigate deeply concerning the present, and to search out the things which have power to save us. Let us therefore flee altogether from all the works of lawlessness, lest the works of lawlessness overpower us; and let us loathe the error of the present time, that we may be loved for that which is to come. Let us give no relaxation to our soul that it should have liberty to consort with sinners and wicked men, lest haply we be made like unto them. The last offence is at hand, concerning which the scripture speaketh, as Enoch saith. For to this end the Master hath cut the seasons and the days short, that His beloved might hasten and come to His inheritance. And the prophet also speaketh on this wise; *Ten reigns shall reign upon the earth, and after them shall arise a little king, who shall bring low three of the kings under one.* In like manner Daniel speaketh concerning the same; *And I saw the fourth beast to be wicked and strong and more intractable than all the beasts of the earth, and how there arose from him ten horns, and from these a little horn an excrescence, and how that it abased under one three of the great horns.* Ye ought therefore to understand. Moreover I ask you this one thing besides, as being one of yourselves and loving you all in particular more than my own soul, to give heed to yourselves now, and not to liken yourselves to certain persons who pile up sin upon sin, saying that our covenant remains to them also. Ours it is; but they lost it in this way for ever, when Moses had just received it. For the scripture saith; *And Moses was in the mountain fasting forty days and forty nights, and he received the covenant from the Lord, even tables of stone written with the finger of the hand of the Lord.* But they lost it by turning unto idols. For thus saith the Lord; *Moses, Moses, come down quickly; for thy people whom thou*

broughtest out of the land of Egypt hath done unlawfully. And Moses understood, and threw the two tables from his hands; and their covenant was broken in pieces, that the covenant of the beloved Jesus might be sealed unto our hearts in the hope which springeth from faith in Him. But though I would fain write many things, not as a teacher, but as becometh one who loveth you not to fall short of that which we possess, I was anxious to write to you, being your devoted slave. Wherefore let us take heed in these last days. For the whole time of our faith shall profit us nothing, unless we now, in the season of lawlessness and in the offences that shall be, as becometh sons of God, offer resistance, that the Black One may not effect an entrance. Let us flee from all vanity, let us entirely hate the works of the evil way. Do not entering in privily stand apart by yourselves, as if ye were already justified, but assemble yourselves together and consult concerning the common welfare. For the scripture saith; *Woe unto them that are wise for themselves, and understanding in their own sight.* Let us become spiritual, let us become a temple perfect unto God. As far as in us lies, let us exercise ourselves in the fear of God, [and] let us strive to keep His commandments, that we may rejoice in His ordinances. The Lord judgeth the world without respect of persons; each man shall receive according to his deeds. If he be good, his righteousness shall go before him in the way; if he be evil, the recompense of his evil-doing is before him; lest perchance, if we relax as men that are called, we should slumber over our sins, and the prince of evil receive power against us and thrust us out from the kingdom of the Lord. Moreover understand this also, my brothers. When ye see that after so many signs and wonders wrought in Israel, even then they were abandoned, let us give heed, lest haply we be found, as the scripture saith, *many called but few chosen.*

5. For to this end the Lord endured to deliver His flesh unto corruption, that by the remission of sins we might be cleansed, which cleansing is through the blood of His sprinkling. For the scripture concerning Him containeth some things relating to Israel, and some things relating to us. And it speaketh thus; *He was wounded for our transgressions, and He hath been bruised for our sins; by His stripes we were healed. As a sheep He was led to the slaughter, and as a lamb that is dumb before his shearer.* We ought therefore to be very thankful unto the Lord, for that He both revealed unto us the past, and made us wise in the present, and as regards the future we are not without understanding. Now the scripture saith; *Not unjustly is the net spread*

for the birds. He meaneth this that a man shall justly perish, who having the knowledge of the way of righteousness forceth himself into the way of darkness. There is yet this also, my brethren ; if the Lord endured to suffer for our souls, though He was Lord of the whole world, unto whom God said from the foundation of the world, *Let us make man after our image and likeness,* how then did He endure to suffer at the hand of men? Understand ye. The prophets, receiving grace from Him, prophesied concerning Him. But He Himself endured that He might destroy death and show forth the resurrection of the dead, for that He must needs be manifested in the flesh; that at the same time He might redeem the promise made to the fathers, and by preparing the new people for Himself might show, while He was on earth, that having brought about the resurrection He will Himself exercise judgment. Yea and further, He preached teaching Israel and performing so many wonders and miracles, and He loved him exceedingly. And when He chose His own apostles who were to proclaim His Gospel, who that He might show that *He came not to call the righteous but sinners* were sinners above every sin, then He manifested Himself to be the Son of God. For if He had not come in the flesh neither would men have looked upon Him and been saved, forasmuch as when they look upon the sun that shall cease to be, which is the work of His own hands, they cannot face its rays. Therefore the Son of God came in the flesh to this end, that He might sum up the complete tale of their sins against those who persecuted and slew His prophets. To this end therefore He endured. For God saith of the wounds of His flesh that they came from them ; *When they shall smite their own shepherd, then shall the sheep of the flock be lost.* But He Himself desired so to suffer; for it was necessary for Him to suffer on a tree. For he that prophesied said concerning Him, *Spare My soul from the sword ;* and, *Pierce My flesh with nails, for the congregations of evil-doers have risen up against Me.* And again He saith ; *Behold I have given My back to stripes, and My cheeks to smitings, and My face did I set as a hard rock.*

6. When then He gave the commandment, what saith He? *Who is he that disputeth with Me? Let him oppose Me. Or who is he that goeth to law with Me? Let him draw nigh unto the servant of the Lord. Woe unto you, for ye all shall wax old as a garment, and the moth shall consume you.* And again the prophet saith, seeing that as a hard stone He was ordained for crushing ; *Behold I will put into the foundations of Zion a stone very precious, elect, a chief corner-stone, honourable.* Then again

what saith He; *And whosoever shall set his hope on Him, shall live for ever*. Is our hope then set upon a stone? Far be it. But it is because the Lord hath set His flesh in strength. For He saith; *And He set Me as a hard rock*. And the prophet saith again; *The stone which the builders rejected, this became the head of the corner*. And again He saith; *This is the great and wonderful day, which the Lord made*. I write to you the more simply, that ye may understand, I who am the offscouring of your love. What then saith the prophet again? *The assembly of evil-doers gathered about Me, they surrounded Me as bees surround a comb;* and; *For My garment they cast a lot*. Forasmuch then as He was about to be manifested in the flesh and to suffer, His suffering was manifested beforehand. For the prophet saith concerning Israel; *Woe unto their soul, for they have counselled evil counsel against themselves saying, Let us bind the righteous one, for he is unprofitable for us*. What saith the other prophet Moses unto them? *Behold, these things saith the Lord God; enter into the good land which the Lord sware unto Abraham, Isaac and Jacob, and inherit it, a land flowing with milk and honey*. But what saith knowledge? Understand ye. Set your hope on Him who is about to be manifested to you in the flesh, even Jesus. For man is earth suffering; for from the face of the earth came the creation of Adam. What then saith He? *Into the good land, a land flowing with milk and honey*. Blessed is our Lord, brethren, who established among us wisdom and understanding of His secret things. For the prophet speaketh a parable concerning the Lord. Who shall comprehend, save he that is wise and prudent and that loveth his Lord? Forasmuch then as He renewed us in the remission of sins, He made us to be a new type, so that we should have the soul of children, as if He were re-creating us. For the scripture saith concerning us, how He saith to the Son; *Let us make man after our image and after our likeness, and let them rule over the beasts of the earth and the fowls of the heaven and the fishes of the sea*. And the Lord said when He saw the fair creation of us men; *Increase and multiply and fill the earth*. These words refer to the Son. Again I will shew thee how the Lord speaketh concerning us. He made a second creation at the last; and the Lord saith; *Behold I make the last things as the first*. In reference to this then the prophet preached; *Enter into a land flowing with milk and honey, and be lords over it*. Behold then we have been created anew, as He saith again in another prophet; *Behold, saith the Lord, I will take out from these*, that is to say, from those whom the Spirit of the

Lord foresaw, *their stony hearts, and will put into them hearts of flesh;* for He Himself was to be manifested in the flesh and to dwell in us. For a holy temple unto the Lord, my brethren, is the abode of our heart. For the Lord saith again; *For wherein shall I appear unto the Lord my God and be glorified? I will make confession unto Thee in the assembly of my brethren, and I will sing unto Thee in the midst of the assembly of the saints.* We therefore are they whom He brought into the good land. What then is the milk and the honey? Because the child is first kept alive by honey, and then by milk. So in like manner we also, being kept alive by our faith in the promise and by the word, shall live and be lords of the earth. Now we have already said above; *And let them increase and multiply and rule over the fishes.* But who is he that is able [now] to rule over beasts and fishes and fowls of the heaven; for we ought to perceive that to rule implieth power, so that one should give orders and have dominion. If then this cometh not to pass now, assuredly He spake to us for the hereafter, when we ourselves shall be made perfect so that we may become heirs of the covenant of the Lord.

7. Understand therefore, children of gladness, that the good Lord manifested all things to us beforehand, that we might know to whom we ought in all things to render thanksgiving and praise. If then the Son of God, being Lord and future Judge of quick and dead, suffered that His wound might give us life, let us believe that the Son of God could not suffer except for our sakes. But moreover when crucified He had vinegar and gall given Him to drink. Hear how on this matter the priests of the temple have revealed. Seeing that there is a commandment in scripture, *Whosoever shall not observe the fast shall surely die,* the Lord commanded, because He was in His own person about to offer the vessel of His Spirit a sacrifice for our sins, that the type also which was given in Isaac who was offered upon the altar should be fulfilled. What then saith He in the prophet? *And let them eat of the goat that is offered at the fast for all their sins.* Attend carefully; *And let all the priests alone eat the entrails unwashed with vinegar.* Wherefore? Since ye are to give Me, who am to offer My flesh for the sins of My new people, gall with vinegar to drink, eat ye alone, while the people fasteth and waileth in sackcloth and ashes; that He might shew that He must suffer at their hands. Attend ye to the commandments which He gave. *Take two goats, fair and alike, and offer them, and let the priest take the one for a whole burnt-offering for sins.* But the

other one—what must they do with it? *Accursed*, saith He, *is the one.* Give heed how the type of Jesus is revealed. *And do ye all spit upon it and goad it, and place scarlet wool about its head, and so let it be cast into the wilderness.* And when it is so done, he that taketh the goat into the wilderness leadeth it, and taketh off the wool, and putteth it upon the branch which is called Rachia, the same whereof we are wont to eat the shoots when we find them in the country. Of this briar alone is the fruit thus sweet. What then meaneth this? Give heed. *The one for the altar, and the other accursed.* And moreover the accursed one crowned. For they shall see Him in that day wearing the long scarlet robe about His flesh, and shall say, Is not this He, Whom once we crucified and set at nought and spat upon; verily this was He, Who then said that He was the Son of God. For how is He like the goat? For this reason it says *the goats shall be fair and alike*, that, when they shall see Him coming then, they may be astonished at the likeness of the goat. Therefore behold the type of Jesus that was to suffer. But what meaneth it, that they place the wool in the midst of the thorns? It is a type of Jesus set forth for the Church, since whosoever should desire to take away the scarlet wool it behoved him to suffer many things owing to the terrible nature of the thorn, and through affliction to win the mastery over it. Thus, He saith, they that desire to see Me, and to attain unto My kingdom, must lay hold on Me through tribulation and affliction.

8. But what think ye meaneth the type, where the commandment is given to Israel that those men, whose sins are full grown, offer an heifer and slaughter and burn it, and then that the children take up the ashes, and cast them into vessels, and twist the scarlet wool on a tree (see here again is the type of the cross and the scarlet wool), and the hyssop, and that this done the children should sprinkle the people one by one, that they may be purified from their sins? Understand ye how in all plainness it is spoken unto you; the calf is Jesus, the men that offer it, being sinners, are they that offered Him for the slaughter. †After this it is no more men (who offer); the glory is no more for sinners.† The children who sprinkle are they that preached unto us the forgiveness of sins and the purification of our heart, they to whom, being twelve in number for a testimony unto the tribes (for there are twelve tribes of Israel), He gave authority over the Gospel, that they should preach it. But wherefore are the children that sprinkle three in number? For a testimony unto Abraham, Isaac and Jacob, because

these are mighty before God. Then there is the placing the wool on
the tree. This means that the kingdom of Jesus is on the cross, and
that they who set their hope on Him shall live for ever. And why is
there the wool and the hyssop at the same time? Because in His
kingdom there shall be evil and foul days, in which we shall be saved;
for he who suffers pain in the flesh is healed through the foulness of the
hyssop. Now to us indeed it is manifest that these things so befel for
this reason, but to them they were dark, because they heard not the
voice of the Lord.

9. Furthermore He saith concerning the ears, how that it is our
heart which He circumcised. The Lord saith in the prophet; *With
the hearing of the ears they listened unto Me.* And again He saith; *They
that are afar off shall hear with their ears, and shall perceive what I
have done.* And; *Be ye circumcised in your hearts,* saith the Lord.
And again He saith; *Hear, O Israel, for thus saith the Lord thy God.
Who is he that desireth to live for ever, let him hear with his ears the
voice of My servant.* And again He saith; *Hear, O heaven, and give
ear, O earth, for the Lord hath spoken these things for a testimony.* And
again He saith; *Hear the word of the Lord, ye rulers of this people.*
And again He saith; *Hear, O my children, the voice of one crying in the
wilderness.* Therefore He circumcised our ears, that hearing the word
we might believe. But moreover the circumcision, in which they have
confidence, is abolished; for He hath said that a circumcision not of
the flesh should be practised. But they transgressed, for an evil angel
taught them cleverness. He saith unto them; *Thus saith the Lord
your God* (so I find the commandment); *sow not upon thorns, be
ye circumcised to your Lord.* And what saith He? *Be ye circumcised
in the hardness of your heart; and then ye will not harden your neck.*
Take this again; *Behold, saith the Lord, all the Gentiles are uncircumcised in their foreskin, but this people is uncircumcised in their
hearts.* But thou wilt say; In truth the people hath been circumcised for a seal. Nay, but so likewise is every Syrian and Arabian
and all the priests of the idols. Do all those then too belong to their
covenant? Moreover the Egyptians also are included among the
circumcised. Learn therefore, children of love, concerning all things
abundantly, that Abraham, who first appointed circumcision, looked
forward in the spirit unto Jesus, when he circumcised having received
the ordinances of three letters. For the scripture saith; *And Abraham
circumcised of his household eighteen males and three hundred.* What

then was the knowledge given unto him? Understand ye that He saith *the eighteen* first, and then after an interval *three hundred.* In the eighteen I stands for ten, H for eight. Here thou hast JESUS (ΙΗΣΟΥΣ). And because the cross in the T was to have grace, He saith also *three hundred.* So He revealeth Jesus in the two letters, and in the remaining one the cross. He who placed within us the innate gift of His covenant knoweth; no man hath ever learnt from me a more genuine word; but I know that ye are worthy.

10. But forasmuch as Moses said; *Ye shall not eat swine nor eagle nor falcon nor crow nor any fish which hath no scale upon it,* he received in his understanding three ordinances. Yea and further He saith unto them in Deuteronomy; *And I will lay as a covenant upon this people My ordinances.* So then it is not a commandment of God that they should not bite with their teeth, but Moses spake it in spirit. Accordingly he mentioned the swine with this intent. Thou shalt not cleave, saith he, to such men who are like unto swine; that is, when they are in luxury they forget the Lord, but when they are in want they recognize the Lord, just as the swine when it eateth knoweth not his lord, but when it is hungry it crieth out, and when it has received food again it is silent. *Neither shalt thou eat eagle nor falcon nor kite nor crow.* Thou shalt not, He saith, cleave unto, or be likened to, such men who know not how to provide food for themselves by toil and sweat, but in their lawlessness seize what belongeth to others, and as if they were walking in guilelessness watch and search about for some one to rob in their rapacity, just as these birds alone do not provide food for themselves, but sit idle and seek how they may eat the meat that belongeth to others, being pestilent in their evil-doings. *And thou shalt not eat,* saith He, *lamprey nor polypus nor cuttle fish.* Thou shalt not, He meaneth, become like unto such men, who are desperately wicked, and are already condemned to death, just as these fishes alone are accursed and swim in the depths, not swimming on the surface like the rest, but dwell on the ground beneath the deep sea. Moreover *thou shalt not eat the hare.* Why so? Thou shalt not be found a corrupter of boys, nor shalt thou become like such persons; for the hare gaineth one passage in the body every year; for according to the number of years it lives it has just so many orifices. Again, *neither shalt thou eat the hyena;* thou shalt not, saith He, become an adulterer or a fornicator, neither shalt thou resemble such persons. Why so? Because this animal changeth its nature year by year, and becometh at

one time male and at another female. Moreover He hath hated the weasel also and with good reason. Thou shalt not, saith He, become such as those men of whom we hear as working iniquity with their mouth for uncleanness, neither shalt thou cleave unto impure women who work iniquity with their mouth. For this animal conceiveth with its mouth. Concerning meats then Moses received three decrees to this effect and uttered them in a spiritual sense; but they accepted them according to the lust of the flesh, as though they referred to eating. And David also receiveth knowledge of the same three decrees, and saith; *Blessed is the man who hath not gone in the counsel of the ungodly*—even as the fishes go in darkness into the depths; *and hath not stood in the path of sinners*—just as they who pretend to fear the Lord sin like swine; *and hath not sat on the seat of the destroyers*— as the birds that are seated for prey. Ye have now the complete lesson concerning eating. Again Moses saith; *Ye shall eat everything that divideth the hoof and cheweth the cud.* What meaneth he? He that receiveth the food knoweth Him that giveth him the food, and being refreshed appeareth to rejoice in him. Well said he, having regard to the commandment. What then meaneth he? Cleave unto those that fear the Lord, with those who meditate in their heart on the distinction of the word which they have received, with those who tell of the ordinances of the Lord and keep them, with those who know that meditation is a work of gladness and who chew the cud of the word of the Lord. But why that which divideth the hoof? Because the righteous man both walketh in this world, and at the same time looketh for the holy world to come. Ye see how wise a lawgiver Moses was. But whence should they perceive or understand these things? Howbeit we having justly perceived the commandments tell them as the Lord willed. To this end He circumcised our ears and hearts, that we might understand these things.

11. But let us enquire whether the Lord took care to signify beforehand concerning the water and the cross. Now concerning the water it is written in reference to Israel, how that they would not receive the baptism which bringeth remission of sins, but would build for themselves. For the prophet saith; *Be astonished, O heaven, and let the earth shudder the more at this, for this people hath done two evil things; they abandoned Me the fountain of life, and they digged for themselves a pit of death. Is My holy mountain of Sinai a desert rock? for ye shall be as the fledglings of a bird, which flutter aloft when deprived of their nest.* And

again the prophet saith; *I will go before thee, and level mountains and crush gates of brass and break in pieces bolts of iron, and I will give thee treasures dark, concealed, unseen, that they may know that I am the Lord God.* And; *Thou shalt dwell in a lofty cave of a strong rock.* And; *His water shall be sure; ye shall see the King in glory, and your soul shall meditate on the fear of the Lord.* And again He saith in another prophet; *And He that doeth these things shall be as the tree that is planted by the parting streams of waters, which shall yield his fruit at his proper season, and his leaf shall not fall off, and all things whatsoever he doeth shall prosper. Not so are the ungodly, not so, but are as the dust which the wind scattereth from the face of the earth. Therefore ungodly men shall not stand in judgment, neither sinners in the counsel of the righteous; for the Lord knoweth the way of the righteous, and the way of the ungodly shall perish.* Ye perceive how He pointed out the water and the cross at the same time. For this is the meaning; Blessed are they that set their hope on the cross, and go down into the water; for He speaketh of the reward *at his proper season;* then, saith He, I will repay. But now what saith He? *His leaves shall not fall off;* He meaneth by this that every word, which shall come forth from you through your mouth in faith and love, shall be for the conversion and hope of many. And again another prophet saith; *And the land of Jacob was praised above the whole earth.* He meaneth this; He glorifieth the vessel of His Spirit. Next what saith He? *And there was a river streaming from the right hand, and beautiful trees rose up from it; and whosoever shall eat of them shall live for ever.* This He saith, because we go down into the water laden with sins and filth, and rise up from it bearing fruit in the heart, resting our fear and hope on Jesus in the spirit. *And whosoever shall eat of these shall live for ever;* He meaneth this; whosoever, saith He, shall hear these things spoken and shall believe, shall live for ever.

12.   In like manner again He defineth concerning the cross in another prophet, who saith; *And when shall these things be accomplished? saith the Lord. Whensoever a tree shall be bended and stand upright, and whensoever blood shall drop from a tree.* Again thou art taught concerning the cross, and Him that was to be crucified. And He saith again in Moses, when war was waged against Israel by men of another nation, and that He might remind them when the war was waged against them that for their sins they were delivered unto death; the Spirit saith to the heart of Moses, that he should make a type of

the cross and of Him that was to suffer, that unless, saith He, they shall set their hope on Him, war shall be waged against them for ever. Moses therefore pileth arms one upon another in the midst of the encounter, and standing on higher ground than any he stretched out his hands, and so Israel was again victorious. Then, whenever he lowered them, they were slain with the sword. Wherefore was this ? That they might learn that they cannot be saved, unless they should set their hope on Him. And again in another prophet He saith ; *The whole day long have I stretched out My hands to a disobedient people that did gainsay My righteous way.* Again Moses maketh a type of Jesus, how that He must suffer, and that He Himself whom they shall think to have destroyed shall make alive in an emblem when Israel was falling. For the Lord caused all manner of serpents to bite them, and they died (forasmuch as the transgression was wrought in Eve through the serpent), that He might convince them that by reason of their transgression they should be delivered over to the affliction of death. Yea and further though Moses gave the commandment ; *Ye shall not have a molten or a carved image for your God,* yet he himself made one that he might shew them a type of Jesus. So Moses maketh a brazen serpent, and setteth it up conspicuously, and summoneth the people by proclamation. When therefore they were assembled together they entreated Moses that he should offer up intercession for them that they might be healed. And Moses said unto them ; Whensoever, said he, one of you shall be bitten, let him come to the serpent which is placed on the tree, and let him believe and hope that the serpent being himself dead can make alive ; and forthwith he shall be saved. And so they did. Here again thou hast in these things also the glory of Jesus, how that in Him and unto Him are all things. What again saith Moses unto Jesus (Joshua) the son of Nun, when he giveth him this name, as being a prophet, that all the people might give ear to him alone, because the Father revealeth all things concerning His Son Jesus ? Moses therefore saith to Jesus the son of Nun, giving him this name, when he sent him as a spy on the land ; *Take a book in thy hands, and write what the Lord saith, how that the Son of God shall cut up by the roots all the house of Amalek in the last days.* Behold again it is Jesus, not a son of man, but the Son of God, and He was revealed in the flesh in a figure. Since then men will say that Christ is the son of David, David himself prophesieth being afraid and understanding the error of sinners ; *The Lord said unto my Lord, Sit thou on My right hand until I set thine enemies for a footstool under Thy feet.* And again thus saith Isaiah; *The Lord said unto my Christ the Lord, of whose right hand I laid hold, that the nations should give ear before Him, and I will break down the strength of kings.* See how David calleth Him Lord, and calleth Him not Son.

13. Now let us see whether this people or the first people hath the inheritance, and whether the covenant had reference to us or to them. Hear then what the scripture saith concerning the people; *And Isaac prayed concerning Rebecca his wife, for she was barren. And she conceived. Then Rebecca went out to enquire of the Lord. And the Lord said unto her; Two nations are in thy womb, and two peoples in thy belly, and one people shall vanquish another people, and the greater shall serve the less.* Ye ought to understand who Isaac is, and who Rebecca is, and in whose case He hath shewn that the one people is greater than the other. And in another prophecy Jacob speaketh more plainly to Joseph his son, saying; *Behold, the Lord hath not bereft me of thy face; bring me thy sons, that I may bless them.* And he brought Ephraim and Manasseh, desiring that Manasseh should be blessed, because he was the elder; for Joseph led him to the right hand of his father Jacob. But Jacob saw in the spirit a type of the people that should come afterwards. And what saith He? *And Jacob crossed his hands, and placed his right hand on the head of Ephraim, the second and younger, and blessed him. And Joseph said unto Jacob, Transfer thy right hand to the head of Manasseh, for he is my first-born son. And Jacob said to Joseph, I know it, my son, I know it; but the greater shall serve the less. Yet this one also shall be blessed.* Mark in whose cases He ordained that this people should be first and heir of the covenant. If then besides this He also recorded it through Abraham, we attain the completion of our knowledge. What then saith he to Abraham when he alone believed, and was ascribed for righteousness? *Behold I have made thee, Abraham, a father of nations that believe in God in uncircumcision.*

14. Yea verily, but as regards the covenant which He sware to the fathers to give it to the people let us see whether He hath actually given it. He hath given it, but they themselves were not found worthy to receive it by reason of their sins. For the prophet saith; *And Moses was fasting in Mount Sinai forty days and forty nights, that he might receive the covenant of the Lord to give to the people. And [Moses] received from the Lord the two tables which were written by the finger of the hand of the Lord in the spirit.* And Moses took them, and brought

them down to give them to the people. And the Lord said unto Moses; *Moses, Moses, come down quickly; for thy people, whom thou leddest forth from the land of Egypt, hath done wickedly. And Moses perceived that they had made for themselves again molten images, and he cast them out of his hands and the tables of the covenant of the Lord were broken in pieces.* Moses received them, but they themselves were not found worthy. But how did we receive them? Mark this. Moses received them being a servant, but the Lord himself gave them to us to be the people of His inheritance, having endured patiently for our sakes. But He was made manifest, in order that at the same time they might be perfected in their sins, and we might receive the covenant through Him who inherited it, even the Lord Jesus, who was prepared beforehand hereunto, that appearing in person He might redeem out of darkness our hearts which had already been paid over unto death and delivered up to the iniquity of error, and thus establish the covenant in us through the word. For it is written how the Father chargeth Him to deliver us from darkness, and to prepare a holy people for Himself. Therefore saith the prophet; *I the Lord thy God called thee in righteousness, and I will lay hold of thy hand and will strengthen thee, and I have given thee to be a covenant of the race, a light to the Gentiles, to open the eyes of the blind, and to bring forth them that are bound from their fetters, and them that sit in darkness from their prison house.* We perceive then whence we were ransomed. Again the prophet saith; *Behold, I have set Thee to be a light to the Gentiles, that Thou shouldest be for salvation unto the ends of the earth; thus saith the Lord that ransomed thee, even God.* Again the prophet saith; *The Spirit of the Lord is upon Me, wherefore He anointed Me to preach good tidings to the humble; He hath sent Me to heal them that are broken-hearted, to preach release to the captives and recovery of sight to the blind, to proclaim the acceptable year of the Lord and the day of recompense, to comfort all that mourn.*

15. Moreover concerning the sabbath likewise it is written in the Ten Words, in which He spake to Moses face to face on Mount Sinai; *And ye shall hallow the sabbath of the Lord with pure hands and with a pure heart.* And in another place He saith; *If My sons observe the sabbath, then I will bestow My mercy upon them.* Of the sabbath He speaketh in the beginning of the creation; *And God made the works of His hands in six days, and He ended on the seventh day, and rested on it, and He hallowed it.* Give heed, children, what this meaneth; *He ended in six days.* He meaneth this, that in six thousand years the Lord shall bring

all things to an end; for the day with Him signifieth a thousand years; and this He himself beareth me witness, saying; *Behold, the day of the Lord shall be as a thousand years.* Therefore, children, in six days, that is in six thousand years, everything shall come to an end. *And He rested on the seventh day.* This He meaneth; when His Son shall come, and shall abolish the time of the Lawless One, and shall judge the ungodly, and shall change the sun and the moon and the stars, then shall He truly rest on the seventh day. Yea and furthermore He saith; *Thou shalt hallow it with pure hands and with a pure heart.* If therefore a man is able now to hallow the day which God hallowed, though he be pure in heart, we have gone utterly astray. But if after all then and not till then shall we truly rest and hallow it, when we shall ourselves be able to do so after being justified and receiving the promise, when iniquity is no more and all things have been made new by the Lord, we shall be able to hallow it then, because we ourselves shall have been hallowed first. Finally He saith to them; *Your new moons and your sabbaths I cannot away with.* Ye see what is His meaning; it is not your present sabbaths that are acceptable [unto Me], but the sabbath which I have made, in the which, when I have set all things at rest, I will make the beginning of the eighth day which is the beginning of another world. Wherefore also we keep the eighth day for rejoicing, in the which also Jesus rose from the dead, and having been manifested ascended into the heavens.

16. Moreover I will tell you likewise concerning the temple, how these wretched men being led astray set their hope on the building, and not on their God that made them, as being a house of God. For like the Gentiles almost they consecrated Him in the temple. But what saith the Lord abolishing the temple? Learn ye. *Who hath measured the heaven with a span, or hath measured the earth with his hand? Have not I, saith the Lord? The heaven is My throne and the earth the footstool of My feet. What manner of house will ye build for Me? Or what shall be My resting-place?* Ye perceive that their hope is vain. Furthermore He saith again; *Behold they that pulled down this temple themselves shall build it.* So it cometh to pass; for because they went to war it was pulled down by their enemies. Now also the very servants of their enemies shall build it up. Again, it was revealed how the city and the temple and the people of Israel should be betrayed. For the scripture saith; *And it shall be in the last days, that the Lord shall deliver up the sheep of the pasture and the fold and the tower*

thereof to destruction. And it came to pass as the Lord spake. But let us enquire whether there be any temple of God. There is; in the place where He Himself undertakes to make and finish it. For it is written; *And it shall come to pass, when the week is being accomplished, the temple of God shall be built gloriously in the name of the Lord.* I find then that there is a temple. How then shall it be built in the name of the Lord? Understand ye. Before we believed on God, the abode of our heart was corrupt and weak, a temple truly built by hands; for it was full of idolatry and was a house of demons, because we did whatsoever was contrary to God. *But it shall be built in the name of the Lord.* Give heed then that the temple of the Lord may be built gloriously. How? Understand ye. By receiving the remission of our sins and hoping on the Name we became new, created afresh from the beginning. Wherefore God dwelleth truly in our habitation within us. How? The word of His faith, the calling of His promise, the wisdom of the ordinances, the commandments of the teaching, He Himself prophesying in us, He Himself dwelling in us, opening for us who had been in bondage unto death the door of the temple, which is the mouth, and giving us repentance leadeth us to the incorruptible temple. For he that desireth to be saved looketh not to the man, but to Him that dwelleth and speaketh in him, being amazed at this that he has never at any time heard these words from the mouth of the speaker, nor himself ever desired to hear them. This is the spiritual temple built up to the Lord.

17. So far as it was possible with all simplicity to declare it unto you, my soul hopeth that I have not omitted anything [of the matters pertaining unto salvation and so failed in my desire]. For if I should write to you concerning things immediate or future, ye would not understand them, because they are put in parables. So much then for this.

18. But let us pass on to another lesson and teaching. There are two ways of teaching and of power, the one of light and the other of darkness; and there is a great difference between the two ways. For on the one are stationed the light-giving angels of God, on the other the angels of Satan. And the one is Lord from all eternity and unto all eternity, whereas the other is Lord of the season of iniquity that now is.

19. This then is the way of light, if any one desiring to travel on the way to his appointed place would be zealous in his works. The

knowledge then which is given to us whereby we may walk therein is as follows. Thou shalt love Him that made thee, thou shalt fear Him that created thee, thou shalt glorify Him that redeemed thee from death; thou shalt be simple in heart and rich in spirit; thou shalt not cleave to those who walk in the way of death; thou shalt hate everything that is not pleasing to God; thou shalt hate all hypocrisy; thou shalt never forsake the commandments of the Lord. Thou shalt not exalt thyself, but shalt be lowly-minded in all things. Thou shalt not assume glory to thyself. Thou shalt not entertain a wicked design against thy neighbour; thou shalt not admit boldness into thy soul. Thou shalt not commit fornication, *thou shalt not commit adultery*, thou shalt not corrupt boys. The word of God shall not come forth from thee where any are unclean. Thou shalt not make a difference in a person to reprove him for a transgression. Thou shalt be meek, thou shalt be *quiet*, thou shalt be *fearing the words* which thou hast heard. Thou shalt not bear a grudge against thy brother. Thou shalt not doubt whether a thing shall be or not be. *Thou shalt not take the name of the Lord in vain.* Thou shalt love thy neighbour more than thine own soul. Thou shalt not murder a child by abortion, nor again shalt thou kill it when it is born. Thou shalt not withhold thy hand from thy son or thy daughter, but from their youth thou shalt teach them the fear of God. Thou shalt not be found coveting thy neighbour's goods; thou shalt not be found greedy of gain. Neither shalt thou cleave with thy soul to the lofty, but shalt walk with the humble and righteous. The accidents that befal thee thou shalt receive as good, knowing that nothing is done without God. Thou shalt not be double-minded nor double-tongued. Thou shalt be subject unto thy masters as to a type of God in shame and fear. Thou shalt not command in bitterness thy bondservant or thine handmaid who set their hope on the same God, lest haply they should cease to fear the God who is over both of you; for He came not to call with respect of persons, but to call those whom the Spirit had prepared. Thou shalt make thy neighbour partake in all things, and shalt not say *that anything is thine own*. For if ye are fellow-partakers in that which is imperishable, how much rather shall ye be in the things which are perishable. Thou shalt not be hasty with thy tongue, for the mouth is a snare of death. So far as thou art able, thou shalt be pure for thy soul's sake. *Be not thou found holding out thy hands to receive, and drawing them in to give.* Thou shalt love as the apple of thine eye every one *that speaketh unto thee the word of the Lord. Thou shalt remember* the day of judgment night and day, and thou shalt seek out day by day the persons of the saints, either labouring by word and going to exhort them and meditating how thou mayst save souls by thy word, or thou shalt work with thy hands for a ransom for thy sins. Thou shall not hesitate to give, neither shalt thou murmur when giving, but thou shalt know who is the good paymaster of thy reward. Thou shalt keep those things which thou hast received, neither adding to them nor taking away from them. Thou shalt utterly hate the Evil One. Thou shalt judge righteously. Thou shalt not make a schism, but thou shalt pacify them that contend by bringing them together. Thou shalt confess thy sins. Thou shalt not betake thyself to prayer with an evil conscience. This is the way of light.

20. But the way of the Black One is crooked and full of a curse. For it is a way of eternal death with punishment wherein are the things that destroy men's souls—idolatry, boldness, exaltation of power, hypocrisy, doubleness of heart, adultery, murder, plundering, pride, transgression, treachery, malice, stubbornness, witchcraft, magic, covetousness, absence of the fear of God; persecutors of good men, hating the truth, loving lies, not perceiving the reward of righteousness, not *cleaving to the good* nor to righteous judgment, paying no heed to the widow and the orphan, wakeful not for the fear of God but for that which is evil; men from whom gentleness and forbearance stand aloof and far off; loving vain things, pursuing a recompense, not pitying the poor man, not toiling for him that is oppressed with toil, ready in slander, not recognizing Him that made them, murderers of children, corrupters of the creatures of God, turning away from him that is in want, oppressing him that is afflicted, advocates of the wealthy, unjust judges of the poor, sinful in all things.

21. It is good therefore to learn the ordinances of the Lord, as many as have been written above, and to walk in them. For he that doeth these things shall be glorified in the kingdom of God; whereas he that chooseth their opposites shall perish together with his works. For this cause is the resurrection, for this the recompense. I entreat those of you who are in higher station, if ye will receive any counsel of good advice from me, keep amongst you those to whom ye may do good. Fail not. The day is at hand, in which everything shall be destroyed together with the Evil One. *The Lord is at hand and His reward.* Again and again I entreat you; be good lawgivers one to another; continue faithful counsellors to yourselves; take away from

you all hypocrisy. And may God, who is Lord of the whole world, give you wisdom, judgment, learning, knowledge of His ordinances, patience. And be ye taught of God, seeking diligently what the Lord requireth of you, and act that ye may be found in the day of judgment. But if you have any remembrance of good, call me to mind when ye practise these things, that both my desire and my watchfulness may lead to some good result. I entreat you asking it as a favour. So long as the good vessel (of the body) is with you, be lacking in none of these things, but search them out constantly, and fulfil every commandment; for they deserve it. For this reason I was the more eager to write to you so far as I was able, that I might give you joy. Fare ye well, children of love and peace. The Lord of glory and of every grace be with your spirit.

THE SHEPHERD

OF

HERMAS

THE SHEPHERD OF HERMAS

THIS work is entitled in the most ancient notices 'The Shepherd', or 'The Shepherd of Hermas'. Hermas is both the narrator and the hero of the narrative. The Shepherd is the divine teacher, who communicates to Hermas, either by precept or by allegory, the lessons which are to be disseminated for the instruction of the Church. Later confusions, which identify Hermas with the Pastor, find no countenance in the work itself. Hermas' own personal and family history are interwoven from time to time into the narrative, and made subservient to the moral purposes of the work. In this case it resembles the *Divina Commedia*, though history plays a much less important part here than in Dante's great poem.

The structure of the work is seriously impaired by the common division into three parts or books, *Visions*, *Mandates*, and *Similitudes*, as if they stood on the same level. It may be convenient to use this mode of division for purposes of reference alone; but we must not suffer it to dominate our conception of the work. The *Visions* are introductory, and the Shepherd does not appear until their close. He delivers his message to Hermas in two parts, (1) *Mandates* or Precepts, (2) *Similitudes* or Parables, i.e., moral lessons taught by allegory.

The person first introduced in the book is one Rhoda (*Vis.* i. 1), to whom Hermas had been sold when brought from Rome as a slave. Her part is somewhat the same as Beatrice's in Dante's poem. She appears to him in the heavens as he is on his way to Cumæ, and reproaches him with his not altogether blameless passion for her. Having thus aroused his conscience, she withdraws. Then he sees before him an aged woman whom (considering the place) he not unnaturally mistakes for the Sibyl (*Vis.* ii. 4), but who proves to be the Church. The object of the *Visions* indeed seems to be to place before the reader the conception of the Church under the guise of an aged woman, whose features become more youthful at each successive appearance. Thus the lessons of a smitten and penitent conscience, of the Church growing and spreading (the Church Militant), lastly, of the Church purified by suffering (the Church Triumphant), and the terrors of the judgment, occupy the four *Visions* properly so called. Hermas is enjoined to write down all that he hears. One copy of his book he is to send to Clement, who is charged with making it known to foreign cities ; another to Grapte, whose business it is to instruct the widows and orphans, and he himself, together with the presbyters, is to read it to the people of 'this city', i.e., Rome (*Vis.* ii. 4).

The fifth *Vision* is different in kind from the preceding four, and indeed is designated, not a Vision (ὅρασις), but a Revelation (ἀποκάλυψις). Hermas is now in his own house. The appearance is no longer the representation of the Church, but a man of glorious visage in a pastoral habit, who has been sent to dwell with him, and teach him to the end of his days. He is 'the Shepherd, the angel of repentance', who delivers to him certain Mandates and Similitudes, which he is ordered to write down, and which form the two remaining books—the main part of the work.

The teaching of the Shepherd then is contained in the twelve *Mandates* and the ten *Similitudes* which follow. But the tenth and last of the latter is not strictly a parable like the rest. It contains a final chapter, summing up the function of the Shepherd and his heavenly associates, in the work of perfecting the instruction of Hermas.

2

The geographical setting of the narrative has its centre in Rome, where evidently the work itself was written. Hermas' home in the city, the road to Cumæ, the *Via Campana,*—these are the localities mentioned by name. There is one exception. Arcadia is chosen as the subject of a Similitude (*Sim.* ix.), the last properly so called, because the mountains visible from a central height by their character and position afford a good subject for the concluding parable, the component elements of the Church (see J. A. Robinson, *The Athos*

Codex of the Shepherd of Hermas, p. 30, where the views of Rendel Harris are discussed and further developed and modified). As he was brought to Rome, and sold as a slave there, Arcadia may have been his native place.

3

The *date* is uncertain. The work is found in general circulation in the Eastern and Western Churches, soon after the middle of the second century. About this time also it must have been translated into Latin. It is quoted by Irenæus in Gaul, by Tertullian in Africa, by Clement and Origen in Alexandria. All these fathers—even Tertullian, before he became a Montanist—either cite it as scripture, or assign to it a special authority as in some sense inspired and quasi-canonical. The same inference as to its early influence may be drawn from the denunciation of Tertullian, who—now become a Montanist—rejects it as repulsive to his puritan tendencies (*de Pudic.* 10), and the author of the *Muratorian Canon* (c. A.D. 180), who denies it a place among either the prophets or the apostles, though apparently allowing it to be read privately for edification. Its canonicity moreover had been the subject of discussion in more than one council, when Tertullian wrote (*l. c.*, not before A.D. 212).

With the date is closely connected the question of *authorship*. On this point there are two ancient traditions.

(1) The author of the 'Shepherd' was the same Hermas, who is greeted by S. Paul as a member of the Roman Church, A.D. 58 (Rom. xvi. 14). This is the view adopted by Origen (IV. p. 683) in his commentary on the passage, where he speaks of the book as 'a very useful scripture, and in my opinion divinely inspired'; but, as he introduces this view of the authorship with 'ut puto' it is plain that he does not fall back on any historical tradition in support of his opinion. His influence had great weight with subsequent writers.

(2) It was written by one Hermas, the brother of pope Pius I (c. A.D. 140—155) during the episcopate of the latter. This is stated in the *Muratorian Canon* (c. A.D. 180) 'sedente cathedram urbis Romae ecclesiae Pio episcopo fratre eius'. This statement, however, is not consistent with the mention of Clement as a contemporary. If it be true, either some other Clement is meant, or the original Greek of the

Canon, of which only the Latin is extant, cannot have stated that Pius was actually bishop at the time when it was written.

This tradition appears likewise in one or two subsequent writings, which however are perhaps not independent. It is somewhat discredited by the fact that its motive in depreciating the value of the work, as being quite recent and having no claim to be read in the Church like the writings of the Apostles and prophets, appears in the context[1].

(3) Besides these two traditional views, a third and intermediate Hermas, not otherwise known, is postulated as the author about A.D. 90—100, to meet the difficulty about Clement. This is the view of several recent critics (Zahn, *Hirt des Hermas* p. 14 sq, followed by Caspari and others). The notices of the Christian ministry, and of the condition of the Church generally, seem to be consistent with either the second or the third view, though they suggest the earlier date rather than the later (*Vis.* ii. 2, 4, iii. 5, 9, *Sim.* ix. 27).

On the whole we may, though not without diffidence, adopt (2) the ancient tradition, which is definite and claims to be almost contemporary, as the safest guide; though confessedly (3) the modern suggestion has stronger support from internal evidence, such as it is.

The Æthiopic version, which identifies the author with S. Paul, ought to be regarded as a blunder, rather than a tradition founded on Acts xiv. 12 τὸν δὲ Παῦλον Ἑρμῆν.

4

The authorities for the text are as follows :

I. GREEK MANUSCRIPTS.

1. The celebrated Sinaitic MS (א) of the fourth century, where, after a gap caused by the loss of six leaves, the Shepherd follows

---

[1] These words are illustrated by the fact that (a) in the Codex Sinaiticus (א) the Shepherd (a fragment, see below, p. 295) appears at the end of the volume, following on the Epistle of Barnabas, which again follows the Apocalypse and the books of the Canonical New Testament ; (b) in the list appended to the Codex Claromontanus (VIth Cent.) again it follows the New Testament proper, of which the closing books are 'Revelation of John ', 'Acts ', and is succeeded by the apocryphal 'Acts of Paul ', and 'Revelation of Peter'; (c) in several MSS of the Latin version it appears in different parts of the Old Testament.

the Epistle of Barnabas at the end of the volume. Unfortunately, however, only a fragment, roughly speaking the first quarter of the text, survives, the manuscript, after several lacunæ, breaking off finally in the middle of *Mand.* iv. 3.

2. The Athos MS (A), written in a very small and cramped hand of the fourteenth century. This consists of three leaves now in the University Library at Leipsic, and six leaves still remaining in the Monastery of Gregory on Mount Athos. The portion of the manuscript now at Leipsic was in 1855 brought from Mount Athos by the famous forger Simonides, who sold it to the University there, as well as what purported to be a copy of six other leaves of the same document. This copy was subsequently edited by Anger. The existence, however, of the original manuscript was questioned until 1880, when Dr Lambros rediscovered it at Mount Athos. His collation of the readings of these six leaves was in 1888 published by J. A. Robinson (*The Athos Codex of the Shepherd of Hermas*). Like the Sinaitic, this manuscript is incomplete, having lost a leaf at the end; but from *Mand.* iv. 3 to *Sim.* ix. 30 (where it fails us), that is to say, for nearly three fourths of the whole work, it is our sole Greek authority for the text.

Besides Simonides' *apographon* mentioned above, another copy was subsequently found among his papers after his arrest, and published by Tischendorf. The publication of Dr Lambros' collation shows us that, whereas the *apographon* edited by Anger was a forgery, the second apographon was truly described as being a transcript of the Athos MS. In passages therefore where the Athos codex has become damaged and illegible between 1855 and 1880, this apographon (A^s) has a certain value.

II. VERSIONS.

1. Latin Versions. These are two in number, (*a*) the so-called *Old Latin Version* (L$_1$), which exists in about twenty manuscripts, the mutual relation of which has not yet been made quite clear. From this version Faber Stapulensis published his *editio princeps* in 1513. (*b*) The *Palatine Version* (L$_2$), found in one manuscript of the fourteenth century, and in 1857 published in full by Dressel. Both these versions give us the text virtually complete.

2. Æthiopic Version (E). This exists in a manuscript discovered in 1847 in the monastery of Guindaguinde by A. d'Abbadie, who procured a transcript, but did not realise the full importance of his

discovery. At length at Dillmann's earnest request he published the text with a Latin translation in 1860. This version likewise contains the Pastor complete.

The mutual relations and comparative value of our authorities are matters of considerable dispute; but a comparison of the early chapters, where the Greek of the Sinaitic MS exists, shows us that ℵ generally agrees with L_1 L_2 against AE, the close connexion of this latter pair of authorities being noticeable throughout. Again, within these groups, L_2 appears to preserve a purer text than L_1, and E than A.

III.   PATRISTIC QUOTATIONS.

Besides these direct authorities for the text, the Shepherd of Hermas is quoted in the Greek by Clement of Alexandria and Origen, while considerable passages have been incorporated into the texts of Antiochus the Monk and ps-Athanasius.

ΠΟΙΜΗΝ

I. Ὁ θρέψας με πέπρακέν με Ῥόδῃ τινὶ εἰς Ῥώμην. μετὰ πολλὰ ἔτη ταύτην ἀνεγνωρισάμην καὶ ἠρξάμην αὐτὴν ἀγαπᾶν ὡς ἀδελφήν. 2. μετὰ χρόνον τινὰ λουομένην εἰς τὸν ποταμὸν τὸν Τίβεριν εἶδον, καὶ ἐπέδωκα αὐτῇ τὴν χεῖρα καὶ ἐξήγαγον αὐτὴν ἐκ τοῦ ποταμοῦ. ταύτης οὖν ἰδὼν τὸ κάλλος διελογιζόμην ἐν τῇ καρδίᾳ μου λέγων· Μακάριος ἤμην εἰ τοιαύτην γυναῖκα εἶχον καὶ τῷ κάλλει καὶ τῷ τρόπῳ. μόνον τοῦτο ἐβουλευσάμην, ἕτερον δὲ οὐδέν. 3. μετὰ χρόνον τινὰ πορευομένου μου εἰς Κούμας καὶ δοξάζοντος τὰς κτίσεις τοῦ Θεοῦ, ὡς μεγάλαι καὶ ἐκπρεπεῖς καὶ δυναταί εἰσιν, περιπατῶν ἀφύπνωσα. καὶ πνεῦμά με ἔλαβεν καὶ ἀπήνεγκέν με δι' ἀνοδίας τινός, δι' ἧς ἄνθρωπος οὐκ ἐδύνατο ὁδεῦσαι· ἦν δὲ ὁ τόπος κρημνώδης καὶ ἀπερρηγὼς ἀπὸ τῶν ὑδάτων. διαβὰς οὖν τὸν ποταμὸν ἐκεῖνον ἦλθον εἰς τὰ ὁμαλά, καὶ τιθῶ τὰ γόνατα καὶ ἠρξάμην προσεύχεσθαι τῷ Κυρίῳ καὶ ἐξομολογεῖσθαί μου τὰς ἁμαρτίας. 4. προσευχομένου δέ μου ἠνοίγη ὁ οὐρανός, καὶ βλέπω τὴν γυναῖκα ἐκείνην ἣν ἐπεθύμησα ἀσπαζομένην με ἐκ τοῦ οὐρανοῦ, λέγουσαν· Ἑρμᾶ, χαῖρε. 5. βλέψας δὲ εἰς αὐτὴν λέγω αὐτῇ· Κυρία, τί σὺ ὧδε ποιεῖς; ἡ δὲ ἀπεκρίθη μοι· Ἀνελήμφθην ἵνα σου τὰς ἁμαρτίας ἐλέγξω πρὸς τὸν Κύριον. 6. λέγω αὐτῇ· Νῦν σύ μου ἔλεγχος εἶ; Οὔ, φησίν, ἀλλὰ ἄκουσον τὰ ῥήματα ἅ σοι μέλλω λέγειν. ὁ Θεὸς ὁ ἐν τοῖς οὐρανοῖς κατοικῶν καὶ κτίσας ἐκ τοῦ μὴ ὄντος τὰ ὄντα καὶ πληθύνας καὶ αὐξήσας ἕνεκεν τῆς ἁγίας ἐκκλησίας αὐτοῦ, ὀργίζεταί σοι ὅτι ἥμαρτες εἰς ἐμέ. 7. ἀποκριθεὶς αὐτῇ λέγω· Εἰς σὲ ἥμαρτον; ποίῳ τρόπῳ; ἢ πότε σοι αἰσχρὸν ῥῆμα

ἐλάλησα; οὐ πάντοτέ σε ὡς θεὰν ἡγησάμην; οὐ πάντοτέ σε
ἐνετράπην ὡς ἀδελφήν; τί μου καταψεύδῃ, ὦ γύναι, τὰ πονηρὰ
ταῦτα καὶ ἀκάθαρτα;   8. γελάσασά μοι λέγει· Ἐπὶ τὴν
καρδίαν σου ἀνέβη ἡ ἐπιθυμία τῆς πονηρίας. ἢ οὐ δοκεῖ σοι
ἀνδρὶ δικαίῳ πονηρὸν πρᾶγμα εἶναι ἐὰν ἀναβῇ αὐτοῦ ἐπὶ τὴν
καρδίαν ἡ πονηρὰ ἐπιθυμία; ἁμαρτία γέ ἐστιν, καὶ μεγάλη,
φησίν. ὁ γὰρ δίκαιος ἀνὴρ δίκαια βουλεύεται. ἐν τῷ οὖν
δίκαια βουλεύεσθαι αὐτὸν κατορθοῦται ἡ δόξα αὐτοῦ ἐν τοῖς
οὐρανοῖς καὶ εὐκατάλλακτον ἔχει τὸν Κύριον ἐν παντὶ πράγματι αὐτοῦ· οἱ δὲ πονηρὰ βουλευόμενοι ἐν ταῖς καρδίαις
αὐτῶν θάνατον καὶ αἰχμαλωτισμὸν ἑαυτοῖς ἐπισπῶνται, μάλιστα οἱ τὸν αἰῶνα τοῦτον περιποιούμενοι καὶ γαυριῶντες ἐν
τῷ πλούτῳ αὐτῶν καὶ μὴ ἀντεχόμενοι τῶν ἀγαθῶν τῶν μελλόντων.   9. μετανοήσουσιν αἱ ψυχαὶ αὐτῶν, οἵτινες οὐκ ἔχουσιν ἐλπίδα, ἀλλὰ ἑαυτοὺς ἀπεγνώκασιν καὶ τὴν ζωὴν αὐτῶν.
ἀλλὰ σὺ προσεύχου πρὸς τὸν Θεόν, καὶ ἰάσεται τὰ ἁμαρτή-
ματά σου καὶ ὅλου τοῦ οἴκου σου καὶ πάντων τῶν ἁγίων.

II.   Μετὰ τὸ λαλῆσαι αὐτὴν τὰ ῥήματα ταῦτα ἐκλείσθη-
σαν οἱ οὐρανοί· κἀγὼ ὅλος ἤμην πεφρικὼς καὶ λυπούμενος.
ἔλεγον δὲ ἐν ἐμαυτῷ· Εἰ αὕτη μοι ἡ ἁμαρτία ἀναγράφεται,
πῶς δυνήσομαι σωθῆναι; ἢ πῶς ἐξιλάσομαι τὸν Θεὸν περὶ
τῶν ἁμαρτιῶν μου τῶν τελείων; ἢ ποίοις ῥήμασιν ἐρωτήσω
τὸν Κύριον ἵνα ἱλατεύσηταί μοι;   2. ταῦτά μου συμβουλευο-
μένου καὶ διακρίνοντος ἐν τῇ καρδίᾳ μου, βλέπω κατέναντί
μου καθέδραν λευκὴν ἐξ ἐρίων χιονίνων γεγονυῖαν μεγάλην·
καὶ ἦλθεν γυνὴ πρεσβῦτις ἐν ἱματισμῷ λαμπροτάτῳ, ἔχουσα
βιβλίον εἰς τὰς χεῖρας, καὶ ἐκάθισεν μόνη, καὶ ἀσπάζεταί με·
Ἑρμᾶ, χαῖρε. κἀγὼ λυπούμενος καὶ κλαίων εἶπον· Κυρία,
χαῖρε.   3. καὶ εἶπέν μοι· Τί στυγνός, Ἑρμᾶ, ὁ μακρόθυμος
καὶ ἀστομάχητος, ὁ πάντοτε γελῶν, τί οὕτω κατηφὴς τῇ ἰδέᾳ
καὶ οὐχ ἱλαρός; κἀγὼ εἶπον αὐτῇ· Ὑπὸ γυναικὸς ἀγαθωτά-
της λεγούσης ὅτι ἥμαρτον εἰς αὐτήν.   4. ἡ δὲ ἔφη· Μηδαμῶς
ἐπὶ τὸν δοῦλον τοῦ Θεοῦ τὸ πρᾶγμα τοῦτο. ἀλλὰ πάντως
ἐπὶ τὴν καρδίαν σου ἀνέβη περὶ αὐτῆς. ἔστιν μὲν τοῖς δού-

λοις τοῦ Θεοῦ ἡ τοιαύτη βουλὴ ἁμαρτίαν ἐπιφέρουσα· πονηρὰ
γὰρ βουλὴ καὶ ἔκπληκτος, εἰς πάνσεμνον πνεῦμα καὶ ἤδη
δεδοκιμασμένον, ἐὰν ἐπιθυμήσῃ πονηρὸν ἔργον, καὶ μάλιστα
Ἑρμᾶς ὁ ἐγκρατής, ὁ ἀπεχόμενος πάσης ἐπιθυμίας πονηρᾶς
καὶ πλήρης πάσης ἁπλότητος καὶ ἀκακίας μεγάλης.

III. Ἀλλ᾽ οὐχ ἕνεκα τούτου ὀργίζεταί σοι ὁ Θεός, ἀλλ᾽
ἵνα τὸν οἶκόν σου τὸν ἀνομήσαντα εἰς τὸν Κύριον καὶ εἰς ὑμᾶς
τοὺς γονεῖς αὐτῶν ἐπιστρέψῃς. ἀλλὰ φιλότεκνος ὢν οὐκ ἐνου-
θέτεις σου τὸν οἶκον, ἀλλὰ ἀφῆκας αὐτὸν καταφθαρῆναι δεινῶς·
διὰ τοῦτό σοι ὀργίζεται ὁ Κύριος· ἀλλὰ ἰάσεταί σου πάντα
τὰ προγεγονότα πονηρὰ ἐν τῷ οἴκῳ σου· διὰ γὰρ τὰς ἐκείνων
ἁμαρτίας καὶ ἀνομήματα σὺ κατεφθάρης ἀπὸ τῶν βιωτικῶν
πράξεων. 2. ἀλλ᾽ ἡ πολυσπλαγχνία τοῦ Κυρίου ἠλέησέν
σε καὶ τὸν οἶκόν σου καὶ ἰσχυροποιήσει σε καὶ θεμελιώσει σε
ἐν τῇ δόξῃ αὐτοῦ. σὺ μόνον μὴ ῥαθυμήσῃς, ἀλλὰ εὐψύχει
καὶ ἰσχυροποίει σου τὸν οἶκον. ὡς γὰρ ὁ χαλκεὺς σφυροκο-
πῶν τὸ ἔργον αὐτοῦ περιγίνεται τοῦ πράγματος οὗ θέλει, οὕτω
καὶ ὁ λόγος ὁ καθημερινὸς ὁ δίκαιος περιγίνεται πάσης πονηρίας. μὴ διαλίπῃς οὖν νουθετῶν σου τὰ τέκνα· οἶδα γὰρ ὅτι
ἐὰν μετανοήσουσιν ἐξ ὅλης καρδίας αὐτῶν, ἐνγραφήσονται εἰς
τὰς βίβλους τῆς ζωῆς μετὰ τῶν ἁγίων. 3. μετὰ τὸ παῆναι
αὐτῆς τὰ ῥήματα ταῦτα λέγει μοι· Θέλεις ἀκοῦσαί μου ἀνα-
γινωσκούσης; λέγω κἀγώ· Θέλω, κυρία. λέγει μοι· Γενοῦ
ἀκροατὴς καὶ ἄκουε τὰς δόξας τοῦ Θεοῦ. ἤκουσα μεγάλως
καὶ θαυμαστῶς ὃ οὐκ ἴσχυσα μνημονεῦσαι· πάντα γὰρ τὰ
ῥήματα ἔκφρικτα, ἃ οὐ δύναται ἄνθρωπος βαστάσαι. τὰ οὖν
ἔσχατα ῥήματα ἐμνημόνευσα· ἦν γὰρ ἡμῖν σύμφορα καὶ ἥμερα·
4. Ἰδοὺ ὁ Θεὸς τῶν δυνάμεων, ὁ ἀοράτῳ δυνάμει καὶ κραταιᾷ
καὶ τῇ μεγάλῃ συνέσει αὐτοῦ κτίσας τὸν κόσμον καὶ τῇ ἐνδόξῳ βουλῇ περιθεὶς τὴν εὐπρέπειαν τῇ κτίσει αὐτοῦ, καὶ τῷ
ἰσχυρῷ ῥήματι πήξας τὸν οὐρανὸν καὶ θεμελιώσας τὴν γῆν
ἐπὶ ὑδάτων, καὶ τῇ ἰδίᾳ σοφίᾳ καὶ προνοίᾳ κτίσας τὴν ἁγίαν
ἐκκλησίαν αὐτοῦ, ἣν καὶ ηὐλόγησεν, ἰδοὺ μεθιστάνει τοὺς
οὐρανοὺς καὶ τὰ ὄρη καὶ τοὺς βουνοὺς καὶ τὰς θαλάσσας, καὶ

πάντα ὁμαλὰ γίνεται τοῖς ἐκλεκτοῖς αὐτοῦ, ἵνα ἀποδῷ αὐτοῖς τὴν ἐπαγγελίαν ἣν ἐπηγγείλατο μετὰ πολλῆς δόξης καὶ χαρᾶς, ἐὰν τηρήσωσιν τὰ νόμιμα τοῦ Θεοῦ ἃ παρέλαβον ἐν μεγάλῃ πίστει.

IV. Ὅτε οὖν ἐτέλεσεν ἀναγινώσκουσα καὶ ἠγέρθη ἀπὸ τῆς καθέδρας, ἦλθαν τέσσαρες νεανίαι καὶ ἦραν τὴν καθέδραν καὶ ἀπῆλθον πρὸς τὴν ἀνατολήν. 2. προσκαλεῖται δέ με καὶ ἥψατο τοῦ στήθους μου καὶ λέγει μοι· Ἤρεσέν σοι ἡ ἀνάγνωσίς μου; καὶ λέγω αὐτῇ· Κυρία, ταῦτά μοι τὰ ἔσχατα ἀρέσκει, τὰ δὲ πρότερα χαλεπὰ καὶ σκληρά. ἡ δὲ ἔφη μοι λέγουσα· Ταῦτα τὰ ἔσχατα τοῖς δικαίοις, τὰ δὲ πρότερα τοῖς ἔθνεσιν καὶ τοῖς ἀποστάταις. 3. λαλούσης αὐτῆς μετ᾽ ἐμοῦ δύο τινὲς ἄνδρες ἐφάνησαν καὶ ἦραν αὐτὴν τῶν ἀγκώνων καὶ ἀπῆλθαν, ὅπου καὶ ἡ καθέδρα, πρὸς τὴν ἀνατολήν. ἱλαρὰ δὲ ἀπῆλθεν, καὶ ὑπάγουσα λέγει μοι· Ἀνδρίζου, Ἑρμᾶ.

Ὅρασις β΄

I. Πορευομένου μου εἰς Κούμας κατὰ τὸν καιρὸν ὃν καὶ πέρυσι, περιπατῶν ἀνεμνήσθην τῆς περυσινῆς ὁράσεως, καὶ πάλιν με αἴρει πνεῦμα καὶ ἀποφέρει εἰς τὸν αὐτὸν τόπον ὅπου καὶ πέρυσι. 2. ἐλθὼν οὖν εἰς τὸν τόπον τιθῶ τὰ γόνατα καὶ ἠρξάμην προσεύχεσθαι τῷ Κυρίῳ καὶ δοξάζειν αὐτοῦ τὸ ὄνομα, ὅτι με ἄξιον ἡγήσατο καὶ ἐγνώρισέν μοι τὰς ἁμαρτίας μου τὰς πρότερον. 3. μετὰ δὲ τὸ ἐγερθῆναί με ἀπὸ τῆς προσευχῆς βλέπω ἀπέναντί μου τὴν πρεσβυτέραν ἣν καὶ πέρυσιν ἑωράκειν, περιπατοῦσαν καὶ ἀναγινώσκουσαν βιβλαρίδιον. καὶ λέγει μοι· Δύνῃ ταῦτα τοῖς ἐκλεκτοῖς τοῦ Θεοῦ ἀναγγεῖλαι; λέγω αὐτῇ· Κυρία, τοσαῦτα μνημονεῦσαι οὐ δύναμαι· δὸς δέ μοι τὸ βιβλίδιον, ἵνα μεταγράψωμαι αὐτό. Λάβε, φησίν, καὶ ἀποδώσεις μοι. 4. ἔλαβον ἐγώ, καὶ εἴς τινα τόπον τοῦ ἀγροῦ ἀναχωρήσας μετεγραψάμην πάντα πρὸς γράμμα· οὐχ ηὕρισκον γὰρ τὰς συλλαβάς. τελέσαντος οὖν μου τὰ γράμματα τοῦ βιβλιδίου ἐξαίφνης ἡρπάγη μου ἐκ τῆς χειρὸς τὸ βιβλίδιον· ὑπὸ τίνος δὲ οὐκ εἶδον.

II. Μετὰ δὲ δέκα καὶ πέντε ἡμέρας νηστεύσαντός μου καὶ
πολλὰ ἐρωτήσαντος τὸν Κύριον ἀπεκαλύφθη μοι ἡ γνῶσις τῆς
γραφῆς. ἦν δὲ γεγραμμένα ταῦτα· 2. Τὸ σπέρμα σου,
Ἑρμᾶ, ἠθέτησαν εἰς τὸν Θεὸν καὶ ἐβλασφήμησαν εἰς τὸν
Κύριον καὶ προέδωκαν τοὺς γονεῖς αὐτῶν ἐν πονηρίᾳ μεγάλῃ,
καὶ ἤκουσαν προδόται γονέων, καὶ προδόντες οὐκ ὠφελήθησαν,
ἀλλὰ ἔτι προσέθηκαν ταῖς ἁμαρτίαις αὐτῶν τὰς ἀσελγείας καὶ
συμφυρμοὺς πονηρίας, καὶ οὕτως ἐπλήσθησαν αἱ ἀνομίαι αὐτῶν. 3. ἀλλὰ γνώρισον ταῦτα τὰ ῥήματα τοῖς τέκνοις σου
πᾶσιν καὶ τῇ συμβίῳ σου τῇ μελλούσῃ σου ἀδελφῇ· καὶ γὰρ
αὕτη οὐκ ἀπέχεται τῆς γλώσσης, ἐν ᾗ πονηρεύεται· ἀλλὰ
ἀκούσασα τὰ ῥήματα ταῦτα ἀφέξεται, καὶ ἕξει ἔλεος. 4. μετὰ
τὸ γνωρίσαι σε ταῦτα τὰ ῥήματα αὐτοῖς ἃ ἐνετείλατό μοι ὁ
δεσπότης ἵνα σοι ἀποκαλυφθῇ, τότε ἀφίενται αὐτοῖς αἱ ἁμαρτίαι πᾶσαι ἃς πρότερον ἥμαρτον, καὶ πᾶσιν τοῖς ἁγίοις τοῖς
ἁμαρτήσασιν μέχρι ταύτης τῆς ἡμέρας, ἐὰν ἐξ ὅλης τῆς καρδίας μετανοήσωσιν καὶ ἄρωσιν ἀπὸ τῆς καρδίας αὐτῶν τὰς
διψυχίας. 5. ὤμοσεν γὰρ ὁ δεσπότης κατὰ τῆς δόξης αὐτοῦ
ἐπὶ τοὺς ἐκλεκτοὺς αὐτοῦ· ἐὰν ὡρισμένης τῆς ἡμέρας ταύτης
ἔτι ἁμάρτησις γένηται, μὴ ἔχειν αὐτοὺς σωτηρίαν· ἡ γὰρ
μετάνοια τοῖς δικαίοις ἔχει τέλος· πεπλήρωνται αἱ ἡμέραι
μετανοίας πᾶσιν τοῖς ἁγίοις· καὶ τοῖς δὲ ἔθνεσιν μετάνοιά
ἐστιν ἕως ἐσχάτης ἡμέρας. 6. ἐρεῖς οὖν τοῖς προηγουμένοις
τῆς ἐκκλησίας ἵνα κατορθώσωνται τὰς ὁδοὺς αὐτῶν ἐν δικαιοσύνῃ, ἵνα ἀπολάβωσιν ἐκ πλήρους τὰς ἐπαγγελίας μετὰ πολλῆς δόξης. 7. ἐμμείνατε οὖν οἱ ἐργαζόμενοι τὴν δικαιοσύνην
καὶ μὴ διψυχήσητε, ἵνα γένηται ὑμῶν ἡ πάροδος μετὰ τῶν
ἀγγέλων τῶν ἁγίων. μακάριοι ὑμεῖς ὅσοι ὑπομένετε τὴν
θλῖψιν τὴν ἐρχομένην τὴν μεγάλην, καὶ ὅσοι οὐκ ἀρνήσονται
τὴν ζωὴν αὐτῶν. 8. ὤμοσεν γὰρ Κύριος κατὰ τοῦ υἱοῦ αὐτοῦ,
τοὺς ἀρνησαμένους τὸν Κύριον αὐτῶν ἀπεγνωρίσθαι ἀπὸ τῆς
ζωῆς αὐτῶν, τοὺς νῦν μέλλοντας ἀρνεῖσθαι ταῖς ἐρχομέναις
ἡμέραις· τοῖς δὲ πρότερον ἀρνησαμένοις διὰ τὴν πολυσπλαγχ-
νίαν ἵλεως ἐγένετο αὐτοῖς.

III. Σὺ δέ, Ἑρμᾶ, μηκέτι μνησικακήσῃς τοῖς τέκνοις σου, μηδὲ τὴν ἀδελφήν σου ἐάσῃς, ἵνα καθαρισθῶσιν ἀπὸ τῶν προτέρων ἁμαρτιῶν αὐτῶν. παιδευθήσονται γὰρ παιδείᾳ δικαίᾳ, ἐὰν σὺ μὴ μνησικακήσῃς αὐτοῖς. μνησικακία θάνατον κατεργάζεται. σὺ δέ, Ἑρμᾶ, μεγάλας θλίψεις ἔσχες ἰδιωτικὰς διὰ τὰς παραβάσεις τοῦ οἴκου σου, ὅτι οὐκ ἐμέλησέν σοι περὶ αὐτῶν. ἀλλὰ παρενεθυμήθης καὶ ταῖς πραγματείαις σου συνανεφύρης ταῖς πονηραῖς· 2. ἀλλὰ σώζει σε τὸ μὴ ἀποστῆναί σε ἀπὸ Θεοῦ ζῶντος, καὶ ἡ ἁπλότης σου καὶ ἡ πολλὴ ἐγκράτεια· ταῦτα σέσωκέν σε, ἐὰν ἐμμείνῃς, καὶ πάντας σώζει τοὺς τὰ τοιαῦτα ἐργαζομένους καὶ πορευομένους ἐν ἀκακίᾳ καὶ ἁπλότητι. οὗτοι κατισχύουσιν πάσης πονηρίας καὶ παραμένουσιν εἰς ζωὴν αἰώνιον. 3. μακάριοι πάντες οἱ ἐργαζόμενοι τὴν δικαιοσύνην· οὐ διαφθαρήσονται ἕως αἰῶνος. 4. ἐρεῖς δὲ Μαξίμῳ· Ἰδοὺ θλῖψις ἔρχεται, ἐάν σοι δόκῃ πάλιν ἀρνεῖσθαι. Ἐγγὺς Κύριος τοῖς ἐπιστρεφομένοις, ὡς γέγραπται ἐν τῷ Ἐλδὰδ καὶ Μωδάτ, τοῖς προφητεύσασιν ἐν τῇ ἐρήμῳ τῷ λαῷ.

IV. Ἀπεκαλύφθη δέ μοι, ἀδελφοί, κοιμωμένῳ ὑπὸ νεανίσκου εὐειδεστάτου λέγοντός μοι· Τὴν πρεσβυτέραν, παρ᾽ ἧς ἔλαβες τὸ βιβλίδιον, τίνα δοκεῖς εἶναι; ἐγώ φημι· Τὴν Σίβυλλαν. Πλανᾶσαι, φησίν, οὐκ ἔστιν. Τίς οὖν ἐστίν; φημί. Ἡ Ἐκκλησία, φησίν. εἶπον αὐτῷ· Διατί οὖν πρεσβυτέρα; Ὅτι, φησίν, πάντων πρώτη ἐκτίσθη· διὰ τοῦτο πρεσβυτέρα, καὶ διὰ ταύτην ὁ κόσμος κατηρτίσθη. 2. μετέπειτα δὲ ὅρασιν εἶδον ἐν τῷ οἴκῳ μου. ἦλθεν ἡ πρεσβυτέρα καὶ ἠρώτησέν με εἰ ἤδη τὸ βιβλίον δέδωκα τοῖς πρεσβυτέροις. ἠρνησάμην δεδωκέναι. Καλῶς, φησίν, πεποίηκας· ἔχω γὰρ ῥήματα προσθεῖναι. ὅταν οὖν ἀποτελέσω τὰ ῥήματα πάντα, διὰ σοῦ γνωρισθήσεται τοῖς ἐκλεκτοῖς πᾶσιν. 3. γράψεις οὖν δύο βιβλαρίδια, καὶ πέμψεις ἓν Κλήμεντι καὶ ἓν Γραπτῇ. πέμψει οὖν Κλήμης εἰς τὰς ἔξω πόλεις, ἐκείνῳ γὰρ ἐπιτέτραπται· Γραπτὴ δὲ νουθετήσει τὰς χήρας καὶ τοὺς ὀρφανούς. σὺ δὲ

2. iii. 4 ἀρνεῖσθαι] conj. Harmer [L₂E]; ἄρνησαι אAL.

ἀναγνώσῃ εἰς ταύτην τὴν πόλιν μετὰ τῶν πρεσβυτέρων τῶν
προϊσταμένων τῆς ἐκκλησίας.

Ὅρασις γ'

I. ἣν εἶδον, ἀδελφοί, τοιαύτη. 2. νηστεύσας πολλάκις
καὶ δεηθεὶς τοῦ Κυρίου ἵνα μοι φανερώσῃ τὴν ἀποκάλυψιν ἥν
μοι ἐπηγγείλατο δεῖξαι διὰ τῆς πρεσβυτέρας ἐκείνης, αὐτῇ τῇ
νυκτὶ ὤφθη μοι ἡ πρεσβυτέρα καὶ εἶπέν μοι· Ἐπεὶ οὕτως
ἐνδεὴς εἶ καὶ σπουδαῖος εἰς τὸ γνῶναι πάντα, ἐλθὲ εἰς τὸν
ἀγρὸν ὅπου χρονίζεις, καὶ περὶ ὥραν πέμπτην ἐμφανισθήσο-
μαί σοι καὶ δείξω σοι ἃ δεῖ σε ἰδεῖν. 3. ἠρώτησα αὐτὴν
λέγων· Κυρία, εἰς ποῖον τόπον τοῦ ἀγροῦ; Ὅπου, φησίν,
θέλεις. ἐξελεξάμην τόπον καλὸν ἀνακεχωρηκότα. πρὶν δὲ
λαλῆσαι αὐτῇ καὶ εἰπεῖν τὸν τόπον, λέγει μοι· Ἥξω ἐκεῖ
ὅπου θέλεις. 4. ἐγενόμην οὖν, ἀδελφοί, εἰς τὸν ἀγρόν, καὶ
συνεψήφισα τὰς ὥρας, καὶ ἦλθον εἰς τὸν τόπον ὅπου διεταξά-
μην αὐτῇ ἐλθεῖν, καὶ βλέπω συμψέλιον κείμενον ἐλεφάντινον,
καὶ ἐπὶ τοῦ συμψελίου ἔκειτο κερβικάριον λινοῦν, καὶ ἐπάνω
λέντιον ἐξηπλωμένον λινοῦν καρπάσιον. 5. ἰδὼν ταῦτα κεί-
μενα καὶ μηδένα ὄντα ἐν τῷ τόπῳ ἔκθαμβος ἐγενόμην, καὶ
ὡσεὶ τρόμος με ἔλαβεν, καὶ αἱ τρίχες μου ὀρθαί· καὶ ὡσεὶ
φρίκη μοι προσῆλθεν, μόνου μου ὄντος. ἐν ἐμαυτῷ οὖν γενόμενος καὶ μνησθεὶς τῆς δόξης τοῦ Θεοῦ καὶ λαβὼν θάρσος,
θεὶς τὰ γόνατα ἐξωμολογούμην τῷ Κυρίῳ πάλιν τὰς ἁμαρτίας
μου ὡς καὶ πρότερον. 6. ἡ δὲ ἦλθεν μετὰ νεανίσκων ἕξ, οὓς
καὶ πρότερον ἑωράκειν, καὶ ἐπεστάθη μοι καὶ κατηκροᾶτο
προσευχομένου μου καὶ ἐξομολογουμένου τῷ Κυρίῳ τὰς ἁμαρτίας μου. καὶ ἁψαμένη μου λέγει· Ἑρμᾶ, παῦσαι περὶ τῶν
ἁμαρτιῶν σου πάντα ἐρωτῶν· ἐρώτα καὶ περὶ δικαιοσύνης,
ἵνα λάβῃς μέρος τι ἐξαυτῆς εἰς τὸν οἶκόν σου. 7. καὶ ἐξε-
γείρει με τῆς χειρὸς καὶ ἄγει με πρὸς τὸ συμψέλιον, καὶ λέγει
τοῖς νεανίσκοις· Ὑπάγετε καὶ οἰκοδομεῖτε. 8. καὶ μετὰ τὸ
ἀναχωρῆσαι τοὺς νεανίσκους καὶ μόνων ἡμῶν γεγονότων λέγει

---

3. i. 6 ἐπεστάθη] conj. Hilgenfeld ; ἐστάθη A ; stetit post L₁E ; def. ℵL₂.

μοι· Κάθισον ὧδε. λέγω αὐτῇ· Κυρία, ἄφες τοὺς πρεσβυτέρους πρῶτον καθίσαι. Ὅ σοι λέγω, φησίν, κάθισον. 9. θέλοντος οὖν μου καθίσαι εἰς τὰ δεξιὰ μέρη οὐκ εἴασέν με, ἀλλ᾽
ἐννεύει μοι τῇ χειρὶ ἵνα εἰς τὰ ἀριστερὰ μέρη καθίσω. διαλο-
γιζομένου μου οὖν καὶ λυπουμένου ὅτι οὐκ εἴασέν με εἰς τὰ
δεξιὰ μέρη καθίσαι, λέγει μοι· Λυπῇ, Ἑρμᾶ; ὁ εἰς τὰ δεξιὰ
μέρη τόπος ἄλλων ἐστίν, τῶν ἤδη εὐαρεστηκότων τῷ Θεῷ καὶ
παθόντων εἵνεκα τοῦ ὀνόματος· σοὶ δὲ πολλὰ λείπει ἵνα μετ᾽
αὐτῶν καθίσῃς· ἀλλ᾽ ὡς ἐμμένεις τῇ ἁπλότητί σου, μεῖνον,
καὶ καθιῇ μετ᾽ αὐτῶν, καὶ ὅσοι ἐὰν ἐργάσωνται τὰ ἐκείνων
ἔργα καὶ ὑπενέγκωσιν ἃ καὶ ἐκεῖνοι ὑπήνεγκαν.

II. Τί, φημί, ὑπήνεγκαν; Ἄκουε, φησίν· μάστιγας,
φυλακάς, θλίψεις μεγάλας, σταυρούς, θηρία εἵνεκεν τοῦ ὀνό-
ματος· διὰ τοῦτο ἐκείνων ἐστὶν τὰ δεξιὰ μέρη τοῦ ἁγιάσματος,
καὶ ὃς ἐὰν πάθῃ διὰ τὸ ὄνομα· τῶν δὲ λοιπῶν τὰ ἀριστερὰ
μέρη ἐστίν. ἀλλὰ ἀμφοτέρων, καὶ τῶν ἐκ δεξιῶν καὶ τῶν ἐξ
ἀριστερῶν καθημένων, τὰ αὐτὰ δῶρα καὶ αἱ αὐταὶ ἐπαγγελίαι·
μόνον ἐκεῖνοι ἐκ δεξιῶν κάθηνται καὶ ἔχουσιν δόξαν τινά.
2. σὺ δὲ κατεπίθυμος εἶ καθίσαι ἐκ δεξιῶν μετ᾽ αὐτῶν, ἀλλὰ
τὰ ὑστερήματά σου πολλά· καθαρισθήσῃ δὲ ἀπὸ τῶν ὑστερη-
μάτων σου· καὶ πάντες δὲ οἱ μὴ διψυχοῦντες καθαρισθήσονται
ἀπὸ πάντων τῶν ἁμαρτημάτων εἰς ταύτην τὴν ἡμέραν. 3.
ταῦτα εἴπασα ἤθελεν ἀπελθεῖν· πεσὼν δὲ αὐτῆς πρὸς τοὺς
πόδας ἠρώτησα αὐτὴν κατὰ τοῦ Κυρίου ἵνα μοι ἐπιδείξῃ ὃ
ἐπηγγείλατο ὅραμα. 4. ἡ δὲ πάλιν ἐπελάβετό μου τῆς
χειρὸς καὶ ἐγείρει με καὶ καθίζει ἐπὶ τὸ συμψέλιον ἐξ εὐω-
νύμων· ἐκαθέζετο δὲ καὶ αὐτὴ ἐκ δεξιῶν. καὶ ἐπάρασα
ῥάβδον τινὰ λαμπρὰν λέγει μοι· Βλέπεις μέγα πρᾶγμα;
λέγω αὐτῇ· Κυρία, οὐδὲν βλέπω. λέγει μοι· [Σύ,] ἰδοὺ οὐχ
ὁρᾷς κατέναντί σου πύργον μέγαν οἰκοδομούμενον ἐπὶ ὑδάτων
λίθοις τετραγώνοις λαμπροῖς; 5. ἐν τετραγώνῳ δὲ ᾠκοδο-
μεῖτο ὁ πύργος ὑπὸ τῶν ἓξ νεανίσκων τῶν ἐληλυθότων μετ᾽
αὐτῆς· ἄλλαι δὲ μυριάδες ἀνδρῶν παρέφερον λίθους, οἱ μὲν ἐκ
τοῦ βυθοῦ, οἱ δὲ ἐκ τῆς γῆς, καὶ ἐπεδίδουν τοῖς ἓξ νεανίσκοις.

ἐκεῖνοι δὲ ἐλάμβανον καὶ ᾠκοδόμουν· 6. τοὺς μὲν ἐκ τοῦ
βυθοῦ λίθους ἑλκομένους πάντας οὕτως ἐτίθεσαν εἰς τὴν
οἰκοδομήν· ἡρμοσμένοι γὰρ ἦσαν καὶ συνεφώνουν τῇ ἁρμογῇ
μετὰ τῶν ἑτέρων λίθων· καὶ οὕτως ἐκολλῶντο ἀλλήλοις, ὥστε
τὴν ἁρμογὴν αὐτῶν μὴ φαίνεσθαι. ἐφαίνετο δὲ ἡ οἰκοδομὴ
τοῦ πύργου ὡς ἐξ ἑνὸς λίθου ᾠκοδομημένη. 7. τοὺς δὲ
ἑτέρους λίθους τοὺς φερομένους ἀπὸ τῆς ξηρᾶς τοὺς μὲν
ἀπέβαλλον, τοὺς δὲ ἐτίθουν εἰς τὴν οἰκοδομήν· ἄλλους δὲ
κατέκοπτον καὶ ἔρριπτον μακρὰν ἀπὸ τοῦ πύργου. 8. ἄλλοι
δὲ λίθοι πολλοὶ κύκλῳ τοῦ πύργου ἔκειντο, καὶ οὐκ ἐχρῶντο
αὐτοῖς εἰς τὴν οἰκοδομήν· ἦσαν γάρ τινες ἐξ αὐτῶν ἐψωριακότες, ἕτεροι δὲ σχισμὰς ἔχοντες, ἄλλοι δὲ κεκολοβωμένοι,
ἄλλοι δὲ λευκοὶ καὶ στρογγύλοι, μὴ ἁρμόζοντες εἰς τὴν οἰκοδομήν. 9. ἔβλεπον δὲ ἑτέρους λίθους ῥιπτομένους μακρὰν
ἀπὸ τοῦ πύργου καὶ ἐρχομένους εἰς τὴν ὁδὸν καὶ μὴ μένοντας
ἐν τῇ ὁδῷ, ἀλλὰ κυλιομένους εἰς τὴν ἀνοδίαν· ἑτέρους δὲ ἐπὶ
πῦρ ἐμπίπτοντας καὶ καιομένους· ἑτέρους δὲ πίπτοντας ἐγγὺς
ὑδάτων καὶ μὴ δυναμένους κυλισθῆναι εἰς τὸ ὕδωρ, καίπερ
θελόντων κυλισθῆναι καὶ ἐλθεῖν εἰς τὸ ὕδωρ.

III. Δείξασά μοι ταῦτα ἤθελεν ἀποτρέχειν. λέγω αὐτῇ·
Κυρία, τί μοι ὄφελος ταῦτα ἑωρακότι καὶ μὴ γινώσκοντι τί
ἐστιν τὰ πράγματα; ἀποκριθεῖσά μοι λέγει· Πανοῦργος εἶ
ἄνθρωπος, θέλων γινώσκειν τὰ περὶ τὸν πύργον. Ναί, φημί,
κυρία, ἵνα τοῖς ἀδελφοῖς ἀναγγείλω, καὶ [ἱλαρώτεροι γένωνται,
καὶ ταῦτα] ἀκούσαντες γινώσκωσιν τὸν Κύριον ἐν πολλῇ δόξῃ.
2. ἡ δὲ ἔφη· Ἀκούσονται μὲν πολλοί· ἀκούσαντες δέ τινες ἐξ
αὐτῶν χαρήσονται, τινὲς δὲ κλαύσονται· ἀλλὰ καὶ οὗτοι, ἐὰν
ἀκούσωσιν καὶ μετανοήσωσιν, καὶ αὐτοὶ χαρήσονται. ἄκουε
οὖν τὰς παραβολὰς τοῦ πύργου· ἀποκαλύψω γάρ σοι πάντα.
καὶ μηκέτι μοι κόπους πάρεχε περὶ ἀποκαλύψεως· αἱ γὰρ
ἀποκαλύψεις αὗται τέλος ἔχουσιν· πεπληρωμέναι γάρ εἰσιν.
ἀλλ᾽ οὐ παύσῃ αἰτούμενος ἀποκαλύψεις· ἀναιδὴς γὰρ εἶ.
3. ὁ μὲν πύργος ὃν βλέπεις οἰκοδομούμενον, ἐγώ εἰμι ἡ
Ἐκκλησία, ἡ ὀφθεῖσά σοι καὶ νῦν καὶ τὸ πρότερον· ὃ ἂν οὖν

θελήσῃς ἐπερώτα περὶ τοῦ πύργου, καὶ ἀποκαλύψω σοι, ἵνα χαρῇς μετὰ τῶν ἁγίων. 4. λέγω αὐτῇ· Κυρία, ἐπεὶ ἅπαξ ἄξιόν με ἡγήσω τοῦ πάντα μοι ἀποκαλύψαι, ἀποκάλυψον. ἡ δὲ λέγει μοι· Ὃ ἐὰν ἐνδέχηταί σοι ἀποκαλυφθῆναι, ἀποκαλυφθήσεται. μόνον ἡ καρδία σου πρὸς τὸν Θεὸν ἤτω καὶ μὴ διψυχήσεις ὃ ἂν ἴδῃς. 5. ἐπηρώτησα αὐτήν· Διατί ὁ πύργος ἐπὶ ὑδάτων ᾠκοδόμηται, κυρία; Εἶπά σοι, φησίν, καὶ τὸ πρότερον, καὶ ἐκζητεῖς ἐπιμελῶς· ἐκζητῶν οὖν εὑρίσκεις τὴν ἀλήθειαν. διατί οὖν ἐπὶ ὑδάτων ᾠκοδόμηται ὁ πύργος, ἄκουε· ὅτι ἡ ζωὴ ὑμῶν διὰ ὕδατος ἐσώθη καὶ σωθήσεται. τεθεμελίωται δὲ ὁ πύργος τῷ ῥήματι τοῦ παντοκράτορος καὶ ἐνδόξου ὀνόματος, κρατεῖται δὲ ὑπὸ τῆς ἀοράτου δυνάμεως τοῦ δεσπότου.

IV. Ἀποκριθεὶς λέγω αὐτῇ· Κυρία, μεγάλως καὶ θαυμαστῶς ἔχει τὸ πρᾶγμα τοῦτο. οἱ δὲ νεανίσκοι οἱ ἓξ οἱ οἰκοδομοῦντες τίνες εἰσίν, κυρία; Οὗτοί εἰσιν οἱ ἅγιοι ἄγγελοι τοῦ Θεοῦ οἱ πρῶτοι κτισθέντες, οἷς παρέδωκεν ὁ Κύριος πᾶσαν τὴν κτίσιν αὐτοῦ, αὔξειν καὶ οἰκοδομεῖν καὶ δεσπόζειν τῆς κτίσεως πάσης. διὰ τούτων οὖν τελεσθήσεται ἡ οἰκοδομὴ τοῦ πύργου. 2. Οἱ δὲ ἕτεροι οἱ παραφέροντες τοὺς λίθους τίνες εἰσίν; Καὶ αὐτοὶ ἅγιοι ἄγγελοι τοῦ Θεοῦ· οὗτοι δὲ οἱ ἓξ ὑπερέχοντες αὐτούς εἰσιν. συντελεσθήσεται οὖν ἡ οἰκοδομὴ τοῦ πύργου, καὶ πάντες ὁμοῦ εὐφρανθήσονται κύκλῳ τοῦ πύργου καὶ δοξάσουσιν τὸν Θεόν, ὅτι ἐτελέσθη ἡ οἰκοδομὴ τοῦ πύργου. 3. ἐπηρώτησα αὐτὴν λέγων· Κυρία, ἤθελον γνῶναι τῶν λίθων τὴν ἔξοδον καὶ τὴν δύναμιν αὐτῶν, ποταπή ἐστιν. ἀποκριθεῖσά μοι λέγει· Οὐχ ὅτι σὺ ἐκ πάντων ἀξιώτερος εἶ ἵνα σοι ἀποκαλυφθῇ· ἄλλοι γάρ σου πρότεροί εἰσιν καὶ βελτίονές σου, οἷς ἔδει ἀποκαλυφθῆναι τὰ ὁράματα ταῦτα· ἀλλ' ἵνα δοξασθῇ τὸ ὄνομα τοῦ Θεοῦ, σοὶ ἀπεκαλύφθη καὶ ἀποκαλυφθήσεται διὰ τοὺς διψύχους, τοὺς διαλογιζομένους ἐν ταῖς καρδίαις αὐτῶν εἰ ἄρα ἔστιν ταῦτα ἢ οὐκ ἔστιν. λέγε αὐτοῖς ὅτι ταῦτα πάντα ἐστὶν ἀληθῆ, καὶ οὐθὲν ἔξωθέν ἐστιν τῆς ἀληθείας, ἀλλὰ πάντα ἰσχυρὰ καὶ βέβαια καὶ τεθεμελιωμένα ἐστίν.

V. Ἄκουε νῦν περὶ τῶν λίθων τῶν ὑπαγόντων εἰς τὴν
οἰκοδομήν. οἱ μὲν οὖν λίθοι οἱ τετράγωνοι καὶ λευκοὶ καὶ
συμφωνοῦντες ταῖς ἁρμογαῖς αὐτῶν, οὗτοί εἰσιν οἱ ἀπόστολοι cf. Apoc.
καὶ ἐπίσκοποι καὶ διδάσκαλοι καὶ διάκονοι οἱ πορευθέντες xxi. 14.
κατὰ τὴν σεμνότητα τοῦ Θεοῦ καὶ ἐπισκοπήσαντες καὶ διδάξαντες καὶ διακονήσαντες ἁγνῶς καὶ σεμνῶς τοῖς ἐκλεκτοῖς
τοῦ Θεοῦ, οἱ μὲν κεκοιμημένοι, οἱ δὲ ἔτι ὄντες· καὶ πάντοτε
ἑαυτοῖς συμφωνήσαντες καὶ ἐν ἑαυτοῖς εἰρήνην ἔσχον καὶ
ἀλλήλων ἤκουον· διὰ τοῦτο ἐν τῇ οἰκοδομῇ τοῦ πύργου συμφωνοῦσιν αἱ ἁρμογαὶ αὐτῶν. 2. Οἱ δὲ ἐκ τοῦ βυθοῦ ἑλκό-
μενοι καὶ ἐπιτιθέμενοι εἰς τὴν οἰκοδομὴν καὶ συμφωνοῦντες
ταῖς ἁρμογαῖς αὐτῶν μετὰ τῶν ἑτέρων λίθων τῶν ἤδη ᾠκοδο-
μημένων τίνες εἰσίν; Οὗτοί εἰσιν οἱ παθόντες ἕνεκεν τοῦ
ὀνόματος τοῦ Κυρίου. 3. Τοὺς δὲ ἑτέρους λίθους τοὺς φερομένους ἀπὸ τῆς ξηρᾶς θέλω γνῶναι τίνες εἰσίν, κυρία. · ἔφη·
Τοὺς μὲν εἰς τὴν οἰκοδομὴν ὑπάγοντας καὶ μὴ λατομουμένους,
τούτους ὁ Κύριος ἐδοκίμασεν, ὅτι ἐπορεύθησαν ἐν τῇ εὐθύτητι
τοῦ Κυρίου καὶ κατωρθώσαντο τὰς ἐντολὰς αὐτοῦ. 4. Οἱ δὲ
ἀγόμενοι καὶ τιθέμενοι εἰς τὴν οἰκοδομὴν τίνες εἰσίν; Νέοι
εἰσὶν ἐν τῇ πίστει καὶ πιστοί. νουθετοῦνται δὲ ὑπὸ τῶν
ἀγγέλων εἰς τὸ ἀγαθοποιεῖν, διότι εὑρέθη ἐν αὐτοῖς πονηρία.
5. Οὓς δὲ ἀπέβαλλον καὶ ἐρίπτουν, τίνες εἰσίν; Οὗτοί εἰσιν
ἡμαρτηκότες καὶ θέλοντες μετανοῆσαι· διὰ τοῦτο μακρὰν οὐκ
ἀπερίφησαν ἔξω τοῦ πύργου, ὅτι εὔχρηστοι ἔσονται εἰς τὴν
οἰκοδομήν, ἐὰν μετανοήσωσιν. οἱ οὖν μέλλοντες μετανοεῖν,
ἐὰν μετανοήσωσιν, ἰσχυροὶ ἔσονται ἐν τῇ πίστει, ἐὰν νῦν
μετανοήσωσιν ἐν ᾧ οἰκοδομεῖται ὁ πύργος. ἐὰν δὲ τελεσθῇ ἡ
οἰκοδομή, οὐκέτι ἔχουσιν τόπον, ἀλλ' ἔσονται ἔκβολοι. μόνον
δὲ τοῦτο ἔχουσιν, παρὰ τῷ πύργῳ κεῖσθαι.

VI. Τοὺς δὲ κατακοπτομένους καὶ μακρὰν ῥιπτομένους
ἀπὸ τοῦ πύργου θέλεις γνῶναι; οὗτοί εἰσιν οἱ υἱοὶ τῆς
ἀνομίας· ἐπίστευσαν δὲ ἐν ὑποκρίσει, καὶ πᾶσα πονηρία οὐκ
ἀπέστη ἀπ' αὐτῶν· διὰ τοῦτο οὐκ ἔχουσιν σωτηρίαν, ὅτι οὐκ
εἰσὶν εὔχρηστοι εἰς οἰκοδομὴν διὰ τὰς πονηρίας αὐτῶν. διὰ

τοῦτο συνεκόπησαν καὶ πόρρω ἀπερίφησαν διὰ τὴν ὀργὴν τοῦ Κυρίου, ὅτι παρώργισαν αὐτόν. 2. τοὺς δὲ ἑτέρους οὓς ἑώρακας πολλοὺς κειμένους, μὴ ὑπάγοντας εἰς τὴν οἰκοδομήν, οὗτοι οἱ μὲν ἐψωριακότες εἰσίν, οἱ ἐγνωκότες τὴν ἀλήθειαν, μὴ ἐπιμείναντες δὲ ἐν αὐτῇ μηδὲ κολλώμενοι τοῖς ἁγίοις· διὰ τοῦτο ἄχρηστοί εἰσιν. 3. Οἱ δὲ τὰς σχισμὰς ἔχοντες τίνες εἰσίν; Οὗτοί εἰσιν οἱ κατ᾽ ἀλλήλων ἐν ταῖς καρδίαις ἔχοντες καὶ μὴ εἰρηνεύοντες ἐν ἑαυτοῖς, ἀλλὰ πρόσωπον εἰρήνης ἔχοντες, ὅταν δὲ ἀπ᾽ ἀλλήλων ἀποχωρήσωσιν, αἱ πονηρίαι αὐτῶν ἐν ταῖς καρδίαις ἐμμένουσιν. αὗται οὖν αἱ σχισμαί εἰσιν ἃς ἔχουσιν οἱ λίθοι. 4. οἱ δὲ κεκολοβωμένοι, οὗτοί εἰσιν πεπιστευκότες μὲν καὶ τὸ πλεῖον μέρος ἔχοντες ἐν τῇ δικαιοσύνῃ, τινὰ δὲ μέρη ἔχουσιν τῆς ἀνομίας· διὰ τοῦτο κολοβοὶ καὶ οὐχ ὁλοτελεῖς εἰσίν. 5. Οἱ δὲ λευκοὶ καὶ στρογγύλοι καὶ μὴ ἁρμόζοντες εἰς τὴν οἰκοδομὴν τίνες εἰσίν, κυρία; ἀποκριθεῖσά μοι λέγει· ῞Εως πότε μωρὸς εἶ καὶ ἀσύνετος, καὶ πάντα ἐπερωτᾷς καὶ οὐδὲν νοεῖς; οὗτοί εἰσιν ἔχοντες μὲν πίστιν, ἔχοντες δὲ καὶ πλοῦτον τοῦ αἰῶνος τούτου. ὅταν γένηται θλῖψις, διὰ τὸν πλοῦτον αὐτῶν καὶ διὰ τὰς πραγματείας ἀπαρνοῦνται τὸν Κύριον αὐτῶν. 6. καὶ ἀποκριθεὶς αὐτῇ λέγω· Κυρία, πότε οὖν εὔχρηστοι ἔσονται εἰς τὴν οἰκοδομήν; ῞Οταν, φησίν, περικοπῇ αὐτῶν ὁ πλοῦτος ὁ ψυχαγωγῶν αὐτούς, τότε εὔχρηστοι ἔσονται τῷ Θεῷ. ὥσπερ γὰρ ὁ λίθος ὁ στρογγύλος ἐὰν μὴ περικοπῇ καὶ ἀποβάλῃ ἐξ αὐτοῦ τι, οὐ δύναται τετράγωνος γενέσθαι, οὕτω καὶ οἱ πλουτοῦντες ἐν τούτῳ τῷ αἰῶνι, ἐὰν μὴ περικοπῇ αὐτῶν ὁ πλοῦτος, οὐ δύνανται τῷ Κυρίῳ εὔχρηστοι γενέσθαι. 7. ἀπὸ [δὲ] σεαυτοῦ πρῶτον γνῶθι· ὅτε ἐπλούτεις, ἄχρηστος ἦς· νῦν δὲ εὔχρηστος εἶ καὶ ὠφέλιμος τῇ ζωῇ. εὔχρηστοι γίνεσθε τῷ Θεῷ· καὶ γὰρ σὺ αὐτὸς χρᾶσαι ἐκ τῶν αὐτῶν λίθων.

VII. Τοὺς δὲ ἑτέρους λίθους, οὓς εἶδες μακρὰν ἀπὸ τοῦ πύργου ῥιπτομένους καὶ πίπτοντας εἰς τὴν ὁδὸν καὶ κυλιομένους ἐκ τῆς ὁδοῦ εἰς τὰς ἀνοδίας· οὗτοί εἰσιν οἱ πεπιστευκότες μέν, ἀπὸ δὲ τῆς διψυχίας αὐτῶν ἀφίουσιν τὴν ὁδὸν αὐτῶν τὴν

ἀληθινήν· δοκοῦντες οὖν βελτίονα ὁδὸν δύνασθαι εὑρεῖν, πλα-
νῶνται καὶ ταλαιπωροῦσιν περιπατοῦντες ἐν ταῖς ἀνοδίαις. 2.
οἱ δὲ πίπτοντες εἰς τὸ πῦρ καὶ καιόμενοι, οὗτοί εἰσιν οἱ εἰς
τέλος ἀποστάντες τοῦ Θεοῦ τοῦ ζῶντος, καὶ οὐκέτι αὐτοῖς
ἀνέβη ἐπὶ τὴν καρδίαν τοῦ μετανοῆσαι διὰ τὰς ἐπιθυμίας τῆς
ἀσελγείας αὐτῶν καὶ τῶν πονηριῶν ὧν εἰργάσαντο. 3. τοὺς δὲ
ἑτέρους τοὺς πίπτοντας ἐγγὺς τῶν ὑδάτων καὶ μὴ δυναμένους
κυλισθῆναι εἰς τὸ ὕδωρ θέλεις γνῶναι τίνες εἰσίν; οὗτοί εἰσιν
οἱ τὸν λόγον ἀκούσαντες καὶ θέλοντες βαπτισθῆναι εἰς τὸ
ὄνομα τοῦ Κυρίου· εἶτα ὅταν αὐτοῖς ἔλθῃ εἰς μνείαν ἡ ἁγνότης
τῆς ἀληθείας, μετανοοῦσιν, καὶ πορεύονται πάλιν ὀπίσω τῶν
ἐπιθυμιῶν αὐτῶν τῶν πονηρῶν. 4. ἐτέλεσεν οὖν τὴν ἐξήγησιν
τοῦ πύργου. 5. ἀναιδευσάμενος ἔτι αὐτὴν ἐπηρώτησα, εἰ ἄρα
πάντες οἱ λίθοι οὗτοι οἱ ἀποβεβλημένοι καὶ μὴ ἁρμόζοντες
εἰς τὴν οἰκοδομὴν τοῦ πύργου, εἰ ἔστιν αὐτοῖς μετάνοια καὶ
ἔχουσιν τόπον εἰς τὸν πύργον τοῦτον. Ἔχουσιν, φησίν, μετάνοιαν, ἀλλὰ εἰς τοῦτον τὸν πύργον οὐ δύνανται ἁρμόσαι. 6.
ἑτέρῳ δὲ τόπῳ ἁρμόσουσιν πολὺ ἐλάττονι, καὶ τοῦτο ὅταν
βασανισθῶσιν καὶ ἐκπληρώσωσιν τὰς ἡμέρας τῶν ἁμαρτιῶν
αὐτῶν. καὶ διὰ τοῦτο μετατεθήσονται, ὅτι μετέλαβον τοῦ
ῥήματος τοῦ δικαίου. καὶ τότε αὐτοῖς συμβήσεται μετατεθῆ-
ναι ἐκ τῶν βασάνων αὐτῶν, ἐὰν ἀναβῇ ἐπὶ τὴν καρδίαν αὐτῶν
τὰ ἔργα ἃ εἰργάσαντο πονηρά. ἐὰν δὲ μὴ ἀναβῇ ἐπὶ τὴν καρδίαν αὐτῶν, οὐ σώζονται διὰ τὴν σκληροκαρδίαν αὐτῶν.

VIII. Ὅτε οὖν ἐπαυσάμην ἐρωτῶν αὐτὴν περὶ πάντων
τούτων, λέγει μοι· Θέλεις ἄλλο ἰδεῖν; κατεπίθυμος ὢν τοῦ
θεάσασθαι περιχαρὴς ἐγενόμην τοῦ ἰδεῖν. 2. ἐμβλέψασά μοι
ὑπεμειδίασεν καὶ λέγει μοι· Βλέπεις ἑπτὰ γυναῖκας κύκλῳ
τοῦ πύργου; Βλέπω, φημί, κυρία. Ὁ πύργος οὗτος ὑπὸ
τούτων βαστάζεται κατ᾽ ἐπιταγὴν τοῦ Κυρίου. 3. ἄκουε νῦν
τὰς ἐνεργείας αὐτῶν. ἡ μὲν πρώτη αὐτῶν, ἡ κρατοῦσα τὰς
χεῖρας, Πίστις καλεῖται· διὰ ταύτης σώζονται οἱ ἐκλεκτοὶ τοῦ
Θεοῦ. 4. ἡ δὲ ἑτέρα, ἡ περιεζωσμένη καὶ ἀνδριζομένη, Ἐγκράτεια καλεῖται· αὕτη θυγάτηρ ἐστὶν τῆς Πίστεως. ὃς ἂν

οὖν ἀκολουθήσῃ αὐτῇ, μακάριος γίνεται ἐν τῇ ζωῇ αὐτοῦ, ὅτι
πάντων τῶν πονηρῶν ἔργων ἀφέξεται, πιστεύων ὅτι, ἐὰν ἀφέξηται πάσης ἐπιθυμίας πονηρᾶς· κληρονομήσει ζωὴν αἰώνιον.
5. Αἱ δὲ ἕτεραι, κυρία, τίνες εἰσίν; Θυγατέρες ἀλλήλων εἰσίν.
καλοῦνται δὲ ἡ μὲν Ἁπλότης, ἡ δὲ Ἐπιστήμη, ἡ δὲ Ἀκακία,
ἡ δὲ Σεμνότης, ἡ δὲ Ἀγάπη. ὅταν οὖν τὰ ἔργα τῆς μητρὸς
αὐτῶν πάντα ποιήσῃς, δύνασαι ζῆσαι. 6. Ἤθελον, φημί,
γνῶναι, κυρία, τίς τίνα δύναμιν ἔχει αὐτῶν. Ἄκουε, φησίν,
τὰς δυνάμεις ἃς ἔχουσιν. 7. κρατοῦνται δὲ ὑπ᾽ ἀλλήλων αἱ
δυνάμεις αὐτῶν καὶ ἀκολουθοῦσιν ἀλλήλαις, καθὼς καὶ γεγεν-
νημέναι εἰσίν. ἐκ τῆς Πίστεως γεννᾶται Ἐγκράτεια, ἐκ τῆς
Ἐγκρατείας Ἁπλότης, ἐκ τῆς Ἁπλότητος Ἀκακία, ἐκ τῆς
Ἀκακίας Σεμνότης, ἐκ τῆς Σεμνότητος Ἐπιστήμη, ἐκ τῆς
Ἐπιστήμης Ἀγάπη. τούτων οὖν τὰ ἔργα ἁγνὰ καὶ σεμνὰ
καὶ θεῖά ἐστιν. 8. ὃς ἂν οὖν δουλεύσῃ ταύταις καὶ ἰσχύσῃ
κρατῆσαι τῶν ἔργων αὐτῶν, ἐν τῷ πύργῳ ἕξει τὴν κατοίκησιν
μετὰ τῶν ἁγίων τοῦ Θεοῦ. 9. ἐπηρώτων δὲ αὐτὴν περὶ τῶν
καιρῶν, εἰ ἤδη συντέλειά ἐστιν. ἡ δὲ ἀνέκραγε φωνῇ μεγάλῃ
λέγουσα· Ἀσύνετε ἄνθρωπε, οὐχ ὁρᾷς τὸν πύργον ἔτι οἰκοδομούμενον; ὡς ἐὰν οὖν συντελεσθῇ ὁ πύργος οἰκοδομούμενος,
ἔχει τέλος. ἀλλὰ ταχὺ ἐποικοδομηθήσεται. μηκέτι με ἐπερώτα μηδέν· ἀρκετή σοι ἡ ὑπόμνησις αὕτη καὶ τοῖς ἁγίοις,
καὶ ἡ ἀνακαίνωσις τῶν πνευμάτων ὑμῶν. 10. ἀλλ᾽ οὐ σοὶ
μόνῳ ἀπεκαλύφθη, ἀλλ᾽ ἵνα πᾶσιν δηλώσῃς αὐτά. 11. μετὰ
τρεῖς ἡμέρας—νοῆσαί σε γὰρ δεῖ πρῶτον, ἐντέλλομαι δέ σοι
πρῶτον, Ἑρμᾶ, τὰ ῥήματα ταῦτα ἅ σοι μέλλω λέγειν—
†λαλῆσαι† αὐτὰ [πάντα] εἰς τὰ ὦτα τῶν ἁγίων, ἵνα ἀκούσαντες αὐτὰ καὶ ποιήσαντες καθαρισθῶσιν ἀπὸ τῶν πονηριῶν
αὐτῶν, καὶ σὺ δὲ μετ᾽ αὐτῶν.

IX. Ἀκούσατέ μου, τέκνα. ἐγὼ ὑμᾶς ἐξέθρεψα ἐν πολλῇ
ἁπλότητι καὶ ἀκακίᾳ καὶ σεμνότητι διὰ τὸ ἔλεος τοῦ Κυρίου
τοῦ ἐφ᾽ ὑμᾶς στάξαντος τὴν δικαιοσύνην, ἵνα δικαιωθῆτε καὶ

viii. 11 λαλῆσαι] ℵA ; but L₁L₂E appear to suggest λάλησον or ἵνα λαλήσῃς.
αὐτὰ πάντα] conj. Hilgenfeld [L₂]; αὐτὰ ℵ; πάντα A; dub. L₁F.

ἁγιασθῆτε ἀπὸ πάσης πονηρίας καὶ ἀπὸ πάσης σκολιότητος.
ὑμεῖς δὲ οὐ θέλετε παῆναι ἀπὸ τῆς πονηρίας ὑμῶν. 2.
νῦν οὖν ἀκούσατέ μου καὶ εἰρηνεύετε ἐν ἑαυτοῖς καὶ ἐπισκέπτεσθε
ἀλλήλους καὶ ἀντιλαμβάνεσθε ἀλλήλων, καὶ μὴ μόνοι τὰ κτί-
σματα τοῦ Θεοῦ μεταλαμβάνετε ἐκ καταχύματος, ἀλλὰ μετα-
δίδοτε καὶ τοῖς ὑστερουμένοις· 3. οἱ μὲν γὰρ ἀπὸ τῶν πολλῶν ἐδεσμάτων ἀσθένειαν τῇ σαρκὶ ἐπισπῶνται καὶ λυμαί-
νονται τὴν σάρκα αὐτῶν· τῶν δὲ μὴ ἐχόντων ἐδέσματα
λυμαίνεται ἡ σὰρξ αὐτῶν διὰ τὸ μὴ ἔχειν τὸ ἀρκετὸν τῆς
τροφῆς, καὶ διαφθείρεται τὸ σῶμα αὐτῶν. 4. αὕτη οὖν ἡ
ἀσυνκρασία βλαβερὰ ὑμῖν τοῖς ἔχουσιν καὶ μὴ μεταδιδοῦσιν
τοῖς ὑστερουμένοις. 5. βλέπετε τὴν κρίσιν τὴν ἐπερχομένην.
οἱ ὑπερέχοντες οὖν ἐκζητεῖτε τοὺς πεινῶντας ἕως οὔπω ὁ
πύργος ἐτελέσθη· μετὰ γὰρ τὸ τελεσθῆναι τὸν πύργον θελή-
σετε ἀγαθοποιεῖν, καὶ οὐχ ἕξετε τόπον. 6. βλέπετε οὖν ὑμεῖς
οἱ γαυρούμενοι ἐν τῷ πλούτῳ ὑμῶν, μήποτε στενάξουσιν οἱ
ὑστερούμενοι, καὶ ὁ στεναγμὸς αὐτῶν ἀναβήσεται πρὸς τὸν
Κύριον, καὶ ἐκκλεισθήσεσθε μετὰ τῶν [ἀσχέτων] ἀγαθῶν ὑμῶν
ἔξω τῆς θύρας τοῦ πύργου. 7. νῦν οὖν ὑμῖν λεγω τοῖς προηγουμένοις τῆς ἐκκλησίας καὶ τοῖς πρωτοκαθεδρίταις· μὴ γίνεσθε ὅμοιοι τοῖς φαρμακοῖς. οἱ φαρμακοὶ μὲν οὖν τὰ φάρμακα
ἑαυτῶν εἰς τὰς πυξίδας βαστάζουσιν, ὑμεῖς δὲ τὸ φάρμακον
ὑμῶν καὶ τὸν ἰὸν εἰς τὴν καρδίαν. 8. ἐνεσκιρωμένοι ἐστὲ καὶ
οὐ θέλετε καθαρίσαι τὰς καρδίας ὑμῶν καὶ συνκεράσαι ὑμῶν
τὴν φρόνησιν ἐπὶ τὸ αὐτὸ ἐν καθαρᾷ καρδίᾳ, ἵνα σχῆτε ἔλεος
παρὰ τοῦ βασιλέως τοῦ μεγάλου. 9. βλέπετε οὖν, τέκνα,
μήποτε αὗται αἱ διχοστασίαι ὑμῶν ἀποστερήσουσιν τὴν ζωὴν
ὑμῶν. 10. πῶς ὑμεῖς παιδεύειν θέλετε τοὺς ἐκλεκτοὺς
Κυρίου, αὐτοὶ μὴ ἔχοντες παιδείαν; παιδεύετε οὖν ἀλλήλους
καὶ εἰρηνεύετε ἐν αὐτοῖς, ἵνα κἀγὼ κατέναντι τοῦ πατρὸς
ἱλαρὰ σταθεῖσα λόγον ἀποδῶ ὑπὲρ ὑμῶν πάντων τῷ Κυρίῳ
ὑμῶν.

X. Ὅτε οὖν ἐπαύσατο μετ᾽ ἐμοῦ λαλοῦσα, ἦλθον οἱ ἐξ
νεανίσκοι οἱ οἰκοδομοῦντες, καὶ ἀπήνεγκαν αὐτὴν πρὸς τὸν

πύργον, καὶ ἄλλοι τέσσαρες ἦραν τὸ συμψέλιον καὶ ἀπήνεγκαν καὶ αὐτὸ πρὸς τὸν πύργον. τούτων τὸ πρόσωπον οὐκ
εἶδον, ὅτι ἀπεστραμμένοι ἦσαν. 2. ὑπάγουσαν δὲ αὐτὴν
ἠρώτων ἵνα μοι ἀποκαλύψῃ περὶ τῶν τριῶν μορφῶν ἐν αἷς
μοι ἐνεφανίσθη. ἀποκριθεῖσά μοι λέγει· Περὶ τούτων ἕτερον
δεῖ σε ἐπερωτῆσαι ἵνα σοι ἀποκαλυφθῇ. 3. ὤφθη δέ μοι,
ἀδελφοί, τῇ μὲν πρώτῃ ὁράσει τῇ περυσινῇ λίαν πρεσβυτέρα
καὶ ἐν καθέδρᾳ καθημένη. 4. τῇ δὲ ἑτέρᾳ ὁράσει τὴν μὲν
ὄψιν νεωτέραν εἶχεν, τὴν δὲ σάρκα καὶ τὰς τρίχας πρεσβυτέρας, καὶ ἑστηκυῖά μοι ἐλάλει. ἱλαρωτέρα δὲ ἦν ἢ τὸ πρότερον. 5. τῇ δὲ τρίτῃ ὁράσει ὅλη νεωτέρα καὶ κάλλει ἐκπρε-
πεστάτη, μόνας δὲ τὰς τρίχας πρεσβυτέρας εἶχεν· ἱλαρὰ δὲ
εἰς τέλος ἦν καὶ ἐπὶ συμψελίου καθημένη. 6. περὶ τούτων
περίλυπος ἤμην λίαν τοῦ γνῶναί με τὴν ἀποκάλυψιν ταύτην.
καὶ βλέπω τὴν πρεσβυτέραν ἐν ὁράματι τῆς νυκτὸς λέγου-
σάν μοι· Πᾶσα ἐρώτησις ταπεινοφροσύνης χρῄζει· νήστευσον
οὖν, καὶ λήμψῃ ὃ αἰτεῖς παρὰ τοῦ Κυρίου. 7. ἐνήστευσα οὖν
μίαν ἡμέραν, καὶ αὐτῇ τῇ νυκτί μοι ὤφθη νεανίσκος καὶ λέγει
μοι· Ὅτι σὺ ὑπὸ χεῖρα αἰτεῖς ἀποκαλύψεις ἐν δεήσει, βλέπε
μήποτε πολλὰ αἰτούμενος βλάψῃς σου τὴν σάρκα. 8. ἀρκοῦ-
σίν σοι αἱ ἀποκαλύψεις αὗται. μήτι δύνῃ ἰσχυροτέρας ἀποκαλύψεις ὧν ἑώρακας ἰδεῖν; 9. ἀποκριθεὶς αὐτῷ λέγω·
Κύριε, τοῦτο μόνον αἰτοῦμαι, περὶ τῶν τριῶν μορφῶν τῆς
πρεσβυτέρας ἵνα ἀποκάλυψις ὁλοτελὴς γένηται. ἀποκριθείς
μοι λέγει· Μέχρι τίνος ἀσύνετοί ἐστε; ἀλλ' αἱ διψυχίαι
ὑμῶν ἀσυνέτους ὑμᾶς ποιοῦσιν καὶ τὸ μὴ ἔχειν τὴν καρδίαν
ὑμῶν πρὸς τὸν Κύριον. 10. ἀποκριθεὶς αὐτῷ πάλιν εἶπον·
Ἀλλ' ἀπὸ σοῦ, κύριε, ἀκριβέστερον αὐτὰ γνωσόμεθα.

XI. Ἄκουε, φησίν, περὶ τῶν τριῶν μορφῶν ὧν ἐπιζητεῖς.
2. τῇ μὲν πρώτῃ ὁράσει διατί πρεσβυτέρα ὤφθη σοι καὶ
ἐπὶ καθέδραν καθημένη; ὅτι τὸ πνεῦμα ὑμῶν πρεσβύτερον
καὶ ἤδη μεμαρασμένον καὶ μὴ ἔχον δύναμιν ἀπὸ τῶν μαλακιῶν
ὑμῶν καὶ διψυχιῶν. 3. ὥσπερ γὰρ οἱ πρεσβύτεροι, μηκέτι
ἔχοντες ἐλπίδα τοῦ ἀνανεῶσαι, οὐδὲν ἄλλο προσδοκῶσιν εἰ μὴ

τὴν κοίμησιν αὐτῶν, οὕτω καὶ ὑμεῖς μαλακισθέντες ἀπὸ τῶν
βιωτικῶν πραγμάτων παρεδώκατε ἑαυτοὺς εἰς τὰς ἀκηδίας,
καὶ οὐκ ἐπερίψατε ἑαυτῶν τὰς μερίμνας ἐπὶ τὸν Κύριον· cf. Ps. lv.
ἀλλὰ ἐθραύσθη ὑμῶν ἡ διάνοια, καὶ ἐπαλαιώθητε ταῖς λύπαις ²². Pet. v. 7.
ὑμῶν. 4. Διατί οὖν ἐν καθέδρᾳ ἐκάθητο, ἤθελον γνῶναι,
κύριε. Ὅτι πᾶς ἀσθενὴς εἰς καθέδραν καθέζεται διὰ τὴν
ἀσθένειαν αὐτοῦ, ἵνα συνκρατηθῇ ἡ ἀσθένεια τοῦ σώματος
αὐτοῦ. ἔχεις τὸν τύπον τῆς πρώτης ὁράσεως.

XII. Τῇ δὲ δευτέρᾳ ὁράσει εἶδες αὐτὴν ἑστηκυῖαν καὶ
τὴν ὄψιν νεωτέραν ἔχουσαν καὶ ἱλαρωτέραν παρὰ τὸ πρότερον, τὴν δὲ σάρκα καὶ τὰς τρίχας πρεσβυτέρας. ἄκουε,
φησίν, καὶ ταύτην τὴν παραβολήν. 2. ὅταν πρεσβύτερός
τις, ἤδη ἀφηλπικὼς ἑαυτὸν διὰ τὴν ἀσθένειαν αὐτοῦ καὶ τὴν
πτωχότητα, οὐδὲν ἕτερον προσδέχεται εἰ μὴ τὴν ἐσχάτην
ἡμέραν τῆς ζωῆς αὐτοῦ· εἶτα ἐξαίφνης κατελείφθη αὐτῷ
κληρονομία, ἀκούσας δὲ ἐξηγέρθη καὶ περιχαρὴς γενόμενος
ἐνεδύσατο τὴν ἰσχύν, καὶ οὐκέτι ἀνάκειται, ἀλλὰ ἔστηκεν, καὶ
ἀνανεοῦται αὐτοῦ τὸ πνεῦμα τὸ ἤδη ἐφθαρμένον ἀπὸ τῶν
προτέρων αὐτοῦ πράξεων, καὶ οὐκέτι κάθηται, ἀλλὰ ἀνδρί-
ζεται· οὕτως καὶ ὑμεῖς, ἀκούσαντες τὴν ἀποκάλυψιν ἣν ὑμῖν
ὁ Κύριος ἀπεκάλυψεν. 3. ὅτι ἐσπλαγχνίσθη ἐφ᾽ ὑμᾶς, καὶ
ἀνενεώσατο τὰ πνεύματα ὑμῶν, καὶ ἀπέθεσθε τὰς μαλακίας
ὑμῶν, καὶ προσῆλθεν ὑμῖν ἰσχυρότης καὶ ἐδυναμώθητε ἐν τῇ
πίστει, καὶ ἰδὼν ὁ Κύριος τὴν ἰσχυροποίησιν ὑμῶν ἐχάρη·
καὶ διὰ τοῦτο ἐδήλωσεν ὑμῖν τὴν οἰκοδομὴν τοῦ πύργου, καὶ
ἕτερα δηλώσει, ἐὰν ἐξ ὅλης καρδίας εἰρηνεύετε ἐν ἑαυτοῖς.

XIII. Τῇ δὲ τρίτῃ ὁράσει εἶδες αὐτὴν νεωτέραν καὶ
καλὴν καὶ ἱλαράν, καὶ καλὴν τὴν μορφὴν αὐτῆς· 2. ὡς ἐὰν
γάρ τινι λυπουμένῳ ἔλθῃ ἀγγελία ἀγαθή τις, εὐθὺς ἐπελάθετο
τῶν προτέρων λυπῶν καὶ οὐδὲν ἄλλο προσδέχεται εἰ μὴ τὴν
ἀγγελίαν ἣν ἤκουσεν, καὶ ἰσχυροποιεῖται λοιπὸν εἰς τὸ ἀγαθόν,
καὶ ἀνανεοῦται αὐτοῦ τὸ πνεῦμα διὰ τὴν χαρὰν ἣν ἔλαβεν·
οὕτως καὶ ὑμεῖς ἀνανέωσιν εἰλήφατε τῶν πνευμάτων ὑμῶν
ἰδόντες ταῦτα τὰ ἀγαθά. 3. καὶ ὅτι ἐπὶ συμψελίου εἶδες

καθημένην, ἰσχυρὰ ἡ θέσις· ὅτι τέσσαρας πόδας ἔχει τὸ συμψέλιον καὶ ἰσχυρῶς ἔστηκεν· καὶ γὰρ ὁ κόσμος διὰ τεσσάρων
στοιχείων κρατεῖται. 4. οἱ οὖν μετανοήσαντες ὁλοτελῶς νέοι
ἔσονται καὶ τεθεμελιωμένοι, οἱ ἐξ ὅλης καρδίας μετανοήσαντες.
ἀπέχεις ὁλοτελῆ τὴν ἀποκάλυψιν· μηκέτι μηδὲν αἰτήσεις
περὶ ἀποκαλύψεως, ἐάν τι δὲ δέῃ, ἀποκαλυφθήσεταί σοι.

"Ορασις δ

I. ἣν εἶδον, ἀδελφοί, μετὰ ἡμέρας εἴκοσι τῆς προτέρας
ὁράσεως τῆς γενομένης, εἰς τύπον τῆς θλίψεως τῆς ἐπερχομένης. 2. ὑπῆγον εἰς ἀγρὸν τῇ ὁδῷ τῇ Καμπανῇ. ἀπὸ τῆς ὁδοῦ
τῆς δημοσίας ἐστὶν ὡσεὶ στάδια δέκα· ῥᾳδίως δὲ ὁδεύεται ὁ
τόπος. 3. μόνος οὖν περιπατῶν ἀξιῶ τὸν Κύριον ἵνα τὰς
ἀποκαλύψεις καὶ τὰ ὁράματα ἅ μοι ἔδειξεν διὰ τῆς ἁγίας
Ἐκκλησίας αὐτοῦ τελειώσῃ, ἵνα με ἰσχυροποιήσῃ καὶ δῷ τὴν
μετάνοιαν τοῖς δούλοις αὐτοῦ τοῖς ἐσκανδαλισμένοις, ἵνα δοξασθῇ τὸ ὄνομα αὐτοῦ τὸ μέγα καὶ ἔνδοξον, ὅτι με ἄξιον ἡγήσατο
τοῦ δεῖξαί μοι τὰ θαυμάσια αὐτοῦ. 4. καὶ δοξάζοντός μου
καὶ εὐχαριστοῦντος αὐτῷ, ὡς ἦχος φωνῆς μοι ἀπεκρίθη· Μὴ
διψυχήσεις, Ἑρμᾶ. ἐν ἐμαυτῷ ἠρξάμην διαλογίζεσθαι καὶ
λέγειν· Ἐγὼ τί ἔχω διψυχῆσαι, οὕτω τεθεμελιωμένος ὑπὸ
τοῦ Κυρίου καὶ ἰδὼν ἔνδοξα πράγματα; 5. καὶ προσέβην
μικρόν, ἀδελφοί, καὶ ἰδοὺ βλέπω κονιορτὸν ὡς εἰς τὸν οὐρανόν,
καὶ ἠρξάμην λέγειν ἐν ἑαυτῷ· Μήποτε κτήνη ἔρχονται καὶ
κονιορτὸν ἐγείρουσιν; οὕτω γὰρ ἦν ἀπ' ἐμοῦ ὡς ἀπὸ σταδίου.
6. γινομένου μείζονος καὶ μείζονος κονιορτοῦ ὑπενόησα εἶναί
τι θεῖον· μικρὸν ἐξέλαμψεν ὁ ἥλιος, καὶ ἰδοὺ βλέπω θηρίον
μέγιστον ὡσεὶ κῆτός τι, καὶ ἐκ τοῦ στόματος αὐτοῦ ἀκρίδες
πύριναι ἐξεπορεύοντο. ἦν δὲ τὸ θηρίον τῷ μήκει ὡσεὶ ποδῶν
ἑκατόν, τὴν δὲ κεφαλὴν εἶχεν ὡς κεράμου. 7. καὶ ἠρξάμην
κλαίειν καὶ ἐρωτᾶν τὸν Κύριον ἵνα με λυτρώσηται ἐξ αὐτοῦ.
καὶ ἐπανεμνήσθην τοῦ ῥήματος οὗ ἀκηκόειν· Μὴ διψυχήσεις,

4. i. 1 τῆς θλίψεως τῆς ἐπερχομένης] [L₁E]; τῶν θλίψεων τῶν ἐπερχομένων A;
usque ad advenientem diem L₂ (ἕως τῆς ἐπερχομένης); def. ℵ.

Ἑρμᾷ. 8. ἐνδυσάμενος οὖν, ἀδελφοί, τὴν πίστιν τοῦ Κυρίου καὶ μνησθεὶς ὧν ἐδίδαξέν με μεγαλείων, θαρσήσας εἰς τὸ θηρίον ἐμαυτὸν ἔδωκα. οὕτω δὲ ἤρχετο τὸ θηρίον ῥοίζῳ, ὥστε δύνασθαι αὐτὸ πόλιν λυμᾶναι. 9. ἔρχομαι ἐγγὺς αὐτοῦ, καὶ τὸ τηλικοῦτο κῆτος ἐκτείνει ἑαυτὸ χαμαὶ καὶ οὐδὲν εἰ μὴ τὴν γλῶσσαν προέβαλλεν, καὶ ὅλως οὐκ ἐκινήθη μέχρις ὅτου παρῆλθον αὐτό· 10. εἶχεν δὲ τὸ θηρίον ἐπὶ τῆς κεφαλῆς χρώματα τέσσαρα· μέλαν, εἶτα πυροειδὲς καὶ αἱματῶδες, εἶτα χρυσοῦν, εἶτα λευκόν.

11. Μετὰ δὲ τὸ παρελθεῖν με τὸ θηρίον καὶ προελθεῖν ὡσεὶ πόδας τριάκοντα, ἰδοὺ ὑπαντᾷ μοι παρθένος κεκοσμημένη ὡς ἐκ νυμφῶνος ἐκπορευομένη, ὅλη ἐν λευκοῖς καὶ ὑποδήμασιν λευκοῖς, κατακεκαλυμμένη ἕως τοῦ μετώπου, ἐν μίτρᾳ δὲ ἦν ἡ κατακάλυψις αὐτῆς· εἶχεν δὲ τὰς τρίχας αὐτῆς λευκάς. 2. ἔγνων ἐγὼ ἐκ τῶν προτέρων ὁραμάτων ὅτι ἡ Ἐκκλησία ἐστίν, καὶ ἱλαρώτερος ἐγενόμην. ἀσπάζεταί με λέγουσα· Χαῖρε σύ, ἄνθρωπε· καὶ ἐγὼ αὐτὴν ἀντησπασάμην· Κυρία, χαῖρε. 3. ἀποκριθεῖσά μοι λέγει· Οὐδέν σοι ἀπήντησεν; λέγω αὐτῇ· Κυρία, τηλικοῦτο θηρίον, δυνάμενον λαοὺς διαφθεῖραι· ἀλλὰ τῇ δυνάμει τοῦ Κυρίου καὶ τῇ πολυσπλαγχνίᾳ αὐτοῦ ἐξέφυγον αὐτό. 4. Καλῶς ἐξέφυγες, φησίν, ὅτι τὴν μέριμνάν cf. Ps. lv. σου ἐπὶ τὸν Θεὸν ἐπέριψας καὶ τὴν καρδίαν σου ἤνοιξας πρὸς 22. 1 Pet. v. 7. τὸν Κύριον, πιστεύσας ὅτι δι' οὐδενὸς δύνῃ σωθῆναι εἰ μὴ διὰ τοῦ μεγάλου καὶ ἐνδόξου ὀνόματος. διὰ τοῦτο ὁ Κύριος ἀπέστειλεν τὸν ἄγγελον αὐτοῦ τὸν ἐπὶ τῶν θηρίων ὄντα, οὗ τὸ ὄνομά ἐστιν Σεγρί, καὶ ἐΝέφραξεΝ τὸ cτόμα αϒτοϒ, ἵΝΑ μΗ cε Daniel λΥμάΝΗ. μεγάλην θλῖψιν ἐκπέφευγας διὰ τὴν πίστιν σου, vi. 22. καὶ ὅτι τηλικοῦτο θηρίον ἰδὼν οὐκ ἐδιψύχησας· 5. ὕπαγε οὖν xi. 33. καὶ ἐξήγησαι τοῖς ἐκλεκτοῖς τοῦ Κυρίου τὰ μεγαλεῖα αὐτοῦ, καὶ εἰπὲ αὐτοῖς ὅτι τὸ θηρίον τοῦτο τύπος ἐστὶν θλίψεως τῆς μελλούσης τῆς μεγάλης· ἐὰν οὖν προετοιμάσησθε καὶ μετανοήσητε ἐξ ὅλης καρδίας ὑμῶν πρὸς τὸν Κύριον, δυνήσεσθε

ii. 4 Σεγρί] conj. Harris (cf. Dan. vi. 22 רגס); Θεγει א*; Θεγρει אᴵ; Θεγρί A; Tegri L₂; Tegeri E; Hegrin L₁.

ἐκφυγεῖν αὐτήν, ἐὰν ἡ καρδία ὑμῶν γένηται καθαρὰ καὶ
ἄμωμος, καὶ τὰς λοιπὰς τῆς ζωῆς ἡμέρας ὑμῶν δουλεύσητε

cf. Ps. lv.
22.
τῷ Κυρίῳ ἀμέμπτως. ἐπιρίψατε τὰς μερίμνας ὑμῶν ἐπὶ τὸν

1 Pet. v. 7. Κύριον, καὶ αὐτὸς κατορθώσει αὐτάς. 6. πιστεύσατε τῷ
Κυρίῳ, οἱ δίψυχοι, ὅτι πάντα δύναται καὶ ἀποστρέφει τὴν
ὀργὴν αὐτοῦ ἀφ᾽ ὑμῶν καὶ ἐξαποστέλλει μάστιγας ὑμῖν τοῖς
διψύχοις. οὐαὶ τοῖς ἀκούσασιν τὰ ῥήματα ταῦτα καὶ παρα-

cf. S. Matt. κούσασιν· αἱρετώτερον ἦν αὐτοῖς τὸ μὴ γεννηθῆναι.
xxvi. 24 ;
S. Mark
xiv. 21.
III. Ἡρώτησα αὐτὴν περὶ τῶν τεσσάρων χρωμάτων ὧν
εἶχεν τὸ θηρίον εἰς τὴν κεφαλήν. ἡ δὲ ἀποκριθεῖσά μοι λέγει·
Πάλιν περίεργος εἶ περὶ τοιούτων πραγμάτων. Ναί, φημί,
κυρία· γνώρισόν μοι τί ἐστιν ταῦτα. 2. Ἄκουε, φησίν· τὸ
μὲν μέλαν οὗτος ὁ κόσμος ἐστίν, ἐν ᾧ κατοικεῖτε. 3. τὸ δὲ
πυροειδὲς καὶ αἱματῶδες, ὅτι δεῖ τὸν κόσμον τοῦτον δι᾽ αἵματος
καὶ πυρὸς ἀπόλλυσθαι· 4. τὸ δὲ χρυσοῦν μέρος ὑμεῖς ἐστε

cf. 1 Pet. i.
7.
οἱ ἐκφυγόντες τὸν κόσμον τοῦτον. ὥσπερ γὰρ τὸ χρυσίον
δοκιμάζεται διὰ τοῦ πυρὸς καὶ εὔχρηστον γίνεται, οὕτως καὶ
ὑμεῖς δοκιμάζεσθε [οἱ κατοικοῦντες] ἐν αὐτοῖς. οἱ οὖν μεί-
ναντες καὶ πυρωθέντες ὑπ᾽ αὐτοῦ καθαρισθήσεσθε. ὥσπερ
τὸ χρυσίον ἀποβάλλει τὴν σκωρίαν αὐτοῦ, οὕτω καὶ ὑμεῖς
ἀποβαλεῖτε πᾶσαν λύπην καὶ στενοχωρίαν, καὶ καθαρισθήσεσθε καὶ χρήσιμοι ἔσεσθε εἰς τὴν οἰκοδομὴν τοῦ πύργου.
5. τὸ δὲ λευκὸν μέρος ὁ αἰὼν ὁ ἐπερχόμενός ἐστιν, ἐν ᾧ κατοικήσουσιν οἱ ἐκλεκτοὶ τοῦ θεοῦ· ὅτι ἄσπιλοι καὶ καθαροὶ
ἔσονται οἱ ἐκλελεγμένοι ὑπὸ τοῦ Θεοῦ εἰς ζωὴν αἰώνιον.
6. σὺ οὖν μὴ διαλίπῃς λαλῶν εἰς τὰ ὦτα τῶν ἁγίων. ἔχετε
καὶ τὸν τύπον τῆς θλίψεως τῆς ἐρχομένης μεγάλης. ἐὰν δὲ
ὑμεῖς θελήσητε, οὐδὲν ἔσται. μνημονεύετε τὰ προγεγραμμένα.
7. ταῦτα εἴπασα ἀπῆλθεν, καὶ οὐκ εἶδον ποίῳ τόπῳ ἀπῆλθεν·
ψόφος γὰρ ἐγένετο· κἀγὼ ἐπεστράφην εἰς τὰ ὀπίσω φοβηθείς,
δοκῶν ὅτι τὸ θηρίον ἔρχεται.

Ἀποκάλυψις εʹ

Προσευξαμένου μου ἐν τῷ οἴκῳ καὶ καθίσαντος εἰς τὴν κλίνην εἰσῆλθεν ἀνήρ τις ἔνδοξος τῇ ὄψει, σχήματι ποιμενικῷ, περικείμενος δέρμα λευκόν, καὶ πήραν ἔχων ἐπὶ τῶν ὤμων καὶ ῥάβδον εἰς τὴν χεῖρα. καὶ ἠσπάσατό με, κἀγὼ ἀντησπασάμην αὐτόν. 2. καὶ εὐθὺς παρεκάθισέν μοι καὶ λέγει μοι· Ἀπεστάλην ὑπὸ τοῦ σεμνοτάτου ἀγγέλου, ἵνα μετὰ σοῦ οἰκήσω τὰς λοιπὰς ἡμέρας τῆς ζωῆς σου. 3. ἔδοξα ἐγὼ ὅτι πάρεστιν ἐκπειράζων με, καὶ λέγω αὐτῷ· Σὺ γὰρ τίς εἶ; ἐγὼ γάρ, φημί, γινώσκω ᾧ παρεδόθην. λέγει μοι· Οὐκ ἐπιγινώσκεις με; Οὔ, φημί. Ἐγώ, φησίν, εἰμὶ ὁ ποιμὴν ᾧ παρεδόθης. 4. ἔτι λαλοῦντος αὐτοῦ ἠλλοιώθη ἡ ἰδέα αὐτοῦ, καὶ ἐπέγνων αὐτόν, ὅτι ἐκεῖνος ἦν ᾧ παρεδόθην, καὶ εὐθὺς συνεχύθην, καὶ φόβος με ἔλαβεν, καὶ ὅλος συνεκόπην ἀπὸ τῆς λύπης, ὅτι οὕτως αὐτῷ ἀπεκρίθην πονηρῶς καὶ ἀφρόνως. 5. ὁ δὲ ἀποκριθείς μοι λέγει· Μὴ συγχύννου, ἀλλὰ ἰσχυροποιοῦ ἐν ταῖς ἐντολαῖς μου, αἷς σοι μέλλω ἐντέλλεσθαι. ἀπεστάλην γάρ, φησίν, ἵνα ἃ εἶδες πρότερον πάντα σοι πάλιν δείξω, αὐτὰ τὰ κεφάλαια τὰ ὄντα ὑμῖν σύμφορα. πρῶτον πάντων τὰς ἐντολάς μου γράψον καὶ τὰς παραβολάς· τὰ δὲ ἕτερα, καθώς σοι δείξω, οὕτως γράψεις· διὰ τοῦτο, φησίν, ἐντέλλομαί σοι πρῶτον γράψαι τὰς ἐντολὰς καὶ παραβολάς, ἵνα ὑπὸ χεῖρα ἀναγινώσκῃς αὐτὰς καὶ δυνηθῇς φυλάξαι αὐτάς. 6. ἔγραψα οὖν τὰς ἐντολὰς καὶ παραβολάς, καθὼς ἐνετείλατό μοι. 7. ἐὰν οὖν ἀκούσαντες αὐτὰς φυλάξητε καὶ ἐν αὐταῖς πορευθῆτε καὶ ἐργάσησθε αὐτὰς ἐν καθαρᾷ καρδίᾳ ἀπολήμψεσθε ἀπὸ τοῦ Κυρίου ὅσα ἐπηγγείλατο ὑμῖν· ἐὰν δὲ ἀκούσαντες μὴ μετανοήσητε, ἀλλ᾽ ἔτι προσθῆτε ταῖς ἁμαρτίαις ὑμῶν, ἀπολήμψεσθε παρὰ τοῦ Κυρίου τὰ ἐναντία. ταῦτά μοι πάντα οὕτως γράψαι ὁ ποιμὴν ἐνετείλατο, ὁ ἄγγελος τῆς μετανοίας.

Ἐντολὴ α΄

Πρῶτον πάντων πίστευσον ὅτι εἷς ἐστὶν ὁ Θεός, ὁ τὰ
πάντα κτίσας καὶ καταρτίσας, καὶ ποιήσας ἐκ τοῦ μὴ ὄντος
εἰς τὸ εἶναι τὰ πάντα, καὶ πάντα χωρῶν, μόνος δὲ ἀχώρητος
ὤν. 2. πίστευσον οὖν αὐτῷ καὶ φοβήθητι αὐτόν, φοβηθεὶς δὲ
ἐγκράτευσαι. ταῦτα φύλασσε καὶ ἀποβαλεῖς πᾶσαν πονηρίαν
ἀπὸ σεαυτοῦ καὶ ἐνδύσῃ πᾶσαν ἀρετὴν δικαιοσύνης καὶ ζήσῃ
τῷ Θεῷ, ἐὰν φυλάξῃς τὴν ἐντολὴν ταύτην.

Ἐντολὴ β΄

Λέγει μοι· Ἁπλότητα ἔχε καὶ ἄκακος γίνου καὶ ἔσῃ ὡς
τὰ νήπια τὰ μὴ γινώσκοντα τὴν πονηρίαν τὴν ἀπολλύουσαν
τὴν ζωὴν τῶν ἀνθρώπων. 2. πρῶτον μὲν μηδενὸς καταλάλει,
μηδὲ ἡδέως ἄκουε καταλαλοῦντος· εἰ δὲ μή, καὶ σὺ ὁ ἀκούων
ἔνοχος ἔσῃ τῆς ἁμαρτίας τοῦ καταλαλοῦντος, ἐὰν πιστεύσῃς
τῇ καταλαλίᾳ ᾗ ἂν ἀκούσῃς· πιστεύσας γὰρ καὶ σὺ αὐτὸς
ἕξεις κατὰ τοῦ ἀδελφοῦ σου. οὕτως οὖν ἔνοχος ἔσῃ τῆς
ἁμαρτίας τοῦ καταλαλοῦντος. 3. πονηρὰ ἡ καταλαλία, ἀκα-
τάστατον δαιμόνιόν ἐστιν, μηδέποτε εἰρηνεῦον, ἀλλὰ πάντοτε
ἐν διχοστασίαις κατοικοῦν. ἀπέχου οὖν ἀπ᾽ αὐτοῦ, καὶ εὐθη-
νίαν πάντοτε ἕξεις μετὰ πάντων. 4. ἔνδυσαι δὲ τὴν σεμνότητα, ἐν ᾗ οὐδὲν πρόσκομμά ἐστιν πονηρόν, ἀλλὰ πάντα
ὁμαλὰ καὶ ἱλαρά. ἐργάζου τὸ ἀγαθόν, καὶ ἐκ τῶν κόπων σου,
ὧν ὁ Θεὸς δίδωσίν σοι, πᾶσιν ὑστερουμένοις δίδου ἁπλῶς, μὴ
διστάζων τίνι δῷς ἢ τίνι μὴ δῷς. πᾶσιν δίδου· πᾶσιν γὰρ ὁ
Θεὸς δίδοσθαι θέλει ἐκ τῶν ἰδίων δωρημάτων. 5. οἱ οὖν λαμβάνοντες ἀποδώσουσιν λόγον τῷ Θεῷ, διατί ἔλαβον καὶ εἰς
τί· οἱ μὲν γὰρ λαμβάνοντες θλιβόμενοι οὐ δικασθήσονται, οἱ
δὲ ἐν ὑποκρίσει λαμβάνοντες τίσουσιν δίκην. 6. ὁ οὖν διδοὺς
ἀθῷός ἐστιν· ὡς γὰρ ἔλαβεν παρὰ τοῦ Κυρίου τὴν διακονίαν
τελέσαι, ἁπλῶς αὐτὴν ἐτέλεσεν, μηθὲν διακρίνων τίνι δῷ ἢ μὴ
δῷ. ἐγένετο οὖν ἡ διακονία αὕτη ἁπλῶς τελεσθεῖσα ἔνδοξος
παρὰ τῷ Θεῷ. ὁ οὖν οὕτως ἁπλῶς διακονῶν τῷ Θεῷ ζήσεται.

7. φύλασσε οὖν τὴν ἐντολὴν ταύτην, ὥς σοι λελάληκα, ἵνα ἡ
μετάνοιά σου καὶ τοῦ οἴκου σου ἐν ἁπλότητι εὑρεθῇ, καὶ ἡ
καρδία [σου] καθαρὰ καὶ ἀμίαντος.

Ἐντολὴ γ΄

Πάλιν μοι λέγει· Ἀλήθειαν ἀγάπα, καὶ πᾶσα ἀλήθεια ἐκ
τοῦ στόματός σου ἐκπορευέσθω, ἵνα τὸ πνεῦμα, ὃ ὁ Θεὸς
κατῴκισεν ἐν τῇ σαρκὶ ταύτῃ, ἀληθὲς εὑρεθῇ παρὰ πᾶσιν
ἀνθρώποις, καὶ οὕτως δοξασθήσεται ὁ Κύριος ὁ ἐν σοὶ κατοι-
κῶν· ὅτι ὁ Κύριος ἀληθινὸς ἐν παντὶ ῥήματι, καὶ οὐδὲν παρ᾽   cf. 1 John
αὐτῷ ψεῦδος· 2. οἱ οὖν ψευδόμενοι ἀθετοῦσι τὸν Κύριον καὶ   ii. 27.
γίνονται ἀποστερηταὶ τοῦ Κυρίου, μὴ παραδιδόντες αὐτῷ τὴν
παρακαταθήκην ἣν ἔλαβον. ἔλαβον γὰρ παρ᾽ αὐτοῦ πνεῦμα
ἄψευστον. τοῦτο ἐὰν ψευδὲς ἀποδώσωσιν, ἐμίαναν τὴν ἐντολὴν τοῦ Κυρίου καὶ ἐγένοντο ἀποστερηταί. 3. ταῦτα οὖν
ἀκούσας ἐγὼ ἔκλαυσα λίαν. ἰδὼν δέ με κλαίοντα λέγει· Τί
κλαίεις; Ὅτι, φημί, κύριε, οὐκ οἶδα εἰ δύναμαι σωθῆναι.
Διατί; φησίν. Οὐδέπω γάρ, φημί, κύριε, ἐν τῇ ἐμῇ ζωῇ
ἀληθὲς ἐλάλησα ῥῆμα, ἀλλὰ πάντοτε πανοῦργος ἔζησα μετὰ
πάντων, καὶ τὸ ψεῦδός μου ἀληθὲς ἐπέδειξα παρὰ πᾶσιν
ἀνθρώποις· καὶ οὐδέποτέ μοι οὐδεὶς ἀντεῖπεν, ἀλλ᾽ ἐπιστεύθη
τῷ λόγῳ μου. πῶς οὖν, φημί, κύριε, δύναμαι ζῆσαι ταῦτα
πράξας; 4. Σὺ μέν, φησί, καλῶς καὶ ἀληθῶς φρονεῖς· ἔδει
γάρ σε ὡς Θεοῦ δοῦλον ἐν ἀληθείᾳ πορεύεσθαι καὶ πονηρὰν
συνείδησιν μετὰ τοῦ πνεύματος τῆς ἀληθείας μὴ κατοικεῖν,
μηδὲ λύπην ἐπάγειν τῷ πνεύματι τῷ σεμνῷ καὶ ἀληθεῖ.
Οὐδέποτε, φημί, κύριε, τοιαῦτα ῥήματα ἀκριβῶς ἤκουσα.
5. Νῦν οὖν, φησίν, ἀκούεις· φύλασσε αὐτά, ἵνα καὶ τὰ πρότερον ἃ ἐλάλησας ψεύδη ἐν ταῖς πραγματείαις σου, τούτων
εὑρεθέντων ἀληθινῶν, κἀκεῖνα πιστὰ γένηται· δύναται γὰρ

2. 7 τὴν ἐντολὴν ταύτην] conj. Gebhardt in marg. [L₁L₂E]; τὰς ἐντόλας
ταύτας A.   ἡ καρδία σου] conj. Hilgenfeld [L₁L₂]; ἀκακία A; om. E; def. א.
3. 1 κατῴκισεν] conj. Gebhardt [L₁L₂E] Ant.; ··τωκησε א; κατῴκησεν A.   3 εἰ δύναμαι] [L₁L₂E]; οὐδὲν ἀγαθόν A; def. א.   ἔζησα] conj.
Gebhardt in marg. [L₁L₂E]; ἐλάλησα A; def. א.

κἀκεῖνα πιστὰ γενέσθαι. ἐὰν ταῦτα φυλάξῃς καὶ ἀπὸ τοῦ
νῦν πᾶσαν ἀλήθειαν λαλήσῃς, δυνήσῃ σεαυτῷ ζωὴν περι-
ποιήσασθαι. καὶ ὃς ἂν ἀκούσῃ τὴν ἐντολὴν ταύτην καὶ
ἀπέχηται τοῦ πονηροτάτου ψεύσματος, ζήσεται τῷ Θεῷ.

Ἐντολὴ δ′

I. Ἐντέλλομαί σοι, φησίν, φυλάσσειν τὴν ἁγνείαν καὶ
μὴ ἀναβαινέτω σου ἐπὶ τὴν καρδίαν περὶ γυναικὸς ἀλλοτρίας
ἢ περὶ πορνείας τινὸς ἢ περὶ τοιούτων τινῶν ὁμοιωμάτων
πονηρῶν. τοῦτο γὰρ ποιῶν μεγάλην ἁμαρτίαν ἐργάζῃ. τῆς
δὲ σῆς μνημονεύων πάντοτε γυναικὸς οὐδέποτε διαμαρτήσεις.
2. ἐὰν γὰρ αὕτη ἡ ἐνθύμησις ἐπὶ [τὴν] καρδίαν σου ἀναβῇ,
διαμαρτήσεις, καὶ ἐὰν ἕτερα οὕτως πονηρά, ἁμαρτίαν ἐργάζῃ·
ἡ γὰρ ἐνθύμησις αὕτη Θεοῦ δούλῳ ἁμαρτία μεγάλη ἐστίν· ἐὰν
δέ τις ἐργάσηται τὸ ἔργον τὸ πονηρὸν τοῦτο, θάνατον ἑαυτῷ
κατεργάζεται. 3. βλέπε οὖν σύ· ἀπέχου ἀπὸ τῆς ἐνθυμήσεως
ταύτης· ὅπου γὰρ σεμνότης κατοικεῖ, ἐκεῖ ἀνομία οὐκ ὀφείλει
ἀναβαίνειν ἐπὶ καρδίαν ἀνδρὸς δικαίου. 4. λέγω αὐτῷ·
Κύριε, ἐπίτρεψόν μοι ὀλίγα ἐπερωτῆσαί σε. Λέγε, φησίν.
Κύριε, φημί, εἰ γυναῖκα ἔχων τις πιστὴν ἐν Κυρίῳ [καὶ] ταύτην
εὕρῃ ἐν μοιχείᾳ τινί, ἆρα ἁμαρτάνει ὁ ἀνὴρ συνζῶν μετ᾽
αὐτῆς; 5. Ἄχρι τῆς ἀγνοίας, φησίν, οὐχ ἁμαρτάνει· ἐὰν δὲ
γνῷ ὁ ἀνὴρ τὴν ἁμαρτίαν αὐτῆς, καὶ μὴ μετανοήσῃ ἡ γυνή,
ἀλλ᾽ ἐπιμένῃ τῇ πορνείᾳ αὐτῆς, καὶ συνζῇ ὁ ἀνὴρ μετ᾽ αὐτῆς,
ἔνοχος γίνεται τῆς ἁμαρτίας αὐτῆς καὶ κοινωνὸς τῆς μοιχείας
αὐτῆς. 6. Τί οὖν, φημί, κύριε, ποιήσῃ ὁ ἀνήρ, ἐὰν ἐπιμείνῃ
τῷ πάθει τούτῳ ἡ γυνή; Ἀπολυσάτω, φησίν, αὐτήν, καὶ ὁ
cf. S. Matt.
xix. 9. ἀνὴρ ἐφ᾽ ἑαυτῷ μενέτω· ἐὰν δὲ ἀπολύσας τὴν γυναῖκα ἑτέραν
γαμήσῃ, καὶ αὐτὸς μοιχᾶται. 7. Ἐὰν οὖν, φημί, κύριε, μετὰ
τὸ ἀπολυθῆναι τὴν γυναῖκα μετανοήσῃ [ἡ γυνὴ] καὶ θελήσῃ
ἐπὶ τὸν ἑαυτῆς ἄνδρα ὑποστρέψαι, οὐ παραδεχθήσεται; 8.
Καὶ μήν, φησίν, ἐὰν μὴ παραδέξηται αὐτὴν ὁ ἀνήρ, ἁμαρτάνει
καὶ μεγάλην ἁμαρτίαν ἑαυτῷ ἐπισπᾶται, ἀλλὰ δεῖ παρα-

3. 5 ἀπέχηται] conj. Hilgenfeld; ··χη· ℵ; ἀφέξηται Α; dub. L₁L₂E.

δεχθῆναι τὸν ἡμαρτηκότα καὶ μετανοοῦντα· μὴ ἐπὶ πολὺ δέ·
τοῖς γὰρ δούλοις τοῦ Θεοῦ μετάνοιά ἐστιν μία. διὰ τὴν μετάνοιαν οὖν οὐκ ὀφείλει γαμεῖν ὁ ἀνήρ. αὕτη ἡ πρᾶξις ἐπὶ
γυναικὶ καὶ ἀνδρὶ κεῖται. 9. οὐ μόνον, φησί, μοιχεία ἐστίν,
ἐάν τις τὴν σάρκα αὐτοῦ μιάνῃ, ἀλλὰ καὶ ὃς ἂν τὰ ὁμοιώματα
ποιῇ τοῖς ἔθνεσιν, μοιχᾶται. ὥστε καὶ ἐν τοῖς τοιούτοις
ἔργοις ἐὰν ἐμμένῃ τις καὶ μὴ μετανοῇ, ἀπέχου ἀπ' αὐτοῦ καὶ
μὴ συνζῆθι αὐτῷ· εἰ δὲ μή, καὶ σὺ μέτοχος εἶ τῆς ἁμαρτίας
αὐτοῦ. 10. διὰ τοῦτο προσετάγη ὑμῖν ἐφ' ἑαυτοῖς μένειν,
εἴτε ἀνὴρ εἴτε γυνή· δύναται γὰρ ἐν τοῖς τοιούτοις μετάνοια
εἶναι. 11. ἐγὼ οὖν, φησίν, οὐ δίδωμι ἀφορμὴν ἵνα αὕτη ἡ
πρᾶξις οὕτως συντελῆται, ἀλλὰ εἰς τὸ μηκέτι ἁμαρτάνειν
τὸν ἡμαρτηκότα. περὶ δὲ τῆς προτέρας ἁμαρτίας αὐτοῦ
ἔστιν ὁ δυνάμενος ἴασιν δοῦναι· αὐτὸς γάρ ἐστιν ὁ ἔχων
πάντων τὴν ἐξουσίαν.

II. Ἠρώτησα αὐτὸν πάλιν λέγων· Ἐπεὶ ὁ Κύριος ἄξιόν
με ἡγήσατο ἵνα μετ' ἐμοῦ πάντοτε κατοικῇς, ὀλίγα μου
ῥήματα ἔτι ἀνασχοῦ, ἐπεὶ οὐ συνίω οὐδέν, καὶ ἡ καρδία μου
πεπώρωται ἀπὸ τῶν προτέρων μου πράξεων· συνέτισόν με,
ὅτι λίαν ἄφρων εἰμὶ καὶ ὅλως οὐθὲν νοῶ. 2. ἀποκριθείς μοι
λέγει· Ἐγώ, φησίν, ἐπὶ τῆς μετανοίας εἰμὶ καὶ πᾶσιν τοῖς
μετανοοῦσιν σύνεσιν δίδωμι. ἢ οὐ δοκεῖ σοι, φησίν, αὐτὸ
τοῦτο τὸ μετανοῆσαι σύνεσιν εἶναι; τὸ μετανοῆσαι, φησί,
σύνεσίς ἐστιν μεγάλη. συνίει γὰρ [ὁ ἀνὴρ] ὁ ἁμαρτήσας ὅτι
πεποίηκεν τὸ πονηρὸν ἔμπροσθεν τοῦ Κυρίου, καὶ ἀναβαίνει
ἐπὶ τὴν καρδίαν αὐτοῦ ἡ πρᾶξις ἣν ἔπραξεν, καὶ μετανοεῖ καὶ
οὐκέτι ἐργάζεται τὸ πονηρόν, ἀλλὰ τὸ ἀγαθὸν πολυτελῶς
ἐργάζεται, καὶ ταπεινοῖ τὴν ἑαυτοῦ ψυχὴν καὶ βασανίζει, ὅτι
ἥμαρτεν. βλέπεις οὖν ὅτι ἡ μετάνοια σύνεσίς ἐστιν μεγάλη.
3. Διὰ τοῦτο οὖν, φημί, κύριε, ἐξακριβάζομαι παρὰ σοῦ
πάντα· πρῶτον μὲν ὅτι ἁμαρτωλός εἰμι, εἶτα ἀγνοῶ ποῖα
ἔργα ἐργαζόμενος ζήσομαι, ὅτι πολλαί μου εἰσὶν αἱ ἁμαρτίαι

---

ii. 3 εἶτα ἀγνοῶ] conj. Harmer [L₂]; ἵνα γνῶ AL₁; scio E; def. א.

καὶ ποικίλαι. 4. Ζήσῃ, φησίν, ἐὰν τὰς ἐντολάς μου φυλάξῃς καὶ πορευθῇς ἐν αὐταῖς· καὶ ὃς ἂν ἀκούσας τὰς ἐντολὰς ταύτας φυλάξῃ, ζήσεται τῷ Θεῷ.

III. Ἔτι, φημί, κύριε, προσθήσω τοῦ ἐπερωτῆσαι. Λέγε, φησίν· Ἤκουσα, φημί, κύριε, παρά τινων διδασκάλων, ὅτι ἑτέρα μετάνοια οὐκ ἔστιν εἰ μὴ ἐκείνη, ὅτε εἰς ὕδωρ κατέβημεν καὶ ἐλάβομεν ἄφεσιν ἁμαρτιῶν ἡμῶν τῶν προτέρων. 2. λέγει μοι· Καλῶς ἤκουσας· οὕτω γὰρ ἔχει. ἔδει γὰρ τὸν εἰληφότα ἄφεσιν ἁμαρτιῶν μηκέτι ἁμαρτάνειν, ἀλλ' ἐν ἁγνείᾳ κατοικεῖν. 3. ἐπεὶ δὲ πάντα ἐξακριβάζῃ, καὶ τοῦτό σοι δηλώσω, μὴ διδοὺς ἀφορμὴν τοῖς μέλλουσι πιστεύειν ἢ τοῖς νῦν πιστεύσασιν εἰς τὸν Κύριον. οἱ γὰρ νῦν πιστεύσαντες ἢ μέλλοντες πιστεύειν μετάνοιαν ἁμαρτιῶν οὐκ ἔχουσιν, ἄφεσιν δὲ ἔχουσι τῶν προτέρων ἁμαρτιῶν αὐτῶν. 4. τοῖς οὖν κληθεῖσι πρὸ τούτων τῶν ἡμερῶν ἔθηκεν ὁ Κύριος μετάνοιαν. καρδιογνώστης γὰρ ὢν ὁ Κύριος, καὶ πάντα προγινώσκων, ἔγνω τὴν ἀσθένειαν τῶν ἀνθρώπων καὶ τὴν πολυπλοκίαν τοῦ διαβόλου, ὅτι ποιήσει τι κακὸν τοῖς δούλοις τοῦ Θεοῦ καὶ πονηρεύσεται εἰς αὐτούς· 5. πολυεύσπλαγχνος οὖν ὢν ὁ Κύριος ἐσπλαγχνίσθη ἐπὶ τὴν ποίησιν αὐτοῦ καὶ ἔθηκεν τὴν μετάνοιαν ταύτην, καὶ ἐμοὶ ἡ ἐξουσία τῆς μετανοίας ταύτης ἐδόθη. 6. ἀλλὰ ἐγώ σοι λέγω, φησί· μετὰ τὴν κλῆσιν ἐκείνην τὴν μεγάλην καὶ σεμνὴν ἐάν τις ἐκπειρασθεὶς ὑπὸ τοῦ διαβόλου ἁμαρτήσῃ, μίαν μετάνοιαν ἔχει. ἐὰν δὲ ὑπὸ χεῖρα ἁμαρτάνῃ καὶ μετανοήσῃ, ἀσύμφορόν ἐστι τῷ ἀνθρώπῳ τῷ τοιούτῳ· δυσκόλως γὰρ ζήσεται. 7. λέγω αὐτῷ· Ἐζωοποιήθην ταῦτα παρὰ σοῦ ἀκούσας οὕτως ἀκριβῶς· οἶδα γὰρ ὅτι, ἐὰν μηκέτι προσθήσω ταῖς ἁμαρτίαις μου, σωθήσομαι. Σωθήσῃ, φησί, καὶ πάντες ὅσοι ἐὰν ταῦτα ποιήσωσιν.

IV. Ἠρώτησα αὐτὸν πάλιν λέγων· Κύριε, ἐπεὶ ἅπαξ

4. iii. 3 μετάνοιαν ἁμαρτιῶν] [L₁E]; μεγάλην ἁμαρτίαν A; al. L₂; def. ℵ.
6 φησί] ℵ finally breaks off in the middle of this word.   κλῆσιν] L₁L₂E;
pref. πνεύματος A.   μετανοήσῃ] L₁L₂E ; pref. οὐ A.   τῷ τοιούτῳ] conj.
Hilgenfeld [L₁L₂E]; τὸ τοιοῦτον A.   iv. 1 κύριε] conj. Hilgenfeld [L₁L₂E];
καὶ A.

ἀνέχῃ μου, ἔτι μοι καὶ τοῦτο δήλωσον. Λέγε, φησίν. Ἐὰν
γυνή, φημί, κύριε, ἢ πάλιν ἀνήρ τις κοιμηθῇ, καὶ γαμήσῃ τις
ἐξ αὐτῶν, μήτι ἁμαρτάνει ὁ γαμῶν; 2. Οὐχ ἁμαρτάνει,
φησίν· ἐὰν δὲ ἐφ' ἑαυτῷ μείνῃ τις, περισσοτέραν ἑαυτῷ τιμὴν cf. 1 Cor.
καὶ μεγάλην δόξαν περιποιεῖται πρὸς τὸν Κύριον· ἐὰν δὲ καὶ vii. 40.
γαμήσῃ, οὐχ ἁμαρτάνει. 3. τήρει οὖν τὴν ἁγνείαν καὶ τὴν
σεμνότητα, καὶ ζήσῃ τῷ Θεῷ. ταῦτά σοι ὅσα λαλῶ καὶ
μέλλω λαλεῖν, φύλασσε ἀπὸ τοῦ νῦν, ἀφ' ἧς μοι παρεδόθης
ἡμέρας, καὶ εἰς τὸν οἶκόν σου κατοικήσω. 4. τοῖς δὲ προτέροις σου παραπτώμασιν ἄφεσις ἔσται, ἐὰν τὰς ἐντολάς μου
φυλάξῃς· καὶ πᾶσι δὲ ἄφεσις ἔσται, ἐὰν τὰς ἐντολάς μου
ταύτας φυλάξωσι καὶ πορευθῶσιν ἐν τῇ ἁγνότητι ταύτῃ.

Ἐντολὴ ε΄

I. Μακρόθυμος, φησί, γίνου καὶ συνετός, καὶ πάντων τῶν
πονηρῶν ἔργων κατακυριεύσεις καὶ ἐργάσῃ πᾶσαν δικαιοσύνην. 2. ἐὰν γὰρ μακρόθυμος ἔσῃ, τὸ πνεῦμα τὸ ἅγιον τὸ
κατοικοῦν ἐν σοὶ καθαρὸν ἔσται, μὴ ἐπισκοτούμενον ὑπὸ ἑτέρου πονηροῦ πνεύματος, ἀλλ' ἐν εὐρυχώρῳ κατοικοῦν ἀγαλλιάσεται καὶ εὐφρανθήσεται μετὰ τοῦ σκεύους ἐν ᾧ κατοικεῖ,
καὶ λειτουργήσει τῷ Θεῷ ἐν ἱλαρότητι πολλῇ, ἔχον τὴν εὐθη-
νίαν ἐν ἑαυτῷ. 3. ἐὰν δὲ ὀξυχολία τις ἐπέλθῃ, εὐθὺς τὸ
πνεῦμα τὸ ἅγιον, τρυφερὸν ὄν, στενοχωρεῖται, μὴ ἔχον [τὸν]
τόπον καθαρόν, καὶ ζητεῖ ἀποστῆναι ἐκ τοῦ τόπου· πνίγεται
γὰρ ὑπὸ τοῦ πονηροῦ πνεύματος, μὴ ἔχον τόπον λειτουργῆσαι
τῷ Κυρίῳ καθὼς βούλεται, μιαινόμενον ὑπὸ τῆς ὀξυχολίας.
ἐν γὰρ τῇ μακροθυμίᾳ ὁ Κύριος κατοικεῖ, ἐν δὲ τῇ ὀξυχολίᾳ ὁ
διάβολος. 4. ἀμφότερα οὖν τὰ πνεύματα ἐπὶ τὸ αὐτὸ κατοικοῦντα, ἀσύμφορόν ἐστιν καὶ πονηρὸν τῷ ἀνθρώπῳ ἐκείνῳ ἐν
ᾧ κατοικοῦσιν. 5. ἐὰν γὰρ λαβὼν ἀψίνθιον μικρὸν εἰς κεράμιον μέλιτος ἐπιχέῃς, οὐχὶ ὅλον τὸ μέλι ἀφανίζεται, καὶ
τοσοῦτον μέλι ὑπὸ τοῦ ἐλαχίστου ἀψινθίου ἀπόλλυται καὶ
ἀπόλλυσι τὴν γλυκύτητα τοῦ μέλιτος, καὶ οὐκέτι τὴν αὐτὴν

iv. 2 ἐφ'] conj. Hilgenfeld [L₁E]; ἐν A; dub. L₂.

χάριν ἔχει παρὰ τῷ δεσπότῃ, ὅτι ἐπικράνθη καὶ τὴν χρῆσιν αὐτοῦ ἀπώλεσεν; ἐὰν δὲ εἰς τὸ μέλι μὴ βληθῇ τὸ ἀψίνθιον, γλυκὺ εὑρίσκεται τὸ μέλι καὶ εὔχρηστον γίνεται τῷ δεσπότῃ αὐτοῦ. 6. βλέπεις [οὖν] ὅτι ἡ μακροθυμία γλυκυτάτη ἐστὶν ὑπὲρ τὸ μέλι καὶ εὔχρηστός ἐστι τῷ Κυρίῳ, καὶ ἐν αὐτῇ κατοικεῖ. ἡ δὲ ὀξυχολία πικρὰ καὶ ἄχρηστός ἐστιν. ἐὰν οὖν μιγῇ ἡ ὀξυχολία τῇ μακροθυμίᾳ, μιαίνεται ἡ μακροθυμία, καὶ οὐκ εὔχρηστός ἐστι τῷ Θεῷ ἡ ἔντευξις αὐτοῦ. 7. Ἤθελον, φημί, κύριε, γνῶναι τὴν ἐνέργειαν τῆς ὀξυχολίας, ἵνα φυλάξωμαι ἀπ᾽ αὐτῆς. Καὶ μήν, φησίν, ἐὰν μὴ φυλάξῃ ἀπ᾽ αὐτῆς σὺ καὶ ὁ οἶκός σου, ἀπώλεσάς σου τὴν πᾶσαν ἐλπίδα. ἀλλὰ φύλαξαι ἀπ᾽ αὐτῆς· ἐγὼ γὰρ μετὰ σοῦ εἰμί. καὶ πάντες δὲ ἀφέξονται ἀπ᾽ αὐτῆς, ὅσοι ἂν μετανοήσωσιν ἐξ ὅλης τῆς καρδίας αὐτῶν· μετ᾽ αὐτῶν γὰρ ἔσομαι καὶ συντηρήσω αὐτούς· ἐδικαιώθησαν γὰρ πάντες ὑπὸ τοῦ σεμνοτάτου ἀγγέλου.

II. Ἄκουε νῦν, φησί, τὴν ἐνέργειαν τῆς ὀξυχολίας, πῶς πονηρά ἐστι, καὶ πῶς τοὺς δούλους τοῦ Θεοῦ καταστρέφει τῇ ἑαυτῆς ἐνεργείᾳ, καὶ πῶς ἀποπλανᾷ αὐτοὺς ἀπὸ τῆς δικαιοσύνης· οὐκ ἀποπλανᾷ δὲ τοὺς πλήρεις ὄντας ἐν τῇ πίστει, οὐδὲ ἐνεργῆσαι δύναται εἰς αὐτούς, ὅτι ἡ δύναμις τοῦ Κυρίου μετ᾽ αὐτῶν ἐστίν· ἀποπλανᾷ δὲ τοὺς ἀποκένους καὶ διψύχους ὄντας. 2. ὅταν γὰρ ἴδῃ τοὺς τοιούτους ἀνθρώπους εὐσταθοῦντας, παρεμβάλλει ἑαυτὴν εἰς τὴν καρδίαν τοῦ ἀνθρώπου, καὶ ἐκ τοῦ μηδενὸς ὁ ἀνὴρ ἢ ἡ γυνὴ πικραίνεται ἕνεκεν βιωτικῶν πραγμάτων, ἢ περὶ ἐδεσμάτων ἢ μικρολογίας τινός, ἢ περὶ φίλου τινός, ἢ περὶ δόσεως ἢ λήψεως, ἢ περὶ τοιούτων μωρῶν πραγμάτων. ταῦτα γὰρ πάντα μωρά ἐστι καὶ κενὰ καὶ ἄφρονα καὶ ἀσύμφορα τοῖς δούλοις τοῦ Θεοῦ. 3. ἡ δὲ μακροθυμία μεγάλη ἐστὶ καὶ ὀχυρά, καὶ ἰσχυρὰν δύναμιν ἔχουσα καὶ στιβαράν, καὶ εὐθηνουμένη ἐν πλατυσμῷ μεγάλῳ, ἱλαρά, ἀγαλλιωμένη, ἀμέριμνος οὖσα, δοξάζουσα τὸν Κύριον

cf. Ps.
xxxiii. 2.

5. i. 7 φυλάξῃ] conj. Gebhardt; φυλάξῃς A; dub. L₁L₂E. ii. 1 νῦν] ins. Gebhardt [L₁L₂E]; om. A; δὲ καὶ ps-Ath. 2 ὁ ἀνὴρ ἢ ἡ γυνὴ] conj. Hilgenfeld [L₁L₂E]; ἡ γυνὴ ἢ ὁ ἀνὴρ A; al. Ant. ps-Ath.

ἐν παντὶ καιρῷ, μηδὲν ἐν ἑαυτῇ ἔχουσα πικρόν, παραμένουσα διὰ παντὸς πραεῖα καὶ ἡσύχιος. αὕτη οὖν ἡ μακροθυμία κατοικεῖ μετὰ τῶν τὴν πίστιν ἐχόντων ὁλόκληρον. 4. ἡ δὲ ὀξυχολία πρῶτον μὲν μωρά ἐστιν, ἐλαφρά τε καὶ ἄφρων. εἶτα ἐκ τῆς ἀφροσύνης γίνεται πικρία, ἐκ δὲ τῆς πικρίας θυμός, ἐκ δὲ τοῦ θυμοῦ ὀργή, ἐκ δὲ τῆς ὀργῆς μῆνις· εἶτα ἡ μῆνις ἐκ τοσούτων κακῶν συνισταμένη γίνεται ἁμαρτία μεγάλη καὶ ἀνίατος. 5. ὅταν γὰρ ταῦτα τὰ πνεύματα πάντα ἐν ἑνὶ ἀγγείῳ κατοικῇ, οὗ καὶ τὸ πνεῦμα τὸ ἅγιον κατοικεῖ, οὐ χωρεῖ τὸ ἄγγος ἐκεῖνο, ἀλλ' ὑπερπλεονάζει. 6. τὸ τρυφερὸν οὖν πνεῦμα, μὴ ἔχον συνήθειαν μετὰ πονηροῦ πνεύματος κατοικεῖν μηδὲ μετὰ σκληρότητος, ἀποχωρεῖ ἀπὸ τοῦ ἀνθρώπου τοῦ τοιούτου καὶ ζητεῖ κατοικεῖν μετὰ πραότητος καὶ ἡσυχίας. 7. εἶτα ὅταν ἀποστῇ ἀπὸ τοῦ ἀνθρώπου ἐκείνου οὗ κατοικεῖ, γίνεται ὁ ἄνθρωπος ἐκεῖνος κενὸς ἀπὸ τοῦ πνεύματος τοῦ δικαίου, καὶ τὸ λοιπὸν πεπληρωμένος τοῖς πνεύμασι τοῖς πονηροῖς ἀκαταστατεῖ ἐν πάσῃ πράξει αὐτοῦ, περισπώμενος ὧδε κἀκεῖ ἀπὸ τῶν πνευμάτων τῶν πονηρῶν, καὶ ὅλως ἀποτυφλοῦται ἀπὸ τῆς διανοίας τῆς ἀγαθῆς. οὕτως οὖν συμβαίνει πᾶσι τοῖς ὀξυχόλοις. 8. ἀπέχου οὖν ἀπὸ τῆς ὀξυχολίας, τοῦ πονηροτάτου πνεύματος· ἔνδυσαι δὲ τὴν μακροθυμίαν καὶ ἀντίστα τῇ ὀξυχολίᾳ καὶ τῇ πικρίᾳ, καὶ ἔσῃ εὑρισκόμενος μετὰ τῆς σεμνότητος τῆς ἠγαπημένης ὑπὸ τοῦ Κυρίου. βλέπε οὖν μήποτε παρενθυμηθῇς τὴν ἐντολὴν ταύτην· ἐὰν γὰρ ταύτης τῆς ἐντολῆς κυριεύσῃς, καὶ τὰς λοιπὰς ἐντολὰς δυνήσῃ φυλάξαι, ἅς σοι μέλλω ἐντέλλεσθαι. ἰσχυροῦ ἐν αὐταῖς καὶ ἐνδυναμοῦ, καὶ πάντες ἐνδυναμούσθωσαν ὅσοι ἐὰν θέλωσιν ἐν αὐταῖς πορεύεσθαι.

Ἐντολὴ ϛ΄

I. Ἐνετειλάμην σοι, φησίν, ἐν τῇ πρώτῃ ἐντολῇ ἵνα φυλάξῃς τὴν πίστιν καὶ τὸν φόβον καὶ τὴν ἐγκράτειαν. Ναί, φημί, κύριε. Ἀλλὰ νῦν θέλω σοι, φησί, δηλῶσαι καὶ τὰς δυνάμεις αὐτῶν, ἵνα νοήσῃς τίς αὐτῶν τίνα δύναμιν ἔχει καὶ ἐνέργειαν. διπλαῖ γάρ εἰσιν αἱ ἐνέργειαι αὐτῶν· κεῖνται οὖν ἐπὶ δικαίῳ καὶ ἀδίκῳ· 2. σὺ οὖν πίστευε τῷ δικαίῳ, τῷ δὲ ἀδίκῳ μὴ πιστεύσῃς· τὸ γὰρ δίκαιον ὀρθὴν ὁδὸν ἔχει, τὸ δὲ ἄδικον στρεβλήν. ἀλλὰ σὺ τῇ ὀρθῇ ὁδῷ πορεύου [καὶ ὁμαλῇ], τὴν δὲ στρεβλὴν ἔασον. 3. ἡ γὰρ στρεβλὴ ὁδὸς τρίβους οὐκ ἔχει, ἀλλ' ἀνοδίας καὶ προσκόμματα πολλά, καὶ τραχεῖά ἐστι καὶ ἀκανθώδης. βλαβερὰ οὖν ἐστὶ τοῖς ἐν αὐτῇ πορευομένοις. 4. οἱ δὲ τῇ ὀρθῇ ὁδῷ πορευόμενοι ὁμαλῶς περιπατοῦσι καὶ ἀπροσκόπτως· οὔτε γὰρ τραχεῖά ἐστιν οὔτε ἀκανθώδης. βλέπεις οὖν ὅτι συμφορώτερόν ἐστι ταύτῃ τῇ ὁδῷ πορεύεσθαι. 5. Ἀρέσκει μοι, φημί, κύριε, ταύτῃ τῇ ὁδῷ πορεύεσθαι.

cf. Jer. xxiv. 7.

Πορεύσῃ, φησί, καὶ ὃς ἂν ἐξ ὅλης καρδίας ἐπιστρέψῃ πρὸς Κύριον πορεύσεται ἐν αὐτῇ.

II. Ἄκουε νῦν, φησί, περὶ τῆς πίστεως. δύο εἰσὶν ἄγγελοι μετὰ τοῦ ἀνθρώπου, εἰς τῆς δικαιοσύνης καὶ εἰς τῆς πονηρίας. 2. Πῶς οὖν, φημί, κύριε, γνώσομαι τὰς αὐτῶν ἐνεργείας, ὅτι ἀμφότεροι ἄγγελοι μετ' ἐμοῦ κατοικοῦσιν; 3. Ἄκουε, φησί, καὶ σύνιε αὐτάς. ὁ μὲν τῆς δικαιοσύνης ἄγγελος τρυφερός ἐστι καὶ αἰσχυντηρὸς καὶ πραῢς καὶ ἡσύχιος. ὅταν οὖν οὗτος ἐπὶ τὴν καρδίαν σου ἀναβῇ, εὐθέως λαλεῖ μετὰ σοῦ περὶ δικαιοσύνης, περὶ ἁγνείας, περὶ σεμνότητος, περὶ αὐταρκείας, περὶ παντὸς ἔργου δικαίου καὶ περὶ πάσης ἀρετῆς ἐνδόξου. ταῦτα πάντα ὅταν εἰς τὴν καρδίαν σου ἀναβῇ, γίνωσκε ὅτι ὁ ἄγγελος τῆς δικαιοσύνης μετὰ σοῦ ἐστί. [ταῦτα οὖν ἐστὶ τὰ ἔργα τοῦ ἀγγέλου τῆς δικαιοσύνης.] τούτῳ οὖν πίστευε καὶ τοῖς ἔργοις αὐτοῦ· 4. ὅρα νῦν καὶ τοῦ ἀγγέλου τῆς πονηρίας τὰ ἔργα. πρῶτον πάντων ὀξύχολός ἐστι καὶ πικρὸς καὶ ἄφρων, καὶ τὰ ἔργα αὐτοῦ πονηρά, καταστρέφοντα τοὺς δούλους τοῦ Θεοῦ· ὅταν οὖν οὗτος ἐπὶ τὴν καρδίαν σου ἀναβῇ, γνῶθι αὐτὸν ἀπὸ τῶν ἔργων αὐτοῦ. 5. Πῶς, φημί, κύριε, νοήσω αὐτόν, οὐκ ἐπίσταμαι. Ἄκουε, φησίν. ὅταν ὀξυχολία

---

6. i. 4 συμφορώτερον] συμφερώτερον A.   ii. 3 σύνιε] conj. Gebhardt
[L₁L₂]; συνιεῖς A; def. E.   4 νῦν] conj. Gebhardt in marg. [L₁L₂E]; οὖν
A ps-Ath.

σοί τις προσπέσῃ ἢ πικρία, γίνωσκε ὅτι αὐτός ἐστιν ἐν σοί·
εἶτα ἐπιθυμία πράξεων πολλῶν καὶ πολυτέλεια ἐδεσμάτων
πολλῶν καὶ μεθυσμάτων καὶ κραιπαλῶν πολλῶν καὶ ποικίλων τρυφῶν καὶ οὐ δεόντων, καὶ ἐπιθυμία γυναικῶν καὶ
πλεονεξία καὶ ὑπερηφανία καὶ ἀλαζονεία, καὶ ὅσα τούτοις
παραπλήσιά ἐστι καὶ ὅμοια. ταῦτα οὖν ὅταν ἐπὶ τὴν καρδίαν
σου ἀναβῇ, γίνωσκε ὅτι ὁ ἄγγελος τῆς πονηρίας ἐστὶ μετὰ σοῦ.
6. σὺ οὖν ἐπιγνοὺς τὰ ἔργα αὐτοῦ ἀπόστα ἀπ' αὐτοῦ καὶ
μηδὲν αὐτῷ πίστευε, ὅτι τὰ ἔργα αὐτοῦ πονηρά εἰσι καὶ ἀσύμφορα τοῖς δούλοις τοῦ Θεοῦ. ἔχεις οὖν ἀμφοτέρων τῶν ἀγγέλων τὰς ἐνεργείας· σύνιε αὐτὰς καὶ πίστευε τῷ ἀγγέλῳ τῆς
δικαιοσύνης· 7. ἀπὸ δὲ τοῦ ἀγγέλου τῆς πονηρίας ἀπόστηθι,
ὅτι ἡ διδαχὴ αὐτοῦ πονηρά ἐστι παντὶ ἔργῳ· ἐὰν γὰρ ᾖ τις
πιστὸς ἀνήρ, καὶ ἡ ἐνθύμησις τοῦ ἀγγέλου τούτου ἀναβῇ ἐπὶ
τὴν καρδίαν αὐτοῦ, δεῖ τὸν ἄνδρα ἐκεῖνον ἢ τὴν γυναῖκα ἐξα-
μαρτῆσαί τι. 8. ἐὰν δὲ πάλιν πονηρότατός τις ᾖ ἀνὴρ ἢ
γυνή, καὶ ἀναβῇ ἐπὶ τὴν καρδίαν αὐτοῦ τὰ ἔργα τοῦ ἀγγέλου
τῆς δικαιοσύνης, ἐξ ἀνάγκης δεῖ αὐτὸν ἀγαθόν τι ποιῆσαι.
9. βλέπεις οὖν, φησίν, ὅτι καλόν ἐστι τῷ ἀγγέλῳ τῆς δικαιοσύνης ἀκολουθεῖν, τῷ δὲ ἀγγέλῳ τῆς πονηρίας ἀποτάξασθαι.
10. τὰ μὲν περὶ τῆς πίστεως αὕτη ἡ ἐντολὴ δηλοῖ, ἵνα τοῖς
ἔργοις τοῦ ἀγγέλου τῆς δικαιοσύνης πιστεύσῃς, καὶ ἐργασάμενος αὐτὰ ζήσῃ τῷ Θεῷ. πίστευε δὲ ὅτι τὰ ἔργα τοῦ ἀγγέλου
τῆς πονηρίας χαλεπά ἐστι· μὴ ἐργαζόμενος οὖν αὐτὰ ζήσῃ
τῷ Θεῷ.

Ἐντολὴ ζ

Φοβήθητι, φησί, τὸν Κύριον καὶ φύλασσε τὰς ἐντολὰς   cf. Eccles.
αὐτοῦ· φυλάσσων οὖν τὰς ἐντολὰς τοῦ Θεοῦ ἔσῃ δυνατὸς ἐν   xii. 13.
πάσῃ πράξει, καὶ ἡ πρᾶξίς σου ἀσύγκριτος ἔσται. φοβούμενος γὰρ τὸν Κύριον πάντα καλῶς ἐργάσῃ· οὗτος δέ ἐστιν
ὁ φόβος, ὃν δεῖ σε φοβηθῆναι καὶ σωθήσῃ. 2. τὸν δὲ διάβολον μὴ φοβηθῇς· φοβούμενος γὰρ τὸν Κύριον κατακυ-

ριεύσεις τοῦ διαβόλου, ὅτι δύναμις ἐν αὐτῷ οὐκ ἔστιν. ἐν ᾧ [δὲ] δύναμις οὐκ ἔστιν, οὐδὲ φόβος· ἐν ᾧ δὲ δύναμις ᾖ ἔνδοξος, καὶ φόβος ἐν αὐτῷ. πᾶς γὰρ ὁ δύναμιν ἔχων φόβον ἔχει· ὁ δὲ μὴ ἔχων δύναμιν ὑπὸ πάντων καταφρονεῖται. 3. φοβή-θητι δὲ τὰ ἔργα τοῦ διαβόλου, ὅτι πονηρά ἐστι. φοβούμενος οὖν τὸν Κύριον φοβηθήσῃ τὰ ἔργα τοῦ διαβόλου, καὶ οὐκ ἐργάσῃ αὐτά, ἀλλ' ἀφέξῃ ἀπ' αὐτῶν. 4. δισσοὶ οὖν εἰσὶν οἱ φόβοι· ἐὰν γὰρ θέλῃς τὸ πονηρὸν ἐργάσασθαι, φοβοῦ τὸν Κύριον καὶ οὐκ ἐργάσῃ αὐτό· ἐὰν δὲ θέλῃς πάλιν τὸ ἀγαθὸν ἐργάσασθαι, φοβοῦ τὸν Κύριον καὶ ἐργάσῃ αὐτό. ὥστε ὁ φόβος τοῦ Κυρίου ἰσχυρός ἐστι καὶ μέγας καὶ ἔνδοξος. φοβήθητι οὖν τὸν Κύριον, καὶ ζήσῃ αὐτῷ· καὶ ὅσοι ἂν φοβηθῶσιν αὐτὸν τῶν φυλασσόντων τὰς ἐντολὰς αὐτοῦ, ζήσονται τῷ Θεῷ. 5. Διατί, φημί, κύριε, εἶπας περὶ τῶν τηρούντων τὰς ἐντολὰς αὐτοῦ· Ζήσονται τῷ Θεῷ; "Ὅτι, φησί, πᾶσα ἡ κτίσις φοβεῖται τὸν Κύριον, τὰς δὲ ἐντολὰς αὐτοῦ οὐ φυλάσσει. τῶν οὖν φοβουμένων αὐτὸν καὶ φυλασ-σόντων τὰς ἐντολὰς αὐτοῦ, ἐκείνων ἡ ζωή ἐστι παρὰ τῷ Θεῷ· τῶν δὲ μὴ φυλασσόντων τὰς ἐντολὰς αὐτοῦ οὐδὲ ζωὴ ἐν αὐτῷ.

Ἐντολὴ η'

Εἶπόν σοι, φησίν, ὅτι τὰ κτίσματα τοῦ Θεοῦ διπλᾶ ἐστί· καὶ γὰρ ἡ ἐγκράτεια διπλῆ ἐστίν. ἐπί τινων γὰρ δεῖ ἐγκρα-τεύεσθαι, ἐπί τινων δὲ οὐ δεῖ. 2. Γνώρισόν μοι, φημί, κύριε, ἐπὶ τίνων δεῖ ἐγκρατεύεσθαι, ἐπὶ τίνων δὲ οὐ δεῖ. Ἄκουε, φησί. τὸ πονηρὸν ἐγκρατεύου, καὶ μὴ ποίει αὐτό· τὸ δὲ ἀγαθὸν μὴ ἐγκρατεύου, ἀλλὰ ποίει αὐτό. ἐὰν | γὰρ ἐγκρα-τεύσῃ τὸ ἀγαθὸν μὴ ποιεῖν, ἁμαρτίαν μεγάλην ἐργάζῃ· ἐὰν | δὲ ἐγκρατεύσῃ τὸ πονηρὸν μὴ ποιεῖν, δικαιοσύνην μεγάλην ἐργάζῃ. ἐγκράτευσαι οὖν ἀπὸ πονηρίας πάσης ἐργαζόμενος τὸ ἀγαθόν. 3. Ποταπαί, φημί, κύριε, εἰσὶν αἱ πονηρίαι ἀφ' ὧν [ἡμᾶς] δεῖ ἐγκρατεύεσθαι; Ἄκουε, φησίν· ἀπὸ

7. 3 ἀφέξῃ] ἀφέξει A.   4 ἐργάσῃ sec.] ἐργάζῃ A.   8. 2 γὰρ...ἐργάζῃ· ἐὰν] ins. Hilgenfeld [L₁L₂E]; om. A by homœot.

μοιχείας καὶ πορνείας, ἀπὸ μεθύσματος ἀνομίας, ἀπὸ τρυφῆς πονηρᾶς, ἀπὸ ἐδεσμάτων πολλῶν καὶ πολυτελείας πλούτου καὶ καυχήσεως καὶ ὑψηλοφροσύνης καὶ ὑπερηφανίας, καὶ ἀπὸ ψεύσματος καὶ καταλαλίας καὶ ὑποκρίσεως [καὶ] μνησικακίας καὶ πάσης βλασφημίας. 4. ταῦτα τὰ ἔργα πάντων πονηρότατά εἰσιν ἐν τῇ ζωῇ τῶν ἀνθρώπων. ἀπὸ τούτων οὖν τῶν ἔργων δεῖ ἐγκρατεύεσθαι τὸν δοῦλον τοῦ Θεοῦ. ὁ γὰρ μὴ ἐγκρατευόμενος ἀπὸ τούτων οὐ δύναται ζῆσαι τῷ Θεῷ. ἄκουε οὖν καὶ τὰ ἀκόλουθα τούτων. 5. Ἔτι γάρ, φημί, κύριε, πονηρὰ ἔργα ἐστί; Καί γε πολλά, φησίν, ἔστιν ἀφ' ὧν δεῖ τὸν δοῦλον τοῦ Θεοῦ ἐγκρατεύεσθαι· κλέμμα, ψεῦδος, ἀποστέρησις, ψευδομαρτυρία, πλεονεξία, ἐπιθυμία πονηρά, ἀπάτη, κενοδοξία, ἀλαζονεία, καὶ ὅσα τούτοις ὅμοιά εἰσιν. 6. οὐ δοκεῖ σοι ταῦτα πονηρὰ εἶναι, καὶ λίαν πονηρά, [φησί,] τοῖς δούλοις τοῦ Θεοῦ; τούτων πάντων δεῖ ἐγκρατεύεσθαι τὸν δουλεύοντα τῷ Θεῷ. ἐγκράτευσαι οὖν ἀπὸ πάντων τούτων, ἵνα ζήσῃ τῷ Θεῷ, καὶ ἐγγραφήσῃ μετὰ τῶν ἐγκρατευομένων αὐτά. ἀφ' ὧν μὲν οὖν δεῖ σε ἐγκρατεύεσθαι, ταῦτά ἐστιν. 7. ἃ δὲ δεῖ σε μὴ ἐγκρατεύεσθαι, φησίν, ἀλλὰ ποιεῖν, ἄκουε. τὸ ἀγαθὸν μὴ ἐγκρατεύου, ἀλλὰ ποίει αὐτό. 8. Καὶ τῶν ἀγαθῶν μοι, φημί, κύριε, δήλωσον τὴν δύναμιν, ἵνα πορευθῶ ἐν αὐτοῖς καὶ δουλεύσω αὐτοῖς, ἵνα ἐργασάμενος αὐτὰ δυνηθῶ σωθῆναι. Ἄκουε, φησί, καὶ τῶν ἀγαθῶν τὰ ἔργα, ἅ σε δεῖ ἐργάζεσθαι καὶ μὴ ἐγκρατεύεσθαι. 9. πρῶτον πάντων πίστις, φόβος Κυρίου, ἀγάπη, ὁμόνοια, ῥήματα δικαιοσύνης, ἀλήθεια, ὑπομονή· τούτων ἀγαθώτερον οὐδέν ἐστιν ἐν τῇ ζωῇ τῶν ἀνθρώπων. ταῦτα ἐάν τις φυλάσσῃ καὶ μὴ ἐγκρατεύηται ἀπ' αὐτῶν, μακάριος γίνεται ἐν τῇ ζωῇ αὐτοῦ. 10. εἶτα τούτων τὰ ἀκόλουθα ἄκουσον· χήραις ὑπηρετεῖν, ὀρφανοὺς καὶ ὑστερουμένους ἐπισκέπτεσθαι, ἐξ ἀναγκῶν λυτροῦσθαι τοὺς δούλους τοῦ Θεοῦ, φιλόξενον εἶναι (ἐν γὰρ τῇ φιλοξενίᾳ εὑρίσκεται ἀγαθοποίησίς ποτε), μηδενὶ ἀντιτάσσεσθαι, ἡσύχιον εἶναι, ἐνδεέστερον γίνεσθαι πάντων

6. ἀφ' ὧν] conj. Harmer; ὧν A.

ἀνθρώπων, πρεσβύτας σέβεσθαι, δικαιοσύνην ἀσκεῖν, ἀδελ-
φότητα συντηρεῖν, ὕβριν ὑποφέρειν, μακρόθυμον εἶναι,
μνησικακίαν μὴ ἔχειν, κάμνοντας τῇ ψυχῇ παρακαλεῖν,
ἐσκανδαλισμένους ἀπὸ τῆς πίστεως μὴ ἀποβάλλεσθαι ἀλλ'
ἐπιστρέφειν καὶ εὐθύμους ποιεῖν, ἁμαρτάνοντας νουθετεῖν,
χρεώστας μὴ θλίβειν ἐνδεεῖς, καὶ εἴ τινα τούτοις ὅμοιά
ἐστι. 11. δοκεῖ σοι, φησί, ταῦτα ἀγαθὰ εἶναι; Τί γάρ,
φημί, κύριε, τούτων ἀγαθώτερον; Πορεύου οὖν, φησίν, ἐν
αὐτοῖς καὶ μὴ ἐγκρατεύου ἀπ' αὐτῶν, καὶ ζήσῃ τῷ Θεῷ.
12. φύλασσε οὖν τὴν ἐντολὴν ταύτην· ἐὰν τὸ ἀγαθὸν ποιῇς
καὶ μὴ ἐγκρατεύσῃ ἀπ' αὐτοῦ, ζήσῃ τῷ Θεῷ, καὶ πάντες
ζήσονται τῷ Θεῷ οἱ οὕτω ποιοῦντες. καὶ πάλιν ἐὰν τὸ
πονηρὸν μὴ ποιῇς καὶ ἐγκρατεύσῃ ἀπ' αὐτοῦ, ζήσῃ τῷ Θεῷ,
καὶ πάντες ζήσονται τῷ Θεῷ ὅσοι ἐὰν ταύτας τὰς ἐντολὰς
φυλάξωσι καὶ πορευθῶσιν ἐν αὐταῖς.

Ἐντολὴ θ'

Λέγει μοι· Ἆρον ἀπὸ σεαυτοῦ τὴν διψυχίαν καὶ μηδὲν
ὅλως διψυχήσῃς αἰτήσασθαι παρὰ τοῦ Θεοῦ, λέγων ἐν
σεαυτῷ ὅτι πῶς δύναμαι αἰτήσασθαί τι παρὰ τοῦ Κυρίου
καὶ λαβεῖν, ἡμαρτηκὼς τοσαῦτα εἰς αὐτόν; 2. μὴ διαλο-
γίζου ταῦτα, ἀλλ' ἐξ ὅλης τῆς καρδίας σου ἐπίστρεψον ἐπὶ
τὸν Κύριον, καὶ αἰτοῦ παρ' αὐτοῦ ἀδιστάκτως, καὶ γνώσῃ
τὴν πολυευσπλαγχνίαν αὐτοῦ, ὅτι οὐ μή σε ἐγκαταλίπῃ, ἀλλὰ
τὸ αἴτημα τῆς ψυχῆς σου πληροφορήσει. 3. οὐκ ἔστι γὰρ
ὁ Θεὸς ὡς οἱ ἄνθρωποι οἱ μνησικακοῦντες, ἀλλ' αὐτὸς ἀμνη-
σίκακός ἐστι καὶ σπλαγχνίζεται ἐπὶ τὴν ποίησιν αὐτοῦ.
4. σὺ οὖν καθάρισόν σου τὴν καρδίαν ἀπὸ πάντων τῶν
ματαιωμάτων τοῦ αἰῶνος τούτου καὶ τῶν προειρημένων σοι
ῥημάτων, καὶ αἰτοῦ παρὰ τοῦ Κυρίου, καὶ ἀπολήψῃ πάντα,
καὶ ἀπὸ πάντων τῶν αἰτημάτων σου ἀνυστέρητος ἔσῃ, ἐὰν
ἀδιστάκτως αἰτήσῃς παρὰ τοῦ Κυρίου. 5. ἐὰν δὲ διστάσῃς
ἐν τῇ καρδίᾳ σου, οὐδὲν οὐ μὴ λήψῃ τῶν αἰτημάτων σου.

cf. Jer.
xxiv. 7.

8. 12 ἀπ' αὐτοῦ sec.] conj. Gebhardt; αὐτὸ A.

οἱ γὰρ διστάζοντες εἰς τὸν Θεόν, οὗτοί εἰσιν οἱ δίψυχοι, καὶ οὐδὲν ὅλως ἐπιτυγχάνουσι τῶν αἰτημάτων αὐτῶν. 6. οἱ δὲ ὁλοτελεῖς ὄντες ἐν τῇ πίστει πάντα αἰτοῦνται πεποιθότες ἐπὶ τὸν Κύριον, καὶ λαμβάνουσιν, ὅτι ἀδιστάκτως αἰτοῦνται, μηδὲν διψυχοῦντες. πᾶς γὰρ δίψυχος ἀνήρ, ἐὰν μὴ μετανοήσῃ, δυσκόλως σωθήσεται. 7. καθάρισον οὖν τὴν καρδίαν σου ἀπὸ τῆς διψυχίας, ἔνδυσαι δὲ τὴν πίστιν, ὅτι ἰσχυρά ἐστι, καὶ πίστευε τῷ Θεῷ ὅτι πάντα τὰ αἰτήματά σου ἃ αἰτεῖς λήψῃ. καὶ ἐὰν αἰτησάμενός ποτε παρὰ τοῦ Κυρίου αἴτημά τι βραδύτερον λαμβάνῃς, μὴ διψυχήσῃς ὅτι ταχὺ οὐκ ἔλαβες τὸ αἴτημα τῆς ψυχῆς σου· πάντως γὰρ διὰ πειρασμόν τινα ἢ παράπτωμά τι, ὃ σὺ ἀγνοεῖς, βραδύτερον λαμβάνεις τὸ αἴτημά σου. 8. σὺ οὖν μὴ διαλίπῃς αἰτούμενος τὸ αἴτημα τῆς ψυχῆς σου, καὶ λήψῃ αὐτό. ἐὰν δὲ ἐκκακήσῃς καὶ διψυχήσῃς αἰτούμενος, σεαυτὸν αἰτιῶ καὶ μὴ τὸν διδόντα σοι. 9. βλέπε τὴν διψυχίαν ταύτην· πονηρὰ γάρ ἐστι καὶ ἀσύνετος, καὶ πολλοὺς ἐκριζοῖ ἀπὸ τῆς πίστεως, καί γε λίαν πιστοὺς καὶ ἰσχυρούς. καὶ γὰρ αὕτη ἡ διψυχία θυγάτηρ ἐστὶ τοῦ διαβόλου, καὶ λίαν πονηρεύεται εἰς τοὺς δούλους τοῦ Θεοῦ. 10. καταφρόνησον οὖν τῆς διψυχίας καὶ κατακυρίευσον αὐτῆς ἐν παντὶ πράγματι, ἐνδυσάμενος τὴν πίστιν τὴν ἰσχυρὰν καὶ δυνατήν. ἡ γὰρ πίστις πάντα ἐπαγγέλλεται, πάντα τελειοῖ· ἡ δὲ διψυχία μὴ καταπιστεύουσα ἑαυτῇ πάντων ἀποτυγχάνει τῶν ἔργων αὐτῆς ὧν πράσσει. 11. βλέπεις οὖν, φησίν, ὅτι ἡ πίστις ἄνωθέν ἐστι παρὰ τοῦ Κυρίου, καὶ ἔχει δύναμιν μεγάλην· ἡ δὲ διψυχία ἐπίγειον πνεῦμά ἐστι παρὰ τοῦ διαβόλου, δύναμιν μὴ ἔχουσα. 12. σὺ οὖν δούλευε τῇ ἐχούσῃ δύναμιν τῇ πίστει, καὶ ἀπὸ τῆς διψυχίας ἀπόσχου τῆς μὴ ἐχούσης δύναμιν, καὶ ζήσῃ τῷ Θεῷ, καὶ πάντες ζήσονται τῷ Θεῷ οἱ ταῦτα φρονοῦντες.

Ἐντολὴ ιʹ

I. Ἆρον ἀπὸ σεαυτοῦ, φησί, τὴν λύπην· καὶ γὰρ αὕτη ἀδελφή ἐστι τῆς διψυχίας καὶ τῆς ὀξυχολίας. 2. Πῶς, φημί, κύριε, ἀδελφή ἐστι τούτων; ἄλλο γάρ μοι δοκεῖ εἶναι ὀξυχολία, καὶ ἄλλο διψυχία, καὶ ἄλλο λύπη. Ἀσύνετος εἶ ἄνθρωπος, φησί, [καὶ] οὐ νοεῖς ὅτι ἡ λύπη πάντων τῶν πνευμάτων πονηροτέρα ἐστί, καὶ δεινοτάτη τοῖς δούλοις τοῦ Θεοῦ, καὶ παρὰ πάντα τὰ πνεύματα καταφθείρει τὸν ἄνθρωπον, καὶ ἐκτρίβει τὸ πνεῦμα τὸ ἅγιον, καὶ πάλιν σώζει. 3. Ἐγώ, φημί, κύριε, ἀσύνετός εἰμι καὶ οὐ συνίω τὰς παραβολὰς ταύτας. πῶς γὰρ δύναται ἐκτρίβειν καὶ πάλιν σώζειν, οὐ νοῶ. 4. Ἄκουε, φησίν· οἱ μηδέποτε ἐρευνήσαντες περὶ τῆς ἀληθείας μηδὲ ἐπιζητήσαντες περὶ τῆς θεότητος, πιστεύσαντες δὲ μόνον, ἐμπεφυρμένοι δὲ πραγματείαις καὶ πλούτῳ καὶ φιλίαις ἐθνικαῖς καὶ ἄλλαις πολλαῖς πραγματείαις τοῦ αἰῶνος τούτου· ὅσοι οὖν τούτοις πρόσκεινται, οὐ νοοῦσι τὰς παραβολὰς τῆς θεότητος· ἐπισκοτοῦνται γὰρ ὑπὸ τούτων τῶν πράξεων καὶ καταφθείρονται καὶ γίνονται κεχερσωμένοι. 5. καθὼς οἱ ἀμπελῶνες οἱ καλοί, ὅταν ἀμελείας τύχωσι, χερσοῦνται ἀπὸ τῶν ἀκανθῶν καὶ βοτανῶν ποικίλων, οὕτως οἱ ἄνθρωποι οἱ πιστεύσαντες καὶ εἰς ταύτας τὰς πράξεις τὰς πολλὰς ἐμπίπτοντες τὰς προειρημένας ἀποπλανῶνται ἀπὸ τῆς διανοίας αὐτῶν καὶ οὐδὲν ὅλως νοοῦσι περὶ τῆς δικαιοσύνης· καὶ γὰρ ὅταν ἀκούσωσι περὶ θεότητος καὶ ἀληθείας, ὁ νοῦς αὐτῶν περὶ τὴν πρᾶξιν αὐτῶν καταγίνεται, καὶ οὐδὲν ὅλως νοοῦσιν. 6. οἱ δὲ φόβον ἔχοντες Θεοῦ καὶ ἐρευνῶντες περὶ θεότητος καὶ ἀληθείας, καὶ τὴν καρδίαν ἔχοντες πρὸς τὸν Κύριον, πάντα τὰ λεγόμενα αὐτοῖς τάχιον νοοῦσι καὶ συνίουσιν, ὅτι ἔχουσι τὸν φόβον τοῦ Κυρίου ἐν ἑαυτοῖς· ὅπου γὰρ ὁ Κύριος κατοικεῖ, ἐκεῖ καὶ σύνεσις πολλή. κολλήθητι οὖν τῷ Κυρίῳ, καὶ πάντα συνήσεις καὶ νοήσεις.

II. Ἄκουε νῦν, φησίν, ἀνόητε, πῶς ἡ λύπη ἐκτρίβει τὸ

---

10. i. 2 ἄνθρωπος, φησί] conj. Harmer [L₂]; illegible in A; ἄνθρωπε (om. φησί) Aˢ; ait L₁; et dixit mihi (om. ἄνθρωπος) E.   5 καθὼς] conj. Hilgenfeld [L₁E]; καὶ ὡς A; def. L₂.   ii. 1 νῦν] conj. Harmer [L₁E]; οὖν A; ergo nunc L₂.

πνεῦμα τὸ ἅγιον καὶ πάλιν σώζει. 2. ὅταν ὁ δίψυχος ἐπι-
βάληται πρᾶξίν τινα, καὶ ταύτης ἀποτύχῃ διὰ τὴν διψυχίαν
αὐτοῦ, ἡ λύπη αὕτη εἰσπορεύεται εἰς τὸν ἄνθρωπον, καὶ λυπεῖ
τὸ πνεῦμα τὸ ἅγιον καὶ ἐκτρίβει αὐτό. 3. εἶτα πάλιν ἡ
ὀξυχολία ὅταν κολληθῇ τῷ ἀνθρώπῳ περὶ πράγματός τινος,
καὶ λίαν πικρανθῇ, πάλιν ἡ λύπη εἰσπορεύεται εἰς τὴν
καρδίαν τοῦ ἀνθρώπου τοῦ ὀξυχολήσαντος, καὶ λυπεῖται ἐπὶ
τῇ πράξει αὐτοῦ ᾗ ἔπραξε, καὶ μετανοεῖ ὅτι πονηρὸν εἰργάσατο. 4. αὕτη οὖν ἡ λύπη δοκεῖ σωτηρίαν ἔχειν, ὅτι τὸ
πονηρὸν πράξας μετενόησεν. ἀμφότεραι οὖν αἱ πράξεις
λυποῦσι τὸ πνεῦμα· ἡ μὲν διψυχία, ὅτι οὐκ ἐπέτυχε τῆς
πράξεως αὐτῆς, ἡ δὲ ὀξυχολία λυπεῖ τὸ πνεῦμα, ὅτι ἔπραξε
τὸ πονηρόν. ἀμφότερα οὖν λυπηρά ἐστι τῷ πνεύματι τῷ
ἁγίῳ, ἡ διψυχία καὶ ἡ ὀξυχολία. 5. ἆρον οὖν ἀπὸ σεαυτοῦ
τὴν λύπην καὶ μὴ θλῖβε τὸ πνεῦμα τὸ ἅγιον τὸ ἐν σοὶ
κατοικοῦν, μήποτε ἐντεύξηται [κατὰ σοῦ] τῷ Θεῷ καὶ
ἀποστῇ ἀπὸ σοῦ. 6. τὸ γὰρ πνεῦμα τοῦ Θεοῦ τὸ δοθὲν εἰς
τὴν σάρκα ταύτην λύπην οὐχ ὑποφέρει οὐδὲ στενοχωρίαν.

III. Ἔνδυσαι οὖν τὴν ἱλαρότητα τὴν πάντοτε ἔχουσαν
χάριν παρὰ τῷ Θεῷ καὶ εὐπρόσδεκτον οὖσαν αὐτῷ, καὶ
ἐντρύφα ἐν αὐτῇ. πᾶς γὰρ ἱλαρὸς ἀνὴρ ἀγαθὰ ἐργάζεται,
καὶ ἀγαθὰ φρονεῖ, καὶ καταφρονεῖ τῆς λύπης· 2. ὁ δὲ
λυπηρὸς ἀνὴρ πάντοτε πονηρεύεται· πρῶτον μὲν πονηρεύεται,
ὅτι λυπεῖ τὸ πνεῦμα τὸ ἅγιον τὸ δοθὲν τῷ ἀνθρώπῳ ἱλαρόν·
δεύτερον δὲ λυπῶν τὸ πνεῦμα τὸ ἅγιον ἀνομίαν ἐργάζεται,
μὴ ἐντυγχάνων μηδὲ ἐξομολογούμενος τῷ Θεῷ. πάντοτε γὰρ
λυπηροῦ ἀνδρὸς ἡ ἔντευξις οὐκ ἔχει δύναμιν τοῦ ἀναβῆναι
ἐπὶ τὸ θυσιαστήριον τοῦ Θεοῦ. 3. Διατί, φημί, οὐκ ἀναβαίνει ἐπὶ τὸ θυσιαστήριον ἡ ἔντευξις τοῦ λυπουμένου· Ὅτι,
φησίν, ἡ λύπη ἐγκάθηται εἰς τὴν καρδίαν αὐτοῦ· μεμιγμένη
οὖν ἡ λύπη μετὰ τῆς ἐντεύξεως οὐκ ἀφίησι τὴν ἔντευξιν
ἀναβῆναι καθαρὰν ἐπὶ τὸ θυσιαστήριον. ὥσπερ γὰρ ὄξος
οἴνῳ μεμιγμένον ἐπὶ τὸ αὐτὸ τὴν αὐτὴν ἡδονὴν οὐκ ἔχει, οὕτω
καὶ ἡ λύπη μεμιγμένη μετὰ τοῦ ἁγίου πνεύματος τὴν αὐτὴν

ἔντευξιν οὐκ ἔχει. 4. καθάρισον οὖν σεαυτὸν ἀπὸ τῆς λύπης τῆς πονηρᾶς ταύτης, καὶ ζήσῃ τῷ Θεῷ· καὶ πάντες ζήσονται τῷ Θεῷ ὅσοι ἂν ἀποβάλωσιν ἀφ᾽ ἑαυτῶν τὴν λύπην καὶ ἐνδύσωνται πᾶσαν ἱλαρότητα.

Ἐντολὴ ια′

Ἔδειξέ μοι ἐπὶ συμψελλίου καθημένους ἀνθρώπους, καὶ ἕτερον ἄνθρωπον καθήμενον ἐπὶ καθέδραν. καὶ λέγει μοι· Βλέπεις τοὺς ἐπὶ τοῦ συμψελλίου καθημένους; Βλέπω, φημί, κύριε. Οὗτοι, φησί, πιστοί εἰσι, καὶ ὁ καθήμενος ἐπὶ τὴν καθέδραν ψευδοπροφήτης ἐστὶν [ὃς] ἀπόλλυσι τὴν διάνοιαν τῶν δούλων τοῦ Θεοῦ· τῶν διψύχων δὲ ἀπόλλυσιν, οὐ τῶν πιστῶν. 2. οὗτοι οὖν οἱ δίψυχοι ὡς ἐπὶ μάγον ἔρχονται, καὶ ἐπερωτῶσιν αὐτὸν τί ἄρα ἔσται αὐτοῖς· κἀκεῖνος ὁ ψευδοπρο-φήτης, μηδεμίαν ἔχων ἐν ἑαυτῷ δύναμιν πνεύματος θείου, λαλεῖ μετ᾽ αὐτῶν κατὰ τὰ ἐπερωτήματα αὐτῶν | [καὶ κατὰ τὰς ἐπιθυμίας τῆς πονηρίας αὐτῶν], καὶ πληροῖ τὰς ψυχὰς αὐτῶν |, καθὼς αὐτοὶ βούλονται. 3. αὐτὸς γὰρ κενὸς ὢν κενὰ καὶ ἀποκρίνεται κενοῖς· ὃ γὰρ ἐὰν ἐπερωτηθῇ, πρὸς τὸ κένωμα τοῦ ἀνθρώπου ἀποκρίνεται. τινὰ δὲ καὶ ῥήματα ἀληθῆ λαλεῖ· ὁ γὰρ διάβολος πληροῖ αὐτὸν τῷ αὐτοῦ πνεύ-ματι, εἴ τινα δυνήσεται ῥῆξαι τῶν δικαίων. 4. ὅσοι οὖν ἰσχυροί εἰσιν ἐν τῇ πίστει τοῦ Κυρίου ἐνδεδυμένοι τὴν ἀλή-θειαν, τοῖς τοιούτοις πνεύμασιν οὐ κολλῶνται, ἀλλ᾽ ἀπέχον-ται ἀπ᾽ αὐτῶν. ὅσοι δὲ δίψυχοί εἰσι καὶ πυκνῶς μετανοοῦσι, μαντεύονται ὡς καὶ τὰ ἔθνη, καὶ ἑαυτοῖς μείζονα ἁμαρτίαν ἐπιφέρουσιν εἰδωλολατροῦντες· ὁ γὰρ ἐπερωτῶν ψευδοπρο-φήτην περὶ πράξεώς τινος εἰδωλολάτρης ἐστὶ καὶ κενὸς ἀπὸ τῆς ἀληθείας καὶ ἄφρων. 5. πᾶν γὰρ πνεῦμα ἀπὸ Θεοῦ δοθὲν οὐκ ἐπερωτᾶται, ἀλλὰ ἔχον τὴν δύναμιν τῆς θεότητος

11. 1 ἔδειξε] [L₁L₂E]; ἔδοξε A.   καθέδραν] καθέραν sic A.   ὅς] ins. Harmer [L₁L₂]; et E; om. A.   2 καὶ κατὰ τὰς ἐπιθυμίας...ψυχὰς αὐτῶν] L₂E; om. A by homœot.; L₁ omits as far as πονηρίας αὐτῶν, perhaps rightly.

ἀφ᾽ ἑαυτοῦ λαλεῖ πάντα, ὅτι ἄνωθέν ἐστιν ἀπὸ τῆς δυνάμεως τοῦ θείου πνεύματος. 6. τὸ δὲ πνεῦμα τὸ ἐπερωτώμενον καὶ λαλοῦν κατὰ τὰς ἐπιθυμίας τῶν ἀνθρώπων ἐπίγειόν ἐστι καὶ ἐλαφρόν, δύναμιν μὴ ἔχον· καὶ ὅλως οὐ λαλεῖ ἐὰν μὴ ἐπερωτηθῇ. 7. Πῶς οὖν, φημί, κύριε, ἄνθρωπος γνώσεται τίς αὐτῶν προφήτης καὶ τίς ψευδοπροφήτης ἐστίν; Ἄκουε, φησί, περὶ ἀμφοτέρων τῶν προφητῶν· καὶ ὥς σοι μέλλω λέγειν, οὕτω δοκιμάσεις τὸν προφήτην καὶ τὸν ψευδοπροφήτην. ἀπὸ τῆς ζωῆς δοκίμαζε τὸν ἄνθρωπον τὸν ἔχοντα τὸ πνεῦμα τὸ θεῖον. 8. πρῶτον μὲν ὁ ἔχων τὸ πνεῦμα [τὸ θεῖον] τὸ ἄνωθεν πραΰς ἐστι καὶ ἡσύχιος καὶ ταπεινόφρων καὶ ἀπεχόμενος ἀπὸ πάσης πονηρίας καὶ ἐπιθυμίας ματαίας τοῦ αἰῶνος τούτου, καὶ ἑαυτὸν ἐνδεέστερον ποιεῖ πάντων τῶν ἀνθρώπων, καὶ οὐδενὶ οὐδὲν ἀποκρίνεται ἐπερωτώμενος, οὐδὲ κατὰ μόνας λαλεῖ—οὐδὲ ὅταν θέλῃ ἄνθρωπος λαλεῖν, λαλεῖ τὸ πνεῦμα τὸ ἅγιον—ἀλλὰ τότε λαλεῖ, ὅταν θελήσῃ αὐτὸν ὁ Θεὸς λαλῆσαι. 9. ὅταν οὖν ἔλθῃ ὁ ἄνθρωπος ὁ ἔχων τὸ πνεῦμα τὸ θεῖον εἰς συναγωγὴν ἀνδρῶν δικαίων τῶν ἐχόντων πίστιν θείου πνεύματος, καὶ ἔντευξις γένηται πρὸς τὸν Θεὸν τῆς συναγωγῆς τῶν ἀνδρῶν ἐκείνων, τότε ὁ ἄγγελος τοῦ προφητικοῦ πνεύματος ὁ κείμενος πρὸς αὐτὸν πληροῖ τὸν ἄνθρωπον, καὶ πληρωθεὶς ὁ ἄνθρωπος τῷ πνεύματι τῷ ἁγίῳ λαλεῖ εἰς τὸ πλῆθος, καθὼς ὁ Κύριος βούλεται. 10. οὕτως οὖν φανερὸν ἔσται τὸ πνεῦμα τῆς θεότητος. ὅση οὖν περὶ τοῦ πνεύματος τῆς θεότητος τοῦ Κυρίου, ἡ δύναμις αὕτη. 11. ἄκουε νῦν, φησί, περὶ τοῦ πνεύματος τοῦ ἐπιγείου καὶ κενοῦ καὶ δύναμιν μὴ ἔχοντος, ἀλλὰ ὄντος μωροῦ. 12. πρῶτον μὲν ὁ ἄνθρωπος ἐκεῖνος ὁ δοκῶν πνεῦμα ἔχειν ὑψοῖ ἑαυτὸν καὶ θέλει πρωτοκαθεδρίαν ἔχειν, καὶ εὐθὺς ἰταμός ἐστι καὶ ἀναιδὴς καὶ πολύλαλος καὶ ἐν τρυφαῖς πολλαῖς ἀναστρεφόμενος καὶ ἐν ἑτέραις πολλαῖς ἀπάταις, καὶ μισθὸν λαμβάνει τῆς προφητείας αὐτοῦ· ἐὰν δὲ μὴ λάβῃ, οὐ προφητεύει. δύναται οὖν πνεῦμα

9 προφητικοῦ πνεύματος] conj. Hilgenfeld [L₂E]; τοῦ προφήτου A: al. L₁.
11 νῦν] conj. Harmer [L₁L₂]; οὖν A; om. E.

θεῖον μισθὸν λαμβάνειν καὶ προφητεύειν; οὐκ ἐνδέχεται
τοῦτο ποιεῖν Θεοῦ προφήτην, ἀλλὰ τῶν τοιούτων προφητῶν
ἐπίγειόν ἐστι τὸ πνεῦμα. 13. εἶτα ὅλως εἰς συναγωγὴν
ἀνδρῶν δικαίων οὐκ ἐγγίζει, ἀλλ᾽ ἀποφεύγει αὐτούς. κολ-
λᾶται δὲ τοῖς διψύχοις καὶ κενοῖς, καὶ κατὰ γωνίαν αὐτοῖς
προφητεύει, καὶ ἀπατᾷ αὐτοὺς λαλῶν κατὰ τὰς ἐπιθυμίας
αὐτῶν πάντα κενῶς· κενοῖς γὰρ καὶ ἀποκρίνεται. τὸ γὰρ
κενὸν σκεῦος μετὰ τῶν κενῶν συντιθέμενον οὐ θραύεται,
ἀλλὰ συμφωνοῦσιν ἀλλήλοις. 14. ὅταν δὲ ἔλθῃ εἰς συναγωγὴν πλήρη ἀνδρῶν δικαίων ἐχόντων πνεῦμα θεότητος, καὶ
ἔντευξις ἀπ᾽ αὐτῶν γένηται, κενοῦται ὁ ἄνθρωπος ἐκεῖνος, καὶ
τὸ πνεῦμα τὸ ἐπίγειον ὑπὸ τοῦ φόβου φεύγει ἀπ᾽ αὐτοῦ, καὶ
κωφοῦται ὁ ἄνθρωπος ἐκεῖνος καὶ ὅλως συνθραύεται, μηδὲν
δυνάμενος λαλῆσαι. 15. ἐὰν γὰρ εἰς ἀποθήκην στιβάσῃς
οἶνον ἢ ἔλαιον καὶ ἐν αὐτοῖς θῇς κεράμιον κενόν, καὶ πάλιν
ἀποστιβάσαι θελήσῃς τὴν ἀποθήκην, τὸ κεράμιον ἐκεῖνο, ὃ
ἔθηκας κενόν, κενὸν καὶ εὑρήσεις· οὕτω καὶ οἱ προφῆται οἱ
κενοί, ὅταν ἔλθωσιν εἰς πνεύματα δικαίων, ὁποῖοι ἦλθον,
τοιοῦτοι καὶ εὑρίσκονται. 16. ἔχεις ἀμφοτέρων τῶν προφητῶν τὴν ζωήν. δοκίμαζε οὖν ἀπὸ τῆς ζωῆς καὶ τῶν ἔργων
τὸν ἄνθρωπον τὸν λέγοντα ἑαυτὸν πνευματοφόρον εἶναι.
17. σὺ δὲ πίστευε τῷ πνεύματι τῷ ἐρχομένῳ ἀπὸ τοῦ Θεοῦ
καὶ ἔχοντι δύναμιν· τῷ δὲ πνεύματι τῷ ἐπιγείῳ καὶ κενῷ
μηδὲν πίστευε, ὅτι ἐν αὐτῷ δύναμις οὐκ ἔστιν· ἀπὸ τοῦ διαβόλου γὰρ ἔρχεται. 18. ἄκουσον [οὖν] τὴν παραβολὴν ἣν
μέλλω σοι λέγειν. λάβε λίθον καὶ βάλε εἰς τὸν οὐρανόν, ἴδε
εἰ δύνασαι ἅψασθαι αὐτοῦ· ἢ πάλιν λάβε σίφωνα ὕδατος
καὶ σιφώνισον εἰς τὸν οὐρανόν, ἴδε εἰ δύνασαι τρυπῆσαι τὸν

11. 13 λαλῶν] λαλοῦν A.   14 θεότητος] conj. Gebhardt [L₁L₂E]; θειό-
τατον A.   ἀπ᾽ αὐτῶν] conj. Hilgenfeld [L₁L₂]; ἀντ᾽ αὐτῆς (sc. τῆς
συναγωγῆς) A; iis E.   ἐπίγειον] conj. [L₁L₂E]; ἅγιον A.   ὑπὸ]
conj. Schmidt [L₂]; ἀπὸ A; def. L₁; dub. E.   κωφοῦται] κουφοῦται A.
μηδὲν] conj. Hollenberg [L₁L₂E]; μὴ A.   16 τῆς ζωῆς καὶ τῶν ἔργων]
conj. Harmer [L₁L₂]; τῶν ἔργων καὶ τῆς ζωῆς AE.   18 οὖν] ins. Hollenberg
[L₁L₂]; om. A; nunc E.   σιφώνισον] συφώνισον A.

οὐρανόν. 19. Πῶς, φημί, κύριε, δύναται ταῦτα γενέσθαι; ἀδύνατα γὰρ ἀμφότερα ταῦτα εἴρηκας. Ὡς ταῦτα οὖν, φησίν, ἀδύνατά ἐστιν, οὕτω καὶ τὰ πνεύματα τὰ ἐπίγεια ἀδύνατά ἐστι καὶ ἀδρανῆ. 20. λάβε νῦν τὴν δύναμιν τὴν ἄνωθεν ἐρχομένην. ἡ χάλαζα ἐλάχιστόν ἐστι κοκκάριον, καὶ ὅταν ἐπιπέσῃ ἐπὶ κεφαλὴν ἀνθρώπου, πῶς πόνον παρέχει; ἢ πάλιν λάβε σταγόνα ἢ ἀπὸ τοῦ κεράμου πίπτει χαμαί, καὶ τρυπᾷ τὸν λίθον. 21. βλέπεις οὖν ὅτι τὰ ἄνωθεν ἐλάχιστα πίπτοντα ἐπὶ τὴν γῆν μεγάλην δύναμιν ἔχει· οὕτω καὶ τὸ πνεῦμα τὸ θεῖον ἄνωθεν ἐρχόμενον δυνατόν ἐστι. τούτῳ οὖν τῷ πνεύματι πίστευε, ἀπὸ δὲ τοῦ ἑτέρου ἀπέχου.

Ἐντολὴ ιβ'

I. Λέγει μοι· Ἀρον ἀπὸ σεαυτοῦ πᾶσαν ἐπιθυμίαν πονηράν, ἔνδυσαι δὲ τὴν ἐπιθυμίαν τὴν ἀγαθὴν καὶ σεμνήν· ἐνδεδυμένος γὰρ τὴν ἐπιθυμίαν ταύτην μισήσεις τὴν πονηρὰν ἐπιθυμίαν καὶ χαλιναγωγήσεις αὐτὴν καθὼς βούλει. 2. ἀγρία γάρ ἐστιν ἡ ἐπιθυμία ἡ πονηρὰ καὶ δυσκόλως ἡμεροῦται· φοβερὰ γάρ ἐστι καὶ λίαν τῇ ἀγριότητι αὐτῆς δαπανᾷ τοὺς ἀνθρώπους· μάλιστα δὲ ἐὰν ἐμπέσῃ εἰς αὐτὴν δοῦλος Θεοῦ καὶ μὴ ᾖ συνετός, δαπανᾶται ὑπ' αὐτῆς δεινῶς. δαπανᾷ δὲ τοὺς τοιούτους τοὺς μὴ ἔχοντας ἔνδυμα τῆς ἐπιθυμίας τῆς ἀγαθῆς, ἀλλὰ ἐμπεφυρμένους τῷ αἰῶνι τούτῳ. τούτους οὖν παραδίδωσιν εἰς θάνατον. 3. Ποῖα, φημί, κύριε, ἔργα ἐστὶ τῆς ἐπιθυμίας τῆς πονηρᾶς τὰ παραδιδόντα τοὺς ἀνθρώπους εἰς θάνατον; γνώρισόν μοι, ἵνα ἀφέξομαι ἀπ' αὐτῶν. Ἄκουσον, [φησίν,] ἐν ποίοις ἔργοις θανατοῖ ἡ ἐπιθυμία ἡ πονηρὰ τοὺς δούλους τοῦ Θεοῦ.

II. Πάντων προέχουσα ἐπιθυμία γυναικὸς ἀλλοτρίας ἢ ἀνδρός, καὶ πολυτελείας πλούτου καὶ ἐδεσμάτων πολλῶν ματαίων καὶ μεθυσμάτων, καὶ ἑτέρων τρυφῶν πολλῶν καὶ μωρῶν· πᾶσα γὰρ τρυφὴ μωρά ἐστι καὶ κενὴ τοῖς δούλοις τοῦ Θεοῦ. 2. αὗται οὖν αἱ ἐπιθυμίαι πονηραί εἰσι, θανατοῦσαι τοὺς δούλους τοῦ Θεοῦ. αὕτη γὰρ ἡ ἐπιθυμία ἡ πονηρὰ τοῦ διαβόλου θυγάτηρ ἐστίν. ἀπέχεσθαι οὖν δεῖ ἀπὸ τῶν ἐπιθυμιῶν τῶν πονηρῶν, ἵνα ἀποσχόμενοι ζήσητε τῷ Θεῷ. 3. ὅσοι δὲ ἂν κατακυριευθῶσιν ὑπ' αὐτῶν καὶ μὴ ἀντισταθῶσιν αὐταῖς, ἀποθανοῦνται εἰς τέλος· θανατώδεις γάρ εἰσιν αἱ ἐπιθυμίαι αὗται. 4. σὺ δὲ ἔνδυσαι τὴν ἐπιθυμίαν τῆς δικαιοσύνης, καὶ καθοπλισάμενος τὸν φόβον τοῦ Κυρίου ἀντίστηθι αὐταῖς. ὁ γὰρ φόβος τοῦ Θεοῦ κατοικεῖ ἐν τῇ ἐπιθυμίᾳ τῇ ἀγαθῇ. ἡ ἐπιθυμία ἡ πονηρά, ἐὰν ἴδῃ σε καθωπλισμένον τῷ φόβῳ τοῦ Θεοῦ καὶ ἀνθεστηκότα αὐτῇ, φεύξεται ἀπὸ σοῦ μακράν, καὶ οὐκ ἔτι σοι ὀφθήσεται φοβουμένη τὰ ὅπλα σου. 5. σὺ οὖν στεφανωθεὶς κατ' αὐτῆς ἐλθὲ πρὸς τὴν ἐπιθυμίαν τῆς δικαιοσύνης, καὶ παραδοὺς αὐτῇ τὸ νῖκος ὃ ἔλαβες, δούλευσον αὐτῇ καθὼς αὐτὴ βούλεται. ἐὰν δουλεύσῃς τῇ ἐπιθυμίᾳ τῇ ἀγαθῇ καὶ ὑποταγῇς αὐτῇ, δυνήσῃ τῆς ἐπιθυμίας τῆς πονηρᾶς κατακυριεῦσαι καὶ ὑποτάξαι αὐτὴν καθὼς βούλει.

III. Ἤθελον, φημί, κύριε, γνῶναι ποίοις τρόποις με δεῖ δουλεῦσαι τῇ ἐπιθυμίᾳ τῇ ἀγαθῇ. Ἄκουε, φησίν· ἔργασαι δικαιοσύνην καὶ ἀρετήν, ἀλήθειαν καὶ φόβον Κυρίου, πίστιν καὶ πραότητα, καὶ ὅσα τούτοις ὅμοιά ἐστιν ἀγαθά. ταῦτα ἐργαζόμενος εὐάρεστος ἔσῃ δοῦλος τοῦ Θεοῦ καὶ ζήσῃ αὐτῷ· καὶ πᾶς ὃς ἂν δουλεύσῃ τῇ ἐπιθυμίᾳ τῇ ἀγαθῇ, ζήσεται τῷ Θεῷ. 2. Συνετέλεσεν οὖν τὰς ἐντολὰς τὰς δώδεκα, καὶ λέγει μοι· Ἔχεις τὰς ἐντολὰς ταύτας· πορεύου ἐν αὐταῖς καὶ τοὺς ἀκούοντας παρακάλει ἵνα ἡ μετάνοια αὐτῶν καθαρὰ γένηται τὰς λοιπὰς ἡμέρας τῆς ζωῆς αὐτῶν. 3. τὴν διακονίαν ταύτην ἥν σοι δίδωμι ἐκτέλει ἐπιμελῶς, καὶ πολὺ ἐργάσῃ· εὑρήσεις γὰρ χάριν ἐν τοῖς μέλλουσι μετανοεῖν, καὶ πεισθήσονταί σου τοῖς ῥήμασιν· ἐγὼ γὰρ μετὰ σοῦ ἔσομαι, καὶ ἀναγκάσω αὐτοὺς πεισθῆναί σοι.

4. Λέγω αὐτῷ· Κύριε, αἱ ἐντολαὶ αὗται μεγάλαι καὶ

καλαὶ καὶ ἔνδοξοί εἰσι καὶ δυνάμεναι εϒφρᾶναι καρδίαν ἀν-

θρώπου τοῦ δυναμένου τηρῆσαι αὐτάς. οὐκ οἶδα δὲ εἰ δύνανται
αἱ ἐντολαὶ αὗται ὑπὸ ἀνθρώπου φυλαχθῆναι, διότι σκληραί
εἰσι λίαν. 5. ἀποκριθεὶς λέγει μοι· Ἐὰν σὺ σεαυτῷ προθῇς
ὅτι δύνανται φυλαχθῆναι, εὐκόλως αὐτὰς φυλάξεις, καὶ οὐκ
ἔσονται σκληραί· ἐὰν δὲ ἐπὶ τὴν καρδίαν σου ἤδη ἀναβῇ μὴ
δύνασθαι αὐτὰς ὑπὸ ἀνθρώπου φυλαχθῆναι, οὐ φυλάξεις
αὐτάς. 6. νῦν δέ σοι λέγω· ἐὰν ταύτας μὴ φυλάξῃς, ἀλλὰ
παρενθυμηθῇς, οὐχ ἕξεις σωτηρίαν, οὔτε τὰ τέκνα σου οὔτε ὁ
οἶκός σου, ἐπεὶ ἤδη σεαυτῷ κέκρικας τοῦ μὴ δύνασθαι τὰς
ἐντολὰς ταύτας ὑπὸ ἀνθρώπου φυλαχθῆναι.

IV. Καὶ ταῦτά μοι λίαν ὀργίλως ἐλάλησεν, ὥστε με συγ-
χυθῆναι καὶ λίαν αὐτὸν φοβηθῆναι· ἡ μορφὴ γὰρ αὐτοῦ
ἠλλοιώθη, ὥστε μὴ δύνασθαι ἄνθρωπον ὑπενεγκεῖν τὴν ὀργὴν
αὐτοῦ. 2. ἰδὼν δέ με τεταραγμένον ὅλον καὶ συγκεχυμένον
ἤρξατό μοι ἐπιεικέστερον [καὶ ἱλαρώτερον] λαλεῖν, καὶ λέγει·
Ἄφρον, ἀσύνετε καὶ δίψυχε, οὐ νοεῖς τὴν δόξαν τοῦ Θεοῦ,
πῶς μεγάλη ἐστὶ καὶ ἰσχυρὰ καὶ θαυμαστή, ὅτι ἔκτισε τὸν
κόσμον ἕνεκα τοῦ ἀνθρώπου καὶ πᾶσαν τὴν κτίσιν αὐτοῦ
ὑπέταξε τῷ ἀνθρώπῳ, καὶ τὴν ἐξουσίαν πᾶσαν ἔδωκεν αὐτῷ
τοῦ κατακυριεύειν τῶν ὑπὸ τὸν οὐρανὸν πάντων; 3. εἰ οὖν,
[φησί,] πάντων ὁ ἄνθρωπος κύριός ἐστι τῶν κτισμάτων τοῦ
Θεοῦ καὶ πάντων κατακυριεύει, οὐ δύναται καὶ τούτων τῶν
ἐντολῶν κατακυριεῦσαι; δύναται, φησί, [πάντων καὶ] πασῶν
τῶν ἐντολῶν τούτων κατακυριεῦσαι ὁ ἄνθρωπος ὁ ἔχων τὸν
Κύριον ἐν τῇ καρδίᾳ αὐτοῦ. 4. οἱ δὲ ἐπὶ τοῖς χείλεσιν ἔχοντες τὸν Κύριον, τὴν δὲ καρδίαν αὐτῶν πεπωρωμένην, καὶ
μακρὰν ὄντες ἀπὸ τοῦ Κυρίου, ἐκείνοις αἱ ἐντολαὶ αὗται σκληραί εἰσι καὶ δύσβατοι. 5. θέσθε οὖν ὑμεῖς, οἱ κενοὶ καὶ
ἐλαφροὶ ὄντες ἐν τῇ πίστει, τὸν Κύριον ὑμῶν εἰς τὴν καρδίαν,
καὶ γνώσεσθε ὅτι οὐδέν ἐστιν εὐκολώτερον τῶν ἐντολῶν τούτων οὔτε γλυκύτερον οὔτε ἡμερώτερον. 6. ἐπιστράφητε ὑμεῖς

---

12. iv. 1 τὴν ὀργὴν αὐτοῦ] Here follows in A a gloss of some forty words.
2 καὶ ἱλαρώτερον] ins. Gebhardt in marg. [L₁E]; om. A; def. L₂.   ὑπὸ
τὸν οὐρανὸν] ὑπὸ τῶν οὐρανῶν A.

οἱ ταῖς ἐντολαῖς πορευόμενοι τοῦ διαβόλου, ταῖς δυσκόλοις καὶ πικραῖς καὶ ἀγρίαις καὶ ἀσελγέσι, καὶ μὴ φοβήθητε τὸν διάβολον, ὅτι ἐν αὐτῷ δύναμις οὐκ ἔστιν καθ᾽ ὑμῶν· 7. ἐγὼ γὰρ ἔσομαι μεθ᾽ ὑμῶν, ὁ ἄγγελος τῆς μετανοίας ὁ κατακυριεύων αὐτοῦ. ὁ διάβολος μόνον φόβον ἔχει, ὁ δὲ φόβος αὐτοῦ τόνον οὐκ ἔχει· μὴ φοβήθητε οὖν αὐτόν, καὶ φεύξεται ἀφ᾽ ὑμῶν.

V. Λέγω αὐτῷ· Κύριε, ἄκουσόν μου ὀλίγων ῥημάτων. Λέγε, φησίν, ὃ βούλει. Ὁ μὲν ἄνθρωπος, φημί, κύριε, πρόθυμός ἐστι τὰς ἐντολὰς τοῦ Θεοῦ φυλάσσειν, καὶ οὐδείς ἐστιν ὁ μὴ αἰτούμενος παρὰ τοῦ Κυρίου, ἵνα ἐνδυναμωθῇ ἐν ταῖς ἐντολαῖς αὐτοῦ καὶ ὑποταγῇ αὐταῖς· ἀλλ᾽ ὁ διάβολος σκληρός ἐστι καὶ καταδυναστεύει αὐτῶν. 2. Οὐ δύναται, φησί, καταδυναστεύειν τῶν δούλων τοῦ Θεοῦ τῶν ἐξ ὅλης καρδίας ἐλπιζόντων ἐπ᾽ αὐτόν. δύναται ὁ διάβολος ἀντιπαλαῖσαι, κατα-

cf. James iv. 7.

παλαῖσαι δὲ οὐ δύναται. ἐὰν οὖν ἀντισταθῆτε αὐτῷ, νικηθεὶς φεύξεται ἀφ᾽ ὑμῶν κατῃσχυμμένος. ὅσοι δέ, φησίν, ἀπόκενοί εἰσι, φοβοῦνται τὸν διάβολον ὡς δύναμιν ἔχοντα. 3. ὅταν ὁ ἄνθρωπος κεράμια ἱκανώτατα γεμίσῃ οἴνου καλοῦ, καὶ ἐν τοῖς κεραμίοις ἐκείνοις ὀλίγα ἀπόκενα ᾖ, ἔρχεται ἐπὶ τὰ κεράμια καὶ οὐ κατανοεῖ τὰ πλήρη· οἶδε γὰρ ὅτι πλήρη εἰσί· κατανοεῖ δὲ τὰ ἀπόκενα, φοβούμενος μήποτε ὤξισαν· ταχὺ γὰρ τὰ ἀπόκενα κεράμια ὀξίζουσι, καὶ ἀπόλλυται ἡ ἡδονὴ τοῦ οἴνου. 4. οὕτω καὶ ὁ διάβολος ἔρχεται ἐπὶ πάντας τοὺς δούλους τοῦ Θεοῦ ἐκπειράζων αὐτούς. ὅσοι οὖν πλήρεις εἰσὶν ἐν τῇ πίστει, ἀνθεστήκασιν αὐτῷ ἰσχυρῶς, κἀκεῖνος ἀποχωρεῖ ἀπ᾽ αὐτῶν μὴ ἔχων τόπον ποῦ εἰσέλθῃ. ἔρχεται οὖν τότε πρὸς τοὺς ἀποκένους, καὶ ἔχων τόπον εἰσπορεύεται εἰς αὐτούς, καὶ ὃ δὲ βούλεται ἐν αὐτοῖς ἐργάζεται, καὶ γίνονται αὐτῷ ὑπόδουλοι.

VI. Ἐγὼ δὲ ὑμῖν λέγω, ὁ ἄγγελος τῆς μετανοίας· μὴ φοβήθητε τὸν διάβολον. ἀπεστάλην γάρ, φησί, μεθ᾽ ὑμῶν εἶναι τῶν μετανοούντων ἐξ ὅλης καρδίας αὐτῶν καὶ ἰσχυροποιῆσαι αὐτοὺς ἐν τῇ πίστει. 2. πιστεύσατε οὖν τῷ Θεῷ ὑμεῖς οἱ διὰ τὰς ἁμαρτίας ὑμῶν ἀπεγνωκότες τὴν ζωὴν ὑμῶν καὶ προστιθέντες ἁμαρτίαις καὶ καταβαρύνοντες τὴν ζωὴν ὑμῶν, ὅτι ἐὰν ἐπιστραφῆτε πρὸς τὸν Κύριον ἐξ ὅλης τῆς καρδίας ὑμῶν καὶ ἐργάσησθε τὴν δικαιοσύνην τὰς λοιπὰς ἡμέρας τῆς ζωῆς ὑμῶν καὶ δουλεύσητε αὐτῷ ὀρθῶς κατὰ τὸ θέλημα αὐτοῦ, ποιήσει ἴασιν τοῖς προτέροις ὑμῶν ἁμαρτήμασι, καὶ ἕξετε δύναμιν τοῦ κατακυριεῦσαι τῶν ἔργων τοῦ διαβόλου. τὴν δὲ ἀπειλὴν τοῦ διαβόλου ὅλως μὴ φοβήθητε· ἄτονος γάρ ἐστιν ὥσπερ νεκροῦ νεῦρα. 3. ἀκούσατε οὖν μου, καὶ φοβήθητε τὸν πάντα ΔΥΝΑΜΕΝΟΝ, cῶcαι κὰ ἀπολέcαι, καὶ τηρεῖτε James iv. τὰς ἐντολὰς ταύτας, καὶ ζήσεσθε τῷ Θεῷ. 4. λέγω αὐτῷ· 12. Κύριε, νῦν ἐνεδυναμώθην ἐν πᾶσι τοῖς δικαιώμασι τοῦ Κυρίου, ὅτι σὺ μετ᾽ ἐμοῦ εἶ· καὶ οἶδα ὅτι συγκόψεις τὴν δύναμιν τοῦ διαβόλου πᾶσαν, καὶ ἡμεῖς αὐτοῦ κατακυριεύσομεν καὶ κατισχύσομεν πάντων τῶν ἔργων αὐτοῦ. καὶ ἐλπίζω, κύριε, δύνασθαί με νῦν τὰς ἐντολὰς ταύτας, ἃς ἐντέταλσαι, τοῦ Κυρίου ἐνδυναμοῦντος φυλάξαι. 5. Φυλάξεις, φησίν, ἐὰν ἡ καρδία σου καθαρὰ γένηται πρὸς Κύριον· καὶ πάντες δὲ φυλάξουσιν ὅσοι ἂν καθαρίσωσιν ἑαυτῶν τὰς καρδίας ἀπὸ τῶν ματαίων ἐπιθυμιῶν τοῦ αἰῶνος τούτου, καὶ ζήσονται τῷ Θεῷ.

ΠΑΡΑΒΟΛΑΙ ΑΣ ΕΛΑΛΗΣΕ ΜΕΤ᾽ ΕΜΟΥ

Λέγει μοι· Οἴδατε ὅτι ἐπὶ ξένης κατοικεῖτε ὑμεῖς οἱ δοῦλοι τοῦ Θεοῦ· ἡ γὰρ πόλις ὑμῶν μακράν ἐστιν ἀπὸ τῆς πόλεως ταύτης· εἰ οὖν οἴδατε τὴν πόλιν ὑμῶν ἐν ᾗ μέλλετε κατοικεῖν, τί ὧδε ὑμεῖς ἐτοιμάζετε ἀγροὺς καὶ παρατάξεις πολυτελεῖς καὶ οἰκοδομὰς καὶ οἰκήματα μάταια ; 2. ταῦτα οὖν ὁ ἑτοιμάζων εἰς ταύτην τὴν πόλιν οὐ διανοεῖται ἐπανα-

κάμψαι εἰς τὴν ἰδίαν πόλιν. 3. ἄφρον καὶ δίψυχε καὶ ταλαί-
πωρε ἄνθρωπε, οὐ νοεῖς ὅτι ταῦτα πάντα ἀλλότριά ἐστι, καὶ
ὑπ' ἐξουσίαν ἑτέρου εἰσίν; ἐρεῖ γὰρ ὁ κύριος τῆς πόλεως
ταύτης· Οὐ θέλω σε κατοικεῖν εἰς τὴν πόλιν μου, ἀλλ' ἔξελθε
ἐκ τῆς πόλεως ταύτης, ὅτι τοῖς νόμοις μου οὐ χρᾶσαι. 4. σὺ
οὖν ἔχων ἀγροὺς καὶ οἰκήσεις καὶ ἑτέρας ὑπάρξεις πολλάς,
ἐκβαλλόμενος ὑπ' αὐτοῦ τί ποιήσεις σου τὸν ἀγρὸν καὶ τὴν
οἰκίαν καὶ τὰ λοιπὰ ὅσα ἡτοίμασας σεαυτῷ; λέγει γάρ σοι
δικαίως ὁ κύριος τῆς χώρας ταύτης· Ἢ τοῖς νόμοις μου χρῶ,
ἢ ἐκχώρει ἐκ τῆς χώρας μου. 5. σὺ οὖν τί μέλλεις ποιεῖν,
ἔχων νόμον ἐν τῇ σῇ πόλει; ἕνεκεν τῶν ἀγρῶν σου καὶ τῆς
λοιπῆς ὑπάρξεως τὸν νόμον σου πάντως ἀπαρνήσῃ καὶ πορεύσῃ τῷ νόμῳ τῆς πόλεως ταύτης; βλέπε μὴ ἀσύμφορόν
ἐστιν ἀπαρνῆσαι τὸν νόμον σου· ἐὰν γὰρ ἐπανακάμψαι θελήσῃς εἰς τὴν πόλιν σου, οὐ μὴ παραδεχθήσῃ, [ὅτι ἀπηρνήσω
τὸν νόμον τῆς πόλεώς σου,] καὶ ἐκκλεισθήσῃ ἀπ' αὐτῆς.
6. βλέπε οὖν σύ· ὡς ἐπὶ ξένης κατοικῶν μηδὲν πλέον ἑτοί-
μαζε σεαυτῷ εἰ μὴ τὴν αὐτάρκειαν τὴν ἀρκετήν σοι, καὶ
ἕτοιμος γίνου, ἵνα ὅταν θέλῃ ὁ δεσπότης τῆς πόλεως ταύτης
ἐκβαλεῖν σε ἀντιταξάμενον τῷ νόμῳ αὐτοῦ, ἐξέλθῃς ἐκ τῆς
πόλεως αὐτοῦ καὶ ἀπέλθῃς εἰς τὴν πόλιν σου, καὶ τῷ σῷ νόμῳ
χρήσῃ ἀνυβρίστως ἀγαλλιώμενος. 7. βλέπετε οὖν ὑμεῖς οἱ
δουλεύοντες τῷ Θεῷ καὶ ἔχοντες αὐτὸν εἰς τὴν καρδίαν· ἐργά-
ζεσθε τὰ ἔργα τοῦ Θεοῦ μνημονεύοντες τῶν ἐντολῶν αὐτοῦ καὶ
τῶν ἐπαγγελιῶν ὧν ἐπηγγείλατο, καὶ πιστεύσατε αὐτῷ ὅτι
ποιήσει αὐτάς, ἐὰν αἱ ἐντολαὶ αὐτοῦ φυλαχθῶσιν. 8. ἀντὶ
ἀγρῶν οὖν ἀγοράζετε ψυχὰς θλιβομένας, καθά τις δυνατός
ἐστι, καὶ χήρας καὶ ὀρφανοὺς ἐπισκέπτεσθε, καὶ μὴ παραβλέ-
πετε αὐτούς, καὶ τὸν πλοῦτον ὑμῶν καὶ τὰς παρατάξεις πάσας
εἰς τοιούτους ἀγροὺς καὶ οἰκίας δαπανᾶτε, ἃς ἐλάβετε παρὰ

1. 4 ὑπάρξεις] conj. Gebhardt [cf. ὑπάρξεως below, § 5]; πράξεις A; dub. E.
6 θέλῃ] conj. Gebhardt [L₁L₂]; ἔλθῃ A; dub. E.   εἰς τὴν πόλιν] conj.
Harmer [L₂E]; ἐν τῇ πόλει A; al. L₁.   ἀγαλλιώμενος] conj. Hollenberg
[L₁L₂E]; καὶ ἀγαλλιωμένως A.   7 θεῷ] conj. Harmer [L₁L₂]; κυρίῳ ΑΕ.

τοῦ Θεοῦ. 9. εἰς τοῦτο γὰρ ἐπλούτισεν ὑμᾶς ὁ δεσπότης, ἵνα
ταύτας τὰς διακονίας τελέσητε αὐτῷ· πολὺ βέλτιόν ἐστι
τοιούτους ἀγροὺς ἀγοράζειν [καὶ κτήματα] καὶ οἴκους, οὓς
εὑρήσεις ἐν τῇ πόλει σου, ὅταν ἐπιδημήσῃς εἰς αὐτήν. 10.
αὕτη ἡ πολυτέλεια καλὴ καὶ ἱλαρά, λύπην μὴ ἔχουσα μηδὲ
φόβον, ἔχουσα δὲ χαράν. τὴν οὖν πολυτέλειαν τῶν ἐθνῶν μὴ
πράσσετε· ἀσύμφορον γάρ ἐστιν ὑμῖν τοῖς δούλοις τοῦ Θεοῦ·
11. τὴν δὲ ἰδίαν πολυτέλειαν πράσσετε, ἐν ᾗ δύνασθε χαρῆ-
ναι· καὶ μὴ παραχαράσσετε, μηδὲ τοῦ ἀλλοτρίου ἅψησθε
μηδὲ ἐπιθυμεῖτε αὐτοῦ· πονηρὸν γάρ ἐστιν ἀλλοτρίων ἐπιθυμεῖν. τὸ δὲ σὸν ἔργον ἐργάζου, καὶ σωθήσῃ.

Ἄλλη παραβολή

1. Περιπατοῦντός μου εἰς τὸν ἀγρὸν καὶ κατανοοῦντος
πτελέαν καὶ ἄμπελον, καὶ διακρίνοντος περὶ αὐτῶν καὶ τῶν
καρπῶν αὐτῶν, φανεροῦταί μοι ὁ ποιμὴν καὶ λέγει· Τί σὺ ἐν
ἑαυτῷ ζητεῖς; Περὶ τῆς πτελέας καὶ τῆς ἀμπέλου συζητῶ,
φημί, [κύριε,] ὅτι εὐπρεπέστατοί εἰσιν ἀλλήλαις. 2. Ταῦτα
τὰ δύο δένδρα, φησίν, εἰς τύπον κεῖνται τοῖς δούλοις τοῦ Θεοῦ.
Ἤθελον, φημί, [κύριε,] γνῶναι τὸν τύπον τῶν δένδρων τούτων
ὧν λέγεις. Βλέπεις, φησί, τὴν πτελέαν καὶ τὴν ἄμπελον;
Βλέπω, φημί, κύριε. 3. Ἡ ἄμπελος, φησίν, αὕτη καρπὸν
φέρει, ἡ δὲ πτελέα ξύλον ἄκαρπόν ἐστιν· ἀλλ' ἡ ἄμπελος
αὕτη, ἐὰν μὴ ἀναβῇ ἐπὶ τὴν πτελέαν, οὐ δύναται καρποφορῆσαι πολὺ ἐρριμμένη χαμαί, καὶ ὃν φέρει καρπόν, σεσηπότα
φέρει μὴ κρεμαμένη ἐπὶ τῆς πτελέας. ὅταν οὖν ἐπιρριφῇ ἡ
ἄμπελος ἐπὶ τὴν πτελέαν, καὶ παρ' ἑαυτῆς φέρει καρπὸν καὶ
παρὰ τῆς πτελέας. 4. βλέπεις οὖν ὅτι καὶ ἡ πτελέα [πολὺν]
καρπὸν δίδωσιν, οὐκ ἐλάσσονα τῆς ἀμπέλου, μᾶλλον δὲ καὶ
πλείονα. | Πῶς, φημί, κύριε, πλείονα; | Ὅτι, φησίν, ἡ ἄμπε-
λος κρεμαμένη ἐπὶ τὴν πτελέαν τὸν καρπὸν πολὺν καὶ καλὸν

10 ἱλαρά] conj. Hilgenfeld [L₂E]; ἱερὰ A; al. L₁.   ἐθνῶν] A perhaps
reads ἐθνικῶν.   2. 1 κύριε] ins. [L₁L₂E]; om. A.   2 κύριε] ins. [L₁L₂E];
om. A.   4 πῶς...πλείονα] ins. Gebhardt [L₁E]; om. AL₂ by homœot.

δίδωσιν, ἐρριμμένη δὲ χαμαὶ σαπρὸν καὶ ὀλίγον φέρει. αὕτη οὖν ἡ παραβολὴ εἰς τοὺς δούλους τοῦ Θεοῦ κεῖται, εἰς πτωχὸν καὶ πλούσιον. 5. Πῶς, φημί, κύριε; γνώρισόν μοι. Ἄκουε, φησίν· ὁ μὲν πλούσιος ἔχει χρήματα πολλά, τὰ δὲ πρὸς τὸν Κύριον πτωχεύει περισπώμενος περὶ τὸν πλοῦτον αὐτοῦ, καὶ λίαν μικρὰν ἔχει τὴν ἐξομολόγησιν καὶ τὴν ἔντευξιν πρὸς τὸν Κύριον, καὶ ἣν ἔχει, μικρὰν καὶ βληχρὰν καὶ ἄνω μὴ ἔχουσαν δύναμιν. ὅταν οὖν ἀναβῇ ὁ πλούσιος ἐπὶ τὸν πένητα καὶ χορηγήσῃ αὐτῷ τὰ δέοντα, πιστεύων ὅτι ὃ ἐργάσεται εἰς τὸν πένητα δυνήσεται τὸν μισθὸν εὑρεῖν παρὰ τῷ Θεῷ—ὅτι ὁ πένης πλούσιός ἐστιν ἐν τῇ ἐντεύξει [καὶ τῇ ἐξομολογήσει,] καὶ δύναμιν μεγάλην ἔχει ἡ ἔντευξις αὐτοῦ παρὰ τῷ Θεῷ— ἐπιχορηγεῖ οὖν ὁ πλούσιος τῷ πένητι πάντα ἀδιστάκτως· 6. ὁ πένης δὲ ἐπιχορηγούμενος ὑπὸ τοῦ πλουσίου ἐντυγχάνει αὐτῷ, τῷ Θεῷ εὐχαριστῶν περὶ τοῦ διδόντος αὐτῷ. κἀκεῖνος ἔτι ἐπισπουδάζει περὶ τοῦ πένητος, ἵνα ἀδιάλειπτος γένηται ἐν τῇ ζωῇ αὐτοῦ· οἶδε γὰρ ὅτι ἡ ἔντευξις τοῦ πένητος προσδεκτή ἐστι καὶ πλουσία πρὸς τὸν Θεόν. 7. ἀμφότεροι οὖν τὸ ἔργον τελοῦσιν· ὁ μὲν πένης ἐργάζεται τὴν ἔντευξιν ἐν ᾗ πλουτεῖ, [ἣν ἔλαβεν ἀπὸ τοῦ Κυρίου·] ταύτην ἀποδίδωσι τῷ Κυρίῳ τῷ ἐπιχορηγοῦντι αὐτῷ. καὶ ὁ πλούσιος ὡσαύτως τὸν πλοῦτον ὃν ἔλαβεν ἀπὸ τοῦ Κυρίου ἀδιστάκτως παρέχει τῷ πένητι. καὶ τοῦτο ἔργον μέγα ἐστὶ καὶ δεκτὸν παρὰ τῷ Θεῷ, ὅτι συνῆκεν ἐπὶ τῷ πλούτῳ αὐτοῦ καὶ εἰργάσατο εἰς τὸν πένητα ἐκ τῶν δωρημάτων τοῦ Κυρίου καὶ ἐτέλεσε τὴν διακονίαν τοῦ Κυρίου ὀρθῶς. 8. παρὰ τοῖς ἀνθρώποις οὖν ἡ πτελέα δοκεῖ καρπὸν μὴ φέρειν, καὶ οὐκ οἴδασιν οὐδὲ νοοῦσιν ὅτι, ἐὰν ἀβροχία γένηται, ἡ πτελέα ὕδωρ ἔχουσα τρέφει τὴν ἄμπελον, καὶ ἡ ἄμπελος ἀδιάλειπτον ἔχουσα ὕδωρ διπλοῦν τὸν καρπὸν δίδωσι, καὶ ὑπὲρ ἑαυτῆς καὶ ὑπὲρ τῆς πτελέας. οὕτω καὶ οἱ πένητες ἐντυγχάνοντες πρὸς τὸν Κύριον ὑπὲρ τῶν πλουσίων

2. 5 βληχρὰν] βλιχρὰν A.   ἄνω] conj. Tischendorf (cf. *apud dominum* L₂); ἀνοῦ (=ἀνθρώπου) A; om. L₁E.   ἀναβῇ] conj. Hollenberg (cf. above, § 3); ἀναπλῇ A; dub. L₂E; om. L₁.

πληροφοροῦσι τὸν πλοῦτον αὐτῶν, καὶ πάλιν οἱ πλούσιοι χορηγοῦντες τοῖς πένησι τὰ δέοντα πληροφοροῦσι τὰς ψυχὰς αὐτῶν. 9. γίνονται οὖν ἀμφότεροι κοινωνοὶ τοῦ ἔργου τοῦ δικαίου. ταῦτα οὖν ὁ ποιῶν οὐκ ἐγκαταλειφθήσεται ὑπὸ τοῦ Θεοῦ, ἀλλ᾽ ἔσται ἐπιγεγραμμένος εἰς τὰς βίβλους τῶν ζώντων. 10. μακάριοι οἱ ἔχοντες καὶ συνιέντες ὅτι παρὰ τοῦ Κυρίου πλουτίζονται· οἱ γὰρ ταῦτα φρονοῦντες δυνήσονται ἀγαθόν τι ἐργάζεσθαι.

Ἄλλη παραβολή

1. Ἔδειξέ μοι δένδρα πολλὰ μὴ ἔχοντα φύλλα, ἀλλ᾽ ὡσεὶ ξηρὰ ἐδόκει μοι εἶναι· ὅμοια γὰρ ἦν πάντα. καὶ λέγει μοι· Βλέπεις τὰ δένδρα ταῦτα; Βλέπω, φημί, κύριε, ὅμοια ὄντα καὶ ξηρά. ἀποκριθείς μοι λέγει· Ταῦτα τὰ δένδρα, ἃ βλέπεις, οἱ κατοικοῦντες εἰσὶν ἐν τῷ αἰῶνι τούτῳ. 2. Διατί οὖν, φημί, κύριε, ὡσεὶ ξηρά εἰσι καὶ ὅμοια; Ὅτι, φησίν, οὔτε οἱ δίκαιοι φαίνονται οὔτε οἱ ἁμαρτωλοὶ ἐν τῷ αἰῶνι τούτῳ, ἀλλ᾽ ὅμοιοί εἰσιν· ὁ γὰρ αἰὼν οὗτος τοῖς δικαίοις χειμών ἐστι, καὶ οὐ φαίνονται μετὰ τῶν ἁμαρτωλῶν κατοικοῦντες. 3. ὥσπερ γὰρ ἐν τῷ χειμῶνι τὰ δένδρα ἀποβεβληκότα τὰ φύλλα ὅμοιά εἰσι, καὶ οὐ φαίνονται τὰ ξηρὰ ποῖά εἰσιν ἢ τὰ ζῶντα, οὕτως ἐν τῷ αἰῶνι τούτῳ οὐ φαίνονται οὔτε οἱ δίκαιοι οὔτε οἱ ἁμαρτωλοί, ἀλλὰ πάντες ὅμοιοί εἰσιν.

Ἄλλη παραβολή

1. Ἔδειξέ μοι πάλιν δένδρα πολλά, ἃ μὲν βλαστῶντα, ἃ δὲ ξηρά, καὶ λέγει μοι· Βλέπεις, φησί, τὰ δένδρα ταῦτα; Βλέπω, φημί, κύριε, τὰ μὲν βλαστῶντα, τὰ δὲ ξηρά. 2. Ταῦτα, φησί, τὰ δένδρα τὰ βλαστῶντα οἱ δίκαιοί εἰσιν οἱ μέλλοντες κατοικεῖν εἰς τὸν αἰῶνα τὸν ἐρχόμενον· ὁ γὰρ αἰὼν ὁ ἐρχόμενος θέρος ἐστὶ τοῖς δικαίοις, τοῖς δὲ ἁμαρτωλοῖς χειμών. ὅταν

9 ὑπὸ] conj. Hollenberg; ἀπὸ A.   10 οἱ γὰρ...ἐργάζεσθαι] L₁L₂E ; om. A.   4. 2 θέρος] conj. Hilgenfeld [L₁L₂E] ; θρόνος A.

οὖν ἐπιλάμψῃ τὸ ἔλεος τοῦ Κυρίου, τότε φανερωθήσονται οἱ δουλεύοντες τῷ Θεῷ, καὶ πάντες φανερωθήσονται· 3. ὥσπερ γὰρ τῷ θέρει ἑνὸς ἑκάστου δένδρου οἱ καρποὶ φανεροῦνται καὶ ἐπιγινώσκονται ποταποί εἰσιν, οὕτω καὶ τῶν δικαίων οἱ καρποὶ φανεροὶ ἔσονται, καὶ γνωσθήσονται πάντες [οἱ ἐλάχιστοι ὄντες] εὐθαλεῖς ὄντες ἐν τῷ αἰῶνι ἐκείνῳ. 4. τὰ δὲ ἔθνη καὶ οἱ ἁμαρτωλοί, οἷα εἶδες τὰ δένδρα τὰ ξηρά, τοιοῦτοι εὑρεθήσονται ξηροὶ καὶ ἄκαρποι ἐν ἐκείνῳ τῷ αἰῶνι, καὶ ὡς ξύλα κατακαυθήσονται καὶ φανεροὶ ἔσονται· ὅτι ἡ πρᾶξις αὐτῶν πονηρὰ γέγονεν ἐν τῇ ζωῇ αὐτῶν. οἱ μὲν γὰρ ἁμαρτωλοὶ καυθήσονται, ὅτι ἥμαρτον καὶ οὐ μετενόησαν· τὰ δὲ ἔθνη καυθήσονται, ὅτι οὐκ ἔγνωσαν τὸν κτίσαντα αὐτούς. 5. σὺ οὖν καρποφόρησον, ἵνα ἐν τῷ θέρει ἐκείνῳ γνωσθῇ σου ὁ καρπός. ἀπέχου δὲ ἀπὸ τῶν πολλῶν πράξεων, καὶ οὐδὲν διαμάρτῃς. οἱ γὰρ τὰ πολλὰ πράσσοντες πολλὰ καὶ ἁμαρτάνουσι, περισπώμενοι περὶ τὰς πράξεις αὐτῶν καὶ μηδὲν δουλεύοντες τῷ Κυρίῳ ἑαυτῶν. 6. Πῶς οὖν, φησίν, ὁ τοιοῦτος δύναταί τι αἰτήσασθαι παρὰ τοῦ Κυρίου καὶ λαβεῖν, μὴ δουλεύων τῷ Κυρίῳ; οἱ [γὰρ] δουλεύοντες αὐτῷ, ἐκεῖνοι λήψονται τὰ αἰτήματα αὐτῶν, οἱ δὲ μὴ δουλεύοντες τῷ Κυρίῳ, ἐκεῖνοι οὐδὲν λήψονται. 7. ἐὰν δὲ μίαν τις πρᾶξιν ἐργάσηται, δύναται καὶ τῷ Κυρίῳ δουλεῦσαι· οὐ γὰρ διαφθαρήσεται ἡ διάνοια αὐτοῦ ἀπὸ τοῦ Κυρίου, ἀλλὰ δουλεύσει αὐτῷ ἔχων τὴν διάνοιαν αὐτοῦ καθαράν. 8. ταῦτα οὖν ἐὰν ποιήσῃς, δύνασαι καρποφορῆσαι εἰς τὸν αἰῶνα τὸν ἐρχόμενον· καὶ ὃς ἂν ταῦτα ποιήσῃ, καρποφορήσει.

Ἄλλη παραβολή

I. Νηστεύων καὶ καθήμενος εἰς ὄρος τι καὶ εὐχαριστῶν τῷ Κυρίῳ περὶ πάντων ὧν ἐποίησε μετ' ἐμοῦ, βλέπω τὸν ποιμένα παρακαθήμενόν μοι καὶ λέγοντα· Τί ὀρθρινὸς ὧδε

4. 3 οἱ ἐλάχιστοι ὄντες] conj. Harmer [L₂]; οἱ εὐθαλεῖς ὄντες A; dub. L₁; om. E.   4 οἷα] conj. Schmidt [L₁L₂]; ἃ A; dub. E.   5 οὐδὲν] L₁L₂; pref. ου...A; def. E.   ἑαυτῶν] ε...A.   6 γὰρ] ins. Hollenberg [L₁L₂]; om. A; def. E.

ἐλήλυθας; Ὅτι, φημί, κύριε, στατίωνα ἔχω. 2. Τί, φησίν,
ἐστὶ στατίων; Νηστεύω, φημί, κύριε. Νηστεία δέ, φησί,
τί ἐστιν αὕτη[, ἣν νηστεύετε]; Ὡς εἰώθειν, φημί, κύριε,
οὕτω νηστεύω. 3. Οὐκ οἴδατε, φησί, νηστεύειν τῷ Κυρίῳ,
οὐδέ ἐστιν νηστεία αὕτη ἡ ἀνωφελὴς ἣν νηστεύετε αὐτῷ.
Διατί, φημί, κύριε, τοῦτο λέγεις; Λέγω σοι, φησίν, ὅτι οὐκ
ἔστιν αὕτη νηστεία, ἣν δοκεῖτε νηστεύειν· ἀλλ' ἐγώ σε διδάξω
τί ἐστι νηστεία πλήρης καὶ δεκτὴ τῷ Κυρίῳ. ἄκουε, φησίν.
4. ὁ Θεὸς οὐ βούλεται τοιαύτην νηστείαν ματαίαν· οὕτω
γὰρ νηστεύων τῷ Θεῷ οὐδὲν ἐργάσῃ τῇ δικαιοσύνῃ. νήστευσον δὲ [τῷ Θεῷ] νηστείαν τοιαύτην· 5. μηδὲν πονηρεύσῃ
ἐν τῇ ζωῇ σου, καὶ δούλευσον τῷ Κυρίῳ ἐν καθαρᾷ καρδίᾳ·
τήρησον τὰς ἐντολὰς αὐτοῦ πορευόμενος ἐν τοῖς προστάγμασιν αὐτοῦ, καὶ μηδεμία ἐπιθυμία πονηρὰ ἀναβήτω ἐν τῇ
καρδίᾳ σου· πίστευσον δὲ τῷ Θεῷ· καὶ ἐὰν ταῦτα ἐργάσῃ καὶ
φοβηθῇς αὐτὸν καὶ ἐγκρατεύσῃ ἀπὸ παντὸς πονηροῦ πράγματος, ζήσῃ τῷ Θεῷ· καὶ ταῦτα ἐὰν ἐργάσῃ, μεγάλην νηστείαν
τελέσεις καὶ δεκτὴν τῷ Θεῷ.

II.   Ἄκουε τὴν παραβολὴν ἣν μέλλω σοι λέγειν ἀνήκουσαν τῇ νηστείᾳ. 2. εἶχέ τις ἀγρὸν καὶ δούλους πολλούς, καὶ
μέρος τι τοῦ ἀγροῦ ἐφύτευσεν ἀμπελῶνα. καὶ ἐκλεξάμενος
δοῦλόν τινα πιστὸν καὶ εὐάρεστον ἔντιμον, προσεκαλέσατο
αὐτὸν καὶ λέγει αὐτῷ· Λάβε τὸν ἀμπελῶνα τοῦτον [ὃν
ἐφύτευσα] καὶ χαράκωσον αὐτὸν [ἕως ἔρχομαι], καὶ ἕτερον δὲ
μὴ ποιήσῃς τῷ ἀμπελῶνι· καὶ ταύτην μου τὴν ἐντολὴν
φύλαξον, καὶ ἐλεύθερος ἔσῃ παρ' ἐμοί. ἐξῆλθε δὲ ὁ δεσπότης
τοῦ δούλου εἰς τὴν ἀποδημίαν. 3. ἐξελθόντος δὲ αὐτοῦ
ἔλαβεν ὁ δοῦλος καὶ ἐχαράκωσε τὸν ἀμπελῶνα. καὶ τελέσας
τὴν χαράκωσιν τοῦ ἀμπελῶνος εἶδε τὸν ἀμπελῶνα βοτανῶν
πλήρη ὄντα. 4. ἐν ἑαυτῷ οὖν ἐλογίσατο λέγων· Ταύτην
τὴν ἐντολὴν τοῦ κυρίου τετέλεκα· σκάψω λοιπὸν τὸν ἀμπελῶνα τοῦτον, καὶ ἔσται εὐπρεπέστερος ἐσκαμμένος, καὶ

βοτάνας μὴ ἔχων δώσει καρπὸν πλείονα, μὴ πνιγόμενος ὑπὸ
τῶν βοτανῶν. λαβὼν ἔσκαψε τὸν ἀμπελῶνα, καὶ πάσας
τὰς βοτάνας τὰς οὔσας ἐν τῷ ἀμπελῶνι ἐξέτιλλε. καὶ
ἐγένετο ὁ ἀμπελὼν ἐκεῖνος εὐπρεπέστατος καὶ εὐθαλής, μὴ
ἔχων βοτάνας πνιγούσας αὐτόν. 5. μετὰ χρόνον ἦλθεν ὁ
δεσπότης τοῦ δούλου [καὶ τοῦ ἀγροῦ], καὶ εἰσῆλθεν εἰς τὸν
ἀμπελῶνα. καὶ ἰδὼν τὸν ἀμπελῶνα κεχαρακωμένον εὐπρεπῶς, ἔτι δὲ καὶ ἐσκαμμένον, καὶ [πάσας] τὰς βοτάνας ἐκτε-
τιλμένας καὶ εὐθαλεῖς οὔσας τὰς ἀμπέλους, ἐχάρη [λίαν]
ἐπὶ τοῖς ἔργοις τοῦ δούλου. 6. προσκαλεσάμενος οὖν τὸν
υἱὸν αὐτοῦ τὸν ἀγαπητόν, ὃν εἶχε κληρονόμον, καὶ τοὺς
φίλους, οὓς εἶχε συμβούλους, λέγει αὐτοῖς ὅσα ἐνετείλατο
τῷ δούλῳ αὐτοῦ, καὶ ὅσα εὗρε γεγονότα. κἀκεῖνοι συνε-
χάρησαν τῷ δούλῳ ἐπὶ τῇ μαρτυρίᾳ ᾗ ἐμαρτύρησεν αὐτῷ ὁ
δεσπότης. 7. καὶ λέγει αὐτοῖς· Ἐγὼ τῷ δούλῳ τούτῳ
ἐλευθερίαν ἐπηγγειλάμην ἐάν μου τὴν ἐντολὴν φυλάξῃ ἣν
ἐνετειλάμην αὐτῷ· ἐφύλαξε δέ μου τὴν ἐντολὴν καὶ προσ-
έθηκε τῷ ἀμπελῶνι ἔργον καλόν, καὶ ἐμοὶ λίαν ἤρεσεν.
ἀντὶ τούτου οὖν τοῦ ἔργου οὗ εἰργάσατο θέλω αὐτὸν συγκλη-
ρονόμον τῷ υἱῷ μου ποιῆσαι, ὅτι τὸ καλὸν φρονήσας οὐ
παρενεθυμήθη, ἀλλ' ἐτέλεσεν αὐτό. 8. ταύτῃ τῇ γνώμῃ ὁ
υἱὸς τοῦ δεσπότου συνηυδόκησεν αὐτῷ, ἵνα συγκληρονόμος
γένηται ὁ δοῦλος τῷ υἱῷ. 9. μετὰ ἡμέρας ὀλίγας δεῖπνον
ἐποίησεν ὁ οἰκοδεσπότης αὐτοῦ, καὶ ἔπεμψεν αὐτῷ ἐκ τοῦ
δείπνου ἐδέσματα πολλά. λαβὼν δὲ ὁ δοῦλος [τὰ ἐδέσματα
τὰ πεμφθέντα αὐτῷ παρὰ τοῦ δεσπότου] τὰ ἀρκοῦντα αὐτῷ
ἦρε, τὰ λοιπὰ δὲ τοῖς συνδούλοις αὐτοῦ διέδωκεν. 10. οἱ δὲ
σύνδουλοι αὐτοῦ λαβόντες τὰ ἐδέσματα ἐχάρησαν, καὶ
ἤρξαντο εὔχεσθαι ὑπὲρ αὐτοῦ ἵνα χάριν μείζονα εὕρῃ παρὰ
τῷ δεσπότῃ, ὅτι οὕτως ἐχρήσατο αὐτοῖς. 11. ταῦτα πάντα
τὰ γεγονότα ὁ δεσπότης αὐτοῦ ἤκουσε, καὶ πάλιν λίαν ἐχάρη

---

5. ii. 6 αὐτοῦ sec.] αὐτῷ A.   7 ἐνετειλάμην] conj. Hollenberg [L₁E];
ἐπηγγειλάμην A; dub. L₂.   9 ὁ οἰκοδεσπότης αὐτοῦ] ins. Hollenberg
[L₁L₂E]; om. A.

ἐπὶ τῇ πράξει αὐτοῦ. συγκαλεσάμενος πάλιν τοὺς φίλους
ὁ δεσπότης καὶ τὸν υἱὸν αὐτοῦ ἀπήγγειλεν αὐτοῖς τὴν πρᾶξιν
αὐτοῦ ἣν ἔπραξεν ἐπὶ τοῖς ἐδέσμασιν αὐτοῦ οἷς ἔλαβεν· οἱ δὲ
ἔτι μᾶλλον συνευδόκησαν γενέσθαι τὸν δοῦλον συγκληρο-
νόμον τῷ υἱῷ αὐτοῦ.

III. Λέγω· Κύριε, ἐγὼ ταύτας τὰς παραβολὰς οὐ γινώσκω οὐδὲ δύναμαι νοῆσαι, ἐὰν μή μοι ἐπιλύσῃς αὐτάς. 2.
Πάντα σοι ἐπιλύσω, φησί, καὶ ὅσα ἂν λαλήσω μετὰ σοῦ,
δείξω σοι. τὰς ἐντολὰς | τοῦ Κυρίου φύλασσε, καὶ ἔσῃ εὐά-
ρεστος τῷ Θεῷ καὶ ἐγγραφήσῃ εἰς τὸν ἀριθμὸν τῶν φυλασ-
σόντων τὰς ἐντολὰς | αὐτοῦ. 3. ἐὰν δέ τι ἀγαθὸν ποιήσῃς
ἐκτὸς τῆς ἐντολῆς τοῦ Θεοῦ, σεαυτῷ περιποιήσῃ δόξαν περισσοτέραν, καὶ ἔσῃ ἐνδοξότερος παρὰ τῷ Θεῷ οὗ ἔμελλες εἶναι.
ἐὰν οὖν φυλάσσων τὰς ἐντολὰς τοῦ Θεοῦ προσθῇς καὶ τὰς
λειτουργίας ταύτας, χαρήσῃ, ἐὰν τηρήσῃς αὐτὰς κατὰ τὴν
ἐμὴν ἐντολήν. 4. λέγω αὐτῷ· Κύριε, ὃ ἐάν μοι ἐντείλῃ,
φυλάξω αὐτό· οἶδα γὰρ ὅτι σὺ μετ᾽ ἐμοῦ εἶ. Ἔσομαι, φησί,
μετὰ σοῦ, ὅτι τοιαύτην προθυμίαν ἔχεις τῆς ἀγαθοποιήσεως,
καὶ μετὰ πάντων δὲ ἔσομαι, φησίν, ὅσοι τοιαύτην προθυμίαν
ἔχουσιν. 5. ἡ νηστεία αὕτη, φησί, τηρουμένων τῶν ἐντολῶν
τοῦ Κυρίου λίαν καλή ἐστιν. οὕτως οὖν φυλάξεις τὴν νηστείαν ταύτην [ἣν μέλλεις τηρεῖν]. 6. πρῶτον πάντων φύλαξαι
ἀπὸ παντὸς ῥήματος πονηροῦ καὶ πάσης ἐπιθυμίας πονηρᾶς,
καὶ καθάρισόν σου τὴν καρδίαν ἀπὸ πάντων τῶν ματαιωμάτων
τοῦ αἰῶνος τούτου. ἐὰν ταῦτα φυλάξῃς, ἔσται σοι αὕτη ἡ
νηστεία τελεία. 7. οὕτω δὲ ποιήσεις· συντελέσας τὰ γεγραμμένα, ἐν ἐκείνῃ τῇ ἡμέρᾳ ᾗ νηστεύεις μηδὲν γεύσῃ εἰ μὴ
ἄρτον καὶ ὕδωρ, καὶ ἐκ τῶν ἐδεσμάτων σου ὧν ἔμελλες
τρώγειν συμψηφίσας τὴν ποσότητα τῆς δαπάνης ἐκείνης τῆς
ἡμέρας ἧς ἔμελλες ποιεῖν, δώσεις αὐτὸ χήρᾳ ἢ ὀρφανῷ ἢ
ὑστερουμένῳ, καὶ οὕτω ταπεινοφρονήσεις, ἵν᾽ ἐκ τῆς ταπεινο-

iii. 1 τὰς] σὰς A.   2 τοῦ κυρίου...ἐντολὰς] ins. Gebhardt [L₁L₂]; om.
AE by homœot.   3 δὲ] conj. Anger [L₁L₂E]; γὲ A.   4 τοιαύτην
sec.] conj. Harmer [L₂]; ταύτην τὴν A; idem (τὴν αὐτὴν) L₁; def. E.

φροσύνης σου ὁ εἰληφὼς ἐμπλήσῃ τὴν ἑαυτοῦ ψυχὴν καὶ εὔξηται ὑπὲρ σοῦ πρὸς τὸν Κύριον. 8. ἐὰν οὖν οὕτω τελέσῃς τὴν νηστείαν ὥς σοι ἐνετειλάμην, ἔσται ἡ θυσία σου δεκτὴ παρὰ τῷ Θεῷ, καὶ ἔγγραφος ἔσται ἡ νηστεία αὕτη, καὶ ἡ λειτουργία οὕτως ἐργαζομένη καλὴ καὶ ἱλαρά ἐστι καὶ εὐπρόσδεκτος τῷ Κυρίῳ. 9. ταῦτα οὕτω τηρήσεις σὺ μετὰ τῶν τέκνων σου καὶ ὅλου τοῦ οἴκου σου· τηρήσας δὲ αὐτὰ μακάριος ἔσῃ· καὶ ὅσοι ἂν ἀκούσαντες αὐτὰ τηρήσωσι, μακάριοι ἔσονται, καὶ ὅσα ἂν αἰτήσωνται παρὰ τοῦ Κυρίου λήψονται.

IV. Ἐδεήθην αὐτοῦ πολλὰ ἵνα μοι δηλώσῃ τὴν παραβολὴν τοῦ ἀγροῦ καὶ τοῦ δεσπότου καὶ τοῦ ἀμπελῶνος καὶ τοῦ δούλου τοῦ χαρακώσαντος τὸν ἀμπελῶνα [καὶ τῶν χαράκων] καὶ τῶν βοτανῶν τῶν ἐκτετιλμένων ἐκ τοῦ ἀμπελῶνος καὶ τοῦ υἱοῦ καὶ τῶν φίλων τῶν συμβούλων. συνῆκα γὰρ ὅτι παραβολή τίς ἐστι ταῦτα πάντα. 2. ὁ δὲ ἀποκριθείς μοι εἶπεν· Αὐθάδης εἶ λίαν εἰς τὸ ἐπερωτᾶν. οὐκ ὀφείλεις, [φησίν,] ἐπερωτᾶν οὐδὲν ὅλως· ἐὰν γάρ σοι δέῃ δηλωθῆναι, δηλωθήσεται. λέγω αὐτῷ· Κύριε, ὅσα ἄν μοι δείξῃς καὶ μὴ δηλώσῃς, μάτην ἔσομαι ἑωρακὼς αὐτὰ καὶ μὴ νοῶν τί ἐστιν· ὡσαύτως καὶ ἐάν μοι παραβολὰς λαλήσῃς καὶ μὴ ἐπιλύσῃς μοι αὐτάς, εἰς μάτην ἔσομαι ἀκηκοώς τι παρὰ σοῦ. 3. ὁ δὲ πάλιν ἀπεκρίθη μοι λέγων· Ὃς ἄν, φησί, δοῦλος ᾖ τοῦ Θεοῦ καὶ ἔχῃ τὸν Κύριον ἑαυτοῦ ἐν τῇ καρδίᾳ, αἰτεῖται παρ᾽ αὐτοῦ σύνεσιν καὶ λαμβάνει, καὶ πᾶσαν παραβολὴν ἐπιλύει, καὶ γνωστὰ αὐτῷ γίνονται τὰ ῥήματα τοῦ Κυρίου τὰ λεγόμενα διὰ παραβολῶν· ὅσοι δὲ βληχροί εἰσι καὶ ἀργοὶ πρὸς τὴν ἔντευξιν, ἐκεῖνοι διστάζουσιν αἰτεῖσθαι παρὰ τοῦ Κυρίου· 4. ὁ δὲ Κύριος πολυεύσπλαγχνός ἐστι, καὶ πᾶσι τοῖς αἰτουμένοις παρ᾽ αὐτοῦ ἀδιαλείπτως δίδωσι. σὺ δὲ ἐνδεδυναμωμένος ὑπὸ τοῦ ἁγίου ἀγγέλου καὶ εἰληφὼς παρ᾽ αὐτοῦ τοιαύτην ἔντευξιν καὶ μὴ ὢν ἀργός, διατί οὐκ αἰτῇ

---

5. iii. 9 αἰτήσωνται] conj. Anger [L₁L₂]; ἀκούσονται A; def. E.   iv. 3
παρ᾽ αὐτοῦ] conj. Gebhardt; παρ᾽ αὐτῷ A.

παρὰ τοῦ Κυρίου σύνεσιν καὶ λαμβάνεις παρ᾽ αὐτοῦ; 5. λέγω αὐτῷ· Κύριε, ἐγὼ ἔχων σὲ μεθ᾽ ἑαυτοῦ ἀνάγκην ἔχω σὲ αἰτεῖσθαι καὶ σὲ ἐπερωτᾶν· σὺ γάρ μοι δεικνύεις πάντα καὶ λαλεῖς μετ᾽ ἐμοῦ· εἰ δὲ ἄτερ σοῦ ἔβλεπον ἢ ἤκουον αὐτά, ἠρώτων ἂν τὸν Κύριον ἵνα μοι δηλωθῇ. V. Εἰπόν σοι, φησί, καὶ ἄρτι, ὅτι πανοῦργος εἶ καὶ αὐθάδης, ἐπερωτῶν τὰς ἐπιλύσεις τῶν παραβολῶν. ἐπειδὴ δὲ οὕτω παράμονος εἶ, ἐπιλύσω σοι τὴν παραβολὴν τοῦ ἀγροῦ καὶ τῶν λοιπῶν τῶν ἀκολούθων πάντων, ἵνα γνωστὰ πᾶσι ποιήσῃς αὐτά. ἄκουε νῦν, φησί, καὶ σύνιε αὐτά. 2. ὁ ἀγρὸς ὁ κόσμος οὗτός ἐστιν· ὁ δὲ κύριος τοῦ ἀγροῦ, ὁ κτίσας τὰ πάντα καὶ ἀπαρτίσας αὐτὰ καὶ ἐνδυναμώσας. ὁ δὲ cf. Ps. δοῦλος ὁ υἱὸς τοῦ Θεοῦ ἐστίν· αἱ δὲ ἄμπελοι ὁ λαὸς [οὗτός] lxvii. (lxviii.) 28. ἐστιν ὃν αὐτὸς ἐφύτευσεν. 3. οἱ δὲ χάρακες οἱ [ἅγιοι] ἄγγελοί εἰσι τοῦ Κυρίου οἱ συγκρατοῦντες τὸν λαὸν αὐτοῦ· αἱ δὲ βοτάναι αἱ ἐκτετιμέναι ἐκ τοῦ ἀμπελῶνος, αἱ ἀνομίαι εἰσὶ τῶν δούλων τοῦ Θεοῦ· τὰ δὲ ἐδέσματα ἃ ἔπεμψεν αὐτῷ ἐκ τοῦ δείπνου, αἱ ἐντολαί εἰσιν ἃς ἔδωκε τῷ λαῷ αὐτοῦ διὰ τοῦ υἱοῦ αὐτοῦ· οἱ δὲ φίλοι καὶ σύμβουλοι, οἱ ἅγιοι ἄγγελοι οἱ πρῶτοι κτισθέντες· ἡ δὲ ἀποδημία τοῦ δεσπότου, ὁ χρόνος ὁ περισσεύων εἰς τὴν παρουσίαν αὐτοῦ. 4. λέγω αὐτῷ· Κύριε, μεγάλως καὶ θαυμαστῶς [πάντα ἐστὶ] καὶ ἐνδόξως πάντα ἔχει. μὴ οὖν, φημί, ἐγὼ ἠδυνάμην ταῦτα νοῆσαι; οὐδὲ ἕτερος τῶν ἀνθρώπων, κἂν λίαν συνετὸς ᾖ τις, οὐ δύναται νοῆσαι αὐτά. ἔτι, φημί, κύριε, δήλωσόν μοι ὃ μέλλω σε ἐπερωτᾶν. 5. Λέγε, φησίν, εἴ τι βούλει. Διατί, φημί, [κύριε,] ὁ υἱὸς τοῦ Θεοῦ εἰς δούλου τρόπον κεῖται ἐν τῇ παραβολῇ;

VI. Ἄκουε, φησίν· εἰς δούλου τρόπον οὐ κεῖται ὁ υἱὸς τοῦ Θεοῦ, ἀλλ᾽ εἰς ἐξουσίαν μεγάλην κεῖται καὶ κυριότητα. Πῶς, φημί, κύριε; οὐ νοῶ. 2. Ὅτι, φησίν, ὁ Θεὸς τὸν ἀμπελῶνα ἐφύτευσε, τοῦτ᾽ ἔστι τὸν λαὸν ἔκτισε, καὶ παρέδωκε τῷ υἱῷ αὐτοῦ· καὶ ὁ υἱὸς κατέστησε τοὺς ἀγγέλους ἐπ᾽

---

v. 3 συγκρατοῦντες] conj. Hilgenfeld [L₁L₂]; συγκροτοῦντες A; def. E. αἱ tert.] ins. Hilgenfeld; om. A. vi. 1 οὐ pri.] ins. Hilgenfeld [L₁L₂E]; om. A.

αὐτοὺς τοῦ συντηρεῖν αὐτούς· καὶ αὐτὸς τὰς ἁμαρτίας αὐτῶν
ἐκαθάρισε πολλὰ κοπιάσας καὶ πολλοὺς κόπους ἠντληκώς·
οὐδεὶς γὰρ δύναται σκαφεῦσαι ἄτερ κόπου ἢ μόχθου. 3. αὐτὸς

cf. Ps. xvi. οὖν καθαρίσας τὰς ἁμαρτίας τοῦ λαοῦ ἔδειξεν αὐτοῖς τὰς
11. τρίβους τῆς ζωῆς, δοὺς αὐτοῖς τὸν νόμον ὃν ἔλαβε παρὰ τοῦ
cf. John x.
18. πατρὸς αὐτοῦ. 4. | βλέπεις, φησίν, ὅτι αὐτὸς κύριός ἐστι
τοῦ λαοῦ, ἐξουσίαν πᾶσαν λαβὼν παρὰ τοῦ πατρὸς αὐτοῦ. |
ὅτι δὲ ὁ κύριος σύμβουλον ἔλαβε τὸν υἱὸν αὐτοῦ καὶ τοὺς
ἐνδόξους ἀγγέλους περὶ τῆς κληρονομίας τοῦ δούλου, ἄκουε.
5. τὸ πνεῦμα τὸ ἅγιον τὸ προόν, τὸ κτίσαν πᾶσαν τὴν
κτίσιν, κατῴκισεν ὁ Θεὸς εἰς σάρκα ἣν ἠβούλετο. αὕτη οὖν
ἡ σάρξ, ἐν ᾗ κατῴκησε τὸ πνεῦμα τὸ ἅγιον, ἐδούλευσε τῷ
πνεύματι καλῶς ἐν σεμνότητι καὶ ἁγνείᾳ πορευθεῖσα, μηδὲν
ὅλως μιάνασα τὸ πνεῦμα. 6. πολιτευσαμένην οὖν αὐτὴν
καλῶς καὶ ἁγνῶς καὶ συγκοπιάσασαν τῷ πνεύματι καὶ
συνεργήσασαν ἐν παντὶ πράγματι, ἰσχυρῶς καὶ ἀνδρείως
ἀναστραφεῖσαν, μετὰ τοῦ πνεύματος τοῦ ἁγίου εἵλατο κοι-
νωνόν· ἤρεσε γὰρ [τῷ Κυρίῳ] ἡ πορεία τῆς σαρκὸς ταύτης,
ὅτι οὐκ ἐμιάνθη ἐπὶ τῆς γῆς ἔχουσα τὸ πνεῦμα τὸ ἅγιον.
7. σύμβουλον οὖν ἔλαβε τὸν υἱὸν καὶ τοὺς ἀγγέλους τοὺς
ἐνδόξους, ἵνα καὶ ἡ σάρξ αὕτη, δουλεύσασα τῷ πνεύματι
ἀμέμπτως, σχῇ τόπον τινὰ κατασκηνώσεως, καὶ μὴ δόξῃ τὸν
μισθὸν | τῆς δουλείας αὐτῆς ἀπολωλεκέναι· πᾶσα γὰρ σὰρξ
ἀπολήψεται μισθὸν | ἡ εὑρεθεῖσα ἀμίαντος καὶ ἄσπιλος, ἐν ᾗ
τὸ πνεῦμα τὸ ἅγιον κατῴκησεν. 8. ἔχεις καὶ ταύτης τῆς
παραβολῆς τὴν ἐπίλυσιν.

VII. Ηὐφράνθην, φημί, κύριε, ταύτην τὴν ἐπίλυσιν
ἀκούσας. Ἄκουε νῦν, φησί· τὴν σάρκα σου ταύτην φύλασσε
καθαρὰν καὶ ἀμίαντον, ἵνα τὸ πνεῦμα τὸ κατοικοῦν ἐν αὐτῇ

---

5. vi. 2 αὐτῶν] conj. Gebhardt [L₁L₂E]; ἡμῶν A.　σκαφεῦσαι] conj. Gebhardt [E]; σκαφῆσαι A; dub. L₁L₂.　4 βλέπεις...αὐτοῦ] conj. Gebhardt
[L₁L₂]; om. AE by homœot.　περὶ] conj. Anger [L₁L₂]; παρὰ A;
def. E.　6 τῷ κυρίῳ] ins. Harmer [L₂E]; deo L₁; om. A.　7 τῆς δουλείας
...μισθὸν] ins. Gebhardt [L₁]; om. A by homœot.; def. E; al. L₂.

μαρτυρήσῃ αὐτῇ, καὶ δικαιωθῇ σου ἡ σάρξ. 2. βλέπε
μήποτε ἀναβῇ ἐπὶ τὴν καρδίαν σου τὴν σάρκα σου ταύτην
φθαρτὴν εἶναι, καὶ παραχρήσῃ αὐτῇ ἐν μιασμῷ τινί. ἐὰν
[γὰρ] μιάνῃς τὴν σάρκα σου, μιανεῖς καὶ τὸ πνεῦμα τὸ ἅγιον·
ἐὰν δὲ μιάνῃς †τὴν σάρκα†, οὐ ζήσῃ. 3. Εἰ δέ τις, φημί,
κύριε, γέγονεν ἄγνοια προτέρα πρὶν ἀκουσθῶσι τὰ ῥήματα
ταῦτα, πῶς σωθῇ ὁ ἄνθρωπος ὁ μιάνας τὴν σάρκα αὐτοῦ ;
Περὶ τῶν προτέρων, φησίν, ἀγνοημάτων τῷ Θεῷ μόνῳ δυνατὸν
ἴασιν δοῦναι· αὐτοῦ γάρ ἐστι πᾶσα ἐξουσία. 4. [ἀλλὰ νῦν
φύλασσε σεαυτόν, καὶ ὁ Κύριος ὁ παντοκράτωρ, πολύ-
σπλαγχνος ὤν, περὶ τῶν προτέρων ἀγνοημάτων ἴασιν δώσει,]
ἐὰν τὸ λοιπὸν μὴ μιάνῃς σου τὴν σάρκα μηδὲ τὸ πνεῦμα·
ἀμφότερα γὰρ κοινά ἐστι καὶ ἄτερ ἀλλήλων μιανθῆναι
οὐ δύναται. ἀμφότερα οὖν καθαρὰ φύλασσε, καὶ ζήσῃ τῷ
Θεῷ.

[Παραβολὴ ϛ´.]

I. Καθήμενος ἐν τῷ οἴκῳ μου καὶ δοξάζων τὸν Κύριον
περὶ πάντων ὧν ἑωράκειν, καὶ συζητῶν περὶ τῶν ἐντολῶν,
ὅτι καλαὶ καὶ δυναταὶ καὶ ἱλαραὶ καὶ ἔνδοξοι καὶ δυνάμεναι cf. James
σῶσαι ψυχὴν ἀνθρώπου, ἔλεγον ἐν ἐμαυτῷ· Μακάριος ἔσομαι i. 21.
ἐὰν ταῖς ἐντολαῖς ταύταις πορευθῶ, καὶ ὃς ἂν ταύταις πορευθῇ,
μακάριος ἔσται. 2. ὡς ταῦτα ἐν ἐμαυτῷ ἐλάλουν, βλέπω
αὐτὸν ἐξαίφνης παρακαθήμενόν μοι καὶ λέγοντα ταῦτα· Τί
διψυχεῖς περὶ τῶν ἐντολῶν ὧν σοι ἐνετειλάμην ; καλαί εἰσιν·
ὅλως μὴ διψυχήσῃς, ἀλλ᾽ ἔνδυσαι τὴν πίστιν τοῦ Κυρίου,
καὶ ἐν αὐταῖς πορεύσῃ· ἐγὼ γάρ σε ἐνδυναμώσω ἐν αὐταῖς.
3. αὗται αἱ ἐντολαὶ σύμφοροί εἰσι τοῖς μέλλουσι μετανοεῖν·
ἐὰν γὰρ μὴ πορευθῶσιν ἐν αὐταῖς, εἰς μάτην ἐστὶν ἡ μετάνοια
αὐτῶν. 4. οἱ οὖν μετανοοῦντες ἀποβάλλετε τὰς πονηρίας
τοῦ αἰῶνος τούτου τὰς ἐκτριβούσας ὑμᾶς· ἐνδυσάμενοι δὲ
πᾶσαν ἀρετὴν δικαιοσύνης δυνήσεσθε τηρῆσαι τὰς ἐντολὰς

---

vii. 2 γὰρ] ins. Gebhardt [L₁L₂]; om. AE. 4 ἀλλὰ νῦν...δώσει] conj.
Gebhardt [L₁L₂]; om. A ; sed nunc custodi te E.

ταύτας καὶ μηκέτι προστιθέναι ταῖς ἁμαρτίαις ὑμῶν. | ἐὰν οὖν μηκέτι μηδὲν προσθῆτε, ἀποστήσεσθε ἀπὸ τῶν προτέρων ἁμαρτιῶν ὑμῶν. | πορεύεσθε οὖν ταῖς ἐντολαῖς μου ταύταις, καὶ ζήσεσθε τῷ Θεῷ. ταῦτα [πάντα] παρ' ἐμοῦ λελάληται ὑμῖν. 5. καὶ μετὰ τὸ ταῦτα λαλῆσαι αὐτὸν μετ' ἐμοῦ, λέγει μοι· Ἄγωμεν εἰς ἀγρόν, καὶ δείξω σοι τοὺς ποιμένας τῶν προβάτων. Ἄγωμεν, φημί, κύριε. καὶ ἤλθομεν εἴς τι πεδίον, καὶ δεικνύει μοι ποιμένα νεανίσκον ἐνδεδυμένον σύνθεσιν ἱματίων, τῷ χρώματι κροκώδη. 6. ἔβοσκε δὲ πρόβατα πολλὰ λίαν, καὶ τὰ πρόβατα ταῦτα ὡσεὶ τρυφῶντα ἦν καὶ λίαν σπαταλῶντα, καὶ ἱλαρὰ ἦν σκιρτῶντα ὧδε κἀκεῖ· καὶ αὐτὸς ὁ ποιμὴν πάνυ ἱλαρὸς ἦν ἐπὶ τῷ ποιμνίῳ αὐτοῦ· καὶ αὐτὴ ἡ ἰδέα τοῦ ποιμένος ἱλαρὰ ἦν λίαν, καὶ ἐν τοῖς προβάτοις περιέτρεχε.

II. Καὶ λέγει μοι· Βλέπεις τὸν ποιμένα τοῦτον; Βλέπω, φημί, κύριε. Οὗτος, φησίν, ἄγγελος τρυφῆς καὶ ἀπάτης ἐστίν. οὗτος ἐκτρίβει τὰς ψυχὰς τῶν δούλων τοῦ Θεοῦ καὶ καταστρέφει αὐτοὺς ἀπὸ τῆς ἀληθείας, ἀπατῶν αὐτοὺς ταῖς ἐπιθυμίαις ταῖς πονηραῖς, ἐν αἷς ἀπόλλυνται. 2. ἐπιλανθάνονται γὰρ τῶν ἐντολῶν τοῦ Θεοῦ τοῦ ζῶντος, καὶ πορεύονται ἀπάταις καὶ τρυφαῖς ματαίαις, καὶ ἀπόλλυνται ὑπὸ τοῦ ἀγγέλου τούτου, τινὰ μὲν εἰς θάνατον, τινὰ δὲ εἰς καταφθοράν. 3. λέγω αὐτῷ· Κύριε, οὐ γινώσκω ἐγὼ τί ἐστιν εἰς θάνατον, καὶ τί εἰς καταφθοράν. Ἄκουε, φησίν· ἃ εἶδες πρόβατα ἱλαρὰ καὶ σκιρτῶντα, οὗτοί εἰσιν οἱ ἀπεσπασμένοι ἀπὸ τοῦ Θεοῦ εἰς τέλος καὶ παραδεδωκότες ἑαυτοὺς ταῖς ἐπιθυμίαις τοῦ αἰῶνος τούτου. ἐν τούτοις οὖν μετάνοια ζωῆς οὐκ ἔστιν· ὅτι καὶ τὸ ὄνομα τοῦ Θεοῦ δι' αὐτοὺς βλασφημεῖται. τῶν τοιούτων ἡ ζωὴ θάνατός ἐστιν. 4. ἃ δὲ

---

6. i. 4 ἐὰν οὖν...ὑμῶν] conj. Gebhardt [L₁L₂]; al. E; om. A by homœot.
5 ἄγωμεν sec.] ἄγομεν A.   καὶ ἤλθομεν κ.τ.λ.] From this point to the end of Sim. vi. (with a few breaks) ps-Ath. (Doctr. ad Antioch. c. 18, 19) becomes an authority for the text.   6 περιέτρεχε] AL₁L₂E; ps-Ath. adds Καὶ ἄλλα πρόβατα εἶδον (MS ἰδιὸν) σπαταλῶντα καὶ τρυφῶντα ἐν τόπῳ ἑνί, οὐ μέντοι σκιρτῶντα.

εἶδες πρόβατα μὴ σκιρτῶντα, ἀλλ' ἐν ἑνὶ τόπῳ βοσκόμενα, οὗτοί εἰσιν οἱ παραδεδωκότες μὲν ἑαυτοὺς ταῖς τρυφαῖς καὶ ἀπάταις, εἰς δὲ τὸν Κύριον οὐδὲν ἐβλασφήμησαν. οὗτοι οὖν κατεφθαρμένοι εἰσὶν ἀπὸ τῆς ἀληθείας· ἐν τούτοις ἐλπίς ἐστι μετανοίας, ἐν ᾗ δύνανται ζῆσαι. ἡ καταφθορὰ οὖν ἐλπίδα ἔχει ἀνανεώσεώς τινος, ὁ δὲ θάνατος ἀπώλειαν ἔχει αἰώνιον. 5. πάλιν προέβημεν μικρόν, καὶ δεικνύει μοι ποιμένα μέγαν ὡσεὶ ἄγριον τῇ ἰδέᾳ, περικείμενον δέρμα αἴγειον λευκόν, καὶ πήραν τινὰ εἶχεν ἐπὶ τῶν ὤμων, καὶ ῥάβδον σκληρὰν λίαν καὶ ὄζους ἔχουσαν, καὶ μάστιγα μεγάλην· καὶ τὸ βλέμμα εἶχε περίπικρον, ὥστε φοβηθῆναί με αὐτόν· τοιοῦτον εἶχε τὸ βλέμμα. 6. οὗτος οὖν ὁ ποιμὴν παρελάμβανε τὰ πρόβατα ἀπὸ τοῦ ποιμένος τοῦ νεανίσκου, ἐκεῖνα τὰ σπαταλῶντα καὶ τρυφῶντα, μὴ σκιρτῶντα δέ, καὶ ἔβαλλεν αὐτὰ εἴς τινα τόπον κρημνώδη καὶ ἀκανθώδη καὶ τριβολώδη, ὥστε ἀπὸ τῶν ἀκανθῶν καὶ τριβόλων μὴ δύνασθαι ἐκπλέξαι τὰ πρόβατα, ἀλλ' [ἐμπλέκεσθαι ταῖς ἀκάνθαις καὶ τριβόλοις· ταῦτα οὖν] ἐμπεπλεγμένα ἐβόσκοντο ἐν ταῖς ἀκάνθαις καὶ τριβόλοις, καὶ λίαν ἐταλαιπώρουν δαιρόμενα ὑπ' αὐτοῦ· καὶ ὧδε κἀκεῖ περιήλαυνεν αὐτά, καὶ ἀνάπαυσιν αὐτοῖς οὐκ ἐδίδου, καὶ ὅλως οὐκ εὐσταθοῦσαν τὰ πρόβατα ἐκεῖνα.

III. Βλέπων οὖν αὐτὰ οὕτω μαστιγούμενα καὶ ταλαιπωρούμενα ἐλυπούμην ἐπ' αὐτοῖς, ὅτι οὕτως ἐβασανίζοντο καὶ ἀνοχὴν ὅλως οὐκ εἶχον. 2. λέγω τῷ ποιμένι τῷ μετ' ἐμοῦ λαλοῦντι· Κύριε, τίς ἐστιν οὗτος ὁ ποιμὴν ὁ [οὕτως] ἄσπλαγχνος καὶ πικρὸς καὶ ὅλως μὴ σπλαγχνιζόμενος ἐπὶ τὰ πρόβατα ταῦτα; Οὗτος, φησίν, ἐστὶν ὁ ἄγγελος τῆς τιμωρίας· ἐκ δὲ τῶν ἀγγέλων τῶν δικαίων ἐστί, κείμενος δὲ ἐπὶ τῆς τιμωρίας. 3. παραλαμβάνει οὖν τοὺς ἀποπλανηθέντας ἀπὸ τοῦ Θεοῦ καὶ πορευθέντας ταῖς ἐπιθυμίαις καὶ ἀπάταις τοῦ αἰῶνος τούτου, καὶ τιμωρεῖ αὐτούς, καθὼς ἄξιοί εἰσι, δειναῖς καὶ ποικίλαις τιμωρίαις. 4. Ἤθελον, φημί, κύριε, γνῶναι τὰς

ii. 4 ἐνὶ] ins. Harmer [L₁L₂E]; om. ps-Ath.; def. A.

ποικίλας ταύτας τιμωρίας, ποταπαί εἰσιν. Ἄκουε, φησίν· αἱ ποικίλαι τιμωρίαι καὶ βάσανοι βιωτικαί εἰσι βάσανοι· τιμωροῦνται γὰρ οἱ μὲν ζημίαις, οἱ δὲ ὑστερήσεσιν, οἱ δὲ ἀσθενείαις ποικίλαις, οἱ δὲ [πάσῃ] ἀκαταστασίᾳ, οἱ δὲ ὑβριζόμενοι ὑπὸ ἀναξίων καὶ ἑτέραις πολλαῖς πράξεσι πάσχοντες· 5. πολλοὶ γὰρ ἀκαταστατοῦντες ταῖς βουλαῖς αὐτῶν ἐπιβάλλονται πολλά, καὶ οὐδὲν αὐτοῖς ὅλως προχωρεῖ. καὶ λέγουσιν ἑαυτοὺς μὴ εὐοδοῦσθαι ἐν ταῖς πράξεσιν αὐτῶν, καὶ οὐκ ἀναβαίνει αὐτῶν ἐπὶ τὴν καρδίαν ὅτι ἔπραξαν πονηρά, ἀλλ᾽ αἰτιῶνται τὸν Κύριον. 6. ὅταν οὖν θλιβῶσι πάσῃ θλίψει, τότε ἐμοὶ παραδίδονται εἰς ἀγαθὴν παιδείαν καὶ ἰσχυροποιοῦνται ἐν τῇ πίστει τοῦ Κυρίου, καὶ τὰς λοιπὰς ἡμέρας τῆς ζωῆς αὐτῶν δουλεύουσι τῷ Κυρίῳ ἐν καθαρᾷ καρδίᾳ· | ἐὰν δὲ μετανοήσωσι, τότε ἀναβαίνει ἐπὶ τὴν καρδίαν αὐτῶν τὰ ἔργα ἃ ἔπραξαν πονηρά, καὶ τότε δοξάζουσι τὸν Θεόν, λέγοντες ὅτι δίκαιος κριτής ἐστι καὶ δικαίως ἔπαθον ἕκαστος κατὰ τὰς πράξεις αὐτοῦ· δουλεύουσι δὲ λοιπὸν τῷ Κυρίῳ ἐν καθαρᾷ καρδίᾳ | αὐτῶν, καὶ εὐοδοῦνται ἐν πάσῃ πράξει αὐτῶν, λαμβάνοντες παρὰ τοῦ Κυρίου πάντα ὅσα ἂν αἰτῶνται· καὶ τότε δοξάζουσι τὸν Κύριον ὅτι ἐμοὶ παρεδόθησαν, καὶ οὐκέτι οὐδὲν πάσχουσι τῶν πονηρῶν.

IV. Λέγω αὐτῷ· Κύριε, ἔτι μοι τοῦτο δήλωσον. Τί, φησίν, ἐπιζητεῖς; Εἰ ἄρα, φημί, κύριε, τὸν αὐτὸν χρόνον βασανίζονται οἱ τρυφῶντες καὶ ἀπατώμενοι, ὅσον τρυφῶσι καὶ ἀπατῶνται; λέγει μοι· Τὸν αὐτὸν χρόνον βασανίζονται. 2. | Ἐλάχιστον, φημί, κύριε, βασανίζονται· | ἔδει γὰρ τοὺς οὕτω τρυφῶντας καὶ ἐπιλανθανομένους τοῦ Θεοῦ ἑπταπλασίως βασανίζεσθαι. 3. λέγει μοι· Ἄφρων εἶ καὶ οὐ νοεῖς τῆς βασάνου τὴν δύναμιν. Εἰ γὰρ ἐνόουν, φημί, κύριε, οὐκ ἂν ἐπηρώτων ἵνα μοι δηλώσῃς. Ἄκουε, φησίν, ἀμφοτέρων τὴν δύναμιν, [τῆς τρυφῆς καὶ τῆς βασάνου]. 4. τῆς τρυφῆς καὶ

---

6. iii. 6 ἐὰν δὲ...καρδίᾳ] conj. Gebhardt [L₁L₂]; def. E; al. ps-Ath.; om. A by homœot. iv. 2 ἐλάχιστον...βασανίζονται] conj. Gebhardt [L₁L₂]; def. E ps-Ath.; om. A by homœot.

ἀπάτης ὁ χρόνος ὥρα ἐστὶ μία· τῆς δὲ βασάνου ἡ ὥρα τριάκοντα ἡμερῶν δύναμιν ἔχει. ἐὰν οὖν μίαν ἡμέραν τρυφήσῃ τις
καὶ ἀπατηθῇ, μίαν δὲ ἡμέραν βασανισθῇ, ὅλον ἐνιαυτὸν ἰσχύει ἡ
ἡμέρα τῆς βασάνου. ὅσας οὖν ἡμέρας τρυφήσῃ τις, τοσούτους
ἐνιαυτοὺς βασανίζεται. βλέπεις οὖν, φησίν, ὅτι τῆς τρυφῆς
καὶ ἀπάτης ὁ χρόνος ἐλάχιστός ἐστι, τῆς δὲ τιμωρίας καὶ
βασάνου πολύς.

V. Ὅτι, φημί, κύριε, οὐ νενόηκα ὅλως περὶ τοῦ χρόνου
τῆς ἀπάτης καὶ τρυφῆς καὶ βασάνου, τηλαυγέστερόν μοι
δήλωσον. 2. ἀποκριθείς μοι λέγει· Ἡ ἀφροσύνη σου παρά-
μονός ἐστι, καὶ οὐ θέλεις σου τὴν καρδίαν καθαρίσαι καὶ
δουλεύειν τῷ Θεῷ. βλέπε, [φησί,] μήποτε ὁ χρόνος πληρωθῇ,
καὶ σὺ ἄφρων εὑρεθῇς. ἄκουε οὖν, [φησί,] καθὼς βούλει, ἵνα
νοήσῃς αὐτά. 3. ὁ τρυφῶν καὶ ἀπατώμενος μίαν ἡμέραν καὶ
πράσσων ἃ βούλεται πολλὴν ἀφροσύνην ἐνδέδυται καὶ οὐ
νοεῖ τὴν πρᾶξιν ἣν ποιεῖ· εἰς τὴν αὔριον ἐπιλανθάνεται
γὰρ τί πρὸ μιᾶς ἔπραξεν· ἡ γὰρ τρυφὴ καὶ ἀπάτη μνήμας
οὐκ ἔχει διὰ τὴν ἀφροσύνην ἣν ἐνδέδυται· ἡ δὲ τιμωρία καὶ ἡ
βάσανος ὅταν κολληθῇ τῷ ἀνθρώπῳ μίαν ἡμέραν, μέχρις
ἐνιαυτοῦ τιμωρεῖται καὶ βασανίζεται· μνήμας γὰρ μεγάλας
ἔχει ἡ τιμωρία καὶ ἡ βάσανος. 4. βασανιζόμενος οὖν καὶ
τιμωρούμενος ὅλον τὸν ἐνιαυτὸν μνημονεύει ποτὲ τῆς τρυφῆς
καὶ ἀπάτης, καὶ γινώσκει ὅτι δι’ αὐτὰ πάσχει τὰ πονηρά.
πᾶς οὖν ἄνθρωπος ὁ τρυφῶν καὶ ἀπατώμενος οὕτω βασανίζεται, ὅτι ἔχοντες ζωὴν εἰς θάνατον ἑαυτοὺς παραδεδώκασι.
5. Ποῖαι, φημί, κύριε, τρυφαί εἰσι βλαβεραί ; Πᾶσα, φησί,
πρᾶξις τρυφή ἐστι τῷ ἀνθρώπῳ, ὃ ἐὰν ἡδέως ποιῇ· καὶ γὰρ
ὁ ὀξύχολος τῷ ἑαυτοῦ πάθει τὸ ἱκανὸν ποιῶν τρυφᾷ· καὶ ὁ
μοιχὸς καὶ ὁ μέθυσος καὶ ὁ κατάλαλος καὶ ὁ ψεύστης καὶ ὁ
πλεονέκτης καὶ ὁ ἀποστερητὴς καὶ ὁ τούτοις τὰ ὅμοια
ποιῶν τῇ ἰδίᾳ νόσῳ τὸ ἱκανὸν ποιεῖ· τρυφᾷ οὖν ἐπὶ τῇ
πράξει αὐτοῦ. 6. αὗται πᾶσαι αἱ τρυφαὶ βλαβεραί εἰσι τοῖς

δούλοις τοῦ Θεοῦ. διὰ ταύτας οὖν τὰς ἀπάτας πάσχουσιν οἱ τιμωρούμενοι καὶ βασανιζόμενοι. 7. εἰσὶν δὲ καὶ τρυφαὶ σώζουσαι τοὺς ἀνθρώπους· πολλοὶ γὰρ ἀγαθὰ ἐργαζόμενοι τρυφῶσι τῇ ἑαυτῶν ἡδονῇ φερόμενοι. αὕτη οὖν ἡ τρυφὴ σύμφορός ἐστι τοῖς δούλοις τοῦ Θεοῦ καὶ ζωὴν περιποιεῖται τῷ ἀνθρώπῳ τῷ τοιούτῳ· αἱ δὲ βλαβεραὶ τρυφαὶ αἱ προειρημέναι βασάνους καὶ τιμωρίας αὐτοῖς περιποιοῦνται· ἐὰν δὲ ἐπιμένωσι καὶ μὴ μετανοήσωσι, θάνατον ἑαυτοῖς περιποιοῦνται.

[Παραβολὴ ζ´.]

Μετὰ ἡμέρας ὀλίγας εἶδον αὐτὸν εἰς τὸ πεδίον τὸ αὐτὸ ὅπου καὶ τοὺς ποιμένας ἑωράκειν, καὶ λέγει μοι· Τί ἐπιζητεῖς; Πάρειμι, φημί, κύριε, ἵνα τὸν ποιμένα τὸν τιμωρητὴν κελεύσῃς ἐκ τοῦ οἴκου μου ἐξελθεῖν, ὅτι λίαν με θλίβει. Δεῖ σε, φησί, θλιβῆναι· οὕτω γάρ, φησί, προσέταξεν ὁ ἔνδοξος ἄγγελος τὰ περὶ σοῦ· θέλει γάρ σε πειρασθῆναι. Τί γάρ, φημί, κύριε, ἐποίησα οὕτω πονηρόν, ἵνα τῷ ἀγγέλῳ τούτῳ παραδοθῶ; 2. Ἄκουε, φησίν· αἱ μὲν ἁμαρτίαι σου πολλαί, ἀλλ᾽ οὐ τοσαῦται ὥστε τῷ ἀγγέλῳ τούτῳ παραδοθῆναι· ἀλλ᾽ ὁ οἶκός σου μεγάλας ἀνομίας καὶ ἁμαρτίας εἰργάσατο, καὶ παρεπικράνθη ὁ ἔνδοξος ἄγγελος ἐπὶ τοῖς ἔργοις αὐτῶν, καὶ διὰ τοῦτο ἐκέλευσέ σε χρόνον τινὰ θλιβῆναι, ἵνα κἀκεῖνοι μετανοήσωσι καὶ καθαρίσωσιν ἑαυτοὺς ἀπὸ πάσης ἐπιθυμίας τοῦ αἰῶνος τούτου. ὅταν οὖν μετανοήσωσι καὶ καθαρισθῶσι, τότε ἀποστήσεται ὁ ἄγγελος τῆς τιμωρίας. 3. λέγω αὐτῷ· Κύριε, εἰ ἐκεῖνοι τοιαῦτα εἰργάσαντο ἵνα παραπικρανθῇ ὁ ἔνδοξος ἄγγελος, τί ἐγὼ ἐποίησα; Ἄλλως, φησίν, οὐ δύνανται ἐκεῖνοι θλιβῆναι, ἐὰν μὴ σὺ ἡ κεφαλὴ τοῦ οἴκου [ὅλου] θλιβῇς· σοῦ γὰρ θλιβομένου ἐξ ἀνάγκης κἀκεῖνοι θλιβήσονται, εὐσταθοῦντος δὲ σοῦ οὐδεμίαν δύνανται θλῖψιν ἔχειν. 4. Ἀλλ᾽ ἰδού, φημί, κύριε, μετανενοήκασιν ἐξ ὅλης καρδίας αὐτῶν. Οἶδα, φησί, κἀγὼ ὅτι μετανενοήκασιν ἐξ

7. 1 πάρειμι] παρ᾽ ἐμοί A.   2 καθαρίσωσιν] καθαρήσωσιν A.   3 ὅλου]
ins. Harmer [L₁L₂]; om. AE.   δὲ σοῦ] conj. Anger [L₁L₂E]; δ...A.

ὅλης καρδίας αὐτῶν· τῶν οὖν μετανοούντων εὐθὺς δοκεῖς τὰς ἁμαρτίας ἀφίεσθαι; οὐ παντελῶς· ἀλλὰ δεῖ τὸν μετανοοῦντα βασανίσαι τὴν ἑαυτοῦ ψυχὴν καὶ ταπεινοφρονῆσαι ἐν πάσῃ πράξει αὐτοῦ ἰσχυρῶς καὶ θλιβῆναι ἐν πάσαις θλίψεσι ποικίλαις· καὶ ἐὰν ὑπενέγκῃ τὰς θλίψεις τὰς ἐπερχομένας αὐτῷ, πάντως σπλαγχνισθήσεται ὁ τὰ πάντα κτίσας καὶ ἐνδυναμώσας καὶ ἴασίν τινα δώσει· 5. καὶ τοῦτο ὅταν [ὁ Θεὸς] τοῦ μετανοοῦντος καθαρὰν ἴδῃ τὴν καρδίαν ἀπὸ παντὸς πονηροῦ πράγματος. σοὶ δὲ συμφέρον ἐστὶ καὶ τῷ οἴκῳ σου νῦν θλιβῆναι. τί δέ σοι πολλὰ λέγω; θλιβῆναί σε δεῖ, καθὼς προσέταξεν ὁ ἄγγελος Κυρίου ἐκεῖνος, ὁ παραδιδούς σε ἐμοί· καὶ τοῦτο εὐχαρίστει τῷ Κυρίῳ ὅτι ἄξιόν σε ἡγήσατο τοῦ προδηλῶσαί σοι τὴν θλῖψιν, ἵνα προγνοὺς αὐτὴν ὑπενέγκῃς ἰσχυρῶς. 6. λέγω αὐτῷ· Κύριε, σὺ μετ᾿ ἐμοῦ γίνου, καὶ [εὐκόλως] δυνήσομαι πᾶσαν θλῖψιν ὑπενεγκεῖν. Ἐγώ, φησίν, ἔσομαι μετὰ σοῦ· ἐρωτήσω δὲ καὶ τὸν ἄγγελον τὸν τιμωρητὴν ἵνα σε ἐλαφροτέρως θλίψῃ· ἀλλ᾿ ὀλίγον χρόνον θλιβήσῃ, καὶ πάλιν ἀποκατασταθήσῃ εἰς τὸν οἶκόν σου· μόνον παράμεινον ταπεινοφρονῶν καὶ λειτουργῶν τῷ Κυρίῳ ἐν καθαρᾷ καρδίᾳ, καὶ τὰ τέκνα σου καὶ ὁ οἶκός σου, καὶ πορεύου ἐν ταῖς ἐντολαῖς μου αἷς σοι ἐντέλλομαι, καὶ δυνήσεταί σου ἡ μετάνοια ἰσχυρὰ καὶ καθαρὰ εἶναι· 7. καὶ ἐὰν ταύτας φυλάξῃς μετὰ τοῦ οἴκου σου, ἀποστήσεται πᾶσα θλῖψις ἀπὸ σοῦ· καὶ ἀπὸ πάντων δέ, φησίν, ἀποστήσεται θλῖψις, ὅσοι ἐὰν ταῖς ἐντολαῖς μου ταύταις πορευθῶσιν.

[Παραβολὴ η΄.]

I. Ἔδειξέ μοι ἰτέαν [μεγάλην] σκεπάζουσαν πεδία καὶ ὄρη, καὶ ὑπὸ τὴν σκέπην τῆς ἰτέας πάντες ἐληλύθασιν οἱ κεκλημένοι τῷ ὀνόματι Κυρίου. 2. εἱστήκει δὲ ἄγγελος τοῦ

---

4 εὐθὺς] ins. Gebhardt [L₁L₂E]; om. A.   ἴασιν] conj. Anger [L₁L₂E]; ἰσχύν A.   5 ὅταν ὁ θεὸς] conj. Harmer; πάντως A; si L₁; si tamen L₂; cum E.   καθαρὰν...τὴν καρδίαν] conj. Harmer [L₁L₂E]; καθαρῶς A.   6 εὐκόλως] ins. Harmer [L₁L₂E]; om. A.   καθαρᾷ] L₁L₂E; pref. πάσῃ A.
7 ἐὰν sec.] conj. Hilgenfeld; ἐν A.

Κυρίου ἔνδοξος λίαν ὑψηλὸς παρὰ τὴν ἰτέαν, δρέπανον ἔχων μέγα, καὶ ἔκοπτε κλάδους ἀπὸ τῆς ἰτέας, καὶ ἐπεδίδου τῷ λαῷ τῷ σκεπαζομένῳ ὑπὸ τῆς ἰτέας· μικρὰ δὲ ῥαβδία ἐπεδίδου αὐτοῖς, ὡσεὶ πηχυαῖα. 3. μετὰ δὲ τὸ πάντας λαβεῖν τὰ ῥαβδία ἔθηκε τὸ δρέπανον ὁ ἄγγελος, καὶ τὸ δένδρον ἐκεῖνο ὑγιὲς ἦν οἷον καὶ ἑωράκειν αὐτό. 4. ἐθαύμαζον δὲ ἐγὼ ἐν ἐμαυτῷ λέγων· Πῶς τοσούτων κλάδων κεκομμένων τὸ δένδρον ὑγιές ἐστι; λέγει μοι ὁ ποιμήν· Μὴ θαύμαζε εἰ τὸ δένδρον ὑγιὲς ἔμεινε τοσούτων κλάδων κοπέντων. ἄφες δὲ ἕως πάντα ἴδῃς, καὶ δηλωθήσεταί σοι τὸ τί ἐστιν. 5. ὁ ἄγγελος ὁ ἐπιδεδωκὼς τῷ λαῷ τὰς ῥάβδους πάλιν ἀπῄτει ἀπ' αὐτῶν· καὶ καθὼς ἔλαβον, οὕτω καὶ ἐκαλοῦντο πρὸς αὐτόν, καὶ εἰς ἕκαστος αὐτῶν ἀπεδίδου τὰς ῥάβδους. ἐλάμβανε δὲ ὁ ἄγγελος τοῦ Κυρίου καὶ κατενόει αὐτάς. 6. παρά τινων ἐλάμβανε τὰς ῥάβδους ξηρὰς καὶ βεβρωμένας ὡς ὑπὸ σητός· ἐκέλευσεν ὁ ἄγγελος τοὺς τὰς τοιαύτας ῥάβδους ἐπιδεδωκότας χωρὶς ἵστασθαι. 7. ἕτεροι δὲ ἐπεδίδοσαν ξηράς, ἀλλ' οὐκ ἦσαν βεβρωμέναι ὑπὸ σητός· καὶ τούτους ἐκέλευσε χωρὶς ἵστασθαι. 8. ἕτεροι δὲ ἐπεδίδουν ἡμιξήρους· καὶ οὗτοι χωρὶς ἵσταντο. 9. ἕτεροι δὲ ἐπεδίδουν τὰς ῥάβδους αὐτῶν ἡμιξήρους καὶ σχισμὰς ἐχούσας· καὶ οὗτοι χωρὶς ἵσταντο. | 10. ἕτεροι δὲ ἐπεδίδουν τὰς ῥάβδους αὐτῶν χλωρὰς καὶ σχισμὰς ἐχούσας· καὶ οὗτοι χωρὶς ἵσταντο. | 11. ἕτεροι δὲ ἐπεδίδουν τὰς ῥάβδους τὸ ἥμισυ ξηρὸν καὶ τὸ ἥμισυ χλωρόν· καὶ οὗτοι χωρὶς ἵσταντο. 12. ἕτεροι δὲ προσέφερον τὰς ῥάβδους αὐτῶν τὰ δύο μέρη τῆς ῥάβδου χλωρά, τὸ δὲ τρίτον ξηρόν· καὶ οὗτοι χωρὶς ἵσταντο. 13. ἕτεροι δὲ ἐπεδίδουν τὰ δύο μέρη ξηρά, τὸ δὲ τρίτον χλωρόν· καὶ οὗτοι χωρὶς ἵσταντο. 14. ἕτεροι δὲ ἐπεδίδουν τὰς ῥάβδους αὐτῶν παρὰ μικρὸν ὅλας χλωράς, ἐλάχιστον δὲ τῶν ῥάβδων αὐτῶν ξηρὸν ἦν, αὐτὸ τὸ ἄκρον· σχισμὰς δὲ εἶχον ἐν αὐταῖς· καὶ οὗτοι χωρὶς ἵσταντο.

8. i. 4 ἄφες δὲ ἕως] conj. Harmer [L₂]; ἀφ' ἧς δὲ φησί A; dub. L₁E.
10 ἕτεροι...ἵσταντο] ins. Hilgenfeld [L₁L₂E]; om. A by homœot.   τὸ pri.] om. A.

15. ἑτέρων δὲ ἦν ἐλάχιστον χλωρόν, τὰ δὲ λοιπὰ τῶν ῥάβδων ξηρά· καὶ οὗτοι χωρὶς ἵσταντο. 16. ἕτεροι δὲ ἤρχοντο τὰς ῥάβδους χλωρὰς φέροντες ὡς ἔλαβον παρὰ τοῦ ἀγγέλου· τὸ δὲ πλεῖον μέρος τοῦ ὄχλου τοιαύτας ῥάβδους ἐπεδίδουν. ὁ δὲ ἄγγελος ἐπὶ τούτοις ἐχάρη λίαν· καὶ οὗτοι χωρὶς ἵσταντο. 17. ἕτεροι δὲ ἐπεδίδουν τὰς ῥάβδους αὐτῶν χλωρὰς καὶ παραφυάδας ἐχούσας· | καὶ οὗτοι χωρὶς ἵσταντο· καὶ ἐπὶ τούτοις δὲ ὁ ἄγγελος λίαν ἐχάρη. 18. ἕτεροι δὲ ἐπεδίδουν τὰς ῥάβδους αὐτῶν χλωρὰς καὶ παραφυάδας ἐχούσας· | αἱ δὲ παραφυάδες αὐτῶν ὡσεὶ καρπόν τινα εἶχον. καὶ λίαν ἱλαροὶ ἦσαν οἱ ἄνθρωποι ἐκεῖνοι, ὧν αἱ ῥάβδοι τοιαῦται εὑρέθησαν. καὶ ὁ ἄγγελος ἐπὶ τούτοις ἠγαλλιᾶτο, καὶ ὁ ποιμὴν λίαν ἱλαρὸς ἦν ἐπὶ τούτοις.

II. Ἐκέλευσε δὲ ὁ ἄγγελος Κυρίου στεφάνους ἐνεχθῆναι. καὶ ἠνέχθησαν στέφανοι ὡσεὶ ἐκ φοινίκων γεγονότες, καὶ ἐστεφάνωσε τοὺς ἄνδρας τοὺς ἐπιδεδωκότας τὰς ῥάβδους τὰς ἐχούσας τὰς παραφυάδας καὶ καρπόν τινα, καὶ ἀπέλυσεν αὐτοὺς εἰς τὸν πύργον. 2. καὶ τοὺς ἄλλους δὲ ἀπέστειλεν εἰς τὸν πύργον, τοὺς τὰς ῥάβδους τὰς χλωρὰς ἐπιδεδωκότας καὶ παραφυάδας ἐχούσας, καρπὸν δὲ μὴ ἐχούσας τὰς παραφυάδας, δοὺς αὐτοῖς σφραγῖδα. 3. ἱματισμὸν δὲ τὸν αὐτὸν πάντες εἶχον λευκὸν ὡσεὶ χιόνα οἱ πορευόμενοι εἰς τὸν πύργον. 4. καὶ τοὺς τὰς ῥάβδους ἐπιδεδωκότας χλωρὰς ὡς ἔλαβον ἀπέλυσε, δοὺς αὐτοῖς ἱματισμὸν [λευκὸν] καὶ σφραγῖδας. 5. μετὰ τὸ ταῦτα τελέσαι τὸν ἄγγελον λέγει τῷ ποιμένι· Ἐγὼ ὑπάγω· σὺ δὲ τούτους ἀπολύσεις εἰς τὰ τείχη καθὼς ἄξιός ἐστί τις κατοικεῖν. κατανόησον δὲ τὰς ῥάβδους αὐτῶν ἐπιμελῶς, καὶ οὕτως ἀπόλυσον· ἐπιμελῶς δὲ κατανόησον. βλέπε μή τίς σε παρέλθῃ, φησίν. ἐὰν δέ τίς σε παρέλθῃ, ἐγὼ αὐτοὺς ἐπὶ τὸ θυσιαστήριον δοκιμάσω. ταῦτα εἰπὼν τῷ ποιμένι ἀπῆλθε. 6. καὶ μετὰ τὸ ἀπελθεῖν τὸν

---

i. 17 καὶ οὗτοι...ἐχούσας] ins. Gebhardt [L₁L₂E]; om. A by homœot.   ii. 2
σφραγῖδα] conj. Gebhardt [L₁L₂E]; σφραγῖδας A.   4 λευκὸν] ins.
Harmer [L₁L₂E] : om. A.

ἄγγελον λέγει μοι ὁ ποιμήν· Λάβωμεν πάντων τὰς ῥάβδους
καὶ φυτεύσωμεν αὐτάς, εἴ τινες ἐξ αὐτῶν δυνήσονται ζῆσαι.
λέγω αὐτῷ· Κύριε, τὰ ξηρὰ ταῦτα πῶς δύνανται ζῆσαι;
7. ἀποκριθείς μοι λέγει· Τὸ δένδρον τοῦτο ἰτέα ἐστὶ καὶ
φιλόζωον τὸ γένος· ἐὰν οὖν φυτευθῶσι καὶ μικρὰν ἰκμάδα
λαμβάνωσιν αἱ ῥάβδοι, ζήσονται πολλαὶ ἐξ αὐτῶν· εἶτα δὲ
πειράσωμεν καὶ ὕδωρ αὐταῖς παραχέειν. ἐάν τις αὐτῶν
δυνηθῇ ζῆσαι, συγχαρήσομαι αὐτῇ· ἐὰν δὲ μὴ ζήσῃ, οὐχ
εὑρεθήσομαι ἐγὼ ἀμελής. 8. ἐκέλευσε δέ μοι ὁ ποιμὴν
καλέσαι καθώς τις αὐτῶν ἐστάθη. ἦλθον τάγματα τάγματα,
καὶ ἐπεδίδουν τὰς ῥάβδους τῷ ποιμένι. ἐλάμβανε δὲ ὁ ποιμὴν
τὰς ῥάβδους, καὶ κατὰ τάγματα ἐφύτευσεν αὐτάς, καὶ μετὰ
τὸ φυτεῦσαι ὕδωρ αὐταῖς πολὺ παρέχεεν, ὥστε ἀπὸ τοῦ
ὕδατος μὴ φαίνεσθαι τὰς ῥάβδους. 9. καὶ μετὰ τὸ ποτίσαι
αὐτὸν τὰς ῥάβδους λέγει μοι· Ἄγωμεν, καὶ μετ᾽ ὀλίγας
ἡμέρας ἐπανέλθωμεν καὶ ἐπισκεψώμεθα τὰς ῥάβδους πάσας·
ὁ γὰρ κτίσας τὸ δένδρον τοῦτο θέλει πάντας ζῆν τοὺς λα-
βόντας ἐκ τοῦ δένδρου τούτου κλάδους. ἐλπίζω δὲ κἀγὼ
ὅτι λαβόντα τὰ ῥαβδία ταῦτα ἰκμάδα καὶ ποτισθέντα ὕδατι
ζήσονται τὸ πλεῖστον μέρος αὐτῶν.

III. Λέγω αὐτῷ· Κύριε, τὸ δένδρον τοῦτο γνώρισόν μοι
τί ἐστιν· ἀπορῦμαι γὰρ περὶ αὐτοῦ, ὅτι τοσούτων κλάδων
κοπέντων ὑγιές ἐστι τὸ δένδρον καὶ οὐδὲν φαίνεται κεκομ-
μένον ἀπ᾽ αὐτοῦ· ἐν τούτῳ οὖν ἀπορῦμαι. 2. Ἄκουε, φησί·
τὸ δένδρον τοῦτο τὸ μέγα τὸ σκεπάζον πεδία καὶ ὄρη καὶ
πᾶσαν τὴν γῆν, νόμος Θεοῦ ἐστιν ὁ δοθεὶς εἰς ὅλον τὸν
κόσμον· ὁ δὲ νόμος οὗτος υἱὸς Θεοῦ ἐστι κηρυχθεὶς εἰς τὰ
πέρατα τῆς γῆς· οἱ δὲ ὑπὸ τὴν σκέπην λαοὶ ὄντες, οἱ ἀκούσαντες τοῦ κηρύγματος καὶ πιστεύσαντες εἰς αὐτόν· 3. ὁ δὲ
ἄγγελος ὁ μέγας καὶ ἔνδοξος, Μιχαὴλ ὁ ἔχων τὴν ἐξουσίαν
τούτου τοῦ λαοῦ καὶ διακυβερνῶν. οὗτος γάρ ἐστιν ὁ διδοὺς
αὐτοῖς τὸν νόμον εἰς τὰς καρδίας τῶν πιστευόντων· ἐπι-

σκέπτεται οὖν αὐτὸς οἷς ἔδωκεν, εἰ ἄρα τετηρήκασιν αὐτόν. 4. βλέπεις δὲ ἑνὸς ἑκάστου τὰς ῥάβδους· αἱ γὰρ ῥάβδοι ὁ νόμος ἐστί. βλέπεις οὖν πολλὰς ῥάβδους ἠχρειωμένας, γνώσῃ δὲ αὐτοὺς πάντας τοὺς μὴ τηρήσαντας τὸν νόμον, καὶ ὄψει ἑνὸς ἑκάστου τὴν κατοικίαν. 5. λέγω αὐτῷ· Κύριε, διατί οὓς μὲν ἀπέλυσεν εἰς τὸν πύργον, οὓς δὲ σοὶ κατέλειψεν; Ὅσοι, φησί, παρέβησαν τὸν νόμον ὃν ἔλαβον παρ᾽ αὐτοῦ, εἰς τὴν ἐμὴν ἐξουσίαν κατέλιπεν αὐτοὺς εἰς μετάνοιαν· ὅσοι δὲ ἤδη εὐηρέστησαν τῷ νόμῳ καὶ τετηρήκασιν αὐτόν, ὑπὸ τὴν ἰδίαν ἐξουσίαν ἔχει αὐτούς. 6. Τίνες οὖν, φημί, κύριε, εἰσὶν οἱ ἐστεφανωμένοι καὶ εἰς τὸν πύργον ὑπάγοντες; [Ὅσοι, φησί, συμπαλαίσαντες τῷ διαβόλῳ ἐνίκησαν αὐτόν, ἐστεφανωμένοι εἰσίν] οὗτοί εἰσιν οἱ ὑπὲρ τοῦ νόμου παθόντες· 7. οἱ δὲ ἕτεροι καὶ αὐτοὶ χλωρὰς τὰς ῥάβδους ἐπιδεδωκότες καὶ παραφυάδας ἐχούσας, καρπὸν δὲ μὴ ἐχούσας, οἱ ὑπὲρ τοῦ νόμου θλιβέντες, μὴ παθόντες δὲ μηδὲ ἀρνησάμενοι τὸν νόμον αὐτῶν. 8. οἱ δὲ χλωρὰς ἐπιδεδωκότες οἵας ἔλαβον, σεμνοὶ καὶ δίκαιοι καὶ λίαν πορευθέντες ἐν καθαρᾷ καρδίᾳ καὶ τὰς ἐντολὰς Κυρίου πεφυλακότες. τὰ δὲ λοιπὰ γνώσῃ, ὅταν κατανοήσω τὰς ῥάβδους ταύτας τὰς πεφυτευμένας καὶ πεποτισμένας.

IV. Καὶ μετὰ ἡμέρας ὀλίγας ἤλθομεν εἰς τὸν τόπον, καὶ ἐκάθισεν ὁ ποιμὴν εἰς τὸν τόπον τοῦ ἀγγέλου, κἀγὼ παρεστάθην αὐτῷ. καὶ λέγει μοι· Περίζωσαι ὠμόλινον, | καὶ διακόνει μοι. καὶ περιεζωσάμην ὠμόλινον | ἐκ σάκκου γεγονὸς καθαρόν. 2. ἰδὼν δέ με περιεζωσμένον καὶ ἕτοιμον ὄντα τοῦ διακονεῖν αὐτῷ, Κάλει, φησί, τοὺς ἄνδρας ὧν εἰσὶν αἱ ῥάβδοι πεφυτευμέναι, κατὰ τὸ τάγμα ὡς ἕκαστος ἔδωκε τὰς ῥάβδους. καὶ ἀπῆλθον εἰς τὸ πεδίον, καὶ ἐκάλεσα πάντας· καὶ ἔστησαν πάντες κατὰ τὰ τάγματα. 3. λέγει αὐτοῖς·

iii. 6 ὅσοι...ἐστεφανωμένοι εἰσίν] ins. Hilgenfeld [L₁L₂E]; om. A.
iv. 1 καὶ διακόνει...ὠμόλινον] conj. Hilgenfeld [L₁L₂E]; om. A by homœot.
2 ὡς ἕκαστος] conj. Harmer; ὅστις A; sicut L₁L₂E.   πάντες κατὰ τὰ τάγματα] conj. Harmer; πάντα τὰ τάγματα A; universi ordinibus suis L₁; locis suis L₂; omnes ex ordine E.

Ἕκαστος τὰς ἰδίας ῥάβδους ἐκτιλάτω καὶ φερέτω πρός με. 4. πρῶτοι ἐπέδωκαν οἱ τὰς ξηρὰς καὶ κεκομμένας ἐσχηκότες, καὶ ὡσαύτως εὑρέθησαν ξηραὶ καὶ κεκομμέναι· ἐκέλευσεν αὐτοὺς χωρὶς σταθῆναι. 5. εἶτα ἐπέδωκαν οἱ τὰς ξηρὰς καὶ μὴ κεκομμένας ἔχοντες· τινὲς δὲ ἐξ αὐτῶν ἐπέδωκαν τὰς ῥάβδους χλωράς, τινὲς δὲ ξηρὰς καὶ κεκομμένας ὡς ὑπὸ σητός. τοὺς ἐπιδεδωκότας οὖν χλωρὰς ἐκέλευσε χωρὶς σταθῆναι, τοὺς δὲ ξηρὰς καὶ κεκομμένας ἐπιδεδωκότας ἐκέλευσε μετὰ τῶν πρώτων σταθῆναι. 6. εἶτα ἐπέδωκαν οἱ τὰς ἡμιξήρους καὶ σχισμὰς ἐχούσας· καὶ πολλοὶ ἐξ αὐτῶν χλωρὰς ἐπέδωκαν καὶ μὴ ἐχούσας σχισμάς· τινὲς δὲ χλωρὰς καὶ παραφυάδας ἐχούσας, καὶ εἰς τὰς παραφυάδας καρπούς, οἵους εἶχον οἱ εἰς τὸν πύργον πορευθέντες ἐστεφανωμένοι· τινὲς δὲ ἐπέδωκαν ξηρὰς καὶ βεβρωμένας, τινὲς δὲ ξηρὰς καὶ ἀβρώτους, τινὲς δὲ οἷαι ἦσαν ἡμίξηροι καὶ σχισμὰς ἔχουσαι. ἐκέλευσεν αὐτοὺς ἕνα ἕκαστον χωρὶς σταθῆναι, τοὺς μὲν πρὸς τὰ ἴδια τάγματα, τοὺς δὲ χωρίς.

V. Εἶτα ἐπεδίδουν οἱ τὰς ῥάβδους χλωρὰς μὲν ἔχοντες, σχισμὰς δὲ ἐχούσας· οὗτοι πάντες χλωρὰς ἐπέδωκαν, καὶ ἔστησαν εἰς τὸ ἴδιον τάγμα. ἐχάρη δὲ ὁ ποιμὴν ἐπὶ τούτοις, ὅτι πάντες ἠλλοιώθησαν καὶ ἀπέθεντο τὰς σχισμὰς αὐτῶν. 2. ἐπέδωκαν δὲ καὶ οἱ τὸ ἥμισυ χλωρόν, τὸ δὲ ἥμισυ ξηρὸν ἔχοντες· τινῶν οὖν εὑρέθησαν αἱ ῥάβδοι ὁλοτελῶς χλωραί, τινῶν ἡμίξηροι, τινῶν ξηραὶ καὶ βεβρωμέναι, τινῶν δὲ χλωραὶ καὶ παραφυάδας ἔχουσαι. οὗτοι πάντες ἀπελύθησαν ἕκαστος πρὸς τὸ τάγμα αὐτοῦ. 3. εἶτα ἐπέδωκαν οἱ τὰ δύο μέρη χλωρὰ ἔχοντες, τὸ δὲ τρίτον ξηρόν· πολλοὶ ἐξ αὐτῶν χλωρὰς ἐπέδωκαν, πολλοὶ δὲ ἡμιξήρους, ἕτεροι δὲ ξηρὰς καὶ βεβρωμένας· οὗτοι πάντες ἔστησαν εἰς τὸ ἴδιον τάγμα. | 4. εἶτα ἐπέδωκαν οἱ τὰ δύο μέρη ξηρὰ ἔχοντες, τὸ δὲ τρίτον χλωρόν. πολλοὶ ἐξ αὐτῶν ἡμιξήρους ἐπέδωκαν, τινὲς δὲ ξηρὰς καὶ

βεβρωμένας, τινὲς δὲ ἡμιξήρους καὶ σχισμὰς ἐχούσας, ὀλίγοι
δὲ χλωράς. οὗτοι πάντες ἔστησαν εἰς τὸ ἴδιον τάγμα.|
5. ἐπέδωκαν δὲ οἱ τὰς ῥάβδους αὐτῶν χλωρὰς ἐσχηκότες,
ἐλάχιστον δὲ [ξηρὸν] καὶ σχισμὰς ἐχούσας. ἐκ τούτων τινὲς
χλωρὰς ἐπέδωκαν, τινὲς δὲ χλωρὰς καὶ παραφυάδας ἐχούσας.
ἀπῆλθον καὶ οὗτοι εἰς τὸ τάγμα αὐτῶν. 6. εἶτα ἐπέδωκαν
οἱ ἐλάχιστον ἔχοντες χλωρόν, τὰ δὲ λοιπὰ μέρη ξηρά· τούτων
αἱ ῥάβδοι εὑρέθησαν τὸ πλεῖστον μέρος χλωραὶ καὶ παραφυάδας ἔχουσαι καὶ καρπὸν ἐν ταῖς παραφυάσι, καὶ ἕτεραι
χλωραὶ ὅλαι. ἐπὶ ταύταις ταῖς ῥάβδοις ἐχάρη ὁ ποιμὴν λίαν
[μεγάλως], ὅτι οὕτως εὑρέθησαν. ἀπῆλθον δὲ οὗτοι ἕκαστος
εἰς τὸ ἴδιον τάγμα.

VI. Μετὰ τὸ πάντων κατανοῆσαι τὰς ῥάβδους [τὸν
ποιμένα] λέγει μοι· Εἶπόν σοι ὅτι τὸ δένδρον τοῦτο φιλό-
ζωόν ἐστι. βλέπεις, φησί, πόσοι μετενόησαν καὶ ἐσώθησαν ;
Βλέπω, φημί, κύριε. Ἵνα ἴδῃς, φησί, τὴν πολυευσπλαγχνίαν
τοῦ Κυρίου, ὅτι μεγάλη καὶ ἔνδοξός ἐστι, καὶ ἔδωκε πνεῦμα
τοῖς ἀξίοις οὖσι μετανοίας. 2. Διατί οὖν, φημί, κύριε, πάντες
οὐ μετενόησαν ; Ὧν εἶδε, φησί, τὴν καρδίαν μέλλουσαν καθαρὰν γενέσθαι καὶ δουλεύειν αὐτῷ ἐξ ὅλης καρδίας, τούτοις
ἔδωκε τὴν μετάνοιαν· ὧν δὲ εἶδε τὴν δολιότητα καὶ πονηρίαν,
μελλόντων ἐν ὑποκρίσει μετανοεῖν, ἐκείνοις οὐκ ἔδωκε μετάνοιαν, μήποτε πάλιν βεβηλώσωσι τὸ ὄνομα αὐτοῦ. 3. λέγω
αὐτῷ· Κύριε, νῦν οὖν μοι δήλωσον τοὺς τὰς ῥάβδους ἐπιδεδωκότας, ποταπός τις αὐτῶν ἐστί, καὶ τὴν τούτων κατοικίαν,
ἵνα ἀκούσαντες οἱ πιστεύσαντες καὶ εἰληφότες τὴν σφραγῖδα
καὶ τεθλακότες αὐτὴν καὶ μὴ τηρήσαντες ὑγιῆ, ἐπιγνόντες
τὰ ἑαυτῶν ἔργα μετανοήσωσι, λαβόντες ὑπὸ σοῦ σφραγῖδα,
καὶ δοξάσωσι τὸν Κύριον, ὅτι ἐσπλαγχνίσθη ἐπ' αὐτοὺς καὶ
ἀπέστειλέ σε τοῦ ἀνακαινίσαι τὰ πνεύματα αὐτῶν. 4. Ἄκουε,
φησίν· ὧν αἱ ῥάβδοι ξηραὶ καὶ βεβρωμέναι ὑπὸ σητὸς εὑρέθησαν, οὗτοί εἰσιν οἱ ἀποστάται καὶ προδόται τῆς ἐκκλησίας

---

v. 5 ἐλάχιστον] ἐλάχιστοι A.   ξηρὸν] ins. Gebhardt [L₂E]; om. A;
def. L₁.   vi. 1 ἴδῃς] εἰδῆς A.   2 διατί] conj. Anger [L₁L₂E]; ·οὗτοι A.

cf. James
ii. 7.
καὶ βλασφημήσαντες ἐν ταῖς ἁμαρτίαις αὐτῶν τὸν Κύριον,
ἔτι δὲ καὶ ἐπαισχυνθέντες τὸ ὄνομα Κυρίου τὸ ἐπικληθὲν
ἐπ᾿ αὐτούς. οὗτοι οὖν εἰς τέλος ἀπώλοντο τῷ Θεῷ. βλέπεις
δὲ ὅτι οὐδὲ εἷς αὐτῶν μετενόησε, καίπερ ἀκούσαντες τὰ ῥήματα
ἃ ἐλάλησας αὐτοῖς, ἅ σοι ἐνετειλάμην· ἀπὸ τῶν τοιούτων ἡ
ζωὴ ἀπέστη. 5. οἱ δὲ τὰς ξηρὰς καὶ ἀσήπτους ἐπιδεδωκότες,
καὶ οὗτοι ἐγγὺς αὐτῶν· ἦσαν γὰρ ὑποκριταὶ καὶ διδαχὰς
ξένας εἰσφέροντες καὶ ἐκστρέφοντες τοὺς δούλους τοῦ Θεοῦ,
μάλιστα δὲ τοὺς ἡμαρτηκότας, μὴ ἀφιέντες μετανοεῖν αὐτούς,
ἀλλὰ ταῖς διδαχαῖς ταῖς μωραῖς πείθοντες αὐτούς. οὗτοι οὖν
ἔχουσιν ἐλπίδα τοῦ μετανοῆσαι. 6. βλέπεις δὲ πολλοὺς
ἐξ αὐτῶν καὶ μετανενοηκότας ἀφ᾿ ἧς ἐλάλησας αὐτοῖς τὰς
ἐντολάς μου· καὶ ἔτι μετανοήσουσιν. ὅσοι δὲ οὐ μετανοήσουσιν, ἀπώλεσαν τὴν ζωὴν αὐτῶν· ὅσοι δὲ μετενόησαν ἐξ
αὐτῶν, ἀγαθοὶ ἐγένοντο, καὶ ἐγένετο ἡ κατοικία αὐτῶν εἰς
τὰ τείχη τὰ πρῶτα· τινὲς δὲ καὶ εἰς τὸν πύργον ἀνέβησαν.
βλέπεις οὖν, [φησίν,] ὅτι ἡ μετάνοια τῶν ἁμαρτιῶν ζωὴν ἔχει,
τὸ δὲ μὴ μετανοῆσαι θάνατον.

VII. Ὅσοι δὲ ἡμιξήρους ἐπέδωκαν καὶ ἐν αὐταῖς σχισμὰς
εἶχον, ἄκουε καὶ περὶ αὐτῶν. ὅσων ἦσαν αἱ ῥάβδοι κατὰ τὸ
αὐτὸ ἡμίξηροι, δίψυχοί εἰσιν· οὔτε γὰρ ζῶσιν οὔτε τεθνήκασιν. 2. οἱ δὲ ἡμιξήρους ἔχοντες καὶ ἐν αὐταῖς σχισμάς,
οὗτοι καὶ δίψυχοι καὶ κατάλαλοί εἰσι, καὶ μηδέποτε εἰρηνεύοντες εἰς ἑαυτούς, ἀλλὰ διχοστατοῦντες πάντοτε. ἀλλὰ
καὶ τούτοις, [φησίν,] ἐπίκειται μετάνοια. βλέπεις, [φησί,]
τινὰς ἐξ αὐτῶν μετανενοηκότας. καὶ ἔτι, φησίν, ἐστὶν ἐν
αὐτοῖς ἐλπὶς μετανοίας. 3. καὶ ὅσοι, φησίν, ἐξ αὐτῶν μετα-
νενοήκασι, τὴν κατοικίαν εἰς τὸν πύργον ἔχουσιν· ὅσοι δὲ ἐξ
αὐτῶν βραδύτερον μετανενοήκασιν, εἰς τὰ τείχη κατοική-
σουσιν· ὅσοι δὲ οὐ μετανοοῦσιν, ἀλλ᾿ ἐμμένουσι ταῖς πράξεσιν
αὐτῶν, θανάτῳ ἀποθανοῦνται. 4. οἱ δὲ χλωρὰς ἐπιδεδωκότες

---

8. vi. 4 καίπερ ἀκούσαντες] conj. Anger [L₁L₂]; καὶ παρακούσαντες A;
dub. E.   ἐλάλησας] conj. Gebhardt [L₂]; ἐλάλησα A; def. L₁E.   vii. 1
κατά] καθά A.   3 ἔχουσιν] conj. Gebhardt [L₁L₂E]; ἕξουσιν A.

τὰς ῥάβδους αὐτῶν καὶ σχισμὰς ἐχούσας, πάντοτε οὗτοι
πιστοὶ καὶ ἀγαθοὶ ἐγένοντο, ἔχοντες [δὲ] ζῆλόν τινα ἐν ἀλλήλοις περὶ πρωτείων καὶ περὶ δόξης τινός· ἀλλὰ πάντες οὗτοι
μωροί εἰσιν, ἐν ἀλλήλοις ἔχοντες περὶ πρωτείων. 5. ἀλλὰ
καὶ οὗτοι ἀκούσαντες τῶν ἐντολῶν μου, ἀγαθοὶ ὄντες, ἐκα-
θάρισαν ἑαυτοὺς καὶ μετενόησαν ταχύ. ἐγένετο οὖν ἡ κατοίκησις αὐτῶν εἰς τὸν πύργον. ἐὰν δέ τις πάλιν ἐπιστρέψῃ
εἰς τὴν διχοστασίαν, ἐκβληθήσεται ἀπὸ τοῦ πύργου, καὶ
ἀπολέσει τὴν ζωὴν αὐτοῦ. 6. ἡ ζωὴ πάντων ἐστὶ τῶν τὰς
ἐντολὰς τοῦ Κυρίου φυλασσόντων· ἐν ταῖς ἐντολαῖς δὲ περὶ
πρωτείων ἢ περὶ δόξης τινὸς οὐκ ἔστιν, ἀλλὰ περὶ μακρο-
θυμίας καὶ περὶ ταπεινοφρονήσεως ἀνδρός. ἐν τοῖς τοιούτοις
οὖν ἡ ζωὴ τοῦ Κυρίου, ἐν τοῖς διχοστάταις δὲ καὶ παρανόμοις
θάνατος.

VIII. Οἱ δὲ ἐπιδεδωκότες τὰς ῥάβδους ἥμισυ μὲν χλωράς, ἥμισυ δὲ ξηράς, οὗτοί εἰσιν οἱ ἐν ταῖς πραγματείαις
ἐμπεφυρμένοι καὶ μὴ κολλώμενοι τοῖς ἁγίοις. διὰ τοῦτο τὸ
ἥμισυ αὐτῶν ζῇ, τὸ δὲ ἥμισυ νεκρόν ἐστι. 2. πολλοὶ οὖν
ἀκούσαντές μου τῶν ἐντολῶν μετενόησαν. ὅσοι γοῦν μετενόησαν, ἡ κατοικία αὐτῶν εἰς τὸν πύργον. τινὲς δὲ αὐτῶν
εἰς τέλος ἀπέστησαν. οὗτοι οὖν μετάνοιαν οὐκ ἔχουσιν· διὰ
γὰρ τὰς πραγματείας αὐτῶν ἐβλασφήμησαν τὸν Κύριον καὶ
ἀπηρνήσαντο. ἀπώλεσαν οὖν τὴν ζωὴν αὐτῶν διὰ τὴν
πονηρίαν ἣν ἔπραξαν. 3. πολλοὶ δὲ ἐξ αὐτῶν ἐδιψύχησαν.
οὗτοι ἔτι ἔχουσι μετάνοιαν, ἐὰν ταχὺ μετανοήσωσι, καὶ ἔσται
αὐτῶν ἡ κατοικία εἰς τὸν πύργον· ἐὰν δὲ βραδύτερον μετανοήσωσι, κατοικήσουσιν εἰς τὰ τείχη· ἐὰν δὲ μὴ μετανοήσωσι,
καὶ αὐτοὶ ἀπώλεσαν τὴν ζωὴν αὐτῶν. 4. οἱ δὲ τὰ δύο μέρη
χλωρά, τὸ δὲ τρίτον ξηρὸν ἐπιδεδωκότες, οὗτοί εἰσιν οἱ ἀρνησάμενοι ποικίλαις ἀρνήσεσι. 5. πολλοὶ οὖν μετενόησαν ἐξ
αὐτῶν, καὶ ἀπῆλθον εἰς τὸν πύργον κατοικεῖν· πολλοὶ δὲ
ἀπέστησαν εἰς τέλος τοῦ Θεοῦ· οὗτοι τὸ ζῆν εἰς τέλος ἀπώ-

---

vii. 4 δὲ sec.] ins. Hilgenfeld [L₁L₂E]; om. A.   viii. 4 χλωρά, ξηρὸν]
conj. Gebhardt [L₁L₂E]; ξηρά, χλωρὸν A.

λεσαν. τινὲς δὲ ἐξ αὐτῶν ἐδιψύχησαν καὶ ἐδιχοστάτησαν.

τούτοις οὖν ἐστὶ μετάνοια, ἐὰν ταχὺ μετανοήσωσι καὶ μὴ ἐπιμείνωσι ταῖς ἡδοναῖς αὐτῶν· ἐὰν δὲ ἐπιμείνωσι ταῖς πράξεσιν αὐτῶν, καὶ οὗτοι θάνατον ἑαυτοῖς κατεργάζονται.

IX. Οἱ δὲ ἐπιδεδωκότες τὰς ῥάβδους τὰ μὲν δύο μέρη ξηρά, τὸ δὲ τρίτον χλωρόν, οὗτοί εἰσι πιστοὶ μὲν γεγονότες, πλουτήσαντες δὲ καὶ γενόμενοι ἔνδοξοι παρὰ τοῖς ἔθνεσιν· ὑπερηφανίαν μεγάλην ἐνεδύσαντο καὶ ὑψηλόφρονες ἐγένοντο, καὶ κατέλιπον τὴν ἀλήθειαν, καὶ οὐκ ἐκολλήθησαν τοῖς δικαίοις, ἀλλὰ κατὰ τὰ ἔθνη συνέζησαν, καὶ αὕτη ἡ ὁδὸς ἡδυτέρα αὐτοῖς ἐγένετο· ἀπὸ δὲ τοῦ Θεοῦ οὐκ ἀπέστησαν, ἀλλ᾿ ἐνέμειναν τῇ πίστει, μὴ ἐργαζόμενοι τὰ ἔργα τῆς πίστεως. 2. πολλοὶ οὖν ἐξ αὐτῶν μετενόησαν, καὶ ἐγένετο ἡ κατοίκησις αὐτῶν ἐν τῷ πύργῳ. 3. ἕτεροι δὲ εἰς τέλος μετὰ τῶν ἐθνῶν συζῶντες καὶ φθειρόμενοι ταῖς κενοδοξίαις τῶν ἐθνῶν ἀπέστησαν ἀπὸ τοῦ Θεοῦ, καὶ ἔπραξαν τὰς πράξεις τῶν ἐθνῶν. οὗτοι μετὰ τῶν ἐθνῶν ἐλογίσθησαν. 4. ἕτεροι δὲ ἐξ αὐτῶν ἐδιψύχησαν μὴ ἐλπίζοντες σωθῆναι διὰ τὰς πράξεις ἃς ἔπραξαν· ἕτεροι δὲ ἐδιψύχησαν καὶ σχίσματα ἐν ἑαυτοῖς ἐποίησαν. τούτοις οὖν τοῖς διψυχήσασι διὰ τὰς πράξεις αὐτῶν μετάνοια ἔτι ἐστίν· ἀλλ᾿ ἡ μετάνοια αὐτῶν ταχινὴ ὀφείλει εἶναι, ἵνα ἡ κατοικία αὐτῶν γένηται ἐντὸς τοῦ πύργου· τῶν δὲ μὴ μετανοούντων, ἀλλ᾿ ἐπιμενόντων ταῖς ἡδοναῖς, ὁ θάνατος ἐγγύς.

X. Οἱ δὲ ἐπιδεδωκότες τὰς ῥάβδους χλωράς, αὐτὰ δὲ τὰ ἄκρα ξηρὰ καὶ σχισμὰς ἔχοντα, οὗτοι πάντοτε ἀγαθοὶ καὶ πιστοὶ καὶ ἔνδοξοι παρὰ τῷ Θεῷ ἐγένοντο, ἐλάχιστον δὲ ἐξήμαρτον διὰ μικρὰς ἐπιθυμίας καὶ μικρὰ κατ᾿ ἀλλήλων ἔχοντες· ἀλλ᾿ ἀκούσαντές μου τῶν ῥημάτων τὸ πλεῖστον μέρος ταχὺ μετενόησαν, καὶ ἐγένετο ἡ κατοικία αὐτῶν εἰς τὸν πύργον. 2. τινὲς δὲ ἐξ αὐτῶν ἐδιψύχησαν, τινὲς δὲ διψυχήσαντες διχοστασίαν μείζονα ἐποίησαν. ἐν τούτοις οὖν ἔτι ἐστὶ μετανοίας ἐλπίς, ὅτι ἀγαθοὶ πάντοτε ἐγένοντο· δυσκόλως δέ τις αὐτῶν ἀποθανεῖται. 3. οἱ δὲ τὰς ῥάβδους αὐτῶν ξηρὰς ἐπι-

δεδωκότες, ἐλάχιστον δὲ χλωρὸν ἐχούσας, οὗτοί εἰσιν οἱ
πιστεύσαντες μέν, τὰ δὲ ἔργα τῆς ἀνομίας ἐργασάμενοι· οὐδέποτε δὲ ἀπὸ τοῦ Θεοῦ ἀπέστησαν, καὶ τὸ ὄνομα ἡδέως ἐβά-
στασαν, καὶ εἰς τοὺς οἴκους αὐτῶν ἡδέως ὑπεδέξαντο τοὺς
δούλους τοῦ Θεοῦ. ἀκούσαντες οὖν ταύτην τὴν μετάνοιαν
ἀδιστάκτως μετενόησαν, καὶ ἐργάζονται πᾶσαν ἀρετὴν καὶ
δικαιοσύνην· 4. τινὲς δὲ ἐξ αὐτῶν καὶ ἑκόντες θλίβονται,
γινώσκοντες τὰς πράξεις αὐτῶν ἃς ἔπραξαν. τούτων οὖν πάντων ἡ κατοικία εἰς τὸν πύργον ἔσται.

XI. Καὶ μετὰ τὸ συντελέσαι αὐτὸν τὰς ἐπιλύσεις πασῶν
τῶν ῥάβδων λέγει μοι· Ὕπαγε, καὶ πᾶσι λέγε ἵνα μετανοήσωσι, καὶ ζήσονται τῷ Θεῷ· ὅτι ὁ Κύριος ἔπεμψέ με
σπλαγχνισθεὶς πᾶσι δοῦναι τὴν μετάνοιαν, καίπερ τινῶν μὴ
ὄντων ἀξίων διὰ τὰ ἔργα αὐτῶν· ἀλλὰ μακρόθυμος ὢν ὁ
Κύριος θέλει τὴν κλῆσιν τὴν γενομένην διὰ τοῦ υἱοῦ αὐτοῦ
σώζεσθαι. 2. λέγω αὐτῷ· Κύριε, ἐλπίζω ὅτι πάντες ἀκούσαντες αὐτὰ μετανοήσουσι. πείθομαι γὰρ ὅτι εἷς ἕκαστος τὰ
ἴδια ἔργα ἐπιγνοὺς καὶ φοβηθεὶς τὸν Θεὸν μετανοήσει.
3. ἀποκριθείς μοι λέγει· Ὅσοι, [φησίν,] ἐξ ὅλης καρδίας
αὐτῶν [μετανοήσωσι καὶ] καθαρίσωσιν ἑαυτοὺς ἀπὸ τῶν
πονηριῶν πασῶν τῶν προειρημένων καὶ μηκέτι μηδὲν προσθῶσι ταῖς ἁμαρτίαις αὐτῶν, λήψονται ἴασιν παρὰ τοῦ
Κυρίου τῶν προτέρων ἁμαρτιῶν, ἐὰν μὴ διψυχήσωσιν ἐπὶ
ταῖς ἐντολαῖς ταύταις, καὶ ζήσονται τῷ Θεῷ. [ὅσοι δέ, φησί,
προσθῶσι ταῖς ἁμαρτίαις αὐτῶν καὶ ἀναστραφῶσιν ἐν ταῖς
ἐπιθυμίαις τοῦ αἰῶνος τούτου, κατακρινοῦσιν ἑαυτοὺς εἰς
θάνατον.] 4. σὺ δὲ πορεύου ἐν ταῖς ἐντολαῖς μου, καὶ ζῆθι
[τῷ Θεῷ· καὶ ὅσοι ἂν πορευθῶσιν ἐν αὐταῖς καὶ κατορθώσωνται, ζήσονται τῷ Θεῷ.] 5. ταῦτά μοι δείξας [καὶ λαλή-

---

x. 3 μέν] conj. Gebhardt [L₁L₂]; μόνον AE.   4 ἑκόντες θλίβονται]
conj. Harmer [L₁L₂]; καὶ φοβοῦνται A; se ipsos afflixerunt E.   xi. 1 πασῶν]
[L₁L₂E]; πάσας A.   3 μετανοήσωσι καὶ] ins. Hilgenfeld [L₁L₂E];
om. A.   καθαρίσωσιν] καθαρίσουσιν A.   πασῶν] conj. Gebhardt [L₁L₂];
αὐτῶν A; hoc E.   ὅσοι δέ...θάνατον] ins. Hilgenfeld [L₁L₂E]; om. A.
4 τῷ Θεῷ...ζήσονται τῷ Θεῷ] ins. Hilgenfeld [L₁L₂E]; om. A.

σας] πάντα λέγει μοι· Τὰ δὲ λοιπὰ ἐπιδείξω μετ' ὀλίγας ἡμέρας.

[Παραβολὴ θ'.]

I. Μετὰ τὸ γράψαι με τὰς ἐντολὰς καὶ παραβολὰς τοῦ ποιμένος, τοῦ ἀγγέλου τῆς μετανοίας, ἦλθε πρός με καὶ λέγει μοι· Θέλω σοι δεῖξαι ὅσα σοι ἔδειξε τὸ πνεῦμα τὸ ἅγιον τὸ λαλῆσαν μετὰ σοῦ ἐν μορφῇ τῆς Ἐκκλησίας· ἐκεῖνο γὰρ τὸ πνεῦμα ὁ υἱὸς τοῦ Θεοῦ ἐστίν. 2. ἐπειδὴ γὰρ ἀσθενέστερος τῇ σαρκὶ ἦς, οὐκ ἐδηλώθη σοι δι' ἀγγέλου. ὅτε οὖν ἐνεδυναμώθης διὰ τοῦ πνεύματος καὶ ἴσχυσας τῇ ἰσχύϊ σου, ὥστε δύνασθαί σε καὶ ἄγγελον ἰδεῖν, τότε μὲν οὖν ἐφανερώθη σοι διὰ τῆς Ἐκκλησίας ἡ οἰκοδομὴ τοῦ πύργου· καλῶς καὶ σεμνῶς πάντα ὡς ὑπὸ παρθένου ἑώρακας. νῦν δὲ ὑπὸ ἀγγέλου βλέπεις, διὰ τοῦ αὐτοῦ μὲν πνεύματος· 3. δεῖ δέ σε παρ' ἐμοῦ ἀκριβέστερον πάντα μαθεῖν. εἰς τοῦτο γὰρ καὶ ἐδόθην ὑπὸ τοῦ ἐνδόξου ἀγγέλου εἰς τὸν οἶκόν σου κατοικῆσαι, ἵνα δυνατῶς πάντα ἴδῃς, μηδὲν δειλαινόμενος ὡς καὶ τὸ πρότερον. 4. καὶ ἀπήγαγέ με εἰς τὴν Ἀρκαδίαν, εἰς ὄρος τι μαστῶδες, καὶ ἐκάθισέ με ἐπὶ τὸ ἄκρον τοῦ ὄρους, καὶ ἔδειξέ μοι πεδίον μέγα, κύκλῳ δὲ τοῦ πεδίου ὄρη δώδεκα, ἄλλην καὶ ἄλλην ἰδέαν ἔχοντα τὰ ὄρη. 5. τὸ πρῶτον ἦν μέλαν ὡς ἀσβόλη· τὸ δὲ δεύτερον ψιλόν, βοτάνας μὴ ἔχον· τὸ δὲ τρίτον ἀκανθῶδες καὶ τριβόλων πλῆρες· 6. τὸ δὲ τέταρτον βοτάνας ἔχον ἡμιξήρους, τὰ μὲν ἐπάνω τῶν βοτανῶν χλωρά, τὰ δὲ πρὸς ταῖς ῥίζαις ξηρά· τινὲς δὲ βοτάναι, ὅταν ὁ ἥλιος ἐπικεκαύκει, ξηραὶ ἐγίνοντο· 7. τὸ δὲ πέμπτον ὄρος ἔχον βοτάνας χλωράς, καὶ τραχὺ ὄν. τὸ δὲ ἕκτον ὄρος σχισμῶν ὅλον ἔγεμεν, ὧν μὲν μικρῶν, ὧν δὲ μεγάλων· εἶχον δὲ βοτάνας αἱ σχισμαί, οὐ λίαν δὲ ἦσαν εὐθαλεῖς αἱ βοτάναι, μᾶλλον δὲ ὡς μεμαρασμέναι ἦσαν. 8. τὸ δὲ ἕβδομον ὄρος εἶχε βοτάνας ἱλαράς, καὶ ὅλον τὸ ὄρος εὐθηνοῦν ἦν, καὶ πᾶν γένος κτηνῶν καὶ ὀρνέων ἐνέμοντο εἰς τὸ ὄρος ἐκεῖνο· καὶ ὅσον ἐβόσκοντο τὰ κτήνη καὶ τὰ πετεινά, μᾶλλον καὶ μᾶλλον αἱ βοτάναι τοῦ ὄρους ἐκείνου ἔθαλλον. τὸ δὲ ὄγδοον ὄρος πηγῶν πλῆρες ἦν, καὶ πᾶν γένος τῆς κτίσεως τοῦ Κυρίου ἐποτίζοντο ἐκ τῶν πηγῶν τοῦ ὄρους ἐκείνου. 9. τὸ δὲ ἔννατον ὄρος ὅλως ὕδωρ οὐκ εἶχε καὶ ὅλον ἐρημῶδες ἦν· εἶχε δὲ ἐν αὐτῷ θηρία καὶ ἑρπετὰ θανάσιμα, διαφθείροντα ἀνθρώπους. τὸ δὲ δέκατον ὄρος εἶχε δένδρα μέγιστα, καὶ ὅλον κατάσκιον ἦν, καὶ ὑπὸ τὴν σκέπην πρόβατα κατέκειντο ἀναπαυόμενα καὶ μαρυκώμενα. 10. τὸ δὲ ἑνδέκατον ὄρος λίαν σύνδενδρον ἦν, καὶ τὰ δένδρα ἐκεῖνα κατάκαρπα ἦν, ἄλλοις καὶ ἄλλοις καρποῖς κεκοσμημένα, ἵνα ἰδών τις αὐτὰ ἐπιθυμήσῃ φαγεῖν ἐκ τῶν καρπῶν αὐτῶν. τὸ δὲ δωδέκατον ὄρος ὅλον ἦν λευκόν, καὶ ἡ πρόσοψις αὐτοῦ ἱλαρὰ ἦν· καὶ εὐπρεπέστατον ἦν ἑαυτῷ τὸ ὄρος.

II. Εἰς μέσον δὲ τοῦ πεδίου ἔδειξέ μοι πέτραν μεγάλην λευκὴν ἐκ τοῦ πεδίου ἀναβεβηκυῖαν. ἡ δὲ πέτρα ὑψηλοτέρα ἦν τῶν ὀρέων, τετράγωνος, ὥστε δύνασθαι ὅλον τὸν κόσμον χωρῆσαι. 2. παλαιὰ δὲ ἦν ἡ πέτρα ἐκείνη, πύλην ἐκκεκομμένην ἔχουσα· ὡς πρόσφατος δὲ ἐδόκει μοι εἶναι ἡ ἐκκόλαψις τῆς πύλης· ἡ δὲ πύλη οὕτως ἔστιλβεν ὑπὲρ τὸν ἥλιον, ὥστε με θαυμάζειν ἐπὶ τῇ λαμπηδόνι τῆς πύλης. 3. κύκλῳ δὲ τῆς πύλης εἱστήκεισαν παρθένοι δώδεκα. αἱ οὖν τέσσαρες αἱ εἰς τὰς γωνίας ἑστηκυῖαι ἐνδοξότεραί μοι ἐδόκουν εἶναι· καὶ αἱ ἄλλαι δὲ ἔνδοξοι ἦσαν. εἱστήκεισαν δὲ εἰς τὰ τέσσαρα μέρη τῆς πύλης, ἀνὰ μέσον αὐτῶν ἀνὰ δύο παρθένοι. 4. ἐνδεδυμέναι δὲ ἦσαν λινοῦς χιτῶνας καὶ περιεζωσμέναι εὐπρεπῶς, ἔξω τοὺς ὤμους ἔχουσαι τοὺς δεξιοὺς ὡς μέλλουσαι φορτίον τι βαστάζειν. οὕτως ἕτοιμοι ἦσαν· λίαν γὰρ ἱλαραὶ ἦσαν καὶ πρόθυμοι. 5. μετὰ τὸ ἰδεῖν με ταῦτα ἐθαύμαζον ἐν ἐμαυτῷ, ὅτι μεγάλα καὶ ἔνδοξα πράγματα βλέπω. καὶ πάλιν διηπό-

i. 9 σκέπην] L₁; add αὐτοῦ πολλὰ A; add arborum L₂; add earum arborum E. μαρυκώμενα] μηρυκώμενα A. 10 σύνδενδρον] σύδενδρον A. ἑαυτῷ] conj. Gebhardt [L₁L₂]; ἐν αὐτῷ A; dub. E. ii. 3 αὐτῶν] [L₂E]; αὐτῆς A; al. L₁.

ρουν ἐπὶ ταῖς παρθένοις, ὅτι τρυφεραὶ οὕτως οὖσαι ἀνδρείως
εἰστήκεισαν ὡς μέλλουσαι ὅλον τὸν οὐρανὸν βαστάζειν. 6.
καὶ λέγει μοι ὁ ποιμήν· Τί ἐν σεαυτῷ διαλογίζῃ καὶ διαπορῇ,
καὶ σεαυτῷ λύπην ἐπισπᾶσαι ; ὅσα γὰρ οὐ δύνασαι νοῆσαι,
μὴ ἐπιχείρει, συνετὸς ὤν, ἀλλ᾽ ἐρώτα τὸν Κύριον, ἵνα λάβῃς
σύνεσιν νοεῖν αὐτά. 7. τὰ ὀπίσω σου ἰδεῖν οὐ δύνῃ, τὰ δὲ
ἔμπροσθέν σου βλέπεις. ἃ οὖν ἰδεῖν οὐ δύνασαι, ἔασον, καὶ
μὴ στρέβλου σεαυτόν· ἃ δὲ βλέπεις, ἐκείνων κατακυρίευε,
καὶ περὶ τῶν λοιπῶν μὴ περιεργάζου· πάντα δέ σοι ἐγὼ
δηλώσω, ὅσα ἐάν σοι δείξω. ἔμβλεπε οὖν τοῖς λοιποῖς.
III. Εἶδον ἐξ ἄνδρας ἐληλυθότας ὑψηλοὺς καὶ ἐνδόξους
καὶ ὁμοίους τῇ ἰδέᾳ· καὶ ἐκάλεσαν πλῆθός τι ἀνδρῶν. κἀκεῖνοι δὲ οἱ ἐληλυθότες ὑψηλοὶ ἦσαν ἄνδρες καὶ καλοὶ καὶ δυνα-
τοί· καὶ ἐκέλευσαν αὐτοὺς οἱ ἐξ ἄνδρες οἰκοδομεῖν ἐπάνω τῆς
πύλης πύργον τινά. ἦν δὲ θόρυβος τῶν ἀνδρῶν ἐκείνων μέγας
τῶν ἐληλυθότων οἰκοδομεῖν τὸν πύργον, ὧδε κἀκεῖσε περιτρε-
χόντων κύκλῳ τῆς πύλης· 2. αἱ δὲ παρθένοι ἑστηκυῖαι κύκλῳ
τῆς πύλης ἔλεγον τοῖς ἀνδράσι σπεύδειν τὸν πύργον οἰκοδομεῖσθαι. ἐκπεπετάκεισαν δὲ τὰς χεῖρας αἱ παρθένοι ὡς μέλ-
λουσαί τι λαμβάνειν παρὰ τῶν ἀνδρῶν. 3. οἱ δὲ ἐξ ἄνδρες
ἐκέλευον ἐκ βυθοῦ τινὸς λίθους ἀναβαίνειν καὶ ὑπάγειν εἰς τὴν
οἰκοδομὴν τοῦ πύργου. ἀνέβησαν δὲ λίθοι δέκα τετράγωνοι
λαμπροί, [μὴ] λελατομημένοι. 4. οἱ δὲ ἐξ ἄνδρες ἐκάλουν τὰς
παρθένους καὶ ἐκέλευσαν αὐτὰς τοὺς λίθους πάντας τοὺς μέλλοντας εἰς τὴν οἰκοδομὴν ὑπάγειν τοῦ πύργου βαστάζειν καὶ
διαπορεύεσθαι διὰ τῆς πύλης, καὶ ἐπιδιδόναι τοῖς ἀνδράσι
τοῖς μέλλουσιν οἰκοδομεῖν τὸν πύργον. 5. αἱ δὲ παρθένοι
τοὺς δέκα λίθους τοὺς πρώτους τοὺς ἐκ τοῦ βυθοῦ ἀναβάντας
ἐπετίθουν ἀλλήλοις καὶ κατὰ ἕνα λίθον ἐβάσταζον ὁμοῦ.
IV. Καθὼς δὲ ἐστάθησαν ὁμοῦ κύκλῳ τῆς πύλης, οὕτως

9. ii. 5 ἐπὶ ταῖς παρθένοις] ἐπὶ τὰς παρθένους A.   6 οὐ δύνασαι]
[L₁L₂E] ; οὐδὲ A.   iii. 1 ἐκάλεσαν] [L₁L₂E] ; ἐκέλευσαν A.   ἐπάνω
τῆς πύλης] conj. Harmer [L₁] ; ἐπάνω τῆς πέτρας AE : supra petram illam et
super portam ipsam L₂.   3 μὴ] ins. Anger (cf. c. v. 3, c. xvi. 7) ;
om. AL₁E ; om. also λελατομημένοι L₂.   5 ἐπετίθουν] conj. Tischendorf
[L₂]; ἐπήνυον A ; al. L₁E.

ἐβάσταζον αἱ δοκοῦσαι δυναταὶ εἶναι καὶ ὑπὸ τὰς γωνίας
τοῦ λίθου ὑποδεδυκυῖαι ἦσαν· αἱ δὲ ἄλλαι ἐκ τῶν πλευρῶν
τοῦ λίθου ὑποδεδύκεισαν καὶ οὕτως ἐβάσταζον πάντας τοὺς
λίθους· διὰ δὲ τῆς πύλης διέφερον αὐτούς, καθὼς ἐκελεύσθη-
σαν, καὶ ἐπεδίδουν τοῖς ἀνδράσιν εἰς τὸν πύργον· ἐκεῖνοι δὲ
ἔχοντες τοὺς λίθους ᾠκοδόμουν. 2. ἡ οἰκοδομὴ δὲ τοῦ πύργου
ἐγένετο ἐπὶ τὴν πέτραν ⸆τὴν μεγάλην καὶ ἐπάνω τῆς πύλης.
ἡρμόσθησαν οὖν οἱ δέκα λίθοι ἐκεῖνοι, | καὶ ἀνέπλησαν ὅλην
τὴν πέτραν. καὶ ἐγένοντο ἐκεῖνοι | θεμέλιος τῆς οἰκοδομῆς τοῦ
πύργου. ἡ δὲ [πέτρα καὶ ἡ] πύλη ἦν βαστάζουσα ὅλον τὸν
πύργον. 3. μετὰ δὲ τοὺς δέκα λίθους ἄλλοι ἀνέβησαν ἐκ τοῦ
βυθοῦ εἴκοσι πέντε λίθοι· καὶ οὗτοι ἡρμόσθησαν εἰς τὴν
οἰκοδομὴν τοῦ πύργου, βασταζόμενοι ὑπὸ τῶν παρθένων καθὼς
καὶ οἱ πρότεροι. μετὰ δὲ τούτους ἀνέβησαν τριάκοντα πέντε·
καὶ οὗτοι ὁμοίως ἡρμόσθησαν εἰς τὸν πύργον. μετὰ δὲ τούτους
ἕτεροι ἀνέβησαν λίθοι τεσσαράκοντα· καὶ οὗτοι πάντες ἐβλή-
.θησαν εἰς τὴν οἰκοδομὴν τοῦ πύργου· | ἐγένοντο οὖν στοῖχοι
τέσσαρες ἐν τοῖς θεμελίοις τοῦ πύργου· | 4. καὶ ἐπαύσαντο
ἐκ τοῦ βυθοῦ ἀναβαίνοντες· ἐπαύσαντο δὲ καὶ οἱ οἰκοδομοῦντες μικρόν. καὶ πάλιν ἐπέταξαν οἱ ἓξ ἄνδρες τῷ πλήθει τοῦ
ὄχλου ἐκ τῶν ὀρέων παραφέρειν λίθους εἰς τὴν οἰκοδομὴν τοῦ
πύργου. 5. παρεφέροντο οὖν ἐκ πάντων τῶν ὀρέων χρόαις
ποικίλαις λελατομημένοι ὑπὸ τῶν ἀνδρῶν καὶ ἐπεδίδοντο ταῖς
παρθένοις· αἱ δὲ παρθένοι διέφερον αὐτοὺς διὰ τῆς πύλης καὶ
ἐπεδίδουν εἰς τὴν οἰκοδομὴν τοῦ πύργου. καὶ ὅταν εἰς τὴν
οἰκοδομὴν ἐτέθησαν οἱ λίθοι οἱ ποικίλοι, ὅμοιοι ἐγένοντο λευ-
κοί, καὶ τὰς χρόας τὰς ποικίλας ἤλλασσον. 6. τινὲς δὲ λίθοι
ἐπεδίδοντο ὑπὸ τῶν ἀνδρῶν εἰς τὴν οἰκοδομήν, καὶ οὐκ ἐγίνοντο λαμπροί, ἀλλ᾽ οἷοι ἐτέθησαν, τοιοῦτοι καὶ εὑρέθησαν·
οὐ γὰρ ἦσαν ὑπὸ τῶν παρθένων ἐπιδεδομένοι, οὐδὲ διὰ τῆς

iv. 2 οὖν] ins. Gebhardt [L₁L₂]; om. A; et E. δέκα] ins. Gebhardt
[L₁L₂E]; om. A (ι′ after οἱ). καὶ ἀνέπλησαν…ἐκεῖνοι] ins. Hilgenfeld
[L₂E, cf. L₁]; om. A·by homœot. 3 εἴκοσι πέντε] conj. Gebhardt [L₁L₂];
εἴκοσι A; quindecem E. ἐγένοντο…τοῦ πύργου] conj. Hilgenfeld [L₁L₂E];
om. A by homœot. 6 ὑπὸ sec.] ἀπὸ A.

πύλης παρενηνεγμένοι. οὗτοι οὖν οἱ λίθοι ἀπρεπεῖς ἦσαν ἐν τῇ οἰκοδομῇ τοῦ πύργου. 7. ἰδόντες δὲ οἱ ἓξ ἄνδρες τοὺς λίθους τοὺς ἀπρεπεῖς ἐν τῇ οἰκοδομῇ ἐκέλευσαν αὐτοὺς ἀρθῆναι καὶ ἀπαχθῆναι [κάτω] εἰς τὸν ἴδιον τόπον ὅθεν ἠνέχθησαν. 8. καὶ λέγουσι τοῖς ἀνδράσι τοῖς παρεμφέρουσι τοὺς λίθους· "Ολως ὑμεῖς μὴ ἐπιδίδοτε εἰς τὴν οἰκοδομὴν λίθους· τίθετε δὲ αὐτοὺς παρὰ τὸν πύργον, ἵνα αἱ παρθένοι διὰ τῆς πύλης παρενέγκωσιν αὐτοὺς καὶ ἐπιδιδῶσιν εἰς τὴν οἰκοδομήν. ἐὰν γάρ, [φασί,] διὰ τῶν χειρῶν τῶν παρθένων τούτων μὴ παρενεχθῶσι διὰ τῆς πύλης, τὰς χρόας αὐτῶν ἀλλάξαι οὐ δύνανται· μὴ κοπιᾶτε οὖν, [φασίν,] εἰς μάτην.

V. Καὶ ἐτελέσθη τῇ ἡμέρᾳ ἐκείνῃ ἡ οἰκοδομή, οὐκ ἀπετελέσθη δὲ ὁ πύργος· ἔμελλε γὰρ [πάλιν] ἐποικοδομεῖσθαι· καὶ ἐγένετο ἀνοχὴ τῆς οἰκοδομῆς. ἐκέλευσαν δὲ οἱ ἓξ ἄνδρες τοὺς οἰκοδομοῦντας ἀναχωρῆσαι μικρὸν [πάντας] καὶ ἀναπαυθῆναι· ταῖς δὲ παρθένοις ἐπέταξαν ἀπὸ τοῦ πύργου μὴ ἀναχωρῆσαι. ἐδόκει δέ μοι τὰς παρθένους καταλελεῖφθαι τοῦ φυλάσσειν τὸν πύργον. 2. μετὰ δὲ τὸ ἀναχωρῆσαι πάντας [καὶ ἀναπαυθῆναι] λέγω τῷ ποιμένι· Διατί, φημί, κύριε, οὐ συνετελέσθη ἡ οἰκοδομὴ τοῦ πύργου; Οὔπω, φησί, δύναται ἀποτελεσθῆναι ὁ πύργος, ἐὰν μὴ ἔλθῃ ὁ κύριος αὐτοῦ καὶ δοκιμάσῃ τὴν οἰκοδομὴν ταύτην, ἵνα ἐάν τινες λίθοι σαπροὶ εὑρεθῶσιν, ἀλλάξῃ αὐτούς· πρὸς γὰρ τὸ ἐκείνου θέλημα οἰκοδομεῖται ὁ πύργος. 3. "Ηθελον, φημί, κύριε, τούτου τοῦ πύργου γνῶναι τί ἐστιν ἡ οἰκοδομὴ αὕτη, καὶ περὶ τῆς πέτρας καὶ πύλης καὶ τῶν ὀρέων καὶ τῶν παρθένων, καὶ τῶν λίθων τῶν ἐκ τοῦ βυθοῦ ἀναβεβηκότων καὶ μὴ λελατομημένων, ἀλλ᾽ οὕτως ἀπελθόντων εἰς τὴν οἰκοδομήν. 4. καὶ διατί πρῶτον εἰς τὰ θεμέλια δέκα λίθοι ἐτέθησαν, εἶτα εἴκοσι πέντε, εἶτα τριάκοντα πέντε, εἶτα τεσσαράκοντα, καὶ περὶ τῶν λίθων τῶν ἀπεληλυθότων εἰς τὴν οἰκοδομὴν καὶ πάλιν ἠρμένων καὶ εἰς τόπον ἴδιον ἀποτεθειμένων· περὶ πάντων τούτων ἀνάπαυσον τὴν ψυχήν μου, κύριε,

9. iv. 8 τοῖς sec.] add τότε A app.; add hos L₁; om. L₂E.   ἐπιδίδοτε] ἐπιδίδωτε A.   v. 2 διατί] conj. Harmer; τί ὅτι A.   4 εἴκοσι πέντε] [L₁L₂]; εἴκοσι A; quindecim E.

καὶ γνώρισόν μοι αὐτά. 5. Ἐάν, φησί, κενόσπουδος μὴ εὑρεθῇς, πάντα γνώσῃ. μετ᾽ ὀλίγας γὰρ ἡμέρας | ἐλευσόμεθα ἐνθάδε, καὶ τὰ λοιπὰ ὄψει τὰ ἐπερχόμενα τῷ πύργῳ τούτῳ, καὶ πάσας τὰς παραβολὰς ἀκριβῶς γνώσῃ. 6. καὶ μετ᾽ ὀλίγας ἡμέρας | ἤλθομεν εἰς τὸν τόπον οὗ κεκαθίκαμεν, καὶ λέγει μοι· Ἄγωμεν πρὸς τὸν πύργον· ὁ γὰρ αὐθέντης τοῦ πύργου ἔρχεται κατανοῆσαι αὐτόν. καὶ ἤλθομεν πρὸς τὸν πύργον· καὶ ὅλως οὐθεὶς ἦν πρὸς αὐτὸν εἰ μὴ αἱ παρθένοι μόναι. 7. καὶ ἐπερωτᾷ ὁ ποιμὴν τὰς παρθένους εἰ ἄρα παρεγεγόνει ὁ δεσπότης τοῦ πύργου. αἱ δὲ ἔφησαν μέλλειν αὐτὸν ἔρχεσθαι κατανοῆσαι τὴν οἰκοδομήν.

VI. Καὶ ἰδοὺ μετὰ μικρὸν βλέπω παράταξιν πολλῶν ἀνδρῶν ἐρχομένων· καὶ εἰς τὸ μέσον ἀνήρ τις ὑψηλὸς τῷ μεγέθει, ὥστε τὸν πύργον ὑπερέχειν. 2. καὶ οἱ ἐξ ἄνδρες οἱ εἰς τὴν οἰκοδομὴν | ἐπιτάξαντες, ἐκ δεξιῶν καὶ ἀριστερῶν μετ᾽ αὐτοῦ περιεπάτουν, καὶ πάντες οἱ εἰς τὴν οἰκοδομὴν | ἐργασάμενοι μετ᾽ αὐτοῦ ἦσαν, καὶ ἕτεροι πολλοὶ κύκλῳ αὐτοῦ ἔνδοξοι. αἱ δὲ παρθένοι αἱ τηροῦσαι τὸν πύργον προσδραμοῦσαι κατεφίλησαν αὐτόν, καὶ ἤρξαντο ἐγγὺς αὐτοῦ περιπατεῖν κύκλῳ τοῦ πύργου. 3. κατενόει δὲ ὁ ἀνὴρ ἐκεῖνος τὴν οἰκοδομὴν ἀκριβῶς, ὥστε αὐτὸν καθ᾽ ἕνα λίθον ψηλαφᾶν. κρατῶν δέ τινα ῥάβδον τῇ χειρὶ κατὰ ἕνα λίθον τῶν ᾠκοδομημένων ἔτυπτε. 4. καὶ ὅταν ἐπάτασσεν, ἐγένοντο αὐτῶν τινὲς μέλανες ὡσεὶ ἀσβόλη, τινὲς δὲ ἐψωριακότες, τινὲς δὲ σχισμὰς ἔχοντες, τινὲς δὲ κολοβοί, τινὲς δὲ οὔτε λευκοὶ οὔτε μέλανες, τινὲς δὲ τραχεῖς καὶ μὴ συμφωνοῦντες τοῖς ἑτέροις λίθοις, τινὲς δὲ σπίλους πολλοὺς ἔχοντες· αὗται ἦσαν αἱ ποικιλίαι τῶν λίθων τῶν σαπρῶν εὑρεθέντων εἰς τὴν οἰκοδομήν. 5. ἐκέλευσεν οὖν πάντας τούτους ἐκ τοῦ πύργου μετενεχθῆναι καὶ τεθῆναι παρὰ τὸν πύργον, καὶ ἑτέρους ἐνεχθῆναι λίθους καὶ ἐμβληθῆναι εἰς τὸν τόπον αὐτῶν. 6. | καὶ ἐπηρώτησαν

---

v. 5 ἐλευσόμεθα...ἡμέρας] ins. Gebhardt [L₁L₂E]; om. A by homœot.
vi. 1 ὥστε] ὡς A.   2 ἐπιτάξαντες...οἰκοδομὴν] ins. Hilgenfeld [L₁L₂E]; om.
A by homœot.   3 ἔτυπτε] L₁E; pref. τρὶς A; def. L₂.

αὐτὸν οἱ οἰκοδομοῦντες, ἐκ τίνος ὄρους θέλῃ ἐνεχθῆναι λίθους καὶ ἐμβληθῆναι εἰς τὸν τόπον αὐτῶν. | καὶ ἐκ μὲν τῶν ὀρέων οὐκ ἐκέλευσεν ἐνεχθῆναι, | ἐκ δέ τινος πεδίου ἐγγὺς ὄντος ἐκέλευσεν ἐνεχθῆναι. | 7. καὶ ὠρύγη τὸ πεδίον, καὶ εὑρέθησαν λίθοι λαμπροὶ τετράγωνοι, τινὲς δὲ καὶ στρογγύλοι. ὅσοι δέ ποτε ἦσαν λίθοι ἐν τῷ πεδίῳ ἐκείνῳ, πάντες ἠνέχθησαν, καὶ διὰ τῆς πύλης ἐβαστάζοντο ὑπὸ τῶν παρθένων. 8. καὶ ἐλατομήθησαν οἱ τετράγωνοι λίθοι καὶ ἐτέθησαν εἰς τὸν τόπον τῶν ἡρμένων· οἱ δὲ στρογγύλοι οὐκ ἐτέθησαν εἰς τὴν οἰκοδομήν, ὅτι σκληροὶ ἦσαν εἰς τὸ λατομηθῆναι αὐτούς, καὶ βραδέως ἐγένετο. ἐτέθησαν δὲ παρὰ τὸν πύργον, ὡς μελλόντων αὐτῶν λατομεῖσθαι καὶ τίθεσθαι εἰς τὴν οἰκοδομήν· λίαν γὰρ λαμπροὶ ἦσαν.

VII. Ταῦτα οὖν συντελέσας ὁ ἀνὴρ ὁ ἔνδοξος καὶ κύριος ὅλου τοῦ πύργου προσεκαλέσατο τὸν ποιμένα, καὶ παρέδωκεν αὐτῷ τοὺς λίθους πάντας τοὺς παρὰ τὸν πύργον κειμένους, τοὺς ἀποβεβλημένους ἐκ τῆς οἰκοδομῆς, καὶ λέγει αὐτῷ· 2. Ἐπιμελῶς καθάρισον τοὺς λίθους τούτους καὶ θὲς αὐτοὺς εἰς τὴν οἰκοδομὴν τοῦ πύργου, τοὺς δυναμένους ἁρμόσαι τοῖς λοιποῖς· τοὺς δὲ μὴ ἁρμόζοντας ῥῖψον μακρὰν ἀπὸ τοῦ πύργου. 3. | ταῦτα κελεύσας τῷ ποιμένι ἀπῄει ἀπὸ τοῦ πύργου | μετὰ πάντων ὧν ἐληλύθει. αἱ δὲ παρθένοι κύκλῳ τοῦ πύργου εἱστήκεισαν τηροῦσαι αὐτόν. 4. λέγω τῷ ποιμένι· Πῶς πάλιν οὗτοι οἱ λίθοι δύνανται εἰς τὴν οἰκοδομὴν τοῦ πύργου ἀπελθεῖν ἀποδεδοκιμασμένοι ; ἀποκριθείς μοι λέγει· Βλέπεις, φησί, τοὺς λίθους τούτους ; Βλέπω, φημί, κύριε. Ἐγώ, φησί, τὸ πλεῖστον μέρος τῶν λίθων τούτων λατομήσω καὶ βαλῶ εἰς τὴν οἰκοδομήν, καὶ ἁρμόσουσι μετὰ τῶν λοιπῶν λίθων. 5. Πῶς, φημί, κύριε, δύνανται περικοπέντες τὸν αὐτὸν τόπον πληρῶσαι ; ἀποκριθεὶς λέγει μοι· "Οσοι μικροὶ εὑρεθήσονται

9. vi. 6 καὶ ἐπηρώτησαν...τόπον αὐτῶν] ins. Gebhardt [L₁L₂E] ; om. A by homœot.   ἐκ δέ τινος...ἐνεχθῆναι] ins. Gebhardt [L₁L₂] ; sed e montibus e proximo iussit apportare E ; om. A by homœot.   vii. 3 ταῦτα...ἀπὸ τοῦ πύργου] ins. Hilgenfeld [L₁L₂E] ; om. A by homœot.   4 πῶς] ins. Harmer [L₁L₂E] ; om. A.   βαλῶ] conj. Anger [L₁L₂E] ; βάλλω A.

εἰς μέσην τὴν οἰκοδομὴν βληθήσονται, ὅσοι δὲ μείζονες, ἐξώτεροι τεθήσονται καὶ συγκρατήσουσιν αὐτούς. 6. ταῦτά μοι λαλήσας λέγει μοι· Ἄγωμεν, καὶ μετὰ ἡμέρας δύο ἔλθωμεν καὶ καθαρίσωμεν τοὺς λίθους τούτους, καὶ βάλωμεν αὐτοὺς εἰς τὴν οἰκοδομήν· τὰ γὰρ κύκλῳ τοῦ πύργου πάντα καθαρισθῆναι δεῖ, μήποτε ὁ δεσπότης ἐξάπινα ἔλθῃ καὶ τὰ περὶ τὸν πύργον ῥυπαρὰ εὕρῃ καὶ προσοχθίσῃ, καὶ οὗτοι οἱ λίθοι οὐκ ἀπελεύσονται εἰς τὴν οἰκοδομὴν τοῦ πύργου, κἀγὼ ἀμελὴς δόξω εἶναι παρὰ τῷ δεσπότῃ. 7. καὶ μετὰ ἡμέρας δύο ἤλθομεν πρὸς τὸν πύργον, καὶ λέγει μοι· Κατανοήσωμεν τοὺς λίθους πάντας, καὶ ἴδωμεν τοὺς δυναμένους εἰς τὴν οἰκοδομὴν ἀπελθεῖν. λέγω αὐτῷ· Κύριε, κατανοήσωμεν.

VIII. Καὶ ἀρξάμενοι πρῶτον τοὺς μέλανας κατενοοῦμεν λίθους. καὶ οἷοι ἐκ τῆς οἰκοδομῆς ἐτέθησαν, τοιοῦτοι καὶ εὑρέθησαν. καὶ ἐκέλευσεν αὐτοὺς ὁ ποιμὴν ἐκ τοῦ πύργου μετενεχθῆναι καὶ χωρισθῆναι. 2. εἶτα κατενόησε τοὺς ἐψωριακότας, καὶ λαβὼν ἐλατόμησε πολλοὺς ἐξ αὐτῶν, καὶ ἐκέλευσε τὰς παρθένους ἆραι αὐτοὺς καὶ βαλεῖν εἰς τὴν οἰκοδομήν. καὶ ἦραν αὐτοὺς αἱ παρθένοι καὶ ἔθηκαν εἰς τὴν οἰκοδομὴν τοῦ πύργου μέσους. τοὺς δὲ λοιποὺς ἐκέλευσε μετὰ τῶν μελάνων τεθῆναι· καὶ γὰρ καὶ οὗτοι μέλανες εὑρέθησαν. 3. εἶτα κατενόει τοὺς τὰς σχισμὰς ἔχοντας· καὶ ἐκ τούτων πολλοὺς ἐλατόμησε καὶ ἐκέλευσε διὰ τῶν παρθένων εἰς τὴν οἰκοδομὴν ἀπενεχθῆναι· ἐξώτεροι δὲ ἐτέθησαν, ὅτι ὑγιέστεροι εὑρέθησαν. οἱ δὲ λοιποὶ διὰ τὸ πλῆθος τῶν σχισμάτων οὐκ ἠδυνήθησαν λατομηθῆναι· διὰ ταύτην οὖν τὴν αἰτίαν ἀπεβλήθησαν ἀπὸ τῆς οἰκοδομῆς τοῦ πύργου. 4. εἶτα κατενόει τοὺς κολοβούς, καὶ εὑρέθησαν πολλοὶ ἐν αὐτοῖς μέλανες, τινὲς δὲ σχισμὰς μεγάλας πεποιηκότες· καὶ ἐκέλευσε καὶ τούτους τεθῆναι μετὰ τῶν ἀποβεβλημένων. τοὺς δὲ περισσεύοντας αὐτῶν καθαρίσας καὶ λατομήσας ἐκέλευσεν

εἰς τὴν οἰκοδομὴν τεθῆναι. αἱ δὲ παρθένοι αὐτοὺς ἄρασαι εἰς
μέσην τὴν οἰκοδομὴν τοῦ πύργου ἥρμοσαν· ἀσθενέστεροι γὰρ
ἦσαν. 5. εἶτα κατενόει τοὺς ἡμίσεις λευκούς, ἡμίσεις δὲ
μέλανας· καὶ πολλοὶ ἐξ αὐτῶν εὑρέθησαν μέλανες. ἐκέλευσε
δὲ καὶ τούτους ἀρθῆναι μετὰ τῶν ἀποβεβλημένων. †οἱ δὲ
λοιποὶ [λευκοὶ] πάντες [εὑρέθησαν καὶ] ἤρθησαν ὑπὸ τῶν
παρθένων· λευκοὶ γὰρ ὄντες ἡρμόσθησαν ὑπ' αὐτῶν [τῶν παρ-
θένων] εἰς τὴν οἰκοδομήν†· ἐξώτεροι δὲ ἐτέθησαν, ὅτι ὑγιεῖς
εὑρέθησαν, ὥστε δύνασθαι αὐτοὺς κρατεῖν τοὺς εἰς τὸ μέσον
τεθέντας· ὅλως γὰρ ἐξ αὐτῶν οὐδὲν ἐκολοβώθη. 6. εἶτα
κατενόει τοὺς σκληροὺς καὶ τραχεῖς, καὶ ὀλίγοι ἐξ αὐτῶν
ἀπεβλήθησαν διὰ τὸ μὴ δύνασθαι λατομηθῆναι· σκληροὶ γὰρ
λίαν εὑρέθησαν. οἱ δὲ λοιποὶ αὐτῶν ἐλατομήθησαν [καὶ
ἤρθησαν ὑπὸ τῶν παρθένων] καὶ εἰς μέσην τὴν οἰκοδομὴν
τοῦ πύργου ἡρμόσθησαν· ἀσθενέστεροι γὰρ ἦσαν. 7. εἶτα
κατενόει τοὺς ἔχοντας τοὺς σπίλους, καὶ ἐκ τούτων ἐλάχιστοι
ἐμελάνησαν, καὶ ἀπεβλήθησαν πρὸς τοὺς λοιπούς. οἱ δὲ
περισσεύοντες λαμπροὶ καὶ ὑγιεῖς εὑρέθησαν· καὶ οὗτοι ἡρμόσθησαν ὑπὸ τῶν παρθένων εἰς τὴν οἰκοδομήν· ἐξώτεροι δὲ
ἐτέθησαν διὰ τὴν ἰσχυρότητα αὐτῶν.

IX. Εἶτα ἦλθε κατανοῆσαι τοὺς λευκοὺς καὶ στρογγύλους
λίθους, καὶ λέγει μοι· Τί ποιοῦμεν περὶ τούτων τῶν λίθων;
Τί, φημί, ἐγὼ γινώσκω, κύριε; [Καὶ λέγει μοι·] Οὐδὲν οὖν
ἐπινοεῖς περὶ αὐτῶν; 2. Ἐγώ, φημί, κύριε, ταύτην τὴν
τέχνην οὐκ ἔχω, οὐδὲ λατόμος εἰμί, οὐδὲ δύναμαι νοῆσαι.
Οὐ βλέπεις αὐτούς, φησί, λίαν στρογγύλους ὄντας; καὶ ἐὰν
θελήσω αὐτοὺς τετραγώνους ποιῆσαι, πολὺ δεῖ ἀπ' αὐτῶν
ἀποκοπῆναι· δεῖ δὲ ἐξ αὐτῶν ἐξ ἀνάγκης τινὰς εἰς τὴν οἰκο-

9. viii. 4 ἀσθενέστεροι] ἀσθενέστεραι A.   5 λευκοὶ] ins. Harmer
[L₁L₂E]; om. A.   εὑρέθησαν καὶ] ins. Harmer [L₁L₂E]; om. A.   Or
perhaps we should keep the text of A, only changing ὄντες ἡρμόσθησαν into
πάντες εὑρέθησαν.   6 σκληροὺς καὶ τραχεῖς] conj. Harmer [L₁L₂E];
τραχεῖς καὶ σκληροὺς A.   ὑπὸ] ἀπὸ A.   ἀσθενέστεροι] ἀσθενέστεραι A app.
7 ἐμελάνησαν] ἐμελάνωσαν A.   ὑγιεῖς] conj. Gebhardt [L₁L₂ integri];
ἐκεῖνοι A; om. E.   ix. 1 καὶ λέγει μοι] ins. Harmer [L₁L₂E]; om. A.

δομὴν τεθῆναι. 3. Εἰ οὖν, φημί, κύριε, ἀναγκη ἐστί, τί σεαυτὸν βασανίζεις καὶ οὐκ ἐκλέγεις εἰς τὴν οἰκοδομὴν οὓς θέλεις, καὶ ἁρμόζεις εἰς αὐτήν; ἐξελέξατο ἐξ αὐτῶν τοὺς μείζονας καὶ λαμπρούς, καὶ ἐλατόμησεν αὐτούς· αἱ δὲ παρθένοι ἄρασαι ἥρμοσαν εἰς τὰ ἐξώτερα μέρη τῆς οἰκοδομῆς. 4. οἱ δὲ λοιποὶ οἱ περισσεύσαντες ἤρθησαν, καὶ ἀπετέθησαν εἰς τὸ πεδίον ὅθεν ἠνέχθησαν· οὐκ ἀπεβλήθησαν δέ, "Ὅτι, φησί, λείπει τῷ πύργῳ ἔτι μικρὸν οἰκοδομηθῆναι. πάντως δὲ θέλει ὁ δεσπότης τοῦ πύργου τούτους ἁρμοσθῆναι τοὺς λίθους εἰς τὴν οἰκοδομήν, ὅτι λαμπροί εἰσι λίαν. 5. ἐκλήθησαν δὲ γυναῖκες δώδεκα, εὐειδέσταται τῷ χαρακτῆρι, μέλανα ἐνδεδυμέναι, [περιεζωσμέναι καὶ ἔξω τοὺς ὤμους ἔχουσαι,] καὶ τὰς τρίχας λελυμέναι. ἐδοκοῦσαν δέ μοι αἱ γυναῖκες αὗται ἄγριαι εἶναι. ἐκέλευσε δὲ αὐτὰς ὁ ποιμὴν ἆραι τοὺς λίθους τοὺς ἀποβεβλημένους ἐκ τῆς οἰκοδομῆς, καὶ ἀπενεγκεῖν αὐτοὺς εἰς τὰ ὄρη ὅθεν καὶ ἠνέχθησαν. 6. αἱ δὲ ἱλαραὶ ἦραν, καὶ ἀπήνεγκαν πάντας τοὺς λίθους, καὶ ἔθηκαν ὅθεν ἐλήφθησαν. καὶ μετὰ τὸ ἀρθῆναι πάντας τοὺς λίθους καὶ μηκέτι κεῖσθαι λίθον κύκλῳ τοῦ πύργου, λέγει μοι ὁ ποιμήν· Κυκλώσωμεν τὸν πύργον, καὶ ἴδωμεν μή τι ἐλάττωμά ἐστιν ἐν αὐτῷ. καὶ ἐκύκλευον ἐγὼ μετ' αὐτοῦ. 7. ἰδὼν δὲ ὁ ποιμὴν τὸν πύργον εὐπρεπῆ ὄντα τῇ οἰκοδομῇ, λίαν ἱλαρὸς ἦν· ὁ γὰρ πύργος οὕτως ἦν ᾠκοδομημένος, ὥστε με ἰδόντα ἐπιθυμεῖν τὴν οἰκοδομὴν αὐτοῦ· οὕτω γὰρ ἦν ᾠκοδομημένος, ὡσὰν ἐξ ἑνὸς λίθου, καὶ ἔχων μίαν ἁρμογὴν ἐν ἑαυτῷ. ἐφαίνετο δὲ ὁ λίθος ὡς ἐκ τῆς πέτρας ἐκκεκολαμμένος· μονόλιθος γάρ μοι ἐδόκει εἶναι.

X. Κἀγὼ περιπατῶν μετ' αὐτοῦ ἱλαρὸς ἤμην τοιαῦτα ἀγαθὰ βλέπων. λέγει δέ μοι ὁ ποιμήν· Ὕπαγε καὶ φέρε ἄσβεστον καὶ ὄστρακον λεπτόν, ἵνα τοὺς τύπους τῶν λίθων

---

ix. 4 πύργῳ] [L₁L₂E]; μικρῷ A.   πάντως] conj. Anger [L₁L₂E];
πάντας A.   5 εὐειδέσταται] εὐειδέστατοι A.   περιεζωσμέναι...ἔχουσαι]
ins. Hilgenfeld [L₁L₂E]; om. A.   7 οὕτως] [L₁L₂]; οὗτος A; dub. E.
ἐκκεκολαμμένος] conj. Anger [L₁L₂]; ἐγκεκολαμμένος AE.

τῶν ἡρμένων καὶ εἰς τὴν οἰκοδομὴν βεβλημένων ἀναπληρώσω· δεῖ γὰρ τοῦ πύργου τὰ κύκλῳ πάντα ὁμαλὰ γενέσθαι. 2. καὶ ἐποίησα καθὼς ἐκέλευσε, καὶ ἤνεγκα πρὸς αὐτόν. Ὑπηρέτει μοι, φησί, καὶ ἐγγὺς τὸ ἔργον τελεσθήσεται. ἐπλήρωσεν οὖν τοὺς τύπους τῶν λίθων τῶν εἰς τὴν οἰκοδομὴν ἀπεληλυθότων, καὶ ἐκέλευσε σαρωθῆναι τὰ κύκλῳ τοῦ πύργου καὶ καθαρὰ γενέσθαι· 3. αἱ δὲ παρθένοι λαβοῦσαι σάρους ἐσάρωσαν, καὶ πάντα τὰ κόπρα ἦραν ἐκ τοῦ πύργου, καὶ ἔρραναν ὕδωρ, καὶ ἐγένετο ὁ τόπος ἱλαρὸς καὶ εὐπρεπέστατος τῷ πύργῳ. 4. λέγει μοι ὁ ποιμήν· Πάντα, φησί, κεκαθάρισται· ἐὰν ἔλθῃ ὁ κύριος ἐπισκέψασθαι τὸν πύργον, οὐκ ἔχει ἡμῖν οὐδὲν μέμ-ψασθαι. ταῦτα εἰπὼν ἤθελεν ὑπάγειν· 5. ἐγὼ δὲ ἐπελαβόμην αὐτοῦ τῆς πήρας καὶ ἠρξάμην αὐτὸν ὁρκίζειν κατὰ τοῦ Κυρίου ἵνα [πάντα] μοι ἐπιλύσῃ ἃ ἔδειξέ μοι. λέγει μοι· Μικρὸν ἔχω ἀκαιρεθῆναι, καὶ πάντα σοι ἐπιλύσω· ἔκδεξαί με ὧδε ἕως ἔρχομαι. 6. λέγω αὐτῷ· Κύριε, μόνος ὢν ὧδε ἐγὼ τί ποιήσω; Οὐκ εἶ, φησί, μόνος· αἱ γὰρ παρθένοι αὗται μετὰ σοῦ εἰσί. Παράδος οὖν, φημί, αὐταῖς με. προσκαλεῖται αὐτὰς ὁ ποιμὴν καὶ λέγει αὐταῖς· Παρατίθεμαι ὑμῖν τοῦτον ἕως ἔρχομαι· καὶ ἀπῆλθεν. 7. ἐγὼ δὲ ἤμην μόνος μετὰ τῶν παρθένων· ἦσαν δὲ ἱλαρώτεραι, καὶ πρὸς ἐμὲ εὖ εἶχον· μάλιστα δὲ αἱ τέσσαρες αἱ ἐνδοξότεραι αὐτῶν.

XI. Λέγουσί μοι αἱ παρθένοι· Σήμερον ὁ ποιμὴν ὧδε οὐκ ἔρχεται. Τί οὖν, φημί, ποιήσω ἐγώ; Μέχρις ὀψέ, φασίν, περίμεινον αὐτόν· καὶ ἐὰν ἔλθῃ, λαλήσει μετὰ σοῦ, ἐὰν δὲ μὴ ἔλθῃ, μενεῖς μεθ' ἡμῶν ὧδε ἕως ἔρχεται. 2. λέγω αὐταῖς· Ἐκδέξομαι αὐτὸν ἕως ὀψέ· ἐὰν δὲ μὴ ἔλθῃ, ἀπελεύσομαι εἰς τὸν οἶκον, καὶ πρωῒ ἐπανήξω. αἱ δὲ ἀποκριθεῖσαι λέγουσί

9. x. 1 ἡρμένων καὶ εἰς τὴν οἰκοδομὴν] conj. Hilgenfeld [L₁]; ἡρμοσμένων εἰς τὴν οἰκοδομὴν καὶ A; dub. L₂E. x. 2 μοι] με A. τελεσθήσεται] [L₁, cf. L₂] E; illeg. in A; τελευθήσεται app. Aˢ. τῶν sec.] om. A. 3 σάρους] conj. Gebhardt [L₁L₂E]; σάρον A. τῷ πύργῳ] conj. Hilgenfeld [L₂E]; τοῦ πύργου A; al. L₁. 5 πάντα] ins. Harmer [L₁L₂E]; om. A. ἀ-καιρεθῆναι] [L₁L₂E]; ἀναιρεθῆναι A. 6 φημί][L₁L₂E]; φησί A. xi. 1 ὀψὲ φασίν] conj. Gebhardt [L₁L₂E]; ὅτέ φησιν ἔλθῃ (sic) A.

μοι· Ἡμῖν παρεδόθης· οὐ δύνασαι ἀφ' ἡμῶν ἀναχωρῆσαι. 3. Ποῦ οὖν, φημί, μενῶ; Μεθ' ἡμῶν, φασί, κοιμηθήσῃ ὡς ἀδελφός, καὶ οὐχ ὡς ἀνήρ. ἡμέτερος γὰρ ἀδελφὸς εἶ, καὶ τοῦ λοιποῦ μέλλομεν μετὰ σοῦ κατοικεῖν· λίαν γάρ σε ἀγαπῶμεν. ἐγὼ δὲ ᾐσχυνόμην μετ' αὐτῶν μένειν. 4. καὶ ἡ δοκοῦσα πρώτη αὐτῶν εἶναι ἤρξατό με καταφιλεῖν καὶ περιπλέκεσθαι· αἱ δὲ ἄλλαι ὁρῶσαι ἐκείνην περιπλεκομένην μοι, καὶ αὐταὶ ἤρξαντό με καταφιλεῖν καὶ περιάγειν κύκλῳ τοῦ πύργου καὶ παίζειν μετ' ἐμοῦ. 5. κἀγὼ ὡσεὶ νεώτερος ἐγεγόνειν καὶ ἠρξάμην καὶ αὐτὸς παίζειν μετ' αὐτῶν. αἱ μὲν γὰρ ἐχόρευον, [αἱ δὲ ὠρχοῦντο,] αἱ δὲ ᾖδον· ἐγὼ δὲ σιγὴν ἔχων μετ' αὐτῶν κύκλῳ τοῦ πύργου περιεπάτουν, καὶ ἱλαρὸς ἤμην μετ' αὐτῶν. 6. ὀψίας δὲ γενομένης ἤθελον εἰς τὸν οἶκον ὑπάγειν· αἱ δὲ οὐκ ἀφῆκαν, ἀλλὰ κατέσχον με. καὶ ἔμεινα μετ' αὐτῶν τὴν νύκτα, καὶ ἐκοιμήθην παρὰ τὸν πύργον. 7. ἔστρωσαν γὰρ αἱ παρθένοι τοὺς λινοῦς χιτῶνας ἑαυτῶν χαμαί, καὶ ἐμὲ ἀνέκλιναν εἰς τὸ μέσον αὐτῶν, καὶ οὐδὲν ὅλως ἐποίουν εἰ μὴ προσηύχοντο· κἀγὼ μετ' αὐτῶν ἀδιαλείπτως προσηυχόμην, καὶ οὐκ ἔλασσον ἐκείνων. καὶ ἔχαιρον αἱ παρθένοι οὕτω μου προσευχομένου. καὶ ἔμεινα ἐκεῖ μέχρι τῆς αὔριον ἕως ὥρας δευτέρας μετὰ τῶν παρθένων. 8. εἶτα παρῆν ὁ ποιμήν, καὶ λέγει ταῖς παρθένοις· Μή τινα αὐτῷ ὕβριν πεποιήκατε; Ἐρώτα, φασίν, αὐτόν. λέγω αὐτῷ· Κύριε, εὐφράνθην μετ' αὐτῶν μείνας. Τί, φησίν, ἐδείπνησας; Ἐδείπνησα, φημί, κύριε, ῥήματα Κυρίου ὅλην τὴν νύκτα. Καλῶς, φησίν, ἔλαβόν σε; Ναί, φημί, κύριε. 9. Νῦν, φησί, τί θέλεις πρῶτον ἀκοῦσαι; Καθώς, φημί, κύριε, ἀπ' ἀρχῆς ἔδειξας, ἐρωτῶ σε, κύριε, ἵνα καθὼς ἄν σε ἐπερωτήσω, οὕτω μοι καὶ δηλώσῃς. Καθὼς βούλει, φησίν, οὕτω σοι καὶ ἐπιλύσω, καὶ οὐδὲν ὅλως ἀποκρύψω ἀπὸ σοῦ.

XII. Πρῶτον, φημί, πάντων, κύριε, τοῦτό μοι δήλωσον· ἡ πέτρα καὶ ἡ πύλη τίς ἐστιν; Ἡ πέτρα, φησίν, αὕτη καὶ ἡ

xi. 4 περιπλέκεσθαι] conj. Harmer [L₁L₂]; περιπ...σθαι A; om. E.
αὐταί] conj. Harmer [L₁L₂E]; αὗται A.   6 γενομένης] γενόμενος A.
9 σε sec.] σου A.

πύλη ὁ υἱὸς τοῦ Θεοῦ ἐστί. Πῶς, φημί, κύριε, ἡ πέτρα
παλαιά ἐστιν, ἡ δὲ πύλη καινή; Ἄκουε, φησί, καὶ σύνιε,
ἀσύνετε. 2. ὁ μὲν υἱὸς τοῦ Θεοῦ πάσης τῆς κτίσεως αὐτοῦ
προγενέστερός ἐστιν, ὥστε σύμβουλον αὐτὸν γενέσθαι τῷ
πατρὶ τῆς κτίσεως αὐτοῦ· διὰ τοῦτο καὶ παλαιός ἐστιν. Ἡ
δὲ πύλη διατί καινή, φημί, κύριε; 3. Ὅτι, φησίν, ἐπ'
ἐσχάτων τῶν ἡμερῶν τῆς συντελείας φανερὸς ἐγένετο, διὰ
τοῦτο καινὴ ἐγένετο ἡ πύλη, ἵνα οἱ μέλλοντες σώζεσθαι δι'
αὐτῆς εἰς τὴν βασιλείαν εἰσέλθωσι τοῦ Θεοῦ. 4. εἶδες, φησί,
τοὺς λίθους τοὺς διὰ τῆς πύλης ἐληλυθότας | ἀπεληλυ-
θότας | εἰς τὴν οἰκοδομὴν τοῦ πύργου, τοὺς δὲ μὴ εἰσεληλυ-
θότας πάλιν ἀποβεβλημένους εἰς τὸν ἴδιον τόπον; Εἶδον,
φημί, κύριε. Οὕτω, φησίν, εἰς τὴν βασιλείαν τοῦ Θεοῦ
οὐδεὶς εἰσελεύσεται, εἰ μὴ λάβοι τὸ ὄνομα τοῦ υἱοῦ αὐτοῦ.
5. ἐὰν γὰρ εἰς πόλιν θελήσῃς εἰσελθεῖν τινά, κἀκείνη ἡ πόλις
περιτετειχισμένη κύκλῳ καὶ μίαν ἔχει πύλην, μήτι δυνήσῃ
εἰς τὴν πόλιν ἐκείνην εἰσελθεῖν εἰ μὴ διὰ τῆς πύλης ἧς ἔχει;
Πῶς γάρ, φημί, κύριε, δύναται ἄλλως; Εἰ οὖν εἰς τὴν
πόλιν οὐ δύνῃ εἰσελθεῖν εἰ μὴ διὰ τῆς πύλης αὐτῆς,
οὕτω, φησί, καὶ εἰς τὴν βασιλείαν τοῦ Θεοῦ ἄλλως εἰσελθεῖν
οὐ δύναται ἄνθρωπος εἰ μὴ διὰ τοῦ ὀνόματος τοῦ υἱοῦ αὐτοῦ
τοῦ ἠγαπημένου ὑπ' αὐτοῦ. 6. εἶδες, φησί, τὸν ὄχλον τὸν
οἰκοδομοῦντα τὸν πύργον; Εἶδον, φημί, κύριε. Ἐκεῖνοι,
φησί, πάντες ἄγγελοι ἔνδοξοί εἰσι. τούτοις οὖν περιτετεί-
χισται ὁ Κύριος. ἡ δὲ πύλη ὁ υἱὸς τοῦ Θεοῦ ἐστίν· αὕτη μία
εἴσοδός ἐστι πρὸς τὸν Κύριον. ἄλλως οὖν οὐδεὶς εἰσελεύσεται
πρὸς αὐτὸν εἰ μὴ διὰ τοῦ υἱοῦ αὐτοῦ. 7. εἶδες, φησί, τοὺς ἐξ
ἄνδρας καὶ τὸν μέσον αὐτῶν ἔνδοξον καὶ μέγαν ἄνδρα τὸν
περιπατοῦντα περὶ τὸν πύργον καὶ τοὺς λίθους ἀποδοκιμά-
σαντα ἐκ τῆς οἰκοδομῆς; Εἶδον, φημί, κύριε. 8. Ὁ ἔνδοξος,
φησίν, ἀνὴρ ὁ υἱὸς τοῦ Θεοῦ ἐστί, κἀκεῖνοι οἱ ἓξ οἱ ἔνδοξοι

9. xii. 2 κτίσεως] κτήσεως A.   3 ἐσχάτων] ἐσχάτου A.   4 ἀπεληλυ-
θότας] ins. Harmer [L₁E, cf. L₂]; om. A by homœot.   τοῦ υἱοῦ] conj.
Gebhardt [L₁L₂E]; τὸ ἅγιον A.   5 διὰ τῆς πύλης] L₁L₂E; om. A.
6 κύριος] [L₁L₂E]; κόσμος A.   7 περὶ] [L₁L₂E]; παρὰ A.

ἄγγελοί εἰσι δεξιὰ καὶ εὐώνυμα συγκρατοῦντες αὐτόν. τούτων, φησί, τῶν ἀγγέλων τῶν ἐνδόξων οὐδεὶς εἰσελεύσεται
πρὸς τὸν Θεὸν ἄτερ αὐτοῦ· ὃς ἂν τὸ ὄνομα αὐτοῦ μὴ λάβῃ,
οὐκ εἰσελεύσεται εἰς τὴν βασιλείαν τοῦ Θεοῦ. XIII. Ὁ δὲ πύργος, φημί, τίς ἐστιν; Ὁ πύργος, φησίν,
οὗτος ἡ Ἐκκλησία ἐστίν. 2. Αἱ δὲ παρθένοι αὗται τίνες
εἰσίν; Αὗται, φησίν, ἅγια πνεύματά εἰσι· καὶ ἄλλως ἄνθρωπος οὐ δύναται εὑρεθῆναι εἰς τὴν βασιλείαν τοῦ Θεοῦ,
ἐὰν μὴ αὗται αὐτὸν ἐνδύσωσι τὸ ἔνδυμα αὐτῶν· ἐὰν γὰρ τὸ
ὄνομα μόνον λάβῃς, τὸ δὲ ἔνδυμα παρὰ τούτων μὴ λάβῃς,
οὐδὲν ὠφελήσῃ· αὗται γὰρ αἱ παρθένοι δυνάμεις εἰσὶ τοῦ υἱοῦ
τοῦ Θεοῦ. ἐὰν [οὖν] τὸ ὄνομα φορῇς, τὴν δὲ δύναμιν μὴ φορῇς
αὐτοῦ, εἰς μάτην ἔσῃ τὸ ὄνομα αὐτοῦ φορῶν. 3. τοὺς δὲ
λίθους, φησίν, οὓς εἶδες ἀποβεβλημένους, οὗτοι τὸ μὲν ὄνομα
ἐφόρεσαν, τὸν δὲ ἱματισμὸν τῶν παρθένων οὐκ ἐνεδύσαντο.
Ποῖος, φημί, ἱματισμὸς αὐτῶν ἐστί, κύριε; Αὐτὰ τὰ ὀνόματα,
φησίν, ἱματισμός ἐστιν αὐτῶν. ὃς ἂν τὸ ὄνομα τοῦ υἱοῦ τοῦ
Θεοῦ φορῇ, καὶ τούτων ὀφείλει φορεῖν τὰ ὀνόματα· καὶ γὰρ
αὐτὸς ὁ υἱὸς τὰ ὀνόματα τῶν παρθένων τούτων φορεῖ. 4. ὅσους,
φησί, λίθους εἶδες εἰς τὴν οἰκοδομὴν | τοῦ πύργου εἰσεληλυ-
θότας, ἐπιδεδομένους διὰ τῶν χειρῶν αὐτῶν καὶ μείναντας εἰς
τὴν οἰκοδομήν, | τούτων τῶν παρθένων τὴν δύναμιν ἐνδεδυ-
μένοι εἰσί. 5. διὰ τοῦτο βλέπεις τὸν πύργον μονόλιθον
γεγονότα [μετὰ] τῆς πέτρας. οὕτω καὶ οἱ πιστεύσαντες τῷ
Κυρίῳ διὰ τοῦ υἱοῦ αὐτοῦ καὶ ἐνδιδυσκόμενοι τὰ πνεύματα
ταῦτα, ἔσονται εἰς ἓν πνεῦμα, καὶ ἓν σῶμα, μιᾷ χρόᾳ τῶν
ἱματίων αὐτῶν. τῶν τοιούτων δὲ τῶν φορούντων τὰ ὀνόματα
τῶν παρθένων ἐστὶν ἡ κατοικία εἰς τὸν πύργον. 6. Οἱ οὖν,
φημί, κύριε, ἀποβεβλημένοι λίθοι διατί ἀπεβλήθησαν; διῆλ-

xii. 8 αὐτοῦ] conj. Anger [L₁L₂E]; τοῦ θεοῦ A.   xiii. 1 ἡ] om. A.
2 ἄλλως] conj. Anger [L₁L₂E]; ἄλλος A.   ὠφελήσῃ] conj. Gebhardt;
ὠφελεῖς A.   οὖν] ins. Gebhardt [L₁L₂]; om. A; et E.   3 οὗτοι]
conj. Hilgenfeld [L₁L₂E]; αὐτοὶ A.   4 τοῦ πύργου...οἰκοδομήν] ins.
Gebhardt [L₁L₂E]; om. A by homœot.   5 μετὰ] ins. Hilgenfeld
[L₁L₂]; om. A; al. E.

θον γὰρ διὰ τῆς πύλης, καὶ διὰ τῶν χειρῶν τῶν παρθένων ἐτέθησαν εἰς τὴν οἰκοδομὴν τοῦ πύργου. Ἐπειδὴ πάντα σοι, φησί, μέλει, καὶ ἀκριβῶς ἐξετάζεις, ἄκουε περὶ τῶν ἀποβεβλημένων λίθων. 7. οὗτοι, [φησί,] πάντες τὸ ὄνομα τοῦ υἱοῦ τοῦ Θεοῦ ἔλαβον, ἔλαβον δὲ καὶ τὴν δύναμιν τῶν παρθένων τούτων. λαβόντες οὖν τὰ πνεύματα ταῦτα ἐνεδυναμώθησαν, καὶ ἦσαν μετὰ τῶν δούλων τοῦ Θεοῦ, καὶ ἦν αὐτῶν ἓν πνεῦμα καὶ ἓν σῶμα [καὶ ἓν ἔνδυμα]· τὰ γὰρ αὐτὰ ἐφρόνουν καὶ δικαιοσύνην εἰργάζοντο. 8. μετὰ οὖν χρόνον τινὰ ἀνεπείσθησαν ὑπὸ τῶν γυναικῶν ὧν εἶδες μέλανα ἱμάτια ἐνδεδυμένων, τοὺς ὤμους ἔξω ἐχουσῶν καὶ τὰς τρίχας λελυμένας καὶ εὐμόρφων. ταύτας ἰδόντες ἐπεθύμησαν αὐτῶν, καὶ ἐνεδύσαντο τὴν δύναμιν αὐτῶν, τῶν δὲ παρθένων ἀπεδύσαντο τὴν δύναμιν. 9. οὗτοι οὖν ἀπεβλήθησαν ἀπὸ τοῦ οἴκου τοῦ Θεοῦ καὶ ἐκείναις παρεδόθησαν. οἱ δὲ μὴ ἀπατηθέντες τῷ κάλλει τῶν γυναικῶν τούτων ἔμειναν ἐν τῷ οἴκῳ τοῦ Θεοῦ. ἔχεις, φησί, τὴν ἐπίλυσιν τῶν ἀποβεβλημένων.

XIV. Τί οὖν, φημί, κύριε, ἐὰν οὗτοι οἱ ἄνθρωποι, τοιοῦτοι ὄντες, μετανοήσωσι καὶ ἀποβάλωσι τὰς ἐπιθυμίας τῶν γυναικῶν τούτων, καὶ ἐπανακάμψωσιν ἐπὶ τὰς παρθένους, καὶ ἐν τῇ δυνάμει αὐτῶν καὶ ἐν τοῖς ἔργοις αὐτῶν πορευθῶσιν, οὐκ εἰσελεύσονται εἰς τὸν οἶκον τοῦ Θεοῦ; 2. Εἰσελεύσονται, φησίν, ἐὰν τούτων τῶν γυναικῶν ἀποβάλωσι τὰ ἔργα, τῶν δὲ παρθένων ἀναλάβωσι τὴν δύναμιν καὶ ἐν τοῖς ἔργοις αὐτῶν πορευθῶσι. διὰ τοῦτο γὰρ καὶ τῆς οἰκοδομῆς ἀνοχὴ ἐγένετο, ἵνα ἐὰν μετανοήσωσιν οὗτοι, ἀπέλθωσιν εἰς τὴν οἰκοδομὴν τοῦ πύργου. ἐὰν δὲ μὴ μετανοήσωσι, τότε ἄλλοι ἀπελεύσονται, καὶ οὗτοι εἰς τέλος ἐκβληθήσονται. 3. ἐπὶ τούτοις πᾶσιν ηὐχαρίστησα τῷ Κυρίῳ, ὅτι ἐσπλαγχνίσθη ἐπὶ πᾶσι τοῖς ἐπικαλουμένοις τὸ ὄνομα αὐτοῦ, καὶ ἐξαπέστειλε τὸν ἄγγελον τῆς μετανοίας εἰς ἡμᾶς τοὺς ἁμαρτήσαντας εἰς αὐτόν, καὶ ἀνεκαίνισεν ἡμῶν τὸ πνεῦμα, καὶ ἤδη κατεφθαρμένων ἡμῶν

9. xiii. 7 τοῦ υἱοῦ] υἱοῦ A. 8 αὐτῶν pri.] αὐτάς A. xiv. 3 τὸν ἄγγελον] [L₁L₂E] ; τοὺς ἀγγέλλους (sic) A.

καὶ μὴ ἐχόντων ἐλπίδα τοῦ ζῆν ἀνενέωσε τὴν ζωὴν ἡμῶν. 4. Νῦν, φημί, κύριε, δήλωσόν μοι, διατί ὁ πύργος χαμαὶ οὐκ ᾠκοδόμηται, ἀλλ᾽ ἐπὶ τὴν πέτραν καὶ ἐπὶ τὴν πύλην. "Ὅτι, φησίν, ἄφρων εἶ καὶ ἀσύνετος, [ἐπερωτᾷς]. Ἀνάγκην ἔχω, φημί, κύριε, πάντα ἐπερωτᾶν σε, ὅτι οὐδ᾽ ὅλως οὐδὲν δύναμαι νοῆσαι· τὰ γὰρ πάντα μεγάλα καὶ ἔνδοξά ἐστι καὶ δυσνόητα τοῖς ἀνθρώποις. 5. Ἄκουε, φησί· τὸ ὄνομα τοῦ υἱοῦ τοῦ Θεοῦ μέγα ἐστὶ καὶ ἀχώρητον, καὶ τὸν κόσμον ὅλον βαστάζει. εἰ οὖν πᾶσα ἡ κτίσις διὰ τοῦ υἱοῦ [τοῦ Θεοῦ] βαστάζεται, τί δοκεῖς τοὺς κεκλημένους ὑπ᾽ αὐτοῦ καὶ τὸ ὄνομα φοροῦντας τοῦ υἱοῦ [τοῦ Θεοῦ] καὶ πορευομένους ταῖς ἐντολαῖς αὐτοῦ; 6. βλέπεις οὖν ποίους βαστάζει; τοὺς ἐξ ὅλης καρδίας φοροῦντας τὸ ὄνομα αὐτοῦ. αὐτὸς οὖν θεμέλιος αὐτοῖς ἐγένετο, καὶ ἡδέως αὐτοὺς βαστάζει, ὅτι οὐκ ἐπαισχύνονται τὸ ὄνομα αὐτοῦ φορεῖν.

XV. Δή⌐λωσόν μοι⌐, φημί, κύριε, τῶν παρθέ⌐νων τ⌐ὰ ὀνόματα | καὶ τῶν γυναικῶν τῶν τὰ μέλανα ἱμάτια ἐνδεδυμένων. Ἄκουε, φησίν, τῶν παρθένων τὰ ὀνόματα | τῶν ἰσχυροτέρων, τῶν εἰς τὰς γωνίας σταθεισῶν. 2. ἡ μὲν πρώτη Πίστις, ἡ δὲ δευτέρα Ἐγκράτεια, ἡ δὲ ⌐τρ⌐ίτη Δύναμις, ἡ δὲ τε⌐τάρ⌐τη Μακροθυμία· αἱ δὲ ἔτεραι ἀνὰ μέσον τούτων σταθεῖσαι ταῦτα ἔχουσι τὰ ὀνόματα· Ἁπλότης, Ἀκακία, Ἁγνεία, Ἱλαρότης, Ἀλήθεια, Σύνεσις, ⌐Ὁ⌐μόνοια, Ἀγάπη. ταῦτα τὰ ὀνόματα ὁ φορῶν καὶ τὸ ὄνομα τοῦ υἱοῦ τοῦ Θεοῦ δυνήσεται εἰς τὴν βασιλείαν τοῦ Θεοῦ εἰσελθεῖν. 3. ἄκουε, φησί, καὶ τὰ ὀνόματα τῶν γυναικῶν τῶν τὰ ἱμάτια μέλανα ἐχουσῶν. καὶ ἐκ τούτων τέσσαρες εἰσὶ δυνατώτεραι· ἡ πρώτη Ἀπιστία, ἡ δευτέρα Ἀκρασία, ἡ δὲ

---

xiv. 3 ἀνενέωσε] [L₁L₂E]; ἀνένευσε A.   4 ἐπερωτᾷς] ins. Harmer [L₁L₂];
om. AE (E read ἔτι for ὅτι).   5 τοῦ θεοῦ sec.] θεοῦ A; ejus L₁; domini E;
om. L₂.   xv. 1 δήλωσόν μοι] Sheet 9 of the Athos MS, which commences
here, is much damaged by worms. The lacunæ, as supplied by Hilgenfeld,
are designated by brackets, thus ⌐ ⌐.   καὶ τῶν γυναικῶν...τὰ ὀνόματα] ins.
Gebhardt [L₁L₂E]; om. A by homœot.   3 ἱμάτια] conj. Hilgenfeld
[L₁L₂E]; ὀνόματα A.

τρίτη Ἀπείθεια, ἡ δὲ τετάρτη Ἀπάτη. αἱ δὲ ἀκόλουθοι αὐτῶν καλοῦνται Λύπη, Πονηρία, Ἀσέλγεια, Ὀξυχολία, Ψεῦδος, Ἀφροσύνη, Καταλαλία, Μῖσος. ταῦτα τὰ ὀνόματα ὁ φορῶν τοῦ Θεοῦ δοῦλος τὴν βασιλείαν μὲν ὄψεται τοῦ Θεοῦ, εἰς αὐτὴν δὲ οὐκ εἰσελεύσεται. 4. Οἱ λίθοι δέ, φημί, κύριε, οἱ ἐκ τοῦ βυθοῦ ἡρμοσμένοι εἰς τὴν οἰκοδομὴν τίνες εἰσίν; Οἱ μὲν πρῶτοι, φησίν, οἱ δέκα οἱ εἰς τὰ θεμέλια τεθειμένοι, πρώτη γενεά· οἱ δὲ εἴκοσι πέντε δευτέρα γενεὰ ἀνδρῶν δικαίων· οἱ δὲ τριάκοντα πέντε προφῆται τοῦ Θεοῦ καὶ διάκονοι αὐτοῦ· οἱ δὲ τεσσαράκοντα ἀπόστολοι καὶ διδάσκαλοι τοῦ κηρύγματος τοῦ υἱοῦ τοῦ Θεοῦ. 5. Διατί οὖν, φημί, κύριε, αἱ παρθένοι καὶ τούτους τοὺς λίθους ἐπέδωκαν εἰς τὴν οἰκοδομὴν τοῦ πύργου, διενέγκασαι διὰ τῆς πύλης; 6. Οὗτοι γάρ, φησί, πρῶτοι ταῦτα τὰ πνεύματα ἐφόρεσαν, καὶ ὅλως ἀπ' ἀλλήλων οὐκ ἀπέστησαν, οὔτε τὰ πνεύματα ἀπὸ τῶν ἀνθρώπων, οὔτε οἱ ἄνθρωποι ἀπὸ τῶν πνευμάτων, ἀλλὰ παρέμειναν τὰ πνεύματα αὐτοῖς μέχρι τῆς κοιμήσεως αὐτῶν. καὶ εἰ μὴ ταῦτα τὰ πνεύματα μετ' αὐτῶν ἐσχήκει⌜σ⌝α⌜ν⌝, ο⌜ὐκ ἂν⌝ εὔχρηστοι γεγόνεισαν τῇ οἰκοδομῇ τοῦ πύργου τούτου.

XVI. Ἔτι μοι, φημί, κύριε, δήλωσον. Τί, φησίν, ἐπιζητεῖς; Διατί, φημί, κύριε, οἱ λίθοι ἐ⌜κ⌝ τοῦ β⌜υ⌝θοῦ ἀνέβησαν καὶ εἰς τὴν οἰκοδομὴν ἐτέθησαν, πεφορηκότες τὰ πνεύματα ταῦτα; 2. Ἀνάγκην, φησίν, εἶχον δι' ὕδατος ἀναβῆναι, ἵνα ζωοποιηθῶσιν· οὐκ ἠδύναντο γὰρ ἄλλως εἰσελθεῖν εἰς τὴν βασιλείαν τοῦ Θεοῦ, εἰ μὴ τὴν νέκρωσιν ἀπέθεντο τῆς ζωῆς αὐτῶν [τῆς προτέρας]. 3. ἔλαβον οὖν καὶ οὗτοι οἱ κεκοιμημένοι τὴν σφραγῖδα τοῦ υἱοῦ τοῦ Θεοῦ | καὶ εἰσῆλθον εἰς τὴν βασιλείαν τοῦ Θεοῦ · | πρὶν γάρ, φησί, φορέσαι τὸν ἄνθρωπον τὸ ὄνομα [τοῦ υἱοῦ] τοῦ Θεοῦ, νεκρός ἐστιν· ὅταν δὲ λάβῃ τὴν σφραγῖδα, ἀποτίθεται τὴν νέκρωσιν καὶ ἀναλαμβάνει τὴν

9. xv. 6 οὐκ ἂν] So Gebhardt supplies the lacuna.   γεγόνεισαν] conj.
Anger; γεγόνασι A.   xvi. 2 τῆς προτέρας] ins. Gebhardt [L₁L₂E] ; om.
A.   3 καὶ εἰσῆλθον...τοῦ θεοῦ] ins. Hilgenfeld [L₁L₂E] ; om. A by
homœot.   τοῦ υἱοῦ sec.] ins. Anger [L₁L₂E] ; om. A.

ζωήν. 4. ἡ σφραγὶς οὖν τὸ ὕδωρ ἐστίν· εἰς τὸ ὕδωρ οὖν
καταβαίνουσι νεκροί, καὶ ἀναβαίνουσι ζῶντες. κἀκείνοις οὖν
ἐκηρύχθη ἡ σφραγὶς αὕτη, καὶ ἐχρήσαντο αὐτῇ, ἵνα εἰσέλ-
θωσιν εἰς τὴν βασιλείαν τοῦ Θεοῦ. 5. Διατί, φημί, κύριε,
καὶ οἱ τεσσαράκοντα λίθοι μετ᾽ αὐτῶν ἀνέβησαν ἐκ τοῦ
βυθοῦ, ἤδη ἐσχηκότες τὴν σφραγῖδα; Ὅτι, φησίν, οὗτοι οἱ
ἀπόστολοι καὶ οἱ διδάσκαλοι οἱ κηρύξαντες τὸ ὄνομα τοῦ
υἱοῦ τοῦ Θεοῦ, κοιμηθέντες ἐν δυνάμει καὶ πίστει τοῦ υἱοῦ
τοῦ Θεοῦ ἐκήρυξαν καὶ τοῖς προκεκοιμημένοις, καὶ αὐτοὶ
ἔδωκαν αὐτοῖς τὴν σφραγῖδα τοῦ κηρύγματος. 6. κατέβησαν
οὖν μετ᾽ αὐτῶν εἰς τὸ ὕδωρ, καὶ πάλιν ἀνέβησαν. | ἀλλ᾽ οὗτοι
ζῶντες κατέβησαν, [καὶ πάλιν ζῶντες ἀνέβησαν]· ἐκεῖνοι δὲ
οἱ προκεκοιμημένοι νεκροὶ κατέβησαν, ζῶντες δὲ ἀνέβησαν.|
7. διὰ τούτων οὖν ἐζωοποιήθησαν καὶ ἐπέγνωσαν τὸ ὄνομα
τοῦ υἱοῦ τοῦ Θεοῦ. διὰ τοῦτο καὶ συνανέβησαν μετ᾽ αὐτῶν
καὶ συνηρμόσθησαν εἰς τὴν οἰκοδομὴν τοῦ πύργου, καὶ ἀλατό-
μητοι συνῳκοδομήθησαν· ἐν δικαιοσύνῃ γὰρ ἐκοιμήθησαν καὶ
ἐν μεγάλῃ ἁγνείᾳ· μόνον δὲ τὴν σφραγῖδα ταύτην οὐκ εἶχον.
ἔχεις οὖν καὶ τὴν τούτων ἐπίλυσιν. Ἔχω, φημί, κύριε.

XVII. Νῦν οὖν, κύριε, περὶ τῶν ὀρέων μοι δήλωσον·
διατί ἄλλαι καὶ ἄλλαι εἰσὶν αἱ ἰδέαι καὶ ποικίλαι; Ἄκουε,
φησί. τὰ ὄρη ταῦτα τὰ δώδεκα [δώδεκα] φυλαί εἰσιν αἱ
κατοικοῦσαι ὅλον τὸν κόσμον. ἐκηρύχθη οὖν εἰς ταύτας ὁ
υἱὸς τοῦ Θεοῦ διὰ τῶν ἀποστόλων. 2. Διατί δὲ ποικίλα, καὶ
ἄλλη καὶ ἄλλη ἰδέα ἐστὶ τὰ ὄρη, δήλωσόν μοι, κύριε. Ἄκουε,
φησίν. αἱ δώδεκα φυλαὶ αὗται αἱ κατοικοῦσαι ὅλον τὸν κόσμον
δώδεκα ἔθνη εἰσί. ποικίλα δέ εἰσι τῇ φρονήσει καὶ τῷ νοΐ·
οἷα οὖν εἶδες τὰ ὄρη ποικίλα, τοιαῦταί εἰσι καὶ τούτων αἱ
ποικιλίαι τοῦ νοὸς τῶν ἐθνῶν καὶ ἡ φρόνησις. δηλώσω δέ
σοι καὶ ἑνὸς ἑκάστου τὴν πρᾶξιν. 3. Πρῶτον, φημί, κύριε,
τοῦτο δήλωσον, διατί οὕτω ποικίλα ὄντα τὰ ὄρη, εἰς τὴν

xvi. 6 ἀλλ᾽ οὗτοι...ζῶντες δὲ ἀνέβησαν] om. A by homœot.; L₂E omit the
words placed within square brackets; L₁ omits κατέβησαν καὶ πάλιν ζῶντες;
the Greek is supplied from Clem. Alex. *Str.* ii. 9, p. 452.   xvii. 1 δώδεκα
sec.] ins. Gebhardt [L₁L₂]; om. with φυλαί A; om. with ὄρη E.

οἰκοδομὴν ὅταν ἐτέθησαν οἱ λίθοι αὐτῶν, μιᾷ χρόᾳ ἐγένοντο λαμπροί, ὡς καὶ οἱ ἐκ τοῦ βυθοῦ ἀναβεβηκότες λίθοι; 4. Ὅτι, φησί, πάντα τὰ ἔθνη τὰ ὑπὸ τὸν οὐρανὸν κατοικοῦντα ἀκούσαντα καὶ πιστεύσαντα ἑνὶ ὀνόματι ἐκλήθησαν [τοῦ υἱοῦ] τοῦ Θεοῦ. λαβόντες οὖν τὴν σφραγῖδα μίαν φρόνησιν ἔσχον καὶ ἕνα νοῦν, καὶ μία πίστις αὐτῶν ἐγένετο καὶ [μία] ἀγάπη, καὶ τὰ πνεύματα τῶν παρθένων μετὰ τοῦ ὀνόματος ἐφόρεσαν· διὰ τοῦτο ἡ οἰκοδομὴ τοῦ πύργου μιᾷ χρόᾳ ἐγένετο λαμπρὰ ὡς ὁ ἥλιος. 5. μετὰ δὲ τὸ εἰσελθεῖν αὐτοὺς ἐπὶ τὸ αὐτὸ καὶ γενέσθαι ἓν σῶμα, τινὲς ἐξ αὐτῶν ἐμίαναν ἑαυτοὺς καὶ ἐξεβλήθησαν ἐκ τοῦ γένους τῶν δικαίων, καὶ πάλιν ἐγένοντο οἷοι πρότερον ἦσαν, μᾶλλον δὲ καὶ χείρονες.

XVIII. Πῶς, φημί, κύριε, ἐγένοντο χείρονες, Θεὸν ἐπεγνωκότες; Ὁ μὴ γινώσκων, φησί, Θεὸν καὶ πονηρευόμενος ἔχει κόλασίν τινα τῆς πονηρίας αὐτοῦ· ὁ δὲ Θεὸν ἐπιγνοὺς οὐκέτι ὀφείλει πονηρεύεσθαι, ἀλλ' ἀγαθοποιεῖν. 2. ἐὰν οὖν ὁ ὀφείλων ἀγαθοποιεῖν πονηρεύηται, οὐ δοκεῖ πλείονα πονηρίαν ποιεῖν παρὰ τὸν μὴ γινώσκοντα τὸν Θεόν; διὰ τοῦτο οἱ μὴ ἐγνωκˈόˈτες Θεὸν καὶ πονηρευόμενοι κεκριμένοι εἰσὶν εἰς θάνατον, οἱ δὲ τὸν Θεὸν ἐγνωκότες καὶ τὰ μεγαλεῖα αὐτοῦ ἑωρακότες καὶ πονηρευόμενοι δισσῶς κολασθήσονται καὶ ἀποθανοῦνται εἰς τὸν αἰῶνα. οὕτως οὖν καθαρισθήσεται ἡ ἐκκλησία τοῦ Θεοῦ. 3. ὡς δὲ εἶδες ἐκ τοῦ πύργου τοὺς λίθους ˈἠρˈμένους καὶ παραδεδομένους τοῖς πνεύμασι τοῖς πονηροῖς, καὶ ἐκεῖνοι ἐκβληθήσονται, καὶ ἔσται ἓν σῶμα τῶν κεκαθαρμένων, ὥσπερ καὶ ὁ πύργος ἐγένετο ὡς ἐξ ἑνὸς λίθου γεγονὼς μετὰ τὸ καθαρισθῆναι αὐτόν. οὕτως ἔσται καὶ ἡ ἐκκλησία τοῦ Θεοῦ μετὰ τὸ καθαρισθῆναι αὐτὴν καὶ ἀποβληθῆναι τοὺς πονηροὺς καὶ ὑποκριτὰς καὶ βλασφήμους καὶ

9. xvii. 4 ἑνὶ] conj. Harmer [L₁]; ἐπὶ τῷ AL₂; om. app. E.   τοῦ υἱοῦ] ins. Gebhardt [L₁L₂E]; om. A.   λαμπρὰ] λαμπρὸς A.   5 ἐξ] ἔξω A. καὶ χείρονες] ἢ χείρονες A.   xviii. 1 θεὸν pri.] conj. Gebhardt [L₂]; X̄ν A ; dominum L₁; dub. E.   2 ὁ ὀφείλων ἀγαθοποιεῖν] conj. Gebhardt [L₁L₂E]; ὁ φιλῶν ἄγαν A.   3 ἠρμένους] conj. Gebhardt ;...μένους A ; eiectos L₁L₂E. ἐκεῖνοι ἐκβληθήσονται] conj. Harmer [L₂]; ἐκεῖθεν ἐκβληθέντας AE ; al. L₁.

διψύχους καὶ πονηρευομένους ποικίλαις πονηρίαις. 4. μετὰ
τὸ τούτους ἀποβληθῆναι ἔσται ἡ ἐκκλησία τοῦ Θεοῦ ἐν σῶμα,
μία φρόνησις, εἰς νοῦς, μία πίστις, μία ἀγάπη. καὶ τότε ὁ
υἱὸς τοῦ Θεοῦ ἀγαλλιάσεται καὶ εὐφρανθήσεται ἐν αὐτοῖς
ἀπειληφὼς τὸν λαὸν αὐτοῦ καθαρόν. Μεγάλως, φημί, κύριε,
καὶ ἐνδόξως πάντα ἔχει. 5. ἔτι, [φημί,] κύριε, τῶν ὀρέων
ἑνὸς ἑκάστου δήλωσόν μοι τὴν δύναμιν καὶ τὰς πράξεις, ἵνα
πᾶσα ψυχὴ πεποιθυῖα ἐπὶ τὸν Κύριον ἀκούσασα δοξάσῃ τὸ
μέγα καὶ θαυμαστὸν καὶ ἔνδοξον ὄνομα αὐτοῦ. Ἄκουε, φησί,
τῶν ὀρέων τὴν ποικιλίαν καὶ τῶν δώδεκα ἐθνῶν.

XIX. Ἐκ τοῦ πρώτου ὄρους τοῦ μέλανος οἱ πιστεύσαντες
τοιοῦτοί εἰσιν· ἀποστάται καὶ βλάσφημοι εἰς τὸν Κύριον
καὶ προδόται τῶν δούλων τοῦ Θεοῦ. τούτοις δὲ μετάνοια οὐκ
ἔστι, θάνατος δὲ ἔστι, καὶ διὰ τοῦτο καὶ μέλανές εἰσι· καὶ
γὰρ τὸ γένος αὐτῶν ἄνομόν ἐστιν. 2. ἐκ δὲ τοῦ δευτέρου
ὄρους τοῦ ψιλοῦ οἱ πιστεύσαντες τοιοῦτοί εἰσιν· ὑποκριταὶ
καὶ διδάσκαλοι πονηρίας. καὶ οὗτοι οὖν τοῖς προτέροις
ὅμοιοί εἰσι, μὴ ἔχοντες καρπὸν δικαιοσύνης· ὡς γὰρ τὸ ὄρος
αὐτῶν ἄκαρπον, οὕτω καὶ οἱ ἄνθρωποι οἱ τοιοῦτοι ὄνομα μὲν
ἔχουσιν, ἀπὸ δὲ τῆς πίστεως κενοί εἰσι, καὶ οὐδεὶς ἐν αὐτοῖς
καρπὸς ἀληθείας. τούτοις οὖν μετάνοια κεῖται, ἐὰν ταχὺ
μετανοήσωσιν· ἐὰν δὲ βραδύνωσι, μετὰ τῶν προτέρων ἔσται
ὁ θάνατος αὐτῶν. 3. Διατί, φημί, κύριε, τούτοις μετάνοιά
ἐστι, τοῖς δὲ προτέροις οὐκ ἔστι; παρά τι γὰρ αἱ αὐταὶ αἱ
πράξεις αὐτῶν εἰσί. Διὰ τοῦτο, φησί, τούτοις μετάνοια
κεῖται, ὅτι οὐκ ἐβλασφήμησαν τὸν Κύριον αὐτῶν οὐδὲ
ἐγένοντο προδόται τῶν δούλων τοῦ Θεοῦ, διὰ δὲ τὴν ἐπιθυμίαν
τοῦ λήμματος ὑπεκρίθησαν καὶ ἐδίδαξεν ἕκαστος [κατὰ] τὰς
ἐπιθυμίας τῶν ἀνθρώπων τῶν ἁμαρτανόντων. ἀλλὰ τίσουσι
δίκην τινά· κεῖται δὲ αὐτοῖς μετάνοια διὰ τὸ μὴ γενέσθαι
αὐτοὺς βλασφήμους μηδὲ προδότας.

xviii. 5 ἑκάστου] L₁L₂E ; add κύριε A.   xix. 2 ψιλοῦ] conj. Anger [L₁];
ὑψηλοῦ AE; arido L₂.   3 προτέροις] conj. Hilgenfeld [L₁L₂E]; πρώτοις A.
αἱ αὐταί] conj. Anger in mg. [L₁L₂E]; καὶ αὗται A.   κατὰ] ins. Hilgenfeld
[L₁L₂E] ; om. A ; L₁E omit the preceding word ἕκαστος.

XX. Ἐκ δὲ τοῦ ὄρους τοῦ τρίτου τοῦ ἔχοντος ἀκάνθας
καὶ τριβόλους οἱ πιστεύσαντες τοιοῦτοί εἰσιν· οἱ μὲν
πλούσιοι, οἱ δὲ πραγματείαις πολλαῖς ἐμπεφυρμένοι. οἱ
μὲν τρίβολοί εἰσιν οἱ πλούσιοι, αἱ δὲ ἄκανθαι οἱ ἐν ταῖς
πραγματείαις ταῖς ποικίλαις ἐμπεφυρμένοι. 2. οὗτοι [οὖν,
οἱ ἐν πολλαῖς καὶ ποικίλαις πραγματείαις ἐμπεφυρμένοι, οὐ]
κολλῶνται τοῖς δούλοις τοῦ Θεοῦ, ἀλλ᾽ ἀποπλανῶνται πνιγό-
μενοι ὑπὸ τῶν πράξεων αὐτῶν· οἱ δὲ πλούσιοι δυσκόλως κολλῶνται τοῖς δούλοις τοῦ Θεοῦ, φοβούμενοι μή τι αἰτιαθῶσιν
ἀπ᾽ αὐτῶν. οἱ τοιοῦτοι οὖν Δ ϹΚΟΛΩϹ Ε ϹΕΛΕ ΎϹΟΝΤΑΙ Ε Ϲ ΤΗΝ
S. Mark x. ΒΑϹΙΛΕΊΑΝ ΤΟ͂Υ ΘΕΟ͂Υ. 3. ὥσπερ γὰρ ἐν τριβόλοις γυμνοῖς ποσὶ
23.   περιπατεῖν δύσκολόν ἐστιν, οὕτω καὶ τοῖς τοιούτοις Δ ΎϹΚΟΛΟΝ
S. Mark x. ἘϹΤΙΝ Ε Ϲ ΤΗΝ ΒΑϹΙΛΕΊΑΝ ΤΟ͂Υ ΘΕΟ͂Υ Ε ϹΕΛΘΕ͂ΙΝ. 4. ἀλλὰ τούτοις πᾶσι
24.   μετάνοιά ἐστι, ταχινὴ δέ, ἵν᾽ ὃ τοῖς προτέροις χρόνοις οὐκ
εἰργάσαντο, νῦν ἀναδράμωσιν ταῖς ἡμέραις καὶ ἀγαθόν τι ποιή-
σωσιν. | ἐὰν οὖν μετανοήσωσι καὶ ἀγαθόν τι ποιήσωσι, | ζή-
σονται τῷ Θεῷ· ἐὰν δὲ ἐπιμείνωσι ταῖς πράξεσιν αὐτῶν, παραδοθήσονται ταῖς γυναιξὶν ἐκείναις, αἵτινες αὐτοὺς θανατώσουσιν.

XXI. Ἐκ δὲ τοῦ τετάρτου ὄρους τοῦ ἔχοντος βοτάνας
πολλάς, τὰ μὲν ἐπάνω τῶν βοτανῶν χλωρά, τὰ δὲ πρὸς ταῖς
ῥίζαις ξηρά, τινὲς δὲ καὶ ἀπὸ τοῦ ἡλίου ξηραινόμεναι, οἱ
πιστεύσαντες τοιοῦτοί εἰσιν· οἱ μὲν δίψυχοι, οἱ δὲ τὸν Κύριον
ἔχοντες ἐπὶ τὰ χείλη, ἐπὶ τὴν καρδίαν δὲ μὴ ἔχοντες. 2. διὰ
τοῦτο τὰ θεμέλια αὐτῶν ξηρά ἐστι καὶ δύναμιν μὴ ἔχοντα,
καὶ τὰ ῥήματα αὐτῶν μόνα ζῶσι, τὰ δὲ ἔργα αὐτῶν νεκρά
ἐστιν. οἱ τοιοῦτοι οὔτε ζῶσιν οὔτε τεθνήκασιν. ὅμοιοι οὖν
εἰσὶ τοῖς διψύχοις· καὶ γὰρ οἱ δίψυχοι οὔτε χλωροί εἰσιν
οὔτε ξηροί· οὔτε γὰρ ζῶσιν οὔτε τεθνήκασιν. 3. ὥσπερ γὰρ
αὐτῶν αἱ βοτάναι ἥλιον ἰδοῦσαι ἐξηράνθησαν, οὕτω καὶ οἱ

9. xx. 1 εἰσιν pri.] L₁L₂; add τινὲς ἐξ αὐτῶν ΑΕ.   2 οὖν...ἐμπεφυρμένοι
οὐ] ins. Gebhardt [L₁L₂, cf. Ε]; om. Α.   4 ταῖς ἡμέραις] pref. ἐν Α.   ἐὰν
οὖν...ποιήσωσι] ins. Hilgenfeld [L₁L₂Ε]; καὶ Α.   γυναιξὶν] conj. Anger
[L₁L₂Ε]; πράξεσιν Α.   xxi. 1 χλωρά, ξηρά] conj. Anger in mg. (cf. c. i. 6);
χλωράς, ξηράς Α; dub. L₁L₂Ε.   2 οὔτε ζῶσιν οὔτε] ins. Anger [L₁L₂Ε]; om. Α.
χλωροί, ξηροί] L₁L₂Ε; ξηροί, χλωροί Α.

δίψυχοι, ὅταν θλῖψιν ἀκούσωσι, διὰ τὴν δειλίαν αὐτῶν
εἰδωλολατροῦσι καὶ τὸ ὄνομα ἐπαισχύνονται τοῦ Κυρίου
αὐτῶν. 4. οἱ τοιοῦτοι οὖν οὔτε | ζῶσιν οὔτε | τεθνήκασιν.
ἀλλὰ καὶ οὗτοι, ἐὰν ταχὺ μετανοήσωσι, | δύνανται ζῆσαι·
ἐὰν δὲ μὴ μετανοήσωσιν, | ἤδη παραδεδομένοι εἰσὶ ταῖς γυναιξὶ
ταῖς ἀποφερομέναις τὴν ζωὴν αὐτῶν.

XXII. Ἐκ δὲ τοῦ ὄρους τοῦ πέμπτου τοῦ ἔχοντος βοτάνας χλωρὰς καὶ τραχέος ὄντος οἱ πιστεύσαντες τοιοῦτοί εἰσι·
πιστοὶ μέν, δυσμαθεῖς δὲ καὶ αὐθάδεις καὶ ἑαυτοῖς ἀρέσκοντες,
θέλοντες πάντα γινώσκειν, καὶ οὐδὲν ὅλως γινώσκουσι.
2. διὰ τὴν αὐθάδειαν αὐτῶν ταύτην ἀπέστη ἀπ' αὐτῶν ἡ
σύνεσις καὶ εἰσῆλθεν εἰς αὐτοὺς ἀφροσύνη μωρά. ἐπαινοῦσι
δὲ ἑαυτοὺς ὡς σύνεσιν ἔχοντας, καὶ θέλουσιν ἐθελοδιδάσκαλοι
εἶναι, ἄφρονες ὄντες. 3. διὰ ταύτην οὖν τὴν ὑψηλοφροσύνην
πολλοὶ ἐκενώθησαν ὑψοῦντες ἑαυτούς· μέγα γὰρ δαιμόν⸢ιόν
ἐστ⸥ιν ⸢ἡ αὐθάδει⸤α ⸢καὶ ἡ κενὴ πεποίθησις⸣· ἐκ τούτων οὖν
πολλοὶ ἀπεβλήθησαν, τινὲς δὲ μετενόησαν καὶ ἐπίστευσαν
καὶ ὑπέταξαν ἑαυτ⸢οὺς τοῖ⸥ς ἔχουσι σύν⸢εσιν, γνόντες τὴν⸣
ἑαυτῶν ἀφροσύνην. 4. καὶ τοῖς λοιποῖς δὲ τοῖς τοιούτοις
κεῖται μετάνοια· οὐκ ἐγένοντο γὰρ πονηροί, μᾶλλον δὲ ⸢μωροὶ
καὶ ἀσύνετοι. οὗτοι οὖν ἐὰν⸣ μετανοήσωσι, ζήσονται τῷ
Θεῷ· ἐὰν δὲ μὴ μετανοήσωσι, κατοικήσουσι μετὰ τῶν γυναικῶν τῶν πονηρευομένων εἰς αὐτούς.

XXIII. Οἱ δὲ ἐκ τ⸢οῦ ὄρους τοῦ⸥ ἕκτου τοῦ ἔχοντος
σχισμὰς μεγάλας καὶ μικρὰς καὶ ἐν ταῖς σχισμαῖς βοτάνας
μεμαρασμένας πιστεύσαντες τοιοῦτοί εἰσιν· 2. οἱ μὲν τὰς
σχισμὰς τὰς μικρὰς ἔχοντες, οὗτοί εἰσιν οἱ κατ' ἀλλήλων
ἔχοντες, καὶ ἀπὸ τῶν καταλαλιῶν ἑαυτῶν μεμαρασμένοι εἰσὶν
ἐν τῇ πίστει· ἀλλὰ μετενό⸢ησαν⸣ ἐκ τούτων πολλοί. καὶ οἱ

xxi. 4 ζῶσιν οὔτε] ins. Anger [L₁L₂E]; om. A by homœot. δύνανται...
μετανοήσωσιν] ins. Hilgenfeld [L₁L₂E]; om. A by homœot. xxii. 3 δαιμόν-
⸢ιόν ἐστ⸥ιν] The brackets ⸢ ⸣ represent the lacunæ in A. The restoration of
the text is Hilgenfeld's, unless the contrary is stated. 4 μωροί] conj.
Hilgenfeld [L₁L₂E]; according to Gebhardt πονηρ... is legible in A.
xxiii. 2 μεμαρασμένοι] μεμωραμένοι A.

λοιποὶ δὲ μετανοήσουσιν, ὅταν ἀκούσωσί μου τὰς ἐντολάς· μικραὶ γὰρ αὐτῶν εἰσιν αἱ καταλαλιαί, καὶ ταχὺ μετανοήσουσιν. 3. οἱ δὲ μεγάλας ἔχοντες σχισμάς, οὗτοι παράμονοί εἰσι ταῖς καταλαλιαῖς αὐτῶν καὶ μνησίκακοι γίνονται μηνιῶντες ἀλλ⌐ήλοις⌐. οὗτοι οὖν ἀπὸ τοῦ πύργου ἀπερρίφησαν καὶ ἀπεδοκιμάσθησαν τῆς οἰκοδομῆς αὐτοῦ. οἱ τοιοῦτοι οὖν δυσκόλως ζήσονται. 4. εἰ ὁ Θεὸς καὶ ὁ Κύριος ἡμῶν ὁ πάντων κυριεύων καὶ ἔχων πάσης τῆς κτίσεως αὐτοῦ τὴν ἐξουσίαν οὐ μνησικακεῖ τοῖς ἐξομολογουμένοις τὰς ἁμαρτίας αὐ⌐τῶν⌐, ἀλλ᾽ ἵλεως γίνεται, ἄνθρωπος φθαρτὸς ὢν καὶ πλήρης ἁμαρτιῶν ἀνθρώπῳ μνησικακεῖ ὡς δυνάμενος ἀπολέσαι ἢ σῶσαι αὐτόν; 5. λέγω δ᾽ ὑ⌐μ⌐ῖν, ὁ⌐ ἄγγελος τῆς μετανοίας, ὅσοι ταύτην ἔχετε τὴν αἵρεσιν, ἀπόθεσθε αὐτὴν καὶ μετανοήσατε, καὶ ὁ Κύριος ἰάσεται ὑμῶν τὰ πρότερ⌐α ἁμαρτήματα⌐, ἐὰν καθαρίσητε ἑαυτοὺς ἀπὸ τούτου τοῦ δαιμονίου· εἰ δὲ μή, παραδοθήσεσθε αὐτῷ εἰς θάνατον.

XXIV. Ἐκ δὲ τοῦ ἑβδόμο⌐υ ὄρους, ἐν ᾧ βότάναι⌐ χλωραὶ ⌐καὶ⌐ ἱλαραί, καὶ ὅλον τὸ ὄρος εὐθηνοῦν, καὶ πᾶν γένος κτηνῶν καὶ τὰ πετεινὰ τοῦ οὐρανοῦ ἐνέμοντο τὰς βοτ⌐άνας ἐν τούτῳ τῷ⌐ ὄρει, καὶ αἱ ⌐βοτ⌐άναι ἃς ἐνέμοντο μᾶλλον εὐθαλεῖς ἐγίνοντο, οἱ πιστεύσαντες τοιοῦτοί εἰσι· 2. πάντοτε ἁπλοῖ ⌐καὶ ἄ⌐κακοι ⌐καὶ μακάριοι ἐ⌐γίνοντο, μηδὲν κατ᾽ ἀλλήλων ἔχοντες, ἀλλὰ πάντοτε ἀγαλλιώμενοι ἐπὶ τοῖς δούλοις τοῦ Θεοῦ καὶ ἐνδεδυμένοι ⌐τὸ⌐ πνεῦμα ⌐τὸ ἅγιον τούτων τῶν πα⌐ρθένων καὶ πάντοτε σπλάγχνον ἔχοντες ἐπὶ πάντα ἄνθρωπον, καὶ ἐκ τῶν κόπων αὐτῶν παντὶ ἀνθρώπῳ ἐχορήγησαν ἀνονειδίστως καὶ ἀδιστάκτως. 3. ⌐ὁ οὖν⌐ Κύριος ἰδὼν τὴν ἁπλότητα αὐτῶν καὶ πᾶσαν νηπιότητα ἐπλήθυνεν αὐτοὺς ἐν τοῖς κόποις τῶν χειρῶν αὐτῶν καὶ ἐχαρίτωσεν αὐτοὺς ἐν πάσῃ πράξει αὐτῶν. 4. λέγω δὲ ὑμῖν τοῖς τοιούτοις οὖσιν ἐγὼ ὁ ἄγγελος τῆς μετανοίας· διαμείνατε τοιοῦτοι, καὶ οὐκ ἐξαλειφθήσεται ⌐τὸ σ⌐πέρμα ὑμῶν ἕως

9. xxiv. 3 νηπιότητα] conj. Gebhardt [L₁L₂, and cf. c. xxix. 1]; ἠπιότητα A; dub. E.

αἰῶνος. ἐδοκίμασε γὰρ ὑμᾶς ὁ Κύριος καὶ ἐνέγραψεν ὑμᾶς εἰς τὸν ἀριθμὸν τὸν ἡμέτερον, καὶ ὅλον τὸ σπέρμα ὑμῶν κατοικήσει μετὰ τοῦ υἱοῦ τοῦ Θεοῦ· ἐκ γὰρ τοῦ πνεύματος αὐτοῦ ἐλάβετε. XXV. Ἐκ δὲ τοῦ ὄρους τοῦ ὀγδόου, οὗ ἦσαν αἱ πολλαὶ πηγαί, καὶ πᾶσα ἡ κτίσις τοῦ Κυρίου ἐποτίζετο ἐκ τῶν πηγῶν, οἱ πιστεύσαντες τοιοῦτοί εἰσιν· 2. ἀπόστολοι καὶ διδάσκαλοι οἱ κηρύξαντες εἰς ὅλον τὸν κόσμον καὶ οἱ διδάξαντες σεμνῶς καὶ ἁγνῶς τὸν λόγον τοῦ Κυρίου, καὶ μηδὲν ὅλως νοσφισάμενοι εἰς ἐπιθυμίαν πονηράν, ἀλλὰ πάντοτε ἐν δικαιοσύνῃ καὶ ἀληθείᾳ πορευθέντες, καθὼς καὶ παρέλαβον τὸ πνεῦμα τὸ ἅγιον. τῶν τοιούτων οὖν ἡ πάροδος μετὰ τῶν ἀγγέλων ἐστίν.

XXVI. Ἐκ δὲ τοῦ ὄρους τοῦ ἐνάτου τοῦ ἐρημώδους, τοῦ ⌈τὰ⌉ ἑρπετὰ καὶ θηρία ἐν αὐτῷ ἔχοντος τὰ διαφθείροντα τοὺς ἀνθρώπους, οἱ πιστεύσαντες τοιοῦτοί εἰσιν· 2. οἱ μὲν τοὺς σπίλους ἔχοντες διάκονοί εἰσι κακῶς διακονήσαντες καὶ διαρπάσαντες χηρῶν καὶ ὀρφανῶν τὴν ζωήν, καὶ ἑαυτοῖς περιποιησάμενοι ἐκ τῆς διακονίας ἧς ἔλαβον διακονῆσ⌈αι⌉· ἐὰν οὖν ἐπιμείνωσι τῇ αὐτῇ ἐπιθυμίᾳ, ἀπέθανον, καὶ οὐδεμία αὐτοῖς ἐλπὶς ζωῆς· ἐὰν δὲ ἐπιστρέψωσι καὶ ἁγνῶς τελειώσωσι τὴν διακονίαν αὐτῶν, δυνήσονται ζῆσαι. 3. οἱ δὲ ἐψωριακότες, οὗτοι οἱ ἀρνησάμενοί εἰσι καὶ μὴ ἐπιστρέψαντες ἐπὶ τὸν κύριον ἑαυτῶν, ἀλλὰ χερσωθέντες καὶ γενόμενοι ἐρημώδεις, μὴ κολλώμενοι τοῖς δούλοις τοῦ Θεοῦ ἀλλὰ μονάζοντες, ἀπολλύουσι τὰς ἑαυτῶν ψυχάς. 4. ὡς γὰρ ἄμπελος ἐν φραγμῷ τινὶ καταλειφθεῖσα ἀμελείας τυγχάνουσα καταφθείρεται καὶ ὑπὸ τῶν βοτανῶν ἐρημοῦται, καὶ τῷ χρόνῳ ἀγρία γίνεται, καὶ οὐκέτι εὔχρηστός ἐστ⌈ι⌉ τῷ δεσπότῃ ἑαυτῆς, οὕτω καὶ οἱ τοιοῦτοι ἄνθρωποι ἑαυτοὺς ἀπεγνώκασι, καὶ γίνονται ἄχρηστοι τῷ κυρίῳ ἑαυτῶν ἀγριωθέντες. 5. τούτοις οὖν μετάνοια γίνεται, ἐὰν μὴ ἐκ καρδίας εὑρεθῶσιν

xxiv. 4 πνεύματος] conj. Anger in mg. [L₁L₂E]; σπέρματος A.   xxvi. 2
διακονῆσαι] supp. Gebhardt.

ἠρνημένοι· ἐὰν δὲ ἐκ καρδίας εὑρεθῇ ἠρνημένος τις, οὐκ οἶδα εἰ δύναται ζῆσαι. 6. καὶ τοῦτο οὐκ εἰς ταύτας τὰς ἡμέρας λέγω, ἵνα τις ἀρνησάμενος μετάνοιαν λάβῃ· ἀδύνατον γάρ ἐστι σωθῆναι τὸν μέλλοντα νῦν ἀρνεῖσθαι τὸν Κύριον ἑαυτοῦ· ἀλλ᾿ ἐκείνοις τοῖς πάλαι ἠρνημένοις δοκεῖ κεῖσθαι μετάνοια. εἴ τις οὖν μέλλει μετανοεῖν, ταχινὸς γενέσθω πρὶν τὸν πύργον ἀποτελεσθῆναι· εἰ δὲ μή, ὑπὸ τῶν γυναικῶν καταφθαρήσεται εἰς θάνατον. 7. καὶ οἱ κολοβοί, οὗτοι δόλιοί εἰσι καὶ κατάλαλοι· καὶ τὰ θηρία ἃ εἶδες εἰς τὸ ὄρος οὗτοί εἰσιν. ὥσπερ γὰρ τὰ θηρία διαφθείρει τῷ ἑαυτῶν ἰῷ τὸν ἄνθρωπον καὶ ἀπολλύει, οὕτω καὶ τῶν τοιούτων ἀνθρώπων τὰ ῥήματα δ⌐ια⌐φθείρει τὸν ἄνθρωπον καὶ ἀπολλύει. 8. οὗτοι οὖν κολοβοί εἰσιν ἀπὸ τῆς πίστεως αὐτῶν διὰ τὴν πρᾶξιν ἣν ἔχουσιν ἐν ἑαυτοῖς· τινὲς δὲ μετενόησαν καὶ ἐσώθησαν. καὶ οἱ λοιποὶ οἱ τοιοῦτοι ὄντες δύνανται σωθῆναι, ἐὰν μετανοήσωσιν· ἐὰν δὲ μὴ μετανοήσωσιν, ἀπὸ τῶν γυναικῶν ἐκείνων, ὧν τὴν δύναμιν ἔχουσιν, ἀποθανοῦνται.

XXVII. Ἐκ δὲ τοῦ ὄρους τοῦ δεκάτου, οὗ ἦσαν δένδρα σκεπάζοντα πρόβατ⌐ά⌐ τινα, οἱ πιστεύσαντες τοιοῦτοί εἰσιν· 2. ἐπίσκοποι φιλόξενοι, οἵτινες ἡδέως εἰς τοὺς οἴκους ἑαυτῶν πάντοτε ὑπεδέξαντο τοὺς δούλους τοῦ Θεοῦ ἄτερ ὑποκρίσεως· [οἱ δὲ ἐπίσκοποι] πάντοτε τοὺς ὑστερημένους καὶ τὰς χήρας τῇ διακονίᾳ ἑαυτῶν ἀδιαλείπτως ἐσκέπασαν καὶ ἁγνῶς ἀνεστράφησαν πάντοτε. 3. οὗτοι οὖν [πάντες] σκεπασθήσονται ὑπὸ τοῦ Κυρίου διαπαντός. οἱ οὖν ταῦτα ἐργασάμενοι ἔνδοξοί εἰσι παρὰ τῷ Θεῷ, καὶ ἤδη ὁ τόπος αὐτῶν μετὰ τῶν ἀγγέλων ἐστίν, ἐὰν ἐπιμείνωσιν ἕως τέλους λειτουργοῦντες τῷ Κυρίῳ.

XXVIII. Ἐκ δὲ τοῦ ὄρους τοῦ ἑνδεκάτου, οὗ ἦσαν δένδρα καρπῶν πλήρη, ἄλλοις καὶ ἄλλοις καρποῖς κεκοσμημένα, οἱ πιστεύσαντες τοιοῦτοί εἰσιν· 2. οἱ παθόντες ὑπὲρ

---

9. xxvi. 7 ὄρος] L₁L₂; pref. θ′ (=ἔννατον) app. A; def. E. xxvii. 2 ἐπίσκοποι φιλόξενοι] conj. Harmer [L₂E]; ἐπίσκοποι καὶ φιλόξενοι A; alii vero hi lapides (hos lapides) L₁, probably a corruption of alienorum hospitales.

τοῦ ὀνόματος [τοῦ υἱοῦ τοῦ Θεοῦ], οἳ καὶ προθύμως ἔπαθον ἐξ
ὅλης τῆς καρδίας καὶ παρέδωκαν τὰς ψυχὰς αὐτῶν. 3. Διατί
οὖν, φημί, κύριε, πάντα μὲν τὰ δένδρα καρποὺς ἔχει, τινὲς δὲ
ἐξ αὐτῶν καρποὶ εὐειδέστεροί εἰσιν; Ἄκουε, φησίν· ὅσοι
ποτὲ ἔπαθον διὰ τὸ ὄνομα, ἔνδοξοί εἰσι παρὰ τῷ Θεῷ, καὶ
πάντων τούτων αἱ ἁμαρτίαι ἀφῃρέθησαν, ὅτι ἔπαθον διὰ τὸ
ὄνομα τοῦ υἱοῦ τοῦ Θεοῦ. διατί δὲ οἱ καρποὶ αὐτῶν ποικίλοι εἰσίν, τινὲς δὲ ὑπερέχοντες, ἄκουε. 4. ὅσοι, φησίν, ἐπ'
ἐξουσίαν ἀχθέντες ἐξητάσθησαν καὶ οὐκ ἠρνήσαντο, ἀλλ'
ἔπαθον προθύμως, οὗτοι μᾶλλον ἐνδοξότεροί εἰσι παρὰ τῷ
Κυρίῳ· τούτων ὁ καρπός ἐστιν ὁ ὑπερέχων. ὅσοι δὲ δειλοὶ
καὶ ἐν δισταγμῷ ἐγένοντο καὶ ἐλογίσαντο ἐν ταῖς καρδίαις
αὐτῶν πότερον ἀρνήσονται ἢ ὁμολογήσουσι, καὶ ἔπαθον,
τούτων οἱ καρποὶ ἐλάττους εἰσίν, ὅτι ἀνέβη ἐπὶ τὴν καρδίαν
αὐτῶν ἡ βουλὴ αὕτη· πονηρὰ γὰρ ἡ βουλὴ αὕτη, ἵνα δοῦλος
κύριον ἴδιον ἀρνήσηται. 5. βλέπετε οὖν ὑμεῖς οἱ ταῦτα
βουλευόμενοι, μήποτε ἡ βουλὴ αὕτη διαμείνῃ ἐν ταῖς καρδίαις ὑμῶν, καὶ ἀποθάνητε τῷ Θεῷ. ὑμεῖς δὲ οἱ πάσχοντες
ἕνεκεν τοῦ ὀνόματος δοξ⌜άζειν⌝ ὀφείλετε τὸν Θεόν, ὅτι ἀξίους
ὑμᾶς ἡγήσατο ὁ Θεὸς ἵνα τοῦτο τὸ ὄνομα βαστάζητε, καὶ
πᾶσαι ὑμῶν αἱ ἁμαρτίαι ἰαθῶσιν. 6. ⌜οὐκοῦν μακα⌝ρίζετε
ἑαυτούς· ἀλλὰ δοκεῖτε ἔργον μέγα πεποιηκέναι, ἐάν τις ὑμῶν
διὰ τὸν Θεὸν πάθῃ. ζωὴν ὑμῖν ὁ Κύριος χαρίζεται, καὶ οὐ νοεῖ-
⌜τε⌝· αἱ γὰρ ἁμαρτίαι ὑμῶν κατεβάρησαν, καὶ εἰ μὴ πεπόνθατε
ἕνεκεν τοῦ ὀνόματος [Κυρίου], διὰ τὰς ἁμαρτίας ὑμῶν τεθνή-
κειτε ⌜ἂν⌝ τῷ Θεῷ. 7. ταῦτα ὑμῖν λέγω τοῖς διστάζουσι
περὶ ἀρνήσεως ἢ ὁμολογήσεως. ὁμολογεῖτε ὅτι Κύριον ἔχετε,
μήποτε ἀρνούμενοι ⌜πα⌝ραδοθ⌜ήσησθε⌝ εἰς δεσμωτήριον. 8. εἰ
τὰ ἔθνη τοὺς δούλους αὐτῶν κολάζουσιν, ἐάν τις ἀρνήσηται
τὸν κύριον ἑαυτοῦ, τί δοκεῖτε ποιήσει ὁ Κύριος ὑμῖν, ὃς ⌜ἔχει⌝

xxviii. 3 εὐειδέστεροι] conj. Hilgenfeld [L₁L₂E] ; ἀηδέστεροι A.   5 ἀπο-
θάνητε] conj. Gebhardt in mg. [L₂E]; ἀποθανῆσθε A ; dub. L₁.   τῷ θεῷ] pref.
ἐν A.   τοῦτο] conj. Gebhardt [L₂] ; τούτου A ; ejus L₁E.   6 οὐκοῦν
μακαρίζετε] supp. Gebhardt.   ἄν] supp. Gebhardt.

πάντων τὴν ἐξουσίαν; ἄρατε τὰς βουλὰς ταύτας ἀπὸ τῶν
καρδιῶν ὑμῶν, ἵνα διαπαντὸς ζήσητε τῷ Θεῷ.

XXIX. Ἐκ δὲ τοῦ ὄρους τοῦ δωδεκάτου τοῦ λευκοῦ
οἱ πιστεύσαντες τοιοῦτοί εἰσιν· ὡς νήπια βρέφη εἰσίν, οἷς
οὐδεμία κακία ἀναβαίνει ἐπὶ τὴν καρδίαν, οὐδὲ ⌜ἔγνω⌝σαν τί
ἐστι πονηρία, ἀλλὰ πάντοτε ἐν νηπιότητι διέμειναν. 2. οἱ
τοιοῦτοι οὖν ἀδιστάκτως κατοικοῦσιν ἐν τῇ βασιλείᾳ τοῦ
Θε⌜οῦ, ὅτι⌝ ἐν οὐδενὶ πράγματι ἐμίαναν τὰς ἐντολὰς τοῦ Θεοῦ,
ἀλλὰ μετὰ νηπιότητος διέμειναν πάσας τὰς ἡμέρας τῆς ζωῆς
αὐτῶν ἐν τῇ αὐτῇ φρονήσει. 3. ὅσοι οὖν διαμενεῖτε, φησί,
καὶ ἔσεσθε ὡς τὰ βρέφη, κακίαν μὴ ἔχοντες, [καὶ] πάντων
τῶν προειρημένων ἐνδοξότεροι ἔ⌜σε⌝σθε· πάντα γὰρ τὰ βρέφη
ἔνδοξά ἐστι παρὰ τῷ Θεῷ καὶ πρῶτα παρ' αὐτῷ. μακάριοι
οὖν ὑμεῖς, ὅσοι ἂν ἄρητε ἀφ' ἑαυτῶν τὴν πονηρίαν, ἐνδύσησθε
δὲ τὴν ἀκακίαν· πρῶτοι πάντων ζήσεσθε τῷ Θεῷ. 4. μετὰ
τὸ συντελέσαι αὐτὸν τὰς παραβολὰς τῶν ὀρέων λέγω αὐτῷ·
Κύριε, νῦν μοι δήλωσον περὶ τῶν λίθων ἡρμένων ἐκ τοῦ
πεδίου καὶ εἰς τὴν οἰκοδομὴν τεθειμένων ἀντὶ τῶν λίθων τῶν
ἡρμένων ⌜ἐκ⌝ τοῦ πύργου, καὶ τῶν στρογγύλων τῶν τεθέντων
εἰς τὴν οἰκοδομήν, καὶ τῶν ἔτι στρογγύλων ὄντων.

XXX. Ἄκουε, φησί, καὶ περὶ τούτων πάντων. οἱ λίθοι
οἱ ἐκ τοῦ ⌜πεδί⌝ου ἡρμένοι καὶ τεθειμένοι εἰς τὴν οἰκοδομὴν
τοῦ πύργου ἀντὶ τῶν ἀποβεβλημένων, αἱ ῥίζαι εἰσὶ τοῦ ὄρους
τοῦ λευκοῦ τούτου. 2. ἐπεὶ οὖν οἱ πιστεύσαντες ἐκ τοῦ
ὄρους τούτου πάντες ἄκακοι εὑρέθησαν, ἐκέλευσεν ὁ κύριος
τοῦ πύργου τούτους ἐκ τῶν ῥιζῶν ὄρους τούτου βληθῆναι
εἰς τὴν οἰκοδομὴν τοῦ πύργου· ἔγνω γὰρ ὅτι, ἐὰν ἀπέλθωσιν
εἰς τὴν οἰκοδομὴν [τοῦ πύργου] οἱ λίθοι οὗτοι, διαμενοῦσι
λαμπροί, καὶ οὐδεὶς αὐτῶν μελανήσει. 3. quodsi de ceteris
montibus adiecisset, necesse habuisset rursus visitare eam
turrem atque purgare. hi autem omnes candidi inventi

9. xxviii. 8 ὑμῶν] conj. Gebhardt [L₁L₂E]; ἡμῶν A.   xxx. 2 τούτου pri.
conj. Harmer [L₁L₂E] ; τοῦ λευκοῦ A.   τῶν ῥιζῶν] ins. Hilgenfeld [L₁L₂E];
om. A.   3 quodsi] The lost Greek ending is supplied from L₁.   inventi]
conj. Gebhardt [=L₂] ; iuvenes L₁ MSS; al. A.

sunt, qui crediderunt et qui credituri sunt; ex eodem enim genere sunt. felix hoc genus, quia innocuum est. 4. audi nunc et de illis rotundis lapidibus et splendidis. hi omnes de hoc candido monte sunt. audi autem quare rotundi sunt reperti. divitiae suae eos pusillum obscuraverunt a veritate atque obfuscaverunt; a Deo vero numquam recesserunt, nec ullum verbum malum processit de ore eorum, sed omnis aequitas et virtus veritatis. 5. horum ergo mentem cum vidisset Dominus, †posse eos veritati favere,† bonos quoque permanere, iussit opes eorum circumcidi, non enim in totum eorum tolli, ut possint aliquid boni facere de eo quod eis relictum est, et vivent Deo, quoniam ex bono genere sunt. ideo ergo pusillum circumcisi sunt et positi sunt in structuram turris huius.

XXXI. Ceteri vero, qui adhuc rotundi remanserunt neque aptati sunt in eam structuram, quia nondum acceperunt sigillum, repositi sunt suo loco; valde enim rotundi reperti sunt. 2. oportet autem circumcidi hoc saeculum ab illis et vanitates opum suarum, et tunc convenient in Dei regnum. necesse est enim eos intrare in dei regnum; hoc enim genus innocuum benedixit Dominus. ex hoc ergo genere non intercidet quisquam. etenim licet quis eorum temptatus a nequissimo diabolo aliquid deliquerit, cito recurret ad dominum suum. 3. felices vos iudico omnes, ego nuntius paenitentiae, quicumque estis innocentes sicut infantes, quoniam pars vestra bona est et honorata apud Deum. 4. dico autem omnibus vobis, quicumque sigillum hoc accepistis, simplicitatem habere neque offensarum memores esse neque in malitia vestra permanere aut in memoria offensarum amaritudinis, in unum quemque spiritum fieri et has malas scissuras permediare ac tollere

---

xxx. 5 *posse...favere*] E (*quod possent...quia beati erant e natura ipsorum*), L₂ (*quod boni nati essent et possint*), and the vv. ll. in L₁ *posses* for *posse*, *favent* for *favere* seem to suggest *posse securitatem* (or *severitatem*) *agentes* as the true reading.

a vobis, ut dominus pecorum gaudeat de his. 5. gaudebit autem, si omnia invenerit sana. sin autem aliqua ex his dissipata invenerit, vae erit pastoribus. 6. quodsi ipsi pastores dissipati reperti fuerint, quid respondebunt [pro] pecoribus his? numquid dicunt a pecore se vexatos? non credetur illis. incredibilis enim res est, pastorem pati posse a pecore; et magis punietur propter mendacium suum. et ego sum pastor, et validissime oportet me de vobis reddere rationem.

XXXII. Remediate ergo vos dum adhuc turris aedificatur. 2. Dominus habitat in viris amantibus pacem; ei enimvero pax cara est; a litigiosis vero et perditis malitiae longe abest. reddite igitur ei spiritum integrum, sicut accepistis. 3. si enim dederis fulloni vestimentum novum integrum, idque integrum iterum vis recipere, fullo autem scissum tibi illud reddet, recipies? nonne statim scandescis et eum convicio persequeris, dicens: Vestimentum integrum tibi dedi ; quare scidisti illud et inutile redegisti? et propter scissuram, quam in eo fecisti, in usu esse non potest. nonne haec omnia verba dices fulloni ergo et de scissura quam in vestimento tuo fecerit? 4. si sic igitur tu doles de vestimento tuo, et quereris quod non illud integrum recipias, quid putas Dominum tibi facturum, qui spiritum integrum tibi dedit, et tu eum totum inutilem redegisti, ita ut in nullo usu esse possit domino suo? inutilis enim esse coepit usus eius, cum sit corruptus a te. nonne igitur dominus spiritus eius propter hoc factum tuum [morte te] adficiet? 5. Plane, inquam, omnes eos, quoscumque invenerit in memoria offensarum permanere, adficiet. Clementiam, inquit, eius calcare nolite, sed potius honorificate eum,

9. xxxi. 6 *pro*] ins. Gebhardt (from ps-Cypr. *de Aleat.* 2); om. L₁ MSS. xxxii. 2 *ei*] conj. Gebhardt [cf. L₂E]; *et* L₁ MSS.   4 *dominus spiritus*] conj. Gebhardt [=E]; the MSS vary between *dominum spiritus, dominus spiritum, dominum spiritum* and *dominum suum spiritui ; dominus* L₂.   *morte te*] ins. Gebhardt ; om. L₁ MSS ; *tradet te morti* L₂ ; *te interficere debebat* E.

quod tam patiens est ad delicta vestra, et non est sicut vos.
agite enim paenitentiam utilem vobis.

XXXIII. Haec omnia quae supra scripta sunt, ego
pastor nuntius paenitentiae ostendi et locutus sum Dei
servis. si credideritis ergo et audieritis verba mea et
ambulaveritis in his et correxeritis itinera vestra, vivere
poteritis. sin autem permanseritis in malitia et memoria
offensarum, nullus ex huiusmodi vivet Deo. haec omnia a
me dicenda dicta sunt vobis. 2. ait mihi ipse pastor:
Omnia a me interrogasti? et dixi: Ita, domine. Quare
ergo non interrogasti me de forma lapidum in structura
repositorum, quod explevimus formas? et dixi: Oblitus
sum, domine. 3. Audi nunc, inquit, de illis. hi sunt qui
nunc mandata mea audierunt et ex totis praecordiis egerunt
paenitentiam. cumque vidisset Dominus bonam atque
puram esse paenitentiam eorum et posse eos in ea permanere, iussit priora peccata eorum deleri. hae enim
formae peccata erant eorum, et exaequata sunt, ne
apparerent.

SIMILITUDO DECIMA

I. Postquam perscripseram librum hunc, venit nuntius
ille, qui me tradiderat huic pastori, in domum in qua eram,
et consedit supra lectum, et adstitit ad dexteram hic pastor.
deinde vocavit me et haec mihi dixit: 2. Tradidi te, inquit,
et domum tuam huic pastori, ut ab eo protegi possis. Ita,
inquam, domine. Si vis ergo protegi, inquit, ab omni
vexatione et ab omni saevitia, successum autem habere in
omni opere bono atque verbo, et omnem virtutem aequita-
tis, in mandatis huius ingredere, quae dedi tibi, et poteris
dominari omni nequitiae. 3. custodienti enim tibi mandata huius subiecta erit omnis cupiditas et dulcedo saeculi
huius, successus vero in omni bono negotio te sequetur.
maturitatem huius et modestiam suscipe in te, et dic

omnibus in magno honore esse eum et dignitate apud
Dominum, et magnae potestatis eum praesidem esse et
potentem in officio suo. huic soli per totum orbem paenitentiae potestas tributa est. potensne tibi videtur esse?
sed vos maturitatem huius et verecundiam quam in vos
habet dispicitis.

II. Dico ei: Interroga ipsum, domine, ex quo in domo
mea est, an aliquid extra ordinem fecerim, in quo eum
offenderim. 2. Et ego, inquit, scio nihil extra ordinem
fecisse te neque esse facturum. et ideo haec loquor tecum,
ut perseveres. bene enim de te hic apud me existimavit.
tu autem ceteris haec verba dices, ut et illi qui egerunt aut
acturi sunt paenitentiam, eadem quae tu sentiant, et hic
apud me his bene interpretetur, et ego apud Dominum.
3. Et ego, inquam, domine, omni homini indico magnalia
Domini; spero autem omnes qui jam antea peccaverunt,
si haec audiant, quod libenter acturi sunt paenitentiam,
vitam recuperantes. 4. Permane ergo, inquit, in hoc
ministerio et consumma illud. quicumque autem mandata
huius efficiunt, habebunt vitam, et hic apud Dominum
magnum honorem. quicumque vero huius mandata non
servant, fugiunt a sua vita et faciunt adversus illum, nec
mandata eius secuntur, sed morti se tradunt, et unusquisque eorum reus fit sanguinis sui. tibi autem dico ut servias
mandatis his, et remedium peccatorum habebis.

III. Misi autem tibi has virgines, ut habitent tecum;
vidi enim eas affabiles tibi esse. habes ergo eas adiutrices,
quo magis possis huius mandata servare; non potest enim
fieri ut sine his virginibus haec mandata serventur. video
autem eas libenter esse tecum. sed ego praecipiam eis ut
omnino a domo tua non discedant. 2. tu tantum con-

---

10. ii. 4 *faciunt*] So ms Dd. iv. 11 in Camb. Univ. Libr.; om. cet. mss.
illum] Here L₁ mss om. some words (as *hic autem apud deum habet honorem
suum. quicumque ergo faciunt adversus illum*) by homœot.; cf. L₂E.

munda domum tuam; in munda enim domo libenter ha-
bitabunt. mundae enim sunt atque castae et industriae, et
omnes habentes gratiam apud Dominum. igitur si habue-
rint domum tuam puram, tecum permanebunt; sin autem
pusillum aliquid inquinationis acciderit, protinus a domo
tua recedent. hae enim virgines nullam omnino diligunt
inquinationem. 3. dico ei: Spero me, domine, placiturum
eis, ita ut in domo mea libenter habitent semper. et sicut
hic, cui me tradidisti, nihil de me queritur, ita neque illae
querentur. 4. ait ad pastorem illum: Video, inquit,
servum Dei velle vivere, et custoditurum haec mandata, et
virgines has habitatione munda conlocaturum. 5. haec
cum dixisset, iterum pastori illi me tradidit, et vocavit eas
virgines et dixit ad eas: Quoniam video vos libenter in
domo huius habitare, conmendo eum vobis et domum eius,
ut a domo eius non recedatis omnino. illae vero haec
verba libenter audierunt.

IV. Ait deinde mihi: Viriliter in ministerio hoc con-
versare, omni homini indica magnalia Domini, et habebis
gratiam in hoc ministerio. quicumque ergo in his mandatis
ambulaverit, vivet et felix erit in vita sua; quicumque vero
neglexerit, non vivet et erit infelix in vita sua. 2. dic
omnibus ut non cessent, quicumque recte facere possunt,
bona opera exercere; utile est illis. dico autem, omnem
hominem de incommodis eripi oportere. et is enim qui
eget et in cotidiana vita patitur incommoda, in magno
tormento est ac necessitate. 3. qui igitur huiusmodi ani-
mam eripit de necessitate, magnum gaudium sibi adquirit.
is enim, qui huiusmodi vexatur incommodo, pari tormento
cruciatur atque torquet se qui in vincula est. multi enim
propter huiusmodi calamitates, cum eas sufferre non
possunt, mortem sibi adducunt. qui novit igitur calamita-
tem huiusmodi hominis et non eripit eum, magnum peccatum admittit et reus fit sanguinis eius. 4. facite igitur

opera bona, quicumque accepistis a Domino, ne, dum tardatis facere, consummetur structura turris. propter vos enim intermissum est opus aedificationis eius. nisi festinetis igitur facere recte, consummabitur turris, et excludemini. 5. postquam vero locutus est mecum, surrexit de lecto, et adprehenso pastore et virginibus abiit, dicens autem mihi, remissurum se pastorem illum et virgines in domum meam.

TRANSLATION

SHEPHERD OF HERMAS

THE SHEPHERD OF HERMAS

THE master, who reared me, had sold me to one Rhoda in Rome. After many years, I met her again, and began to love her as a sister. After a certain time I saw her bathing in the river Tiber; and I gave her my hand, and led her out of the river. So, seeing her beauty, I reasoned in my heart, saying, 'Happy were I, if I had such an one to wife both in beauty and in character.' I merely reflected on this and nothing more. After a certain time, as I was journeying to Cumæ, and glorifying God's creatures for their greatness and splendour and power, as I walked I fell asleep. And a Spirit took me, and bore me away through a pathless tract, through which no man could pass: for the place was precipitous, and broken into clefts by reason of the waters. When then I had crossed the river, I came into the level country, and knelt down, and began to pray to the Lord and to confess my sins. Now, while I prayed, the heaven was opened, and I see the lady, whom I had desired, greeting me from heaven, saying, 'Good morrow, Hermas.' And, looking at her, I said to her, 'Lady, what doest *thou* here?' Then she answered me, 'I was taken up, that I might convict thee of thy sins before the Lord.' I said to her, 'Dost thou now convict me?' 'Nay, not so,' said she, 'but hear the words, that I shall say to thee. God, Who dwelleth in the heavens, and created out of nothing the things which are, and increased and multiplied them for His holy Church's sake, is wroth with thee, for that thou didst sin against me.' I answered her and said, 'Sin against thee? In what way? Did I ever speak an unseemly word unto thee? Did I not always regard thee as a goddess? Did I not always respect thee as a sister? How couldst thou falsely charge me, lady, with such villainy and uncleanness?' Laughing she saith unto me, 'The desire after evil entered into thine heart. Nay, thinkest thou not that it is an evil deed for a righteous man, if the evil desire should enter into his heart? It is indeed a sin and a great one too,' saith she; 'for the righteous man entertaineth righteous purposes. While then his purposes are righteous, his repute stands stedfast in the heavens, and he finds the Lord easily propitiated in all that he does. But they that entertain evil purposes in their hearts, bring upon themselves death and captivity, especially they that claim for themselves this present world, and boast in its riches, and cleave not to the good things that are to come. Their souls shall rue it, seeing that they have no hope, but have abandoned themselves and their life. But do thou pray unto God, and He shall heal thine own sins, and those of thy whole house, and of all the saints.'

2. As soon as she had spoken these words the heavens were shut; and I was given over to horror and grief. Then I said within myself, 'If this sin is recorded against me, how can I be saved? Or how shall I propitiate God for my sins which are full-blown? Or with what words shall I entreat the Lord that He may be propitious unto me?' While I was advising and discussing these matters in my heart, I see before me a great white chair of snow-white wool; and there came an aged lady in glistening raiment, having a book in her hands, and she sat down alone, and she saluted me, 'Good morrow, Hermas.' Then I, grieved and weeping, said, 'Good morrow, lady.' And she said to me, 'Why so gloomy, Hermas, thou that art patient and good-tempered, and art always smiling? Why so downcast in thy looks, and far from cheerful?' And I said to her, 'Because of an excellent lady's saying that I had sinned against her.' Then she said, 'Far be this thing from the servant of God! Nevertheless the thought did enter into thy heart concerning her. Now to the servants of God such a purpose bringeth sin. For it is an evil and mad purpose to overtake a devout spirit that hath been already approved, that it should desire an evil deed, and especially if it be Hermas the temperate, who abstaineth from every evil desire, and is full of all simplicity and of great guilelessness.

3. 'Yet it is not for this that God is wroth with thee, but that thou mayest convert thy family, that hath done wrong against the Lord and against you their parents. But out of fondness for thy children thou didst not admonish thy family, but didst suffer it to become fearfully corrupt. Therefore the Lord is wroth with thee. But He will heal all thy past sins, which have been committed in thy family; for by reason of their sins and iniquities thou hast been corrupted by the affairs of this world. But the great mercy of the Lord had pity on thee and thy

family, and will strengthen thee, and establish thee in His glory. Only be not thou careless, but take courage, and strengthen thy family. For as the smith hammering his work conquers the task which he wills, so also doth righteous discourse repeated daily conquer all evil. Cease not therefore to reprove thy children; for I know that if they shall repent with all their heart, they shall be written in the books of life with the saints.' After these words of hers had ceased, she saith unto me, 'Wilt thou listen to me as I read?' Then say I, 'Yes, lady.' She saith to me, 'Be attentive, and hear the glories of God.' I listened with attention and with wonder to that which I had no power to remember; for all the words were terrible, such as man cannot bear. The last words however I remembered, for they were suitable for us and gentle. 'Behold, the God of Hosts, Who by His invisible and mighty power and by His great wisdom created the world, and by His glorious purpose clothed His creation with comeliness, and by His strong word fixed the heaven, and founded the earth upon the waters, and by His own wisdom and providence formed His holy Church, which also He blessed—behold, He removeth the heavens and the mountains and the hills and the seas, and all things are made level for His elect, that He may fulfil to them the promise which He promised with great glory and rejoicing, if so be that they shall keep the ordinances of God, which they received, with great faith.'

4. When then she finished reading and arose from her chair, there came four young men, and they took away the chair, and departed towards the East. Then she calleth me unto her, and she touched my breast, and saith to me, 'Did my reading please thee?' And I say unto her, 'Lady, these last words please me, but the former were difficult and hard.' Then she spake to me, saying, 'These last words are for the righteous, but the former are for the heathen and the rebellious.' While she yet spake with me, two men appeared, and took her by the arms, and they departed, whither the chair also had gone, towards the East. And she smiled as she departed and, as she was going, she saith to me, 'Play the man, Hermas.'

VISION 2

1. I was on the way to Cumæ, at the same season as last year, and I called to mind my last year's vision as I walked; and again a Spirit taketh me, and carrieth me away to the same place as last year. When then I arrived at the place, I fell upon my knees, and began to pray to

the Lord, and to glorify His name, for that he counted me worthy, and made known unto me my former sins. But after I had risen up from prayer, I behold before me the aged lady, whom also I had seen last year, walking and reading a little book. And she saith to me, 'Canst thou report these things to the elect of God?' I say unto her, 'Lady, I cannot recollect so much; but give me the little book, that I may copy it.' 'Take it,' saith she, 'and be sure and return it to me.' I took it, and retiring to a certain spot in the country I copied it letter for letter: for I could not make out the syllables. When then I had finished the letters of the book, suddenly the book was snatched out of my hand; but by whom I did not see.

2. Now after fifteen days, when I had fasted and entreated the Lord earnestly, the knowledge of the writing was revealed to me. And this is what was written:—

'Thy seed, Hermas, have sinned against God, and have blasphemed the Lord, and have betrayed their parents through great wickedness, yea, they have got the name of betrayers of parents, and yet they did not profit by their betrayal; and they still further added to their sins wanton deeds and reckless wickedness; and so the measure of their transgressions was filled up. But make these words known to all thy children, and to thy wife who shall be as thy sister; for she too refraineth not from using her tongue, wherewith she doeth evil. But, when she hears these words, she will refrain, and will find mercy. After that thou hast made known unto them all these words, which the Master commanded me that they should be revealed unto thee, then all their sins which they sinned aforetime are forgiven to them; yea, and to all the saints that have sinned unto this day, if they repent with their whole heart, and remove double-mindedness from their heart. For the Master sware by His own glory, as concerning His elect; that if, now that this day has been set as a limit, sin shall hereafter be committed, they shall not find salvation; for repentance for the righteous hath an end; the days of repentance are accomplished for all the saints; whereas for the Gentiles there is repentance until the last day. Thou shalt therefore say unto the rulers of the Church, that they direct their paths in righteousness, that they may receive in full the promises with abundant glory. Ye therefore that work righteousness be stedfast, and be not double-minded, that ye may have admission with the holy angels. Blessed are ye, as many as endure patiently the great tribulation that cometh, and as many as shall not deny their life. For the

Lord sware concerning His Son, that those who denied their Lord should be rejected from their life, even they that are now about to deny Him in the coming days; but to those who denied Him aforetime, to them mercy was given of His great lovingkindness.

3. 'But do thou, Hermas, no longer bear a grudge against thy children, neither suffer thy sister to have her way, so that they may be purified from their former sins. For they shall be chastised with a righteous chastisement, unless thou bear a grudge against them thyself. The bearing of a grudge worketh death. But thou, Hermas, hast had great tribulations of thine own, by reason of the transgressions of thy family, because thou hadst no care for them. For thou wast neglectful of them, and wast mixed up with thine evil transactions. But herein is thy salvation, in that thou didst not depart from the living God, and in thy simplicity and thy great continence. These have saved thee, if thou abidest therein; and they save all who do such things, and walk in guilelessness and simplicity. These men prevail over all wickedness, and continue unto life eternal. Blessed are all they that work righteousness. They shall never be destroyed. But thou shalt say to Maximus, "Behold tribulation cometh (upon thee), if thou think fit to deny a second time. *The Lord is nigh unto them that turn unto Him*, as it is written in Eldad and Modat, who prophesied to the people in the wilderness."'

4. Now, brethren, a revelation was made unto me in my sleep by a youth of exceeding fair form, who said to me, 'Whom thinkest thou the aged woman, from whom thou receivedst the book, to be?' I say, 'The Sibyl.' 'Thou art wrong,' saith he, 'she is not.' 'Who then is she?' I say. 'The Church,' saith he. I said unto him, 'Wherefore then is she aged?' 'Because,' saith he, 'she was created before all things; therefore is she aged; and for her sake the world was framed.' And afterwards I saw a vision in my house. The aged woman came, and asked me, if I had already given the book to the elders. I said that I had not given it. 'Thou hast done well,' she said, 'for I have words to add. When then I shall have finished all the words, it shall be made known by thy means to all the elect. Thou shalt therefore write two little books, and shalt send one to Clement, and one to Grapte. So Clement shall send to the foreign cities, for this is his duty; while Grapte shall instruct the widows and the orphans. But thou shalt read (the book) to this city along with the elders that preside over the Church.

Vision 3.

The third vision, which I saw, brethren, was as follows. After fasting often, and entreating the Lord to declare unto me the revelation which He promised to show me by the mouth of the aged woman, that very night the aged woman was seen of me, and she said to me, 'Seeing that thou art so importunate and eager to know all things, come into the country where thou abidest, and about the fifth hour I will appear, and will show thee what thou oughtest to see.' I asked her, saying, 'Lady, to what part of the country?' 'Where thou wilt,' saith she. I selected a beautiful and retired spot; but before I spoke to her and named the spot, she saith to me, 'I will come, whither thou willest.' I went then, brethren, into the country, and I counted up the hours, and came to the place where I appointed her to come, and I see an ivory couch placed there, and on the couch there lay a linen cushion, and on the cushion was spread a coverlet of fine linen of flax.

When I saw these things so ordered, and no one in the place, I was amazed, and a fit of trembling seized me, and my hair stood on end; and a fit of shuddering came upon me, because I was alone. When then I recovered myself, and remembered the glory of God, and took courage, I knelt down and confessed my sins to the Lord once more, as I had done on the former occasion.

Then she came with six young men, the same whom I had seen before, and she stood by me, and listened attentively to me, as I prayed and confessed my sins to the Lord. And she touched me, and said: 'Hermas, make an end of constantly entreating for thy sins; entreat also for righteousness, that thou mayest take some part forthwith to thy family.' Then she raiseth me by the hand, and leadeth me to the couch, and saith to the young men, 'Go ye, and build.' And after the young men had retired and we were left alone, she saith to me, 'Sit down here.' I say to her, 'Lady, let the elders sit down first.' 'Do as I bid thee,' saith she, 'sit down.' When then I wanted to sit down on the right side, she would not allow me, but beckoned me with her hand that I should sit on the left side. As then I was musing thereon, and was sad because she would not permit me to sit on the right side, she saith to me, 'Art thou sad, Hermas? The place on the right side is for others, even for those who have already been well-pleasing to God, and have suffered for the Name's sake. But thou lackest much that thou shouldest sit with them; but as thou abidest in thy simplicity, even so continue, and thou shalt sit with them, thou and as many as shall have done their deeds, and have suffered what they suffered.'

2. 'What did they suffer?' say I. 'Listen,' saith she. 'Stripes, imprisonments, great tribulations, crosses, wild beasts, for the Name's sake. Therefore to them belongs the right side of the Holiness—to them, and to all who shall suffer for the Name. But for the rest is the left side. Howbeit, to both, to them that sit on the right, and to them that sit on the left, are the same gifts, and the same promises, only they sit on the right and have a certain glory. Thou indeed art very desirous to sit on the right with them, but thy shortcomings are many; yet thou shalt be purified from thy shortcomings; yea, and all that are not double-minded shall be purified from all their sins unto this day.'

When she had said this, she wished to depart; but, falling at her feet, I entreated her by the Lord that she would show me the vision which she promised. Then she again took me by the hand, and raiseth me, and seateth me on the couch at the left hand, while she herself sat on the right. And lifting up a certain glistening rod, she saith to me, 'Seest thou a great thing?' I say to her, 'Lady, I see nothing.' She saith to me, 'Look thou; dost thou not see in front of thee a great tower being builded upon the waters, of glistening square stones?' Now the tower was being builded foursquare by the six young men that came with her. And countless other men were bringing stones, some of them from the deep, and others from the land, and were handing them to the six young men. And they took them and builded. The stones that were dragged from the deep they placed in every case, just as they were, into the building, for they had been shaped, and they fitted in their joining with the other stones; and they adhered so closely one with another that their joining could not possibly be detected; and the building of the tower appeared as if it were built of one stone. But of the other stones which were brought from the dry land, some they threw away, and some they put into the building; and others they broke in pieces, and threw to a distance from the tower. Now many other stones were lying round the tower, and they did not use them for the building; for some of them were mildewed, and others had cracks in them, and others were too short, and others were white and round, and did not fit into the building. And I saw other stones thrown to a distance from the tower, and coming to the way, and yet not staying in the way, but rolling to where there was no way; and others falling into the fire and burning there; and others falling near the waters, and yet not able to roll into the water, although they desired to roll and to come to the water.

3. When she had shown me these things, she wished to hurry away. I say to her, 'Lady, what advantage is it to me to have seen these things, and yet not to know what the things mean?' She answered and said unto me, 'Thou art an over-curious fellow, in desiring to know all that concerns the tower.' 'Yea, lady,' I said, 'that I may announce it to my brethren, and that they [may be the more gladdened and] when they hear [these things] may know the Lord in great glory.' Then said she, 'Many shall hear; but when they hear, some of them shall be glad, and others shall weep. Yet even these latter, if they hear and repent, shall likewise be glad. Hear thou therefore the parables of the tower; for I will reveal all things unto thee. And trouble me no more about revelation; for these revelations have an end, seeing that they have been completed. Nevertheless thou wilt not cease asking for revelations; for thou art shameless.

'The tower, which thou seest building, is myself, the Church, which was seen of thee both now and aforetime. Ask, therefore, what thou willest concerning the tower, and I will reveal it unto thee, that thou mayest rejoice with the saints.' I say unto her, 'Lady, since thou didst hold me worthy once for all, that thou shouldest reveal all things to me, reveal them.' Then she saith to me, 'Whatsoever is possible to be revealed to thee, shall be revealed. Only let thy heart be with God, and doubt not in thy mind about that which thou seest.' I asked her, 'Wherefore is the tower builded upon waters, lady?' 'I told thee so before,' said she, 'and indeed thou dost enquire diligently. So by thy enquiry thou discoverest the truth. Hear then why the tower is builded upon waters; it is because your life is saved and shall be saved by water. But the tower has been founded by the word of the Almighty and Glorious Name, and is strengthened by the unseen power of the Master.'

4. I answered and said unto her, 'Lady, this thing is great and marvellous. But the six young men that build, who are they, lady?'

'These are the holy angels of GOD, that were created first of all, unto whom the Lord delivered all His creation to increase and to build it, and to be masters of all creation. By their hands therefore the building of the tower will be accomplished.' 'And who are the others who are bringing the stones?' 'They also are holy angels of God; but these six are superior to them. The building of the tower then shall be accomplished, and all alike shall rejoice in the (completed) circle of the tower, and shall glorify God that the building of the tower was accomplished.' I enquired of her, saying, 'Lady, I could wish to know concerning the end of the stones, and their power, of what kind it is.' She answered and said unto me, 'It is not that thou of all men art especially worthy that it should be revealed to thee; for there are others before thee, and better than thou art, unto whom these visions ought to have been revealed. But that the name of God may be glorified, it hath been revealed to thee, and shall be revealed, for the sake of the doubtful-minded, who question in their hearts whether these things are so or not. Tell them that all these things are true, and that there is nothing beside the truth, but that all are stedfast, and valid, and established on a firm foundation.

5. 'Hear now concerning the stones that go to the building. The stones that are squared and white, and that fit together in their joints, these are the apostles and bishops and teachers and deacons, who walked after the holiness of God, and exercised their office of bishop and teacher and deacon in purity and sanctity for the elect of God, some of them already fallen on sleep, and others still living. And because they always agreed with one another, they both had peace among themselves and listened one to another. Therefore their joinings fit together in the building of the tower.' 'But they that are dragged from the deep, and placed in the building, and that fit together in their joinings with the other stones that are already builded in, who are they?' 'These are they that suffered for the name of the Lord.' 'But the other stones that are brought from the dry land, I would fain know who these are, lady.' She said, 'Those that go to the building, and yet are not hewn, these the Lord hath approved because they walked in the uprightness of the Lord, and rightly performed His commandments.' 'But they that are brought and placed in the building, who are they?' 'They are young in the faith, and faithful; but they are warned by the angels to do good, because wickedness was found in them.' 'But those whom they rejected and threw away, who are they?' 'These have sinned, and desire to repent, therefore they were not cast to a great distance from the tower, because they will be useful for the building, if they repent. They then that shall repent, if they repent, will be strong in the faith, if they repent now while the tower is building. But if the building shall be finished, they have no more any place, but shall be castaways. This privilege only they have, that they lie near the tower.

6. 'But wouldst thou know about them that are broken in pieces, and cast away far from the tower? These are the sons of lawlessness. They received the faith in hypocrisy, and no wickedness was absent from them. Therefore they have not salvation, for they are not useful for building by reason of their wickednesses. Therefore they were broken up and thrown far away by reason of the wrath of the Lord, for they excited Him to wrath. But the rest whom thou hast seen lying in great numbers, not going to the building, of these they that are mildewed are they that knew the truth, but did not abide in it, nor cleave to the saints. Therefore they are useless.'

'But they that have the cracks, who are they?' 'These are they that have discord in their hearts against one another, and are not at peace among themselves; who have an appearance of peace, but when they depart from one another, their wickednesses abide in their hearts. These are the cracks which the stones have. But they that are broken off short, these have believed, and have their greater part in righteousness, but have some parts of lawlessness; therefore they are too short, and are not perfect.'

'But the white and round stones, which did not fit into the building, who are they, lady?' She answered and said to me, 'How long art thou foolish and stupid, and enquirest everything, and understandest nothing? These are they that have faith, but have also riches of this world. When tribulation cometh, they deny their Lord by reason of their riches and their business affairs.' And I answered and said unto her, 'When then, lady, will they be useful for the building?' 'When,' she replied, 'their wealth, which leadeth their souls astray, shall be cut away, then will they be useful for God. For just as the round stone, unless it be cut away, and lose some portion of itself, cannot become square, so also they that are rich in this world, unless their riches be cut away, cannot become useful to the Lord. Learn first from thyself. When thou hadst riches, thou wast useless; but now thou art useful and profitable unto life. Be ye useful unto God, for thou thyself also art taken from the same stones.

7. 'But the other stones which thou sawest cast far away from the tower and falling into the way and rolling out of the way into the regions where there is no way, these are they that have believed, but by reason of their double heart they abandon their true way. Thus thinking that they can find a better way, they go astray and are sore distressed, as they walk about in the regions where there is no

way. But they that fall into the fire and are burned, these are they
that finally rebelled from the living God, and it no more entered into
their hearts to repent by reason of the lusts of their wantonness and
of the wickednesses which they wrought. But the others, which fall
near the waters and yet cannot roll into the water, wouldest thou know
who are they? These are they that heard the word, and would be
baptized unto the name of the Lord. Then, when they call to their
remembrance the purity of the truth, they change their minds, and go
back again after their evil desires.' So she finished the explanation of
the tower. Still importunate, I asked her further, whether for all these
stones that were rejected and would not fit into the building of the tower
there was repentance, and they had a place in this tower. 'They can
repent,' she said, 'but they cannot be fitted into this tower. Yet they
shall be fitted into another place much more humble, but not until they
have undergone torments, and have fulfilled the days of their sins.
And they shall be changed for this reason, because they participated in
the Righteous Word; and then shall it befal them to be relieved from
their torments, if the evil deeds, that they have done, come into
their heart; but if these come not into their heart, they are not saved
by reason of the hardness of their hearts.'

8. When then I ceased asking her concerning all these things, she
saith to me; 'Wouldest thou see something else?' Being very desirous
of beholding, I was greatly rejoiced that I should see it. She looked
upon me, and smiled, and she saith to me, 'Seest thou seven women
round the tower?' 'I see them, lady,' say I. 'This tower is supported
by them by commandment of the Lord. Hear now their employments.
The first of them, the woman with the strong hands, is called Faith;
through her are saved the elect of God. And the second, that is girded
about and looketh like a man, is called Continence; she is the daughter
of Faith. Whosoever then shall follow her, becometh happy in his life,
for he shall refrain from all evil deeds, believing that, if he refrain from
every evil desire, he shall inherit eternal life.' 'And the others, lady,
who be they?' 'They are daughters one of the other. The name of
the one is Simplicity, of the next, Knowledge, of the next, Guilelessness,
of the next, Reverence, of the next, Love. When then thou shalt do all
the works of their mother, thou canst live.' 'I would fain know, lady,'
I say, 'what power each of them possesseth.' 'Listen then,' saith she, 'to
the powers which they have. Their powers are mastered each by the
other, and they follow each other, in the order in which they were born.

From Faith is born Continence, from Continence Simplicity, from Simplicity Guilelessness, from Guilelessness Reverence, from Reverence Knowledge, from Knowledge Love. Their works then are pure and reverent and divine. Whosoever therefore shall serve these women, and shall have strength to master their works, shall have his dwelling in the tower with the saints of God.' Then I asked her concerning the seasons, whether the consummation is even now. But she cried aloud, saying, 'Foolish man, seest thou not that the tower is still a-building? Whensoever therefore the tower shall be finished building, the end cometh; but it shall be built up quickly. Ask me no more questions: this reminder is sufficient for you and for the saints, and is the renewal of your spirits. But it was not revealed to thyself alone, but in order that thou mightest show these things unto all. After three days—for thou must understand first, and I charge thee, Hermas, first with these words, which I am about to speak to thee—(I charge thee to) tell all these things into the ears of the saints, that hearing them and doing them they may be purified from their wickednesses, and thyself also with them.

9. 'Hear me, my children. I brought you up in much simplicity and guilelessness and reverence, through the mercy of the Lord, Who instilled righteousness into you, that ye might be justified and sanctified from all wickedness and all crookedness. But ye will not to cease from your wickedness. Now then hear me and be at peace among yourselves, and have regard one to another, and assist one another, and do not partake of the creatures of God alone in abundance, but share them also with those that are in want. For some men through their much eating bring weakness on the flesh, and injure their flesh: whereas the flesh of those who have nought to eat is injured by their not having sufficient nourishment, and their body is ruined. This exclusiveness therefore is hurtful to you that have and do not share with them that are in want. Look ye to the judgment that cometh. Ye then that have more than enough, seek out them that are hungry, while the tower is still unfinished; for after the tower is finished, ye will desire to do good, and will find no place for it. Look ye therefore, ye that exult in your wealth, lest they that are in want shall moan, and their moaning shall go up unto the Lord, and ye with your [abundance of] good things be shut outside the door of the tower. Now therefore I say unto you that are rulers of the Church, and that occupy the chief seats; be not ye like unto the sorcerers. The sorcerers indeed carry their

drugs in boxes, but ye carry your drug and your poison in your heart. Ye are case-hardened, and ye will not cleanse your hearts and mix your wisdom together in a clean heart, that ye may obtain mercy from the Great King. Look ye therefore, children, lest these divisions of yours deprive you of your life. How is it that ye wish to instruct the elect of the Lord, while ye yourselves have no instruction? Instruct one another therefore, and have peace among yourselves, that I also may stand gladsome before the Father, and give an account concerning you all to your Lord.'

10. When then she ceased speaking with me, the six young men, who were building, came, and took her away to the tower, and other four lifted the couch, and took it also away to the tower. I saw not the face of these, for they were turned away. And, as she went, I asked her to reveal to me concerning the three forms, in which she had appeared to me. She answered and said to me; 'As concerning these things thou must ask another, that they may be revealed to thee.' Now she was seen of me, brethren, in my first vision of last year, as a very aged woman and seated on a chair. In the second vision her face was youthful, but her flesh and her hair were aged, and she spake to me standing; and she was more gladsome than before. But in the third vision she was altogether youthful and of exceeding great beauty, and her hair alone was aged; and she was gladsome exceedingly and seated on a couch. Touching these things I was very greatly anxious to learn this revelation. And I see the aged woman in a vision of the night, saying to me, 'Every enquiry needs humility. Fast therefore, and thou shalt receive what thou askest from the Lord.' So I fasted one day; and that very night there appeared unto me a young man, and he saith to me, 'Seeing that thou askest me revelations offhand with entreaty, take heed lest by thy much asking thou injure thy flesh. Sufficient for thee are these revelations. Canst thou see mightier revelations than those thou hast seen?' I say unto him in reply, 'Sir, this one thing alone I ask, concerning the three forms of the aged woman, that a complete revelation may be vouchsafed me.' He saith to me in answer, 'How long are ye without understanding? It is your double-mindedness that maketh you of no understanding, and because your heart is not set towards the Lord.' I answered and said unto him again, 'From thee, Sir, we shall learn the matters more accurately.'

11. 'Listen,' saith he, 'concerning the three forms, of which thou enquirest. In the first vision wherefore did she appear to thee an aged

woman and seated on a chair? Because your spirit was aged, and already decayed, and had no power by reason of your infirmities and acts of double-mindedness. For as aged people, having no longer hope of renewing their youth, expect nothing else but to fall asleep, so ye also, being weakened with the affairs of this world, gave yourselves over to repining, and cast not your cares on the Lord; but your spirit was broken, and ye were aged by your sorrows.' 'Wherefore then she was seated on a chair, I would fain know, Sir.' 'Because every weak person sits on a chair by reason of his weakness, that the weakness of his body may be supported. So thou hast the symbolism of the first vision.

12. 'But in the second vision thou sawest her standing, and with her countenance more youthful and more gladsome than before; but her flesh and her hair aged. Listen to this parable also,' saith he. 'Imagine an old man, who has now lost all hope of himself by reason of his weakness and his poverty, and expecteth nothing else save the last day of his life. Suddenly an inheritance is left him. He heareth the news, riseth up and full of joy clothes himself with strength, and no longer lieth down, but standeth up, and his spirit, which was now broken by reason of his former circumstances, is renewed again, and he no longer sitteth, but taketh courage; so also was it with you, when ye heard the revelation which the Lord revealed unto you. For He had compassion on you, and renewed your spirits, and ye laid aside your maladies, and strength came to you, and ye were made powerful in the faith, and the Lord rejoiced to see you put on your strength. And therefore He showed you the building of the tower; yea, and other things also shall He show you, if with your whole heart ye be at peace among yourselves.

13. 'But in the third vision ye saw her younger and fair and gladsome, and her form fair. For just as when to some mourner cometh some piece of good tidings, immediately he forgetteth his former sorrows, and admitteth nothing but the tidings which he hath heard, and is strengthened thenceforth unto that which is good, and his spirit is renewed by reason of the joy which he hath received; so also ye have received a renewal of your spirits by seeing these good things. And whereas thou sawest her seated on a couch, the position is a firm one; for the couch has four feet and standeth firmly; for the world too is upheld by means of four elements. They then that have fully repented shall be young again, and founded firmly, seeing that they have re-

pented with their whole heart. There thou hast the revelation entire
and complete. Thou shalt ask nothing more as touching revelation;
but if anything be lacking still, it shall be revealed unto thee.'

[VISION 4.]

1. The fourth vision which I saw, brethren, twenty days after the
former vision which came unto me, for a type of the impending tribulation. I was going into the country by the Campanian Way. From the
high road, it is about ten stades; and the place is easy for travelling.
While then I am walking alone, I entreat the Lord that He will accomplish the revelations and the visions which He showed me through
His holy Church, that He may strengthen me and may give repentance
to His servants which have stumbled, that His great and glorious Name
may be glorified, for that He held me worthy that He should show me
His marvels. And as I gave glory and thanksgiving to Him, there
answered me as it were the sound of a voice, 'Be not of doubtful mind,
Hermas.' I began to question in myself and to say, 'How can I be of
doubtful mind, seeing that I am so firmly founded by the Lord, and
have seen glorious things?' And I went on a little, brethren, and
behold, I see a cloud of dust rising as it were to heaven, and I began to
say within myself, 'Can it be that cattle are coming, and raising a cloud
of dust?' for it was just about a stade from me. As the cloud of
dust waxed greater and greater, I suspected that it was something
supernatural. Then the sun shone out a little, and behold, I see a huge
beast like some sea-monster, and from its mouth fiery locusts issued
forth. And the beast was about a hundred feet in length, and its head
was as it were of pottery. And I began to weep, and to entreat the Lord
that He would rescue me from it. And I remembered the word which
I had heard, 'Be not of doubtful mind, Hermas.' Having therefore,
brethren, put on the faith of the Lord and called to mind the mighty
works that He had taught me, I took courage and gave myself up to the
beast. Now the beast was coming on with such a rush, that it might
have ruined a city. I come near it, and, huge monster as it was, it
stretcheth itself on the ground, and merely put forth its tongue, and
stirred not at all until I had passed by it. And the beast had on its
head four colours; black, then fire and blood colour, then gold, then
white.

2. Now after I had passed the beast, and had gone forward about thirty feet, behold, there meeteth me a virgin arrayed as if she were going forth from a bride-chamber, all in white and with white sandals, veiled up to her forehead, and her head-covering consisted of a turban, and her hair was white. I knew from the former visions that it was the Church, and I became more cheerful. She saluteth me, saying, 'Good morrow, my good man'; and I saluted her in turn, 'Lady, good morrow.' She answered and said unto me, 'Did nothing meet thee?' I say unto her, 'Lady, such a huge beast, that could have destroyed whole peoples : but, by the power of the Lord and by His great mercy, I escaped it.' 'Thou didst escape it well,' saith she, 'because thou didst cast thy care upon God, and didst open thy heart to the Lord, believing that thou canst be saved by nothing else but by His great and glorious Name. Therefore the Lord sent His angel, which is over the beasts, whose name is Segri, and *shut its mouth, that it might not hurt thee.* Thou hast escaped a great tribulation by reason of thy faith, and because, though thou sawest so huge a beast, thou didst not doubt in thy mind. Go therefore, and declare to the elect of the Lord His mighty works, and tell them that this beast is a type of the great tribulation which is to come. If therefore ye prepare yourselves beforehand, and repent (and turn) unto the Lord with your whole heart, ye shall be able to escape it, if your heart be made pure and without blemish, and if for the remaining days of your life ye serve the Lord blamelessly. Cast your cares upon the Lord and He will set them straight. Trust ye in the Lord, ye men of doubtful mind, for He can do all things, yea, He both turneth away His wrath from you, and again He sendeth forth His plagues upon you that are of doubtful mind. Woe to them that hear these words and are disobedient; it were better for them that they had not been born.'

3. I asked her concerning the four colours, which the beast had upon its head. Then she answered me and said, 'Again thou art curious about such matters.' 'Yes, lady,' said I, 'make known unto me what these things are.' 'Listen,' said she ; 'the black is this world in which ye dwell; and the fire and blood colour showeth that this world must perish by blood and fire ; and the golden part are ye that have escaped from this world. For as the gold is tested by the fire and is made useful, so ye also [that dwell in it] are being tested in yourselves. Ye then that abide and pass through the fire will be purified by it. For as the gold loses its dross, so ye also shall cast away all sorrow and

tribulation, and shall be purified, and shall be useful for the building of the tower. But the white portion is the coming age, in which the elect of God shall dwell; because the elect of God shall be without spot and pure unto life eternal. Wherefore cease not thou to speak in the ears of the saints. Ye have now the symbolism also of the tribulation which is coming in power. But if ye be willing, it shall be nought. Remember ye the things that are written beforehand.' With these words she departed, and I saw not in what direction she departed; for a noise was made ; and I turned back in fear, thinking that the beast was coming.

REVELATION 5

As I prayed in the house, and sat on the couch, there entered a man glorious in his visage, in the garb of a shepherd, with a white skin wrapped about him, and with a wallet on his shoulders and a staff in his hand. And he saluted me, and I saluted him in return. And he immediately sat down by my side, and he saith unto me, 'I was sent by the most holy angel, that I might dwell with thee the remaining days of thy life.' I thought he came to tempt me, and I say unto him, 'Why, who art thou? For I know,' say I, 'unto whom I was delivered.' He saith to me, 'Dost thou not recognise me?' 'No,' I say. 'I,' saith he, 'am the shepherd, unto whom thou wast delivered.' While he was still speaking, his form was changed, and I recognised him as being the same, to whom I was delivered; and straightway I was confounded, and fear seized me, and I was altogether overwhelmed with distress that I had answered him so wickedly and senselessly. But he answered and said unto me, 'Be not confounded, but strengthen thyself in my commandments which I am about to command thee. For I was sent,' saith he, 'that I might show thee again all the things which thou didst see before, merely the heads which are convenient for you. First of all, write down my commandments and my parables ; and the other matters thou shalt write down as I shall show them to thee. The reason why,' saith he, 'I command thee to write down first the commandments and parables is, that thou mayest read them off-hand, and mayest be able to keep them.' So I wrote down the commandments and parables, as he commanded me. If then, when ye hear them, ye keep them and walk in them, and do them with a pure heart, ye shall receive from the Lord all things that He promised you ; but if, when ye hear them, ye do not repent, but still add to your sins, ye shall receive from the Lord the opposite. All these the shepherd, the angel of repentance, commanded me so to write.

Mandate the First

'First of all, believe that God is One, even He Who created all things and set them in order, and brought all things from non-existence into being, Who comprehendeth all things, being alone incomprehensible. Believe Him therefore, and fear Him, and in this fear be continent. Keep these things, and thou shalt cast off all wickedness from thyself, and shalt clothe thyself with every excellence of righteousness, and shalt live unto God, if thou keep this commandment.'

Mandate the Second

He saith to me; 'Keep simplicity and be guileless, and thou shalt be as little children, that know not the wickedness which destroyeth the life of men. First of all, speak evil of no man, neither take pleasure in listening to a slanderer. Otherwise thou that hearest too shalt be responsible for the sin of him that speaketh the evil, if thou believest the slander, which thou hearest; for in believing it thou thyself also wilt have a grudge against thy brother. So then shalt thou be responsible for the sin of him that speaketh the evil. Slander is evil; it is a restless demon, never at peace, but always having its home among factions. Refrain from it therefore, and thou shalt have success at all times with all men. But clothe thyself in reverence, wherein is no evil stumbling-block, but all things are smooth and gladsome. Work that which is good, and of thy labours, which God giveth thee, give to all that are in want freely, not questioning to whom thou shalt give, and to whom thou shalt not give. Give to all; for to all God desireth that there should be given of His own bounties. They then that receive shall render an account to God why they received it, and to what end; for they that receive in distress shall not be judged, but they that receive by false pretence shall pay the penalty. He then that giveth is guiltless; for as he received from the Lord the ministration to perform it, he hath performed it in sincerity, by making no distinction to whom to give or not to give. This ministration then, when sincerely performed, becomes glorious in the sight of God. He therefore that ministereth thus sincerely shall live unto God. Therefore keep this commandment, as I have told thee, that thine own repentance and that of thy house-hold may be found to be sincere, and [thy] heart pure and undefiled.'

Mandate the Third

Again he saith to me; 'Love truth, and let nothing but truth proceed out of thy mouth, that the Spirit which God made to dwell in this flesh, may be found true in the sight of all men; and thus shall the Lord, Who dwelleth in thee, be glorified; for the Lord is true in every word, and with Him there is no falsehood. They therefore that speak lies set the Lord at nought, and become robbers of the Lord, for they do not deliver up to Him the deposit which they received. For they received of Him a spirit free from lies. This if they shall return a lying spirit, they have defiled the commandment of the Lord and have become robbers.' When then I heard these things, I wept bitterly. But seeing me weep he saith, 'Why weepest thou?' 'Because, Sir,' say I, 'I know not if I can be saved.' 'Why so?' saith he. 'Because, Sir,' I say, 'never in my life spake I a true word, but I always lived deceitfully with all men and dressed up my falsehood as truth before all men; and no man ever contradicted me, but confidence was placed in my word. How then, Sir,' say I, 'can I live, seeing that I have done these things?' 'Your supposition,' he saith, 'is right and true, for it behoved thee as a servant of God to walk in truth, and no complicity with evil should abide with the Spirit of truth, nor bring grief to the Spirit which is holy and true.' 'Never, Sir,' say I, 'heard I clearly words such as these.' 'Now then,' saith he, 'thou hearest. Guard them, that the former falsehoods also which thou spakest in thy business affairs may themselves become credible, now that these are found true; for they too can become trustworthy. If thou keep these things, and from henceforward speak nothing but truth, thou shalt be able to secure life for thyself. And whosoever shall hear this command, and abstain from falsehood, that most pernicious habit, shall live unto God.'

Mandate the Fourth

1. 'I charge thee,' saith he, 'to keep purity, and let not a thought enter into thy heart concerning another's wife, or concerning fornication, or concerning any such like evil deeds; for in so doing thou committest a great sin. But remember thine own wife always, and thou shalt never go wrong. For should this desire enter into thine heart, thou wilt go wrong, and should any other as evil as this, thou committest sin. For this desire in a servant of God is a great sin; and if any man doeth this evil deed, he worketh out death for himself. Look to it

therefore. Abstain from this desire; for, where holiness dwelleth, there lawlessness ought not to enter into the heart of a righteous man.' I say to him, 'Sir, permit me to ask thee a few more questions.' 'Say on,' saith he. 'Sir,' say I, 'if a man who has a wife that is faithful in the Lord detect her in adultery, doth the husband sin in living with her?' 'So long as he is ignorant,' saith he, 'he sinneth not; but if the husband know of her sin, and the wife repent not, but continue in her fornication, and her husband live with her, he makes himself responsible for her sin and an accomplice in her adultery.' 'What then, Sir,' say I, 'shall the husband do, if the wife continue in this case?' 'Let him divorce her,' saith he, 'and let the husband abide alone: but if after divorcing his wife he shall marry another, he likewise committeth adultery.' 'If then, Sir,' say I, 'after the wife is divorced, she repent and desire to return to her own husband, shall she not be received?' 'Certainly,' saith he, 'if the husband receiveth her not, he sinneth and bringeth great sin upon himself; nay, one who hath sinned and repented must be received, yet not often; for there is but one repentance for the servants of God. For the sake of her repentance therefore the husband ought not to marry. This is the manner of acting enjoined on husband and wife. Not only,' saith he, 'is it adultery, if a man pollute his flesh, but whosoever doeth things like unto the heathen committeth adultery. If therefore in such deeds as these likewise a man continue and repent not, keep away from him, and live not with him. Otherwise, thou also art a partaker of his sin. For this cause ye were enjoined to remain single, whether husband or wife; for in such cases repentance is possible. I,' said he, 'am not giving an excuse that this matter should be concluded thus, but to the end that the sinner should sin no more. But as concerning his former sin, there is One Who is able to give healing; it is He Who hath authority over all things.'

2. I asked him again, saying, 'Seeing that the Lord held me worthy that thou shouldest always dwell with me, suffer me still to say a few words, since I understand nothing, and my heart has been made dense by my former deeds. Make me to understand, for I am very foolish, and I apprehend absolutely nothing.' He answered and said unto me, 'I,' saith he, 'preside over repentance, and I give understanding to all who repent. Nay, thinkest thou not,' saith he, 'that this very act of repentance is understanding? To repent is great understanding,' saith he. 'For the man that hath sinned understandeth that he hath done evil before the Lord, and the deed which he hath done entereth into his

heart, and he repenteth, and doeth no more evil, but doeth good lavishly, and humbleth his own soul and putteth it to torture because it sinned. Thou seest then that repentance is great understanding.' 'It is on this account therefore, Sir,' say I, 'that I enquire everything accurately of thee; first, because I am a sinner; secondly, because I know not what deeds I must do that I may live, for my sins are many and various.' 'Thou shalt live,' saith he, 'if thou keep my commandments and walk in them; and whosoever shall hear these commandments and keep them, shall live unto God.'

3. 'I will still proceed, Sir,' say I, 'to ask a further question.' 'Speak on,' saith he. 'I have heard, Sir,' say I, 'from certain teachers, that there is no other repentance, save that which took place when we went down into the water and obtained remission of our former sins.' He saith to me; 'Thou hast well heard; for so it is. For he that hath received remission of sins ought no longer to sin, but to dwell in purity. But, since thou enquirest all things accurately, I will declare unto thee this also, so as to give no excuse to those who shall hereafter believe, or those who have already believed, on the Lord. For they that have already believed, or shall hereafter believe, have not repentance for sins, but have only remission of their former sins. To those then that were called before these days the Lord has appointed repentance. For the Lord, being a discerner of hearts and foreknowing all things, perceived the weakness of men and the manifold wiles of the devil, how that he will be doing some mischief to the servants of God, and will deal wickedly with them. The Lord then, being very compassionate, had pity on His handiwork, and appointed this (opportunity of) repentance, and to me was given the authority over this repentance. But I say unto you,' saith he, 'if after this great and holy calling any one, being tempted of the devil, shall commit sin, he hath only one (opportunity of) repentance. But if he sin off-hand and repent, repentance is unprofitable for such a man; for he shall live with difficulty.' I say unto him, 'I was quickened into life again, when I heard these things from thee so precisely. For I know that, if I shall add no more to my sins, I shall be saved.' 'Thou shalt be saved,' he saith, 'thou and all, as many as shall do these things.'

4. I asked him again, saying, 'Sir, since once thou dost bear with me, declare unto me this further matter also.' 'Say on,' saith he. 'If a wife, Sir,' say I, 'or, it may be, a husband fall asleep, and one of them marry, doth the one that marrieth sin?' 'He sinneth not,' saith he, 'but if he remain single, he investeth himself with more exceeding honour

and with great glory before the Lord; yet even if he should marry, he sinneth not. Preserve purity and holiness therefore, and thou shalt live unto God. All these things, which I speak and shall hereafter speak unto thee, guard from this time forward, from the day when thou wast committed unto me, and I will dwell in thy house. But for thy former transgressions there shall be remission, if thou keepest my commandments. Yea, and all shall have remission, if they keep these my commandments, and walk in this purity.'

MANDATE THE FIFTH

1. 'Be thou long-suffering and understanding,' he saith, 'and thou shalt have the mastery over all evil deeds, and shalt work all righteousness. For if thou art long-suffering, the Holy Spirit that abideth in thee shall be pure, not being darkened by another evil spirit, but dwelling in a large room shall rejoice and be glad with the vessel in which he dwelleth, and shall serve God with much cheerfulness, having prosperity in himself. But if any angry temper approach, forthwith the Holy Spirit, being delicate, is straitened, not having [the] place clear, and seeketh to retire from the place; for he is being choked by the evil spirit, and has no room to minister unto the Lord, as he desireth, being polluted by angry temper. For the Lord dwelleth in long-suffering, but the devil in angry temper. Thus that both the spirits then should be dwelling together is inconvenient and evil for that man in whom they dwell. For if you take a little wormwood, and pour it into a jar of honey, is not the whole of the honey spoiled, and all that honey ruined by a very small quantity of wormwood? For it destroyeth the sweetness of the honey, and it no longer hath the same attraction for the owner, because it is rendered bitter and hath lost its use. But if the wormwood be not put into the honey, the honey is found sweet and becomes useful to its owner. Thou seest [then] that long-suffering is very sweet, beyond the sweetness of honey, and is useful to the Lord, and He dwelleth in it. But angry temper is bitter and useless. If then angry temper be mixed with long-suffering, long-suffering is polluted and the man's intercession is no longer useful to God.' 'I would fain know, Sir,' say I, 'the working of angry temper, that I may guard myself from it.' 'Yea, verily,' saith he, 'if thou guard not thyself from it—thou and thy family—thou hast lost all thy hope. But guard thyself from it; for I am with thee. Yea,

and all men shall hold aloof from it, as many as have repented with their whole heart. For I will be with them and will preserve them; for they all were justified by the most holy angel.

2. 'Hear now,' saith he, 'the working of angry temper, how evil it is, and how it subverteth the servants of God by its own working, and how it leadeth them astray from righteousness. But it doth not lead astray them that are full in the faith, nor can it work upon them, because the power of the Lord is with them; but them that are empty and double-minded it leadeth astray. For when it seeth such men in prosperity it insinuates itself into the heart of the man, and for no cause whatever the man or the woman is embittered on account of worldly matters, either about meats, or some triviality, or about some friend, or about giving or receiving, or about follies of this kind. For all these things are foolish and vain and senseless and inexpedient for the servants of God. But long-suffering is great and strong, and has a mighty and vigorous power, and is prosperous in great enlargement, gladsome, exultant, free from care, glorifying the Lord at every season, having no bitterness in itself, remaining always gentle and tranquil. This long-suffering therefore dwelleth with those whose faith is perfect. But angry temper is in the first place foolish, fickle and senseless; then from foolishness is engendered bitterness, and from bitterness wrath, and from wrath anger, and from anger spite; then spite being composed of all these evil elements becometh a great sin and incurable. For when all these spirits dwell in one vessel, where the Holy Spirit also dwelleth, that vessel cannot contain them, but overfloweth. The delicate spirit therefore, as not being accustomed to dwell with an evil spirit nor with harshness, departeth from a man of that kind, and seeketh to dwell with gentleness and tranquillity. Then, when it hath removed from that man, in whom it dwells, that man becometh emptied of the righteous spirit, and henceforward, being filled with the evil spirits, he is unstable in all his actions, being dragged about hither and thither by the evil spirits, and is altogether blinded and bereft of his good intent. Thus then it happeneth to all persons of angry temper. Refrain therefore from angry temper, the most evil of evil spirits. But clothe thyself in long-suffering, and resist angry temper and bitterness, and thou shalt be found in company with the holiness which is beloved of the Lord. See then that thou never neglect this commandment; for if thou master this commandment, thou shalt be able likewise to keep the remaining commandments, which I am about to give thee. Be strong in them and

endowed with power; and let all be endowed with power, as many as desire to walk in them.'

MANDATE THE SIXTH

1. ' I charged thee,' saith he, ' in my first commandment to guard faith and fear and temperance.' ' Yes, Sir,' say I. ' But now,' saith he, ' I wish to show thee their powers also, that thou mayest understand what is the power and effect of each one of them. For their effects are twofold. Now they are prescribed alike to the righteous and the unrighteous. Do thou therefore trust righteousness, but trust not unrighteousness; for the way of righteousness is straight, but the way of unrighteousness is crooked. But walk thou in the straight [and level] path, and leave the crooked one alone. For the crooked way has no tracks, but only pathlessness and many stumbling-stones, and is rough and thorny. So it is therefore harmful to those who walk in it. But those who walk in the straight way walk on the level and without stumbling: for it is neither rough nor thorny. Thou seest then that it is more expedient to walk in this way.' ' I am pleased, Sir,' say I, ' to walk in this way.' ' Thou shalt walk,' he saith, ' yea, and whosoever shall turn unto the Lord with his whole heart shall walk in it.

2. ' Hear now,' saith he, ' concerning faith. There are two angels with a man, one of righteousness and one of wickedness.' ' How then, Sir,' say I, ' shall I know their workings, seeing that both angels dwell with me?' ' Hear,' saith he, ' and understand their workings. The angel of righteousness is delicate and bashful and gentle and tranquil. When then this one enters into thy heart, forthwith he speaketh with thee of righteousness, of purity, of holiness, and of contentment, of every righteous deed and of every glorious virtue. When all these things enter into thy heart, know that the angel of righteousness is with thee. [These then are the works of the angel of righteousness.] Trust him therefore and his works. Now see the works of the angel of wickedness also. First of all, he is quick-tempered and bitter and senseless, and his works are evil, overthrowing the servants of God. Whenever then he entereth into thy heart, know him by his works.' ' How I shall discern him, Sir,' I reply, ' I know not.' ' Listen,' saith he. ' When a fit of angry temper or bitterness comes upon thee, know that he is in thee. Then the desire of much business and the costliness of many viands and drinking bouts and of many drunken fits and of various

luxuries which are unseemly, and the desire of women, and avarice, and haughtiness and boastfulness, and whatsoever things are akin and like to these—when then these things enter into thy heart, know that the angel of wickedness is with thee. Do thou therefore, recognising his works, stand aloof from him, and trust him in nothing, for his works are evil and inexpedient for the servants of God. Here then thou hast the workings of both the angels. Understand them, and trust the angel of righteousness. But from the angel of wickedness stand aloof, for his teaching is evil in every matter ; for though one be a man of faith, and the desire of this angel enter into his heart, that man, or that woman, must commit some sin. And if again a man or a woman be exceedingly wicked, and the works of the angel of righteousness come into that man's heart, he must of necessity do something good. Thou seest then,' saith he, ' that it is good to follow the angel of righteousness, and to bid farewell to the angel of wickedness. This commandment declareth what concerneth faith, that thou mayest trust the works of the angel of righteousness, and doing them mayest live unto God. But believe that the works of the angel of wickedness are difficult ; so by not doing them thou shalt live unto God.'

MANDATE THE SEVENTH

' Fear the Lord,' saith he, ' and keep His commandments. So keeping the commandments of God thou shalt be powerful in every deed, and thy doing shall be incomparable. For whilst thou fearest the Lord, thou shalt do all things well. But this is the fear wherewith thou oughtest to be afraid, and thou shalt be saved. But fear not the devil ; for, if thou fear the Lord, thou shalt be master over the devil, for there is no power in him. [For] in whom is no power, neither is there fear of him ; but in whom power is glorious, of him is fear likewise. For every one that hath power hath fear, whereas he that hath no power is despised of all. But fear thou the works of the devil, for they are evil. While then thou fearest the Lord, thou wilt fear the works of the devil, and wilt not do them, but abstain from them. Fear therefore is of two kinds. If thou desire to do evil, fear the Lord, and thou shalt not do it. If again thou desire to do good, fear the Lord and thou shalt do it. Therefore the fear of the Lord is powerful and great and glorious. Fear the Lord then, and thou shalt live unto Him ; yea, and as many of them that keep His commandments as shall fear Him, shall live unto God.'   ' Wherefore, Sir,' say I, 'didst thou say concerning those that keep His commandments, "They shall live unto God"?' 'Because,' saith he, 'every creature feareth the Lord, but not every one keepeth His commandments. Those then that fear Him and keep His commandments, they have life unto God; but they that keep not His commandments have no life in them.'

Mandate the Eighth

'I told thee,' saith he, 'that the creatures of God are twofold; for temperance also is twofold. For in some things it is right to be temperate, but in other things it is not right.' 'Make known unto me, Sir,' say I, 'in what things it is right to be temperate, and in what things it is not right.' 'Listen,' saith he. 'Be temperate as to what is evil, and do it not; but be not temperate as to what is good, but do it. For if thou be temperate as to what is good, so as not to do it, thou committest a great sin; but if thou be temperate as to what is evil, so as not to do it, thou doest great righteousness. Be temperate therefore in abstaining from all wickedness, and do that which is good.' 'What kinds of wickedness, Sir,' say I, 'are they from which we must be temperate and abstain?' 'Listen,' saith he; 'from adultery and fornication, from the lawlessness of drunkenness, from wicked luxury, from many viands and the costliness of riches, and vaunting and haughtiness and pride, and from falsehood and evil-speaking and hypocrisy, malice and all blasphemy. These works are the most wicked of all in the life of men. From these works therefore the servant of God must be temperate and abstain; for he that is not temperate so as to abstain from these cannot live unto God. Listen then to what follows upon these.' 'Why, are there still other evil deeds, Sir?' say I. 'Aye,' saith he, 'there are many, from which the servant of God must be temperate and abstain; theft, falsehood, deprivation, false witness, avarice, evil desire, deceit, vain-glory, boastfulness, and whatsoever things are like unto these. Thinkest thou not that these things are wrong, yea, very wrong,' [saith he,] 'for the servants of God? In all these things he that serveth God must exercise temperance. Be thou temperate, therefore, and refrain from all these things, that thou mayest live unto God, and be enrolled among those who exercise self-restraint in them. These then are the things from which thou shouldest restrain thyself. Now hear,' saith he, 'the things, in which thou shouldest not exercise self-restraint, but do them. Exercise no self-restraint in that which is good, but do it.' 'Sir,' say I, 'show me the power of the good also, that I may walk in them and serve them, that doing them it may be possible for me to be saved.' 'Hear,' saith he, 'the works of the good likewise, which thou must do, and towards which thou must exercise no self-restraint. First of all, there is faith, fear of the Lord, love, concord, words of righteousness, truth, patience; nothing is better than these in the life of men. If a man keep these, and exercise not self-restraint from them, he becomes blessed in his life. Hear now what follow upon these; to minister to widows, to visit the orphans and the needy, to ransom the servants of God from their afflictions, to be hospitable (for in hospitality benevolence from time to time has a place), to resist no man, to be tranquil, to show yourself more submissive than all men, to reverence the aged, to practise righteousness, to observe brotherly feeling, to endure injury, to be long-suffering, to bear no grudge, to exhort those who are sick at soul, not to cast away those that have stumbled from the faith, but to convert them and to put courage into them, to reprove sinners, not to oppress debtors and indigent persons, and whatsoever actions are like these. Do these things,' saith he, 'seem to thee to be good?' 'Why, what, Sir,' say I, 'can be better than these?' 'Then walk in them,' saith he, 'and abstain not from them, and thou shalt live unto God. Keep this commandment therefore. If thou do good and abstain not from it, thou shalt live unto God; yea, and all shall live unto God who act so. And again if thou do not evil, and abstain from it, thou shalt live unto God; yea, and all shall live unto God, who shall keep these commandments, and walk in them.'

MANDATE THE NINTH

He saith to me; 'Remove from thyself a doubtful mind and doubt not at all whether to ask of God, saying within thyself, " How can I ask a thing of the Lord and receive it, seeing that I have committed so many sins against Him?" Reason not thus, but turn to the Lord with thy whole heart, and ask of Him nothing wavering, and thou shalt know His exceeding compassion, that He will surely not abandon thee, but will fulfil the petition of thy soul. For God is not as men who bear a grudge, but Himself is without malice and hath compassion on His creatures. Do thou therefore cleanse thy heart from all the vanities of this life, and from the things mentioned before; and ask of the Lord, and thou shalt receive all things, and shalt lack nothing of all thy petitions, if thou ask of the Lord nothing wavering. But if thou waver in thy heart, thou shalt surely receive none of thy petitions. For they that waver towards God, these are the doubtful-minded, and they never obtain any of their petitions. But they that are complete in the faith make all their petitions trusting in the Lord, and they receive, because they ask without wavering, nothing doubting; for every doubtful-minded man, if he repent not, shall hardly be saved. Cleanse therefore thy heart from doubtful-mindedness, and put on faith, for it is strong, and trust God that thou wilt receive all thy petitions which thou askest; and if after asking anything of the Lord, thou receive thy petition somewhat tardily, be not of doubtful mind because thou didst not receive the petition of thy soul at once. For assuredly it is by reason of some temptation or some transgression, of which thou art ignorant, that thou receivest thy petition so tardily. Do thou therefore cease not to make thy soul's petition, and thou shalt receive it. But if thou grow weary, and doubt as thou askest, blame thyself and not Him that giveth unto thee. See to this doubtful-mindedness; for it is evil and senseless, and uprooteth many from the faith, yea, even very faithful and strong men. For indeed this doubtful-mindedness is a daughter of the devil, and worketh great wickedness against the servants of God. Therefore despise doubtful-mindedness and gain the mastery over it in everything, clothing thyself with faith which is strong and powerful. For faith promiseth all things, accomplisheth all things; but doubtful-mindedness, as having no confidence in itself, fails in all the works which it doeth. Thou seest then,' saith he, 'that faith is from above from the Lord, and hath great power; but doubtful-mindedness is an earthly spirit from the devil, and hath no power. Do thou therefore serve that faith which hath power, and hold aloof from the doubtful-mindedness which hath no power; and thou shalt live unto God; yea, and all those shall live unto God who are so minded.'

MANDATE THE TENTH

1. 'Put away sorrow from thyself,' saith he, 'for she is the sister of doubtful-mindedness and of angry temper.' 'How, Sir,' say I, 'is she the sister of these? For angry temper seems to me to be one thing, doubtful-mindedness another, sorrow another.' 'Thou art a foolish fellow,' saith he, '[and] perceivest not that sorrow is more evil than all the spirits, and is most fatal to the servants of God, and beyond all the spirits destroys a man, and crushes out the Holy Spirit, and yet again saves it.' 'I, Sir,' say I, 'am without understanding, and I understand

not these parables. For how it can crush out and again save, I do not comprehend.' 'Listen,' saith he. 'Those who have never investigated concerning the truth, nor enquired concerning the deity, but have merely believed, and have been mixed up in business affairs and riches and heathen friendships, and many other affairs of this world—as many, I say, as devote themselves to these things, comprehend not the parables of the deity; for they are darkened by these actions, and are corrupted and become barren. As good vineyards, when they are treated with neglect, are made barren by the thorns and weeds of various kinds, so men who after they have believed fall into these many occupations which were mentioned before, lose their understanding and comprehend nothing at all concerning righteousness; for if they hear concerning the deity and truth, their mind is absorbed in their occupations, and they perceive nothing at all. But they that have the fear of God, and investigate concerning deity and truth, and direct their heart towards the Lord, perceive and understand everything that is said to them more quickly, because they have the fear of the Lord in themselves; for where the Lord dwelleth, there too is great understanding. Cleave therefore unto the Lord, and thou shalt understand and perceive all things.

2. 'Hear now, senseless man,' saith he, 'how sorrow crusheth out the Holy Spirit, and again saveth it. When the man of doubtful mind sets his hand to any action, and fails in it owing to his doubtful-mindedness, grief at this entereth into the man, and grieveth the Holy Spirit, and crusheth it out. Then again when angry temper cleaveth to a man concerning any matter, and he is much embittered, again sorrow entereth into the heart of the man that was ill-tempered, and he is grieved at the deed which he hath done, and repenteth that he did evil. This sadness therefore seemeth to bring salvation, because he repented at having done the evil. So both the operations sadden the Spirit; first, the doubtful mind saddens the Spirit, because it succeeded not in its business, and the angry temper again, because it did what was evil. Thus both are saddening to the Holy Spirit, the doubtful mind and the angry temper. Put away therefore from thyself sadness, and afflict not the Holy Spirit that dwelleth in thee, lest haply He intercede with God [against thee], and depart from thee. For the Spirit of God, that was given unto this flesh, endureth not sadness neither constraint.

3. 'Therefore clothe thyself in cheerfulness, which hath favour with God always, and is acceptable to Him, and rejoice in it. For every

cheerful man worketh good, and thinketh good, and despiseth sadness ; but the sad man is always committing sin.   In the first place he committeth sin, because he grieveth the Holy Spirit, which was given to the man being a cheerful spirit; and in the second place, by grieving the Holy Spirit he doeth lawlessness, in that he doth not intercede with neither confess unto God.   For the intercession of a sad man hath never at any time power to ascend to the altar of God.'   'Wherefore,' say I, 'doth not the intercession of him that is saddened ascend to the altar?'   'Because,' saith he, 'sadness is seated at his heart. Thus sadness mingled with the intercession doth not suffer the intercession to ascend pure to the altar.   For as vinegar when mingled with wine in the same (vessel) hath not the same pleasant taste, so likewise sadness mingled with the Holy Spirit hath not the same intercession. Therefore cleanse thyself from this wicked sadness, and thou shalt live unto God ; yea, and all they shall live unto God, who shall cast away sadness from themselves and clothe themselves in all cheerfulness.'

MANDATE THE ELEVENTH

He shewed me men seated on a couch, and another man seated on a chair.   And he saith to me, 'Seest thou those that are seated on the couch?'   'I see them, Sir,' say I.   'These,' saith he, 'are faithful, but he that sitteth on the chair is a false prophet who destroyeth the mind of the servants of God—I mean, of the doubtful-minded, not of the faithful.   These doubtful-minded ones then come to him as to a soothsayer and enquire of him what shall befall them.   And he, the false prophet, having no power of a divine Spirit in himself, speaketh with them according to their enquiries [and according to the lusts of their wickedness], and filleth their souls as they themselves wish.   For being empty himself he giveth empty answers to empty enquirers ; for whatever enquiry may be made of him, he answereth according to the emptiness of the man.   But he speaketh also some true words ; for the devil filleth him with his own spirit, if so be he shall be able to break down some of the righteous.   So many therefore as are strong in the faith of the Lord, clothed with the truth, cleave not to such spirits, but hold aloof from them ; but as many as are doubters and frequently change their minds, practise soothsaying like the Gentiles, and bring upon themselves greater sin by their idolatries.   For he that consulteth a false prophet on any matter is an idolater and emptied of the truth, and senseless.   For no Spirit given of God needeth to be consulted ; but, having the power of deity, speaketh all things of itself, because it is from above, even from the power of the divine Spirit. But the spirit which is consulted, and speaketh according to the desires of men, is earthly and fickle, having no power; and it speaketh not at all, unless it be consulted.' 'How then, Sir,' say I, 'shall a man know who of them is a prophet, and who a false prophet?' 'Hear,' saith he, 'concerning both the prophets; and, as I shall tell thee, so shalt thou test the prophet and the false prophet. By his life test the man that hath the divine Spirit. In the first place, he that hath the [divine] Spirit, which is from above, is gentle and tranquil and humble-minded, and abstaineth from all wickedness and vain desire of this present world, and holdeth himself inferior to all men, and giveth no answer to any man when enquired of, nor speaketh in solitude (for neither doth the Holy Spirit speak when a man wisheth Him to speak); but the man speaketh then when God wisheth him to speak. When then the man who hath the divine Spirit cometh into an assembly of righteous men, who have faith in a divine Spirit, and intercession is made to God by the gathering of those men, then the angel of the prophetic spirit, who is attached to him, filleth the man, and the man, being filled with the Holy Spirit, speaketh to the multitude, according as the Lord willeth. In this way then the Spirit of the deity shall be manifest. This then is the greatness of the power as touching the Spirit of the deity of the Lord. Hear now,' saith he, 'concerning the earthly and vain spirit, which hath no power but is foolish. In the first place, that man who seemeth to have a spirit exalteth himself, and desireth to have a chief place, and straight-way he is impudent and shameless and talkative and conversant in many luxuries and in many other deceits, and receiveth money for his prophesying, and if he receiveth not, he prophesieth not. Now can a divine Spirit receive money and prophesy? It is not possible for a prophet of God to do this, but the spirit of such prophets is earthly. In the next place, it never approacheth an assembly of righteous men; but avoideth them, and cleaveth to the doubtful-minded and empty, and prophesieth to them in corners, and deceiveth them, speaking all things in emptiness to gratify their desires; for they too are empty whom it answereth. For the empty vessel placed together with the empty is not broken, but they agree one with the other. But when he comes into an assembly full of righteous men who have a Spirit of deity, and intercession is made from them, that man is emptied, and the earthly spirit fleeth from him in fear, and that man is struck dumb and is altogether broken in pieces, being unable to utter a word. For, if you pack wine or oil into a closet, and place an empty vessel among them, and again desire to unpack the closet, the vessel which you placed there empty, empty in like manner you will find it. Thus also the empty prophets, whenever they come unto the spirits of righteous men, are found just such as they came. I have given thee the life of both kinds of prophets. Therefore test, by his life and his works, the man who says that he is moved by the Spirit. But do thou trust the Spirit that cometh from God, and hath power; but in the earthly and empty spirit put no trust at all; for in it there is no power, for it cometh from the devil. Listen [then] to the parable which I shall tell thee. Take a stone, and throw it up to heaven—see if thou canst reach it; or again, take a squirt of water, and squirt it up to heaven—see if thou canst bore through the heaven.' 'How, Sir,' say I, 'can these things be? For both these things which thou hast mentioned are beyond our power.' 'Well then,' saith he, 'just as these things are beyond our power, so likewise the earthly spirits have no power and are feeble. Now take the power which cometh from above. The hail is a very small grain, and yet, when it falleth on a man's head, what pain it causeth! Or again, take a drop which falls on the ground from the tiles, and bores through the stone. Thou seest then that the smallest things from above falling on the earth have great power. So likewise the divine Spirit coming from above is powerful. This Spirit therefore trust, but from the other hold aloof.'

MANDATE THE TWELFTH

1. He saith to me; 'Remove from thyself all evil desire, and clothe thyself in the desire which is good and holy; for clothed with this desire thou shalt hate the evil desire, and shalt bridle and direct it as thou wilt. For the evil desire is wild, and only tamed with difficulty; for it is terrible, and by its wildness is very costly to men; more especially if a servant of God get entangled in it, and have no understanding, he is put to fearful costs by it. But it is costly to such men as are not clothed in the good desire, but are mixed up with this life. These men then it hands over to death.' 'Of what sort, Sir,' say I, 'are the works of the evil desire, which hand over men to death? Make them known to me, that I may hold aloof from them.' 'Listen,' [saith he,] 'through what works the evil desire bringeth death to the servants of God.

2. 'Before all is desire for the wife or husband of another, and for
extravagance of wealth, and for many needless dainties, and for drinks
and other luxuries, many and foolish. For every luxury is foolish and
vain for the servants of God. These desires then are evil, and bring
death to the servants of God. For this evil desire is a daughter of the
devil. Ye must, therefore, abstain from the evil desires, that so abstaining
ye may live unto God. But as many as are mastered by them, and resist
them not, are done to death utterly ; for these desires are deadly. But
do thou clothe thyself in the desire of righteousness, and, having armed
thyself with the fear of the Lord, resist them. For the fear of God
dwelleth in the good desire. If the evil desire shall see thee armed
with the fear of God and resisting itself, it shall flee far from thee, and
shall no more be seen of thee, being in fear of thine arms. Do thou
therefore, when thou art crowned for thy victory over it, come to the
desire of righteousness, and deliver to her the victor's prize which thou
hast received, and serve her, according as she herself desireth. If thou
serve the good desire, and art subject to her, thou shalt have power to
master the evil desire, and to subject her, according as thou wilt.'

3. 'I would fain know, Sir,' say I, 'in what ways I ought to serve
the good desire.' 'Listen,' saith he; 'practise righteousness and virtue,
truth and the fear of the Lord, faith and gentleness, and as many good
deeds as are like these. Practising these thou shalt be well-pleasing as
a servant of God, and shalt live unto Him ; yea, and every one who
shall serve the good desire shall live unto God.'

So he completed the twelve commandments, and he saith to me ;
'Thou hast these commandments ; walk in them, and exhort thy hearers
that their repentance may become pure for the rest of the days of their
life. This ministration, which I give thee, fulfil thou with all diligence
to the end, and thou shalt effect much. For thou shalt find favour
among those who are about to repent, and they shall obey thy words.
For I will be with thee, and will compel them to obey thee.'

I say to him ; 'Sir, these commandments are great and beautiful
and glorious, and are able *to gladden the heart of* the *man* who is able
to observe them. But I know not whether these commandments can
be kept by a man, for they are very hard.' He answered and said unto
me ; 'If thou set it before thyself that they can be kept, thou wilt
easily keep them, and they will not be hard ; but if it once enter into
thy heart that they cannot be kept by a man, thou wilt not keep them.
But now I say unto thee; if thou keep them not, but neglect them,

thou shalt not have salvation, neither thy children nor thy household, since thou hast already pronounced judgment against thyself that these commandments cannot be kept by a man.'

4. And these things he said to me very angrily, so that I was confounded, and feared him exceedingly ; for his form was changed, so that a man could not endure his anger. And when he saw that I was altogether disturbed and confounded, he began to speak more kindly [and cheerfully] to me, and he saith; 'Foolish fellow, void of understanding and of doubtful mind, perceivest thou not the glory of God, how great and mighty and marvellous it is, how that He created the world for man's sake, and subjected all His creation to man, and gave all authority to him, that he should be master over all things under the heaven ? If then,' [he saith,] 'man is lord of all the creatures of God and mastereth all things, cannot he also master these commandments ? Aye,' saith he, 'the man that hath the Lord in his heart can master [all things and] all these commandments. But they that have the Lord on their lips, while their heart is hardened, and are far from the Lord, to them these commandments are hard and inaccessible. Therefore do ye, who are empty and fickle in the faith, set your Lord in your heart, and ye shall perceive that nothing is easier than these commandments, nor sweeter, nor more gentle. Be ye converted, ye that walk after the commandments of the devil, (the commandments which are so) difficult and bitter and wild and riotous ; and fear not the devil, for there is no power in him against you. For I will be with you, I, the angel of repentance, who have the mastery over him. The devil hath fear alone, but his fear hath no force. Fear him not therefore ; and he will flee from you.'

5. I say to him, 'Sir, listen to a few words from me.' 'Say what thou wilt,' saith he. 'Man, Sir,' I say, 'is eager to keep the commandments of God, and there is no one that asketh not of the Lord, that he may be strengthened in His commandments, and be subject to them ; but the devil is hard and overmastereth them.' 'He cannot,' saith he, 'overmaster the servants of God, who set their hope on Him with their whole heart. The devil can wrestle with them, but he cannot overthrow them. If then ye resist him, he will be vanquished, and will flee from you disgraced. But as many,' saith he, 'as are utterly empty, fear the devil as if he had power. When a man has filled amply sufficient jars with good wine, and among these jars a few are quite empty, he comes to the jars, and does not examine the full

ones, for he knows that they are full ; but he examineth the empty ones, fearing lest they have turned sour. For empty jars soon turn sour, and the taste of the wine is spoilt. So also the devil cometh to all the servants of God tempting them. As many then as are complete in the faith, oppose him mightily, and he departeth from them, not having a place where he can find an entrance. So he cometh next to the empty ones, and finding a place goeth into them, and further he doeth what he willeth in them, and they become submissive slaves to him.

6. 'But I, the angel of repentance, say unto you ; Fear not the devil ; for I was sent,' saith he, 'to be with you who repent with your whole heart, and to strengthen you in the faith. Believe, therefore, on God, ye who by reason of your sins have despaired of your life, and are adding to your sins, and weighing down your life ; for if ye turn unto the Lord with your whole heart, and work righteousness the remaining days of your life, and serve Him rightly according to His will, He will give healing to your former sins, and ye shall have power to master the works of the devil.. But of the threatening of the devil fear not at all ; for he is unstrung, like the sinews of a dead man. Hear me therefore, and fear Him, *Who is able* to do all things, *to save and to destroy*, and observe these commandments, and ye shall live unto God.' I say to him, 'Sir, now am I strengthened in all the ordinances of the Lord, because thou art with me ; and I know that thou wilt crush all the power of the devil, and we shall be masters over him, and shall prevail over all his works. And I hope, Sir, that I am now able to keep these commandments which thou hast commanded, the Lord enabling me.' 'Thou shalt keep them,' saith he, 'if thy heart be found pure with the Lord ; yea, and all shall keep them, as many as shall purify their hearts from the vain desires of this world, and shall live unto God.'

PARABLES WHICH HE SPAKE WITH ME.

He saith to me ; 'Ye know that ye, who are the servants of God, are dwelling in a foreign land ; for your city is far from this city. If then ye know your city, in which ye shall dwell, why do ye here prepare fields and expensive displays and buildings and dwelling-chambers which are superfluous? He, therefore, that prepareth these things for this city does not purpose to return to his own city. O foolish and double-minded and miserable man, perceivest thou not that all these things are foreign, and are under the power of another? For the lord of this city shall say, " I do not wish thee to dwell in my city; go forth from this city, for thou dost not conform to my laws." Thou, therefore, who hast fields and dwellings and many other possessions, when thou art cast out by him, what wilt thou do with thy field and thy house and all the other things that thou preparedst for thyself? For the lord of this country saith to thee justly, " Either conform to my laws, or depart from my country." What then shalt thou do, who art under law in thine own city? For the sake of thy fields and the rest of thy possessions wilt thou altogether repudiate thy law, and walk according to the law of this city? Take heed, lest it be inexpedient to repudiate thy law; for if thou shouldest desire to return again to thy city, thou shalt surely not be received [because thou didst repudiate the law of thy city], and shalt be shut out from it. Take heed therefore; as dwelling in a strange land prepare nothing more for thyself but a competency which is sufficient for thee, and make ready that, whensoever the master of this city may desire to cast thee out for thine opposition to his law, thou mayest go forth from his city and depart into thine own city, and use thine own law joyfully, free from all insult. Take heed therefore, ye that serve God and have Him in your heart : work the works of God being mindful of His commandments and of the promises which He made, and believe Him that He will perform them, if His commandments be kept. Therefore, instead of fields buy ye souls that are in trouble, as each is able, and visit widows and orphans, and neglect them not; and spend your riches and all your displays, which ye received from God, on fields and houses of this kind. For to this end the Master enriched you, that ye might perform these ministrations for Him. It is much better to purchase fields [and possessions] and houses of this kind, which thou wilt find in thine own city, when thou visitest it. This lavish expenditure is beautiful and joyous, not bringing sadness or fear, but bringing joy. The expenditure of the heathen then practise not ye; for it is not convenient for you the servants of God. But practise your own expenditure, in which ye can rejoice; and do not corrupt, neither touch that which is another man's, nor lust after it; for it is wicked to lust after other men's possessions. But perform thine own task, and thou shalt be saved.'

ANOTHER PARABLE

As I walked in the field, and noticed an elm and a vine, and was distinguishing them and their fruits, the shepherd appeareth to me and

saith; 'What art thou meditating within thyself?' 'I am thinking,
[Sir,]' say I, 'about the elm and the vine, that they are excellently
suited the one to the other.' 'These two trees,' saith he, 'are appointed
for a type to the servants of God.' 'I would fain know, [Sir,]' say I,
'the type contained in these trees, of which thou speakest.' 'Seest
thou,' saith he, 'the elm and the vine?' 'I see them, Sir,' say I. 'This
vine,' saith he, 'beareth fruit, but the elm is an unfruitful stock. Yet
this vine, except it climb up the elm, cannot bear much fruit when it is
spread on the ground; and such fruit as it beareth is rotten, because it is
not suspended upon the elm. When then the vine is attached to the elm,
it beareth fruit both from itself and from the elm. Thou seest then that
the elm also beareth [much] fruit, not less than the vine, but rather more.'
'How more, Sir?' say I. 'Because,' saith he, 'the vine, when hanging
upon the elm, bears its fruit in abundance, and in good condition; but,
when spread on the ground, it beareth little fruit, and that rotten.
This parable therefore is applicable to the servants of God, to poor
and to rich alike.' 'How, Sir?' say I; 'instruct me.' 'Listen,' saith he;
'the rich man hath much wealth, but in the things of the Lord he is
poor, being distracted about his riches, and his confession and intercession with the Lord is very scanty; and even that which he giveth is
small and weak and hath not power above. When then the rich man
goeth up to the poor, and assisteth him in his needs, believing that for
what he doth to the poor man he shall be able to obtain a reward with
God—because the poor man is rich in intercession [and confession],
and his intercession hath great power with God—the rich man then
supplieth all things to the poor man without wavering. But the poor
man being supplied by the rich maketh intercession for him, thanking
God for him that gave to him. And the other is still more zealous to
assist the poor man, that he may be continuous in his life: for he
knoweth that the intercession of the poor man is acceptable and rich
before God. They both then accomplish their work; the poor man
maketh intercession, wherein he is rich [which he received of the
Lord]; this he rendereth again to the Lord Who supplieth him with it.
The rich man too in like manner furnisheth to the poor man, nothing
doubting, the riches which he received from the Lord. And this work
is great and acceptable with God, because (the rich man) hath understanding concerning his riches, and worketh for the poor man from the
bounties of the Lord, and accomplisheth the ministration of the Lord
rightly. In the sight of men then the elm seemeth not to bear fruit,

and they know not, neither perceive, that if there cometh a drought, the elm having water nurtureth the vine, and the vine having a constant supply of water beareth fruit twofold, both for itself and for the elm. So likewise the poor, by interceding with the Lord for the rich, establish their riches, and again the rich, supplying their needs to the poor, establish their souls. So then both are made partners in the righteous work. He then that doeth these things shall not be abandoned of God, but shall be written in the books of the living. Blessed are the rich, who understand also that they are enriched from the Lord. For they that have this mind shall be able to do some good work.'

ANOTHER PARABLE

He showed me many trees which had no leaves, but they seemed to me to be, as it were, withered; for they were all alike. And he saith to me; 'Seest thou these trees?' 'I see them, Sir,' I say, 'they are all alike, and are withered.' He answered and said to me; 'These trees that thou seest are they that dwell in this world.' 'Wherefore then, Sir,' say I, 'are they as if they were withered, and alike?' 'Because,' saith he, 'neither the righteous are distinguishable, nor the sinners in this world, but they are alike. For this world is winter to the righteous, and they are not distinguishable, as they dwell with the sinners. For as in the winter the trees, having shed their leaves, are alike, and are not distinguishable, which are withered, and which alive, so also in this world neither the just nor the sinners are distinguishable, but they are all alike.'

ANOTHER PARABLE

He showed me many trees again, some of them sprouting, and others withered, and he saith to me; 'Seest thou,' saith he, 'these trees?' 'I see them, Sir,' say I, 'some of them sprouting, and others withered.' 'These trees,' saith he, 'that are sprouting are the righteous, who shall dwell in the world to come; for the world to come is summer to the righteous, but winter to the sinners. When then the mercy of the Lord shall shine forth, then they that serve God shall be made manifest; yea, and all men shall be made manifest. For as in summer the fruits of each several tree are made manifest, and are recognised of what sort they are, so also the fruits of the righteous shall be manifest, and all [even the very smallest] shall be known to be flourishing in that world. But the Gentiles and the sinners, just as thou sawest the trees which were withered, even such shall they be found, withered and unfruitful in that world, and shall be burnt up as fuel, and shall be manifest, because their practice in their life hath been evil. For the sinners shall be burned, because they sinned and repented not; and the Gentiles shall be burned, because they knew not Him that created them. Do thou therefore bear fruit, that in that summer thy fruit may be known. But abstain from overmuch business, and thou shalt never fall into any sin. For they that busy themselves overmuch, sin much also, being distracted about their business, and in no wise serving their own Lord. How then,' saith he, 'can such a man ask anything of the Lord and receive it, seeing that he serveth not the Lord? [For] they that serve Him, these shall receive their petitions, but they that serve not the Lord, these shall receive nothing. But if any one work one single action, he is able also to serve the Lord; for his mind shall not be corrupted from (following) the Lord, but he shall serve Him, because he keepeth his mind pure. If therefore thou doest these things, thou shalt be able to bear fruit unto the world to come; yea, and whosoever shall do these things, shall bear fruit.'

ANOTHER PARABLE

1. As I was fasting and seated on a certain mountain, and giving thanks to the Lord for all that He had done unto me, I see the shepherd seated by me and saying; 'Why hast thou come hither in the early morn?' 'Because, Sir,' say I, 'I am keeping a station.' 'What,' saith he, 'is a station?' 'I am fasting, Sir,' say I. 'And what,' saith he, 'is this fast [that ye are fasting]?' 'As I was accustomed, Sir,' say I, 'so I fast.' 'Ye know not,' saith he, 'how to fast unto the Lord, neither is this a fast, this unprofitable fast which ye make unto Him.' 'Wherefore, Sir,' say I, 'sayest thou this?' 'I tell thee,' saith he, 'that this is not a fast, wherein ye think to fast; but I will teach thee what is a complete fast and acceptable to the Lord. Listen,' saith he; 'God desireth not such a vain fast; for by so fasting unto God thou shalt do nothing for righteousness. But fast thou [unto God] such a fast as this; do no wickedness in thy life, and serve the Lord with a pure heart; observe His commandments and walk in His ordinances, and let no evil desire rise up in thy heart; but believe God. Then, if thou shalt do these things, and fear Him, and control thyself from every evil deed, thou shalt live unto God; and if thou do these things, thou shalt accomplish a great fast, and one acceptable to God.

2. 'Hear the parable which I shall tell thee relating to fasting. A certain man had an estate, and many slaves, and a portion of his estate he planted as a vineyard; and choosing out a certain slave who was trusty and well-pleasing (and) held in honour, he called him to him and saith unto him; "Take this vineyard [which I have planted], and fence it [till I come], but do nothing else to the vineyard. Now keep this my commandment, and thou shalt be free in my house." Then the master of the servant went away to travel abroad. When then he had gone away, the servant took and fenced the vineyard; and having finished the fencing of the vineyard, he noticed that the vineyard was full of weeds. So he reasoned within himself, saying, "This command of my lord I have carried out. I will next dig this vineyard, and it shall be neater when it is digged; and when it hath no weeds it will yield more fruit, because not choked by the weeds." He took and digged the vineyard, and all the weeds that were in the vineyard he plucked up. And that vineyard became very neat and flourishing, when it had no weeds to choke it. After a time the master of the servant [and of the estate] came, and he went into the vineyard. And seeing the vineyard fenced neatly, and digged as well, and [all] the weeds plucked up, and the vines flourishing, he rejoiced [exceedingly] at what his servant had done. So he called his beloved son, who was his heir, and the friends who were his advisers, and told them what he had commanded his servant, and how much he had found done. And they rejoiced with the servant at the testimony which his master had borne to him. And he saith to them; "I promised this servant his freedom, if he should keep the commandment which I commanded him; but he kept my commandment and did a good work besides to my vineyard, and pleased me greatly. For this work therefore which he has done, I desire to make him joint-heir with my son, because, when the good thought struck him, he did not neglect it, but fulfilled it." In this purpose the son of the master agreed with him, that the servant should be made joint-heir with the son. After some few days, his master made a feast, and sent to him many dainties from the feast. But when the servant received [the dainties sent to him by the master], he took what was sufficient for him, and distributed the rest to his fellow-servants. And his fellow-servants, when they received the dainties, rejoiced, and began to pray for him, that he might find greater favour with the master, because he had treated them so handsomely. All these things which had taken place his master heard, and again rejoiced greatly at his deed. So the master

called together again his friends and his son, and announced to them the deed that he had done with regard to his dainties which he had received; and they still more approved of his resolve, that his servant should be made joint-heir with his son.'

3. I say, 'Sir, I understand not these parables, neither can I apprehend them, unless thou explain them for me.' 'I will explain everything to thee,' saith he; 'and will show thee whatsoever things I shall speak with thee. Keep the commandments of the Lord, and thou shalt be well-pleasing to God, and shalt be enrolled among the number of them that keep His commandments. But if thou do any good thing outside the commandment of God, thou shalt win for thyself more exceeding glory, and shalt be more glorious in the sight of God than thou wouldest otherwise have been. If then, while thou keepest the commandments of God, thou add these services likewise, thou shalt rejoice, if thou observe them according to my commandment.' I say to him, 'Sir, whatsoever thou commandest me, I will keep it; for I know that thou art with me.' 'I will be with thee,' saith he, 'because thou hast so great zeal for doing good; yea, and I will be with all,' saith he, 'whosoever have such zeal as this. This fasting,' saith he, 'if the commandments of the Lord are kept, is very good. This then is the way, that thou shalt keep this fast [which thou art about to observe]. First of all, keep thyself from every evil word and every evil desire, and purify thy heart from all the vanities of this world. If thou keep these things, this fast shall be perfect for thee. And thus shalt thou do. Having fulfilled what is written, on that day on which thou fastest thou shalt taste nothing but bread and water; and from thy meats, which thou wouldest have eaten, thou shalt reckon up the amount of that day's expenditure, which thou wouldest have incurred, and shalt give it to a widow, or an orphan, or to one in want, and so shalt thou humble thy soul, that he that hath received from thy humiliation may satisfy his own soul, and may pray for thee to the Lord. If then thou shalt so accomplish this fast, as I have commanded thee, thy sacrifice shall be acceptable in the sight of God, and this fasting shall be recorded; and the service so performed is beautiful and joyous and acceptable to the Lord. These things thou shalt so observe, thou and thy children and thy whole household; and, observing them, thou shalt be blessed; yea, and all those, who shall hear and observe them, shall be blessed, and whatsoever things they shall ask of the Lord, they shall receive.'

4. I entreated him earnestly, that he would show me the parable

of the estate, and of the master, and of the vineyard, and of the servant that fenced the vineyard, [and of the fence,] and of the weeds which were plucked up out of the vineyard, and of the son, and of the friends, the advisers.   For I understood that all these things are a parable. But he answered and said unto me; 'Thou art exceedingly importunate in enquiries.   Thou oughtest not,' [saith he,] 'to make any enquiry at all; for if it be right that a thing be explained unto thee, it shall be explained.' I say to him; 'Sir, whatsoever things thou showest unto me and dost not explain, I shall have seen them in vain, and without understanding what they are.   In like manner also, if thou speak parables to me and interpret them not, I shall have heard a thing in vain from thee.'   But he again answered, and said unto me; 'Whosoever,' saith he, 'is a servant of God, and hath his own Lord in his heart, asketh understanding of Him, and receiveth it, and interpreteth every parable, and the words of the Lord which are spoken in parables are made known unto him.   But as many as are sluggish and idle in intercession, these hesitate to ask of the Lord.   But the Lord is abundant in compassion, and giveth to them that ask of Him without ceasing.   But thou who hast been strengthened by the holy angel, and hast received from him such (powers of) intercession and art not idle, wherefore dost thou not ask understanding of the Lord, and obtain it from Him?' I say to him, 'Sir, I that have thee with me have (but) need to ask thee and enquire of thee; for thou showest me all things, and speakest with me; but if I had seen or heard them apart from thee I should have asked of the Lord, that they might be shown to me.'

5.   'I told thee just now,' saith he, 'that thou art unscrupulous and importunate, in enquiring for the interpretations of the parables.   But since thou art so obstinate, I will interpret to thee the parable of the estate and all the accompaniments thereof, that thou mayest make them known unto all.   Hear now,' saith he, 'and understand them.   The estate is this world, and the lord of the estate is He that created all things, and set them in order, and endowed them with power; and the servant is the Son of God, and the vines are this people whom He Himself planted; and the fences are the [holy] angels of the Lord who keep together His people; and the weeds, which are plucked up from the vineyard, are the transgressions of the servants of God; and the dainties which He sent to him from the feast are the commandments which He gave to His people through His Son; and the friends and advisers are the holy angels which were first created; and the

absence of the master is the time which remaineth over until His coming.' I say to him; 'Sir, great and marvellous are all things and all things are glorious; was it likely then,' say I, 'that I could have apprehended them?' 'Nay, nor can any other man, though he be full of understanding, apprehend them.' 'Yet again, Sir,' say I, 'explain to me what I am about to enquire of thee.' 'Say on,' he saith, 'if thou desirest anything.' 'Wherefore, [Sir,]' say I, 'is the Son of God represented in the parable in the guise of a servant?'

6. 'Listen,' said he; 'the Son of God is not represented in the guise of a servant, but is represented in great power and lordship.' 'How, Sir?' say I; 'I comprehend not.' 'Because,' saith he, 'God planted the vineyard, that is, He created the people, and delivered them over to His Son. And the Son placed the angels in charge of them, to watch over them; and the Son Himself cleansed their sins, by labouring much and enduring many toils; for no one can dig without toil or labour. Having Himself then cleansed the sins of His people, He showed them the paths of life, giving them the law which He received from His Father. Thou seest,' saith he, 'that He is Himself Lord of the people, having received all power from His Father. But how that the lord took his son and the glorious angels as advisers concerning the inheritance of the servant, listen. The Holy Pre-existent Spirit, Which created the whole creation, God made to dwell in flesh that He desired. This flesh, therefore, in which the Holy Spirit dwelt, was subject unto the Spirit, walking honourably in holiness and purity, without in any way defiling the Spirit. When then it had lived honourably in chastity, and had laboured with the Spirit, and had cooperated with it in everything, behaving itself boldly and bravely, He chose it as a partner with the Holy Spirit; for the career of this flesh pleased [the Lord], seeing that, as possessing the Holy Spirit, it was not defiled upon the earth. He therefore took the son as adviser and the glorious angels also, that this flesh too, having served the Spirit unblameably, might have some place of sojourn, and might not seem to have lost the reward for its service; for all flesh, which is found undefiled and unspotted, wherein the Holy Spirit dwelt, shall receive a reward. Now thou hast the interpretation of this parable also.'

7. 'I was right glad, Sir,' say I, 'to hear this interpretation.' 'Listen now,' saith he. 'Keep this thy flesh pure and undefiled, that the Spirit which dwelleth in it may bear witness to it, and thy flesh may be justified. See that it never enter into thine heart that this flesh of

thine is perishable, and so thou abuse it in some defilement. [For] if thou defile thy flesh, thou shalt defile the Holy Spirit also; but if thou defile †the flesh†, thou shalt not live.' 'But if, Sir,' say I, 'there has been any ignorance in times past, before these words were heard, how shall a man who has defiled his flesh be saved?' 'For the former deeds of ignorance,' saith he, 'God alone hath power to give healing; for all authority is His. [But now keep thyself, and the Lord Almighty, Who is full of compassion, will give healing for thy former deeds of ignorance,] if henceforth thou defile not thy flesh, neither the Spirit; for both share in common, and the one cannot be defiled without the other. Therefore keep both pure, and thou shalt live unto God.'

[PARABLE THE SIXTH.]

1. As I sat in my house, and glorified the Lord for all things that I had seen, and was considering concerning the commandments, how that they were beautiful and powerful and gladsome and glorious and able to save a man's soul, I said within myself; 'Blessed shall I be, if I walk in these commandments; yea, and whosoever shall walk in them shall be blessed.' As I spake these things within myself, I see him suddenly seated by me, and saying as follows; 'Why art thou of a doubtful mind concerning the commandments, which I commanded thee? They are beautiful. Doubt not at all; but clothe thyself in the faith of the Lord, and thou shalt walk in them. For I will strengthen thee in them. These commandments are suitable for those who meditate repentance; for if they walk not in them, their repentance is in vain. Ye then that repent, cast away the evil doings of this world which crush you; and, by putting on every excellence of righteousness, ye shall be able to observe these commandments, and to add no more to your sins. If then ye add no further sin at all, ye will depart from your former sins. Walk then in these my commandments, and ye shall live unto God. These things have [all] been told you from me.' And after he had told these things to me, he saith to me, 'Let us go into the country, and I will show thee the shepherds of the sheep.' 'Let us go, Sir,' say I. And we came to a certain plain, and he showeth me a young man, a shepherd, clothed in a light cloak, of saffron colour; and he was feeding a great number of sheep, and these sheep were, as it were, well fed and very frisky, and were gladsome as they skipped about hither and thither; and the shepherd himself was all gladsome

over his flock; and the very visage of the shepherd was exceedingly gladsome; and he ran about among the sheep.

2. And he saith to me; 'Seest thou this shepherd?' 'I see him, Sir,' I say. 'This,' saith he, 'is the angel of self-indulgence and of deceit. He crusheth the souls of the servants of God, and perverteth them from the truth, leading them astray with evil desires, wherein they perish. For they forget the commandments of the living God, and walk in vain deceits and acts of self-indulgence, and are destroyed by this angel, some of them unto death, and others unto corruption.' I say to him, 'Sir, I comprehend not what means "unto death," and what "unto corruption".' 'Listen,' saith he; 'the sheep which thou sawest gladsome and skipping about, these are they who have been turned asunder from God utterly, and have delivered themselves over to the lusts of this world. In these, therefore, there is not repentance unto life. For the Name of God is being blasphemed through them. The life of such persons is death. But the sheep, which thou sawest not skipping about, but feeding in one place, these are they that have delivered themselves over to acts of self-indulgence and deceit, but have not uttered any blasphemy against the Lord. These then have been corrupted from the truth. In these there is hope of repentance, wherein they can live. Corruption then hath hope of a possible renewal, but death hath eternal destruction.' Again we went forward a little way, and he showeth me a great shepherd like a wild man in appearance, with a white goatskin thrown about him; and he had a kind of wallet on his shoulders, and a staff very hard and with knots in it, and a great whip. And his look was very sour, so that I was afraid of him because of his look. This shepherd then kept receiving from the young man, the shepherd, those sheep that were frisky and well-fed, but not skipping about, and putting them in a certain spot, which was precipitous and covered with thorns and briars, so that the sheep could not disentangle themselves from the thorns and briars, but [became entangled among the thorns and briars. And so they] pastured entangled in the thorns and briars, and were in great misery with being beaten by him; and he kept driving them about to and fro, and giving them no rest, and altogether those sheep had not a happy time.

3. When then I saw them so lashed with the whip and vexed, I was sorry for their sakes, because they were so tortured and had no rest at all. I say to the shepherd who was speaking with me; 'Sir, who is this shepherd, who is [so] hard-hearted and severe, and has no compassion

at all for these sheep?' 'This,' saith he, 'is the angel of punishment, and he is one of the just angels, and presides over punishment. So he receiveth those who wander away from God, and walk after the lusts and deceits of this life, and punisheth them, as they deserve, with fearful and various punishments.' 'I would fain learn, Sir,' say I, 'of what sort are these various punishments.' 'Listen,' saith he; 'the various tortures and punishments are tortures belonging to the present life; for some are punished with losses, and others with want, and others with divers maladies, and others with [every kind] of unsettlement, and others with insults from unworthy persons and with suffering in many other respects. For many, being unsettled in their plans, set their hands to many things, and nothing ever goes forward with them. And then they say that they do not prosper in their doings, and it doth not enter into their hearts that they have done evil deeds, but they blame the Lord. When then they are afflicted with every kind of affliction, then they are delivered over to me for good instruction, and are strengthened in the faith of the Lord, and serve the Lord with a pure heart the remaining days of their life. But, if they repent, the evil works which they have done rise up in their hearts, and then they glorify God, saying that He is a just Judge, and that they suffered justly each according to his doings. And they serve the Lord thenceforward with a pure heart, and are prosperous in all their doings, receiving from the Lord whatsoever things they may ask; and then they glorify the Lord because they were delivered over unto me, and they no longer suffer any evil thing.'

4. I say unto him; 'Sir, declare unto me this further matter.' 'What enquirest thou yet?' saith he. 'Whether, Sir,' say I, 'they that live in self-indulgence and are deceived undergo torments during the same length of time as they live in self-indulgence and are deceived.' He saith to me, 'They undergo torments for the same length of time.' 'Then, Sir,' say I, 'they undergo very slight torments; for those who are living thus in self-indulgence and forget God ought to have been tormented sevenfold.' He saith to me, 'Thou art foolish, and comprehendest not the power of the torment.' 'True,' say I, 'for if I had comprehended it, I should not have asked thee to declare it to me.' 'Listen,' saith he, 'to the power of both, [of the self-indulgence and of the torment]. The time of the self-indulgence and deceit is one hour. But an hour of the torment hath the power of thirty days. If then one live in self-indulgence and be deceived for one day, and be tormented for one day,

the day of the torment is equivalent to a whole year. For as many days then as a man lives in self-indulgence, for so many years is he tormented. Thou seest then,' saith he, 'that the time of the self-indulgence and deceit is very short, but the time of the punishment and torment is long.'

5. 'Inasmuch, Sir,' say I, 'as I do not quite comprehend concerning the time of the deceit and self-indulgence and torment, show me more clearly.' He answered and said unto me; 'Thy stupidity cleaveth to thee; and thou wilt not cleanse thy heart and serve God. Take heed,' [saith he,] 'lest haply the time be fulfilled, and thou be found in thy foolishness. Listen then,' [saith he,] 'even as thou wishest, that thou mayest comprehend the matter. He that liveth in self-indulgence and is deceived for one day, and doeth what he wisheth, is clothed in much folly and comprehendeth not the thing which he doeth; for on the morrow he forgetteth what he did the day before. For self-indulgence and deceit have no memories, by reason of the folly, wherewith each is clothed; but when punishment and torment cling to a man for a single day, he is punished and tormented for a whole year long; for punishment and torment have long memories. So being tormented and punished for the whole year, the man remembers at length the self-indulgence and deceit, and perceiveth that it is on their account that he is suffering these ills. Every man, therefore, that liveth in self-indulgence and is deceived, is tormented in this way because, though possessing life, they have delivered themselves over unto death.' 'What kinds of self-indulgence, Sir,' say I, 'are harmful?' 'Every action,' saith he, 'is self-indulgence to a man, which he does with pleasure; for the irascible man, when he gives the reins to his passion, is self-indulgent; and the adulterer and the drunkard and the slanderer and the liar and the miser and the defrauder and he that doeth things akin to these, giveth the reins to his peculiar passion; therefore he is self-indulgent in his action. All these habits of self-indulgence are harmful to the servants of God; on account of these deceits therefore they so suffer who are punished and tormented. But there are habits of self-indulgence likewise which save men; for many are self-indulgent in doing good, being carried away by the pleasure it gives to themselves. This self-indulgence then is expedient for the servants of God, and bringeth life to a man of this disposition; but the harmful self-indulgencies afore-mentioned bring to men torments and punishments; and if they continue in them and repent not, they bring death upon themselves.'

[PARABLE THE SEVENTH.]

After a few days I saw him on the same plain, where also I had seen the shepherds, and he saith to me, 'What seekest thou?' 'I am here, Sir,' say I, 'that thou mayest bid the shepherd that punisheth go out of my house; for he afflicteth me much.' 'It is necessary for thee,' saith he, 'to be afflicted; for so,' saith he, 'the glorious angel ordered as concerning thee, for he wisheth thee to be proved.' 'Why, what so evil thing have I done, Sir,' say I, 'that I should be delivered over to this angel?' 'Listen,' saith he. 'Thy sins are many, yet not so many that thou shouldest be delivered over to this angel; but thy house has committed great iniquities and sins, and the glorious angel was embittered at their deeds, and for this cause he bade thee be afflicted for a certain time, that they also might repent and cleanse themselves from every lust of this world. When therefore they shall repent and be cleansed, then shall the angel of punishment depart.' I say to him; 'Sir, if they perpetrated such deeds that the glorious angel is embittered, what have I done?' 'They cannot be afflicted otherwise,' saith he, 'unless thou, the head of the [whole] house, be afflicted; for if thou be afflicted, they also of necessity will be afflicted; but if thou be prosperous, they can suffer no affliction.' 'But behold, Sir,' say I, 'they have repented with their whole heart.' 'I am quite aware myself,' saith he, 'that they have repented with their whole heart; well, thinkest thou that the sins of those who repent are forgiven forthwith? Certainly not; but the person who repents must torture his own soul, and must be thoroughly humble in his every action, and be afflicted with all the divers kinds of affliction; and if he endure the afflictions which come upon him, assuredly He Who created all things and endowed them with power will be moved with compassion and will bestow some remedy. And this (will God do), if in any way He perceive the heart of the penitent pure from every evil thing. But it is expedient for thee and for thy house that thou shouldest be afflicted now. But why speak I many words to thee? Thou must be afflicted as the angel of the Lord commanded, even he that delivered thee unto me; and for this give thanks to the Lord, in that He deemed thee worthy that I should reveal unto thee beforehand the affliction, that foreknowing it thou mightest endure it with fortitude.' I say to him; 'Sir, be thou with me, and I shall be able to endure all affliction [easily].' 'I will be with thee,' saith he; 'and I will ask the angel that punisheth to afflict thee more lightly; but thou shalt be afflicted for a short time, and thou shalt be' restored

again to thy house. Only continue to be humble and to minister unto
the Lord with a pure heart, thou and thy children and thy house, and
walk in my commandments which I command thee, and thus it will be
possible for thy repentance to be strong and pure. And if thou keep
these commandments with thy household, all affliction shall hold aloof
from thee; yea, and affliction,' saith he, ' shall hold aloof from all whosoever shall walk in these my commandments.'

[PARABLE THE EIGHTH.]

1. He showed me a [great] willow, overshadowing plains and
mountains, and under the shadow of the willow all have come who
are called by the name of the Lord. And by the willow there stood
an angel of the Lord, glorious and very tall, having a great sickle, and
he was lopping branches from the willow, and giving them to the people
that sheltered beneath the willow; and he gave them little rods about
a cubit long. And after all had taken the rods, the angel laid aside
the sickle, and the tree was sound, just as I had seen it. Then I
marvelled within myself, saying, ' How is the tree sound after so many
branches have been lopped off?' The shepherd saith to me, ' Marvel
not that the tree remained sound, after so many branches were lopped
off; but wait until thou seest all things, and it shall be shown to thee
what it is.' The angel who gave the rods to the people demanded
them back from them again; and according as they had received
them, so also they were summoned to him, and each of them returned
the several rods. But the angel of the Lord took them, and examined
them. From some he received the rods withered and eaten as it were
by grubs: the angel ordered those who gave up rods like these to
stand apart. And others gave them up withered, but not grub-eaten; and
these again he ordered to stand apart. And others gave them up half-
withered; these also stood apart. And others gave up their rods half-
withered and with cracks; these also stood apart. And others gave up
their rods green and with cracks; these also stood apart. And others
gave up their rods one half withered and one half green; these also stood
apart. And others brought their rods two parts of the rod green, and
the third part withered; these also stood apart. And others gave them
up two parts withered, and the third part green; these also stood apart.
And others gave up their rods nearly all green, but a very small portion
of their rods was withered, just the end; but they had cracks in them;
these also stood apart. And in those of others there was a very small

portion green, but the rest of the rods was withered; these also stood apart. And others came bringing their rods green, as they received them from the angel; and the most part of the multitude gave up their rods in this state; and the angel rejoiced exceedingly at these; these also stood apart. And others gave up their rods green and with shoots; these also stood apart; and at these again the angel rejoiced exceedingly. And others gave up their rods green and with shoots; and their shoots had, as it were, a kind of fruit. And those men were exceeding gladsome, whose rods were found in this state. And over them the angel exulted, and the shepherd was very gladsome over them.

2. And the angel of the Lord commanded crowns to be brought. And crowns were brought, made as it were of palm-branches; and he crowned the men that had given up the rods which had the shoots and some fruit, and sent them away into the tower. And the others also he sent into the tower, even those who had given up the rods green and with shoots, but the shoots were without fruit; and he set a seal upon them. And all they that went into the tower had the same raiment, white as snow. And those that had given up their rods green as they received them, he sent away, giving them a [white] robe, and seals. After the angel had finished these things, he saith to the shepherd; 'I go away; but these thou shalt send away to (their places within) the walls, according as each deserveth to dwell; but examine their rods carefully, and so send them away. But be careful in examining them. Take heed lest any escape thee,' saith he. 'Still if any escape thee, I will test them at the altar.' When he had thus spoken to the shepherd, he departed. And, after the angel had departed, the shepherd saith to me; 'Let us take the rods of all and plant them, to see whether any of them shall be able to live.' I say unto him, 'Sir, these withered things, how can they live?' He answered and said unto me; 'This tree is a willow, and this class of trees clingeth to life. If then the rods shall be planted and get a little moisture, many of them will live. And afterwards let us try to pour some water also over them. If any of them shall be able to live, I will rejoice with it; but if it live not, I at least shall not be found neglectful.' So the shepherd bade me call them, just as each one of them was stationed. And they came row after row, and they delivered up the rods to the shepherd. And the shepherd took the rods, and planted them in rows, and after he had planted them, he poured much water over them, so that the rods could not be seen for the water. And after he had watered the rods, he saith to me; 'Let us go now, and after a

few days let us return and inspect all the rods; for He Who created this tree willeth that all those who have received rods from this tree should live. And I myself hope that these little rods, after they have got moisture and been watered, will live the greater part of them.'

3. I say to him; 'Sir, inform me what this tree is. For I am perplexed herewith, because, though so many branches were cut off, the tree is sound, and nothing appears to have been cut from it; I am therefore perplexed thereat.' 'Listen,' saith he; 'this great tree which overshadows plains and mountains and all the earth is the law of God which was given to the whole world; and this law is the Son of God preached unto the ends of the earth. But the people that are under the shadow are they that have heard the preaching, and believed on Him; but the great and glorious angel is Michael, who hath the power over this people and is their captain. For this is he that putteth the law into the hearts of the believers; therefore he himself inspecteth them to whom he gave it, to see whether they have observed it. But thou seest the rods of every one; for the rods are the law. Thou seest these many rods rendered useless, and thou shalt notice all those that have not observed the law, and shalt see the abode of each severally.' I say unto him; 'Sir, wherefore did he send away some into the tower, and leave others for thee?' 'As many,' saith he, 'as transgressed the law which they received from him, these he left under my authority for repentance; but as many as already satisfied the law and have observed it, these he has under his own authority.' 'Who then, Sir,' say I, 'are they that have been crowned and go into the tower?' ['As many,' saith he, ' as wrestled with the devil and overcame him in their wrestling, are crowned:] these are they that suffered for the law. But the others, who likewise gave up their rods green and with shoots, though not with fruit, are they that were persecuted for the law, but did not suffer nor yet deny their law. But they that gave them up green just as they received them, are sober and righteous men, who walked altogether in a pure heart and have kept the commandments of the Lord. But all else thou shalt know, when I have examined these rods that have been planted and watered.'

4. And after a few days we came to the place, and the shepherd sat down in the place of the angel, while I stood by him. And he saith to me; 'Gird thyself with a garment of raw flax, and minister to me.' So I girded myself with a clean garment of raw flax made of coarse material. And when he saw me girded and ready to minister to him,

'Call,' saith he, 'the men whose rods have been planted, according
to the rank as each presented their rods.' And I went away to the
plain, and called them all; and they stood all of them according
to their ranks. He saith to them; 'Let each man pluck out his
own rod, and bring it to me.' Those gave them up first, who had
had the withered and chipped rods, and they were found accordingly
withered and chipped. He ordered them to stand apart. Then those
gave them up, who had the withered but not chipped; and some of
them gave up the rods green, and others withered and chipped as by
grubs. Those then that gave them up green he ordered to stand apart;
but those that gave them up withered and chipped he ordered to stand
with the first. Then those gave them up who had had the half-withered
and with cracks; and many of them gave them up green and without
cracks; and some gave them up green and with shoots, and fruits on the
shoots, such as those had who went into the tower crowned; and some
gave them up withered and eaten, and some withered and uneaten, and
some such as they were, half-withered and with cracks. He ordered them
to stand each one apart, some in their proper ranks, and others apart.

5. Then those gave them up who had their rods green, but with
cracks. These all gave them up green, and stood in their own
company. And the shepherd rejoiced over these, because they all were
changed and had put away their cracks. And those gave them up
likewise who had the one half green and the other half withered. The
rods of some were found entirely green, of some half-withered, of some
withered and eaten, and of some green and with shoots. These were
all sent away each to his company. Then those gave them up who had
two parts green and the third withered; many of them gave them up
green, and many half-withered, and others withered and eaten. These
all stood in their own company. Then those gave them up who
had two parts withered and the third part green. Many of them
gave them up half-withered, but some withered and eaten, others half-
withered and with cracks, and a few green. These all stood in their own
company. Then those gave them up who had had their rods green, but
a very small part [withered] and with cracks. Of these some gave them
up green, and others green and with shoots. These also went away to
their own company. Then those gave them up who had a very small
part green and the other parts withered. The rods of these were found
for the most part green and with shoots and fruit on the shoots,
and others altogether green. At these rods the shepherd rejoiced very

[greatly], because they were found so. And these went away each to his own company.

6. After [the shepherd] had examined the rods of all, he saith to me, 'I told thee that this tree clingeth to life. Seest thou,' saith he, 'how many repented and were saved?' 'I see, Sir,' say I. 'It is,' saith he, 'that thou mayest see the abundant compassion of the Lord, how great and glorious it is, and He hath given (His) Spirit to those that are worthy of repentance.' 'Wherefore then, Sir,' say I, 'did they not all repent?' 'To those, whose heart He saw about to become pure and to serve Him with all the heart, to them He gave repentance; but those whose craftiness and wickedness He saw, who intend to repent in hypocrisy, to them He gave not repentance, lest haply they should again profane His name.' I say unto him, 'Sir, now then show me concerning those that have given up their rods, what manner of man each of them is, and their abode, that when they hear this, they that believed and have received the seal and have broken it and did not keep it sound may fully understand what they are doing, and repent, receiving from thee a seal, and may glorify the Lord, that He had compassion upon them and sent thee to renew their spirits.' 'Listen,' saith he; 'those whose rods were found withered and grub-eaten, these are the renegades and traitors to the Church, that blasphemed the Lord in their sins, and still further were ashamed of the Name of the Lord, which was invoked upon them. These then perished altogether unto God. But thou seest how not one of them repented, although they heard the words which thou spakest to them, which I commanded thee. From men of this kind life departed. But those that gave up the green and undecayed (rods), these also are near them; for they were hypocrites, and brought in strange doctrines, and perverted the servants of God, especially them that had sinned, not permitting them to repent, but persuading them with their foolish doctrines. These then have hope of repenting. But thou seest that many of them have indeed repented from the time when thou spakest to them my commandments; yea, and (others) still will repent. And as many as shall not repent, have lost their life; but as many of them as repented, became good; and their dwelling was placed within the first walls, and some of them even ascended into the tower. Thou seest then,' [saith he,] 'that repentance from sins bringeth life, but not to repent bringeth death.

7. 'But as many as gave up (the rods) half-withered, and with cracks in them, hear also concerning these. Those whose rods were half-

withered throughout are the double-minded; for they neither live nor are dead. But those that have them half-withered and cracks in them, these are both double-minded and slanderers, and are never at peace among themselves but always causing dissensions. Yet even to these,' [saith he,] 'repentance is given. Thou seest,' [saith he,] 'that some of them have repented; and there is still,' saith he, 'hope of repentance among them. And as many of them,' saith he, 'as have repented, have their abode within the tower; but as many of them as have repented tardily shall abide within the walls; and as many as repent not, but continue in their doings, shall die the death. But they that have given up their rods green and with cracks, these were found faithful and good at all times, [but] they have a certain emulation one with another about first places and about glory of some kind or other; but all these are foolish in having (emulation) one with another about first places. Yet these also, when they heard my commandments, being good, purified themselves and repented quickly. They have their habitation, therefore, within the tower. But if any one shall again turn to dissension, he shall be cast out from the tower and shall lose his life. Life is for all those that keep the commandments of the Lord. But in the commandments there is nothing about first places, or about glory of any kind, but about long-suffering and humility in man. In such men, therefore, is the life of the Lord, but in factious and lawless men is death.

8. 'But they that gave up their rods half green and half withered, these are they that are mixed up in business and cleave not to the saints. Therefore the one half of them liveth, but the other half is dead. Many then when they heard my commandments repented. As many then as repented, have their abode within the tower. But some of them altogether stood aloof. These then have no repentance; for by reason of their business affairs they blasphemed the Lord and denied Him. So they lost their life for the wickedness that they committed. But many of them were doubtful-minded. These still have place for repentance, if they repent quickly, and their dwelling shall be within the tower; and if they repent tardily, they shall dwell within the walls; but if they repent not, they too have lost their life. But they that have given up two parts green and the third part withered, these are they that have denied with manifold denials. Many of them therefore repented, and departed to dwell inside the tower; but many utterly rebelled from God; these lost their life finally. And some of them were double-minded and caused dissensions. For these then

there is repentance, if they repent speedily and continue not in their pleasures; but if they continue in their doings, they likewise procure for themselves death.

9. 'But they that have given up their rods two thirds withered and one third green, these are men who have been believers, but grew rich and became renowned among the Gentiles. They clothed themselves with great pride and became high-minded, and abandoned the truth and did not cleave to the righteous, but lived together after the manner of the Gentiles, and this path appeared the more pleasant unto them; yet they departed not from God, but continued in the faith, though they wrought not the works of the faith. Many of them therefore repented, and they had their habitation within the tower. But others at the last living with the Gentiles, and being corrupted by the vain opinions of the Gentiles, departed from God, and worked the works of the Gentiles. These therefore were numbered with the Gentiles. But others of them were doubtful-minded, not hoping to be saved by reason of the deeds that they had done; and others were double-minded and made divisions among themselves. For these then that were double-minded by reason of their doings there is still repentance; but their repentance ought to be speedy, that their dwelling may be within the tower; but for those who repent not, but continue in their pleasures, death is nigh.

10. 'But they that gave up their rods green, yet with the extreme ends withered and with cracks; these were found at all times good and faithful and glorious in the sight of God, but they sinned to a very slight degree by reason of little desires and because they had somewhat against one another. But, when they heard my words, the greater part quickly repented, and their dwelling was assigned within the tower. But some of them were double-minded, and some being double-minded made a greater dissension. In these then there is still a hope of repentance, because they were found always good; and hardly shall one of them die. But they that gave up their rods withered, yet with a very small part green, these are they that believed, but practised the works of lawlessness. Still they never separated from God, but bore the Name gladly, and gladly received into their houses the servants of God. So hearing of this repentance they repented without wavering, and they practise all excellence and righteousness. And some of them even suffer persecution willingly, knowing the deeds that they did. All these then shall have their dwelling within the tower.'

11. And after he had completed the interpretations of all the rods,

he saith unto me; 'Go, and tell all men to repent, and they shall live
unto God; for the Lord in His compassion sent me to give repentance
to all, though some of them do not deserve it for their deeds; but being
long-suffering the Lord willeth them that were called through His Son
to be saved.' I say to him; 'Sir, I hope that all when they hear these
words will repent; for I am persuaded that each one, when he fully
knows his own deeds and fears God, will repent.' He answered and
said unto me; 'As many,' [saith he,] 'as [shall repent] from their whole
heart [and] shall cleanse themselves from all the evil deeds afore-mentioned, and shall add nothing further to their sins, shall receive healing
from the Lord for their former sins, unless they be double-minded
concerning these commandments, and they shall live unto God. [But
as many,' saith he, 'as shall add to their sins and walk in the lusts of
this world, shall condemn themselves to death.] But do thou walk in
my commandments, and live [unto God; yea, and as many as shall
walk in them and shall do rightly, shall live unto God.'] Having shown
me all these things [and told me them] he saith to me; 'Now the rest
will I declare (unto thee) after a few days.'

[PARABLE THE NINTH.]

1. After I had written down the commandments and parables of the
shepherd, the angel of repentance, he came to me and saith to me; 'I
wish to show thee all things that the Holy Spirit, Which spake with
thee in the form of the Church, showed unto thee. For that Spirit is
the Son of God. For when thou wast weaker in the flesh, it was not
declared unto thee through an angel; but when thou wast enabled
through the Spirit, and didst grow mighty in thy strength so that thou
couldest even see an angel, then at length was manifested unto thee,
through the Church, the building of the tower. In fair and seemly
manner hast thou seen all things, (instructed) as it were by a virgin; but
now thou seest (being instructed) by an angel, though by the same Spirit;
yet must thou learn everything more accurately from me. For to this
end also was I appointed by the glorious angel to dwell in thy house,
that thou mightest see all things mightily, in nothing terrified, even as
before.' And he took me away into Arcadia, to a certain rounded
mountain, and set me on the top of the mountain, and showed me a
great plain, and round the plain twelve mountains, the mountains having
each a different appearance. The first was black as soot; the second
was bare, without vegetation; the third was thorny and full of briars;

the fourth had the vegetation half-withered, the upper part of the grass green, but the part by the roots withered, and some of the grass became withered, whenever the sun had scorched it; the fifth mountain had green grass and was rugged; the sixth mountain was full with clefts throughout, some small and some great, and the clefts had vegetation, but the grass was not very luxuriant, but rather as if it had been withered; the seventh mountain had smiling vegetation, and the whole mountain was in a thriving condition, and cattle and birds of every kind did feed upon that mountain; and the more the cattle and the birds did feed, so much the more did the herbage of that mountain flourish. The eighth mountain was full of springs, and every kind of creature of the Lord did drink of the springs on that mountain. The ninth mountain had no water at all, and was entirely desert; and it had in it wild beasts and deadly reptiles, which destroy mankind. The tenth mountain had very large trees and was umbrageous throughout, and beneath the shade lay sheep resting and feeding. The eleventh mountain was thickly wooded all over, and the trees thereon were very productive, decked with divers kinds of fruits, so that one seeing them would desire to eat of their fruits. The twelfth mountain was altogether white and its aspect was cheerful; and the mountain was most beauteous in itself.

2. And in the middle of the plain he showed me a great white rock, rising up from the plain. The rock was loftier than the mountains, being four-square, so that it could contain the whole world. Now this rock was ancient, and had a gate hewn out of it; but the gate seemed to me to have been hewed out quite recently. And the gate glistened beyond the brightness of the sun, so that I marvelled at the brightness of the gate. And around the gate stood twelve virgins. The four then that stood at the corners seemed to me to be more glorious (than the rest); but the others likewise were glorious; and they stood at the four quarters of the gate, and virgins stood in pairs between them. And they were clothed in linen tunics and girt about in seemly fashion, having their right shoulders free, as if they intended to carry some burden. Thus were they prepared, for they were very cheerful and eager. After I had seen these things, I marvelled in myself at the greatness and the glory of what I was seeing. And again I was perplexed concerning the virgins, that delicate as they were they stood up like men, as if they intended to carry the whole heaven. And the shepherd saith unto me; 'Why questionest thou within thyself and art perplexed, and bringest sadness on thyself? For whatsoever things thou canst not

comprehend, attempt them not, if thou art prudent; but entreat the Lord, that thou mayest receive understanding to comprehend them. What is behind thee thou canst not see, but what is before thee thou beholdest. The things therefore which thou canst not see, let alone, and trouble not thyself (about them); but the things which thou seest, these master, and be not over curious about the rest; but I will explain unto thee all things whatsoever I shall show thee. Have an eye therefore to what remaineth.'

3.   I saw six men come, tall and glorious and alike in appearance; and they summoned a multitude of men. And the others also which came were tall men and handsome and powerful. And the six men ordered them to build a tower above the gate. And there arose a great noise from those men who had come to build the tower, as they ran hither and thither round the gate. For the virgins standing round the gate told the men to hasten to build the tower. Now the virgins had spread out their hands, as if they would take something from the men. And the six men ordered stones to come up from a certain deep place, and to go to the building of the tower. And there went up ten stones square and polished, [not] hewn from a quarry. And the six men called to the virgins, and ordered them to carry all the stones which should go unto the building of the tower, and to pass through the gate and to hand them to the men that were about to build the tower. And the virgins laid the first ten stones that rose out of the deep on each other, and they carried them together, stone by stone.

4.   And just as they stood together around the gate, in that order they carried them that seemed to be strong enough and had stooped under the corners of the stone, while the others stooped at the sides of the stone. And so they carried all the stones. And they carried them right through the gate, as they were ordered, and handed them to the men for the tower; and these took the stones and builded. Now the building of the tower was upon the great rock and above the gate. Those ten stones then were joined together, and they covered the whole rock. And these formed a foundation for the building of the tower. And [the rock and] the gate supported the whole tower. And, after the ten stones, other twenty-five stones came up from the deep, and these were fitted into the building of the tower, being carried by the virgins, like the former. And after these thirty-five stones came up. And these likewise were fitted into the tower. And after these came up other forty stones, and these all were put into the building of the tower. So

four rows were made in the foundations of the tower. And (the stones) ceased coming up from the deep, and the builders likewise ceased for a little. And again the six men ordered the multitude of the people to bring in stones from the mountains for the building of the tower. They were brought in accordingly from all the mountains, of various colours, shaped by the men, and were handed to the virgins; and the virgins carried them right through the gate, and handed them in for the building of the tower. And when the various stones were placed in the building, they became all alike and white, and they lost their various colours. But some stones were handed in by the men for the building, and these did not become bright; but just as they were placed, such likewise were they found; for they were not handed in by the virgins, nor had they been carried in through the gate. These stones then were unsightly in the building of the tower. Then the six men, seeing the stones that were unsightly in the building, ordered them to be removed and carried [below] into their own place whence they were brought. And they say to the men who were bringing the stones in; 'Abstain for your parts altogether from handing in stones for the building; but place them by the tower, that the virgins may carry them through the gate, and hand them in for the building. For if,' [say they,] 'they be not carried in through the gate by the hands of these virgins, they cannot change their colours. Labour not therefore,' [say they,] 'in vain.'

5. And the building was finished on that day, yet was not the tower finally completed, for it was to be carried up [still] higher; and there was a cessation in the building. And the six men ordered the builders to retire for a short time [all of them], and to rest; but the virgins they ordered not to retire from the tower. And methought the virgins were left to guard the tower. And after all had retired [and rested], I say to the shepherd; 'How is it, Sir,' say I, 'that the building of the tower was not completed?' 'The tower,' he saith, 'cannot yet be finally completed, until its master come and test this building, that if any stones be found crumbling, he may change them; for the tower is being built according to His will.' 'I would fain know, Sir,' say I, 'what is this building of this tower, and concerning the rock and gate, and the mountains, and the virgins, and the stones that came up from the deep, and were not shaped, but went just as they were into the building; and wherefore ten stones were first placed in the foundations, then twenty-five, then thirty-five, then forty, and concerning the stones that had gone to the building and were removed again and put away in their own

place—concerning all these things set my soul at rest, Sir, and explain them to me.' 'If,' saith he, 'thou be not found possessed of an idle curiosity, thou shalt know all things. For after a few days we shall come here, and thou shalt see the sequel that overtaketh this tower and shalt understand all the parables accurately.' And after a few days we came to the place where we had sat, and he saith to me, 'Let us go to the tower; for the owner of the tower cometh to inspect it.' And we came to the tower, and there was no one at all by it, save the virgins alone. And the shepherd asked the virgins whether the master of the tower had arrived. And they said that he would be there directly to inspect the building.

6. And, behold, after a little while I see an array of many men coming, and in the midst a man of such lofty stature that he overtopped the tower. And the six men who superintended the building walked with him on the right hand and on the left, and all they that worked at the building were with him, and many other glorious attendants around him. And the virgins that watched the tower ran up and kissed him, and they began to walk by his side round the tower. And that man inspected the building so carefully, that he felt each single stone; and he held a rod in his hand and struck each single stone that was built in. And when he smote, some of the stones became black as soot, others mildewed, others cracked, others broke off short, others became neither white nor black, others rough and not fitting in with the other stones, and others with many spots; these were the varied aspects of the stones which were found unsound for the building. So he ordered all these to be removed from the tower, and to be placed by the side of the tower, and other stones to be brought and put into their place. And the builders asked him from what mountain he desired stones to be brought and put into their place. And he would not have them brought from the mountains, but ordered them to be brought from a certain plain that was nigh at hand. And the plain was dug, and stones were found there bright and square, but some of them too were round. And all the stones which there were anywhere in that plain were brought every one of them, and were carried through the gate by the virgins. And the square stones were hewed, and set in the place of those which had been removed; but the round ones were not placed in the building, because they were too hard to be shaped, and to work on them was slow. So they were placed by the side of the tower, as though they were intended to be shaped and placed in the building; for they were very bright.

7. So then, having accomplished these things, the glorious man who was lord of the whole tower called the shepherd to him, and delivered unto him all the stones which lay by the side of the tower, which were cast out from the building, and saith unto him; 'Clean these stones carefully, and set them in the building of the tower, these, I mean, which can fit with the rest; but those which will not fit, throw far away from the tower.' Having given these orders to the shepherd, he departed from the tower with all those with whom he had come. And the virgins stood round the tower watching it. I say to the shepherd, ' How can these stones go again to the building of the tower, seeing that they have been disapproved?' He saith unto me in answer; 'Seest thou,' saith he, ' these stones?' ' I see them, Sir,' say I. ' I myself,' saith he, ' will shape the greater part of these stones and put them into the building, and they shall fit in with the remaining stones.' ' How, Sir,' say I, ' can they, when they are chiseled, fill the same space?' He saith unto me in answer, ' As many as shall be found small, shall be put into the middle of the building; but as many as are larger, shall be placed nearer the outside, and they will bind them together.' With these words he saith to me, ' Let us go away, and after two days let us come and clean these stones, and put them into the building; for all things round the tower must be made clean, lest haply the master come suddenly and find the circuit of the tower dirty, and he be wroth, and so these stones shall not go to the building of the tower, and I shall appear to be careless in my master's sight.'

And after two days we came to the tower, and he saith unto me; ' Let us inspect all the stones, and see those which can go to the building.' I say to him, 'Sir, let us inspect them.'

8. And so commencing first we began to inspect the black stones; and just as they were when set aside from the building, such also they were found. And the shepherd ordered them to be removed from the tower and to be put on one side. Then he inspected those that were mildewed, and he took and shaped many of them, and ordered the virgins to take them up and put them into the building. And the virgins took them up and placed them in the building of the tower in a middle position. But the rest he ordered to be placed with the black ones; for these also were found black. Then he began to inspect those that had the cracks; and of these he shaped many, and he ordered them to be carried away by the hands of the virgins for the building. And they were placed towards the outside, because they were found to be

sounder. But the rest could not be shaped owing to the number of the cracks. For this reason therefore they were cast aside from the building of the tower. Then he proceeded to inspect the stunted (stones), and many among them were found black, and some had contracted great cracks; and he ordered these also to be placed with those that had been cast aside. But those of them which remained he cleaned and shaped, and ordered to be placed in the building. So the virgins took them up, and fitted them into the middle of the building of the tower; for they were somewhat weak. Then he began to inspect those that were half white and half black, and many of them were (now) found black; and he ordered these also to be taken up with those that had been cast aside. †But all the rest were [found white, and were] taken up by the virgins; for being white they were fitted by [the virgins] them[selves] into the building.† But they were placed towards the outside, because they were found sound, so that they could hold together those that were placed in the middle; for not a single one of them was too short. Then he began to inspect the hard and rough; and a few of them were cast away, because they could not be shaped; for they were found very hard. But the rest of them were shaped [and taken up by the virgins] and fitted into the middle of the building of the tower; for they were somewhat weak. Then he proceeded to inspect those that had the spots, and of these some few had turned black and were cast away among the rest; but the remainder were found bright and sound, and these were fitted by the virgins into the building; but they were placed towards the outside, owing to their strength.

9. Then he came to inspect the white and round stones, and he saith unto me; 'What shall we do with these stones?' 'How do I know, Sir?' say I. [And he saith to me,] 'Perceivest thou nothing concerning them?' 'I, Sir,' say I, 'do not possess this art, neither am I a mason, nor can I understand.' 'Seest thou not,' saith he, 'that they are very round; and if I wish to make them square, very much must needs be chiseled off from them? Yet some of them must of necessity be placed into the building.' 'If then, Sir,' say I, 'it must needs be so, why distress thyself, and why not choose out for the building those thou willest, and fit them into it?' He chose out from them the large and the bright ones, and shaped them; and the virgins took them up, and fitted them into the outer parts of the building. But the rest, which remained over, were taken up, and put aside into the plain whence they were brought; they were not however cast away, 'Because,' saith he,

'there remaineth still a little of the tower to be builded. And the master
of the tower is exceedingly anxious that these stones be fitted into the
building, for they are very bright.' So twelve women were called, most
beautiful in form, clad in black, [girded about and having the shoulders
bare,] with their hair hanging loose. And these women, methought,
had a savage look. And the shepherd ordered them to take up the stones
which had been cast away from the building, and to carry them off to
the same mountains from which also they had been brought; and they
took them up joyfully, and carried away all the stones and put them in
the place whence they had been taken. And after all the stones had
been taken up, and not a single stone still lay round the tower, the
shepherd saith unto me; 'Let us go round the tower, and see that there
is no defect in it.' And I proceeded to go round it with him. And when
the shepherd saw that the tower was very comely in the building, he was
exceedingly glad; for the tower was so well builded, that when I saw it
I coveted the building of it; for it was builded, as it were, of one stone,
having one fitting in it. And the stone-work appeared as if hewn out
of the rock; for it seemed to me to be all a single stone.

10. And I, as I walked with him, was glad to see so brave a sight.
And the shepherd saith to me; 'Go and bring plaster and fine clay,
that I may fill up the shapes of the stones that have been taken up and
put into the building; for all the circuit of the tower must be made
smooth.' And I did as he bade, and brought them to him. 'Assist
me,' saith he, 'and the work will speedily be accomplished.' So he
filled in the shapes of the stones which had gone to the building, and
ordered the circuit of the tower to be swept and made clean. And the
virgins took brooms and swept, and they removed all the rubbish from
the tower, and sprinkled water, and the site of the tower was made
cheerful and very seemly. The shepherd saith unto me, 'All,' saith
he, 'hath now been cleaned. If the lord come to inspect the tower,
he hath nothing for which to blame us.' Saying this, he desired to go
away. But I caught hold of his wallet, and began to adjure him by the
Lord that he would explain to me [all] what he had showed me. He
saith to me; 'I am busy for a little while, and then I will explain
everything to thee. Await me here till I come.' I say to him; 'Sir,
when I am here alone what shall I do?' 'Thou art not alone,' saith he;
'for these virgins are here with thee.' 'Commend me then to them,'
say I. The shepherd calleth them to him and saith to them; 'I commend this man to you till I come,' and he departed. So I was alone

with the virgins; and they were most cheerful, and kindly disposed to me, especially the four of them that were the more glorious in appearance.

11. The virgins say to me; 'Today the shepherd cometh not here.' 'What then shall I do?' say I. 'Stay for him,' say they, 'till eventide; and if he come, he will speak with thee; but if he come not, thou shalt stay here with us till he cometh.' I say to them; 'I will await him till evening, and if he come not, I will depart home and return early in the morning.' But they answered and said unto me; 'To us thou wast entrusted; thou canst not depart from us.' 'Where then,' say I, 'shall I remain?' 'Thou shalt pass the night with us,' say they, 'as a brother, not as a husband; for thou art our brother, and henceforward we will dwell with thee; for we love thee dearly.' But I was ashamed to abide with them. And she that seemed to be the chief of them began to kiss and to embrace me; and the others seeing her embrace me, they too began to kiss me, and to lead me round the tower, and to sport with me. And I had become as it were a younger man, and I commenced myself likewise to sport with them. For some of them began to dance, [others to skip,] others to sing. But I kept silence and walked with them round the tower, and was glad with them. But when evening came I wished to go away home; but they would not let me go, but detained me. And I stayed the night with them, and I slept by the side of the tower. For the virgins spread their linen tunics on the ground, and made me lie down in the midst of them, and they did nothing else but pray; and I prayed with them without ceasing, and not less than they. And the virgins rejoiced that I so prayed. And I stayed there with the virgins until the morning till the second hour. Then came the shepherd, and saith to the virgins; 'Have ye done him any injury?' 'Ask him,' say they. I say to him, 'Sir, I was rejoiced to stay with them.' 'On what didst thou sup?' saith he. 'I supped, Sir,' say I, 'on the words of the Lord the whole night through.' 'Did they treat thee well?' saith he. 'Yes, Sir,' say I. 'Now,' saith he, 'what wouldest thou hear first?' 'In the order as thou showedst to me, Sir, from the beginning,' say I; 'I request thee, Sir, to explain to me exactly in the order that I shall enquire of thee.' 'According as thou desirest,' saith he, 'even so will I interpret to thee, and I will conceal nothing whatever from thee.'

12. 'First of all, Sir,' say I, 'explain this to me. The rock and the gate, what is it?' 'This rock,' saith he, 'and gate is the Son of God.' 'How, Sir,' say I, 'is the rock ancient, but the gate recent?'

'Listen,' saith he, 'and understand, foolish man. The Son of God is older than all His creation, so that He became the Father's adviser in His creation. Therefore also He is ancient.' 'But the gate, why is it recent, Sir?' say I. 'Because,' saith he, 'He was made manifest in the last days of the consummation; therefore the gate was made recent, that they which are to be saved may enter through it into the kingdom of God. Didst thou see,' saith he, 'that the stones which came through the gate have gone to the building of the tower, but those which came not through it were cast away again to their own place?' 'I saw, Sir,' say I. 'Thus,' saith he, 'no one shall enter into the kingdom of God, except he receive the name of His Son. For if thou wishest to enter into any city, and that city is walled all round and has one gate only, canst thou enter into that city except through the gate which it hath?' 'Why, how, Sir,' say I, 'is it possible otherwise?' 'If then thou canst not enter into the city except through the gate itself, even so,' saith he, 'a man cannot enter into the kingdom of God except by the name of His Son that is beloved by Him. Didst thou see,' saith he, 'the multitude that is building the tower?' 'I saw it, Sir,' say I. 'They,' saith he, 'are all glorious angels. With these then the Lord is walled around. But the gate is the Son of God; there is this one entrance only to the Lord. No one then shall enter in unto Him otherwise than through His Son. Didst thou see,' saith he, 'the six men, and the glorious and mighty man in the midst of them, him that walked about the tower and rejected the stones from the building?' 'I saw him, Sir,' say I. 'The glorious man,' saith he, 'is the Son of God, and those six are the glorious angels who guard Him on the right hand and on the left. Of these glorious angels not one,' saith he, 'shall enter in unto God without Him; whosoever shall not receive His name, shall not enter into the kingdom of God.'

13. 'But the tower,' say I, 'what is it?' 'The tower,' saith he, 'why, this is the Church. 'And these virgins, who are they?' 'They,' saith he, 'are holy spirits; and no man can otherwise be found in the kingdom of God, unless these shall clothe him with their garment; for if thou receive only the name, but receive not the garment from them, thou profitest nothing. For these virgins are powers of the Son of God. If [therefore] thou bear the Name, and bear not His power, thou shalt bear His Name to none effect. And the stones,' saith he, 'which thou didst see cast away, these bare the Name, but clothed not themselves with the raiment of the virgins.' 'Of what sort, Sir,' say I, 'is their raiment?' 'The names themselves,' saith he, 'are their raiment. Who-

soever beareth the Name of the Son of God, ought to bear the names of these also ; for even the Son Himself beareth the names of these virgins. As many stones,' saith he, 'as thou sawest enter into the building of the tower, being given in by their hands and waiting for the building, they have been clothed in the power of these virgins. For this cause thou seest the tower made a single stone with the rock. So also they that have believed in the Lord through His Son and clothe themselves in these spirits, shall become one spirit and one body, and their garments all of one colour. But such persons as bear the names of the virgins have their dwelling in the tower.' 'The stones then, Sir,' say I, 'which are cast aside, wherefore were they cast aside? For they passed through the gate and were placed in the building of the tower by the hands of the virgins.' 'Since all these things interest thee,' saith he, 'and thou enquirest diligently, listen as touching the stones that have been cast aside. These all,' [saith he,] 'received the name of the Son of God, and received likewise the power of these virgins. When then they received these spirits, they were strengthened, and were with the servants of God, and they had one spirit and one body [and one garment]; for they had the same mind, and they wrought righteousness. After a certain time then they were persuaded by the women whom thou sawest clad in black raiment, and having their shoulders bare and their hair loose, and beautiful in form. When they saw them they desired them, and they clothed themselves with their power, but they stripped off from themselves the power of the virgins. They then were cast away from the house of God, and delivered to these (women). But they that were not deceived by the beauty of these women remained in the house of God. So thou hast,' saith he, 'the interpretation of them that were cast aside.'

14. 'What then, Sir,' say I, 'if these men, being such as they are, should repent and put away their desire for these women, and return unto the virgins, and walk in their power and in their works? Shall they not enter into the house of God?' 'They shall enter,' saith he, 'if they shall put away the works of these women, and take again the power of the virgins, and walk in their works. For this is the reason why there was also a cessation in the building, that, if these repent, they may go into the building of the tower; but if they repent not, then others will go, and these shall be cast away finally.' For all these things I gave thanks unto the Lord, because He had compassion on all that called upon His name, and sent forth the angel of repentance to us

that had sinned against Him, and refreshed our spirit, and, when we were already ruined and had no hope of life, restored our life. 'Now, Sir,' say I, 'show me why the tower is not built upon the ground, but upon the rock and upon the gate.' 'Because thou art senseless,' saith he, 'and without understanding [thou askest the question].' 'I am obliged, Sir,' say I, 'to ask all questions of thee, because I am absolutely unable to comprehend anything at all; for all are great and glorious and difficult for men to understand.' 'Listen,' saith he. 'The name of the Son of God is great and incomprehensible, and sustaineth the whole world. If then all creation is sustained by the Son [of God], what thinkest thou of those that are called by Him, and bear the name of the Son of God, and walk according to His commandments? Seest thou then what manner of men He sustaineth? Even those that bear His name with their whole heart. He Himself then is become their foundation, and He sustaineth them gladly, because they are not ashamed to bear His name.'

15. 'Declare to me, Sir,' say I, 'the names of the virgins, and of the women that are clothed in the black garments.' 'Hear,' saith he, 'the names of the more powerful virgins, those that are stationed at the corners. The first is Faith, and the second, Continence, and the third, Power, and the fourth, Longsuffering. But the others stationed between them have these names—Simplicity, Guilelessness, Purity, Cheerfulness, Truth, Understanding, Concord, Love. He that beareth these names and the name of the Son of God shall be able to enter into the kingdom of God. Hear,' saith he, 'likewise the names of the women that wear the black garments. Of these also four are more powerful than the rest; the first is Unbelief; the second, Intemperance; the third, Disobedience; the fourth, Deceit; and their followers are called, Sadness, Wickedness, Wantonness, Irascibility, Falsehood, Folly, Slander, Hatred. The servant of God that beareth these names shall see the kingdom of God, but shall not enter into it.' 'But the stones, Sir,' say I, 'that came from the deep, and were fitted into the building, who are they?' 'The first,' saith he, 'even the ten, that were placed in the foundations, are the first generation; the twenty-five are the second generation of righteous men; the thirty-five are God's prophets and His ministers; the forty are apostles and teachers of the preaching of the Son of God.' 'Wherefore then, Sir,' say I, 'did the virgins give in these stones also for the building of the tower and carry them through the gate?' 'Because these first,' saith he, 'bore these spirits, and they

never separated the one from the other, neither the spirits from the men nor the men from the spirits, but the spirits abode with them till they fell asleep; and if they had not had these spirits with them, they would not have been found useful for the building of this tower.'

16. 'Show me still further, Sir,' say I. 'What desirest thou to know besides?' saith he. 'Wherefore, Sir,' say I, 'did the stones come up from the deep, and wherefore were they placed into the building, though they bore these spirits?' 'It was necessary for them,' saith he, 'to rise up through water, that they might be made alive; for otherwise they could not enter into the kingdom of God, except they had put aside the deadness of their [former] life. So these likewise that had fallen asleep received the seal of the Son of God and entered into the kingdom of God. For before a man,' saith he, 'has borne the name of [the Son of] God, he is dead; but when he has received the seal, he layeth aside his deadness, and resumeth life. The seal then is the water: so they go down into the water dead, and they come up alive. Thus to them also this seal was preached, and they availed themselves of it that they might enter into the kingdom of God.' 'Wherefore, Sir,' say I, 'did the forty stones also come up with them from the deep, though they had already received the seal?' 'Because,' saith he, 'these, the apostles and the teachers who preached the name of the Son of God, after they had fallen asleep in the power and faith of the Son of God, preached also to them that had fallen asleep before them, and themselves gave unto them the seal of the preaching. Therefore they went down with them into the water, and came up again. But these went down alive [and again came up alive]; whereas the others that had fallen asleep before them went down dead and came up alive. So by their means they were quickened into life, and came to the full knowledge of the name of the Son of God. For this cause also they came up with them, and were fitted with them into the building of the tower and were builded with them, without being shaped; for they fell asleep in righteousness and in great purity. Only they had not this seal. Thou hast then the interpretation of these things also.' 'I have, Sir,' say I.

17. 'Now then, Sir, explain to me concerning the mountains. Wherefore are their forms diverse the one from the other, and various?' 'Listen,' saith he. 'These twelve mountains are [twelve] tribes that inhabit the whole world. To these (tribes) then the Son of God was preached by the Apostles.' 'But explain to me, Sir, why they are various—these mountains—and each has a different appearance.' 'Listen,' saith he.

'These twelve tribes which inhabit the whole world are twelve nations ; and they are various in understanding and in mind. As various, then, as thou sawest these mountains to be, such also are the varieties in the mind of these nations, and such their understanding. And I will show unto thee the conduct of each.' 'First, Sir,' say I, 'show me this, why the mountains being so various, yet, when their stones were set into the building, became bright and of one colour, just like the stones that had come up from the deep.' 'Because,' saith he, 'all the nations that dwell under heaven, when they heard and believed, were called by the one name of [the Son of] God. So having received the seal, they had one understanding and one mind, and one faith became theirs and [one] love, and they bore the spirits of the virgins along with the Name ; therefore the building of the tower became of one colour, even bright as the sun. But after they entered in together, and became one body, some of them defiled themselves, and were cast out from the society of the righteous, and became again such as they were before, or rather even worse.'

18. 'How, Sir,' say I, 'did they become worse, after they had fully known God ?' 'He that knoweth not God,' saith he, 'and committeth wickedness, hath a certain punishment for his wickedness ; but he that knoweth God fully ought not any longer to commit wickedness, but to do good. If then he that ought to do good committeth wickedness, does he not seem to do greater wickedness than the man that knoweth not God ? Therefore they that have not known God, and commit wickedness, are condemned to death ; but they that have known God and seen His mighty works, and yet commit wickedness, shall receive a double punishment, and shall die eternally. In this way therefore shall the Church of God be purified. And as thou sawest the stones removed from the tower and delivered over to the evil spirits, they too shall be cast out; and there shall be one body of them that are purified, just as the tower, after it had been purified, became made as it were of one stone. Thus shall it be with the Church of God also, after she hath been purified, and the wicked and hypocrites and blasphemers and double-minded and they that commit various kinds of wickedness have been cast out. When these have been cast out, the Church of God shall be one body, one understanding, one mind, one faith, one love. And then the Son of God shall rejoice and be glad in them, for that He hath received back His people pure.' 'Great and glorious, Sir,' say I, 'are all these things. Once more, Sir,' [say I,] 'show me the force and the doings of each one of the mountains, that every soul that

trusteth in the Lord, when it heareth, may glorify His great and marvellous and glorious name.' 'Listen,' saith he, 'to the variety of the mountains and of the twelve nations.

19. 'From the first mountain, which was black, they that have believed are such as these; rebels and blasphemers against the Lord, and betrayers of the servants of God. For these there is no repentance, but there is death. For this cause also they are black; for their race is lawless. And from the second mountain, the bare one, they that believed are such as these; hypocrites and teachers of wickedness. And these then are like the former in not having the fruit of righteousness. For, even as their mountain is unfruitful, so likewise such men as these have a name indeed, but they are void of the faith, and there is no fruit of truth in them. For these then repentance is offered, if they repent quickly; but if they delay, they will have their death with the former.' 'Wherefore, Sir,' say I, 'is repentance possible for them, but not for the former? For their doings are almost the same.' 'On this account,' he saith, 'is repentance offered for them, because they blasphemed not their Lord, nor became betrayers of the servants of God; yet from desire of gain they played the hypocrite, and taught each other [after] the desires of sinful men. But they shall pay a certain penalty; yet repentance is ordained for them, because they are not become blasphemers or betrayers.

20. 'And from the third mountain, which had thorns and briars, they that believed are such as these; some of them are wealthy and others are entangled in many business affairs. The briars are the wealthy, and the thorns are they that are mixed up in various business affairs. These [then, that are mixed up in many and various business affairs,] cleave [not] to the servants of God, but go astray, being choked by their affairs, but the wealthy unwillingly cleave to the servants of God, fearing lest they may be asked for something by them. Such men therefore *shall hardly enter into the kingdom of God.* For as it is difficult to walk on briars with bare feet, so also *it is difficult* for such men *to enter into the kingdom of God.* But for all these repentance is possible, but it must be speedy, that in respect to what they omitted to do in the former times, they may now revert to (past) days, and do some good. If then they shall repent and do some good, they shall live unto God; but if they continue in their doings, they shall be delivered over to those women, the which shall put them to death.

21. 'And from the fourth mountain, which had much vegetation,

the upper part of the grass green and the part towards the roots withered, and some of it dried up by the sun, they that believed are such as these ; the double-minded, and they that have the Lord on their lips, but have Him not in their heart.   Therefore their foundations are dry and without power, and their words only live, but their works are dead.   Such men are neither alive nor dead.   They are, therefore, like unto the double-minded; for the double-minded are neither green nor withered; for they are neither alive nor dead.   For as their grass was withered up when it saw the sun, so also the double-minded, when they hear of tribulation, through their cowardice worship idols and are ashamed of the name of their Lord.   Such are neither alive nor dead.   Yet these also, if they repent quickly, shall be able to live ; but if they repent not, they are delivered over already to the women who deprive them of their life.

22.   'And from the fifth mountain, which had green grass and was rugged, they that believed are such as these ; they are faithful, but slow to learn and stubborn and self-pleasers, desiring to know all things, and yet they know nothing at all.   By reason of this their stubbornness, understanding stood aloof from them, and a foolish senselessness entered into them ; and they praise themselves as having understanding, and they desire to be self-appointed teachers, senseless though they are. Owing then to this pride of heart many, while they exalted themselves, have been made empty ; for a mighty demon is stubbornness and vain confidence.   Of these then many were cast away, but some repented and believed, and submitted themselves to those that had understanding, having learnt their own senselessness.   Yea, and to the rest that belong to this class repentance is offered ; for they did not become wicked, but rather foolish and without understanding.   If these then shall repent, they shall live unto God; but if they repent not, they shall have their abode with the women who work evil against them.

23.   'But they that believed from the sixth mountain, which had clefts great and small, and in the clefts herbage withered, are such as these ; they that have the small clefts, these are they that have aught against one another, and from their backbitings they are withered in the faith ; but many of these repented.   Yea, and the rest shall repent, when they hear my commandments ; for their backbitings are but small, and they shall quickly repent.   But they that have great clefts, these are persistent in their backbitings and bear grudges, nursing wrath against one another.   These then were thrown right away from the tower and rejected from its building.   Such persons therefore shall with difficulty

live. If God and our Lord, Who ruleth over all things and hath the authority over all His creation, beareth no grudge against them that confess their sins, but is propitiated, doth man, who is mortal and full of sins, bear a grudge against man, as though he were able to destroy or save him? I say unto you—I, the angel of repentance—unto as many as hold this heresy, put it away from you and repent, and the Lord shall heal your former sins, if ye shall purify yourselves from this demon; but if not, ye shall be delivered unto him to be put to death.

24. 'And from the seventh mountain, on which was herbage green and smiling, and the whole mountain thriving, and cattle of every kind and the fowls of heaven were feeding on the herbage on that mountain, and the green herbage, on which they fed, only grew the more luxuriant, they that believed are such as these; they were ever simple and guileless and blessed, having nothing against one another, but rejoicing always in the servants of God, and clothed in the Holy Spirit of these virgins, and having compassion always on every man, and out of their labours they supplied every man's need without reproach and without misgiving. The Lord then seeing their simplicity and entire childliness made them to abound in the labours of their hands, and bestowed favour on them in all their doings. But I say unto you that are such—I, the angel of repentance—remain to the end such as ye are, and your seed shall never be blotted out. For the Lord hath put you to the proof, and enrolled you among our number, and your whole seed shall dwell with the Son of God; for of His Spirit did ye receive.

25. 'And from the eighth mountain, where were the many springs, and all the creatures of the Lord did drink of the springs, they that believed are such as these; apostles and teachers, who preached unto the whole world, and who taught the word of the Lord in soberness and purity, and kept back no part at all for evil desire, but walked always in righteousness and truth, even as also they received the Holy Spirit. Such therefore shall have their entrance with the angels.

26. 'And from the ninth mountain, which was desert, which had [the] reptiles and wild beasts in it which destroy mankind, they that believed are such as these; they that have the spots are deacons that exercised their office ill, and plundered the livelihood of widows and orphans, and made gain for themselves from the ministrations which they had received to perform. If then they abide in the same evil desire, they are dead and there is no hope of life for them; but if they turn again and fulfil their ministrations in purity, it shall be possible for them to live.

But they that are mildewed, these are they that denied and turned not again unto their Lord, but having become barren and desert, because they cleave not unto the servants of God but remain alone, they destroy their own souls.   For as a vine left alone in a hedge, if it meet with neglect, is destroyed and wasted by the weeds, and in time becometh wild and is no longer useful to its owner, so also men of this kind have given themselves up in despair and become useless to their Lord, by growing wild.   To these then repentance cometh, unless they be found to have denied from the heart ; but if a man be found to have denied from the heart, I know not whether it is possible for him to live. And this I say not in reference to these days, that a man after denying should receive repentance ; for it is impossible for him to be saved who shall now deny his Lord ; but for those who denied Him long ago repentance seemeth to be possible.   If a man therefore will repent, let him do so speedily before the tower is completed ; but if not, he shall be destroyed by the women and put to death.   And the stunted, these are the treacherous and backbiters ; and the wild beasts which thou sawest on the mountain are these.   For as wild beasts with their venom poison and kill a man, so also do the words of such men poison and kill a man.   These then are broken off short from their faith through the conduct which they have in themselves ; but some of them repented and were saved ; and the rest that are of this kind can be saved, if they repent ; but if they repent not, they shall meet their death from those women of whose power they are possessed.

27. 'And from the tenth mountain, where were trees sheltering certain sheep, they that believed are such as these ; bishops, hospitable persons, who gladly received into their houses at all times the servants of God without hypocrisy. [These bishops] at all times without ceasing sheltered the needy and the widows in their ministration and conducted themselves in purity at all times.   These [all] then shall be sheltered by the Lord for ever.   They therefore that have done these things are glorious in the sight of God, and their place is even now with the angels, if they shall continue unto the end serving the Lord.

28. 'And from the eleventh mountain, where were trees full of fruit, decked with divers kinds of fruits, they that believed are such as these ; they that suffered for the Name [of the Son of God], who also suffered readily with their whole heart, and yielded up their lives.'   'Wherefore then, Sir,' say I, 'have all the trees fruits, but some of their fruits are more beautiful than others?'   'Listen,' saith he ; 'all as many as ever suffered

for the Name's sake are glorious in the sight of God, and the sins of all these were taken away, because they suffered for the name of the Son of God. Now hear why their fruits are various, and some surpassing others. As many,' saith he, ' as were tortured and denied not, when brought before the magistracy, but suffered readily, these are the more glorious in the sight of the Lord ; their fruit is that which surpasseth. But as many as became cowards, and were lost in uncertainty, and considered in their hearts whether they should deny or confess, and yet suffered, their fruits are less, because this design entered into their heart ; for this design is evil, that a servant should deny his own lord. See to it, therefore, ye who entertain this idea, lest this design remain in your hearts, and ye die unto God. But ye that suffer for the Name's sake ought to glorify God, because God deemed you worthy that ye should bear this name, and that all your sins should be healed. Reckon yourselves blessed therefore ; yea, rather think that ye have done a great work, if any of you shall suffer for God's sake. The Lord bestoweth life upon you, and ye perceive it not; for your sins weighed you down, and if ye had not suffered for the Name [of the Lord], ye had died unto God by reason of your sins. These things I say unto you that waver as touching denial and confession. Confess that ye have the Lord, lest denying Him ye be delivered into prison. If the Gentiles punish their slaves, if any one deny his lord, what think ye the Lord will do unto you, He Who hath the authority over all things? Away with these designs from your hearts, that ye may live for ever unto God.

29. ' And from the twelfth mountain, which was white, they that believed are such as these ; they are as very babes, into whose heart no guile entereth, neither learnt they what wickedness is, but they remained as babes for ever. Such as these then dwell without doubt in the kingdom of God, because they defiled the commandments of God in nothing, but continued as babes all the days of their life in the same mind. As many of you therefore as shall so continue,' saith he, ' and shall be as infants not having guile, shall be more glorious [even] than all them that have been mentioned before ; for all infants are glorious in the sight of God, and stand first in His sight. Blessed then are ye, as many as have put away wickedness from you, and have clothed yourselves in guilelessness : ye shall live unto God chiefest of all.'

After he had finished the parables of the mountains, I say unto him, ' Sir, now explain to me concerning the stones that were taken from the plain and placed in the building in the room of the stones that were taken from the tower, and concerning the round (stones) which were placed in the building, and concerning those that were still round.'

30. 'Hear,' saith he, 'likewise concerning all these things. The stones which were taken from the plain and placed in the building of the tower in the room of those that were rejected, are the roots of this white mountain. When then they that believed from this mountain were all found guileless, the lord of the tower ordered these from the roots of this mountain to be put into the building of the tower. For He knew that if these stones should go to the building [of the tower], they would remain bright and not one of them would turn black. But if he had added (stones) from the other mountains, he would have been obliged to visit that tower again, and to purify it. Now all these have been found white, who have believed and who shall believe; for they are of the same kind. Blessed is this kind, for it is innocent! Hear now likewise concerning those round and bright stones. All these are from this white mountain. Now hear wherefore they have been found round. Their riches have darkened and obscured them a little from the truth, yet they never departed from God, nor did any evil word proceed from their mouth, but all equity and virtue which comes from the truth. When therefore the Lord perceived their mind, †that they could favour the truth,† and likewise remain good, He commanded their possessions to be cut from off them, yet not to be taken away altogether, so that they might be able to do some good with that which hath been left to them, and might live unto God, for that they come of a good kind. So therefore they have been cut away a little, and placed in the building of this tower.

31. 'But the other (stones), which have remained round and have not been fitted into the building, because they have not yet received the seal, have been replaced in their own position, for they were found very round. For this world and the vanities of their possessions must be cut from off them, and then they will fit into the kingdom of God. For it is necessary that they should enter into the kingdom of God; because the Lord hath blessed this innocent kind. Of this kind then not one shall perish. Yea, even though any one of them being tempted by the most wicked devil have committed any fault, he shall return speedily unto his Lord. Blessed I pronounce you all to be— I, the angel of repentance—whoever of you are guileless as infants, because your part is good and honourable in the sight of God. More-over I bid all of you, whoever have received this seal, keep guilelessness,

and bear no grudge, and continue not in your wickedness nor in the memory of the offences of bitterness; but become of one spirit, and heal these evil clefts and take them away from among you, that the owner of the flocks may rejoice concerning them. For he will rejoice, if he find all things whole. But if he find any part of the flock scattered, woe unto the shepherds. For if the shepherds themselves shall have been found scattered, how will they answer for the flocks? Will they say that they were harassed by the flock? No credence will be given them. For it is an incredible thing that a shepherd should be injured by his flock; and he will be punished the more because of his falsehood. And I am the shepherd, and it behoveth me most strongly to render an account for you.

32. 'Amend yourselves therefore, while the tower is still in course of building. The Lord dwelleth in men that love peace; for to Him peace is dear; but from the contentious and them that are given up to wickedness He keepeth afar off. Restore therefore to Him your spirit whole as ye received it. For suppose thou hast given to a fuller a new garment whole, and desirest to receive it back again whole, but the fuller give it back to thee torn, wilt thou receive it thus? Wilt thou not at once blaze out and attack him with reproaches, saying; "The garment which I gave thee was whole; wherefore hast thou rent it and made it useless? See, by reason of the rent, which thou hast made in it, it cannot be of use." Wilt thou not then say all this to a fuller even about a rent which he has made in thy garment? If therefore thou art thus vexed in the matter of thy garment, and complainest because thou receivest it not back whole, what thinkest thou the Lord will do to thee, He, Who gave thee the spirit whole, and thou hast made it absolutely useless, so that it cannot be of any use at all to its Lord? For its use began to be useless, when it was corrupted by thee. Will not therefore the Lord of this spirit for this thy deed punish [thee with death]?' 'Certainly,' I said, 'all those, whomsoever He shall find continuing to bear malice, He will punish.' 'Trample not,' said he, 'upon His mercy, but rather glorify Him, because He is so long-suffering with your sins, and is not like unto you. Practise then repentance which is expedient for you.

33. 'All these things which are written above I, the shepherd, the angel of repentance, have declared and spoken to the servants of God. If then ye shall believe and hear my words, and walk in them, and amend your ways, ye shall be able to live. But if ye continue in wickedness and in bearing malice, no one of this kind shall live unto God.

All things which were to be spoken by me have (now) been spoken to you.' The shepherd said to me, 'Hast thou asked me all thy questions?' And I said, 'Yes, Sir.' 'Why then hast thou not enquired of me concerning the shape of the stones placed in the building, in that we filled up their shapes?' And I said, 'I forgot, Sir.' 'Listen now,' said he, 'concerning them. These are they that have heard my commandments now, and have practised repentance with their whole heart. So when the Lord saw that their repentance was good and pure, and that they could continue therein, he ordered their former sins to be blotted out. These shapes then were their former sins, and they have been chiseled away that they might not appear.'

PARABLE THE TENTH.

1. After I had written out this book completely, the angel who had delivered me to the shepherd came to the house where I was, and sat upon a couch, and the shepherd stood at his right hand. Then he called me, and spake thus unto me; 'I delivered thee,' said he, 'and thy house to this shepherd, that thou mightest be protected by him.' 'True, Sir,' I said. 'If therefore,' said he, 'thou desirest to be protected from all annoyance and all cruelty, to have also success in every good work and word, and all the power of righteousness, walk in his commandments, which I have given thee, and thou shalt be able to get the mastery over all wickedness. For if thou keep his commandments, all evil desire and the sweetness of this world shall be subject unto thee ; moreover success shall attend thee in every good undertaking. Embrace his gravity and self-restraint, and tell it out unto all men that he is held in great honour and dignity with the Lord, and is a ruler of great authority, and powerful in his office. To him alone in the whole world hath authority over repentance been assigned. Seemeth he to thee to be powerful? Yet ye despise the gravity and moderation which he useth towards you.'

2. I say unto him; 'Ask him, Sir, himself, whether from the time that he hath been in my house, I have done ought out of order, whereby I have offended him.' 'I myself know,' said he, 'that thou hast done nothing out of order, nor art about to do so. And so I speak these things unto thee, that thou mayest persevere. For he hath given a good account of thee unto me. Thou therefore shalt speak these words to others, that they too who have practised or shall practise repentance may be of the same mind as thou art; and he may give a good report of

them to me, and I unto the Lord.' 'I too, Sir,' I say, 'declare to every man the mighty works of the Lord; for I hope that all who have sinned in the past, if they hear these things, will gladly repent and recover life.' 'Continue therefore,' said he, 'in this ministry, and complete it unto the end. For whosoever fulfil his commandments shall have life; yea such a man (shall have) great honour with the Lord. But whosoever keep not his commandments, fly from their life, and oppose him, and follow not his commandments, but deliver themselves over to death; and each one becometh guilty of his own blood. But I bid thee obey these commandments, and thou shalt have a remedy for thy sins.

3. 'Moreover, I have sent these virgins unto thee, that they may dwell with thee; for I have seen that they are friendly towards thee. Thou hast them therefore as helpers, that thou mayest be the better able to keep his commandments; for it is impossible that these commandments be kept without the help of these virgins. I see too that they are glad to be with thee. But I will charge them that they depart not at all from thy house. Only do thou purify thy house; for in a clean house they will gladly dwell. For they are clean and chaste and industrious, and all have favour in the sight of the Lord. If, therefore, they shall find thy house pure, they will continue with thee; but if the slightest pollution arise, they will depart from thy house at once. For these virgins love not pollution in any form.' I say unto him, 'I hope, Sir, that I shall please them, so that they may gladly dwell in my house for ever; and just as he to whom thou didst deliver me maketh no complaint against me, so they likewise shall make no complaint.' He saith unto the shepherd, 'I perceive,' saith he, 'that he wishes to live as the servant of God, and that he will keep these commandments, and will place these virgins in a clean habitation.' With these words he again delivered me over to the shepherd, and called the virgins, and said to them; 'Inasmuch as I see that ye are glad to dwell in this man's house, I commend to you him and his house, that ye depart not at all from his house.' But they heard these words gladly.

4. He said then to me, 'Quit you like a man in this ministry; declare to every man the mighty works of the Lord, and thou shalt have favour in this ministry. Whosoever therefore shall walk in these commandments, shall live and be happy in his life; but whosoever shall neglect them, shall not live, and shall be unhappy in his life. Charge all men who are able to do right, that they cease not to practise

good works ; for it is useful for them. I say moreover that every man ought to be rescued from misfortune ; for he that hath need, and suffereth misfortune in his daily life, is in great torment and want. Whosoever therefore rescueth from penury a life of this kind, winneth great joy for himself. For he who is harassed by misfortune of this sort is afflicted and tortured with equal torment as one who is in chains. For many men on account of calamities of this kind, because they can bear them no longer, lay violent hands on themselves. He then who knows the calamity of a man of this kind and rescueth him not, committeth great sin, and becometh guilty of the man's blood. Do therefore good works, whoever of you have received (benefits) from the Lord, lest, while ye delay to do them, the building of the tower be completed. For it is on your account that the work of the building has been interrupted. Unless then ye hasten to do right, the tower will be completed, and ye shut out.'

When then he had finished speaking with me, he rose from the couch and departed, taking with him the shepherd and the virgins. He said however unto me, that he would send the shepherd and the virgins back again to my house.

THE EPISTLE

TO

DIOGNETUS

THE EPISTLE TO DIOGNETUS

I

WE owe the text of this work to a single MS of the thirteenth or possibly the fourteenth century, now no longer extant. This MS had originally belonged to Joann. Reuchlin († 1522), and ultimately found a home in the Strassburg Library, where it perished by fire during the Franco-German war in 1870 together with the other manuscript treasures contained therein. Two transcripts however had been made at the close of the sixteenth century, one by H. Stephens (in 1586), who first edited the Epistle to Diognetus (Paris, 1592), and another by Beurer (1587—1591), who however did not publish it. Stephens' copy is now at Leyden; that of Beurer is lost, but some of its readings are preserved by Stephens and by Sylburg (1593). Happily the portion of the Strassburg MS containing this Epistle was carefully collated by E. Cunitz in 1842 for Otto's first edition of Justin Martyr (1843), and again by E. Reuss still more accurately in 1861 for the same editor's third edition (1879).

The Strassburg MS contained several spurious or doubtful writings of Justin Martyr, at the close of which was the Epistle to Diognetus, likewise ascribed to him, τοῦ αὐτοῦ ['Ιουστίνου φιλοσόφου καὶ μάρτυρος] πρὸς Διόγνητον, besides other works following—some of them in a later hand—with which we are not concerned. Hence subsequent writers ascribed it unhesitatingly to Justin. Tillemont was the first (1691) who threw any doubt on this ascription. More recently critics, one and all, have agreed to assign it to some other author. It is not mentioned by Eusebius, or in any other ancient account of Justin's works; and its style is wholly different from that of Justin.

The most diverse opinions have been held respecting its date. Almost every epoch from the middle of the second century to the reign of Constantine in the beginning of the fourth has been assigned to it; nor indeed is any certainty possible. On the whole, however, the earlier date (c. A.D. 150) seems the more probable. Its ascription to Justin Martyr and its companionship with early writings in the MS suggest an epoch not later than the first half of the second century. The person meant by Diognetus is not improbably the tutor of Marcus Aurelius, here addressed as an enquirer after truth. The reference to the emperor commissioning his son (c. 7 ὡς βασιλεὺς πέμπων υἱὸν βασιλέα), as illustrating the great truth of Christian theology, may not improbably have been suggested by such events as the adoption of M. Aurelius by Antoninus Pius into the tribunician power (A.D. 147), or the association of his adopted son L. Aelius (A.D. 161) or of his own son Commodus (A.D. 176, 177) in the empire by M. Aurelius himself. The simplicity in the mode of stating theological truths, and the absence of all reference to the manifold heresies of later times, both point to a somewhat early date. Whenever it was written, it is one of the noblest and most impressive of early Christian apologies in style and treatment.

The dream of some very recent writers who suppose it to have been written, or rather forged, at the revival of learning in the sixteenth century may be dismissed at once as inconsistent alike with its style and contents, and with the history of the documents as given above.

2

The Epistle to Diognetus, however, does not reach beyond the tenth chapter, where it ends abruptly. The two remaining chapters belong to some different work, which has been accidentally attached to it, just as in most of the extant MSS the latter part of the Epistle of Polycarp is attached to the former part of the Epistle of Barnabas (see above, pp. 166 sq, 242), so as to form in appearance one work. Probably in this case also an archetypal MS had lost some leaves. Of this there seems to have been some indication in the Strassburg MS itself.

Who then was the author of this latter work? May we not hazard a conjecture which may be taken for what it is worth? The writer was Pantænus, the master of Clement (c. A.D. 180—210). Clearly it is Alexandrian, as its phraseology and its sentiments alike show. More especially he treats the account of the creation and the garden of Eden

(c. 12 παράδεισος τρυφῆς κ.τ.λ.) spiritually of the Church of Christ; and Pantænus is singled out with two or three other early fathers by Anastasius of Sinai in two passages as exhibiting this mode of treatment (ed. Migne, p. 860, p. 962). Nor indeed could any one more appropriately use the words (c. 11) ἀποστόλων γενόμενος μαθητὴς γίνομαι διδάσκαλος ἐθνῶν of himself than Pantænus the Apostle of the Indies. The first part of the sentence, ἀποστόλων μαθητής, wrongly understood, has given a place to the Epistle to Diognetus as a whole among the Apostolical Fathers, though (as we have shown) the last two chapters form no part of that Epistle. It is perhaps this very sentence also, or similar language of Pantænus elsewhere, which has led to the impossible statement in Photius (*Bibl.* 118) that Pantænus himself had listened to the preaching of the apostles.

ΠΡΟΣ ΔΙΟΓΝΗΤΟΝ

I. ἘΠΕΙΔΗ ὁρῶ, κράτιστε Διόγνητε, ὑπερεσπουδακότα
σε τὴν θεοσέβειαν τῶν Χριστιανῶν μαθεῖν καὶ πάνυ σαφῶς
καὶ ἐπιμελῶς πυνθανόμενον περὶ αὐτῶν, τίνι τε Θεῷ πεποιθότες καὶ πῶς θρησκεύοντες αὐτὸν τόν τε κόσμον ὑπερορῶσι
πάντες καὶ θανάτου καταφρονοῦσι, καὶ οὔτε τοὺς νομιζομένους
ὑπὸ τῶν Ἑλλήνων θεοὺς λογίζονται οὔτε τὴν Ἰουδαίων δεισιδαιμονίαν φυλάσσουσι, καὶ τίνα τὴν φιλοστοργίαν ἔχουσι
πρὸς ἀλλήλους, καὶ τί δήποτε καινὸν τοῦτο γένος ἢ ἐπι-
τήδευμα εἰσῆλθεν εἰς τὸν βίον νῦν καὶ οὐ πρότερον· ἀπο-
δέχομαί γε τῆς προθυμίας σε ταύτης καὶ παρὰ τοῦ Θεοῦ,
τοῦ καὶ τὸ λέγειν καὶ τὸ ἀκούειν ἡμῖν χορηγοῦντος, αἰτοῦμαι
δοθῆναι ἐμοὶ μὲν εἰπεῖν οὕτως ὡς μάλιστα ἂν ἀκούσαντά σε
βελτίω γενέσθαι, σοί τε οὕτως ἀκοῦσαι ὡς μὴ λυπηθῆναι
τὸν εἰπόντα.

II. Ἄγε δὴ καθάρας σεαυτὸν ἀπὸ πάντων τῶν προκατε-
χόντων σου τὴν διάνοιαν λογισμῶν, καὶ τὴν ἀπατῶσάν σε
cf. Eph. iv.
22—24. συνήθειαν ἀποσκευασάμενος, καὶ γενόμενος ὥσπερ ἐξ ἀρχῆς
καινὸς ἄνθρωπος, ὡς ἂν καὶ λόγου καινοῦ, καθάπερ καὶ αὐτὸς
ὡμολόγησας, ἀκροατὴς ἐσόμενος· ἴδε μὴ μόνον τοῖς ὀφθαλμοῖς
ἀλλὰ καὶ τῇ φρονήσει τίνος ὑποστάσεως ἢ τίνος εἴδους
τυγχάνουσιν οὓς ἐρεῖτε καὶ νομίζετε θεούς. 2. οὐχ ὁ μέν
τις λίθος ἐστὶν ὅμοιος τῷ πατουμένῳ, ὁ δ' ἐστὶ χαλκὸς οὐ
κρείσσων τῶν εἰς τὴν χρῆσιν ἡμῖν κεχαλκευμένων σκευῶν,

i. αὐτὸν τόν τε] conj. Lachmann; αὐτόν τε MS.   ἀκούσαντα] conj.
Stephens; ἀκοῦσαι MS.

ὁ δὲ ξύλον ἤδη καὶ σεσηπός, ὁ δὲ ἄργυρος χρῄζων ἀνθρώπου
τοῦ φυλάξαντος ἵνα μὴ κλαπῇ, ὁ δὲ σίδηρος ὑπὸ ἰοῦ διε-
φθαρμένος, ὁ δὲ ὄστρακον, οὐδὲν τοῦ κατεσκευασμένου πρὸς
τὴν ἀτιμοτάτην ὑπηρεσίαν εὐπρεπέστερον; 3. οὐ φθαρτῆς
ὕλης ταῦτα πάντα; οὐχ ὑπὸ σιδήρου καὶ πυρὸς κεχαλ-
κευμένα; οὐχ ὃ μὲν αὐτῶν λιθοξόος ὃ δὲ χαλκεὺς ὃ δὲ
ἀργυροκόπος ὃ δὲ κεραμεὺς ἔπλασεν; οὐ πρὶν ἢ ταῖς τέχναις
τούτων εἰς τὴν μορφὴν ταύτην ἐκτυπωθῆναι ἦν ἕκαστον
αὐτῶν ἑκάστῳ εἰκάζειν μεταμεμορφωμένον; οὐ τὰ νῦν ἐκ
τῆς αὐτῆς ὕλης ὄντα σκεύη γένοιτ᾽ ἄν, εἰ τύχοι τῶν αὐτῶν
τεχνιτῶν, ὅμοια τοιούτοις; 4. οὐ ταῦτα πάλιν τὰ νῦν ὑφ᾽
ὑμῶν προσκυνούμενα δύναιτ᾽ ἂν ὑπὸ ἀνθρώπων σκεύη ὅμοια
γενέσθαι τοῖς λοιποῖς; οὐ κωφὰ πάντα, οὐ τυφλά, οὐκ
ἄψυχα, οὐκ ἀναίσθητα, οὐκ ἀκίνητα; οὐ πάντα σηπόμενα, οὐ
πάντα φθειρόμενα; 5. ταῦτα θεοὺς καλεῖτε, τούτοις δου-
λεύετε, τούτοις προσκυνεῖτε· τέλεον δ᾽ αὐτοῖς ἐξομοιοῦσθε.
6. διὰ τοῦτο μισεῖτε Χριστιανούς, ὅτι τούτους οὐχ ἡγοῦνται
θεούς. 7. ὑμεῖς γὰρ οἱ νῦν νομίζοντες καὶ σεβόμενοι, οὐ
πολὺ πλέον αὐτῶν καταφρονεῖτε; οὐ πολὺ μᾶλλον αὐτοὺς
χλευάζετε καὶ ὑβρίζετε, τοὺς μὲν λιθίνους καὶ ὀστρακίνους
σέβοντες ἀφυλάκτως, τοὺς δὲ ἀργυρέους καὶ χρυσοῦς ἐγκλεί-
οντες ταῖς νυξί, καὶ ταῖς ἡμέραις φύλακας παρακαθιστάντες,
ἵνα μὴ κλαπῶσιν; 8. αἷς δὲ δοκεῖτε τιμαῖς προσφέρειν, εἰ
μὲν αἰσθάνονται, κολάζετε μᾶλλον αὐτούς· εἰ δὲ ἀναισθη-
τοῦσιν, ἐλέγχοντες αἵματι καὶ κνίσαις αὐτοὺς θρησκεύετε.
9. ταῦθ᾽ ὑμῶν τις ὑπομεινάτω, ταῦτα ἀνασχέσθω τις ἑαυτῷ
γενέσθαι. ἀλλὰ ἄνθρωπος μὲν οὐδὲ εἷς ταύτης τῆς κολάσεως
ἑκὼν ἀνέξεται, αἴσθησιν γὰρ ἔχει καὶ λογισμόν· ὁ δὲ λίθος
ἀνέχεται, ἀναισθητεῖ γάρ. οὐκοῦν τὴν αἴσθησιν αὐτοῦ ἐλέγχετε. 10. περὶ μὲν οὖν τοῦ μὴ δεδουλῶσθαι Χριστιανοὺς

ii. 3 ταύτην] conj. Böhl; τούτων MS.   ἕκαστον] conj. S. Maur; ἕκαστος
MS.   εἰκάζειν] conj. Lachmann; ἔτι καὶ νῦν MS.   4 ὑμῶν] ἡμῶν MS.
7 σεβόμενοι] conj. Lachmann; οἰόμενοι MS.   παρακαθιστάντες] conj. Krenkel;
παρακαθίσαντες MS.

τοιούτοις θεοῖς πολλὰ μὲν [ἂν] καὶ ἄλλα εἰπεῖν ἔχοιμι· εἰ δέ τινι μὴ δοκοίη κἂν ταῦτα ἱκανά, περισσὸν ἡγοῦμαι καὶ τὸ πλείω λέγειν. III. Ἑξῆς δὲ περὶ τοῦ μὴ κατὰ τὰ αὐτὰ Ἰουδαίοις θεοσεβεῖν αὐτοὺς οἶμαί σε μάλιστα ποθεῖν ἀκοῦσαι. 2. Ἰουδαῖοι τοίνυν εἰ μὲν ἀπέχονται ταύτης τῆς προειρημένης λατρείας, καλῶς Θεὸν ἕνα τῶν πάντων σέβειν καὶ δεσπότην ἀξιοῦσι φρονεῖν· εἰ δὲ τοῖς προειρημένοις ὁμοιοτρόπως τὴν θρησκείαν προσάγουσιν αὐτῷ ταύτην, διαμαρτάνουσιν. 3. ἃ γὰρ τοῖς ἀναισθήτοις καὶ κωφοῖς προσφέροντες οἱ Ἕλληνες ἀφροσύνης δεῖγμα παρέχουσι, ταῦθ' οὗτοι καθάπερ προσδεομένῳ τῷ θεῷ λογιζόμενοι παρέχειν μωρίαν εἰκὸς μᾶλλον ἡγοῖντ' ἄν, οὐ θεοσέβειαν. 4. ὁ γὰρ ποιήσας τὸν οὐρανὸν καὶ τὴν γῆν καὶ πάντα τὰ ἐν αὐτοῖς καὶ πᾶσιν ἡμῖν χορηγῶν ὧν προσδεόμεθα, οὐδενὸς ἂν αὐτὸς προσδέοιτο τούτων ὧν τοῖς οἰομένοις διδόναι παρέχει αὐτός. 5. οἱ δέ γε θυσίας αὐτῷ δι' αἵματος καὶ κνίσης καὶ ὁλοκαυτωμάτων ἐπιτελεῖν οἰόμενοι καὶ ταύταις ταῖς τιμαῖς αὐτὸν γεραίρειν, οὐδέν μοι δοκοῦσι διαφέρειν τῶν εἰς τὰ κωφὰ τὴν αὐτὴν ἐνδεικνυμένων φιλοτιμίαν· τῶν [μὲν] μὴ δυναμένοις τῆς τιμῆς μεταλαμβάνειν, τῶν δὲ δοκούντων παρέχειν τῷ μηδενὸς προσδεομένῳ. IV. Ἀλλὰ μὴν τό γε περὶ τὰς βρώσεις αὐτῶν ψοφοδεές, καὶ τὴν περὶ τὰ σάββατα δεισιδαιμονίαν, καὶ τὴν τῆς περιτομῆς ἀλαζονείαν, καὶ τὴν τῆς νηστείας καὶ νουμηνίας εἰρωνείαν, καταγέλαστα καὶ οὐδενὸς ἄξια λόγου [οὐ] νομίζω σε χρῄζειν παρ' ἐμοῦ μαθεῖν. 2. τό τε γὰρ τῶν ὑπὸ τοῦ Θεοῦ κτισθέντων εἰς χρῆσιν ἀνθρώπων ἃ μὲν ὡς καλῶς κτισθέντα παραδέχεσθαι, ἃ δ' ὡς ἄχρηστα καὶ περισσὰ παραιτεῖσθαι, πῶς οὐκ ἀθέμιστον; 3. τὸ δὲ καταψεύδεσθαι

cf. Acts
xvii. 24,25.

ii. 10 ἂν] ins. Lachmann.   iii. 2 καλῶς] conj. Hilgenfeld; καὶ εἰς MS.
5 ἐνδεικνυμένων] conj. Stephens; ἐνδεικνύμενοι MS.   μὲν] ins. Gebhardt.
δυναμένοις] conj. Gebhardt; δυναμένων MS.   τῶν δὲ δοκούντων] conj.
Lachmann; τὸ δὲ δοκεῖν τινα MS.   iv. 1 οὐ] ins. Stephens.   2 οὐκ
ἀθέμιστον] conj. Gebhardt; οὐ θέμις ἐστὶ MS.

Θεοῦ ὡς κωλύοντος ἐν τῇ τῶν σαββάτων ἡμέρα καλόν τι ποιεῖν, πῶς οὐκ ἀσεβές; 4. τὸ δὲ καὶ τὴν μείωσιν τῆς σαρκὸς μαρτύριον ἐκλογῆς ἀλαζονεύεσθαι ὡς διὰ τοῦτο ἐξαιρέτως ἠγαπημένους ὑπὸ Θεοῦ, πῶς οὐ χλεύης ἄξιον; 5. τὸ δὲ παρεδρεύοντας αὐτοὺς ἄστροις καὶ σελήνῃ τὴν παρατήρησιν τῶν μηνῶν καὶ τῶν ἡμερῶν ποιεῖσθαι, καὶ τὰς οἰκονομίας Θεοῦ καὶ τὰς τῶν καιρῶν ἀλλαγὰς καταδιαιρεῖν πρὸς τὰς αὐτῶν ὁρμάς, ἃς μὲν εἰς ἑορτάς, ἃς δὲ εἰς πένθη· τίς ἂν θεοσεβείας καὶ οὐκ ἀφροσύνης πολὺ πλέον ἡγήσαιτο δεῖγμα; 6. τῆς μὲν οὖν κοινῆς εἰκαιότητος καὶ ἀπάτης καὶ τῆς Ἰουδαίων πολυπραγμοσύνης καὶ ἀλαζονείας [ὡς] ὀρθῶς ἀπέχονται Χριστιανοί, ἀρκούντως σε νομίζω μεμαθηκέναι· τὸ δὲ τῆς ἰδίας αὐτῶν θεοσεβείας μυστήριον μὴ προσδοκήσῃς δύνασθαι παρὰ ἀνθρώπου μαθεῖν.

V. Χριστιανοὶ γὰρ οὔτε γῇ οὔτε φωνῇ οὔτε ἔθεσι διακεκριμένοι τῶν λοιπῶν εἰσὶν ἀνθρώπων. 2. οὔτε γάρ που πόλεις ἰδίας κατοικοῦσιν οὔτε διαλέκτῳ τινὶ παρηλλαγμένῃ χρῶνται οὔτε βίον παράσημον ἀσκοῦσιν. 3. οὐ μὴν ἐπινοίᾳ τινὶ καὶ φροντίδι πολυπραγμόνων ἀνθρώπων μάθημα τοιοῦτ' αὐτοῖς ἐστιν εὑρημένον, οὐδὲ δόγματος ἀνθρωπίνου προεστᾶσιν ὥσπερ ἔνιοι. 4. κατοικοῦντες δὲ πόλεις Ἑλληνίδας τε καὶ βαρβάρους ὡς ἕκαστος ἐκληρώθη, καὶ τοῖς ἐγχωρίοις ἔθεσιν ἀκολουθοῦντες ἔν τε ἐσθῆτι καὶ διαίτῃ καὶ τῷ λοιπῷ βίῳ, θαυμαστὴν καὶ ὁμολογουμένως παράδοξον ἐνδείκνυνται τὴν κατάστασιν τῆς ἑαυτῶν πολιτείας. 5. πατρίδας οἰκοῦσιν ἰδίας, ἀλλ' ὡς πάροικοι· μετέχουσι πάντων ὡς πολῖται, καὶ πάνθ' ὑπομένουσιν ὡς ξένοι· πᾶσα ξένη πατρίς ἐστιν αὐτῶν, καὶ πᾶσα πατρὶς ξένη. 6. γαμοῦσιν ὡς πάντες, τεκνογονοῦσιν· ἀλλ' οὐ ῥίπτουσι τὰ γεννώμενα. 7. τράπεζαν κοινὴν παρατίθενται, ἀλλ' οὐ κοίτην. 8. ἐν σαρκὶ τυγχάνουσιν,

---

iv. 5 καταδιαιρεῖν] καταδ....εῖν MS.　　　ἡγήσαιτο] conj. Lachmann;
ἡγήσεται τὸ MS.　　　6 ὡς] ins. Bunsen.　　　v. 3 μάθημα τοιοῦτ'] conj. van
Hengel; μαθήματι τοῦτ' MS.　　　εὑρημένον] conj. Stephens; εἰρημένον MS.
4 καὶ sec.] conj. Otto; ἐν MS.　　　7 κοιτήν] conj. S. Maur; κοινήν MS.-

cf. Phil.
iii. 20.

cf. 2 Cor.
vi. 9, 10.

cf. 1 Cor.
iv. 12.

cf. S. John
xvii. 11, 14.

ἀλλ' οὐ κατὰ σάρκα ζῶσιν. 9. ἐπὶ γῆς διατρίβουσιν, ἀλλ'
ἐν οὐρανῷ πολιτεύονται. 10. πείθονται τοῖς ὡρισμένοις
νόμοις, καὶ τοῖς ἰδίοις βίοις νικῶσι τοὺς νόμους. 11. ἀγα-
πῶσι πάντας, καὶ ὑπὸ πάντων διώκονται. 12. ἀγνοοῦνται,
καὶ κατακρίνονται· θανατοῦνται, καὶ ζωοποιοῦνται. 13.
πτωχεύουσι, καὶ πλουτίζουσι πολλούς· πάντων ὑστεροῦνται,
καὶ ἐν πᾶσι περισσεύουσιν. 14. ἀτιμοῦνται, καὶ ἐν ταῖς
ἀτιμίαις δοξάζονται· βλασφημοῦνται, καὶ δικαιοῦνται. 15.
λοιδοροῦνται, καὶ εὐλογοῦσιν· ὑβρίζονται, καὶ τιμῶσιν. 16.
ἀγαθοποιοῦντες ὡς κακοὶ κολάζονται· κολαζόμενοι χαίρουσιν
ὡς ζωοποιούμενοι. 17. ὑπὸ Ἰουδαίων ὡς ἀλλόφυλοι πολε-
μοῦνται καὶ ὑπὸ Ἑλλήνων διώκονται, καὶ τὴν αἰτίαν τῆς
ἔχθρας εἰπεῖν οἱ μισοῦντες οὐκ ἔχουσιν.

VI. Ἁπλῶς δ' εἰπεῖν, ὅπερ ἐστὶν ἐν σώματι ψυχή, τοῦτ'
εἰσὶν ἐν κόσμῳ Χριστιανοί. 2. ἔσπαρται κατὰ πάντων τῶν
τοῦ σώματος μελῶν ἡ ψυχή, καὶ Χριστιανοὶ κατὰ τὰς τοῦ
κόσμου πόλεις. 3. οἰκεῖ μὲν ἐν τῷ σώματι ψυχή, οὐκ ἔστι
δὲ ἐκ τοῦ σώματος· καὶ Χριστιανοὶ ἐν κόσμῳ οἰκοῦσιν,
οὐκ εἰσὶ δὲ ἐκ τοῦ κόσμου. 4. ἀόρατος ἡ ψυχὴ ἐν ὁρατῷ
φρουρεῖται τῷ σώματι· καὶ Χριστιανοὶ γινώσκονται μὲν
ὄντες ἐν τῷ κόσμῳ, ἀόρατος δὲ αὐτῶν ἡ θεοσέβεια μένει.
5. μισεῖ τὴν ψυχὴν ἡ σὰρξ καὶ πολεμεῖ μηδὲν ἀδικουμένη,
διότι ταῖς ἡδοναῖς κωλύεται χρῆσθαι· μισεῖ καὶ Χριστιανοὺς
ὁ κόσμος μηδὲν ἀδικούμενος, ὅτι ταῖς ἡδοναῖς ἀντιτάσσονται.
6. ἡ ψυχὴ τὴν μισοῦσαν ἀγαπᾷ σάρκα καὶ τὰ μέλη· καὶ
Χριστιανοὶ τοὺς μισοῦντας ἀγαπῶσιν. 7. ἐγκέκλεισται μὲν
ἡ ψυχὴ τῷ σώματι, συνέχει δὲ αὐτὴ τὸ σῶμα· καὶ Χριστιανοὶ
κατέχονται μὲν ὡς ἐν φρουρᾷ τῷ κόσμῳ, αὐτοὶ δὲ συνέχουσι
τὸν κόσμον. 8. ἀθάνατος ἡ ψυχὴ ἐν θνητῷ σκηνώματι
κατοικεῖ· καὶ Χριστιανοὶ παροικοῦσιν ἐν φθαρτοῖς, τὴν
ἐν οὐρανοῖς ἀφθαρσίαν προσδεχόμενοι. 9. κακουργουμένη
σιτίοις καὶ ποτοῖς ἡ ψυχὴ βελτιοῦται· καὶ Χριστιανοὶ
κολαζόμενοι καθ' ἡμέραν πλεονάζουσι μᾶλλον. 10. εἰς

vi. 4 μὲν ὄντες] conj. Stephens; μένοντες MS.

τοσαύτην αὐτοὺς τάξιν ἔθετο ὁ Θεός, ἣν οὐ θεμιτὸν αὐτοῖς
παραιτήσασθαι. VII. Οὐ γὰρ ἐπίγειον, ὡς ἔφην, εὕρημα τοῦτ᾽ αὐτοῖς
παρεδόθη, οὐδὲ θνητὴν ἐπίνοιαν φυλάσσειν οὕτως ἀξιοῦσιν
ἐπιμελῶς, οὐδὲ ἀνθρωπίνων οἰκονομίαν μυστηρίων πεπίσ-
τευνται. 2. ἀλλ᾽ αὐτὸς ἀληθῶς ὁ παντοκράτωρ καὶ παντο-
κτίστης καὶ ἀόρατος Θεός, αὐτὸς ἀπ᾽ οὐρανῶν τὴν ἀλήθειαν
καὶ τὸν λόγον τὸν ἅγιον καὶ ἀπερινόητον ἀνθρώποις ἐνίδρυσε
καὶ ἐγκατεστήριξε ταῖς καρδίαις αὐτῶν, οὐ καθάπερ ἄν τις
εἰκάσειεν ἄνθρωπος, ὑπηρέτην τινὰ πέμψας ἢ ἄγγελον ἢ
ἄρχοντα ἤ τινα τῶν διεπόντων τὰ ἐπίγεια ἤ τινα τῶν πεπιστευμένων τὰς ἐν οὐρανοῖς διοικήσεις, ἀλλ᾽ αὐτὸν τὸν τεχνίτην
καὶ δημιουργὸν τῶν ὅλων, ᾧ τοὺς οὐρανοὺς ἔκτισεν, ᾧ τὴν
θάλασσαν ἰδίοις ὅροις ἐνέκλεισεν, οὗ τὰ μυστήρια πιστῶς
πάντα φυλάσσει τὰ στοιχεῖα, παρ᾽ οὗ τὰ μέτρα τῶν τῆς ἡμέρας δρόμων [ἥλιος] εἴληφε φυλάσσειν, ᾧ πειθαρχεῖ σελήνη
νυκτὶ φαίνειν κελεύοντι, ᾧ πειθαρχεῖ τὰ ἄστρα τῷ τῆς
σελήνης ἀκολουθοῦντα δρόμῳ, ᾧ πάντα διατέτακται καὶ
διώρισται καὶ ὑποτέτακται, οὐρανοὶ καὶ τὰ ἐν οὐρανοῖς, γῆ
καὶ τὰ ἐν τῇ γῇ, θάλασσα καὶ τὰ ἐν τῇ θαλάσσῃ, πῦρ, ἀήρ,
ἄβυσσος, τὰ ἐν ὕψεσι, τὰ ἐν βάθεσι, τὰ ἐν τῷ μεταξύ· τοῦτον
πρὸς αὐτοὺς ἀπέστειλεν. 3. ἆρά γε, ὡς ἀνθρώπων ἄν τις
λογίσαιτο, ἐπὶ τυραννίδι καὶ φόβῳ καὶ καταπλήξει; 4.
οὐμενοῦν· ἀλλ᾽ ἐν ἐπιεικείᾳ [καὶ] πραΰτητι ὡς βασιλεὺς πέμπων υἱὸν βασιλέα ἔπεμψεν, ὡς Θεὸν ἔπεμψεν, ὡς [ἄνθρωπον]
πρὸς ἀνθρώπους ἔπεμψεν, ὡς σώζων ἔπεμψεν, ὡς πείθων, οὐ
βιαζόμενος· βία γὰρ οὐ πρόσεστι τῷ Θεῷ. 5. ἔπεμψεν ὡς
καλῶν, οὐ διώκων· ἔπεμψεν ὡς ἀγαπῶν, οὐ κρίνων. 6. πέμ- cf. S. John
ψει γὰρ αὐτὸν κρίνοντα, καὶ τίς αὐτοῦ τὴν παρουσίαν ὑπο- iii. 17.
στήσεται;.... 7. [Οὐχ ὁρᾶς] παραβαλλομένους θηρίοις,

---

vii. 2 ἄνθρωπος] conj. Bunsen ; ἀνθρώποις MS.   ἥλιος] ins. Hefele.
4 καὶ] ins. Stephens.   ἄνθρωπον] ins. Bunsen.   6 ὑποστήσεται] Here the
MS marks a lacuna and adds in marg. οὕτως καὶ ἐν τῷ ἀντιγράφῳ εὗρον ἐγκο-
πήν, παλαιοτάτου ὄντος.   7 οὐχ ὁρᾷς] ins. Stephens.

ἵνα ἀρνήσωνται τὸν Κύριον, καὶ μὴ νικωμένους; 8. οὐχ ὁρᾷς ὅσῳ πλείονες κολάζονται, τοσούτῳ πλεονάζοντας ἄλλους; 9. ταῦτα ἀνθρώπου οὐ δοκεῖ τὰ ἔργα, ταῦτα δύναμίς ἐστι Θεοῦ· ταῦτα τῆς παρουσίας αὐτοῦ δείγματα. VIII. Τίς γὰρ ὅλως ἀνθρώπων ἠπίστατο τί ποτ' ἐστὶ Θεός, πρὶν αὐτὸν ἐλθεῖν; 2. ἢ τοὺς κενοὺς καὶ ληρώδεις ἐκείνων λόγους ἀποδέχῃ τῶν ἀξιοπίστων φιλοσόφων; ὧν οἱ μέν τινες πῦρ ἔφασαν εἶναι τὸν θεόν (οὗ μέλλουσι χωρήσειν αὐτοί, τοῦτο καλοῦσι θεόν), οἱ δὲ ὕδωρ, οἱ δ' ἄλλο τι τῶν στοιχείων τῶν ἐκτισμένων ὑπὸ Θεοῦ. 3. καίτοι γε εἴ τις τούτων τῶν λόγων ἀπόδεκτός ἐστι, δύναιτ' ἂν καὶ τῶν λοιπῶν κτισμάτων ἓν ἕκαστον ὁμοίως ἀποφαίνεσθαι Θεόν. 4. ἀλλὰ ταῦτα μὲν τερατεία καὶ πλάνη τῶν γοήτων ἐστίν· 5. ἀνθρώπων δὲ οὐδεὶς οὔτε εἶδεν οὔτε ἐγνώρισεν, αὐτὸς δὲ ἑαυτὸν ἐπέδειξεν. 6. ἐπέδειξε δὲ διὰ πίστεως, ᾗ μόνῃ Θεὸν ἰδεῖν συγκεχώρηται. 7. ὁ γὰρ δεσπότης καὶ δημιουργὸς τῶν ὅλων Θεός, ὁ ποιήσας τὰ πάντα καὶ κατὰ τάξιν διακρίνας, οὐ μόνον φιλάνθρωπος ἐγένετο ἀλλὰ καὶ μακρόθυμος. 8. ἀλλ' οὗτος ἦν μὲν ἀεὶ τοιοῦτος, καὶ ἔστι, καὶ ἔσται· χρηστὸς καὶ ἀγαθὸς καὶ ἀόργητος καὶ ἀληθής, καὶ μόνος ἀγαθός ἐστιν· 9. ἐννοήσας δὲ μεγάλην καὶ ἄφραστον ἔννοιαν ἀνεκοινώσατο μόνῳ τῷ παιδί. 10. ἐν ὅσῳ μὲν οὖν κατεῖχεν ἐν μυστηρίῳ καὶ διετήρει τὴν σοφὴν αὐτοῦ βουλήν, ἀμελεῖν ἡμῶν καὶ ἀφρονιστεῖν ἐδόκει· 11. ἐπεὶ δὲ ἀπεκάλυψε διὰ τοῦ ἀγαπητοῦ παιδὸς καὶ ἐφανέρωσε τὰ ἐξ ἀρχῆς ἡτοιμασμένα, πάνθ' ἅμα παρέσχεν ἡμῖν, καὶ μετασχεῖν τῶν εὐεργεσιῶν αὐτοῦ καὶ ἰδεῖν καὶ νοῆσαι ἃ τίς ἂν πώποτε προσεδόκησεν ἡμῶν;

IX. Πάντ' οὖν ἤδη παρ' ἑαυτῷ σὺν τῷ παιδὶ οἰκονομηκώς, μέχρι μὲν τοῦ πρόσθεν χρόνου εἴασεν ἡμᾶς ὡς ἐβου-

---

vii. 9 δείγματα] conj. Stephens; δόγματα MS.   viii. 5 εἶδεν] conj. Stephens; εἶπεν MS.   6 μόνῃ] conj. Stephens; μόνον MS.   9 ἀνεκοινώσατο] conj. Stephens; ἣν ἐκοινώσατο MS.   11 νοῆσαι ἃ τίς] conj. Lachmann; ποιῆσαι τις MS.   ix. 1 ἤδη, οἰκονομηκώς, μέχρι μὲν] conj. Lachmann; ᾔδει, οἰκονομιεῖς, μέχρι μὲν οὖν MS.

λόμεθα ἀτάκτοις φοραῖς φέρεσθαι, ἡδοναῖς καὶ ἐπιθυμίαις
ἀπαγομένους, οὐ πάντως ἐφηδόμενος τοῖς ἁμαρτήμασιν ἡμῶν,
ἀλλ᾽ ἀνεχόμενος, οὐδὲ τῷ τότε τῆς ἀδικίας καιρῷ συνευδοκῶν,
ἀλλὰ τὸν νῦν τῆς δικαιοσύνης δημιουργῶν, ἵνα ἐν τῷ τότε
χρόνῳ ἐλεγχθέντες ἐκ τῶν ἰδίων ἔργων ἀνάξιοι ζωῆς νῦν
ὑπὸ τῆς τοῦ Θεοῦ χρηστότητος ἀξιωθῶμεν καὶ τὸ καθ᾽ ἑαυτοὺς
φανερώσαντες ἀδύνατον εἰσελθεῖν εἰς τὴν βασιλείαν τοῦ Θεοῦ
τῇ δυνάμει τοῦ Θεοῦ δυνατοὶ γενηθῶμεν. 2. ἐπεὶ δὲ πεπλή-
ρωτο μὲν ἡ ἡμετέρα ἀδικία, καὶ τελείως πεφανέρωτο ὅτι ὁ
μισθὸς αὐτῆς κόλασις καὶ θάνατος προσεδοκᾶτο, ἦλθε δὲ ὁ
καιρὸς ὃν Θεὸς προέθετο λοιπὸν φανερῶσαι τὴν ἑαυτοῦ cf. Tit. iii.
χρηστότητα καὶ δύναμιν (ὢ τῆς ὑπερβαλλούσης φιλανθρω- 4.
πίας καὶ ἀγάπης τοῦ Θεοῦ), οὐκ ἐμίσησεν ἡμᾶς οὐδὲ ἀπώσατο
οὐδὲ ἐμνησικάκησεν, ἀλλὰ ἐμακροθύμησεν, ἠνέσχετο, ἐλεῶν
αὐτὸς τὰς ἡμετέρας ἁμαρτίας ἀνεδέξατο, αὐτὸς τὸν ἴδιον
υἱὸν ἀπέδοτο λύτρον ὑπὲρ ἡμῶν, τὸν ἅγιον ὑπὲρ ἀνόμων, τὸν
ἄκακον ὑπὲρ τῶν κακῶν, τὸν δίκαιον ὑπὲρ τῶν ἀδίκων, τὸν 1 Pet.
ἄφθαρτον ὑπὲρ τῶν φθαρτῶν, τὸν ἀθάνατον ὑπὲρ τῶν θνητῶν. iii. 18.
3. τί γὰρ ἄλλο τὰς ἁμαρτίας ἡμῶν ἠδυνήθη καλύψαι ἢ
ἐκείνου δικαιοσύνη ; 4. ἐν τίνι δικαιωθῆναι δυνατὸν τοὺς
ἀνόμους ἡμᾶς καὶ ἀσεβεῖς ἢ ἐν μόνῳ τῷ υἱῷ τοῦ Θεοῦ ;
5. ὢ τῆς γλυκείας ἀνταλλαγῆς, ὢ τῆς ἀνεξιχνιάστου δη-
μιουργίας, ὢ τῶν ἀπροσδοκήτων εὐεργεσιῶν· ἵνα ἀνομία
μὲν πολλῶν ἐν δικαίῳ ἑνὶ κρυβῇ, δικαιοσύνη δὲ ἑνὸς πολλοὺς
ἀνόμους δικαιώσῃ. 6. ἐλέγξας οὖν ἐν μὲν τῷ πρόσθεν
χρόνῳ τὸ ἀδύνατον τῆς ἡμετέρας φύσεως εἰς τὸ τυχεῖν ζωῆς,
νῦν δὲ τὸν σωτῆρα δείξας δυνατὸν σώζειν καὶ τὰ ἀδύνατα, ἐξ
ἀμφοτέρων ἐβουλήθη πιστεύειν ἡμᾶς τῇ χρηστότητι αὐτοῦ,
αὐτὸν ἡγεῖσθαι τροφέα, πατέρα, διδάσκαλον, σύμβουλον,
ἰατρόν, νοῦν, φῶς, τιμήν, δόξαν, ἰσχύν, ζωήν.

X. Ταύτην καὶ σὺ τὴν πίστιν ἐὰν ποθήσῃς, κατάλαβε

---

ix. 1 νῦν pri.] conj. Hefele ; νοῦν MS.   2 ὦ] conj. Otto ; ὡς MS.   καὶ
ἀγάπης] conj. Stephens ; μία ἀγάπη MS.   ἐλεῶν] conj. Lachmann ; λέγων MS.
6 ζωήν] add περὶ ἐνδύσεως καὶ τροφῆς μὴ μεριμνᾶν MS.   x. 1 κατάλαβε] conj.
Gebhardt ; καὶ λάβῃς MS.

S. John
iii. 16.

1 John
iv. 9.

cf. 1 John
iv. 19.

πρῶτον μὲν ἐπίγνωσιν πατρός. 2. ὁ γὰρ Θεὸς τοὺς ἀνθρώπους ἠγάπησε, δι᾽ οὓς ἐποίησε τὸν κόσμον, οἷς ὑπέταξε πάντα τὰ ἐν τῇ γῇ, οἷς λόγον ἔδωκεν, οἷς νοῦν, οἷς μόνοις ἄνω πρὸς οὐρανὸν ὁρᾶν ἐπέτρεψεν, οὓς ἐκ τῆς ἰδίας εἰκόνος ἔπλασε, πρὸς οὓς ἀπέϲτειλε τὸν γἱὸν ᾱγτοῦ τὸν μονοϲενῆ, οἷς τὴν ἐν οὐρανῷ βασιλείαν ἐπηγγείλατο καὶ δώσει τοῖς ἀγαπήσασιν αὐτόν. 3. ἐπιγνοὺς δέ, τίνος οἴει πληρωθήσεσθαι χαρᾶς; ἢ πῶς ἀγαπήσεις τὸν οὕτως προαγαπήσαντά σε; 4. ἀγαπήσας δὲ μιμητὴς ἔσῃ αὐτοῦ τῆς χρηστότητος. καὶ μὴ θαυμάσῃς εἰ δύναται μιμητὴς ἄνθρωπος γενέσθαι Θεοῦ· δύναται θέλοντος αὐτοῦ. 5. οὐ γὰρ τὸ καταδυναστεύειν τῶν πλησίον οὐδὲ τὸ πλέον ἔχειν βούλεσθαι τῶν ἀσθενεστέρων οὐδὲ τὸ πλουτεῖν καὶ βιάζεσθαι τοὺς ὑποδεεστέρους εὐδαιμονεῖν ἐστίν, οὐδὲ ἐν τούτοις δύναταί τις μιμήσασθαι Θεόν, ἀλλὰ ταῦτα ἐκτὸς τῆς ἐκείνου μεγαλειότητος· 6. ἀλλ᾽ ὅστις τὸ τοῦ πλησίον ἀναδέχεται βάρος, ὃς ἐν ᾧ κρείσσων ἐστὶν ἕτερον τὸν ἐλαττούμενον εὐεργετεῖν ἐθέλει, ὃς ἃ παρὰ τοῦ Θεοῦ λαβὼν ἔχει, ταῦτα τοῖς ἐπιδεομένοις χορηγῶν Θεὸς γίνεται τῶν λαμβανόντων, οὗτος μιμητής ἐστι Θεοῦ. 7. τότε θεάσῃ τυγχάνων ἐπὶ γῆς ὅτι Θεὸς ἐν οὐρανοῖς πολιτεύεται, τότε μυστήρια Θεοῦ λαλεῖν ἄρξῃ, τότε τοὺς κολαζομένους ἐπὶ τῷ μὴ θέλειν ἀρνήσασθαι Θεὸν καὶ ἀγαπήσεις καὶ θαυμάσεις, τότε τῆς ἀπάτης τοῦ κόσμου καὶ τῆς πλάνης καταγνώσῃ, ὅταν τὸ ἀληθῶς ἐν οὐρανῷ ζῆν ἐπιγνῷς, ὅταν τοῦ δοκοῦντος ἐνθάδε θανάτου καταφρονήσῃς, ὅταν τὸν ὄντως θάνατον φοβηθῇς, ὃς φυλάσσεται τοῖς κατακριθησομένοις εἰς τὸ πῦρ τὸ αἰώνιον, ὃ τοὺς παραδοθέντας αὐτῷ μέχρι τέλους κολάσει. 8. τότε τοὺς ὑπομένοντας ὑπὲρ δικαιοσύνης θαυμάσεις τὸ πῦρ τὸ πρόσκαιρον, καὶ μακαρίσεις, ὅταν ἐκεῖνο τὸ πῦρ ἐπιγνῷς…

*　　*　　*　　*　　*

x. 2 ἐν τῇ γῇ] conj. Stephens; ἐν… MS.　　　ἄνω] a.. MS (so Cunitz and Stephens, but Beurer ἄνω).　　οὐρανὸν] conj. Lachmann; αὐτὸν MS.　　6 ὃς ἅ] conj. van Hengel; ὅσα MS.　　7 ἐπιγνῶς] conj. Lachmann; ἐπιγνώσῃ MS.　　8 πρόσκαιρον] conj. Sylburg; προς… app. MS.　　ἐπιγνῶς] The MS marks a lacura and adds καὶ ὧδε ἐγκοπὴν εἶχε τὸ ἀντίγραφον.

XI. Οὐ ξένα ὁμιλῶ οὐδὲ παραλόγως ζητῶ, ἀλλὰ ἀποστόλων γενόμενος μαθητὴς γίνομαι διδάσκαλος ἐθνῶν, τὰ παραδοθέντα ἀξίως ὑπηρετῶν γινομένοις ἀληθείας μαθηταῖς. 2. τίς γὰρ ὀρθῶς διδαχθεὶς καὶ Λόγῳ προσφιλὴς γενηθεὶς οὐκ ἐπιζητεῖ σαφῶς μαθεῖν τὰ διὰ Λόγου δειχθέντα φανερῶς μαθηταῖς; οἷς ἐφανέρωσεν ὁ Λόγος φανείς, παρρησίᾳ λαλῶν, ὑπὸ cf. 1 Tim. ἀπίστων μὴ νοούμενος, μαθηταῖς δὲ διηγούμενος, οἳ πιστοὶ λο- iii. 16. γισθέντες ὑπ᾿ αὐτοῦ ἔγνωσαν πατρὸς μυστήρια. 3. οὗ χάριν ἀπέστειλε Λόγον, ἵνα κόσμῳ φανῇ, ὃς ὑπὸ λαοῦ ἀτιμασθείς, διὰ ἀποστόλων κηρυχθείς, ὑπὸ ἐθνῶν ἐπιστεύθη. 4. οὗτος cf. S. John ὁ ἀπ᾿ ἀρχῆς, ὁ καινὸς φανεὶς καὶ παλαιὸς εὑρεθεὶς καὶ πάντοτε i. 1. νέος ἐν ἁγίων καρδίαις γεννώμενος· 5. οὗτος ὁ ἀεί, [ὁ] σήμερον υἱὸς λογισθείς, δι᾿ οὗ πλουτίζεται ἡ ἐκκλησία καὶ χάρις ἁπλουμένη ἐν ἁγίοις πληθύνεται, παρέχουσα νοῦν, φανεροῦσα μυστήρια, διαγγέλλουσα καιρούς, χαίρουσα ἐπὶ πιστοῖς, ἐπιζητοῦσι δωρουμένη, οἷς ὅρκια πίστεως οὐ θραύεται οὐδὲ ὅρια πατέρων παρορίζεται. 6. εἶτα φόβος νόμου ᾄδεται καὶ προφητῶν χάρις γινώσκεται καὶ εὐαγγελίων πίστις ἵδρυται καὶ ἀποστόλων παράδοσις φυλάσσεται καὶ ἐκκλησίας χαρὰ σκιρτᾷ. 7. ἣν χάριν μὴ λυπῶν ἐπιγνώσῃ ἃ Λόγος ὁμιλεῖ δι᾿ ὧν βούλεται, ὅτε θέλει. 8. ὅσα γὰρ θελήματι τοῦ κελεύοντος Λόγου ἐκινήθημεν ἐξειπεῖν μετὰ πόνου, ἐξ ἀγάπης τῶν ἀποκαλυφθέντων ἡμῖν γινόμεθα ὑμῖν κοινωνοί.

XII. Οἷς ἐντυχόντες καὶ ἀκούσαντες μετὰ σπουδῆς εἴσεσθε ὅσα παρέχει ὁ Θεὸς τοῖς ἀγαπῶσιν ὀρθῶς, οἱ γενόμενοι παράδεισος τρυφῆς, πάγκαρπον ξύλον, εὐθαλοῦν, ἀνατείλαντες ἐν ἑαυτοῖς, ποικίλοις καρποῖς κεκοσμημένοι. 2. ἐν γὰρ τούτῳ τῷ χωρίῳ ξύλον γνώσεως καὶ ξύλον ζωῆς πεφύτευται· ἀλλ᾿ οὐ τὸ τῆς γνώσεως ἀναιρεῖ, ἀλλ᾿ ἡ παρακοὴ ἀναιρεῖ. 3. οὐδὲ γὰρ ἄσημα τὰ γεγραμμένα, ὡς Θεὸς ἀπ᾿ ἀρχῆς ξύλον

---

xi. 1 ἀξίως] conj. Hollenberg; ἀξίοις MS.   2 προσφιλῆς] conj. S. Maur;
προσφιλεῖ app. MS.   γενηθεὶς] conj. Bunsen; γεννηθεὶς MS.   5 ὁ sec.]
ins. Lachmann.   ὅρκια] conj. Lachmann; ὅρια MS.   6 χαρᾷ] conj.
Lachmann; χάρις MS.

| γνώσεως καὶ ξύλον | ζωῆς ἐν μέσῳ παραδείσου ἐφύτευσε, διὰ γνώσεως ζωὴν ἐπιδεικνύς. ἢ μὴ καθαρῶς χρησάμενοι οἱ ἀπ᾽ ἀρχῆς πλάνῃ τοῦ ὄφεως γεγύμνωνται. 4. οὐδὲ γὰρ ζωὴ ἄνευ γνώσεως, οὐδὲ γνῶσις ἀσφαλὴς ἄνευ ζωῆς ἀληθοῦς· διὸ πλησίον ἑκάτερον πεφύτευται. 5. ἢν δύναμιν ἐνιδὼν ὁ ἀπόστολος τήν τε ἄνευ ἀληθείας προστάγματος εἰς ζωὴν ἀσκουμένην γνῶσιν μεμφόμενος λέγει· Ἡ ΓΝῶϲιϲ φΥϲιοῖ, ἡ Δὲ ἀΓάπΗ οἰκοΔομεῖ. 6. ὁ γὰρ νομίζων εἰδέναι τι ἄνευ γνώσεως ἀληθοῦς καὶ μαρτυρουμένης ὑπὸ τῆς ζωῆς, οὐκ ἔγνω· ὑπὸ τοῦ ὄφεως πλανᾶται, μὴ ἀγαπήσας τὸ ζῆν. ὁ δὲ μετὰ φόβου ἐπιγνοὺς καὶ ζωὴν ἐπιζητῶν ἐπ᾽ ἐλπίδι φυτεύει, καρπὸν προσδοκῶν. 7. ἤτω σοι καρδία γνῶσις, ζωὴ δὲ λόγος ἀληθής, χωρούμενος. 8. οὗ ξύλον φέρων καὶ καρπὸν αἱρῶν τρυγήσεις ἀεὶ τὰ παρὰ Θεῷ ποθούμενα, ὧν ὄφις οὐχ ἅπτεται οὐδὲ πλάνη συγχρωτίζεται· οὐδὲ Εὖα φθείρεται, ἀλλὰ παρθένος πιστεύεται· 9. καὶ σωτήριον δείκνυται, καὶ ἀπόστολοι συνετίζονται, καὶ τὸ Κυρίου πάσχα προέρχεται, καὶ κλῆροι συνάγονται καὶ [πάντα] μετὰ κόσμου ἁρμόζεται, καὶ διδάσκων ἁγίους ὁ Λόγος εὐφραίνεται, δι᾽ οὗ Πατὴρ δοξάζεται· ᾧ ἡ δόξα εἰς τοὺς αἰῶνας. ἀμήν.

1 Cor.
viii. 1.

xii. 3 γνώσεως καὶ ξύλον] ins. Bunsen; om. MS by homœot.   8 αἱρῶν]
conj. Otto; ...ρῶν MS.   9 κλῆροι] conj. Bunsen; κηροὶ MS.   πάντα] ins.
Bunsen.

TRANSLATION

OF THE

EPISTLE TO DIOGNETUS

THE EPISTLE TO DIOGNETUS

SINCE I see, most excellent Diognetus, that thou art exceedingly anxious to understand the religion of the Christians, and that thy enquiries respecting them are distinctly and carefully made, as to what God they trust and how they worship Him, that they all disregard the world and despise death, and take no account of those who are regarded as gods by the Greeks, neither observe the superstition of the Jews, and as to the nature of the affection which they entertain one to another, and of this new development or interest, which has entered into men's lives now and not before: I gladly welcome this zeal in thee, and I ask of God, Who supplieth both the speaking and the hearing to us, that it may be granted to myself to speak in such a way that thou mayest be made better by the hearing, and to thee that thou mayest so listen that I the speaker may not be disappointed.

2. Come then, clear thyself of all the prepossessions which occupy thy mind, and throw off the habit which leadeth thee astray, and become a new man, as it were, from the beginning, as one who would listen to a new story, even as thou thyself didst confess. See not only with thine eyes, but with thine intellect also, of what substance or of what form they chance to be whom ye call and regard as gods. Is not one of them stone, like that which we tread under foot, and another bronze, no better than the vessels which are forged for our use, and another wood, which has already become rotten, and another silver, which needs a man to guard it lest it be stolen, and another iron, which is corroded with rust, and another earthenware, not a whit more comely than that which is supplied for the most dishonourable service? Are not all these of perishable matter? Are they not forged by iron and fire? Did not the sculptor make one, and the brass-founder another, and the silversmith another, and the potter

another? Before they were moulded into this shape by the crafts of these several artificers, was it not possible for each one of them to have been changed in form and made to resemble these several utensils? Might not the vessels which are now made out of the same material, if they met with the same artificers, be made like unto such as these? Could not these things which are now worshipped by you, by human hands again be made vessels like the rest? Are not they all deaf and blind, are they not soul-less, senseless, motionless? Do they not all rot and decay? These things ye call gods, to these ye are slaves, these ye worship; and ye end by becoming altogether like unto them. Therefore ye hate the Christians, because they do not consider these to be gods. For do not ye yourselves, who now regard and worship them, much more despise them? Do ye not much rather mock and insult them, worshipping those that are of stone and earthenware unguarded, but shutting up those that are of silver and gold by night, and setting guards over them by day, to prevent their being stolen? And as for the honours which ye think to offer to them, if they are sensible of them, ye rather punish them thereby, whereas, if they are insensible, ye reproach them by propitiating them with the blood and fat of victims. Let one of yourselves undergo this treatment, let him submit to these things being done to him. Nay, not so much as a single individual will willingly submit to such punishment, for he has sensibility and reason; but a stone submits, because it is insensible. Therefore ye convict his sensibility. Well, I could say much besides concerning the Christians not being enslaved to such gods as these; but if any one should think what has been said insufficient, I hold it superfluous to say more.

3. In the next place, I fancy that thou art chiefly anxious to hear about their not practising their religion in the same way as the Jews. The Jews then, so far as they abstain from the mode of worship described above, do well in claiming to reverence one God of the universe and to regard Him as Master; but so far as they offer Him this worship in methods similar to those already mentioned, they are altogether at fault. For whereas the Greeks, by offering these things to senseless and deaf images, make an exhibition of stupidity, the Jews considering that they are presenting them to God, as if He were in need of them, ought in all reason to count it folly and not religious worship. For He that made the heaven and the earth and all things that are therein, and furnisheth

us all with what we need, cannot Himself need any of these things which He Himself supplieth to them that imagine they are giving them to Him. But those who think to perform sacrifices to Him with blood and fat and whole burnt offerings, and to honour Him with such honours, seem to me in no way different from those who show the same respect towards deaf images; for the one class think fit to make offerings to things unable to participate in the honour, the other class to One Who is in need of nothing.

4. But again their scruples concerning meats, and their super-stition relating to the sabbath and the vanity of their circumcision and the dissimulation of their fasting and new moons, I do [not] suppose you need to learn from me, are ridiculous and unworthy of any consideration. For of the things created by God for the use of man to receive some as created well, but to decline others as useless and superfluous, is not this impious? And again to lie against God, as if He forbad us to do any good thing on the sabbath day, is not this profane? Again, to vaunt the mutilation of the flesh as a token of election as though for this reason they were particularly beloved by God, is not this ridiculous? And to watch the stars and the moon and to keep the observance of months and of days, and to distinguish the arrangements of God and the changes of the seasons according to their own impulses, making some into festivals and others into times of mourning, who would regard this as an exhibition of godliness and not much more of folly? That the Christians are right therefore in holding aloof from the common silliness and error of the Jews and from their excessive fussiness and pride, I consider that thou hast been sufficiently instructed; but as regards the mystery of their own religion, expect not that thou canst be instructed by man.

5. For Christians are not distinguished from the rest of mankind either in locality or in speech or in customs. For they dwell not somewhere in cities of their own, neither do they use some different language, nor practise an extraordinary kind of life. Nor again do they possess any invention discovered by any intelligence or study of ingenious men, nor are they masters of any human dogma as some are. But while they dwell in cities of Greeks and barbarians as the lot of each is cast, and follow the native customs in dress and food and the other arrangements of life, yet the constitution of their own citizenship, which they set forth, is marvellous, and

confessedly contradicts expectation. They dwell in their own countries, but only as sojourners; they bear their share in all things as citizens, and they endure all hardships as strangers. Every foreign country is a fatherland to them, and every fatherland is foreign. They marry like all other men and they beget children; but they do not cast away their offspring. They have their meals in common, but not their wives. They find themselves in the flesh, and yet they live not after the flesh. Their existence is on earth, but their citizenship is in heaven. They obey the established laws, and they surpass the laws in their own lives. They love all men, and they are persecuted by all. They are ignored, and yet they are condemned. They are put to death, and yet they are endued with life. They are in beggary, and yet they make many rich. They are in want of all things, and yet they abound in all things. They are dishonoured, and yet they are glorified in their dishonour. They are evil spoken of, and yet they are vindicated. They are reviled, and they bless; they are insulted, and they respect. Doing good they are punished as evil-doers; being punished they rejoice, as if they were thereby quickened by life. War is waged against them as aliens by the Jews, and persecution is carried on against them by the Greeks, and yet those that hate them cannot tell the reason of their hostility.

6. In a word, what the soul is in a body, this the Christians are in the world. The soul is spread through all the members of the body, and Christians through the divers cities of the world. The soul hath its abode in the body, and yet it is not of the body. So Christians have their abode in the world, and yet they are not of the world. The soul which is invisible is guarded in the body which is visible: so Christians are recognised as being in the world, and yet their religion remaineth invisible. The flesh hateth the soul and wageth war with it, though it receiveth no wrong, because it is forbidden to indulge in pleasures; so the world hateth Christians, though it receiveth no wrong from them, because they set themselves against its pleasures. The soul loveth the flesh which hateth it, and the members: so Christians love those that hate them. The soul is enclosed in the body, and yet itself holdeth the body together; so Christians are kept in the world as in a prison-house, and yet they themselves hold the world together. The soul though itself immortal dwelleth in a mortal tabernacle; so Christians sojourn amidst perishable things, while they look for the imperishability which is in the heavens. The soul when hardly treated

in the matter of meats and drinks is improved; and so Christians when punished increase more and more daily. So great is the office for which God hath appointed them, and which it is not lawful for them to decline.

7. For it is no earthly discovery, as I said, which was committed to them, neither do they care to guard so carefully any mortal invention, nor have they entrusted to them the dispensation of human mysteries. But truly the Almighty Creator of the Universe, the Invisible God Himself from heaven planted among men the truth and the holy teaching which surpasseth the wit of man, and fixed it firmly in their hearts, not as any man might imagine, by sending (to mankind) a subaltern, or angel, or ruler, or one of those that direct the affairs of earth, or one of those who have been entrusted with the dispensations in heaven, but the very Artificer and Creator of the Universe Himself, by Whom He made the heavens, by Whom He enclosed the sea in its proper bounds, Whose mysteries all the elements faithfully observe, from Whom [the sun] hath received even the measure of the courses of the day to keep them, Whom the moon obeys as He bids her shine by night, Whom the stars obey as they follow the course of the moon, by Whom all things are ordered and bounded and placed in subjection, the heavens and the things that are in the heavens, the earth and the things that are in the earth, the sea and the things that are in the sea, fire, air, abyss, the things that are in the heights, the things that are in the depths, the things that are between the two. Him He sent unto them. Was He sent, think you, as any man might suppose, to establish a sovereignty, to inspire fear and terror? Not so. But in gentleness [and] meekness has He sent Him, as a king might send his son who is a king. He sent Him, as sending God; He sent Him, as [a man] unto men; He sent Him, as Saviour, as using persuasion, not force: for force is no attribute of God. He sent Him, as summoning, not as persecuting; He sent Him, as loving, not as judging. For He will send Him in judgment, and who shall endure His presence? ...[Dost thou not see] them thrown to wild beasts that so they may deny the Lord, and yet not overcome? Dost thou not see that the more of them are punished, just so many others abound? These look not like the works of a man; they are the power of God; they are proofs of His presence.

8. For what man at all had any knowledge what God was, before He came? Or dost thou accept the empty and nonsensical statements of those pretentious philosophers: of whom some said that God was fire

(they call that God, whereunto they themselves shall go), and others water, and others some other of the elements which were created by God? And yet if any of these statements is worthy of acceptance, any one other created thing might just as well be made out to be God. Nay, all this is the quackery and deceit of the magicians; and no man has either seen or recognised Him, but He revealed Himself. And He revealed (Himself) by faith, whereby alone it is given to see God. For God, the Master and Creator of the Universe, Who made all things and arranged them in order, was found to be not only friendly to men, but also long-suffering. And such indeed He was always, and is, and will be, kindly and good and dispassionate and true, and He alone is good. And having conceived a great and unutterable scheme He communicated it to His Son alone. For so long as He kept and guarded His wise design as a mystery, He seemed to neglect us and to be careless about us. But when He revealed it through His beloved Son, and manifested the purpose which He had prepared from the beginning, He gave us all these gifts at once, participation in His benefits, and sight and understanding of (mysteries) which none of us ever would have expected.

9. Having thus planned everything already in His mind with His Son, He permitted us during the former time to be borne along by disorderly impulses as we desired, led astray by pleasures and lusts, not at all because He took delight in our sins, but because He bore with us, not because He approved of the past season of iniquity, but because He was creating the present season of righteousness, that, being convicted in the past time by our own deeds as unworthy of life, we might now be made deserving by the goodness of God, and having made clear our inability to enter into the kingdom of God of ourselves, might be enabled by the ability of God. And when our iniquity had been fully accomplished, and it had been made perfectly manifest that punishment and death were expected as its recompense, and the season came which God had ordained, when henceforth He should manifest His goodness and power (O the exceeding great kindness and love of God), He hated us not, neither rejected us, nor bore us malice, but was long-suffering and patient, and in pity for us took upon Himself our sins, and Himself parted with His own Son as a ransom for us, the holy for the lawless, the guileless for the evil, *the just for the unjust*, the incorruptible for the corruptible, the immortal for the mortal. For what else but His righteousness would have covered our sins? In whom was

it possible for us lawless and ungodly men to have been justified, save only in the Son of God? O the sweet exchange, O the inscrutable creation, O the unexpected benefits; that the iniquity of many should be concealed in One Righteous Man, and the righteousness of One should justify many that are iniquitous! Having then in the former time demonstrated the inability of our nature to obtain life, and having now revealed a Saviour able to save even creatures which have no ability, He willed that for both reasons we should believe in His goodness and should regard Him as nurse, father, teacher, counsellor, physician, mind, light, honour, glory, strength and life.

10. This faith if thou also desirest, apprehend first full knowledge of the Father. *For God loved* men for whose sake He made the world, to whom He subjected all things that are in the earth, to whom He gave reason and mind, whom alone He permitted to look up to heaven, whom He created after His own image, to whom *He sent His only begotten Son*, to whom He promised the kingdom which is in heaven, and will give it to those that have loved Him. And when thou hast attained to this full knowledge, with what joy thinkest thou that thou wilt be filled, or how wilt thou love Him that so loved thee before? And loving Him thou wilt be an imitator of His goodness. And marvel not that a man can be an imitator of God. He can, if God willeth it. For happiness consisteth not in lordship over one's neighbours, nor in desiring to have more than weaker men, nor in possessing wealth and using force to inferiors; neither can any one imitate God in these matters; nay, these lie outside His greatness. But whosoever taketh upon himself the burden of his neighbour, whosoever desireth to benefit one that is worse off in that in which he himself is superior, whosoever by supplying to those that are in want possessions which he received from God becomes a God to those who receive them from him, he is an imitator of God. Then, though thou art placed on earth, thou shalt behold that God liveth in heaven; then shalt thou begin to declare the mysteries of God; then shalt thou both love and admire those that are punished because they will not deny God; then shalt thou condemn the deceit and error of the world; when thou shalt perceive the true life which is in heaven, when thou shalt despise the apparent death which is here on earth, when thou shalt fear the real death, which is reserved for those that shall be condemned to the eternal fire that shall punish those delivered over to it unto the end. Then shalt thou admire those who endure for righteousness' sake the

fire that is for a season, and shalt count them blessed when thou perceivest that fire...

    *   *   *   *   *   *

11. Mine are no strange discourses nor perverse questionings, but
having been a disciple of Apostles I come forward as a teacher of the
Gentiles, ministering worthily to them, as they present themselves disciples of the truth, the lessons which have been handed down. For
who that has been rightly taught and has entered into friendship with
the Word does not seek to learn distinctly the lessons revealed openly
by the Word to the disciples; to whom the Word appeared and declared them, speaking plainly, not perceived by the unbelieving, but
relating them to disciples who being reckoned faithful by Him were
taught the mysteries of the Father? For which cause He sent forth
the Word, that He might appear unto the world, Who being dishonoured by the people, and preached by the Apostles, was believed
in by the Gentiles. This Word, Who was from the beginning, Who
appeared as new and yet was proved to be old, and is engendered always young in the hearts of saints, He, I say, Who is eternal, Who
to-day was accounted a Son, through Whom the Church is enriched and
grace is unfolded and multiplied among the saints, grace which confers
understanding, which reveals mysteries, which announces seasons,
which rejoices over the faithful, which is bestowed upon those who seek
her, even those by whom the pledges of faith are not broken, nor the
boundaries of the fathers overstepped. Whereupon the fear of the law
is sung, and the grace of the prophets is recognised, and the faith of the
gospels is established, and the tradition of the apostles is preserved, and
the joy of the Church exults. If thou grieve not this grace, thou shalt
understand the discourses which the Word holds by the mouth of those
whom He desires when He wishes. For in all things, that by the will of
the commanding Word we were moved to utter with much pains, we
become sharers with you, through love of the things revealed unto us.

12. Confronted with these truths and listening to them with attention, ye shall know how much God bestoweth on those that love (Him)
rightly, who become a Paradise of delight, a tree bearing all manner of
fruits and flourishing, growing up in themselves and adorned with various
fruits. For in this garden a tree of knowledge and a tree of life hath
been planted; yet the tree of knowledge does not kill, but disobedience
kills; for the scriptures state clearly how God from the beginning planted
a tree [of knowledge and a tree] of life in the midst of Paradise, revealing

life through knowledge; and because our first parents used it not genuinely they were made naked by the deceit of the serpent. For neither is there life without knowledge, nor sound knowledge without true life; therefore the one (tree) is planted near the other. Discerning the force of this and blaming the knowledge which is exercised apart from the truth of the injunction which leads to life, the apostle says, *Knowledge puffeth up, but charity edifieth.* For the man who supposes that he knows anything without the true knowledge which is testified by the life, is ignorant, he is deceived by the serpent, because he loved not life; whereas he who with fear recognises and desires life plants in hope expecting fruit. Let your heart be knowledge, and your life true reason, duly comprehended. Whereof if thou bear the tree and pluck the fruit, thou shalt ever gather the harvest which God looks for, which serpent toucheth not, nor deceit infecteth, neither is Eve corrupted, but is believed on as a virgin, and salvation is set forth, and the apostles are filled with understanding, and the passover of the Lord goes forward, and the congregations are gathered together, and [all things] are arranged in order, and as He teacheth the saints the Word is gladdened, through Whom the Father is glorified, to Whom be glory for ever and ever. Amen.

THE FRAGMENTS

OF

PAPIAS

THE following extracts contain not only the fragments of Papias' writings which survive, but also the scanty notices of his life and theological opinions which have come down to us. As therefore all the facts about him are placed before the reader herewith, it will only be necessary to add that Papias was born probably between A.D. 60—70, and published his *Exposition of Oracles of the Lord* late in life (c. A.D. 130—140). For a full account of the man, and of his evidence to the Canon of the New Testament, the reader is referred to Dr Lightfoot's *Essays on the Work entitled Supernatural Religion*, pp. 142—216 (Macmillan and Co. 1889). Reasons are there given (p. 194 sq.) for assigning to Papias the two anonymous fragments quoted by Irenæus, which appear below (pp. 548, 549) among the Reliques of the Elders (Nos. XIII, XVII).

For convenience of reference the actual quotations from Papias are given in larger type than the introductory matter and personal notices.

FRAGMENTS OF PAPIAS

I.

Ἰωάννην τὸν θεολόγον καὶ ἀπόστολον Εἰρηναῖος καὶ ἄλλοι ἱστοροῦσι παραμεῖναι τῷ βίῳ ἕως τῶν χρόνων Τραϊανοῦ· μεθ᾽ ὃν Παπίας Ἱεραπολίτης καὶ Πολύκαρπος Σμύρνης ἐπίσκοπος ἀκουσταὶ αὐτοῦ ἐγνωρίζοντο.

EUSEBIUS *Chronicon* (Syncell. 655, 14) for Olymp. 220, *ed.* A. Schoene (1866) II. p. 162.

II.

Διέπρεπέ γε μὴν κατὰ τούτους ἐπὶ τῆς Ἀσίας τῶν ἀποστόλων ὁμιλητὴς Πολύκαρπος, τῆς κατὰ Σμύρναν ἐκκλησίας πρὸς τῶν ΑΥΤΟΠΤΩΝ καὶ S.Lukei.2. ΥΠΗΡΕΤΩΝ τοῦ Κυρίου τὴν ἐπισκοπὴν ἐγκεχειρισμένος. καθ᾽ ὃν ἐγνωρίζετο Παπίας τῆς ἐν Ἱεραπόλει παροικίας καὶ αὐτὸς ἐπίσκοπος.

EUSEBIUS *Hist. Eccl.* iii. 36. 1. 2, *ed.* Heinichen (1868) I. p. 141.

III.

Τοῦ δὲ Παπία συγγράμματα πέντε τὸν ἀριθμὸν φέρεται, ἃ καὶ ἐπιγέγραπται λογίων κυριακῶν ἐξηγήσεις. τούτων καὶ Εἰρηναῖος ὡς μόνων αὐτῷ γραφέντων μνημονεύει, ὧδέ πως λέγων· Ταῦτα δὲ καὶ Παπίας ὁ Ἰωάννου μὲν ἀκουστής, Πολυκάρπου δὲ ἑταῖρος γεγονώς, ἀρχαῖος ἀνήρ, ἐγγράφως ἐπιμαρτυρεῖ ἐν τῇ τετάρτῃ τῶν ἑαυτοῦ βιβλίων· ἔστι γὰρ αὐτῷ πέντε βιβλία συντεταγμένα. 2. Καὶ ὁ μὲν Εἰρηναῖος ταῦτα. Αὐτός γε μὴν ὁ Παπίας κατὰ τὸ προοίμιον τῶν αὐτοῦ λόγων ἀκροατὴν μὲν καὶ αὐτόπτην οὐδαμῶς ἑαυτὸν γενέσθαι τῶν ἱερῶν ἀποστόλων ἐμφαίνει, παρειληφέναι δὲ τὰ τῆς πίστεως παρὰ τῶν ἐκείνοις γνωρίμων διδάσκει δι᾽ ὧν φησι λέξεων·

3. Οὐκ ὀκνήσω δέ σοι καὶ ὅσα ποτὲ παρὰ τῶν πρεσβυτέρων καλῶς ἔμαθον καὶ καλῶς ἐμνημόνευσα, συγκατατάξαι ταῖς ἑρμηνείαις, διαβεβαιούμενος ὑπὲρ αὐτῶν ἀλήθειαν. οὐ γὰρ τοῖς τὰ πολλὰ λέγουσιν ἔχαιρον ὥσπερ οἱ πολλοί, ἀλλὰ τοῖς τἀληθῆ διδάσκουσιν, οὐδὲ τοῖς τὰς ἀλλοτρίας ἐντολὰς μνημονεύουσιν, ἀλλὰ τοῖς τὰς παρὰ τοῦ Κυρίου τῇ πίστει δεδομένας καὶ ἀπ' αὐτῆς παραγινομένοις τῆς ἀληθείας. 4. Εἰ δέ που καὶ παρηκολουθηκώς τις τοῖς πρεσβυτέροις ἔλθοι, τοὺς τῶν πρεσβυτέρων ἀνέκρινον λόγους· τί Ἀνδρέας ἢ τί Πέτρος εἶπεν ἢ τί Φίλιππος ἢ τί Θωμᾶς ἢ Ἰάκωβος ἢ τί Ἰωάννης ἢ Ματθαῖος ἤ τις ἕτερος τῶν τοῦ Κυρίου μαθητῶν, ἅ τε Ἀριστίων καὶ ὁ πρεσβύτερος Ἰωάννης, οἱ τοῦ Κυρίου μαθηταί, λέγουσιν. οὐ γὰρ τὰ ἐκ τῶν βιβλίων τοσοῦτόν με ὠφελεῖν ὑπελάμβανον, ὅσον τὰ παρὰ ζώσης φωνῆς καὶ μενούσης. 5. Ἔνθα καὶ ἐπιστῆσαι ἄξιον δὶς καταριθμοῦντι αὐτῷ τὸ Ἰωάννου ὄνομα, ὧν τὸν μὲν πρότερον Πέτρῳ καὶ Ἰακώβῳ καὶ Ματθαίῳ καὶ τοῖς λοιποῖς ἀποστόλοις συγκαταλέγει, σαφῶς δηλῶν τὸν εὐαγγελιστήν, τὸν δ' ἕτερον Ἰωάννην διαστείλας τὸν λόγον ἑτέροις παρὰ τὸν τῶν ἀποστόλων ἀριθμὸν κατατάσσει, προτάξας αὐτοῦ τὸν Ἀριστίωνα, 6. σαφῶς τε αὐτὸν πρεσβύτερον ὀνομάζει· ὡς καὶ διὰ τούτων ἀποδείκνυσθαι τὴν ἱστορίαν ἀληθῆ τῶν δύο κατὰ τὴν Ἀσίαν ὁμωνυμίᾳ κεχρῆσθαι εἰρηκότων, δύο τε ἐν Ἐφέσῳ γενέσθαι μνήματα καὶ ἑκάτερον Ἰωάννου ἔτι νῦν λέγεσθαι. Οἷς καὶ ἀναγκαῖον προσέχειν τὸν νοῦν· εἰκὸς γὰρ τὸν δεύτερον, εἰ μή τις ἐθέλοι τὸν πρῶτον, τὴν ἐπ' ὀνόματος φερομένην Ἰωάννου ἀποκάλυψιν ἑωρακέναι. 7. Καὶ ὁ νῦν δὲ ἡμῖν δηλούμενος Παπίας τοὺς μὲν τῶν ἀποστόλων λόγους παρὰ τῶν αὐτοῖς παρηκολουθηκότων ὁμολογεῖ παρειληφέναι, Ἀριστίωνος δὲ καὶ τοῦ πρεσβυτέρου Ἰωάννου αὐτήκοον ἑαυτόν φησι γενέσθαι. Ὀνομαστὶ γοῦν πολλάκις αὐτῶν μνημονεύσας, ἐν τοῖς αὐτοῦ συγγράμμασι τίθησιν αὐτῶν καὶ παραδόσεις. Καὶ ταῦτα δ' ἡμῖν οὐκ εἰς τὸ ἄχρηστον εἰρήσθω. 8. Ἄξιον δὲ ταῖς ἀποδοθείσαις τοῦ Παπία φωναῖς προσάψαι λέξεις ἑτέρας αὐτοῦ, δι' ὧν παράδοξά τινα ἱστορεῖ καὶ ἄλλα, ὡσὰν ἐκ παραδόσεως εἰς αὐτὸν ἐλθόντα. 9. Τὸ μὲν οὖν κατὰ τὴν Ἱεράπολιν Φίλιππον τὸν ἀπόστολον ἅμα ταῖς θυγατράσι διατρῖψαι, διὰ τῶν πρόσθεν δεδήλωται, ὡς δὲ κατὰ τοὺς αὐτοὺς ὁ Παπίας γενόμενος διήγησιν παρειληφέναι θαυμασίαν ὑπὸ τῶν τοῦ Φιλίππου θυγατέρων μνημονεύει, τὰ νῦν σημειωτέον. Νεκροῦ γὰρ ἀνάστασιν κατ' αὐτὸν γεγονυῖαν ἱστορεῖ, καὶ αὖ πάλιν ἕτερον παράδοξον περὶ Ἰοῦστον τὸν ἐπικληθέντα Βαρσαββᾶν γεγονός, ὡς δηλητήριον φάρμακον ἐμπιόντος καὶ μηδὲν ἀηδὲς διὰ τὴν τοῦ Κυρίου χάριν ὑπομείναντος. 10. Τοῦτον δὲ τὸν Ἰοῦστον μετὰ τὴν τοῦ Σωτῆρος ἀνάληψιν τοὺς ἱεροὺς ἀποστόλους μετὰ Ματθία στῆσαί τε καὶ ἐπεύξασθαι ἀντὶ τοῦ προδό-

τοῦ Ἰούδα ἐπὶ τὸν κλῆρον τῆς ἀναπληρώσεως τοῦ αὐτῶν ἀριθμοῦ, ἡ τῶν πράξεων ὧδέ πως ἱστορεῖ γραφή· Καὶ ἔϲτηϲαν Δγο, Ἰωϲὴφ τὸν καλογ- Acts i. 23. μενον Βαρϲαββᾶν, ὃϲ ἐπεκλήθη Ἰογϲτοϲ, καὶ Ματθίαν· καὶ προϲ-εγξάμενοι εἶπαν. 11. Καὶ ἄλλα δὲ ὁ αὐτὸς ὡσὰν ἐκ παραδόσεως ἀγρά-φου εἰς αὐτὸν ἥκοντα παρατέθειται, ξένας τέ τινας παραβολὰς τοῦ Σωτῆρος καὶ διδασκαλίας αὐτοῦ, καί τινα ἄλλα μυθικώτερα. 12. Ἐν οἷς καὶ χιλιάδα τινά φησιν ἐτῶν ἔσεσθαι μετὰ τὴν ἐκ νεκρῶν ἀνάστασιν, σωματικῶς τῆς Χριστοῦ βασιλείας ἐπὶ ταυτησὶ τῆς γῆς ὑποστησομένης. Ἃ καὶ ἡγοῦμαι τὰς ἀποστολικὰς παρεκδεξάμενον διηγήσεις ὑπολαβεῖν, τὰ ἐν ὑποδείγμασι πρὸς αὐτῶν μυστικῶς εἰρημένα μὴ συνεωρακότα. 13. Σφόδρα γάρ τοι σμικρὸς ὢν τὸν νοῦν, ὡσὰν ἐκ τῶν αὐτοῦ λόγων τεκμηράμενον εἰπεῖν, φαίνεται· πλὴν καὶ τοῖς μετ᾽ αὐτὸν πλείστοις ὅσοις τῶν ἐκκλησιαστικῶν τῆς ὁμοίας αὐτῷ δόξης παραίτιος γέγονε, τὴν ἀρχαιότητα τἀνδρὸς προβεβλημένοις, ὥσπερ οὖν Εἰρηναίῳ, καὶ εἴ τις ἄλλος τὰ ὅμοια φρονῶν ἀναπέφηνεν. 14. Καὶ ἄλλας δὲ τῇ ἑαυτοῦ γραφῇ παραδίδωσιν Ἀριστίωνος τοῦ πρόσθεν δεδηλωμένου τῶν τοῦ Κυρίου λόγων διηγήσεις καὶ τοῦ πρεσβυτέρου Ἰωάννου παραδόσεις, ἐφ᾽ ἃς τοὺς φιλομαθεῖς ἀναπέμψαντες, ἀναγκαίως νῦν προσ-θήσομεν ταῖς προεκτεθείσαις αὐτοῦ φωναῖς παράδοσιν, ἣν περὶ Μάρκου τοῦ τὸ εὐαγγέλιον γεγραφότος ἐκτέθειται διὰ τούτων·

15. Καὶ τοῦτο ὁ πρεσβύτερος ἔλεγε· Μάρκος μὲν ἑρμη-νευτὴς Πέτρου γενόμενος, ὅσα ἐμνημόνευσεν, ἀκριβῶς ἔγραψεν, οὐ μέντοι τάξει, τὰ ὑπὸ τοῦ Χριστοῦ ἢ λεχθέντα ἢ πραχθέντα. οὔτε γὰρ ἤκουσε τοῦ Κυρίου, οὔτε παρηκολούθησεν αὐτῷ, ὕστερον δέ, ὡς ἔφην, Πέτρῳ, ὃς πρὸς τὰς χρείας ἐποιεῖτο τὰς διδασκαλίας, ἀλλ᾽ οὐχ ὥσπερ σύνταξιν τῶν κυριακῶν ποιού-μενος λόγων, ὥστε οὐδὲν ἥμαρτε Μάρκος, οὕτως ἔνια γράψας ὡς ἀπεμνημόνευσεν. ἑνὸς γὰρ ἐποιήσατο πρόνοιαν, τοῦ μηδὲν ὧν ἤκουσε παραλιπεῖν ἢ ψεύσασθαί τι ἐν αὐτοῖς.

Ταῦτα μὲν οὖν ἱστόρηται τῷ Παπίᾳ περὶ τοῦ Μάρκου. 16. Περὶ δὲ τοῦ Ματθαίου ταῦτ᾽ εἴρηται·

Ματθαῖος μὲν οὖν Ἑβραΐδι διαλέκτῳ τὰ λόγια συνεγρά-ψατο, ἡρμήνευσε δ᾽ αὐτὰ ὡς ἦν δυνατὸς ἕκαστος.

Κέχρηται δ᾽ αὐτὸς μαρτυρίαις ἀπὸ τῆς Ἰωάννου προτέρας ἐπιστολῆς καὶ ἀπὸ τῆς Πέτρου ὁμοίως. ἐκτέθειται δὲ καὶ ἄλλην ἱστορίαν περὶ γυναικὸς ἐπὶ πολλαῖς ἁμαρτίαις διαβληθείσης ἐπὶ τοῦ Κυρίου, ἣν τὸ κατ᾽ Ἑβραίους εὐαγγέλιον περιέχει. Καὶ ταῦτα δ᾽ ἡμῖν ἀναγκαίως πρὸς τοῖς ἐκτεθεῖσιν ἐπιτετηρήσθω.

EUSEBIUS *Hist. Eccl.* iii. 39 (Heinichen I. p. 147 sq.).

IV.

Καὶ ἐπορεύθησαν ἕκαστος εἰς τὸν οἶκον αὐτοῦ, Ἰησοῦς δὲ
ἐπορεύθη εἰς τὸ Ὄρος τῶν Ἐλαιῶν. ὄρθρου δὲ πάλιν
παρεγένετο εἰς τὸ ἱερόν, [καὶ πᾶς ὁ λαὸς ἤρχετο πρὸς αὐτόν,
καὶ καθίσας ἐδίδασκεν αὐτούς]. ἄγουσιν δὲ οἱ γραμματεῖς
καὶ οἱ Φαρισαῖοι γυναῖκα ἐπὶ μοιχείᾳ κατειλημμένην, καὶ
στήσαντες αὐτὴν ἐν μέσῳ λέγουσιν αὐτῷ Διδάσκαλε, αὕτη ἡ
γυνὴ κατείληπται ἐπ᾽ αὐτοφώρῳ μοιχευομένη· ἐν δὲ τῷ νόμῳ
[ἡμῖν] Μωυσῆς ἐνετείλατο τὰς τοιαύτας λιθάζειν· σὺ οὖν τί
λέγεις; [τοῦτο δὲ ἔλεγον πειράζοντες αὐτόν, ἵνα ἔχωσιν
κατηγορεῖν αὐτοῦ.] ὁ δὲ Ἰησοῦς κάτω κύψας τῷ δακτύλῳ
κατέγραφεν εἰς τὴν γῆν. ὡς δὲ ἐπέμενον ἐρωτῶντες [αὐτόν],
ἀνέκυψεν καὶ εἶπεν [αὐτοῖς] Ὁ ἀναμάρτητος ὑμῶν πρῶτος
ἐπ᾽ αὐτὴν βαλέτω λίθον· καὶ πάλιν κατακύψας ἔγραφεν εἰς
τὴν γῆν. οἱ δὲ ἀκούσαντες ἐξήρχοντο εἷς καθ᾽ εἷς ἀρξάμενοι
ἀπὸ τῶν πρεσβυτέρων, καὶ κατελείφθη μόνος, καὶ ἡ γυνὴ ἐν
μέσῳ οὖσα. ἀνακύψας δὲ ὁ Ἰησοῦς εἶπεν αὐτῇ Γύναι, ποῦ
εἰσίν; οὐδείς σε κατέκρινεν; ἡ δὲ εἶπεν Οὐδείς, κύριε. εἶπεν
δὲ ὁ Ἰησοῦς Οὐδὲ ἐγώ σε κατακρίνω· πορεύου, ἀπὸ τοῦ νῦν
μηκέτι ἁμάρτανε.

PERICOPE ADULTERAE ; see Westcott and Hort *The
New Testament in the original Greek* I. p. 241,
II. pp. 82 sq, 91 ; Lightfoot *Essays on Super-
natural Religion* p. 203 sq.

V.

Παπίας Ἱεροπόλεως ἐπίσκοπος ἀκουστὴς τοῦ θεολόγου Ἰωάννου γενόμενος, Πολυκάρπου δὲ ἑταῖρος, πέντε λόγους κυριακῶν λογίων ἔγραψεν,
ἐν οἷς ἀπαρίθμησιν ἀποστόλων ποιούμενος μετὰ Πέτρον καὶ Ἰωάννην, Φίλιππον καὶ Θωμᾶν καὶ Ματθαῖον εἰς μαθητὰς τοῦ Κυρίου ἀνέγραψεν Ἀριστίωνα
καὶ Ἰωάννην ἕτερον, ὃν καὶ πρεσβύτερον ἐκάλεσεν. ὥς τινας οἴεσθαι,
ὅτι [ins. τούτου] τοῦ Ἰωάννου εἰσὶν αἱ δύο ἐπιστολαὶ αἱ μικραὶ καὶ καθολικαί,
αἱ ἐξ ὀνόματος Ἰωάννου φερόμεναι, διὰ τὸ τοὺς ἀρχαίους τὴν πρώτην μόνην
ἐγκρίνειν· τινὲς δὲ καὶ τὴν ἀποκάλυψιν τούτου πλανηθέντες ἐνόμισαν. καὶ
Παπίας δὲ περὶ τὴν χιλιονταετηρίδα σφάλλεται, ἐξ οὗ καὶ ὁ Εἰρηναῖος.
Παπίας ἐν τῷ δευτέρῳ λόγῳ λέγει, ὅτι Ἰωάννης ὁ θεολόγος καὶ Ἰάκωβος ὁ

ἀδελφὸς αὐτοῦ ὑπὸ Ἰουδαίων ἀνῃρέθησαν. Παπίας ὁ εἰρημένος ἱστόρησεν ὡς παραλαβὼν ἀπὸ τῶν θυγατέρων Φιλίππου, ὅτι Βαρσαβᾶς ὁ καὶ Ἰοῦστος δοκιμαζόμενος ὑπὸ τῶν ἀπίστων ἰὸν ἐχίδνης πιὼν ἐν ὀνόματι τοῦ Χριστοῦ ἀπαθὴς διεφυλάχθη. ἱστορεῖ δὲ καὶ ἄλλα θαύματα καὶ μάλιστα τὸ κατὰ τὴν μητέρα Μαναΐμου τὴν ἐκ νεκρῶν ἀναστᾶσαν· περὶ τῶν ὑπὸ τοῦ Χριστοῦ ἐκ νεκρῶν ἀναστάντων, ὅτι ἕως Ἀδριανοῦ ἔζων.

PHILIPPUS SIDETES (?) *Hist. Christ.* (published by De Boor *Texte und Untersuchungen* v. 2 p. 170 from cod. Baroccianus 142 in the Bodleian Library).

VI.

Μετὰ δὲ Δομετιανὸν ἐβασίλευσε Νερούας ἔτος ἕν, ὃς ἀνακαλεσάμενος Ἰωάννην ἐκ τῆς νήσου ἀπέλυσεν οἰκεῖν ἐν Ἐφέσῳ. μόνος τότε περιὼν τῷ βίῳ ἐκ τῶν δώδεκα μαθητῶν καὶ συγγραψάμενος τὸ κατ᾽ αὐτὸν εὐαγγέλιον μαρτυρίου κατηξίωται. Παπίας γὰρ ὁ Ἱεραπόλεως ἐπίσκοπος, αὐτόπτης τούτου γενόμενος, ἐν τῷ δευτέρῳ λόγῳ τῶν κυριακῶν λογίων φάσκει, ὅτι ὑπὸ Ἰουδαίων ἀνῃρέθη· πληρώσας δηλαδὴ μετὰ τοῦ ἀδελφοῦ τὴν τοῦ Χριστοῦ περὶ αὐτῶν πρόρρησιν καὶ τὴν ἑαυτῶν ὁμολογίαν περὶ τούτου καὶ συγκατάθεσιν· εἰπὼν γὰρ ὁ Κύριος πρὸς αὐτούς· Δýνασθε πιεῖν τὸ S. Mark x. ποτήριον ὃ ἐγὼ πίνω; καὶ κατανευσάντων προθύμως καὶ συνθεμένων· 38, 39. Τὸ ποτήριόν μογ, φησίν, πίεσθε καὶ τὸ Βάπτισμα ὃ ἐγὼ Βαπτίζομαι Βαπτισθήσεσθε. καὶ εἰκότως. ἀδύνατον γὰρ Θεὸν ψεύσασθαι. οὕτω δὲ καὶ ὁ πολυμαθὴς Ὠριγένης ἐν τῇ κατὰ Ματθαῖον ἑρμηνείᾳ διαβεβαιοῦται, ὡς ὅτι μεμαρτύρηκεν Ἰωάννης, ἐκ τῶν διαδόχων τῶν ἀποστόλων ὑποσημαινάμενος τοῦτο μεμαθηκέναι. καὶ μὲν δὴ καὶ ὁ πολυΐστωρ Εὐσέβιος ἐν τῇ ἐκκλησιαστικῇ ἱστορίᾳ φησί· Θωμᾶς μὲν τὴν Παρθίαν εἴληχεν, Ἰωάννης δὲ τὴν Ἀσίαν, πρὸς οὓς καὶ διατρίψας ἐτελεύτησεν ἐν Ἐφέσῳ.

GEORGIUS HAMARTOLUS *Chronicon* (published by Nolte *Tüb. Theol. Quartalschr.* 1862 p. 466 sq. from cod. Coisl.); see Lightfoot *Essays on Supernatural Religion* p. 211 sq.

VII.

Papias, Iohannis auditor, Hierapolitanus in Asia episcopus, quinque tantum scripsit volumina, quae praenotavit Explanatio Sermonum Domini. In quibus quum se in praefatione asserat non varias opiniones sequi, sed apostolos habere auctores, ait: Considerabam, quid Andreas, quid Petrus dixissent, quid Philippus, quid Thomas, quid Iacobus, quid Iohannes, quid Matthaeus, vel alius quilibet discipulorum Domini: quid etiam Aristion et senior Iohannes, discipuli Domini, loquebantur. Non enim tantum mihi libri ad legendum prosunt, quantum viva vox usque hodie in suis auctoribus personans.

Ex quo apparet in ipso catalogo nominum, alium esse Iohannem, qui inter apostolos ponitur, et alium seniorem Iohannem, quem post Aristionem enumerat. Hoc autem diximus propter superiorem opinionem, quam a plerisque retulimus traditam, duas posteriores epistulas Iohannis non apostoli esse, sed presbyteri. Hic dicitur mille annorum Iudaicam edidisse δευτέρωσιν, quem secuti sunt Irenaeus et Apollinarius et caeteri, qui post resurrectionem aiunt in carne cum sanctis Dominum regnaturum.

HIERONYMUS de vir. illust. 18, ed. Vallarsi II. p. 845.

VIII.

Porro Iosephi libros et sanctorum Papiae et Polycarpi volumina falsus ad te rumor pertulit a me esse translata : quia nec otii mei nec virium est tantas res eadem in alteram linguam exprimere venustate.

HIERONYMUS ad Lucinium Ep. 71 (28) c. 5.
(Vallarsi I. p. 432.)

IX.

Refert Irenaeus...... Papiae auditoris evangelistae Iohannis discipulus.....

HIERONYMUS ad Theodoram Ep. 75 (29) c. 3.
(Vallarsi I. p. 450.)

X.

Περὶ μέντοι τοῦ θεοπνεύστου τῆς βίβλου (sc. τῆς ἀποκαλύψεως Ἰωάννου) περιττὸν μηκύνειν τὸν λόγον ἡγούμεθα, τῶν μακαρίων Γρηγορίου φημὶ τοῦ θεολόγου καὶ Κυρίλλου, προσέτι δὲ καὶ τῶν ἀρχαιοτέρων Παπίου, Εἰρηναίου, Μεθοδίου καὶ Ἱππολύτου ταύτῃ προσμαρτυρούντων τὸ ἀξιόπιστον.

ANDREAS CAESARIENSIS praef. in Apocalypsin (in Morel's edition of S. Chrysostom, p. 2).

XI.

Παπίας δὲ οὕτως ἐπὶ λέξεως· Ἐνίοις δὲ αὐτῶν, δηλαδὴ τῶν πάλαι θείων ἀγγέλων, καὶ τῆς περὶ τὴν γῆν διακοσμήσεως ἔδωκεν ἄρχειν καὶ καλῶς ἄρχειν παρηγγύησε. καὶ ἑξῆς φησίν· Εἰς οὐδὲν δέον συνέβη τελευτῆσαι τὴν τάξιν αὐτῶν. Καὶ ἐβλήθη ὁ δράκων ὁ μέγας, ὁ ὄφις ὁ ἀρχαῖος ὁ καλούμενος διάβολος καὶ ὁ Σατανᾶς, ὁ πλανῶν τὴν οἰκουμένην ὅλην ἐβλήθη εἰς τὴν γῆν, καὶ οἱ ἄγγελοι αὐτοῦ.

ANDREAS CAESARIENSIS *in Apocalypsin* c. 34, serm. 12.
(Morel *l.c.* p. 52.)

XII.

Λαβόντες τὰς ἀφορμὰς ἐκ Παπίου τοῦ πάνυ τοῦ Ἱεραπολίτου, τοῦ ἐν τῷ ἐπιστηθίῳ φοιτήσαντος, καὶ Κλήμεντος, Πανταίνου τῆς Ἀλεξανδρέων ἱερέως καὶ Ἀμμωνίου σοφωτάτου, τῶν ἀρχαίων καὶ πρώτων συνῳδῶν ἐξηγητῶν, εἰς Χριστὸν καὶ τὴν ἐκκλησίαν πᾶσαν τὴν ἑξαήμερον νοησάντων.

ANASTASIUS SINAITA *Contempl. Anagog. in Hexaëm.* i
(Migne *P. G.* LXXXIX. p. 860); the Greek was
given first by Halloix *Ill. Eccl. Orient.* II. p. 851.

XIII.

Οἱ μὲν οὖν ἀρχαιότεροι τῶν ἐκκλησιῶν ἐξηγητῶν, λέγω δὴ Φίλων ὁ φιλόσοφος καὶ τῶν ἀποστόλων ὁμόχρονος καὶ Παπίας ὁ πολὺς ὁ Ἰωάννου τοῦ εὐαγγελιστοῦ φοιτητὴς ὁ Ἱεραπολίτης..... καὶ οἱ ἀμφ' αὐτοὺς πνευματικῶς τὰ περὶ παραδείσου ἐθεώρησαν εἰς τὴν Χριστοῦ ἐκκλησίαν ἀναφερόμενοι.

ANASTASIUS SINAITA *l.c.* vii (Migne *P. G.* LXXXIX.
p. 961); the Greek was given first by Nolte *Tüb.
Theol. Quartalschr.* (1867) p. 56.

XIV.

Praedicta itaque benedictio ad tempora regni sine contradictione pertinet, quando regnabunt iusti surgentes a mortuis; quando et creatura renovata et liberata multitudinem fructificabit universae escae, *ex rore caeli et ex fertilitate terrae:* quemadmodum presbyteri Genesis meminerunt, qui Iohannem discipulum Domini viderunt, audisse se ab xxvii. 28. eo, quemadmodum de temporibus illis docebat Dominus et dicebat:

Venient dies, in quibus vineae nascentur, singulae decem millia palmitum habentes, et in uno palmite dena millia brachiorum, et in uno vero palmite [*l.* brachio] dena millia flagellorum, et in unoquoque flagello dena millia botruum, et in unoquoque botro dena millia acinorum, et unumquodque acinum expressum dabit vigintiquinque metretas vini. Et cum eorum apprehenderit aliquis sanctorum botrum, alius clamabit: Botrus ego melior sum, me sume, per me Dominum benedic. Similiter et granum tritici decem millia spicarum generaturum, et unamquamque spicam habituram decem millia granorum, et unumquodque granum quinque bilibres similae clarae mundae: et reliqua autem poma et semina et herbam secundum congruentiam iis consequentem: et omnia animalia iis cibis utentia, quae a terra accipiuntur, pacifica et consentanea invicem fieri, subiecta hominibus cum omni subiectione.

Haec autem et Papias Iohannis auditor, Polycarpi autem contubernalis, vetus homo, per scripturam testimonium perhibet in quarto librorum suorum : sunt enim illi quinque libri conscripti.

Ταῦτα δὲ καὶ Παπίας ὁ Ἰωάννου μὲν ἀκουστής, Πολυκάρπου δὲ ἑταῖρος γεγονώς, ἀρχαῖος ἀνήρ, ἐγγράφως ἐπιμαρτυρεῖ ἐν τῇ τετάρτῃ τῶν ἑαυτοῦ βιβλίων· ἔστι γὰρ αὐτῷ πέντε βιβλία συντεταγμένα (see above, No. III.).

Et adiecit dicens :

Haec autem credibilia sunt credentibus. Et Iuda, inquit, proditore non credente et interrogante: Quomodo ergo tales geniturae a Domino perficientur? dixisse Dominum: Videbunt qui venient in illa.

IRENÆUS *Haer.* V. 33. 3, 4, *ed.* Stieren (1853) I. p. 809 sq.

XV.

Τοὺς κατὰ θεὸν ἀκακίαν ἀσκοῦντας παῖδας ἐκάλουν, ὡς καὶ Παπίας δηλοῖ βιβλίῳ πρώτῳ τῶν κυριακῶν ἐξηγήσεων καὶ Κλήμης ὁ Ἀλεξανδρεὺς ἐν τῷ Παιδαγωγῷ.

MAXIMUS CONFESSOR *Schol. in libr. Dionys. Areopag.*
de eccl. hierarch. c. 2, *ed.* Corder. (1755) I. p. 32.

XVI.

Ταῦτά φησιν αἰνιττόμενος οἶμαι Παπίαν τὸν Ἱεραπόλεως τῆς κατ᾽ Ἀσίαν
τότε γενόμενον ἐπίσκοπον καὶ συνακμάσαντα τῷ θείῳ εὐαγγελιστῇ Ἰωάννῃ.
οὗτος γὰρ ὁ Παπίας ἐν τῷ τετάρτῳ αὐτοῦ βιβλίῳ τῶν κυριακῶν ἐξηγήσεων τὰς διὰ βρωμάτων εἶπεν ἐν τῇ ἀναστάσει ἀπολαύσεις....καὶ Εἰρηναῖος δὲ ὁ Λουγδούνου ἐν τῷ κατὰ αἱρέσεων πέμπτῳ λόγῳ τὸ αὐτό φησι καὶ
παράγει μάρτυρα τῶν ὑπ᾽ αὐτοῦ εἰρημένων τὸν λεχθέντα Παπίαν.

MAXIMUS CONFESSOR *l. c.* (Corder. I. p. 422 *de eccl. hierarch.* c. 7).

XVII.

Οὐ μὴν ἀλλ᾽ οὐδὲ Παπίαν τὸν Ἱεραπόλεως ἐπίσκοπον καὶ μάρτυρα,
οὐδὲ Εἰρηναῖον τὸν ὅσιον ἐπίσκοπον Λουγδούνων (sc. ἀποδέχεται Στέ-
φανος), ἐν οἷς λέγουσιν αἰσθητῶν τινῶν βρωμάτων ἀπόλαυσιν εἶναι τὴν
τῶν οὐρανῶν βασιλείαν.

PHOTIUS *Biblioth.* 232, speaking of Stephanus Gobarus,
ed. Bekker (1824) p. 291.

XVIII.

Ἀπολιναρίου· Οὐκ ἀπέθανε τῇ ἀγχόνῃ Ἰούδας, ἀλλ᾽ ἐπεβίω καθαιρεθεὶς
πρὸ τοῦ ἀποπνιγῆναι. καὶ τοῦτο δηλοῦσιν αἱ τῶν ἀποστόλων πράξεις, ὅτι
ΠΡΗΝΗϹ ΓΕΝΟΜΕΝΟϹ ἘΛΑΚΗϹΕ ΜΕϹΟϹ, ΚΑΙ ἘΞΕΧΥΘΗ ΤΑ ϹΠΛΑΓΧΝΑ Acts i. 18.
ΑΥΤΟΥ. τοῦτο δὲ σαφέστερον ἱστορεῖ Παπίας ὁ Ἰωάννου μαθητὴς λέγων
οὕτως ἐν τῷ τετάρτῳ τῆς ἐξηγήσεως τῶν κυριακῶν λόγων·

Μέγα δὲ ἀσεβείας ὑπόδειγμα ἐν τούτῳ τῷ κόσμῳ περιε-
πάτησεν ὁ Ἰούδας πρησθεὶς ἐπὶ τοσοῦτον τὴν σάρκα, ὥστε
μηδὲ ὁπόθεν ἅμαξα ῥᾳδίως διέρχεται ἐκεῖνον δύνασθαι διελ-
θεῖν, ἀλλὰ μηδὲ αὐτὸν μόνον τὸν τῆς κεφαλῆς ὄγκον αὐτοῦ.
τὰ μὲν γὰρ βλέφαρα τῶν ὀφθαλμῶν αὐτοῦ φασὶ τοσοῦτον
ἐξοιδῆσαι, ὡς αὐτὸν μὲν καθόλου τὸ φῶς μὴ βλέπειν, τοὺς
ὀφθαλμοὺς δὲ αὐτοῦ μηδὲ ὑπὸ ἰατροῦ [διὰ] διόπτρας ὀφθῆναι
δύνασθαι· τοσοῦτον βάθος εἶχον ἀπὸ τῆς ἔξωθεν ἐπιφανείας·
τὸ δὲ αἰδοῖον αὐτοῦ πάσης μὲν ἀσχημοσύνης ἀηδέστερον καὶ
μεῖζον φαίνεσθαι, φέρεσθαι δὲ δι᾽ αὐτοῦ ἐκ παντὸς τοῦ σώματος συρρέοντας ἰχῶράς τε καὶ σκώληκας εἰς ὕβριν δι᾽

αὐτῶν μόνων τῶν ἀναγκαίων. μετὰ πολλὰς δὲ βασάνους καὶ τιμωρίας ἐν ἰδίῳ, φασί, χωρίῳ τελευτήσαντος, ἀπὸ τῆς ὀδμῆς ἔρημον καὶ ἀοίκητον τὸ χωρίον μέχρι τῆς νῦν γενέσθαι, ἀλλ᾽ οὐδὲ μέχρι τῆς σήμερον δύνασθαί τινα ἐκεῖνον τὸν τόπον παρελθεῖν, ἐὰν μὴ τὰς ῥῖνας ταῖς χερσὶν ἐπιφράξῃ. τοσαύτη διὰ τῆς σαρκὸς αὐτοῦ καὶ ἐπὶ τῆς γῆς ἔκρυσις ἐχώρησεν.

Compiled from Cramer *Catena ad Acta SS. Apost.*
(1838) p. 12 sq. and other sources given in
Gebhardt, Harnack and Zahn, 1877, p. 73.

XIX.

Incipit argumentum secundum Iohannem.

Evangelium Iohannis manifestatum et datum est ecclesiis ab Iohanne adhuc in corpore constituto ; sicut Papias nomine Hierapolitanus, discipulus Iohannis carus, in exotericis (*l.* exegeticis)—id est in extremis (*l.* externis)—quinque libris retulit. Descripsit vero evangelium dictante Iohanne recte. Verum Martion haereticus, cum ab eo fuisset improbatus, eo quod contraria sentiebat, abiectus est a Iohanne. Is vero scripta vel epistolas ad eum pertulerat a fratribus, qui in Ponto fuerunt.

Codex Vatic. Alex. Nr. 14 Bibl. Lat. (Evv.) [IX], *ed.*
I. M. Thomasius Cardinalis (Opp. I. p. 344
Romae 1747); see Lightfoot *Essays on Super-
natural Religion* p. 210.

XX.

Ὕστατος γὰρ τούτων Ἰωάννης ὁ τῆς βροντῆς υἱὸς μετακληθείς, πάνυ γηραλέου αὐτοῦ γενομένου, ὡς παρέδοσαν ἡμῖν ὅ τε Εἰρηναῖος καὶ Εὐσέβιος καὶ ἄλλοι πιστοὶ κατὰ διαδοχὴν γεγονότες ἱστορικοί, κατ᾽ ἐκεῖνο καιροῦ αἱρέσεων ἀναφυεισῶν δεινῶν ὑπηγόρευσε τὸ εὐαγγέλιον τῷ ἑαυτοῦ μαθητῇ Παπίᾳ εὐβιώτῳ (*l.* εὐβιότῳ) τῷ Ἱεραπολίτῃ, πρὸς ἀναπλήρωσιν τῶν πρὸ αὐτοῦ κηρυξάντων τὸν λόγον τοῖς ἀνὰ πᾶσαν τὴν οἰκουμένην ἔθνεσιν.

Catena *Patr. Graec. in S. Joan.* Procem. first published
by B. Corder (Antwerp 1630).

TRANSLATION

OF THE

FRAGMENTS OF PAPIAS

I.

Irenæus and others record that John the Divine and Apostle survived until the times of Trajan; after which time Papias of Hierapolis and Polycarp, bishop of Smyrna, his hearers, became well known.

EUSEBIUS *Chronicon* (Syncell. 655, 14) for Olymp. 220.

II.

At this time flourished in Asia Polycarp, a disciple of the Apostles, who had received the bishopric of the church in Smyrna at the hands of *the eye-witnesses and ministers* of the Lord. At which time Papias, who was himself also bishop of the diocese of Hierapolis, became distinguished.

EUSEBIUS *Hist. Eccl.* iii. 36. 1. 2.

III.

Five books of Papias are extant, which bear the title Expositions of Oracles of the Lord. Of these Irenæus also makes mention as the only works written by him, in the following words : ' These things Papias, who was a hearer of John and a companion of Polycarp, an ancient worthy, witnesseth in writing in the fourth of his books. For there are five books composed by him.' So far Irenæus.

Yet Papias himself, in the preface to his discourses, certainly does not declare that he himself was a hearer and eye-witness of the holy Apostles, but he shows, by the language which he uses, that he received the matters of the faith from those who were their friends :—

But I will not scruple also to give a place for you along with my interpretations to everything that I learnt carefully and remembered carefully in time past from the elders, guaranteeing its truth. For, unlike the many, I did not take pleasure in those who have so very much to say, but in those who teach the truth ; nor in those who relate foreign commandments, but in those (who record) such as were given from the Lord to the Faith, and are derived from the Truth itself. And again, on any occasion when a person came (in my way) who had been a follower of the Elders, I would inquire about the discourses of the elders—what was said by Andrew, or by Peter, or by Philip, or by Thomas or James, or by John or Matthew or any other of the Lord's disciples, and what Aristion and the Elder John, the disciples of the Lord, say. For I did not think that I could get so much profit from the contents of books as from the utterances of a living and abiding voice.

Here it is worth while to observe that he twice enumerates the name of John. The first he mentions in connexion with Peter and James and Matthew and the rest of the Apostles, evidently meaning the Evangelist, but the other John he mentions after an interval and classes with others outside the number of the Apostles, placing Aristion before him, and he distinctly calls him an Elder. So that he hereby makes it quite evident that their statement is true who say that there were two persons of that name in Asia, and that there are two tombs in Ephesus, each of which even now is called (the tomb) of John. And it is important to notice this ; for it is probable that it was the second, if one will not admit that it was the first, who saw the Revelation which is ascribed by name to John. And Papias, of whom we are now speaking, confesses that he had received the words of the Apostles from those who had followed them, but says that he was himself a hearer of Aristion and the Elder John. At all events he mentions them frequently by name, and besides records their traditions in his writings. So much for these points which I trust have not been uselessly adduced.

It is worth while however to add to the words of Papias given above other passages from him, in which he records some other wonderful events likewise, as having come down to him by tradition. That Philip the Apostle resided in Hierapolis with his daughters has been already stated ; but how Papias, their contemporary, relates that he had heard a marvellous tale from the daughters of Philip, must be noted here. For he relates that in his time a man rose from the dead, and again he gives another wonderful story about Justus who was surnamed Barsabas, how that he drank a deadly poison, and yet, by the grace of the Lord, suffered no inconvenience. Of this Justus the Book of the Acts records that after the ascension of the Saviour the holy Apostles put him forward with Matthias, and prayed for the (right) choice, in place of the traitor Judas, that should make their number complete. The passage is somewhat as follows ; ‘ *And they put forward two, Joseph, called Barsabas, who was surnamed Justus, and Matthias ; and they prayed, and said.'* The same writer has recorded other notices as having come down to him from oral tradition, certain strange parables of the Saviour and teachings of His, and some other statements of a rather mythical character. Among which he says that there will be a period of some ten thousand years after the resurrection, and that the kingdom of Christ will be set up in material form on this earth. These ideas I suppose he got through a misunderstanding of the apostolic accounts, not perceiving that the things recorded there in figures were spoken by them mystically. For he evidently was a man of very mean capacity, as one may say judging from his own statements : yet it was owing to him that so many church fathers after him adopted a like opinion, urging in their own support the antiquity of the man, as for instance Irenæus and whoever else they were who declared that they held like views. Papias also gives in his own work other accounts of the words of the Lord on the authority of Aristion who has been mentioned above, and traditions of the Elder John. To these we refer the curious, and for our present purpose we will merely add to his words, which have been quoted above, a tradition, which has been set forth through these sources concerning Mark who wrote the Gospel :—

And the Elder said this also : Mark, having become the interpreter of Peter, wrote down accurately everything that he remembered, without however recording in order what was either said or done by Christ. For neither did he hear the Lord, nor did he follow Him ; but afterwards, as I said, (attended) Peter, who adapted his instructions to the needs (of his hearers) but had no design of giving a connected account of the Lord's oracles. So then Mark made no mistake, while he thus wrote down some things as he remembered them ; for he made it his one care not to omit anything that he heard, or to set down any false statement therein.

Such then is the account given by Papias concerning Mark. But concerning Matthew, the following statement is made (by him) :

So then Matthew composed the oracles in the Hebrew language, and each one interpreted them as he could.

The same writer employed testimonies from the First Epistle of John, and likewise from that of Peter. And he has related another story about a woman accused of many sins before the Lord, which the Gospel according to the Hebrews contains.

EUSEBIUS *Hist. Eccl.* iii. 39.

IV.

And they went every man unto his own house; but Jesus went unto the mount of Olives. And early in the morning He came again unto the temple, [and all the people came unto Him; and He sat down, and taught them]. And the Scribes and the Pharisees bring a woman taken in adultery; and having set her in the midst, they say unto Him, Master, this woman hath been taken in adultery, in the very act. Now in the law Moses commanded [us] to stone such: what then sayest thou? [And this they said, tempting Him, that they might have (whereof) to accuse Him.] But Jesus stooped down, and with His finger wrote on the ground. But when they continued asking [Him], He lifted up Himself, and said [unto them], He that is without sin among you, let him first cast a stone at her. And again He stooped down, and wrote on the ground. And they, when they heard it, went out one by one, beginning from the eldest: and He was left alone, and the woman, where she was, in the midst. And Jesus lifted up Himself, and said unto her, Woman, where are they? Did no man condemn thee? And she said, No man, Lord. And Jesus said, Neither do I condemn thee: go thy way; from henceforth sin no more.

PERICOPE ADULTERAE; see Westcott and Hort
The New Testament in the Original Greek
I. p. 241, II. pp. 82 sq, 91; Lightfoot *Essays
on Supernatural Religion* p. 203 sq.

V.

Papias, bishop of Hierapolis, who was a disciple of John the Divine, and a companion of Polycarp, wrote five books of Oracles of the Lord, wherein, when giving a list of the Apostles, after Peter and John, Philip and Thomas and Matthew he included among the disciples of the Lord Aristion and a second John, whom also he called 'The Elder.' [He says] that some think that this John is the author of the two short and catholic Epistles, which are published in the name of John; and he gives as the reason that the primitive (fathers) only accept the first epistle. Some too have wrongly considered the Apocalypse also to be his (i.e. the Elder John's) work. Papias too is in error about the Millennium, and from him Irenæus also. Papias in his second book says that John the Divine and James his brother were killed by the Jews. The aforesaid Papias stated on the authority of the daughters of Philip that Barsabas, who is also called Justus, when challenged by the unbelievers drank serpent's poison in the name of the Lord, and was shielded from all harm. He makes also other marvellous statements, and particularly about the mother of Manaim who was raised from the dead. As for those who were raised from the dead by Christ, (he states) that they survived till the time of Hadrian.

PHILIPPUS OF SIDE (?) Hist. Christ.

VI.

After Domitian Nerva reigned one year, who recalled John from the island (i.e. Patmos), and allowed him to dwell in Ephesus. He was at that time the sole survivor of the twelve Apostles, and after writing his Gospel received the honour of martyrdom. For Papias, bishop of Hierapolis, who was an eye-witness of him, in the second book of the Oracles of the Lord says that he was killed by the Jews, and thereby evidently fulfilled, together with his brother, Christ's prophecy concerning them, and their own confession and undertaking on His behalf. For when the Lord said to them; Are ye able to drink of the cup that I drink of?, and they readily assented and agreed, He said; My cup shall ye drink, and with the baptism that I am baptized shall ye be baptized. And reasonably so, for it is impossible for God to lie. So too the learned Origen affirms in his interpretation of S. Matthew's Gospel that John was martyred, declaring that he had learnt the fact from the successors of the Apostles. And indeed the well-informed Eusebius also in his Ecclesiastical History says; 'Thomas received by lot Parthia, but John, Asia, where also he made his residence and died at Ephesus.'

GEORGIUS HAMARTOLUS Chronicon.

VII.

Papias, a hearer of John, (and) bishop of Hierapolis in Asia, wrote only five books, which he entitled An Exposition of Discourses of the Lord. Wherein, when he asserts in his preface that he is not following promiscuous statements, but has the Apostles as his authorities, he says :—

I used to inquire what had been said by Andrew, or by Peter, or by Philip, or by Thomas or James, or by John or Matthew or any other of the Lord's disciples, and what Aristion and the Elder John, the disciples of the Lord, were saying. For books to read do not profit me so much as the living voice clearly sounding up to the present day in (the persons of) their authors.

From which it is clear that in his list of names itself there is one John who is reckoned among the Apostles, and another the Elder John, whom he enumerates after Aristion. We have mentioned this fact on account of the statement made above, which we have recorded on the authority of very many, that the two later epistles of John are not (the work) of the Apostle, but of the Elder. This (Papias) is said to have promulgated the Jewish tradition of a Millennium, and he is followed by Irenæus, Apollinarius and the others, who say that after the resurrection the Lord will reign in the flesh with the saints.

JEROME de vir. illust. 18.

VIII.

Further a false rumour has reached me that the books of Josephus and the writings of Papias and Polycarp have been translated by me ; but I have neither leisure nor strength to render such works as these with corresponding elegance into another tongue.

JEROME ad Lucinium Epist. 71 (28) c. 5.

IX.

Irenæus, a disciple of Papias who was a hearer of John the Evangelist, relates.

JEROME ad Theodoram Epist. 75 (29) c. 3.

X.

With regard however to the inspiration of the book (i.e. the Apocalypse) we hold it superfluous to speak at length ; since the blessed Gregory (I mean, the Divine) and Cyril, and men of an older generation as well, Papias, Irenæus, Methodius and Hippolytus, bear testimony to its genuineness.

ANDREAS OF CÆSAREA preface to the Apocalypse.

XI.

But thus says Papias, (I quote him) word for word :—

To some of them, clearly the angels which at first were holy, He gave dominion also over the arrangement of the universe, and He commissioned them to exercise their dominion well.

And he says next :—

But it so befel that their array came to nought; for the great dragon, the old serpent, who is also called Satan and the devil, was cast down, yea, and was cast down to the earth, he and his angels.

ANDREAS OF CÆSAREA in Apocalypsin c. 34 serm. 12.

XII.

Taking their start from Papias the great, of Hierapolis, the disciple of the Apostle who leaned on Christ's bosom, and Clement, Pantænus the priest of the Alexandrians and Ammonius, the great scholar, those ancient and first expositors who agree with each other in understanding all the work of the six days (as referring) to Christ and His Church.

ANASTASIUS OF SINAI *Contempl. Anagog. in Hexaëm.* i.

XIII.

So then the more ancient expositors of the churches, I mean Philo, the philosopher, and contemporary of the Apostles, and the famous Papias of Hierapolis, the disciple of John the Evangelist...and their associates, interpreted the sayings about Paradise spiritually, and referred them to the Church of Christ.

ANASTASIUS OF SINAI *Contempl. Anagog. in Hexaëm.* vii.

XIV.

The blessing thus foretold belongs undoubtedly to the times of the Kingdom, when the righteous shall rise from the dead and reign, when too creation renewed and freed from bondage shall produce a wealth of food of all kinds *from the dew of heaven and from the fatness of the earth;* as the elders, who saw John the disciple of the Lord, relate, that they had heard from him, how the Lord used to teach concerning those times, and to say,

The days will come, in which vines shall grow, each having ten thousand shoots, and on each shoot ten thousand branches, and on each branch again ten thousand twigs, and on each twig ten thousand clusters, and on each cluster ten thousand grapes, and each grape when pressed shall yield five-and-twenty measures of wine. And when any of the saints shall have taken hold of one of their clusters, another shall cry, I am a better cluster; take me, bless the Lord through me. Likewise also a grain of wheat shall produce ten thousand heads, and every head shall have ten thousand grains, and every grain ten pounds of fine flour, bright and clean, and the other fruits, seeds and the grass shall produce in similar proportions, and all the animals, using these fruits which are products of the soil, shall become in their turn peaceable and harmonious, obedient to man in all subjection. These things Papias, who was a hearer of John and a companion of Polycarp, an ancient worthy, witnesseth in writing in the fourth of his books, for there are five books composed by him. And he added, saying,

But these things are credible to them that believe. And when Judas the traitor did not believe, and asked, How shall such growths be accomplished by the Lord? he relates that the Lord said, They shall see, who shall come to these (times).

IRENÆUS *Haer.* v. 33. 3, 4.

XV.

Those who practised guilelessness towards God they used to call children, as Papias also shows in the first book of the Expositions of the Lord, and Clement of Alexandria in the Paedagogue.

MAXIMUS THE CONFESSOR *Schol. in libr. Dionys. Areopag. de eccl. hierarch.* c. 2.

XVI.

This he says, darkly indicating, I suppose, Papias of Hierapolis in Asia, who was a bishop at that time and flourished in the days of the holy Evangelist John. For this Papias in the fourth book of his Dominical Expositions mentioned viands among the sources of delights in the resurrection.... And Irenæus of Lyons says the same thing in his fifth book against heresies, and produces in support of his statements the aforesaid Papias.

MAXIMUS THE CONFESSOR *Schol. in libr. Dionys. Areopag. de eccl. hierarch.* c. 7.

XVII.

Nor again (does Stephanus follow) Papias, the bishop and martyr of Hierapolis, nor Irenæus, the holy bishop of Lyons, when they say that the kingdom of heaven will consist in enjoyment of certain material foods.

PHOTIUS *Bibliotheca* 232, on Stephanus Gobarus.

XVIII.

Apollinarius. 'Judas did not die by hanging, but lived on, having been cut down before he was suffocated. And the Acts of the Apostles show this, that *falling headlong he burst asunder in the midst, and all his bowels gushed out.* This fact is related more clearly by Papias, the disciple of John, in the fourth (book) of the Exposition of the Oracles of the Lord as follows :—

Judas walked about in this world a terrible example of impiety; his flesh swollen to such an extent that, where a waggon can pass with ease, he was not able to pass, no, not even the mass of his head merely. They say that his eyelids swelled to such an extent that he could not see the light at all, while as for his eyes they were not visible even by a physician looking through an instrument, so far had they sunk from the surface....'

> Compiled from Cramer *Catena ad Acta SS. Apost.* (1838) p. 12 sq. and other sources.

XIX.

Here beginneth the argument to the Gospel according to John.

The Gospel of John was made known and given to the Churches by John, while he yet remained in the body; as (one) Papias by name, of Hierapolis, a beloved disciple of John, has related in his five exoteric (*read* exegetical) books; but he wrote down the Gospel at the dictation of John, correctly.

> A Vatican MS of the ninth century.

XX.

For, last of these, John, surnamed the Son of Thunder, when he was now a very old man, as Irenæus and Eusebius and a succession of trustworthy historians have handed down to us, about the time when terrible heresies had cropped up, dictated the Gospel to his own disciple, the virtuous Papias of Hierapolis, to fill up what was lacking in those who before him had proclaimed the word to the nations throughout all the earth.

> Catena *Patr. Graec. in S. Joan.* published by B. Corder.

THE RELIQUES

OF THE

ELDERS

PRESERVED IN IRENÆUS

I.

Καθὼς ὑπὸ τοῦ κρείττονος ἡμῶν εἴρηται ἐπὶ τῶν τοιούτων ὅτι

λίθον τὸν τίμιον
σμάραγδον ὄντα καὶ πολυτίμητόν τισιν
ὕαλος ἐνυβρίζει διὰ τέχνης

παρομοιουμένη, ὁπόταν μὴ παρῇ ὁ σθένων δοκιμάσαι καὶ
τέχνῃ διελέγξαι τὴν πανούργως γενομένην·

ὅταν δὲ
ἐπιμιγῇ
ὁ χαλκὸς εἰς τὸν ἄργυρον, τίς εὐκόλως
δυνήσεται τοῦτον ἀκέραιος δοκιμάσαι;

IRENÆUS *Haer.*, *preface to Bk. i.* The Greek is preserved in Epiphanius *Haer.* xxxi. 9 (*ed.* Dindorf,
1859-62, II. p. 148).

II.

Καθὼς ὁ κρείσσων ἡμῶν ἔφη περὶ τῶν τοιούτων, ὅτι τολμηρὸν καὶ
ἀναιδὲς ψυχὴ κενῷ ἀέρι θερμαινομένη.

IRENÆUS i. 13. 3. The Greek from Epiphanius *Haer.*
xxxiv. 2 (Dindorf II. p. 220).

III.

Διὸ καὶ δικαίως ... ὁ θεῖος πρεσβύτης καὶ κῆρυξ τῆς ἀληθείας
ἐμμέτρως ἐπιβεβόηκέ σοι, εἰπὼν οὕτως·

εἰδωλοποιὲ Μάρκε καὶ τερατοσκόπε,
ἀστρολογικῆς ἔμπειρε καὶ μαγικῆς τέχνης

δι' ὧν κρατύνεις τῆς πλάνης τὰ διδάγματα,
σημεῖα δεικνὺς τοῖς ὑπὸ σοῦ πλανωμένοις,
ἀποστατικῆς δυνάμεος ἐγχειρήματα,
ἅ σοι χορηγεῖ σὸς πατὴρ Σατὰν ἀεί,
δι' ἀγγελικῆς δυνάμεος Ἀζαζὴλ ποιεῖν,
ἔχων σε πρόδρομον ἀντιθέου πανουργίας.
Καὶ ταῦτα μὲν ὁ θεοφιλὴς πρεσβύτης.

IRENÆUS i. 15. 6. The Greek in Epiphanius *Haer.*
xxxiv. 11·(Dindorf II. p. 233).

IV.

Quia autem triginta annorum aetas prima indolis est iuvenis, et extenditur usque ad quadragesimum annum, omnis quilibet confitebitur; a quadragesimo autem et quinquagesimo anno declinat iam in aetatem seniorem, quam habens Dominus noster docebat, sicut evangelium καὶ πάντες οἱ πρεσβύτεροι μαρτυροῦσιν, οἱ κατὰ τὴν Ἀσίαν Ἰωάννῃ τῷ τοῦ Κυρίου μαθητῇ συμβεβληκότες, παραδεδωκέναι ταῦτα τὸν Ἰωάννην. Παρέμεινε γὰρ αὐτοῖς μέχρι τῶν Τραϊανοῦ χρόνων. Quidam autem eorum non solum Ioannem, sed et alios apostolos viderunt, et haec eadem ab ipsis audierunt, et testantur de huiusmodi relatione.

IRENÆUS ii. 22. 5 (*ed.* Stieren, 1853, I. p. 359). The
Greek from Eusebius *Hist. Eccl.* iii. 23. 3.

V.

Sicut quidam dixit superior nobis, de omnibus qui quolibet modo depravant quae sunt Dei, et adulterant veritatem: In Dei lacte gypsum male miscetur.

IRENÆUS iii. 17. 4 (Stieren I. p. 516).

VI.

Quemadmodum ex veteribus quidam ait: Quoniam quidem transtulit Deus maledictum in terram, ut non perseveraret in homine.

IRENÆUS iii. 23. 3 (Stieren I. p. 547).

VII.

Quapropter hi qui ante nos fuerunt, et quidem multo nobis
meliores, non tamen satis potuerunt contradicere his qui sunt a
Valentino, quia ignorabant regulam ipsorum, quam nos cum omni
diligentia in primo libro tibi tradidimus.

IRENÆUS *preface to Bk. iv.* (Stieren I. p. 558).

VIII.

Ἅπαντα μέτρῳ καὶ τάξει ὁ Θεὸς ποιεῖ, καὶ οὐδὲν ἄμετρον παρ᾽ αὐτῷ,
ὅτι μηδὲν ἀναρίθμητον. Et bene qui dixit ipsum immensum Patrem
in Filio mensuratum: mensura enim Patris Filius, quoniam et capit
eum.

IRENÆUS iv. 4. 2 (Stieren I. p. 568).   The Greek
from the *Parallela* of John Damascene.

IX.

Quemadmodum audivi a quodam presbytero, qui audierat ab
his qui apostolos viderant, et ab his qui didicerant: suffi-
cere veteribus, de his quae sine consilio Spiritus egerunt, eam quae
ex scripturis esset correptionem. Cum enim non sit personarum
acceptor Deus, quae sunt non secundum eius placitum facta, his
inferebat congruam correptionem. [Quemadmodum sub David,
quando persecutionem quidem patiebatur a Saul propter iustitiam,
et regem Saul fugiebat, et inimicum non ulciscebatur, et Christi adventum psallebat et sapientia instruebat gentes, et omnia secundum
consilium faciebat Spiritus, placebat Deo. Quando autem propter
concupiscentiam ipse sibi accepit Bersabee Uriae uxorem, dixit
scriptura de eo: *Nequam autem visus est sermo quem fecit David in*   2 Sam. xi.
oculis domini; et mittitur ad eum Nathan propheta, ostendens ei   27.
peccatum eius, ut ipse dans sententiam de semetipso, et semetipsum
adiudicans, misericordiam consequeretur et remissionem a Christo:
et dixit ei : *Duo viri fuerunt in civitate una, unus dives et unus*   2 Sam. xii.
pauper; diviti erant greges ovium et boum multi valde, et pauperi   1 sq.
nihil aliud nisi ovicula una, quam habebat et nutriebat et fuerat cum
eo et cum filiis eius pariter; de pane suo manducabat, et de calice
bibebat, et erat ei quasi filia. Et venit hospes homini diviti, et pepercit
accipere de grege ovicularum suarum et de gregibus boum suorum, et
facere hospiti; et accepit oviculam viri pauperis, et apposuit viro qui

venerat ad eum. Iratus est autem David super hominem illum valde, et dixit ad Nathan: Vivit Dominus, quoniam filius mortis est homo ille qui fecit hoc; et oviculam reddet quadruplum pro eo quod fecit factum hoc, et pro eo quod non pepercit pauperi. Et ait ad eum Nathan: *Tu es vir, qui fecisti hoc;* et deinceps reliqua exsequitur, exprobrans eum et enumerans in eum Dei beneficia, et quoniam exacerbavit Dominum cum fecisset hoc. Non enim placere Deo huiusmodi operationem, sed iram magnam imminere domui eius. Compunctus est autem David ad haec, et ait : *Peccavi Domino;* et psalmum exhomologeseos post psallebat, adventum Domini sustinens, qui abluit et emundat eum hominem qui peccato fuerat obstrictus.

Similiter autem et de Salomone, cum perseveraret iudicare recte et sapientiam enarrare, et typum veri templi aedificabat, et glorias exponebat Dei, et adventuram pacem gentibus annuntiabat, et Christi regnum praefigurabat, et loquebatur tria millia parabolarum in adventum Domini, et quinque millia canticorum, hymnum dicens Deo, et eam quae est in conditione sapientiam Dei exponebat physiologice ex omni ligno et de omni herba et volatilibus omnibus et de quad-rupedibus et de piscibus, et dicebat : *Si vere Deus, quem caeli non capiunt, super terram habitabit cum hominibus?* et placebat Deo, et omnes eum admirabantur, et omnes reges terrae quaerebant faciem eius, ut audirent sapientiam eius, quam dederat illi Deus, et regina Austri a finibus terrae veniebat ad eum, sapientiam, quae in eo erat, scitura ; quam et Dominus ait in iudicio resurrecturam cum eorum natione qui audiunt sermones eius et non credunt in eum, et ad-iudicaturam eos : quoniam illa quidem subiecta est annuntiatae sapientiae per servum Dei, hi vero eam quae a Filio Dei dabatur contemserunt sapientiam. Salomon enim servus erat, Christus vero Filius Dei et Dominus Salomonis. Cum igitur sine offensa serviret Deo et ministraret dispositionibus eius, tunc glorificabatur : cum autem uxores accipiebat ab universis gentibus, et permittebat eis erigere idola in Israel, dixit scriptura de eo : *Et rex Salomon erat amator mulierum, et accepit sibi mulieres alienigenas; et factum est in tempore senectutis Salomonis, non erat cor eius perfectum cum Domino Deo suo. Et diverterunt mulieres alienigenae cor eius post Deos alienos. Et fecit Salomon malignum in conspectu Domini; non abiit post Dominum, quemadmodum David pater eius. Et iratus est Dominus in Salomonem: non enim erat cor eius perfectum in Domino, secundum cor David patris eius.*] Sufficienter increpavit eum scrip-tura, sicut dixit presbyter, ut non glorietur universa caro in conspectu Domini.

Et propter hoc Dominum in ea quae sunt sub terra descendisse, evangelizantem et illis adventum suum, remissione peccatorum ex-sistente his qui credunt in eum. [Crediderunt autem in eum omnes qui

1 Kings viii. 27.
1 Kings xi. 1 sq.

sperabant in eum, id est qui adventum eius praenuntiaverunt et dispositionibus eius servierunt, iusti et prophetae et patriarchae : quibus similiter ut nobis remisit peccata, quae non oportet nos imputare his, si quominus contemnimus gratiam Dei. Quemadmodum enim illi non imputabant nobis incontinentias nostras, quas operati sumus priusquam Christus in nobis manifestaretur ; sic et nos non est iustum imputare ante adventum Christi his qui peccaverunt. *Omnes* enim Rom. iii. homines *egent gloria Dei,* iustificantur autem non a semetipsis, sed 23. a Domini adventu, qui intendunt lumen eius.] In nostram autem correptionem conscriptos esse actus eorum, ut sciremus primum quidem, quoniam unus est Deus noster et illorum, cui non placeant peccata, etiamsi a claris fiant ; deinde, ut abstineamus a malis. [Si enim hi qui praecesserunt nos in charismatibus veteres, propter quos nondum Filius Dei passus erat, delinquentes in aliquo et concupiscentiae carnis servientes, tali affecti sunt ignominia : quid passuri sunt qui nunc sunt, qui contemserunt adventum Domini et deservierunt voluptatibus suis? Et illis quidem curatio et remissio peccatorum mors Domini fuit ; propter eos vero qui nunc peccant Christus non iam morietur, iam enim mors non dominabitur eius ; sed veniet Filius in gloria Patris, exquirens ab actoribus et dispensatoribus suis pecuniam quam eis credidit, cum usuris : et quibus plurimum dedit, plurimum ab eis exiget.] Non debemus ergo, inquit ille senior, superbi esse, neque reprehendere veteres ; sed ipsi timere, ne forte post agnitionem Christi agentes aliquid quod non placeat Deo, remissionem ultra non habeamus delictorum, sed excludamur a regno eius. Et ideo Paulum dixisse : *Si enim naturalibus ramis non* Rom. xi. *pepercit, ne forte (nec) tibi parcat, qui cum esses oleaster, insertus es* 21, 17. *in pinguedinem olivae, et socius factus es pinguedinis eius.*

Similiter et plebis praevaricationes vides descriptas esse, non propter illos qui tunc transgrediebantur, sed in correptionem nostram, et ut sciremus unum et eundem Deum, in quem illi delinquebant et in quem nunc delinquunt quidam ex his qui credidisse dicuntur. Et hoc autem apostolum in epistola quae est ad Corinthios manifestissime ostendisse, dicentem : *Nolo enim vos ignorare, fratres, quoniam* 1 Cor. x. *patres nostri omnes sub nube fuerunt, et omnes in Mose baptizati sunt* 1 sq. *in nube et in mari, omnes eandem escam spiritalem manducaverunt, et omnes eundem potum spiritalem biberunt : bibebant autem enim de spiritali consequente eos petra : petra autem erat Christus. Sed non in pluribus eorum bene sensit Deus : prostrati sunt enim in deserto. Haec in figuram nostri fuerunt, ut non simus concupiscentes malorum, quemadmodum et illi concupierunt ; neque idololatrae sitis, quemadmodum quidam eorum ; sicut scriptum est : Sedit populus manducare et bibere, et surrexerunt ludere. Neque fornicemur, sicut quidam ex illis fornicati sunt, et corruerunt una die viginti tria millia. Nec tentemus Christum, quemadmodum quidam eorum tentaverunt, et a serpentibus perierunt. Neque murmuraveritis, sicuti quidem eorum murmuraverunt et perierunt ab exterminatore. Haec autem omnia in figura fiebant illis; scripta sunt autem ad correptionem nostram, in quos finis saeculorum devenit. Quapropter qui putat se stare, videat ne cadat.*

[Sine dubitatione igitur et sine contradictione ostendente apostolo, unum et eundem esse Deum, qui et illa iudicavit et ea, quae nunc sunt, exquirit, et caussam descriptionis eorum demonstrante ; indocti et audaces, adhuc etiam imprudentes inveniuntur omnes, qui propter transgressionem eorum qui olim fuerunt, et propter plurimorum indicto audientiam, alterum quidem aiunt illorum fuisse Deum, et hunc esse mundi fabricatorem, et esse in diminutione ; alterum vero a Christo traditum Patrem, et hunc esse qui sit ab unoquoque eorum mente conceptus : non intelligentes, quoniam quemadmodum ibi in pluribus eorum, qui peccaverunt, non bene sensit Deus ; sic et hic

S. Matt. xx. 16. *vocati multi, pauci vero electi:* quemadmodum ibi iniusti et idololatrae et fornicatores vitam perdiderunt ; sic et hic : et Domino quidem

1 Cor. vi. 9, 10. praedicante, in ignem aeternum mitti tales, et apostolo dicente : *An ignoratis, quoniam iniusti regnum Dei non hereditabunt? Nolite seduci: neque fornicatores neque idololatrae neque adulteri neque molles neque masculorum concubitores neque fures neque avari neque ebriosi neque maledici neque raptores regnum Dei possidebunt.* Et quoniam non ad eos, qui extra sunt, hoc dicit, sed ad nos ne proiiciamur extra

1 Cor. vi. 11. regnum Dei, tale aliquid operantes, intulit : *Et haec quidem fuistis; sed abluti estis, sed sanctificati estis in nomine Domini Jesu Christi et in Spiritu Dei nostri.* Et quemadmodum illic condemnabantur et proiiciebantur hi, qui male operabantur, et reliquos exterminabant ; similiter et hic oculus quoque effoditur scandalizans et pes et manus,

1 Cor. v. 11. ne reliquum corpus pariter pereat. Et habemus praeceptum : *Si quis frater nominatur fornicator aut avarus aut idololatra aut maledicus aut ebriosus aut rapax, cum huiusmodi nec cibum sumere.* Et iterum

Eph. v. 6, 7. ait apostolus : *Nemo vos seducat inanibus verbis; propter haec enim venit ira Dei in filios diffidentiae. Nolite ergo fieri participes eorum.* Et quemadmodum ibi peccantium damnatio participabat et reliquos, quoniam placebant eis et una cum eis conversabantur ; sic et hic

1 Cor. v. 6. *modicum fermentum totam massam corrumpit.* Et quemadmodum ibi adversus iniustos ira descendebat Dei, et hic similiter apostolus

Rom. i. 18. ait : *Revelabitur enim ira Dei de caelo super omnem impietatem et iniustitiam eorum hominum qui veritatem in iniustitia detinent.* Et quemadmodum ibi in Aegyptios, qui iniuste puniebant Israel, vindicta

S. Luke xviii. 7, 8. a Deo fiebat ; sic et hic, Domino quidem dicente : *Deus autem non faciet vindictam electorum suorum, quicunque clamant ad eum die et nocte? Etiam dico vobis, faciet vindictam eorum cito;* et apostolo in

ea, quae est ad Thessalonicenses, epistola ista praedicante : *Si quidem* 2 Thess. i.
iustum est apud Deum retribuere retributionem his qui tribulant vos, et 6 sq.
vobis qui tribulamini, refrigerium nobiscum, in revelatione Domini
nostri Iesu Christi de caelo cum angelis virtutis eius, et in flamma
ignis, dare vindictam in eos qui non noverunt Deum, et in eos qui
non obediunt evangelio Domini nostri Iesu Christi; qui etiam poenas
pendent interitus aeternas a facie Domini et a gloria virtutis eius,
cum venerit magnificari in sanctis suis et admirabilis esse omnibus
qui crediderunt in eum.]

Cum ergo hic et illic eadem sit in vindicando Deo iustitia
Dei, et illic quidem typice et temporaliter et mediocrius ; hic vero
vere et semper et austerius ; ignis enim aeternus et quae a caelo
revelabitur ira Dei a facie Domini nostri, (quemadmodum et David
ait : *Vultus autem Domini super facientes mala, ut perdat de terra* Psalm
memoriam ipsorum), maiorem poenam praestat iis qui incidunt in xxxiii
eam ; valde insensatos ostendebant presbyteri eos qui ex his (xxxiv). 17.
quae acciderunt his, qui olim Deo obtemperabant, tentant alterum
Patrem introducere, e contrario opponentes quanta Dominus ad sal-
vandos eos, qui receperunt eum, veniens fecisset, miserans eorum ;
tacentes autem de iudicio eius, et quaecunque provenient his qui
audierunt sermones eius, et non fecerunt, et quoniam expediebat eis cf. S. Matt.
si non essent nati, et quoniam tolerabilius Sodomae et Gomorrae erit xxvi. 24;
in iudicio, quam civitati illi quae non recepit sermones discipulorum x. 15.
eius.

IRENÆUS iv. 27. 1—28. 1 (Stieren I. p. 648 sq.).

X.

Qui vero exprobrant et imputant quod profecturus populus iussu
Dei vascula omnis generis et vestimenta acceperit ab Aegyptiis et sic
abierit, ex quibus et tabernaculum factum est in eremo, ignorantes
iustificationes Dei et dispositiones eius, semetipsos arguunt, sicut et
presbyter dicebat. [Si enim non in typica profectione hoc consen-
sisset Deus, hodie in vera nostra profectione, id est, in fide in qua
sumus constituti, per quam de numero gentilium exemti sumus, nemo
poterat salvari. Omnes enim nos aut modica aut grandis sequitur
possessio, quam ex mammona iniquitatis acquisivimus. Unde enim
domus in quibus habitamus, et vestimenta quibus induimur, et vasa
quibus utimur, et reliqua omnis ad diuturnam vitam nostram mini-
stratio, nisi ex his quae, cum ethnici essemus, de avaritia acquisivimus,
vel ab ethnicis parentibus aut cognatis aut amicis de iniustitia acqui-
rentibus percepimus? ut non dicamus quia et nunc in fide exsistentes
acquirimus. Quis enim vendit, et non lucrari vult ab eo qui emit?

Quis autem emit, et non vult utiliter secum agi ab eo qui vendit? Quis autem negotians non propterea negociatur, ut inde alatur? Quid autem et hi, qui in regali aula sunt, fideles, nonne ex eis, quae Caesaris sunt, habent utensilia, et his, qui non habent, unusquisque eorum secundum virtutem suam praestat? Aegyptii populi erant debitores non solum rerum sed et vitae suae propter patriarchae Ioseph praecedentem benignitatem: nobis autem secundum quid debitores sunt ethnici, a quibus et lucra et utilitates percipimus? quaecunque illi cum labore comparant, his nos, in fide cum simus, sine labore utimur.

Ad hoc populus pessimam servitutem serviebat Aegyptiis, quem-admodum scriptura ait: *Et cum vi potestatem exercebant Aegyptii in filios Israel, et in odium eis adducebant vitam in operibus duris, luto et latere et omnibus operibus, quae faciebant in campis, per omnia opera quibus eos deprimebant cum vi;* et aedificaverunt eis civitates munitas, multum laborantes et augentes eorum substantias annis multis et per omnem modum servitutis, cum illi non solum ingrati essent adversus eos, verum et universos perdere vellent. Quid igitur iniuste gestum est, si ex multis pauca sumserunt, et qui potuerunt multas substantias habere, si non servissent eis, et divites abire, paucissimam mercedem pro magna servitute accipientes, inopes abierunt? Quemadmodum si quis liber, abductus ab aliquo per vim, et serviens ei annis multis et augens substantiam eius, post deinde aliquod adminiculum consecutus, putetur quidem modica quaedam eius habere, revera autem ex multis laboribus suis, et ex acquisitione magna, pauca percipiens discedat, et hoc ab aliquo imputetur ei, quasi non recte fecerit; ipse magis iniustus iudex apparebit ei, qui per vim in servitium fuerit deductus. Sic ergo sunt et huiusmodi qui imputant populo parva de multis accipienti sibi; et ipsis non imputant, qui nullam gratiam ex merito parentum debitam reddiderunt, immo et in gravissimam servitutem redigentes, maximam ab eis consecuti sunt utilitatem; et illos quidem non signatum aurum et argentum in paucis vasculis, quemadmodum praediximus, accipientes, iniuste fecisse dicunt; semetipsos autem, (dicetur enim quod verum est, licet ridiculum quibusdam esse videatur) ex alienis laboribus insigne aurum et argentum et aeramentum, cum inscriptione et imagine Caesaris in zonis suis ferentes, iuste (se) facere dicunt.

Si autem comparatio fiat nostra et illorum; qui iustius apparebunt accepisse? utrumne populus ab Aegyptiis, qui erant per omnia debitores; an nos a Romanis et reliquis gentibus, et a quibus nihil tale nobis debeatur? Sed et mundus pacem habet per eos, et nos sine timore in viis ambulamus et navigamus quocunque voluerimus. Adversus igitur huiusmodi aptus erit sermo Domini: *Hypocrita*, dicens, *exime primo trabem de oculo tuo, et tunc perspicies auferre festucam de oculo fratris tui.* Etenim si is qui tibi haec imputat et gloriatur in

Ex. i. 13, 14.

S. Matt. vii. 5.

sua scientia, separatus est a gentilium coetu et nihil est alienorum apud eum, sed est simpliciter nudus et nudis pedibus et sine domo in montibus conversatur, quemadmodum aliquod ex his animalibus, quae herbis vescuntur; veniam merebitur ideo quod ignoret necessitates nostrae conversationis. Si autem ab hominibus quae dicuntur aliena esse, participatur, et arguit typum eorum; semetipsum iniustissimum ostendit, retorquens in se eiusmodi accusationem.] Invenietur enim aliena circumferens, et ea quae eius non sunt concupiscens; et propter hoc dixisse Dominum: *Nolite iudicare, ne iudicemini: in quo* S. Matt. *enim iudicio iudicabitis, iudicabitur de vobis.* [Non utique ut peccantes vii. 1, 2. non corripiamus, nec ut his quae male fiunt consentiamus; sed ut Dei dispositiones non iudicemus iniuste, cum ille omnia iuste profutura providerit. Quoniam enim sciebat nos de nostra substantia, quam ab alio accipientes haberemus, bene acturos: *Qui enim habet,* S. Luke inquit, *duas tunicas, det ei qui non habet; et qui habet escam, similiter* iii. 11. *faciat.* Et: *Esurivi enim, et dedistis mihi manducare; et nudus fui,* S. Matt. *et vestistis me.* Et: *Cum facis misericordiam, non sciat sinistra tua* S. Matt. xxv. 35, 36. *quid faciat dextra tua;* et reliqua quaecumque benefacientes iustifi- vi. 3. camur, velut de alienis nostra redimentes; de alienis autem ita dico, non quasi mundus alienus sit a Deo, sed quoniam huiusmodi dationes ab aliis accipientes habemus, similiter velut illi ab Aegyptiis qui non sciebant Deum, et per haec ipsa erigimus nobismetipsis tabernaculum Dei: cum bene enim facientibus habitat Deus; quemadmodum Dominus ait: *Facite vobis amicos de mammona iniquitatis, ut hi, quando* S. Luke *fugati fueritis, recipiant vos in aeterna tabernacula.* Quaecunque xvi. 9. enim, cum essemus ethnici, de iniustitia acquisivimus, haec, cum crediderimus, in dominicas utilitates conversantes iustificamur.

Necessarie igitur haec in typo praemeditabantur, et tabernaculum Dei ex his fabricatur: illis quidem iuste accipientibus, quemadmodum ostendimus; nobis autem praeostensis, qui inciperemus per aliena Deo deservire. Universa enim quae ex Aegypto profectio fiebat populi a Deo typus et imago fuit profectionis ecclesiae, quae erat futura ex gentibus: propter hoc et in fine educens eam hinc in suam heredi-tatem, quam non Moyses quidem famulus Dei, sed Iesus Filius Dei, in hereditatem dabit. Si quis autem diligentius intendat his, quae a prophetis dicuntur de fine, et quaecunque Ioannes discipulus Domini vidit in Apocalypsi, inveniet easdem plagas universaliter accipere gentes, quas tunc particulatim accepit Aegyptus.]

Talia quaedam enarrans de antiquis **presbyter** reficiebat nos et dicebat de his quidem delictis, de quibus ipsae scripturae increpant patriarchas et prophetas, nos non oportere exprobrare eis, neque fieri similes Cham, qui irrisit turpitudinem patris sui et in maledictionem decidit, sed gratias agere pro illis Deo, quoniam in adventu Domini nostri remissa sunt eis peccata: etenim illos dicebat gratias agere et

gloriari in nostra salute. De quibus autem scripturae non increpant,
sed simpliciter sunt positae, nos non debere fieri accusatores; non
enim sumus diligentiores Deo, neque super magistrum possumus esse,
sed typum quaerere. Nihil enim otiosum est eorum quaecunque inac-
cusabilia posita sunt in scripturis.

IRENÆUS iv. 30. 1—31. 1 (Stieren I. p. 658 sq.).

XI.

Huiusmodi quoque de duobus testamentis senior apostolorum
discipulus disputabat, ab uno quidem et eodem Deo utraque ostendens : nec esse alterum Deum praeter unum qui fecit et plasmavit
nos, nec firmitatem habere sermonem eorum qui dicunt aut per angelos
aut per quamlibet virtutem aut ab alio Deo factum esse hunc mundum,
qui est secundum nos. [Si enim semel quis transmoveatur a factore
omnium, et concedat ab aliquo altero aut per alium factam condi-
tionem, quae est secundum nos, multam incongruentiam et plurimas
contradictiones necesse est incidat huiusmodi, ad quas nullas dabit
rationes neque secundum verisimile, neque secundum veritatem. Et
propter hoc hi qui alias doctrinas inferunt, abscondunt a nobis quam
habent ipsi de Deo sententiam; scientes quassum et futile doctrinae
suae, et timentes ne victi salvari periclitentur.]

IRENÆUS iv. 32. 1 (Stieren I. p. 664).

XII.

Filius enim, quemadmodum et quidam ante nos dixit, dupliciter
intelligitur: alius quidem secundum naturam, eo quod natus sit filius;
alius autem secundum id quod factus est, reputatur filius: licet sit
differentia inter natum et factum.

IRENÆUS iv. 41. 2 (Stieren I. p. 709).

XIII.

Ποῦ οὖν ἐτέθη ὁ πρῶτος ἄνθρωπος; ἐν τῷ παραδείσῳ δηλονότι, καθὼς
γέγραπται· καὶ ἐκεῖθεν ἐξεβλήθη εἰς τόνδε τὸν κόσμον παρακούσας. Διὸ
καὶ λέγουσιν οἱ πρεσβύτεροι, τῶν ἀποστόλων μαθηταί, τοὺς μετα-
τεθέντας ἐκεῖσε μετατεθῆναι· (δικαίοις γὰρ ἀνθρώποις καὶ πνευματοφόροις
ἡτοιμάσθη ὁ παράδεισος, ἐν ᾧ καὶ Παῦλος ἀπόστολος εἰσκομισθεὶς ἬΚΟΥϹΕΝ
ἌΡΡΗΤΑ ῬΉΜΑΤΑ, ὡς πρὸς ἡμᾶς ἐν τῷ παρόντι), κἀκεῖ μένειν τοὺς μετατε-
θέντας ἕως συντελείας, προοιμιαζομένους τὴν ἀφθαρσίαν.

2 Cor.
xii. 4.

IRENÆUS v. 5. 1 (Stieren I. p. 727). The Greek
from the *Parallela* of John Damascene.

XIV.

Ἐπεὶ γὰρ διὰ ξύλου ἀπεβάλομεν αὐτόν, διὰ ξύλου πάλιν φανερὸν
(l. φανερὸς) τοῖς πᾶσιν ἐγένετο, ἐπιδεικνύων τὸ μῆκος καὶ ὕψος καὶ βάθος
καὶ πλάτος ἐν ἑαυτῷ, καὶ ὡς ἔφη τις τῶν προβεβηκότων, διὰ τῆς
θείας ἐκτάσεως τῶν χειρῶν τοὺς δύο λαοὺς εἰς ἕνα Θεὸν
συνάγων.

IRENÆUS v. 17. 4 (Stieren I. p. 765). The Greek
from Cod. Coisl. 211.

XV.

Τούτων δὲ οὕτως ἐχόντων, καὶ ἐν πᾶσι τοῖς σπουδαίοις καὶ ἀρχαίοις
ἀντιγράφοις τοῦ ἀριθμοῦ τούτου κειμένου, καὶ μαρτυρούντων αὐτῶν ἐκείνων
τῶν κατ᾽ ὄψιν τὸν Ἰωάννην ἑωρακ ότων, καὶ τοῦ λόγου διδάσκοντος
ἡμᾶς, ὅτι ὁ ἀριθμὸς τοῦ ὀνόματος τοῦ θηρίου κατὰ τὴν τῶν Ἑλλήνων ψῆφον cf. Apoc.
διὰ τῶν ἐν αὐτῷ γραμμάτων sexcentos habebit et sexaginta et sex.... xiii. 18.
οὐκ οἶδα πῶς ἐσφάλησάν τινες ἐπακολουθήσαντες ἰδιωτισμῷ καὶ τὸν μέσον
ἠθέτησαν ἀριθμὸν τοῦ ὀνόματος, ν᾽ ψήφισμα ὑφελόντες καὶ ἀντὶ τῶν ἑξ
δεκάδων μίαν δεκάδα βουλόμενοι εἶναι.

IRENÆUS v. 30. 1 (Stieren I. p. 798). The Greek
from Eusebius Hist. Eccl. v. 8. 5, and the
Parallela of John Damascene.

XVI.

Quemadmodum presbyteri meminerunt qui Ioannem discipulum Domini viderunt, audisse se ab eo, quemadmodum de
temporibus illis docebat Dominus et dicebat.

IRENÆUS v. 33. 3 (Stieren I. p. 809). See above,
Fragments of Papias, No. XIV. p. 521.

XVII,

Ὡς οἱ πρεσβύτεροι λέγουσι, τότε καὶ οἱ μὲν καταξιωθέντες τῆς ἐν
οὐρανῷ διατριβῆς, ἐκεῖσε χωρήσουσιν, οἱ δὲ ΤΗϹ ΤΟΫ ΠΑΡΑΔΕΊϹΟΥ ΤΡΥΦΆϹ Ezek.
ἀπολαύσουσιν, οἱ δὲ τὴν λαμπρότητα τῆς πόλεως καθέξουσιν· πανταχοῦ xxviii. 13.
γὰρ ὁ Σωτὴρ ὁραθήσεται, [καὶ] καθὼς ἄξιοι ἔσονται οἱ ὁρῶντες αὐτόν. εἶναι
δὲ τὴν διαστολὴν ταύτην τῆς οἰκήσεως τῶν τὰ ἑκατὸν καρποφορούντων καὶ
τῶν τὰ ἑξήκοντα καὶ τῶν τὰ τριάκοντα· ὧν οἱ μὲν εἰς τοὺς οὐρανοὺς ἀνα-
ληφθήσονται, οἱ δὲ ἐν τῷ παραδείσῳ διατρίψουσιν, οἱ δὲ τὴν πόλιν κατοι-

S. John
xiv. 2.

κήσουσιν· καὶ διὰ τοῦτο εἰρηκέναι τὸν Κύριον, ἐν τοῖc τοῦ πατρόc μογ μονὰc εἶναι πολλάc. τὰ πάντα γὰρ τοῦ Θεοῦ, ὃς τοῖς πᾶσι τὴν ἁρμόζουσαν οἴκησιν παρέχει· [quemadmodum Verbum eius ait, omnibus divisum esse a Patre secundum quod quis est dignus aut erit. Et hoc est triclinium in quo recumbent ii qui epulantur vocati ad nuptias.] Hanc esse adordinationem et dispositionem eorum qui salvantur, dicunt presbyteri apostolorum discipuli; et per huiusmodi gradus proficere, et per Spiritum quidem ad Filium, per Filium autem ascendere ad Patrem; Filio deinceps cedente Patri opus suum, quem-

1 Cor. xv.
25.

admodum et ab Apostolo dictum est: *Quoniam oportet regnare eum, quoadusque ponat omnes inimicos sub pedibus eius.*

IRENÆUS v. 36. 1, 2 (Stieren 1. p. 818). The Greek from the Appendix to Anastasius *Quaestiones in S. Scripturam* No. 74.

TRANSLATION

RELIQUES OF THE ELDERS

PRESERVED IN IRENÆUS

I.

According to what was said of such cases by one better than we are:

the precious stone,
The emerald, accounted of much worth,
Is shamed by artful mimicry in glass,

whenever he is not by, who hath power to prove it, and

Detect the craft so cunningly devised.

Again, when

alloy of brass
Is mixed with silver, who that simple is
Shall easily be able to assay?

IRENÆUS *Heresies, preface to Bk.* i.

II.

As he that was better than we are affirmed of such persons, A daring and shameless thing is a soul heated with empty air.

IRENÆUS i. 13. 3.

III.

Wherefore also justly did the divine Elder and herald of the truth exclaim against thee in verse, thus saying:

Thou idol-framer, Mark, and portent-gazer,
Skill'd in the astrologer's and wizard's art,
Strengthening thereby the words of thy false lore,
Dazzling with signs whome'er thou lead'st astray,
Strange handywork of God-defying power
Such to perform thy father Satan still
Affords thee might, by an angelic Power
Azazel:—thee, by the destroyer mark'd
Chosen forerunner of the impious craft.

Thus far that Elder, beloved of God.

IRENÆUS i. 15. 6.

IV.

But that the age of thirty years is the prime of a young man's ability, and that it reaches even to the fortieth year, every one will allow ; but after the fortieth and fiftieth year, it begins to verge towards elder age : which our Lord was of when He taught, as the Gospel and all the Elders witness, who in Asia conferred with John the Lord's disciple, to the effect that John had delivered these things unto them : for he abode with them until the times of Trajan. And some of them saw not only John, but others also of the Apostles, and had this same account from them, and witness to the aforesaid account.

IRENÆUS ii. 22. 5.

V.

As was said by one who was before us, concerning all who in any way deprave the things of God, and adulterate the truth, It is evil mingling chalk in the milk of God.

IRENÆUS iii. 17. 4.

VI.

As one of the ancients saith, God for His part transferred the curse unto the earth, that it might not continue in the man.

IRENÆUS iii. 23. 3.

VII.

For which cause they who have been before us, yea, and much better men than we, were nevertheless unable to dispute against the Valentinians, as not knowing their system : which we in our first Book have very diligently expounded unto thee.

IRENÆUS *preface to Bk. iv.*

VIII.

For God doeth all things in measure and order, and nothing with Him wants measure, since nothing is unnumbered. And well spake he who said that the Immeasurable Father Himself was measured in the Son : for the measure of the Father is the Son, since He even contains Him.

IRENÆUS iv. 4. 2.

IX.

As I have heard from a certain Elder, who had heard from those who had seen the Apostles, and from their scholars :—that it is enough for the ancients to be reproved, as they are by the Scriptures, for what they did without counsel from the Spirit. For God, being no respecter of persons, upon things not done to His pleasure brings such reproof as is suitable. [Thus in the case of David, when on the one hand he was suffering persecution from Saul for righteousness' sake, and flying from king Saul, and avenged not himself on his enemy, and was singing of Christ's Advent, and teaching the nations wisdom, and doing all by the suggestion of the Spirit, he pleased God. But when for lust he took to his own self Bathsheba Uriah's wife, the scripture hath said of him, *But the thing etc.* (2 Sam. xi. 27) : and Nathan the prophet is sent unto him, to shew him his sin, that he, passing sentence on himself, and judging himself, may find mercy and forgiveness from Christ.

And he said unto him etc. (2 Sam. xii. 1—7); and goes over the rest in order, upbraiding him, and reckoning up God's favours towards him, and how he had provoked the Lord in having done this. For that such conduct pleases not God, rather great anger is hanging over his house.

And hereupon David was pricked to the heart, and said, *I have sinned against the Lord* (2 Sam. xii. 13), and afterwards he chanted the psalm of confession, waiting for the coming of the Lord, Who washes and cleanses the man who had been bound in sin.

And so it is also concerning Solomon ; as long as he went on to judge rightly, and to declare wisdom, and was building the figure of the true Temple, and setting forth the glories of God, and announcing the peace which should come to the Gentiles, and prefiguring the Kingdom of Christ, and was speaking his three thousand parables on the coming of the Lord, and his five thousand songs, by way of hymn to God, and gathering accounts of God's wisdom in the Creation, after the manner of a natural philosopher, from every tree, and from every herb, and from all fowls and quadrupeds and fishes, and saying, *Will God indeed etc.* (1 Kings viii. 27), he both pleased God, and was admired by all, and all the kings of the Earth sought his face, to hear his wisdom which God had given him, and the Queen of the South came to him from the ends of the earth, to know the wisdom which was in him ; who also, as the Lord saith, will rise again in the judgment with the generation of those who hear His words and believe not in Him, and will pass sentence upon them : because, while she submitted herself to the wisdom declared by the servant of God, they despised that wisdom which was given by the Son of God. For Solomon was a servant; but Christ the Son of God, and the Lord of Solomon. Well then, as long as he served God without offence, and ministered to His purposes, so long he was glorified : but when he took wives of all nations, and permitted them to set up idols in Israel, the Scripture hath said of him, *And King Solomon was a lover etc.* (1 Kings xi. 1, 4, 6, 9).] The rebuke laid on him by Scripture was sufficient, as that Elder affirmed, that no flesh might glory before the Lord.

And therefore, he said, the Lord descended to the parts under the earth, announcing to them also the good news of His coming ; there being remission of sins for such as believe on Him. [And those all believed on Him, who were hoping for Him : i.e., who foretold His coming and ministered to His purposes, righteous men and prophets and patriarchs : whose sins He forgave, even as He forgave ours, neither ought we to impute the same unto them, unless we despise the grace of God. For as they did not charge us with our irregularities, which we wrought before Christ was manifested in us ; so neither is it just for us to charge the like, before the coming of Christ, on such as sinned. For *all* men *need the glory of God* (Rom. iii. 23), and are justified not of themselves, but by the coming of the Lord—those I mean who look steadily on His Light.

And their deeds, he said, were written for our admonition : to teach us, first of all, that our God and theirs is one and the same ; a God, Whom sins please not, though wrought by renowned persons : and next that we should abstain from evils. [For if those of old time who went before us in God's special graces, for whom the Son of God had not yet suffered, were visited with such disgrace, if they transgressed in some one thing, and became slaves to fleshly concupiscence ; what shall this generation suffer, as many as have despised the coming of the Lord, and turned utter slaves to their own pleasures?

And they indeed had our Lord's death for the healing and remission of their sins : but for those who now sin Christ shall no more die, for death shall no more have dominion over Him ; but the Son shall come in the glory of the Father, exacting from His agents and stewards the money which He lent them, with usury : and to whom He gave most, of them will He require most.]

We ought not therefore, said that Elder, to be proud, nor to reproach the ancients, but ourselves to fear, lest haply, after the knowledge of Christ, if we do anything which pleases not God, we no longer have remission of our sins, but find ourselves shut out of His Kingdom. And to this he referred Paul's saying, *For if He spared not etc.* (Rom. xi. 17, 21).

In like manner again the transgressions of the people, you see, are written down, not for their sake who did then transgress, but for our rebuke, and that we might know that it is one and the same God, against Whom they sinned, and against Whom sin even now certain of those who are said to have believed. And this again, he said, the Apostle did most clearly point out, saying in the Epistle to the Corinthians, *For I would not have etc.* (1 Cor. x. 1—12).

[Whereas therefore the Apostle declares, in a way which admits not of doubt or gainsaying, that it is one and the same God, Who both judged the things which then were, and searches out those which now are, and since he tells us the purpose of their being set down : unlearned and daring and senseless withal are all those proved to be, who take occasion from the sin of them of old time, and the disobedience of the greater part of them, to affirm that their God (Who is also the Maker of the world) is a different Being from the Father taught by Christ, and is in decay, and that it is this latter who is mentally received by every one of them. Because they consider not, that as in that case God was not well pleased with the greater part of them, being sinners, so also in this case *many are called but few chosen* (S. Matt. xx. 16): as among them the unjust and idolaters and fornicators lost their life, so also among us. For both the Lord proclaims that such are sent into the eternal fire, and the Apostle saith, *Know ye not etc.* (1 Cor. vi. 9, 10).

And in proof that he said this not to those who are without, but to us, lest we be cast out of the Kingdom of God, for doing some such thing, he hath subjoined, *And these things etc.* (1 Cor. vi. 11).

And as in that case those were condemned and cast out, who did evil, and led the rest astray, so in this case also the very eye is dug out which gives offence, and the foot, and the hand, that the rest of the body perish not alike. And we have it ordained, *If any is named etc.* (1 Cor. v. 11). And again the Apostle saith, *Let no man deceive you etc.* (Eph. v. 6, 7).

And as then the condemnation of them that sinned imparted itself also to the rest, in that they were pleased with them, and they held converse together : so here also *a little leaven corrupteth the whole mass* (1 Cor. v. 6). And as there God's anger came down against the unrighteous, here also saith the Apostle in like manner, *For the wrath of God etc.* (Rom. i. 18). And as there upon the Egyptians, who were punishing Israel unjustly, vengeance from God took place, so here also ; since both the Lord saith, *And shall not God etc.* (S. Luke xviii. 7, 8), and the Apostle in the Epistle to the Thessalonians declares as follows, *Since it is a righteous thing etc.* (2 Thess. i. 6—10).]

Both here therefore and there is the same righteousness of God in maintaining God's cause. There indeed it is done typically, and for a certain time, and with comparative moderation ; but here truly, and for ever, and more severely. For the fire is eternal ; and the anger of God which shall be revealed from heaven from the countenance of our Lord brings a greater penalty on those who incur it : as David also saith, *But the countenance etc.* (Ps. xxxiv. 16). This being so, the Elders used to declare those persons to be very senseless, who from what befel God's disobedient people of old try to bring in another Father: objecting the great things which the Lord when He came had done to save those who received Him, in His pity for them ; but saying nothing of His judgment and of all that is to happen to such as have heard His words and fulfilled them not; and how it were good for them if they had not been born: and how it shall be more tolerable for Sodom and Gomorrah in the judgment than for that city which received not the words of His disciples.

IRENÆUS iv. 27. 1—28. 1.

X.

Those again who upbraid and charge us with the circumstance, that the people by command of God, on point of departure, received of the Egyptians vessels of all sorts and apparel, and so went away, from which stores the Tabernacle also was made in the wilderness, prove themselves ignorant of God's ways of justification, and of His providences; as that Elder likewise used to say. [Since, had not God permitted this in the typical journey, no man could at this day be saved in our real journey, i.e., in the faith wherein we are established, whereby we have been taken out of the number of the Gentiles. For we are all accompanied by some property, moderate or large, which we have gotten out of the Mammon of iniquity. For whence are the houses in which we dwell, and the garments which we put on, and the furniture which we use, and all the rest of what serves us for our daily life, but out of what in our Gentile state we gained by avarice, or what we have received from Gentile parents, or kinsmen, or friends, who acquired it by injustice? Not to say that even now, while we are in the faith, we gain. For who sells, and desires not to gain from the buyer? And who buys, and would not fain be dealt with by the seller to his profit? Again, what person in business does not carry on his business, that so he may get his bread thereby? And how is it with those believers who are in the royal court? Have they not goods from among the things which are Cæsar's, and doth not each one of them according to his ability impart unto such as have not? The Egyptians were debtors to the people not only for their goods but for their life also, through the former kindness of the Patriarch Joseph: but in what respect are the Gentiles debtors to us, from whom we receive both profit and the commodities of life? Whatsoever they gain with toil, that we, being in the faith, use without toil.

Besides, the people were serving the Egyptians in the worst of servitude, as saith the Scripture, *And the Egyptians violently etc.* (Exod. i. 13, 14); and with much toil they built them fortified cities, adding to their stores for many years, and in every kind of servitude; whereas the others, over and above their ingratitude toward them, were fain even to destroy them utterly.

What then was unrighteously done, if they took a little out of much, and if those who might have had much property, and gone away rich, had they not served them, went away poor, receiving for their heavy servitude very scanty wages? So, if any free person, carried away violently by some one, and serving him many years and increasing his goods, should afterwards, upon gaining some little support, be suspected of having some small portion of his master's property (whereas in fact he goes off with a very little, out of his own many toils and of the other's great gain) and if this were charged on him by any one as a wrong ; the judge himself will rather appear unjust towards him who had been reduced to slavery by force. Now of like sort are the aforesaid, who blame the people for taking to themselves a little out of much, yet blame not themselves, who have made no due return according to the merit of their parents, but rather, reducing them into most heavy servitude, have obtained from them very great advantage. And while they charge the Jews with unjust dealings, for receiving, as we said before, in a few little vessels uncoined gold and silver ; of themselves (for the truth shall be spoken, ridiculous as it may appear to some) they say that they do justly in bearing about in their girdles stamped gold and silver and copper from others' toils, with the inscription and image of Cæsar upon it.

But if we and they are compared, which will seem to have received more honestly ? The people from the Egyptians, who were in all their debtors, or we from the Romans and other Gentiles, those even who owe us no such debt ? Rather by them the world hath peace, and we walk on the highways and sail whithersoever we will without fear. Against this sort of objector then, our Lord's saying will be applicable, *Thou hypocrite etc.* (S. Matt. vii. 5).

For, if he who lays this to thy charge, and glories in his knowledge, is cut off from the assembly of the Gentiles, and there is nothing of others' property with him ; if he be simply naked and barefoot, and haunt the mountains without a home, like some of those animals which eat grass : he will obtain pardon, as not knowing what is needed in our manner of life. But if he take from men his share in the property of others, as it is called, while he finds fault with the type of the same, he proves himself to be most unjust, and turns back on himself the aforesaid accusation.] For he will be convicted of carrying about what is another's, and of desiring what is not his own : and with a view to this, they report, the Lord said, *Judge not that ye etc.* (S. Matt. vii. 1, 2). [Not of course that we rebuke not sinners, or consent to things done amiss, but that we judge not unfairly God's ways of ordering things, whereas He hath provided in righteousness whatsoever shall be profitable. Thus, because He knew that we would make a good use of our substance, which we should have, receiving it from another, *He that hath two coats*, saith He, *let him impart etc.* (S. Luke iii. 11). Again, *For I was an hungred etc.* (S. Matt. xxv. 35, 36). Again, *When thou doest alms etc.* (S. Matt. vi. 3) : and all other acts of bounty upon which we are justified, redeeming our own as it were by what was another's. And when I say, Another's, I do not mean that the world is alien from God, but that we receive from others and possess the aforesaid gifts, even as they from the Egyptians who knew not God ; and by these same we build up for ourselves the tabernacle of God. For with doers of good God dwelleth : as saith the Lord, *Make to yourselves friends etc.* (S. Luke xvi. 9). For whatsoever things we had acquired, when we were heathens, by unrighteousness, those same, now we have believed, we turn to the Lord's service, and so are justified.

These things were then of necessity practised in type beforehand, and out of those materials the tabernacle of God is wrought ; in which matter, as we have explained, both they received justly, and we were prophetically indicated, how that we should begin to wait on God with things not our own. For all that journey of the people, whereby God brought them out of Egypt, was the type and image of the Church's journey, which was to take place from among the Gentiles ; which journey accordingly ends also with leading her hence into her inheritance, which not indeed Moses the servant of God, but Jesus the Son of God, will give her to inherit. And if any one will look more carefully at what the Prophets say of the end, and at all that John the Lord's disciple saw in the Apocalypse, he will find the Gentiles generally enduring the same plagues, which at that time Egypt in particular endured.]

By statements of this kind touching the ancients did that Elder console us, and say that concerning those faults, which the Scriptures themselves have laid to the charge of Patriarchs and Prophets, we must not reproach them, nor be like Ham, who scoffed at the disgrace of his father, and fell into the curse ; but we must give thanks to God for them, inasmuch as their sins were forgiven them in the coming of our Lord. For that (his word it is) they give thanks and exult in our salvation.

But in respect of those things, for which the Scriptures reprove them not, but simply state the facts, we must not, he said, become accusers (for we are not more exact than God, nor can we be above our master), but look out for the typical meaning. For none of all the things, which are set down in the Scriptures without definite censure, is without its force.

IRENÆUS iv. 30. 1—31. 1.

XI.

In the same way also did that older disciple of the Apostles reason about the two Testaments : declaring that both are indeed from one and the same God ; and that there is no other God, besides Him Who made and formed us, nor any strength in their argument, who say that this world of ours was made either by Angels, or by any kind of Power, or by some other God. [For if a person once withdraw himself from the Creator of all things, and grant that the world with which we are concerned is made by some different God, or through another, such an one must needs fall into much absurdity and many contradictions ; for which he will render no reasons with either appearance or substance of truth. And therefore such as introduce other doctrines, hide from us the opinion which they themselves have concerning God; knowing the unsoundness and futility of their own doctrine, and fearing to be overcome, and so to have their salvation endangered.]

IRENÆUS iv. 32. 1.

XII.

For the word 'son,' as a certain person also before us hath said, has two meanings: one is naturally such, as being born a son; while another is counted for a son, because he is made such: notwithstanding the difference between the born and the made.

IRENÆUS iv. 41. 2.

XIII.

Where then was the first man placed? In paradise plainly, as it is written; and he was cast out thence into this world, owing to his disobedience. Wherefore also the Elders, disciples of the Apostles, say that those who were translated were translated thither (for paradise was prepared for righteous and inspired men, whither also the Apostle Paul was carried and *heard words unspeakable*, to us at least in this present life), and that they who are translated remain there until the end of all things, preluding immortality.

IRENÆUS v. 5. 1.

XIV.

For since by wood we lost Him, by wood again He was made manifest unto all, shewing forth the length and height and depth and breadth in Himself; and as one of those who have gone before said, by the divine extension of His Hands gathering the two peoples together unto one God.

IRENÆUS v. 17. 4.

XV.

Now such being the state of the case, and this number being set down in all the good and old copies, and testimony being given by the persons themselves who had seen John with their eyes, and reason teaching us that the number of the name of the Beast, according to the reckoning of the Greeks, by the letters therein, will have 600, and 60, and 6......some, I know not how, have erred, following a particular reading, and have taken liberties with the middle number of the name, subtracting the value of fifty, and choosing to have one decade instead of six.

IRENÆUS v. 30. 1.

XVI.

As the Elders, who saw John the disciple of the Lord, relate that they had heard from him, how the Lord used to teach concerning those times, and to say......

IRENÆUS v. 33. 3. See above, *Fragments of Papias*, No. XIV. p. 533.

XVII.

As the Elders say, then also shall they which have been deemed worthy of the abode in heaven go thither, while others shall enjoy *the delight of paradise*, and others again shall possess the brightness of the city ; for in every place the Saviour shall be seen, according as they shall be worthy who see Him.   They say moreover that this is the distinction between the habitation of them that bring forth a hundred-fold, and them that bring forth sixty-fold, and them that bring forth thirty-fold ; of whom the first shall be taken up into the heavens, and the second shall dwell in paradise, and the third shall inhabit the city ; and that therefore our Lord has said, *In My Father's abode are many mansions ;* for all things are of God, Who giveth to all their appropriate dwelling, [according as His Word saith that allotment is made unto all by the Father, according as each man is, or shall be, worthy.   And this is the banqueting-table at which those shall recline who are called to the marriage and take part in the feast.]   The Elders, the disciples of the Apostles, say that this is the arrangement and disposal of them that are being saved, and that they advance by such steps, and ascend through the Spirit to the Son, and through the Son to the Father, the Son at length yielding His work to the Father, as it is said also by the Apostle, *For He must reign until He putteth all enemies under His feet.*

IRENÆUS v. 36. 1, 2.

SYMBOLS AND ABBREVIATIONS

The following symbols and abbreviations have been employed in this volume :

add. ⎫ Where a word (or words) is (or are) added, or prefixed, in the
pref. ⎭ authority subjoined.

al. Where the divergence is so great in a version that no inference can be drawn as to the reading which the author of the version had before him. This will also include passages which are so corrupt as to be worthless for determining a reading.

app. Apparently.

cf. Where an authority, or another passage in the text, may be claimed indirectly in support of a reading.

conj. ⎫ The editor whose name follows this abbreviation has conjectured,
ins. ⎭ or inserted, the reading which precedes the abbreviation.

def. When the context, in which the word or words should occur, is wanting in the MS or version stated.

dub. Where a word or expression is so translated or paraphrased that the reading which it represents is uncertain.

homœot. Where a passage has been inadvertently omitted by a scribe, because it ends with the same word which closed the preceding sentence.

illeg. Illegible.

in marg. Where an editor has stated a conjectural emendation in his notes, but has not placed it in his text.

pri. ⎫ Whenever the same word or expression occurs more than once
sec. ⎬ in the same chapter or section, these abbreviations signify
tert. ⎭ that the note refers to the first, second or third occurrence (respectively) of such word or expression.

supp.   The editor whose name follows this abbreviation has filled up a
lacuna in the text by supplying the word or words which pre-
cede the abbreviation.

[ ]   In the Greek text or English translation, words placed between
square brackets have only a modified textual authority, and are
probably the result of a gloss or of a second recension.   In
the footnotes, an authority placed between square brackets
after the name of an editor represents a version, the reading of
which has helped the editor in question to emend the Greek
text as specified.   In the Reliques of the Elders, passages
thus included may perhaps be nothing more than Irenæus'
own comments.

| | Words included within perpendicular lines are conjectural read-
ings, inserted where there is preponderating evidence that
words have fallen out of the Greek text by homœoteleuton.
This symbol is only used where (as in the case of the Epistle
to Diognetus and of the greater part of the Shepherd of
Hermas) the Greek text is extant in a single MS.

( )   Brackets of this form include words in the English translation
which have been supplied to help the sense of the passage, and
are not represented in the Greek or Latin original.

⌐ ¬   These symbols exhibit the restoration of the text of the Shepherd
of Hermas, where lacunae exist in the Athos MS.

† †   Corruptions in the text are indicated by daggers placed on each
side of the corrupt passage.

The symbols which represent the authorities for the text in any document are explained in the introduction which precedes that document.

References to patristic authorities are abbreviated as follows :

Anon-Syr.   The anonymous Syriac writer of the *Demonstrationes Patrum*
[VI or VII].
Ant.   Antiochus the Monk [VII].
Clem. Alex.   Clement of Alexandria [II].
ps-Ath.   The anonymous author of the *Doctrina ad Antiochum
ducem*, wrongly assigned to Athanasius.
Sev.   Severus of Antioch [VI].
Tim.   Timotheus of Alexandria [V].

The century in which the writer lived is given within square brackets.

INDEX OF SCRIPTURAL PASSAGES

WHERE the reference to a patristic passage is printed in italics, the resemblance to the corresponding scriptural passage is less close than in the other instances.

The following are the abbreviations employed:—B=the Epistle of Barnabas; C=the Genuine Epistle of Clement; 2 C=the Spurious Epistle of Clement; D=the Epistle to Diognetus; Δ=the Didache; E=the Reliques of the Elders preserved in Irenæus; H=the Shepherd of Hermas; I=the Epistles of Ignatius; P=the Epistle of Polycarp; II=the Fragments of Papias; MP=the Martyrdom of Polycarp.

The Epistles of Ignatius are indicated as follows in italics:—*E*=Ephesians; *M*=Magnesians; *T*=Trallians; *R*=Romans; *Ph*=Philadelphians; *Sm*=Smyrnæans; *Pol*=Polycarp; the subdivisions of the Shepherd of Hermas thus:—*V*=Visions; *M*=Mandates; *S*=Similitudes.

The patristic references are to the chapters, except in the case of Papias and the Elders, where they refer to the number of the fragment: in the case of references to the Epistle of Barnabas and the Shepherd of Hermas the subsections also are given, as shewn in the Greek text.